s, and

ONE WEEK LOAN

D0528777

OXFORD SERIES IN HUMAN–TECHNOLOGY INTERACTION

SERIES EDITOR

Alex Kirlik

Adaptive Perspectives on Human–Technology Interaction: Methods and Models for Cognitive Engineering and Human–Computer Interaction
Edited by Alex Kirlik

Computers, Phones, and the Internet: Domesticating Information Technology
Edited by Robert Kraut, Malcolm Brynin, and Sara Kiesler

Computers, Phones, and the Internet

Domesticating Information Technology

EDITED BY

Robert Kraut

Malcolm Brynin

Sara Kiesler

OXFORD

UNIVERSITY PRESS

2006

OXFORD
UNIVERSITY PRESS

Oxford University Press, Inc., publishes works that further
Oxford University's objective of excellence
in research, scholarship, and education.

Oxford   New York
Auckland   Cape Town   Dar es Salaam   Hong Kong   Karachi
Kuala Lumpur   Madrid   Melbourne   Mexico City   Nairobi
New Delhi   Shanghai   Taipei   Toronto

With offices in
Argentina   Austria   Brazil   Chile   Czech Republic   France   Greece
Guatemala   Hungary   Italy   Japan   Poland   Portugal   Singapore
South Korea   Switzerland   Thailand   Turkey   Ukraine   Vietnam

Published by Oxford University Press, Inc.
198 Madison Avenue, New York, New York 10016

www.oup.com

Oxford is a registered trademark of Oxford University Press

Library of Congress Cataloging-in-Publication Data
Computers, phones, and the Internet / edited by Robert Kraut, Malcolm Brynin, Sara Kiesler.
p. cm. — (Oxford series in human-technology interaction ; 2)
Includes bibliographic references and index.
ISBN-13 978-0-19-517963-7; 978-0-19-531280-5 (pbk.)
ISBN 0-19-517963-3; 0-19-531280-5 (pbk.)
1. Information society.   2. Information technology—Social aspects.   3. Technological
innovations—Social aspects.   I. Kraut, Robert E.   II. Brynin, Malcolm.   III. Kiesler, Sara.
IV. Series.
HM851.C665 2006
303.48'33—dc22   2006007261

9 8 7 6 5 4 3 2 1

Printed in the United States of America
on acid-free paper

Contents

III New Technology in Teenage Life

IV The Internet and Social Relationships

Contributors

Ben Anderson is currently deputy director of Chimera, a research institute of the University of Essex, and he is also a visiting researcher at the University of Essex's Institute for Social and Economic Research (ISER). His general research interests include longitudinal time-use data analysis and e-social science and spatial microsimulation. More specifically, he is interested in the application of behavioral science techniques to the study of technology-mediated human communication; the co-evolution of people and the technology they use; and the relationship among ICT, social capital, and quality of life. He has a BSc in biology and computer science (Southampton University, United Kingdom) and a PhD in computer studies (Loughborough University, United Kingdom).

Maria Bakardjieva is associate professor at the Faculty of Communication and Culture at the University of Calgary. She holds a PhD in sociology from the Bulgarian Academy of Sciences (1995) and a PhD in communication from Simon Fraser University, Burnaby, British Columbia (2000). Her research interests focus on the social processes of integrating new communication media into everyday practices and diverse cultures. Ethnographic studies of Internet use in the home, virtual communities, and online education have been among her primary research projects in the past 10 years. She is author of *Internet Society: The Internet in Everyday Life* (2005) and coeditor of *How Canadians*

Communicate (2003). More information is available at http://www.ucalgary.ca/UofC/faculties/COMCUL/Web/instr/bakardjieva.html

Gretchen Barbatsis earned a PhD in speech communication from the University of Minnesota, 1979. She is currently a professor in the Department of Telecommunication, Information Studies, and Media at Michigan State University and has previously held positions at Middle Tennessee State University and the University of Nebraska. Professor Barbatsis served as director of the Mass Media in Britain Program, Office of Overseas Studies, Michigan State University, and has participated in numerous international research projects, most recently in Nigeria. Her research interests include sense-making aesthetics, hypermediated telepresence, and the social consequences of digital exclusion for opportunities for transformative interactivity of being "voiced" in cyberspace.

Frank Biocca earned a PhD in mass communication from the University of Wisconsin in 1989. He is currently SBC Chair of Telecommunication, Information Studies and Media at Michigan State University. Previous positions include professor, researcher, and lecturer at the University of California–Berkeley, Stanford University, University of North Carolina, and University of Wisconsin. Professor Biocca is interested in how mind and media interfaces can be coupled to extend human cognition and enhance human performance. He directs the networked Media Interface and Network Design (MIND) Lab, an international, multiuniversity human–computer interaction and communication research lab with seven facilities spanning five countries. Among his books is the award-winning *Communication in the Age of Virtual Reality*. Professor Biocca is on the editorial board of several journals including *MIT Presence: Teleoperators and Virtual Environments, Journal of Communication, Journal of Computer-Mediated Communication,* and *Media Psychology*.

Bonka S. Boneva died tragically in September 2004. She was a lecturer at the University of Pittsburgh, holding an MS in personality psychology (University of Pittsburgh) and a PhD in social psychology (University of Sofia) and she had finished a postdoctoral fellowship at the Human–Computer Interaction Institute at Carnegie Mellon University. Her most recent research and publications were focused on two main issues: the psychological effect of computer-mediated communication and the personality profile associated with geographic relocation.

Malcolm Brynin, who holds sociology degrees from London, Reading, and City Universities, is the principal research officer at the Institute for Social and Economic Research at the University of Essex. His research interests there focus on the use of large-scale data sets to examine the relationship between education and employment, the social effects of technology at work, and, when time permits, the relationship between social status and political behavior.

John M. Carroll is Edward Frymoyer Chair Professor of Information Sciences and Technology at the Pennsylvania State University. His research interests include methods and theory in human–computer interaction, particularly as applied to networking tools for collaborative learning and problem solving and the design of interactive information systems. Recent books include *Making Use* (2000) and *HCI Models, Theories, and Frameworks* (2003). Carroll is a member of the U.S. National Research Council's Committee on Human Factors and editor-in-chief of the *ACM Transactions on Computer–Human Interaction*. He received the Rigo Award and the CHI Lifetime Achievement Award from ACM, the Silver Core Award from IFIP, and the Goldsmith Award from IEEE and is a Fellow in ACM, HFES, and IEEE. More information is available at http://faculty.ist.psu .edu/jcarroll/.

Steven Chen is a PhD student at the Graduate School of Management, University of California-Irvine, having received his BA in visual arts from UC-Irvine. His research interest is in the aesthetics and design of new technologies in different user environments. He was a research assistant and visual artist for the Center for Research on Information Technology in Organizations (CRITO) and Project NOAH (National Outlook for Automation in the Home) at UC-Irvine before joining the graduate program.

Jonathon N. Cummings (jonathon.cummings@duke .edu) is an associate professor of management at the Fuqua School of Business at Duke University. He received a PhD in organization science from Carnegie Mellon University. His research focuses on social networks and teams in organizations and the role of knowledge-sharing in the distributed innovation process. His recent papers are available at http://netvis.fu qua .duke.edu/papers/.

Daniel Dunlap is a faculty researcher in the Center for Human-Computer Interaction at Virginia Tech. He received his PhD in science and technology studies from Virginia Tech in 2002. He has taught and conducted research in public schools and the local community since 1987. Dr. Dunlap is particularly interested in the social impacts of computing, technologies in teaching and education, community computing, computer-supported collaborative learning, and technology studies. More information is available at http:// www.teacherbridge.org/users/dunlapd.

Alexander von Eye earned a PhD in psychology from the University of Trier, Germany, in 1976. He has held positions at the University of Trier, the University of Erlangen-Nürnberg, the Max Planck Institute for Human Development, and Pennsylvania State University and is currently a professor at Michigan State University. His research focuses on the development and application of statistical methods for analysis of categorical data, longitudinal data, classification, computational statistics, and structural equations modeling. Current work focuses on configural frequency analysis, a method for searching for structure in cross-classifications of categorical data. Professor von Eye also conducts simulation studies on the behavior of statistical methods. Substantively, he is a developmental psychologist with a life-span perspective.

Hiram E. Fitzgerald earned a PhD in experimental child psychology from the University of Denver in 1967. He is currently assistant provost for University Outreach and Engagement and a University Distinguished Professor of Psychology at Michigan State University. His research focuses on the etiology of alcoholism and co-active psychopathology, the impact of early childhood community-based prevention programs, the role that fathers play in early child development, the development of successful models of community-university research partnerships, and Internet accessibility issues. He has collaborated extensively with colleagues across a variety of disciplines and nations.

Victor M. Gonzalez is a research fellow at the Center for Research on Information Technology (CRITO) at the University of California-Irvine. He conducts theoretical and empirical research on information technology usage to support activity management. His studies have focused on office and home settings. Currently he is studying the strategies that information workers use to manage multiple projects under fast-paced conditions. He received a PhD in information and computer science from UC-Irvine; an MS in telecommunication and information systems from the University of Essex, UK; and a BS in electronic communication from the Institute of Technology of Monterrey, Mexico (ITESM).

Patricia Greenfield received her PhD from Harvard University and is professor of psychology at University of California-Los Angeles, where she is a member of the developmental group and directs the Children's Digital Media Center. Her central theoretical and research interest is in the relationship between culture and human development. She is a past recipient of the American Association for the Advancement of Science Award for Behavioral Science Research and has received teaching awards from UCLA and the American Psychological Association. Professor Greenfield has held fellowships at the Bunting Institute, Radcliffe College, the School of American Research, Santa Fe, and the Center for Advanced Study in the Behavioral Sciences, Stanford. Her books include *Mind and Media: The Effects of Television, Video Games, and Computers* (1984), which has been translated into nine languages. In the 1990s she coedited (with R.R. Cocking) *Interacting with Video* (1996) and *Cross-Cultural Roots of Minority Child Development* (1994). She has done field research on child development, social change, and weaving apprenticeship in Chiapas, Mexico, since 1969. This cumulative work is presented in a new book entitled *Weaving Generations Together* (2004). A project in Los Angeles investigates how cultural values influence relationships on multiethnic high school sports teams. Another project, "Bridging Cultures," utilizes research on cross-cultural value conflict between Latino immigrant parents and the schools as the basis for teacher and parent training.

Elisheva Gross is a doctoral candidate at the University of California-Los Angeles. After earning her bachelor's degree at Yale University in 1995, she developed and directed new media projects in nonprofit community organizations dedicated to developing communication, technical and creative skills among youth from diverse backgrounds. Since beginning graduate school, she has continued to collaborate with community educators and artists (in Oakland, Los Angeles, New York and Taipei) to promote public dialogue, education and media for and by youth. Her research focuses on the influences of social and cultural contexts on adolescents' psychological adjustment and experiences among peers.

Jos de Haan received a PhD in sociology from Utrecht University in 1960 (thesis: Research groups in Dutch sociology) and has worked since 1994 with the Social and Cultural Planning Office (SCP) in the Hague, the Netherlands, where he carries out research dealing with culture, media, and information and communication technology (ICT). His research into the spread, use, and consequences of new ICTs include investigations of the digital divide, of digital skills among the young, and of the rise of e-culture. He is editor of the Dutch yearbook *ICT and Society* and has published in several English journals, including *IT&Society* (http://www.stanford.edu/group/siqss/itandsociety/). More information is available at http://www.scp.nl or just send an e-mail to j.de.haan@scp.nl.

John B. Horrigan has a PhD in public policy from the Lyndon B. Johnson School of Public Affairs at the University of Texas-Austin. He has been associate director of research at the Pew Internet and American Life Project since 2000. Horrigan has authored over a dozen reports while at Pew, focusing on the online behavior of broadband users, the Internet's social and economic impact on communities, e-government, and emerging technology behaviors. Before working at Pew, he was a program officer at National Research Council's Board on Science, Technology, and Economic Policy. Horrigan is also an adjunct professor of government at the University of Texas-Austin's Washington Campus, the Bill Archer Center.

Philip L. Isenhour is a senior research associate with the Center for Human-Computer Interaction at Virginia Tech. He received an MS in computer science from Virginia Tech in 1998. His research focuses on adaptable component technologies for collaboration and distributed interaction, with a particular interest in applications for classroom and community computing.

Mizuko (Mimi) Ito is a cultural anthropologist of technology use, focusing on children and youth's changing relationships to media and communications. She is co-editor of the book *Personal, Portable, Pedestrian: Mobile Phones in Japanese Life*. She is a research scientist at the Annenberg Center for Communication at the

University of Southern California and a visiting associate professor at Keio University in Japan. Past workplaces include the Institute for Research on Learning, Xerox PARC, Tokyo University, the National Institute for Educational Research in Japan, and Apple Computer. Her web page is at http://www.itofisher.com/mito.

Linda A. Jackson earned a PhD in psychology from the University of Rochester, New York, in 1981. She is a professor of psychology at Michigan State University and Principal Investigator for the HomeNetToo Project. Her research interests include cultural and social-psychological factors that influence use and consequences of using information and communication technology (ICT); children's use of ICT and cultural factors that influence its impact on developmental outcomes; culture, cognition and learning in ICT environments; and gender and cultural influences on ICT use and career choice. Her recent research focuses on issues surrounding the digital "use" divide. Professor Jackson has over 100 publications in professional journals, books, book chapters, and conference proceedings.

Andrea L. Kavanaugh, a Cunningham Fellow and Fulbright scholar, is senior research scientist and associate director of the Center for Human-Computer Interaction at Virginia Tech. Her research focuses on educational and social computing, including the use and social impact of community computer networks on social relations and civic engagement. She is the former director of research for the Blacksburg Electronic Village (BEV), a community computer network project of Information Systems, at Virginia Tech. She also studies communication behavior and effects in developing countries, primarily the Middle East. She is the author of *The Social Control of Technology: Information in the Global Economy; Community Networks: Lessons from Blacksburg, Virginia* (edited with Andrew Cohill); and *The Wired Homestead* (edited with Joseph Turow). She serves on the board of directors of the International Telecommunications Society. Her research is supported by grants from the U.S. Department of Commerce, the World Bank and the National Science Foundation. More information is available at http://java.cs.vt.edu/public/users/kavan.

Sara Kiesler is Hillman Professor of Computer Science and Human-Computer Interaction at Carnegie Mellon University. She has a PhD in psychology. She has held positions at Yale, Connecticut College, University of Kansas, the National Research Council, Interval Research, and Carnegie Mellon University. Her research aims at understanding the design and social impact of computer and telecommunications technologies. Professor Kiesler has studied social aspects of communi-

cating through computer networks and has published papers on individuals, groups, and organizations using communication technologies. With Lee Sproull, she co-authored *Connections: New Ways of Working in the Networked Organization*, and she edited *Culture of the Internet*. Her current research also includes studies of collaborations and distributed work arrangements in organizations, and studies of human-robot interaction.

Robert Kraut is Herbert A. Simon Professor of Human-Computer Interaction at Carnegie Mellon University. He received a PhD in social psychology from Yale University in 1973 and previously taught at the University of Pennsylvania and Cornell University. He was a research scientist at AT&T Bell Laboratories and Bell Communications Research for twelve years. Dr. Kraut has broad interests in the design and social impact of computing and conducts research on everyday use of the Internet, technology and conversation, collaboration in small work groups, computing in organizations and contributions to online communities. More information is available at http://www.cs.cmu.edu/~kraut.

John Lee is a Paul F. Lazarsfeld Fellow in the Department of Sociology at Columbia University. Mr. Lee earned his BS in Social Science and Statistics from Carnegie Mellon University in 2001. He is currently pursuing broad interests in discourse and communication, models of social network formation, and identity.

Christian Licoppe is a professor of sociology of information and communication technologies at the Ecole Nationale Supérieure des Télécommunications in Paris. Trained in the history of science and technology, he is the author of a book on experimental laboratory practices in the modern period. His current research focusses on the sociological analysis of the contemporary uses of ICTs within a pragmatic, activity-based perspective.

Rich Ling is a sociologist at Telenor's research institute located near Oslo, Norway, and a visiting professor at the University of Michigan-Ann Arbor. He also the author of a book on the social consequences of mobile telephony, *The Mobile Connection: The Cell Phone's Impact on Society*. He received a PhD in sociology from the University of Colorado-Boulder in his native United States. Upon completion of his doctorate, he taught at the University of Wyoming in Laramie before coming to Norway on a Marshall Foundation grant. Since that time he has worked at the Gruppen for Ressursstudier (the Resource Study Group) and has been a partner in a consulting firm, Ressurskonsult, which focused on studies of energy, technology and society. For the past ten years, he has worked at Telenor R&D and has been active in researching issues associated with new information communication technology and society, with a particular focus on mobile telephony.

Sonia Livingstone is professor of social psychology in the Department of Media and Communications at the London School of Economics. She is the author *of Making Sense of Television* (1990, 1998); *Mass Consumption and Personal Identity* (with Peter Lunt, 1992); *Talk on Television* (with Peter Lunt, 1994); *Children and Their Changing Media Environment* (edited with Moira Bovill, 2001); *The Handbook of New Media* (edited with Leah Lievrouw, 2002, 2005); *Young People and New Media* (2002), and *Audiences and Publics* (2005, edited). Her current work concerns children, young people, and the Internet, as part of a broader interest in the domestic, familial, and educational contexts of new media access and use (see http://www.children-go-online.net).

Katelyn Y. A. McKenna is assistant professor in the Department of Communication at Ben Gurion University in Israel. Since fall 2005, she has also been a professor in the new Department of Communications at the Interdisciplinary Center, Herzliya, Israel. She received her BA with honors from Tulane University and her PhD from Ohio University in 1998. She is the co-editor of a forthcoming book and the author of numerous publications concerning social and psychological processes on the Internet. Her research interests focus on relationship cognition and social identity processes, especially as these unfold over the Internet.

Daisuke Okabe is a cognitive psychologist specializing in situated learning theory. His focus is interactional studies of learning and education in relation to new media technologies, and he is co-editor of the book *Personal, Portable, Pedestrian: Mobile Phones in Japanese Life*. He works as a research associate at Keio University in Japan.

Amy Quinn is currently a user experience specialist at User Centric, Inc., a consulting firm in Oakbrook Terrace, Illinois, specializing in analyzing user experiences and designing usable interfaces. She has worked with clients such as the American Society of Clinical Oncology, Cox Communications, Microsoft Consulting Services, and CDW. She earned a Masters of Human-Computer Interaction degree at Carnegie Mellon University in August 2003. Previously, Ms. Quinn held research and software development positions at SPSS, Inc. and Columbia University. She graduated from New York University in 1995 with a BA in psychology and history. She has a variety of interests that include the social impact of computers, the integration of software development and HCI processes, and the design of software systems.

Yoel Raban is a senior research fellow at ICTAF, Tel Aviv University. Dr. Raban has a PhD in marketing from the Leon Recanati Graduate School of Business Administration, Tel Aviv University, and an MA in economics from the Eitan Berglas School of Economics, Tel Aviv University. He has extensive research and consulting experience in the area of socioeconomic impacts of technology. He is currently involved in several European projects, such as the e-Living study on the impact of ICTs on our daily life.

John P. Robinson is professor of sociology at the University of Maryland and past director of the Americans' Use of Time Project. He is primarily interested in the study of time and is co-author of several books dealing with the use of time and the quality of life, including *Time for Life* (with G. Godbey, 1999). Professor Robinson has also published widely on the social implications of the Internet. This work, undertaken under the auspices of a grant from the National Science Foundation, has led to the creation of a website, http://www.webuse.umd.edu, which contains a wide variety of Internet-related data as well as an online statistical tool for analysis of the data. Professor Robinson co-founded, along with Stanford Professor Norman Nie, the journal *IT&Society* (http://www.itandsociety.org), jointly published with the Stanford Institute for the Quantitative Study of Society, which publishes up-to-date Internet research. In addition, over the past three years Professor Robinson has conducted an annual summer Webshop, where 40–50 top graduate students are given the opportunity to interact with leading Internet scholars and researchers. More information is available at http://www.bsos.umd.edu/socy/faculty/jrobinson.html.

Mary Beth Rosson is professor of information sciences and technology at Pennsylvania State University. Before joining Penn State in 2003, she was a professor of computer science at Virginia Tech for 10 years and a research staff member at IBM's T. J. Watson Research Center for 11 years. Professor Rosson's research interests include scenario-based design and evaluation; the use of network technology to support collaboration, especially in learning contexts; and the psychological issues associated with use of high-level programming languages and tools. She is co-author of *Usability Engineering: Scenario-Based Development of Human-Computer Interaction* (2002) and author of *Instructor's Guide to Object-Oriented Analysis and Design with Application* (1994), as well as numerous articles, book chapters, and tutorials. More information is available at http://ist.psu.edu/rosson.

Wendy Schafer is a postdoctoral researcher with the Computer-Supported Collaboration and Learning

Laboratory at the School of Information Sciences and Technology of Pennsylvania State University. She completed her PhD in computer science with a focus on human-computer interaction at Virginia Tech in 2004. Her research interests include collaborative software, geospatial software, emergency management, and collaborative virtual environments.

Gwendolyn Seidman is a graduate student in the Social-Personality Program in the Department of Psychology at New York University. She earned a BA with a double major in psychology and statistics from The College of New Jersey in 2001, and an MA in psychology from New York University in 2004. Her research focuses on relationship processes, particularly social support processes and the development of Internet relationships.

Irina Shklovski is a PhD candidate in the Human-Computer Interaction Institute at Carnegie Mellon University. Her research interests include residential mobility, everyday use of information communication technologies and their impact on sociability and psychological well-being, and issues of survey methodology as they relate to Internet research. She recently spent a summer working with the Intel People and Practices research group studying long-distance movers and their patterns of technology use. Her research is supported by an NSF graduate fellowship.

Zbigniew Smoreda is a senior researcher in the Social Sciences Laboratory (SUSI) at France Telecom Research & Development Division. He previously taught Social Psychology at the Warsaw University and the University of Paris 8. His research interests include the study of the social link via social network configurations, personal identity transformations, life cycle influence on individual and family communication practices, and, more recently, daily personal mobility and communication patterns using monitoring systems via GSM devices.

Jason Snook is an IT Consultant for Captech Ventures in Richmond, VA. He received a PhD in Computer Science at Virginia Tech in May 2005. His research interests focus on user psychology and behavior on the Internet. Within this area he studies social influence, subjective perception, and adoption as they relate to software usage.

Kaveri Subrahmanyam received a PhD in psychology from University of California-Los Angeles in 1993 and is an associate professor in the Department of Child and Family Studies at California State University-Los Angeles. She is also the associate director of the Children's Digital Media Center at UCLA. She is interested in studying the in-

fluence of cultural tools such as language, computers, and the Internet on children's development. Dr. Subrahmanyam has conducted research on children's use of syntactic cues when learning nouns and on the impact of computer use on children's cognitive skills. In her research on the culture of teen chat rooms, she has studied the linguistic codes, strategies for coherence, and construction of sexuality and gender found within these online spaces. Her current research on adolescents and the Internet includes a study of online blogs maintained and updated by teens.

Lalita K. Suzuki received a BA in psychology from Stanford University (1993) and a PhD in psychology from University of California-Los Angeles (2000). She is senior research analyst at a nonprofit organization called HopeLab in Palo Alto, California, where she conducts research relevant to the development of interactive technologies for adolescents with chronic illnesses. Before joining the research team at HopeLab, she was a Visiting Scholar at the UCLA Children's Digital Media Center, where she conducted studies on the Internet and teen health. She has also served as a consultant for the Children's Television Workshop (now Sesame Workshop) on a pilot evaluation of an educational television program for preschoolers and was the author and producer of an educational CD-ROM entitled *Stuart Little's Learning Adventures*.

Brendesha Tynes is an assistant professor of African-American Studies and Educational Psychology at the University of Illinois-Urbana-Champaign, where she teaches adolescent development and African-American psychology. Her research interests include race, identity, and intergroup communication online and the uses of multicultural curricula to reduce prejudice. She received a Ford Pre-doctoral Diversity Fellowship and an American Educational Researchers Association postdoctoral fellowship. Tynes has published several articles and book chapters that explore online discourse, including "Children, Adolescents and the Culture of Online Hate," in the *Handbook of Children, Culture and Violence*.

Alladi Venkatesh is professor and associate director of the Center for Research on Information Technology (CRITO), University of California-Irvine. His primary research areas are home informatics and networking, consumers and electronic environments, and technology diffusion. Over the years, under funding from the NSF, he has directed Project NOAH (National Outlook for Automation in the Home), which looks at various issues concerning computer adoption and use in the home environment. In addition to studying households in the United States, he has also examined similar issues in Sweden and India. A detailed list of his publications and other information is available at http://www.crito.uci.edu/noah.

Brigitte Yttri is research manager for the User Requirements Group at Telenor Research and Development in Oslo, Norway. She finished her studies in sociology in 1998, writing her thesis on the relationship between the private and public sphere among home-based teleworkers. Since that time she has conducted research on information technologies in their social context, and especially the use of current and future mobile services in both the business and mass markets.

Yong Zhao earned a PhD in education from the University of Illinois- Urbana-Champaign in 1996. He is an associate professor in the Department of Technology in Teaching and Learning, Michigan State University, where he is also director of the Center for Teaching and Technology. His research interests include technology integration in schools, teacher adoption of technology, technology-rich learning environments, and online education. Professor Zhao has directed several multimillion-dollar federal and state projects to explore the diffusion of technology-supported innovation in schools. He has published extensively on the design, development, implementation, and diffusion of technology-supported education innovations, focusing on the interactions of existing practices and innovations. Dr. Zhao is a recipient of the prestigious Raymond B. Cattell Early Career Award from the American Educational Research Association.

Computers, Phones, and the Internet

Malcolm Brynin and Robert Kraut

Social Studies of Domestic Information and Communication Technologies

Why Study the New Information and Communication Technologies?

In the 20th century, new information technology has the potential to influence the lives of ordinary citizens as much as it has influenced business, education, and government. In many of the countries in Europe, North America, and Asia, the majority of individuals and households are using personal computers, the Internet, and mobile telephones. In the United States, this equipment is often referred to as information technology. In Europe, the phrase "information and communication technologies" is more commonly used and is abbreviated to ICTs. This book is about the potential effect of these new technologies, as they enter our homes and our daily lives, to change the range of activities we pursue, the way we perform old activities, our relationships with other people, and our personal and economic welfare. But will the new ICTs have a significant social effect, and if they do, will the change be positive? This book contributes to the investigations needed to answer these questions.

Toward the end of his book *The Coming of Post-Industrial Society*, Daniel Bell (1973) argues that before the industrial revolution, humankind confronted nature; through the industrial revolution,

we confronted a sort of "fabricated nature." However, the "post-industrial society is essentially a game between persons" (p. 488). In the new knowledge society, there is at one level simply more social interaction, but at another level, we also face new social challenges. The new technologies we discuss in this volume are a part of this new social and human environment.

In a sense, of course, nothing is new. Although computers, the Internet, and mobile phones are new technologies, the debate over the effects of technology on personal lives is old. In *The Republic*, Plato warned against the pernicious effects of consuming the mass media of the day (drama and poetry), because viewers and readers might have difficulty distinguishing fact from fiction and might emulate the worst rather than the best behavior of the tragic heroes. Such ancient concerns are a strange echo of current social science research findings and argument; for instance, it is said that television and computer games promote violence or other negative behavior (Anderson et al., 2003).

Psychologists, sociologists, and communication scholars have long been interested in the effect on everyday life of broadcast media such as radio and television (e.g., Janowitz & Hirsch, 1981; Ball-Rokeach & Cantor, 1986; Gurevitch & Levy, 1987;

Huston et al., 1992), as well as interpersonal communications media such as the telephone. The telephone was invented in 1876; by the turn of the 20th century, it was reducing the isolation of farm families and helping extended families keep in touch (Fischer, 1992). Today, wireless technology, miniaturization, and new pricing plans are changing the telephone's capabilities, how it is used, and the types of people who use it. A major consequence is that the telephone has become more a personal device—even a fashion accessory—than a household appliance used in common by a family. Now telephones are extensively used for social communication, for household logistics, for providing families with a sense of security, for just-in-time coordination among people on the go, and for providing friends and loved ones a continual sense of being in contact. How are these changes in capabilities, services, and usages influencing everyday life?

As older technologies have evolved and newer ones have been accepted by the general public, social scientists have added personal computers, the Internet, and mobile telephones to the mix of technologies whose effect they seek to assess. At the heart of this enquiry is the digital revolution. From the dawn of computing in World War II to the late 1980s, this revolution primarily influenced organizational life. As a result, in the 1980s and 1990s, researchers debated and documented the influence that computerization was having on such domains as organizational productivity, interorganizational coordination, employment levels, distributed work, and the quality of individual work life (Brynjolfsson, 1993; Hartmann, Kraut & Tilly, 1986; McLoughlin & Clark, 1994).

In the late 1990s, low-cost personal computers and an extensive, relatively easy to use Internet helped computers spread to the majority of households in many developed countries. Less than 9% of U.S. households had computers in 1985, but by 2001 that number had risen to 57% (U.S. Department of Commerce, 2002). Horrigan reports in his chapter in this book that by the end of 2003, 64% of American adults had Internet access, and on a typical day, 50–60% went online. In the United Kingdom, 10% of households had Internet access in 1999, but by the beginning of 2003, that number had risen to 45% (U.K. Office for National Statistics, 2004). In chapter 3, Anderson reports that 59% of Britons aged 14 years and over currently use the Internet, with 89% of these accessing the

Internet from home. From the beginning, social scientists have been documenting these developments and examining how individual lives are changing as a result (e.g., Venkatesh, Vitalari, & Gronhaug, 1985).

The growing availability of mobile telephones, personal computers, and the Internet, as well as the expansion in the range of services they offer, could lead to changes in the lives of the average citizen as profound as those that have affected organizations and economic life. As the chapters in this book document, these technologies are being used in a wide variety of ways to make everyday activities more efficient, more convenient, or just more fun. Figure 1.1, adapted from the Pew Internet and American Life project, shows the percentage of Internet users who perform various online activities on a typical day. For example, of the approximately 63% of American adults with Internet access, 48% of them send electronic mail in a typical day. Using the Internet to access news or information about hobbies, weather, and reference questions is very common.

Many of the activities for which people use the Internet are long standing and well rooted in our social system. For instance, one can maintain contacts with friends and family though telephone calls, visits, and letters or can meet new people by joining formal organizations. One can turn to the newspaper for the news or weather, go to the library for research on a variety of topics, look at advertisements and buy consumer magazines for product information, or visit the bank to conduct financial transactions. New technology perhaps makes these activities easier to perform, but it does not change their fundamental nature.

Other uses of new technology, however, seem qualitatively new. The wholesale sharing of music among strangers is one example. Even though listening to music and other entertainment is routine among teens, giving music from one's own collection to people whom one does not know is a new phenomenon. So, too, is the use of web logs ("blogs," or online diaries) to publicly broadcast what in the past would have been private writings about one's emotions and experiences. People, of course, continue to hold neighborhood yard and jumble sales to sell used merchandise, but the extension of these sales to reach a national market via online auction sites, such as eBay, makes them different in kind.

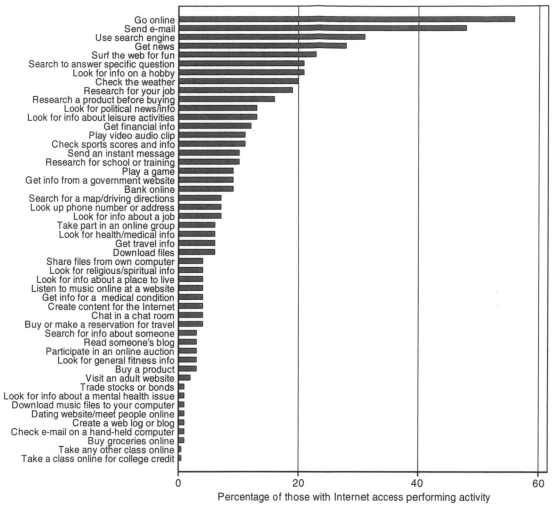

Figure 1.1. Daily Internet activities. Bars represent the percentage of U.S. adults with Internet access who perform the listed activities on a randomly selected day. As of 2005, approximately 62% of U.S. adults had Internet access. From the Pew Internet and American Life Project (2004).

By definition, this penetration of the Internet and mobile telecommunications into the way we achieve fundamental goals of connecting to other people, finding information, or entertaining ourselves is changing how we live our lives. Do these changes have larger consequences, beyond the activities that are directly affected? Does using the Internet change the amount of time people spend on the other activities they engage in? Does performing an activity online take time from comparable offline activities or from different ones? Does the use of mobile phones and online communication change people's social resources—the number of people they communicate with, the type of social ties they start and maintain, and the quality of the relationships they have with other people? Does the time people spend online or using mobile phones influence their commitment and contribution to their local communities? What, in sum, are the social effects of the new information and communication technologies? Our goal in this book is to explore these questions by examining the diverse uses, channels, and people involved with the new ICTs.

What Do We Mean by Social Impact?

We identify four broad approaches to describe what researchers mean by the phrase "social impact of information technology." One can think of these approaches as arrayed in concentric circles around the activities that the technology directly supports, with the narrowest approach directly concerned with changes in how particular tasks are performed and the broadest considering the effect on society as a whole.

Technology as a Tool

In the first and narrowest of these approaches, the new ICTs are seen as mere tools that allow people to achieve relatively static goals and to perform old activities in slightly new ways. In the process, people may change their efficiency in performing these activities. Using the Internet to find product information, to research health information, to make vacation plans, or to bank online are examples of a new technology seeming to change the efficiency of routine transactions, although not all commentators agree that personal efficiency is necessarily increasing (e.g., Landauer, 1996). The use of e-mail to exchange birthday greetings or news of the day illustrates this model in the interpersonal realm. Listening to music online serves the same ends as listening to it over the radio with a small shift in mechanism. In these cases, the new technologies are displacing one activity with a functionally equivalent alternative. Although this switch might have important consequences for the companies and institutions involved—as the recording industry's legal moves to prohibit the downloading of music from the Internet demonstrate—from the individual's point of view, downloading music rather than listening to the radio or buying a CD merely swaps one medium for another. The main effects are on cost and convenience. The empirical research reported in chapters 5 and 6 by Robinson and de Haan, and by Kraut, Kiesler, Boneva, and Shklovski, suggests that the Internet is used in part to substitute among functionally equivalent activities in this manner. For instance, much of the time people spend online seems to come from time previously spent watching television.

Technology That Shifts Goals

A second approach to research on the social effects of new technologies emphasizes the ways they allow or encourage qualitative changes in daily life. People use the technology to accomplish new goals, not just to achieve the old ones more efficiently.

Turkle (1997), for example, describes how young adults use the anonymity of online communication as a resource, allowing them to experiment with identities, such as playing at being another gender. To document this type of social impact, researchers often use qualitative research techniques to create rich descriptions of how new technology is used. In chapter 16, Ito and Okabe's account of the use of mobile telephones in Japan suggests that teens use these devices to carve out a sphere of privacy in a country where family relationships, architectural styles, and living arrangements otherwise constrict it.

A substantial body of research, much reviewed in this text, has examined how the Internet and the mobile phone are expanding and altering our social networks. In this case, the new technologies do not simply influence users' social life but shape it to a substantial degree. It can even be argued that the technologies allow people to enact new kinds of social relationships, therefore bringing a qualitative change to their lives. In addition to chapter 16, chapter 15 by Ling and Yttri emphasizes the way mobile phones allow young people to achieve a new intimacy with their close friends, and in chapter 14, Boneva, Quinn, Kraut, Kiesler, and Shklovski focus on how instant messaging allows friends to feel part of a larger peer group. McKenna and Seidman's chapter 19 describes how people, especially those who are shy or socially awkward, slowly develop online social relationships from which they might otherwise be excluded, and in chapter 18, Cummings, Lee and Kraut demonstrate that Internet communications help high school students prevent their friendships from fading when they move away to college.

Personal Welfare Outcomes

The third approach to social impact stretches beyond the activity itself to emphasize how changes in people's behavior, as a result of using new ICTs, have consequences for their more general well-being. Researchers consider the effect on personal welfare in many spheres, including physical and mental health, privacy, educational attainments, and even income. As a central example, researchers are interested in how new computer- and phone-based technologies change the social relationships for which they are used. The researchers are interested in this change not simply because interpersonal communication is one of the most frequent uses of these new technologies (e.g., e-mail is the most frequent use of the Internet, as seen in figure 1.1; see Kraut et al., 1999, for a fuller discussion), though this aspect plays a role in their interest. Rather, a major source of the fascination with the effect of new technologies on social relationships is that these relationships have important consequences for both physical and psychological health (Cohen, Underwood, & Gottlieb, 2000). People with stronger social networks tend to be both healthier and happier (e.g., Diener, Lucas & Oishi, 2002). If the new ICTs enable larger or more diverse social networks, or if they change the quality of relationships among people who communicate using them, then these technologies could significantly affect well-being.

Many of the chapters in this book focus on how social relationships are supported by the new technologies, on how using the Internet and mobile phones translates into social capital, and on the benefits that often result from having social support. Shklovski, Kiesler and Kraut's chapter 17 is a quantitative review of the literature, asking whether Internet use leads to changes in social interaction. Licoppe and Smoreda's chapter 20 examines how people use mobile phones to keep up with people who are both nearby and far away, Boneva, Kraut and Shklovski's chapter 14 asks how online communication helps teens feel a connection to their peer groups, and McKenna and Seidman's chapter 19 examines how different types of people benefit from online relationships.

Educational researchers have long tried to assess the benefits that students gain from various types of computer-aided instruction in the classroom (see Fletcher-Flinn & Gravatt, 1995, for a review). Computing is now used frequently at home and in other settings outside of the classroom by children for communicating, playing games, and seeking information about hobbies or other leisure interests, as well as for explicitly educational purposes. Researchers want to know whether the noneducational uses influence educational success. Because Internet use in particular is such a text-intensive experience, there is reason to think that a wide range of computing and Internet use will have educational outcomes. Surveys indicate that having a home personal computer (PC) increases students' performance on standardized tests, at least modestly (Attewell & Battle, 1999). Chapter 11, by

Jackson, von Eye, Bocca, Barbatsis, Zhao, and Fitzgerald, presents results from an experiment suggesting that spending time online can increase children's scores on standardized reading tests, as well as their school grades.

Societal Impact

The fourth approach to social impact again extends beyond the specifics of the activity, but this time it examines the consequences for the larger society. Sproull and Kiesler (1991) describe these as secondary effects of new technology. As an example, although individual consumers may use the telephone to increase business or household efficiency or to enrich their social networks and reduce isolation, the wholesale adoption of telephony might also have influenced both the development of high-rise office buildings concentrated in urban areas and the suburbanization of residential choice (Pool, 1977).

A related area of change involves the relationship between the development of new ICTs and economic growth (Organization for Economic Co-operation and Development, 2003). The knowledge society requires new skills, especially perhaps computer skills, but also a greater acceptance of the role of technology in our lives. We need not only to use the new formats but to have a greater adaptability in relation to them. This issue is examined in chapter 7, where Brynin suggests that computer usage and skills, as well as positive attitudes to computer technology, are associated with higher wages for both men and women. This is a significant social effect, if true (see, e.g., Kling, 1996, for an alternative view), because historically men have held a technological advantage in employment.

In an influential book, Putnam (2000) documented a broad decline over recent decades in civic engagement and social participation in the United States. Citizens vote less, go to church less, discuss government with their neighbors less, are members of fewer voluntary organizations, have fewer dinner parties, and generally get together less for civic and social purposes. Putnam argues that this social disengagement has major consequences for the social fabric, leading to, among other things, a more corrupt, less efficient government and to more crime. Further, Putnam provides evidence to suggest that the introduction and diffusion of television in the 1950s had a major role in causing this social disengagement. In an age of the privatization of entertainment, people spend more time at home compared to earlier generations—isolating themselves from other people and removing them from opportunities for civic dialog.

Although elements of this theory are contested, researchers have a concern that the widespread use of computing and the Internet might have similar effects on community and civic engagement. Chapter 12 considers whether personal uses of the Internet for communication and information gathering have wider effects on the links between citizens and their communities. The authors suggest a model with two paths. People who were already concerned about community recruit the Internet for the purposes of networking within the community and enhancing its goals. In contrast, the researchers suggest that those who use the Internet heavily but do not have already existing concerns about community may become less engaged because of their Internet use.

A Theoretical Framework for Understanding the Social Impact of Technology

We have just identified four approaches to understanding the social impact of new technology, suggesting that use of new information and communication technology can change what people do or how they do it. They can have effects both on individual well-being and on society as a whole. This book concentrates mostly on the first three types of impact. The fourth and most general type of impact is often difficult to discern, as such a change could take decades to become visible. In addition, major societal change of this sort has many sources. For example, although telecommunication technology might have contributed to suburbanization, so did transportation and climate control technologies. In addition, this demographic tread was also influenced by population growth, tax policies, and shifts in the location of jobs.

The chapters in this book display a diversity of theoretical and empirical approaches, some of which even conflict with each other. Yet there is more agreement among them than appears on the surface, in terms both of theory and of substantive conclusion. All of the chapters are empirical. Their observations and conclusions about the effects of new technolo-

gies are grounded in systematically collected data. Most subscribe to a common, albeit implicit, theoretical framework that postulates that technology can have substantial effects—both on the individual and on society—resulting from an aggregation of small and seemingly inconsequential changes. Substantively, there is some agreement that new information and communication technologies are having a moderate impact, especially in terms of qualitative changes in the way users are achieving both old and new goals (see Wellman and Haythornthwaite, 2002). There is less agreement, however, about the personal and social outcomes to which these changes in behavior may be leading.

Although technologies "can open, close, and otherwise shape social choices" (Dutton, 1996, p. 9), the authors of this volume's chapters all acknowledge that people shape the impact that technology has on their lives. People influence the technology itself, directly as inventors and indirectly through market feedback. More important, people shape the impact that technology has on their lives by choosing which technology to use and how to use it. New technologies are incorporated into people's lives, merging with their old manner of doing things; in the process, these new technologies are producing, whether by design or by accident, new ways of achieving goals, new forms of association, and new expectations. This incorporation leads to a potential for wider personal and social impact.

The preceding discussion implies an adaptive model of social change, similar to the one spelled out in Fischer's analysis of the effect of the introduction of the residential telephone, *America Calling* (1992). According to this model, people have relatively stable motives, wants, and needs. The stability may come about because of institutional forces, such as the pursuit by wage earners in their peak earning years of more efficient use of their time, or of personal forces, like the needs of teenagers and adults for different types of social contact. When a new technology is perceived as relevant, individuals and organizations appropriate it to serve their old motives. As the chapters in part III show, people are concerned with exploring social relationships; when new technologies become available, people exploit those same technologies for this purpose.

This adaptive view of the social impact of the new technologies is related to the long tradition of research into the social effects of the mass media. Although some early accounts suggested that the mass media have strong effects (e.g., Marcuse, 1972), and a less strong version of this view still has adherents (Signorielli & Morgan, 1990; Iyengar, 1997), a common finding of research in this area is that media content is selected, absorbed, and used in ways that are meaningful to consumers or to groups of consumers, and that media content in turn adapts to this usage. Social effects are therefore limited.

Yet, paradoxically, the small changes in behavior enabled by new technology can have much larger personal and social consequences. The difficulty or ease of performing certain actions via particular technologies leads to nondeliberate or, perhaps more accurately, nonmindful shifts in activity. This fundamental property of human behavior has been documented since at least the 1940s, following Zipf's *Human Behavior and the Principle of Least Effort* (1949). In particular, we believe that new information and communication technologies typically have features that make them easier and more convenient to use than previous tools, and these features lead to shifts in how people use time. A clear example can be seen in the ability of television to "steal" time from activities that its users really prefer doing. Most research shows that people strongly prefer visiting and conversing with friends to watching television (e.g., Kubey & Csikszentmihalyi, 1990). However, because television programming is always available, does not require coordination with others, and is packaged to be consumed in small chunks, watching television can be a less deliberate act than alternative behaviors. Broadcasters exploit this feature by scheduling unproven shows after highly popular ones, knowing that viewers will typically continue watching their channel without deliberately choosing to do so—simply because it requires no explicit action. Television is an easy way to kill time, and therefore people perhaps use it more than they want to. This type of nondeliberate choice about time can have large personal and social consequences. The sedentary leisure associated with television viewing is one component of the epidemic of obesity affecting most developed societies (see Kaiser Family Foundation, 2004, for a review of research on television viewing and childhood obesity). As previously discussed, Putnam (2000) argues that television viewing is also one cause of the lack of

civic participation that has characterized America since the 1950s.

Scholars are concerned with whether such new ways of communicating have larger consequences on users' health and happiness. The research literature to date on this issue is mixed. For example, longitudinal research by Kraut and others, using samples of the general population (Kraut et al., 1998; Bessiére et al., under review), indicates that heavy use of the Internet increases depression, but this finding has not been replicated with college-student samples using cross-sectional research designs (e.g., Sanders, Field, Diego, & Kaplan, 2000; LaRose, Eastin, & Gregg, 2001; Waestlund, Norlander, & Archer, 2001).

As technology's features change, however, its potential effect on psychological and social outcomes can also change. In the case of the Internet, we have recently seen three developments that could influence the amount and type of social impact it can have on people who use it. First, although Kraut and his colleagues (Kraut et al., 1999) observed that the early Internet was used primarily for social purposes, before 1995, features of both the user-base and the technology favored communication with relative strangers and other weak social ties. Too few people were online in those early days for most people to be able to communicate with their own friends and family. In addition, besides e-mail, the popular communication applications of the day were distribution lists, Usenet groups, and chat rooms, all of which brought together strangers interested in common topics. Today, the growth of the web has expanded options from using the Internet primarily for social purposes to more individualistic, recreational, and informational uses. Second, the growth in the number of people online also means that if people use it socially, they have more options to connect to others about whom they care (expressing or reinforcing strong ties) than they had several years ago. Third, the growth of services like Instant Messenger over older services like chat and multiuser dimensions may allow users to increase contacts that are characterized by strong ties rather than by weak ones. Thus, the potential for social adaptation of the Internet has increased enormously.

Our conceptualization builds on the interweaving of three distinct elements: technology, social networks, and the content of what passes within and between the networks via this technology. Each influences the other; none is dominant. It is even difficult to disentangle technology from society, as new outcomes evolve through the continuous translation of meaning between the two (Latour, 2000). Machines are neither slaves nor merely imposed, but increasingly live in symbiosis with us. In the notion of the "cyborg" this integration is within the individual (Haraway, 1991), as we become increasingly dependent even physiologically on technology. But there is no need to go that far. Society and technology are also closely integrated, so much so that we must not only avoid technological determinism but be wary of how we construct our pictures of the social determination of technology. Indeed, ideally "the boundary between the social and the technical is part of the phenomenon to be investigated" (Grint & Woolgar, 1997, p. 37). However, empirically this is difficult. What we see in the world is a range of evolving relationships between society and its technologies that build incrementally on the previous forms of these relationships. This book describes and analyzes some of these incremental changes.

How Do We Determine That the New Technologies Have a Social Impact?

The goal of the chapters selected for this book is to understand how everyday use of mobile phones, computers, and the Internet is changing the lives of their users and those around them. Rather than relying on speculation or on the elaboration of possibilities, which are so frequent in the technology and popular media, the chapters all bring empirical evidence to bear on this question. They address factors that can have a direct domestic or community effect and that are potentially measurable. We say "potentially measurable" because there are both theoretical and methodological hurdles to overcome before we can effectively assess the social impact of the new ICTs. We outline these hurdles in this section before going on to describe the contribution this book makes to understanding the social impact of new technologies.

The theoretical framework described previously leads to some ambiguity in assessing the social impact of new technology. It would be easier to write about and to measure the effect of technology if technological determinism were true. If telephones and computers were similar to medications prescribed by a doctor in standardized doses, then assessing their effects would be relatively straightforward. One could conduct a randomized trial in which there are two groups—one randomly assigned to use a new technology and the other not. After a suitable period, it would be possible to measure how the groups spend their time, the number of friends they have, their grades in school, their income, their knowledge of local political issues, their likelihood of voting, their depression, and other outcomes of interest.

In reality, people choose and appropriate the technologies whose putative impact we are trying to assess. As a result, people's choices influence how the technology is used and, indirectly though market feedback, change what is available to be used. These conditions undercut the rationale for experiments, because interventions such as the adoption or specific usage of a technology are not exogenous events controlled by an experimenter. To a large degree, these interventions are controlled by the user. It is then empirically difficult to distinguish changes associated with use of a technology from changes that are endogenous, caused by the users themselves in deciding how to use technology.

Researchers have adopted a variety of techniques, both qualitative and quantitative, to assess the effect of the new technologies under these circumstances. The qualitative research method used by a number of chapters in this book is especially suited to understanding how people have incorporated new technologies into their lives. The chapters in part III of this volume, focusing on teenagers' use of the Internet and mobile phones, use qualitative techniques to illustrate how teens are expanding the times and places in which they exercise their need to be social with both intimate partners and peer groups. These qualitative studies are also crucial in assessing the effect of new technology on welfare outcomes. For example, we need to understand to whom people are talking online, and what they are talking about, to understand the effect that Internet use is having on the types of social support available to them.

However, both qualitative and quantitative analyses have difficulties in determining causality. One technique that both methods use is to ask respondents to assess the impact the technology is having on their lives. Yet people find it very hard to compare their states before and after some event, such as the introduction of technology (Bem & McConnell, 1971). In addition, they are often unable to distinguish their theories of what the impact should be from what has actually happened (McArthur, 1980). These well-known problems in participants' accounts of social change apply to their assessment of the impact of new technology as well. Take chapter 2 as an example. Although respondents in the Pew studies report that e-mail caused them to increase their interaction with friends and family, longitudinal data from the Pew project actually show that visits with friends and family decrease more for Internet users than for non-Internet users (Shklovski, Kraut, & Rainie, 2004).

Although quantitative research and especially large-scale survey-based analyses are needed to test statistical models and to generalize conclusions from a small sample to the population as a whole, using quantitative technologies to determine the causal impact of the new technologies is fraught with ambiguity. The aim of much of the quantitative research is often the same: to relate change in technology use (e.g., acquisition of the Internet) to change in behavior (e.g., social networks' size or technological skill) or to relate change in behavior with some measure of well-being (e.g., depression or income). For example, in assessing how Internet use affects time that people spend on other activities, one technique is to correlate these variables through regression analysis while controlling for other factors that might influence time use. However, even if we see an association between Internet use and time devoted to other activities, the resulting cause-and-effect relationships may still be ambiguous. Because certain types of people select into high or low usage or into particular types of usage, it is difficult to assess the extent to which their Internet use per se is responsible for the final time use we observe. We might instead be observing the effects of unmeasured personal and social characteristics that influence the selection process.

The debate over the effects that Internet use has on social capital illustrates the ambiguities in interpreting correlations between technology use and either behavioral or welfare outcomes. In chapter 2 Horrigan notes that a "consistent finding in the body of work produced by the Pew Internet and American Life Project has been that the Internet enhances social connectivity in a variety of ways" (p. 22). Horrigan also notes that "those who go online have more robust social lives than non-us-

ers" (p. 22). This assertion, however, is based on cross-sectional comparisons of Internet users to nonusers, or on respondents' own claims about the effect that e-mail is having on their social relationships. Although the association between Internet use and a robust social life might be correct, the causal conclusion is not clear.

Differences other than Internet use between Internet users and nonusers may account for differences in total social contact. As an example, Internet users are younger and richer than nonusers and may be more extraverted as well (see chapter 12). These attributes are themselves associated with social interaction. A similar causal ambiguity occurs if one claims that Internet use is associated with reductions in social contact (Nie, 2001). Here, too, we often cannot tell whether the Internet causes this, or whether more socially isolated people are drawn into certain types of Internet use.

In general, cross-sectional data are ill-suited for drawing causal conclusions. Longitudinal data that describe how each person in a sample changes over time are needed to model change (Singer & Willet, 2003). Panel data, for which the same person is interviewed more than once, create the opportunity to test causality through "before and after" measures. For instance, Gershuny (2003), responding to the hypothesis that Internet use leads to declines in social contact, uses panel data on changes in time use among both Internet users and nonusers to show that time spent online does not reduce sociability. As Shklovski, Kiesler, and Kraut note in chapter 17 and Kraut, Kiesler, Boneva, and Shklovski note in chapter 6, longitudinal and cross-sectional analyses of the same data can lead to different conclusions about the effect of new technology in people's lives. The researchers also observe, however, that panel data are no panacea for the ambiguities in assessing causation. Panel designs are subject to attrition, learning effects, and sometimes confounding factors. Nevertheless, when panel and cross-sectional results diverge, the former provide stronger inferences about causal impact (Shklovski et al., 2004).

Even if one could identify an unambiguous causal link between use of a new technology and change in behavior, this still leaves open the issue of the value of the change. It is granted that the new technologies have some social effect, but many scholars contest their value and meaning. To some extent, this issue can be seen as an extension of older concerns about the mass media. Although it was seen as essential to a functioning democracy, some early critics saw only the negative effects of mass media—for instance, through globalization and standardization. Although many see the increased flow of information as essential to freedom, others have seen in this growth only a sort of information overload, so that the fundamental becomes banal and trivial, reducing real freedom. As Marcuse (1972) wrote in the case of religious choice in the modern age, "Why not try God?" (p. 25). The new social system reduces and dissipates meaning. There are parallels with Putnam's view, already discussed, except that for Marcuse the media can be said to provide "too much" society, whereas in Putnam's view there is too little.

The argument continues into the age of the Internet. On the one hand, new developments lead to greater flexibility and choice. For instance, people have greater personal control over their lives through the creation of a "networked individualism" (Haythornthwaite & Wellman, 2002, p. 32). On the other hand, the massive expansion of networks, and networks of networks, may simply be an indicator of a postmodern world characterized by "ephemerality and fragmentation" (Harvey, 1990, p. 328), by a "deculturation of culture" (Baudrillard, 1990, p. 92). Although Castells (2000) acknowledges the ability of the decentralized Internet to cross-cut traditional flows of information and power, societies "are finally and truly disenchanted because all wonders are on-line" (p. 406).

These arguments give some idea of the different theoretical conclusions that can be extracted from the empirical work currently underway. Scholars, technologists, and social critics currently debate whether the new technologies, and the Internet in particular, are positively or negatively transforming economic and social life (e.g., Anderson, Bikson, Law, & Mitchell, 1995). For instance, some argue that Internet use cuts people off from genuine social relationships, as they sit alone at their terminals or communicate with anonymous strangers through a socially impoverished medium (e.g., Stoll, 1995; Turkle, 1997). Others argue that the Internet leads to more and better social relationships by freeing people from the constraints of geography or from isolation brought on by stigma, illness, or schedule. Some claim the Internet allows people to join groups on the basis of common interests rather than convenience and that this com-

munity building has a positive value (e.g., Katz & Aspden, 1997; Rheingold, 2000); others worry about cyber-ghettoization and Balkanization (Ebo, 1998).

However, there is an empirical quandary: How can we confidently conclude that the effects we observe are good or bad? We have limited theoretical means for such an evaluation of social or psychological welfare. This problem does not apply to "harder" outcomes such as the effects of social change on people's incomes or health. With the softer aspects of social welfare, however, it is difficult to relate the outcomes that we observe to real needs or even to preferences. The solution we instinctively adopt is to assume that almost everyone prefers socially desirable outcomes (such as having either many friends or close friends). Yet people vary in the degree to which they as individuals need or value these same outcomes.

These concerns are not mere caveats but serve to place some limit on what researchers can expect to be able to say. Yet, as this discussion has demonstrated, the range of questions that research is beginning to address is quite startling. Underlying these inquiries are the much larger questions that we asked at the outset: Will the new information and communication technologies have a significant social effect, and if they do, will the change be positive? The following chapters seek to respond to these questions.

The Contribution of This Book

Information Technology and Social Change

Part I of this book provides a quantitative introduction, first to the extent to which people are using the new information and communication technologies in the United States and in Europe; second, to the significance of this new behavior in the context of the full range of things that people do in their daily lives; and third, to some of the distributional effects of technological change. The chapters together indicate that many technological outcomes are complex but also have potentially important implications for social change.

In chapter 2, Horrigan summarizes research that the Pew Internet and American Life project has been conducting since 2000, in particular describing the diffusion of the Internet in terms of both users and domains of use. Because The Pew Internet Project has conducted national cross-sectional telephone interviews of a sample of Americans since 2000, it can examine how Internet use has changed over this period. Internet use is still growing, although growth is slowing as a large proportion of the U.S. population already has access. By the end of 2003, approximately two-thirds of adults in the United States used the Internet at least occasionally, with most logging in from home. The Pew project paints a detailed description of the domains in which people use the Internet: developing and maintaining social ties, seeking health care information for themselves and those for whom they care, maintaining involvement in national and local civic issues, seeking government information and services, searching for product information and making commercial transactions, and creating content that others can read and download. Figure 1.1 in this introduction comes from the Pew Internet Project.

In chapter 3, Anderson makes good use of panel data. He shows the diffusion of information and communication technologies in Europe. For example, from 1998 to 2001, Internet adoption rates in U.K. households more than doubled from 24% to 51%. Mobile phone use grew even faster, almost tripling from 24% in 1998 to 69% in 2001. However, this aggregate growth conceals some complexities, which form the heart of the chapter. In particular, a minority of those who began to use the Internet or a mobile phone dropped this service. Although adoption easily outstrips churn, the result indicates that we cannot view diffusion of technology as a uniform process. It is much more erratic. Moreover, adoption and dropout are distinct processes, influenced by quite different needs. Those who move in or out of access do not jointly form an intermediate category of less committed users.

In chapter 4, Raban and Brynin use some of the same European data that Anderson analyses to examine the social distribution of diffusion, concentrating on differences in ICT use that are dependent on age. Although adoption of new technologies declines with age, and "technophobic" attitudes increase, there is considerable variation within age groups. We should not dismiss the older population as being technologically illiterate. In fact, the key distinction determining use or nonuse is not age itself but resources. Older people tend to be poorer. In addition to the effects of age itself, their relative lack of resources determines their use of the new information technologies.

The differences in the amount and type of use of the Internet by different demographic groups can have consequences both for the other activities in which people engage and for aspects of their social welfare. Robinson and de Haan ask in chapter 5, where does people's online time come from? Prior research showed that time for television watching came from functionally equivalent activities: listening to the radio, reading newspapers, attending movies, and so on. Robinson and de Haan's research uses time-diary data from the United States and from the Netherlands to examine the source of Internet time. According to their functional equivalence hypothesis, one should expect decreases in daily activities that perform the same functions as the Internet. Because the Internet enhances communication, the retrieval of information, and entertainment, displacement effects might be expected in time spent on social activities and mass-media use. By comparing Internet users with nonusers, both the U.S. and Dutch research indicates that Internet use is displacing television viewing but not social activities or reading.

Chapter 6, by Kraut, Kiesler, Boneva, and Shklovski, partially replicates Robinson and de Haan's results. Using longitudinal data, this research indicates that people who use the Internet most also show the largest decline in television viewing. However, this fall is not steepest among those who use the Internet for entertainment or information seeking, as the functional equivalence argument would imply. Rather, the largest drop in television viewing occurs among people who use the Internet to meet new people and communicate in online groups.

In chapter 7, Brynin's research goes a step beyond the examination of how the use of new technology influences time spent on other activities by examining its effect on users' income, specifically looking at gender differences. The goal here is to test the extent to which technology usage is inherently gendered. Using panel data from the United Kingdom and cross-sectional surveys from other European countries, Brynin shows that although there are a number of differences between men and women in their technology behavior and attitudes, these are rather superficial. The data indicate, for instance, that attitudes toward computers are highly malleable and follow usage of computers at least as much as they cause it. Moreover, the gender differences in attitudes are declining; younger women's ICT adoption rates are little different from those of young men. The most important finding concerns the welfare effects, here measured by the effect of computer attitudes on wages. Positive attitudes toward computers are associated with higher wages, and this effect is somewhat greater for men than for women. However, when the author looks at the effect of computer skills rather than actual usage or attitudes, the effect is about equal by gender, though very slightly greater for women. Familiarity with computers through the work environment has a potentially significant welfare impact, but the effects of skills and motivation need not exactly coincide.

Technology in Context: Home, Family, and Community

Some of the chapters in the previous section indicate in the aggregate a measure of uncertainty in the adoption of new ICTs. For instance, people drop in or out of usage in rather complicated ways. Bakardjieva's chapter 8, which is based on qualitative research, looks at this uncertainty in a different way, through the detailed history of people's decisions to use a computer or the Internet for the first time.

Here we can see that a range of influences, which are not easy to predict, need to be taken into account. In Bakardjieva's view, it is possible to discern patterns in usage (e.g., in how people use technology as an interface with the real world, and how other people mediate this relationship). Bakardjieva finds that we cannot see either the technology or the individual user as an "enclosed" entity. Computer behavior is a complex package of interrelationships.

Venkatesh, Chen, and Gonzalez, in chapter 9, also use qualitative methods to examine how new technology varies between individual and family usage. Computers are primarily individual tools, but this research team believes that a family portal device would be desirable for the home because it is a shared technology, supporting, for example, facilities like a shared mailbox. Families have mixed feelings toward this shared resource compared to their feelings toward individualized PCs. The results suggest an important finding: domestication of services through new home technologies does not have

to run in parallel with individualization. It is possible to design new technologies for groups, like the family, rather than for individuals.

In chapter 10, Livingstone also looks at the family, but in this case, because of the importance of privacy, sharing is out of the question. Livingstone's concern is with children and the imposition of "sharing" by parents who assert a right to oversee children's use of the Internet. Although parents have a rationale for this supervision—to protect children from sexual or financial pressures—the danger is that there is then no boundary around a child's private life. The online world of children is different from the world of adults. Although we wish to ensure that adults online cannot harm our children, the rights of children as individuals need to be respected.

Jackson and colleagues, in chapter 11, present data from the HomeNetToo project, an in-depth study that examines use of computers and the Internet over 16 months among 140 children and their parents. The sample population was primarily lower income and African American. As in Anderson's research, there was churn in Internet use among the children in Jackson's study, with 8% stopping Internet use entirely over the course of the study and 38% stopping e-mail. The research examines the factors predicting the extent to which children in the sample used the Internet. However, perhaps, the most interesting facet of this research is the examination of consequences of Internet use in terms of social relationships, time allocation, and academic achievement. Among other findings, the research indicates that children who use the Internet most improve their performance on standardized reading exams and on their school grade point averages.

Chapter 12, by Carroll, Rosson, Kavanaugh, Dunlap, Schafer, Snook et al., moves the focus of attention from the individual in the household to the larger community. Their field site is a midsized American university town in a rural setting, which has had one of the longest standing community networks in the United States. Eighty-seven percent of the town's residents use the Internet on a regular basis, and 75% of the town's businesses advertise online. In this well-connected community, approximately 5% of web traffic is local, connecting to Internet hosts located in the area. Although by no means the dominant focus of Internet activity in the town, use of local Internet services and content is strong. The researchers conclude that many residents recruit Internet technology in the service of their community-oriented goals (e.g., activism, staying informed, participating in groups). Yet when people do not have these community-oriented goals, increased use of the Internet may actually decrease their level of activity in the community. The Internet can therefore both complement and displace community activities, with the effects being different for different people.

New Technology in Teenage Life

As many researchers have noted both in this book and elsewhere, youth is a major predictor of use of new ICTs. Young people in their teens and early twenties have adopted new ICTs *en masse*, integrating computers, mobile phones, and the Internet into their daily routines and then expanding these routines to new uses. The commercial success of some of the most interesting service innovations—instant messaging, music downloads, and cellular telephones with prepaid minutes, among others—were fueled by the special needs of this demographic group. The chapters in this section use both qualitative and quantitative data to examine in detail how young people are using these new technologies. The dominant theme in all of the chapters is that teenagers and young adults incorporate the new technologies to handle developmental problems that uniquely characterize their age groups.

In chapter 13, Greenfield et al. attempt to give a detailed examination of the functions for which teenagers use the Internet. They report that interpersonal communication and downloading music dominate teens' time online. Almost all of their online communication is with other teens whom they know from school and other local contexts, although online gaming and participation in chat rooms puts them in contact with strangers. By analyzing the multiple conversational threads intertwined in an online chat room, this chapter provides a rich description of how teenagers use online conversation to cope with the perennial concerns of adolescent life, such as gender and racial identity, sexual development, and romantic partners.

Boneva and colleagues, in chapter 14, also examine how teenagers use Internet communication to deal with traditional concerns in adolescent life. These researchers review a range of data to compare instant messaging communication with com-

munication by phone calls and in-person visits. Although most teen communication is with local friends and acquaintances, instant messaging supports more communication at a distance than do other modalities. A central question that this chapter addresses is why teens use instant messaging so frequently even though they report enjoying instant messaging conversations substantially less than those conducted by phone or in person. The answer seems to be that instant messaging allows young people to build and maintain social ties with particular friends as well as to create a sense of belonging with groups of peers with whom they do not necessarily feel close.

The graphs by Ling and Yttri in Chapter 15 show that in Europe, young people in their teens and early twenties are the ones mostly likely to have Internet access and to own a mobile phone. These young people use these technologies to create a lifestyle distinct from that of the adult world and even in opposition to it. The technologies therefore play a part in a sort of domestic power play. Ling and Yttri examine this tension in the case of mobile phones; this tension is also apparent in chapter 10, where the focus is the Internet.

In chapter 16, Ito and Okabe describe how teenagers' easy access to mobile phones (compared to a home landline phone) frees them from reserving the phone for consequential communication. Teens can then use their mobile phones to exchange moment-by-moment experiences in their daily lives with special partners, and thus to have a more continuous sense of connection with friends. The technology can shift how much time users spend with others and alter the nature of their interaction with them. Although Ito and Okabe describe problems of adolescence, they go beyond this to identify how mobile telephones are used to handle some concerns that may be unique to Japanese life, and how previous generations of pagers and other technologies paved the way for mobile phones.

The Internet and Social Relationships

One of the central questions animating much social science research on the social impact of new technology is the specific effect this has on social relationships. Chapters by Horrigan and by Robinson and de Haan address this theme through a general overview of how people use the Internet, and of its influence on how they spend their time.

Chapters by Greenfield and colleagues, by Boneva and colleagues, and by Ito and Okabe provide rich descriptions of how teens are incorporating both Internet and mobile telephone technology into their lives to communicate with friends and to solve problems of social relationships. The chapters in the final part of this book focus on the consequences of Internet use for social interaction and social relationships.

In chapter 17, Shklovski, Kiesler, and Kraut provide a quantitative literature review, a meta-analysis, of 16 empirical studies investigating the association of Internet use with measures of social activity. They reach both substantive and methodological conclusions. Collectively, the data show little influence of Internet use on social activities. Effect sizes were generally small and inconsistent. However, research methods make a difference in the conclusions one draws. The results depend both on the type of social relationship analyzed (family versus friend) and the type of research method deployed (cross-sectional versus panel surveys). For instance, studies using panels indicate that Internet use increases social interaction with friends more than interaction in other types of relationships.

Cummings, Lee, and Kraut, in chapter 18, examine use of the Internet by young people to maintain social ties after they move from high school to college. The researchers find that when young adults move away from home to go to college, technology-mediated communication retards the natural decline in social relationships that young adults often experience as a result of the move. However, this effect varies by type of technology. Even though speaking by phone with a partner is a much stronger predictor of a close personal relationship than Internet-based communication, the latter is most likely to help young people maintain relationships. However, the authors argue that this effect of communication on psychological closeness does not reflect intrinsic properties of the communication media but instead reflects the marketing and regulatory decisions in the United States that lower the cost of Internet communications. If it is possible to generalize from this, in recent years and in the United States at least, Internet communication rather than telephone communication has had the largest effect on preserving friendships.

In chapter 19, McKenna and Seidman review several of their own studies on the mechanisms though which computer-mediated communication influences the development of social relationships. Unlike the other research presented in this volume, their research includes laboratory experiments as well as surveys. Experiments, in which participants are randomly assigned to communication either over the computer or through another modality, have the advantage of unraveling the causal direction in the link between communication modality and strength of social relationships. They are able to show that students who are assigned to meet in an Internet chat room grow to like each other more than those who first meet face-to-face. Whether the very short-term interactions that participants have in the laboratory experiment can be generalized to the longer-term development of social relationships, however, is an open question. McKenna and Seidman's main conclusion is that there are few unqualified effects of using the Internet. Although they believe Internet communication can have transformational effects, these depend on individual differences in personality and motivations and on the nature of the online groups to which they become attached.

We argued above that it is difficult to evaluate the real welfare significance of the new technologies, and in particular those which relate to social ties. Are strong ties "better" than weak ties? Licoppe and Smoreda, in chapter 20, go further in breaking the concept of social ties into more revealing formulations. They show that people use technologies in different ways to support different types of relationships. Each has its different mode. For instance, a "connected presence" is maintained not through the communication of information in detail and depth but through little gestures, which are easier with some technologies than with others. Technology is used to enable people to find an effective "rhythm" to their social lives. Although most of this research is qualitative, the authors use quantitative data to show that the frequency of phone calls decreases—and their duration increases—when people move further away from those they are emotionally close to, but frequency increases and duration falls when the distance decreases. People try to maintain their strong ties, but they also use different techniques depending on the behavioral costs of communication. If communication is cheap, they can maintain their ties with large quantities of relatively meaningless chitchat. When it is expensive, each communication episode is made to count more.

Acknowledgments. This book was based on a workshop supported by the National Science Foundation under grant 0227969. This chapter was partially supported by National Foundation grant ISS 9900449.

References

Anderson, C. A., Berkowitz, L., Donnerstein, E., Huesmann, L. R., Johnson, J. D., Linz, D., Malamuth, N. M., & Wartella, E. (2003). The influence of media violence on youth. *Psychological Science in the Public Interest, 4*(3), 81–110.

Anderson, R., Bikson, T., Law, S., & Mitchell, B. (1995). *Universal access to e-mail*. Santa Monica, CA: RAND.

Attewell, P., & Battle, J. (1999). Home computers and school performance. *The Information Society, 15*(1). 1–10.

Ball-Rokeach, S., & Cantor, M. (Eds.) (1986). *Media, audience and social structure*. Thousand Oaks, CA: Sage.

Baudrillard, J. (1990). *Revenge of the crystal*. London: Pluto.

Bell, D. 1973. *The coming of post-industrial society*. New York: Basic Books.

Bem, D. J., & McConnell, H. K. (1971). Testing the self-perception explanation of dissonance phenomena: On the salience of premanipulation attitudes. *Journal of Personality and Social Psychology, 14*, 23–31.

Bessiére, K., Kraut, R., & Kiesler, S. (Under review). *Social integration, Internet use, and depressive affect: A social resources approach*. Pittsburgh, PA: Carnegie Mellon University.

Brynjolfsson, E. (1993). The productivity paradox of information technology. *Communications of the ACM, 36*(12), 66–77.

Castells, M. (2000). *The rise of the network society*. Malden, MA: Blackwell.

Cohen, S., Underwood, L. G., & Gottlieb, B. (2000). Social relationships and health. In S. Cohen, L. G. Underwood, & B. Gottlieb (Eds.), *Social support measurement and interventions: A guide for health and social scientists* (pp. 3–25). New York: Oxford University Press.

Diener, E., Lucas, R. E., & Oishi, S. (2002). Subjective well-being: The science of happiness and life satisfaction. In C. R. Snyder & S. J. Lopez (Eds.), *Handbook of positive psychology* (pp. 463–473). London: Oxford University Press.

Dutton, W. (Ed). (1996). *Information and communication technologies: visions and realities*. Oxford: Oxford University Press.

Ebo, B. (Ed.). (1998). *Cyberghetto or Cybertopia?* Westport, CT: Praeger.

Fischer, C.S. (1992). *America calling: A social history of the telephone to 1940*. Berkeley: University of California Press.

Fletcher-Flinn, C. M., & Gravatt, B. (1995). The efficacy of computer assisted instruction (CAI): A meta-analysis. *Journal of Educational Computing Research, 13*(3), 219–241.

Gershuny, J. (2003). Web use and net nerds: A neofunctionalist analysis of the impact of information technology in the home. *Social Forces, 83*(1), 141–168.

Grint, K., & Woolgar, S. (1997). *The machine at work: Technology, work and organization*. Cambridge, U.K.: Polity.

Gurevitch, M., & Levy, M. (Eds.). (1987). *Mass communication yearbook* (vol. 6). Thousand Oaks, CA: Sage.

Haraway, D. J. (1991). *Simians, Cyborgs and Women: The Reinvention of Nature*. London: Free Association Books.

Hartmann, H., Kraut, R. E., & Tilly, L. (1986). *Computer chips and paper clips: Technology and women's employment*. Washington, DC: National Academy Press.

Harvey, D. (1990). *The condition of postmodernity*. Oxford, U.K.: Blackwell.

Haythornthwaite, C., & Wellman, B. (2002). Moving the Internet out of cyberspace. In B. Wellman & C. Haythornthwaite (Eds.) *The Internet in everyday life* (pp. 2–41). Oxford, UK: Blackwell.

Huston, A. C., Donnerstein, E., Fairchild, H. H., Feshbach, N. D., Katz, P. A., Murray, J. P., et al. (1992). *Big world, small screen: The role of television in American society*. Lincoln: University of Nebraska Press.

Iyengar, S. (1997). Overview. In S. Iyengar & R. Reeves (Eds.), *Do the media govern?* (pp. 3–8). Thousand Oaks, CA: Sage.

Janowitz, M., & Hirsch, P. (Eds.) (1981). *Reader in public opinion and mass communication*. New York: Free Press.

Kaiser Family Foundation. (2004). *The role of media in childhood obesity*. Menlo Park, CA: Kaiser Family Foundation.

Katz, J., & Aspden, P. (1997). A nation of strangers? *Communications of the ACM, 40*(12), 81–86.

Kling, R. (1996). The shifting balance between privacy and social control. In R. Kling (Ed.), *Computerization and controversy: Value conflicts and social choices* (pp. 614–636). San Diego, CA: Academic Press.

Kraut, R., Mukhopadhyay, T., Szczypula, J., Kiesler, S., & Scherlis, W. (1999). Communication and information: Alternative uses of the Internet in households. *Information Systems Research, 10*(4), 287–303.

Kraut, R., Patterson, M., Lundmark, V., Kiesler, S., Mukhopadhyay, T., & Scherlis, W. (1998). Internet paradox: A social technology that reduces social involvement and psychological well-being? *American Psychologist, 53*(9), 1017–1031.

Kubey, R., & Csikszentmihalyi, M. (1990). *Television and the quality of life: How viewing shapes everyday experience*. Hillsdale, NJ: Lawrence Erlbaum.

Landauer, T. K. (1996). *The trouble with computers*. Cambridge, MA: MIT Press.

LaRose, R., Eastin, M. S., & Gregg, J. (2001). Reformulating the Internet paradox: Social cognitive explanations of Internet use and depression. *Journal of Online Behavior, 1*(2), NP.

Latour, B. 2000. Technology is society made durable. In K. Grint (Ed), *Work and society: A reader* (pp. 41–53) Cambridge, UK: Polity.

Marcuse, H. (1972). *Counterrevolution and revolt*. Boston, MA: Beacon.

McArthur, L. Z. (1980). Illusory causation and illusory correlation: Two epistemological accounts. *Personality & Social Psychology Bulletin, 6*(4), 507–519.

McLoughlin, I., & Clark, J. (1994). *Technological change at work*. Buckingham, UK: Open University Press.

Nie, N. H. (2001). Sociability, interpersonal relations, and the Internet: Reconciling conflicting findings. *American Behavioral Scientist, 45*(3), 420–435.

Organization for Economic Co-operation and Development (2003). *ICT and Economic Growth*. Paris: Organization for Economic Co-operation and Development.

Pool, I. d. S. (Ed.). (1977). *The social impact of the telephone*. Cambridge, MA: MIT Press.

Putnam, R. (2000). *Bowling alone: The collapse and revival of American community*. New York: Simon & Schuster.

Rheingold, H. (2000). *The virtual community: Homesteading on the electronic frontier* (Rev., 1st ed.). Cambridge, MA: MIT Press.

Sanders, C. E., Field, T. M., Diego, M., & Kaplan, M. (2000). The relationship of Internet use to depression and social isolation among adolescents. *Adolescence, 35*(138), 237–242.

Shklovski, I., Kraut, R., & Rainie, L. (2004). The Internet and social participation: Contrasting sross-sectional and longitudinal analyses. *Journal of Computer Mediated Communication, 10*(1), np.

Signorielli, N. & Morgan, M. (1990). *Cultivation analysis: new direction in media effects research*. Newbury Park, CA: Sage.

Singer, J. D., & Willett, J. B. (2003). *Applied longitudinal data analysis*. New York: Oxford University Press.

Sproull, L., & Kiesler, S. B. (1991). *Connections: New ways of working in the networked organization*. Cambridge, MA: The MIT Press.

Stoll, C. (1995). *Silicon snake oil*. New York: Doubleday.

Turkle, S. (1997). *Life on the screen*. New York: Touchstone Books.

U.K. Office for National Statistics. (2004). *Social trends*, London: The Stationery Office.

U.S. Department of Commerce. (2002). A nation online: How Americans are expanding their use of the Internet. Washington, DC: Government Printing Office.

Venkatesh, A., Vitalari, N. P., & Gronhaug, K. (1985). Computing in the home: Shifts in the time allocation patterns of households. *Communications in the ACM, 28*(5), 512–522.

Waestlund, E., Norlander, T., & Archer, T. (2001). Internet blues revisited: Replication and extension of an Internet paradox study. *CyberPsychology & Behavior, 4*(3), 385–391.

Wellman, B. & Haythornthwaite, C. (Eds.) (2002). *The Internet in everyday life*, Oxford: Blackwell.

Zipf, G. (1949). *Human behavior and the principle of least effort*. Cambridge, MA: Addison-Wesley.

Information Technology and Social Change

John B. Horrigan

Portraits of American Internet Use

Findings from the Pew Internet and American Life Project

The purpose of this chapter is to outline the scope and patterns of Internet usage among Americans as seen through the eyes of the Pew Internet and American Life Project, which has conducted periodic surveys of Americans' Internet use since early 2000. The series of studies produced by the Pew Internet Project has, with one exception, provided snapshots of respondents' online behavior. This series has the advantage of pursuing a wide range of topics and identifying trends over time. By producing research reports designed to appeal to a broad swath of the interested public, press, and policy makers, the objective of the Pew Internet Project's research is to provide unbiased information about the Internet and its effect on people's social lives. This research approach brings with it limitations; namely, the ability to delve in depth into some topics and, absent a panel of respondents, to pin down precisely the causal links between Internet use and outcomes in people's lives. Nonetheless, casting the net widely in a series of research reports allows the Pew Internet Project to see trends in net usage that yield insight into the Internet's effect on people's lives.

With this in mind, this chapter will summarize the Pew Internet Project's findings in the following areas:

- Social connectedness
- Online health care information
- Community and civic engagement
- How users shape the Internet

Before proceeding, here are some basic facts about Internet penetration and trends over the past several years. When the Pew Internet Project conducted its first survey in March 2000, 46% of Americans 18 years of age and older identified themselves as Internet users, meaning they had access at home, work, or from some other place. At that time, 81% of adult Americans had access at home and 48% at work. By the end of 2003, 64% of American adults had Internet access—88% at home and 52% at work; about 4% of Internet users have Internet access only at a place other than home or work. Throughout the life of the project, between 50% and 60% of online Americans say that they go online on the typical day, a number that tends to fluctuate seasonally, with fewer people logging on during the average day in the summer months and more logging on in the winter. For teens (ages 12 to 17 years), 73% were online as of the end of 2000—a figure that rose to 79% by middle of 2003. Between teens and adults, about 148 million Americans were Internet users by the end of 2003.

As Internet penetration saw a steady increase over the course of 3 years, means of access changed quite substantially. In June 2000, only a handful of Internet users with access at home—5%—had high-speed Internet connections in the house. By December 2003, that number had increased to 35% (or about 30% of all Internet users). Between population growth and increase in the share of online access at home (from 81% to 88%), there has been nearly an eightfold increase in the number of home high-speed Internet surfers in the United States from mid-2000 to the end of 2003. Figures 2.1 and 2.2 show the increases in the overall number of American adult Internet users and those with broadband connections at home from mid-2003 to the end of 2003. The number of adult Internet users has risen from approximately 86 million to 128 million from 2000 to 2003, whereas the number of Americans with high-speed connections at home has risen from 5 million to approximately 38 million.

Social Connectedness

The Internet's role in people's social lives remains a topic of ongoing debate among scholars and the general public, and the debate animated early research by the Pew Internet Project. A landmark study by Kraut, Scherlis, Patterson, Kiesler, and Mukhopadhyay (1998) found that heavy Internet users report higher levels of depression and isolation than non-Internet users. In a similar vein, Nie (2000) worried that time spent online takes people away from everyday face-to-face interactions with family and friends, thereby undermining social life.

There is controversy, however. Subsequent research by Kraut et al. (2002) was unable to replicate the earlier finding that the Internet had an isolating effect on people.

In contrast, the consistent finding in the body of work produced by the Pew Internet and American Life Project has been that the Internet enhances social connectivity in a variety of ways. The project's first report, *Tracking Life Online* (Rainie, 2000), found that the Internet generally broadens people's social worlds. Those who go online have more robust social lives than nonusers, but even within this context, e-mail helps users connect to family and friends—often in ways that would not have happened without the Internet. A majority of Internet users report that e-mail improves connections to family and friends and that the Internet has increased the frequency of communication with family and friends.

The Pew Internet Project explored this issue in a richer fashion in our panel study entitled *Getting serious online* (Horrigan, 2002a). The survey for *Tracking life online* was conducted in March 2000. In March 2001, we reinterviewed about 40% of our March 2000 respondents, asking them the same questions we did a year earlier. During that time frame, Internet penetration rose from 46% to 57% among respondents. We found some interesting cross currents in this longitudinal study. First, people were a bit less likely to sing the socially connective praises of e-mail the second time around, and they also reported less frequent e-mailing with key friends or family members. Internet users in this time interval also reported a drop in the frequency of visiting family or friends and of calling people

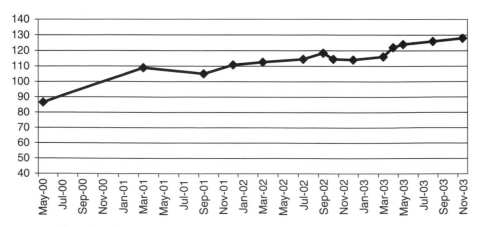

Figure 2.1. Number of adult American Internet users.

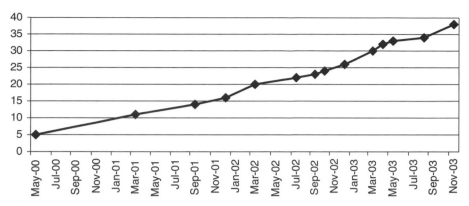

Figure 2.2. Number of Americans with broadband connections at home.

just to talk. The decrease was from 74% of Internet users in March 2000 saying they had visited a family or friend to 66% in March 2001. However, levels of satisfaction with e-mail as a means of communicating with family and friends remained high: 79% of users said e-mail was a useful way to communicate with family in 2001, although that number was down from 88% in 2000. For frequency of e-mailing family, this number dropped from 21% of respondents who said they e-mailed key family members every day in 2000 to 12% who said this in 2001. People's assessment of whether the Internet improved connections with family and friends also fell modestly. Three in five (60%) said the Internet improved "a lot" or "somewhat" connections with family members in 2000, and this number fell to 56% a year later; the numbers with respect to friends fell from 69% to 65%.

Second, and in a bit of a contrast, people reported that the content of their e-mail became more serious over the course of the year. This very robust conclusion came about through four questions. Respondents were asked to think of a family member with whom they frequently e-mail and also a friend they frequently e-mail. They were then asked whether they send e-mails seeking advice from this particular family member and friend and whether they send e-mails sharing worries. Uniformly, there was a reported surge in the amount of e-mailing to seek advice and to share worries. In March 2000, 45% of respondents said they e-mailed a family member for advice—a figure that rose to 56% a year later; with respect to e-mailing a friend for advice, the share doing this rose from 48% to 56% in the same time frame. When asked whether they had e-mailed a family member regarding some-

thing they were worried about, 44% said this in March 2001, up from 37% in 2000. When asked the same question regarding friends, 47% said they had sent an e-mail about a worry in 2001 compared with 39% in 2000.

Third, there was an increase in a number of online activities that require that the user trust the reliability of the Internet. Use of the Internet for job-related research grew substantially from March 2000 to March 2001, from 25% to 36% among respondents with access at work. Online transactions also witnessed strong growth in this period; 47% of Internet users said they had bought something online in March 2000, and this number increased to 53% in March 2001. For travel services, 34% of respondents had purchased a travel service online in March 2000, with that number growing to 42% a year later. Growth was strong in all categories of users, from novice to veteran, but was particularly rapid for people who were inexperienced net users in March 2000. In general, online users showed a greater predilection to expand the set of online activities undertaken in a year's time. The Pew Internet survey asked about 24 different online activities, and Internet users had tried, on average, 11 of them in March 2000. A year later, when asked about the same 24 activities, users had tried an average of 14 of them.

What to make of this? We conclude that as people gain online experience, it appears that the dazzle of the Internet fades a bit as it becomes the norm. However, its importance does not fade, as indicated by the growth in serious e-mails, as well as other trusting online activities, such as transactions. The findings also indicate that the Internet shifts the mores of communication in time—whereas people might have picked up the phone to share serious news, in time they turn to the Internet. These findings point to the social nature of technology adoption and even to the Internet's "network effect"—the more people are online doing socially connective things, the more others do the same.

Finally, it is important to point out that the longitudinal study found similar e-mailing patterns among early and late adopters of the net. In the debate about whether the Internet is socially isolating, some have argued that whatever connective effects were found were a function of early adopters who, it was argued, have larger social universes anyway. As late adopters populate the Internet, the argument was that the connective effects would vanish. Our longitudinal study did not support these contentions. The patterns in the growth of serious e-mailing and trusting activities such as online transactions were roughly the same for people who were new to the net in 2000 as they were for online veterans from 2000. In fact, the surge in serious online activities was greatest for year 2000 newcomers.

Online Health Care Information

One of the most striking findings of the Pew Internet Project is in the area of online health care. Lots of Internet users go online for health care information—about 62% in 2003 reported doing so when asked whether they go online to look for health or medical information; this is up from 55% in 2000. In the Pew Internet Project's July 2003 study, respondents were asked whether they had used the Internet for any of 16 health care topics, ranging from queries about specific diseases or medical problems to fitness or health insurance problems. Not surprisingly, when prompted with topics the total number of "yes" responses to online health care questions grew: fully 80% of online Americans have searched for at least one of the 16 health topics (Fox, 2003).

In addition to tracking the size of the online "health seeker" population, the Pew Internet Project also looks into detail on how and for what reason people conduct online health searches. For instance, more people go online for health care information on behalf of someone else (54%) than they do for themselves (43%). The web has also become a way to get a second opinion—or at a

minimum, supplementary information—about a condition. About 70% of online health information seekers say that their last health search had to do with a specific condition or illness. Typically, if the health seeker is searching on his or her own behalf, the online search is conducted before a visit to the doctor. If a person is searching on behalf of someone else, the search more often occurs after a doctor's visit. Overall, health seekers greatly value the convenience of getting more information when they want it, and about half of all health seekers said that online health searching improved how they take care of themselves and led to them asking more questions of their doctor.

The outcomes of health care searches are only as good as the data available on the Internet, and the Pew Internet Project's 2002 report *Vital Decisions* (Fox, 2002) asked respondents about the process they undergo in assessing online health care information. Though many health care experts recommend that users check out the sponsor of a health care site, check the date of the information, and go to as many as six sites for health care information, *Vital Decisions* found that few health care searchers adhere to such a rigorous search regimen. Online health searchers typically start at a search engine (as opposed to a medical site), and they usually visit between two and five sites. Only one-quarter of health seekers check the source of the information and timeliness of its posting on the site, and half say they rely on their own common sense to assess the reliability of online health information. Fortunately, very few people self-diagnose using online information or use online health information in lieu of a visit to the doctor. Finally, three-quarters (73%) of online health seekers have rejected health care information from a site at one time, usually because the information seemed too commercial or the source and timeliness of the information was hard to determine.

The wealth of health care information online is substantially reshaping how people interact with the health care system, and for some health seekers, it is probably not an overstatement to characterize this change as revolutionary. Patients usually spend only 10 or 15 minutes with a doctor in a typical visit, and the ability to enter the session armed with additional questions can have a powerful effect. Three-quarters (73%) of online health seekers say that online information has improved the quality of health information and services they receive. Most cite convenience as a principle benefit of online health care information: They can search when they want in the comfort and security of their home. One reason that the effect of the Internet for some health seekers has been possible is the existence of online support groups—either formally constituted ones or informal ones among friends and family. Nearly one-third (32%) of e-mail users say they have exchanged e-mails with family and friends about health care matters, and 54% of Internet users have visited a web site that provides information or support for specific conditions.

Overall, 62% of online health seekers reported in December 2002 that the Internet had improved how they manage their health care—an increase from about 50% in late 2000. These two snapshots, which show a beneficial and growing sense of satisfaction with the value of online health care information, do not mean that online health care information is leading to better health care outcomes. However, health care problems introduce uncertainty into people's lives, and the existence of conveniently accessible information helps many people reduce that uncertainty. That, in turn, leads at a minimum to a perception of improvement in health care experiences for people and, often through the exchange of information with professionals or similarly afflicted people, to real improvements in treatment.

Community and Civic Engagement

The idea of online or virtual communities is one of the oldest promises of the Internet. Through online bulletin boards, e-mail chats, or listservs, the many-to-many character of the Internet, many forecast, would connect people with common interests over distance. The Internet was established initially to connect a community—academic researchers—and as the net expanded its reach, early online communities such as the Well put people who mainly wanted to communicate with each other together over distance (Hafner, 2001). Online communities, many argued, give individuals new opportunities, give new life to geographic communities, improve democratic deliberation, and even improve government functions. The Pew Internet Project has investigated online communities and their effect directly and indirectly in studies that look at the following topic areas:

- General online community activity
- Political involvement
- E-government

Online Communities

A Pew Internet Project survey conducted in February 2001 assessed the scope of online community activity in the United States, and the survey found that fully 84% of Internet users have visited an online group or community at one time (Horrigan, 2001). About one in five Internet users (i.e., 22% of net users, or 23 million people) are active in a specific online group, meaning they e-mail their principle online group several times a week. We call net users who have been to online groups "Cyber Groupies," and they are most engaged with trade or professional groups online (21% say such groups are the main ones they contact) and hobbies (17% say they most frequently contact these kinds of group). The February 2001 survey also examined how online groups might affect local communities, and it found that 28 million Americans (25% of Internet users) have used the Internet to deepen ties with the places where they live. For local online groups, users most often gravitate to groups having to do with their local church or synagogue, a social club or charitable organization, with neighborhood groups and local youth groups trailing slightly.

Online groups seem to encourage chatter and connection among many users. About half of active online Cyber Groupies say they have met face to face people they first encountered online, and about one-third who connect to local groups say they have met people they otherwise would not have. A substantial number (about one-third) of Cyber Groupies say that the net has helped them meet people of different ages and different economic and ethnic backgrounds.

Beyond the sizable population of Cyber Groupies, online groups seem to attract new people to groups. Many online groups existed in the "real" world before the Internet, and many people simply maintain established patterns of contact with their group via the net. In part of the survey, respondents were asked about the online group they most frequently contacted via the Internet and whether they belonged to this group before they started using the Internet. More than half of Cyber Groupies (56%) joined the group after having begun communicating with it over the Internet. For local groupies, 20% joined the group after they begun communicating with it on the Internet. These findings are based on respondents self-reporting whether they joined a group after making online contact, but the findings nonetheless indicate that the Internet, perhaps because of its anonymity, provides a comfort zone for some people that draws them to group membership. Those who discover a group online and then become a member of it tend to be more ethnically and economically diverse than other Internet users. This indicates that the Internet may foster cooperation by letting people try out groups in a way that is initially nonthreatening. By reducing uncertainties inherent in joining a new group, the Internet may prompt people to join a group they might not otherwise join.

Politics Online

A subset of the broader issue of online community is how the Internet may affect democratic participation. The ability for people to use the Internet to organize for political purposes, deliver messages to public officials (and perhaps get responses), and be more informed about political issues will contribute to a more vibrant democracy, and ultimately a better community—or so goes the hope. The buzz about Howard Dean using the Internet to give momentum to his long-shot candidacy is only the latest movement in the discourse about the net's potentially transformative effect on politics.

The Pew Internet Project, in its report *Untuned Keyboards*, looked at Internet surfers use the net in the 2002 political season to see to what use people put the net during the run-up to the November election (Cornfield, Rainie, & Horrigan, 2002). About 43% of Internet users in the October–November 2002 survey said they had ever gone online for news about politics, and 22% said they had done so specifically for information about the 2002 election. Most Internet users who had gone online for political information were basic information searchers—64% sought information on candidates and their positions on issues in the 2002 election cycle. Roughly one-third got information about a candidate's voting record, participated in an electronic poll, or went online to see how an organization had rated a candidate. For fairly sophisticated activities, such as participating in an online chat about the election or donating money, only about one in 20

online political information seekers (the 43% of net users who had ever looked for political information online) did these things.

More recently, findings from the Pew Research Center for the People and the Press and the Pew Internet Project show a growing reliance on the Internet as a source for political news (Pew Research Center, 2004). Just before the start of the 2004 primary season for Democrats, 22% of Internet users had gone online for news about the 2004 election. This matches the share of Internet users doing this at about the time of the 2002 midterm election. With the hotly contested 2004 election, the share of Internet users who went online for news or information about politics was up sharply compared to 2000; in 2000, 33% of Internet users said they got political news online, a number that rose to 52% by November 2004 (Rainie, Cornfield, and Horrigan 2005). Moreover, the share of Americans who say they regularly learn something about the political campaign from the Internet rose to 13% in January 2004 from 9% in 2000, at a time during which Internet penetration grew from 46% to 64%. For all Americans, local television news, cable television news, nightly news, and the daily newspaper remain the main way by which people learn about political campaigns (at a rate about three times that of the Internet). However, for young people (between the ages of 18 and 29 years), the Internet rivals the daily newspaper, national nightly news, and, intriguingly, comedy shows—a regular source for political news. Cable television news is the leader, with 37% of those between 18 and 29 years of age saying that they regularly learn something about the campaign from this source, versus 20% who say the Internet.

Untuned Keyboards also asked whether searching for political information online was associated with higher rates of voting in 2002. In a nutshell, merely being an Internet user is not associated with higher rates of voting, but having sought out information online about the 2002 midterm election was associated with higher voting rates, even controlling for demographic characteristics, socioeconomic status, age, gender, self-reported level of interest in the election, and past voting behavior. It is possible that other factors are more the cause of higher voting rates among searchers of online political information than the act of doing a search. The findings, therefore, do not show conclusively that online political information will increase political participation; at best, it indicates that the availability of online information may draw a few additional people who already have a predisposition to vote to the polls. The findings do not say anything about what leads people to do these searches or how to get them to do them. Some intervention to encourage people to do online political searches might in itself diminish any positive effect on voting the searches may have. Nonetheless, the findings at least do not dash the hopes of advocates who hope the Internet will enhance political participation.

Electronic Government

Connected to the idea that the Internet can revive democracy is the idea that the Internet may help reinvent government—with a corresponding improvements, it is hoped, in a community's level of social capital (Fountain, 2002). By improving how government functions, how citizens communicate with government, and how nonprofits and government can cooperate to address problems, e-government holds out the possibility of a more effective institutional structure for government. Pew Internet Project research on e-government has focused on characterizing the frequency with which Internet users go to government web sites and how local government officials use the web to connect with citizens. Most recently, a cross-channel comparison was conducted of the different means by which people contact government and success rates in people's interactions with government, using different means.

When asked whether they had ever visited a government web site of any sort, 47% of Internet users said they had done this in March 2000. This figure rose to 56% in Pew Internet Project's November 2002 survey and 66% in the August 2003 survey. With Internet penetration rising overall from 46% to 63% of American adults in that time frame, use of e-government web sites rose sharply in this time frame. Online users do a wide range of things when going to government web sites, with tourism and recreational information topping the list and research, downloading forms, and inquiring about services also being popular. In each case, more than 50% of online users have done these things. In the August 2003 survey, respondents were probed more deeply about their pursuits of government information online, much like was done with respect to online health and medical information. When asked about e-mailing government, looking

for information about health or safety issues, getting recreational or tourist information from the government, researching official government records, or applying for benefits, fully 77% of Internet users had tried at least one of these things online. An increase in supply of e-government web sites (both in terms of quantity and quality) during this period is probably an important driver of the growth in the use of government resources online.

In addition to looking at users, the Pew Internet Project also conducted a survey in cooperation with the National League of Cities to see how local government officials use the Internet in the course of their duties. The survey of 520 local officials in 2002 found that the Internet is widely used in local government; 88% of the officials said they use e-mail as part of their duties. Most (73%) say that e-mail helps them better understand public opinion, 56% say e-mail has improved relations with the community, and 32% say e-mail has influenced a policy decision. Still, local officials said that the telephone remains the primary means for connecting with citizens (Larsen, 2002).

Partly because of this last finding from local government officials, the Pew Internet Project embarked on an e-government study that compared the different channels—letter, telephone, Internet, and in-person visits—that people use to contact government, and asked respondents whether they were satisfied and successful in their interactions with government. The survey found that, excluding mailing tax filings, 54% of all Americans contacted the government in the year before the survey, with a variety of reasons cited. Some 30% contacted the government to carry out a transaction, 25% to get information about a specific question, 19% to express an opinion, and 11% to get help solving a problem. Nearly three-quarters (72%) of Internet users contacted the government in the prior year compared with just 23% of non-Internet users. In terms of self-reported success in the contact from government, 63% of all respondents said they were successful in accomplishing what they wanted; 65% of Internet users and 53% of non-Internet users were successful.

One question that immediately arises from these results is whether the different contact and success rates with the government for Internet users and nonusers have something to do with the Internet. Multivariate analysis finds that Internet use is associated with higher rates of contacting the government, holding a number of demographic and socioeconomic factors constant. The finding that the Internet has an independent effect on the frequency of contacting the government withstands concerns about bias in survey design. A source of concern for a survey that asks people about different means of government contact, with an Internet theme throughout, is that responses will inflate the incidence of government contact using the Internet. In the August 2003 survey, however, respondents were asked before the series of Internet-related questions whether they contacted the government in the past year, and by what non-Internet means. The finding that Internet users contact government more often than nonusers holds up when analyzing non-Internet means of contact. About 24% of non-Internet users said they contacted the government last year (by phone, by writing a letter, or in person); 47% of Internet users did this. As noted, when asked about all means of contact, including using the Internet, online users are three times as likely to make contact as nonusers. This indicates that two things are going on. First, Internet users, for whatever reason (even when income and education are taken into account) are inherently more likely to contact the government, and second, the Internet, as an additional channel for contact, encourages more frequent contact with government.

When it comes to pinning down whether Internet use has an independent effect on different outcomes, there are a number of things in motion that make it difficult. Different channels are used for different types of government interactions, and different reasons for government contact are inherently more likely to be successful (e.g., it is probably easier to successfully conclude a transaction than to say that one's expression of opinion about a policy matter successfully influenced the outcome). Nonetheless, multivariate analysis shows that Internet use in itself is not associated with successful outcomes with government—irrespective of why a person has contacted the government (i.e., whether performing a transaction or inquiring about a service). The multivariate analysis showed that those who preferred the Internet and the telephone as a means of contact with government were more likely to be successful than those who preferred letter or in-person contact—again, regardless of the reason for contact. Finally, though about one-quarter of Internet users say the Internet has improved their interactions with the government, people are more likely to prefer contacting the government by telephone than by e-mail or through the web.

Because Internet use seems strongly associated with higher rates of contact with the government, it seems fair to conclude that the Internet is an additive channel. People have an additional way to contact the government, with obvious conveniences, and they use it for contacts they might not otherwise make. Whether or not this additional means of contact is a help is another matter.

As noted, it perhaps helps the constituents feel better about government, at least for one-quarter of Internet users, but the Internet is not associated with higher success rates when it comes to people's interactions with government. The Internet does not appear to help people's capacity to address the matters that bring them into contact with government. Those who prefer the Internet to contact government are more successful in resolving the reason for the contact, but it seems likely that this is because these people bring better problem solving skills to the issue.

Users Shaping the Internet

Focusing on users invites the temptation to concentrate on what people get off of the Internet—whether it is news, music, health care information, or other entertainment content such as videos. Inquiring about e-mail patterns or frequency of posting to online chat rooms begins to get at how people shape the Internet in terms of content they put online. There is, in fact, a small, but arguably influential set of Internet users who post information to the web, thereby shaping the contours of cyberspace. The role of content creation among Internet users first came to light in Pew Internet Project research in *The Broadband Difference* report, released in June 2002, which focused on home broadband users, who represented about 20% of American Internet users at the time (Horrigan, 2002b). When asked whether they had ever created content on the Internet, such as updating a web site or posting to news groups, 39% of broadband users said they had done this—twice the rate of dial-up Internet users. On the typical day, 16% of broadband users said they had created online content, which is about three times the rate of dial-up users. The speed and "always on" convenience is a likely reason that the numbers for content creation are much higher among broadband users than those who have dial-up connections. Broadband users, as early technology adopters, also have a higher predilection for doing sophisticated Internet activities such as updating web pages.[1]

To further disentangle the issue of content creation, the Pew Internet Project April 2003 survey asked a more detailed series of questions about the types of content creation. Users were asked about whether they have their own web site, update a web site for their family or an organization to which they belong, have their own web diary (or "blog"), or post to the web photos, audio files, video files, artwork, or their writing. Overall, 44% of Internet users say they have tried at least one of these content-creating activities. This represents an upper bound of the share of Internet users who have created online content, though the average number of activities attempted of these nine categories is low (1.8 activities). For home broadband users, 54% have done content creation of some sort, with average users having done 2.1 content creation activities. Looking at specific activities, 8% of Internet users say they have their own web site (20% of broadband users say this), 3% have blogs (4% for broadband users), and 21% post photos online (31% for high-speed home surfers). For a grouping of young Internet users, with a mean age of 25 years, online self-expression plays an important role in their Internet experience. Many of them (30%) have their own web site, 12% have their own blog, and 29% read the blogs of others (compared with 11% of all net users).

The creative activity associated with online content creation can have greater meaning for particular segments of the population. The Pew Internet Project conducted a callback survey in November 2003 of 809 Americans who identify themselves as artists. In the general population, about 30% of Americans say they practice some artistic activity, and approximately 10% say they get income from their art. Among the general artistic population surveyed in late 2003, 16% have their own web site (twice the rate of the general population of Internet users), with most posting samples of their art online. For paid artists, 24% have their own web site, and another 15% market their art via another web site. About half of paid artists use the Internet to collaborate with other artists, and 13% say the Internet is their most important source of ideas and inspiration; 36% say purchased or borrowed media are their most important source of inspiration, and 26% say performance, shows, or museums. For a significant portion of America's artistic community, the Internet is part of their creative process, an important means of connecting with other artists, and a way to market to potential buyers.

The existence of a set of online users who are ardent content creators has two implications for the Internet. First, a significant set of users will likely demand robust high-speed capacity in both directions on the network. Not unlike electric utilities who must have enough generating capacity to handle peak electric demand on a seasonal basis, providers of network services may need to provide enough bandwidth to accommodate users who have high demand for uploading information to the Internet. Second, individual content creators seem to value an Internet where "open access" is the rule. These users—particularly the home broadband surfers—would seem to value extensive connectivity to the web and not prefer "wall gardens" as determined by Internet service providers.

Conclusions

Examining the studies conducted by the Pew Internet and American Life Project that have been summarized here, several crosscutting themes emerge.

1. *The Internet reduces uncertainty in important contexts.* The wealth of information online can serve to reduce uncertainty for Internet users in important ways, with online health care information perhaps being the best example. Issues pertaining to health care, depending on their severity, introduce uncertainty into people's lives, and the typically brief face time that people have with health care providers can contribute to additional informational uncertainty. The ability to obtain information online—either from health care sites or online support groups from similarly afflicted people—is a source of both comfort and the capacity to ask better questions of a health care professional. Being able to surf for health care information at their own convenience is greatly valued by users and helps explain why many Internet users say health care information online has improved how they manage their health. The way in which online communities seem to draw people is another example of this phenomenon. When asked about the online community in which they were most involved, about half of Internet users say they

found the group online first and only later considered themselves as belonging to the group. These joiners were more ethnically and economically diverse than other online group members. Coupled with the fact that a sizable number of online groupies say they have met people of different ages and socioeconomic backgrounds in cyber groups, it would appear that the anonymity of the net and the ability to repeatedly interact with a group helps some people come to a place where they feel they belong to a group.

2. *The Internet as information utility is an encouragement to civic engagement for some users.* Examining news gathering about politics online and e-government, the Internet offers an avenue for engagement with civic life for some users who are probably on the edge of civic engagement anyway. The act of going online for political news during the 2002 election cycle was associated with a higher rate of voting for users, holding other things constant. Similarly, Internet use does seem to foster additional contact with government, though not higher success rates in solving problems (except for those who, for whatever reason, prefer online means to solve problems). However, this conclusion needs some caveats. Net users who have problem-solving skills bring them to their preferences for the Internet to deal with government, and the consequent higher success rate with using these means to address problems. The survey results about early 2004 online election surfing indicate that people (especially the young) are more reliant on the Internet as a source for election news and less so on radio and nightly national news broadcast. For e-government and politics, this probably reflects substitution effects more than real Internet effects. Nonetheless—especially when it comes to increased voting rates in 2002 and additional government contact among Internet users when looking at the various channels people use to communicate with government—it does seem that the Internet gets at least a few additional interested people involved with civic life.

3. *The Internet as societal connective tissue.* The results from the Pew Internet longitudinal survey show that the Internet seems to become a substitute for some face-to-face visits among users, but that users also, in time, shift discussion of some weighty matters to e-mail. Respondents in the longitudinal survey reported a decrease in frequency of contact with friends and family in a year's time (both in terms of frequency of visits and e-mails) but a sizable increase in e-mails sharing worries or seeking advice. Other trusting online activities also increased, such as doing transactions online and relying on the Internet for work-related research. Evidence from other Pew Internet surveys indicates a connective role for the Internet in times of crisis. Following September 11, Internet users were active in e-mailing about the events (72% of all users e-mailed about September 11), with many using the tragedy to connect with friends with whom they had lost contact. One-third posted comments to a chat room, with most reporting that discourse in chat rooms were civil. It is not possible to connect the flurry of e-mailing to outcomes (e.g., whether it helped people cope better with the crisis), but the large numbers of net users turning to e-mail indicate that, at a minimum, there is a perceived benefit to using e-mail and chat rooms during times of crisis.

4. *Internet users shape the net; they do not just consume online information.* The predilection among some Internet users to post information online, whether through images or audio files, suggests the importance of the Internet as a vehicle for creativity, not just for the exchange of information in e-mails and online forums. The Internet is clearly a two-way street for many, especially those with broadband connections at home. With the growing penetration of broadband to the home, this indicates that an Internet that is open and with fast uploading speeds will be of value to many users, particularly those with a creative bent.

In closing, it is important to note that the Internet effects identified in Pew Internet research—whether in online health care information or community life—rest largely on the self-reports of survey respondents. This is an important limitation, as it does not prove that the Internet is causing an improvement in people's health or communities. People's perceptions about the Internet's effect are not the same as measurable impacts. However, positive perceptions of the Internet's benefits may be considered a beneficial impact, particularly in cases such as health care, where online information helps reduce uncertainties and increase convenience in people's lives.

It also appears to be the case that the Internet effects identified fall predominantly on people with an existing predilection in a particular area. Those who searched for political information online in 2002 were more likely to vote than others, but this says nothing about what got them to surf the web for political information. Similarly, those who prefer the Internet as a means to deal with government may be more successful in resolving issues than those who do not, but how Internet users come by these preferences is indeterminate. The nature of the Internet's impact seems to stand on its head the old saying about being able to lead a horse to water, but not being able to make it drink. The Internet doesn't lead people to water, but for those who have already gotten there, the Internet is a tool that helps a few additional people take a drink.

Note

1. Even so, multivariate analysis comparing intensity of Internet use of broadband and dial-up users (measured by amount of time spent online on the average day, frequency of logging on, and number of Internet activities done on a typical day) indicates that the broadband connection is independently associated with greater Internet use. The analysis holds constant demographic and socioeconomic characteristics and online experience.

References

Cornfield, M., Rainie, L., & Horrigan, J. (2002). *Untuned keyboards: Online campaigners, citizens, and portals in the 2002 elections.* Washington, DC: Pew Internet and American Life Project. Retrieved on September 20, 2005 from http://www.pewinternet.org/reports/toc.asp?Report=85.

Fountain, J. (2002), *Information, institutions, and governance.* Boston: Harvard University, National Center for Digital Government.

Fox, S. (2002). *Vital decisions: How Internet users decide what information to trust when they or their loved ones are sick.* Washington, DC: Pew Internet and American Life Project. Retrieved on September 20, 2005 from http://www.pewinternet.org/reports/toc.asp?Report=59.

Fox, S. (2003). *Internet health resources: Health searches and e-mail have become more commonplace, but there is room for improvement in searches and overall Internet access.* Washington, DC: Pew Internet and American Life Project. Retrieved on September 20, 2005 from http://www.pewinternet.org/reports/toc.asp?Report=95.

Hafner, K. (2001). *The well: A story of love, death & real life in the seminal online community.* New York: Carroll and Graf.

Horrigan, J. B. (2001). *Online communities: Networks that nurture long-distance relationships and local ties.* Washington, DC: Pew Internet and American Life Project. Retrieved on September 20, 2005 from http://www.pewinternet.org/reports/toc.asp?Report=47.

Horrigan, J. B. (2002a). *Getting serious online: As Americans gain experience, they use the web more at work, write e-mails with more significant content, perform more online transactions, and pursue more serious activities.* Washington, DC: Pew Internet and American Life Project. Retrieved on September 20, 2005 from http://www.pewinternet.org/reports/toc.asp?Report=55.

Horrigan, J. B. (2002b). *The broadband difference: How online Americans' behavior changes with high-speed Internet connections at home.* Washington, DC: Pew Internet and American Life Project. Retrieved on September 20, 2005 from http://www.pewinternet.org/reports/toc.asp?Report=63.

Kraut, R., Kiesler, S., Boneva, B., Cummings, J., Helgeson, V., & Crawford, A. (2002). Internet paradox revisited *Journal of Social Issues, 58*(1), 49–74.

Kraut, R. E., Scherlis, W., Patterson, M., Kiesler, S., & Mukhopadhyay, T. (1998). *Social impact of the Internet: What does it mean? Communications of the ACM, 41*(12), 21–22.

Larsen, E. (2002). *Digital Town Hall: How local officials use the Internet and the civic benefits they cite from dealing with constituents online.* Washington, DC: Pew Internet and American Life Project. Retrieved on September 20, 2005 from http://www.pewinternet.org/reports/toc.asp?Report=74.

Nie, N. (2001). *Sociability, interpersonal relations, and the Internet: Reconciling conflicting findings. American Behavioral Scientist, 45*(3), 420–435.

Pew Research Center for the People and the Press (2004). *Cable and Internet loom large in fragmented political news universe.* Washington, DC: Pew Research Center. Retrieved on September 20, 2005 from http://people-press.org/reports/display.php3?ReportID=200.

Rainie, L. (2000). *Tracking life online: How women use the Internet to cultivate relationships with family and friends.* Washington, DC: Pew Internet and American Life Project. Retrieved on September 20, 2005 from http://www.pewinternet.org/reports/toc.asp?Report=11.

Rainie, L., Cornfield, M., & Horrigan, J. (2005). *The Internet and Campaign 2004.* Washington, DC: Pew Internet and American Life Project. Retrieved on September 20, 2005. from http://www.pewinternet.org/PPF/r/150/report_display.asp.

3

Ben Anderson

Passing By and Passing Through

It is by now quite well known that there are funda-mental differences between those who undergo brief but transitory periods of poverty and those who are in poverty, however defined, for some considerable length of time (Layte & Whelan, 2002). Transient poverty is actually fairly common: it is quite likely that many of us will, at some stage in our lives, undergo a period of poverty. However, it is far less likely that we will suffer from persis-tent poverty. If the kinds of people who suffer from transient versus persistent poverty are substantially different, then policy responses to these two phe-nomena also need to be different. Differentiating between these two phenomena requires a certain kind of survey design. This is the longitudinal panel design in which the same individuals are followed over time; it can therefore show who is currently in poverty, for how long they have been in poverty, and what factors might affect their movements in and out of poverty.

There are some obvious parallels with current approaches to measuring the incidence of informa-tion and communication technology (ICT) adop-tion rates. Cross-sectional surveys are frequently used to measure overall ICT "diffusion," and it is often assumed that such adoption rates are a one-way street. However, these measures can give a very

misleading picture of the dynamics of ICT diffu-sion, with no guidance as to who might move in and out of access to ICTs, who might be persistent nonadopters, or who might be persistently ex-cluded. The study of poverty dynamics, as opposed to poverty incidence, has produced extremely im-portant results of relevance to poverty-alleviation policy-making. Might the same be true of the study of ICT adoption dynamics?

The extent to which such an analysis might matter can be seen in the United Kingdom and Eu-rope by reference to statements about participation for all in the European Knowledge Society (CEC, 2002) and the U.K. e-Society (Office of the e-Envoy, 2003). Clearly, patterns of uptake, use, and nonuse are critical to the achievement of any policy objec-tives that rely on a close to 100% universality of ac-cess to ICTs (and in most cases, ICT is conflated with Internet). The government of the United Kingdom has recently congratulated itself on the progress made with household- and individual-level Internet access (Office of the e-Envoy, 2003), citing a recent aca-demic survey (Rose, 2003) indicating that only 4% of the U.K. population does not have a reasonably accessible location from which they can access the net (home, school, work, public library). Is this rea-sonable, given that the same survey shows that 89%

of Internet users access the Internet from home and that only 48% of U.K. households had Internet access in June 2003 (Office of the e-Envoy, 2003)? Leaving aside the issue of what kind of access constitutes "useful and usable access," the report goes further in stating that, "With 61% of the population now reporting that they have used the Internet at some time, 'e-citizens' now make up a majority of the adult population" (p. 6).

As we can see, there is an explicit assumption that those who have ever used the Internet are still "cyber-minded," an assumption that clearly also pervades the European Commission's thinking in this regard. One of their most recent estimates of Internet penetration and use in Europe was based on a survey that did not ask nonusers whether they had ever been users (Gallup Europe, 2002). Contrast this with recent research on Internet dropouts, which has shown quite clearly that there are large numbers who would be in the "e-citizen" group but who, for one reason or another, either no longer use or no longer have access to the Internet. It should therefore be apparent that in any group of those who "have ever used" the Internet, some considerable proportion will be ex-users who have simply passed through. The first to notice the existence of Internet dropouts were Katz and Apsden (1998), who have since reported a consistent 10% per annum Internet dropout rate in the United States through the later 1990s (Rice & Katz, 2003). Others such as Wyatt, Thomas & Terranova (2002) and Rose (2003) for the United Kingdom, Thomas (2002) for several European countries, and Lenhart (2002) for the United States, have all either reported or analyzed the factors that might potentially affect ICT users dropping out. Thus, we are starting to understand who is most likely to become "ICT poor" or, to put it differently, who is most at risk. Indications are that loss of PC access, cost, and low perceived utility may all play a role, as may demographics (lower educational attainment, certain household types, age, gender) and historical Internet usage and experience.

It is not only in public policy that the existence of dropouts matters. Customer churn is an ever-present risk or opportunity for commercial service providers; this is especially true in a maturing market in which totally new customers are increasingly rare. Profit flows not from increasing the overall market and the company's share thereof, but through attracting customers from competitors, retaining them, and driving up the revenue they provide. At the time of this writing, the mobile telephony market in Europe is in exactly this situation. As we will see, in most northern European countries, further market growth is unlikely. In Rogers' terms (Rogers, 1995) the "late majority" are now mobile phone owners, and only the laggards (as well as the dropouts—a phenomenon he terms "discontinuance") remain. In contrast, the Internet market is still in the middle of the late majority stage in many European countries, although as we will see there is evidence that this period is ending much earlier and at lower penetration rates than many pundits had predicted.

In both the commercial and the public policy contexts, it is important to understand the overall significance of those who move in and out of ICT "poverty" and of those who are more permanently ICT poor, because there may well be important and significant differences between them. Those who are transitory may come back to ICTs, or they may be about to become persistent ex-users because of bad experiences, low perceived utility, or other life-stage and lifestyle changes. Understanding these dynamics will be critical to the "Digital Divide" debates in the same way that poverty dynamics were critical to the debates on the persistence of poverty. If certain vulnerable groups are persistently ICT poor, and we believe that such poverty, or exclusion, could be socially problematic, then certain kinds of actions may be required.

It may also be that different ICTs exhibit different rates of poverty. Given that all ICTs are not created equal in terms of the social benefits that they afford or the profitable services that they can support, it may be that public and commercial policy can justifiably ignore some types of ICT poverty but not others. In addition, such analysis might start to indicate which ICTs, and which services they support, have greatest value to their users. If drop-out rates for mobile telephones are significantly lower than for PC-based Internet access, then perhaps this tells us something about the utility and value of mobiles compared to the Internet, either in general or for specific social groups.

Research Questions

In this context there are a number of important questions we need to ask.

1. What are the rates of passing by (not taking up a new technology or service) and passing through (take-up followed by churn), and do they vary between different ICTs?
2. Do these rates differ between different groups of people and between countries?
3. Are these rates changing over time?
4. What are the factors that seem to best predict passing through and persistent nonuse?
5. Who is therefore most at risk and what might be done about it?

This chapter presents a preliminary analysis of two data sets to start to answer some of these questions using two specific forms of ICT poverty —household Internet access and the personal ownership of a mobile telephone. In analyzing these two ICTs in a comparative manner and across a number of European countries, we can directly contrast our results with those of Rice and Katz (2003). In addition, by introducing analysis of longitudinal as opposed to cross-sectional data, we can provide a more powerful analysis both of movements in and out of ICT poverty and of the factors that are associated with—and that may even contribute to—passing through.

The next section describes these data sets. The results section begins by reporting mainly descriptive data in response to questions 1–3 and then reports the results of multivariate statistical analysis. The discussion section draws together and synthesizes the results, and the concluding section draws out preliminary implications for public and commercial strategy as well as pointing toward further work.

Data

The data comprise the results of two separate household panel studies. The first, Home OnLine, was a three-wave, ICT-focused household panel conducted in the United Kingdom between 1998 and 2001 (Anderson & Tracey, 2001; Gershuny, 2003). The second, e-Living, was a two-wave panel conducted in six European countries (United Kingdom, Norway, Germany, Italy, Bulgaria, and Israel) in 2001 and 2002 (Raban, 2004). Both surveys carried extensive items on ICT ownership and use as well as labor market activity, education and skills, social networks, attitudes, and well-being, plus

standard sociodemographic variables such as income, age, gender, household type, housing tenure, and so on. Both data sets are now in the public domain via the United Kingdom's Social Science Data Archive (http://www.data-archive.ac.uk).

Results

First we turn to the three-wave, U.K. Home OnLine data to describe who is most likely to be persistently ICT poor and who is only transiently ICT poor. We use this data set because the three waves allow us to see how many members of our longitudinal sample move in and out of ICT poverty over the 3 years. By pooling adjacent years, we increase the number of respondents who underwent a transition, thus making the group more amenable to statistical analysis. This is a standard method in panel analysis and has already been used with the same data set to analyze the effects on time-use of acquiring household Internet access (Gershuny, 2003).

Figure 3.1 shows the incidence of transitions in and out of household Internet access; figure 3.2 shows the incidence of transitions in and out of personal mobile ownership over the 3 years. These figures give some prehistory to the results presented below from the chronologically later e-Living survey and also indicate the extent to which a lot of dynamic processes underpin the apparently smooth growth of ICT diffusion.

In the case of household Internet access, we can see the rapid increase in penetration over the 3 years of the panel so that by 2001, around 50% of the longitudinal panel had access. However, by looking at the longitudinal dynamics we can see that 45% of the longitudinal sample did not have household Internet access at any wave—they were in persistent ICT poverty. Nineteen percent had Internet access at all waves (bearing in mind that household Internet access in 1998 was roughly 24%); in wave 2, 23% (19% + 4%) of the sample had some sort of transitional status (consisting of take-up and churn).

The transitions between waves 2 and 3 are more complex. Some 36% of the sample underwent an Internet-related transition of some sort between the two waves. In the case of personal mobile ownership, we can see again the rapid increase in penetration over the 3 years of the panel, so that by

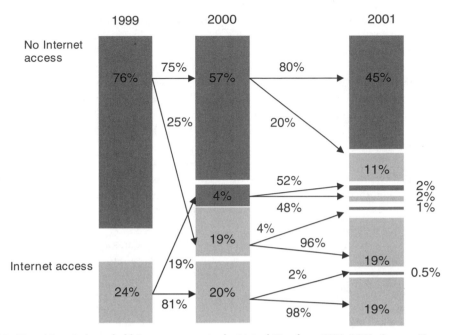

Figure 3.1. Transitions in household Internet access in the United Kingdom, 1998–2001. Source: Home OnLine waves 1–3, longitudinal sample only, unweighted.

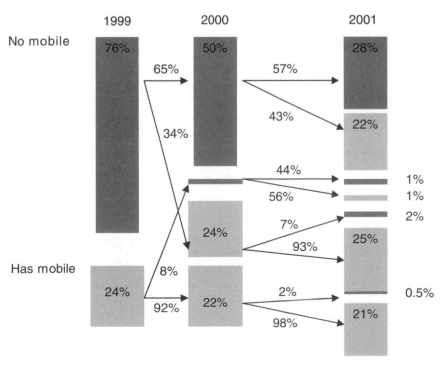

Figure 3.2. Transitions in the personal ownership of mobiles in the UK 1998–2001. Source: Home OnLine waves 1–3, longitudinal sample only, unweighted.

2001, around 70% of the longitudinal sample had a mobile phone. In contrast to Internet access, only 28% were in persistent mobile phone poverty, but equally, 21% had a mobile at all waves. Again, transitions from wave 2 to wave 3 are more complex; for instance, 7% of those who acquired a mobile between waves 1 and 2 then dropped out again. Overall, some 51% of the sample underwent a mobile ownership transition of some sort over the entire period.

The similarities between these descriptive patterns are more obvious than their differences. Overall mobile penetration is higher in 2001 than is household Internet access from a similar starting position in 1999, reflected for the most part by the higher rates at which those who had never had a mobile acquired one. This results in fewer individuals exhibiting persistent mobile poverty than persistent household Internet access poverty over the three waves of the panel. Both pictures argue against a simple one-way diffusion theory. However, take-up is clearly more substantial than churn at any point in time, even if routes through the process are

complex. This raises the question of whether the factors underlying take-up are also complex. For example, do people who adopt a new technology have similar characteristics to those who already have it, or are transitions a distinctive process, so that those who adopt and those who drop out are similar?

Who, then, are the persistently ICT poor, and what factors are associated with dropping out? These people must be the focus of digital divide concerns, as it is they who are missing out on whatever economic and social benefits may follow from household Internet access and ownership of a mobile phone.

We analyze this information below, using longitudinal regression modelling techniques but before presenting that analysis, and as we know that age is an important factor in ICT adoption rates, we introduce a descriptive figure showing the distribution of transitions by age.

As we can see in figure 3.3, older people are significantly more at risk of being persistently ICT poor but are no more at risk of dropping out. Of course it

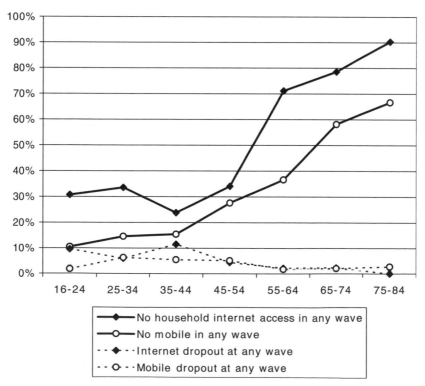

Figure 3.3. Proportion of age groups who were persistently ICT poor and who were ICT dropouts over three waves of the Home On-Line panel survey. Unweighted, age at wave 1 (1999).

is difficult to drop out of using something if it is not used in the first place, as occurs with both the Internet and mobile phones among older people. This means that at older ages, ICT poverty is more likely than experimentation. However, also of note is that at earlier ages, drop-outs are a fairly high proportion of total nonusers at any specific time.

Comparative Rates: Evidence from a Two-Wave European Panel

Having looked at the United Kingdom alone, in this section we present comparative descriptive data on the rates of passing through for household Internet access and for personal ownership of the mobile telephone in six European countries, including the United Kingdom.

Tables 3.1 and 3.2 summarize these results in terms of the six key indicators that are of interest to this discussion. These are the proportion of the population who did not have household Internet access or own a mobile phone at either wave as a proportion of the wave 2 respondents; the proportion of those who did not have household Internet access or did not personally own a mobile phone at wave 1 who did so at wave 2; and the proportion of those who did have household Internet access or personally own a mobile phone at wave 1 but did not at wave 2 ("dropouts"). In the final column, we show the number of dropouts as a percentage of the number of acquirers.

These tables show distinct differences between countries in terms of the proportion of individuals who are persistently ICT poor. For example, 29% of Norwegians did not have household Internet

access in each wave compared with 52% of Italians and 96% of Bulgarians. However, apart from Bulgaria, the rate of acquisition is remarkably similar, with between 16% (Italy) and 20% (United Kingdom) of those who did not have access at wave 1 acquiring it by wave 2. The rates of Internet dropping out are also remarkably consistent, ranging from 4% in Germany to 10% in Israel. The last column showing the number of dropouts as a proportion of the number of adopters indicates why Norway and Israel's Internet penetration growth may have slowed.

In terms of personal mobile ownership, we can see that there are more or less the same intercountry differences, with Norway having the fewest respondents who did not have a mobile phone at either wave (29%) and Bulgaria the most (84%). However, Germany has a comparatively high rate (29%), which may reflect recent market conditions in Germany and, in particular, the relatively late introduction of prepaid mobile subscriptions. These subscriptions are known to have contributed to the diffusion of mobiles across lower-income groups and among young people (P. Stollenmayer, personal communication, 2004). Again, the rates of mobile dropping out are remarkably consistent at between 3% and 5%, with the notable exception of Bulgaria, which is much higher, at 24%. Given that only 95 of the Bulgarian wave 1 respondents personally owned a mobile phone, this may not be a reliable result.

It is noticeable that with the exception of Bulgaria, the mobile phone dropout rate is equal to or marginally lower than for household Internet access, with the largest difference occurring in Israel,

Table 3.1. Summary of rates of passing through Internet access for each country.

	No household Internet access in either wave[a]	Acquired household Internet access w1–w2[b]	Household Internet dropout w1–w2[c]	Dropouts as a % of take up
UK	43%	20%	5%	22%
Italy	52%	16%	6%	23%
Germany	47%	18%	4%	18%
Norway	29%	19%	5%	50%
Bulgaria	96%	2%	7%	6%
Israel	49%	19%	10%	33%

Source: e-Living wave 1 and 2, unweighted.
[a]Percentage of all respondents in country.
[b]Percentage of all those who did not have it/did not own one at wave 1.
[c]Percentage of those who did have it/did own one at wave 1.

Table 3.2. Summary of rates of passing through personal mobile phone ownership for each country.

	No personal mobile phone at either wave[a]	Acquired mobile phone w1–w2[b]	Mobile dropout w1–w2[c]	Dropouts as a % of take up
UK	21%	51%	5%	12%
Italy	14%	56%	3%	11%
Germany	29%	39%	3%	9%
Norway	14%	58%	4%	12%
Bulgaria	84%	10%	24%	18%
Israel	18%	48%	5%	21%

Source: e-Living wave 1 and 2, unweighted.
[a]Percentage all respondents in country.
[b]Percentage of all those who did not have it/did not own one at wave 1.
[c]Percentage of those who did have it/did own one at wave 1.

where the mobile dropout rate is half that of the Internet rate.

Understanding Flux

Having established that such flux exists, we now need to know what factors might be associated with being either persistently ICT poor or dropping out. To do this, we construct two models in which the outcomes are binary. In model 1, either a person suffered persistent ICT poverty over the three waves or they did not, meaning in the latter case that they had ICT access at some point. In model 2, either a person dropped out at some point over the three waves or they did not, so the comparison here is between those who dropped out by time T_2 and those who still had access at T_2. As mentioned above, we pool the three waves to develop model 2 so that those who dropped out between waves 1 and 2 and those who dropped out between waves 2 and 3 are analyzed together as a single group. We label the models 1.1 for persistent Internet poverty, 1.2 for the equivalent in the case of mobile phones, 2.1 for Internet drop-outs, and 2.2 for mobile drop-outs.

We use a range of household level variables to understand the influence that some of the background sociodemographic variables have, and we include two wealth proxies (we do not include income because of item nonresponse): the household fixed line telephone bill and the number of cars, relative to the number of individuals in the household. We also include a range of ICT usage and attitudinal and experience indicators, together with

indicators of social networks and, in the case of models 2.1 and 2.2, ICT, household, and work transitions. The results, which are reported in detail elsewhere (Anderson, 2004), indicate that the best predictors of persistent Internet poverty are either being in a couple or being a lone parent, especially with older children; living alone and being over 55 years of age; low educational qualifications; and having strong negative attitudes to personal computers. Being female is also a good predictor, confirming that women are more at risk of being persistently Internet poor. The number of cars in the home and the household phone bill are both good predictors (negative effects), indicating that wealth or income may also play a role. Of the working status variables, being in full-time education appears to reduce the likelihood of being in persistent household Internet poverty. Overall, income differentials, educational level, gender, and age seem to underlie the patterns we observe.

With respect to persistent mobile poverty, we see a mostly similar picture but with less marked effects. Those in younger childless couples, but also those couples aged 45–54 years and older, are most likely to be in this group. Wealth, represented by the number of cars in the home, is a significant negative predictor; having no formal qualifications was a strong positive predictor. The more likely a person is to state that they only used the telephone when they had to, the more likely they are not to have a mobile phone at any wave. Interestingly, perceptions of cost did not show any effects, nor did any of the social network measures.

Turning to the dropouts, we find that the models perform just as well, if not slightly better. Model 2.1 indicates that those who either have little Internet experience or, in particular, who are nonusers in an Internet household are most at risk from losing household Internet access. In addition, those aged 24–54 years are least at risk of becoming dropouts. We see no evidence that changing work or household circumstances plays any role. In contrast to several previous studies (Lenhart, 2002; Rice & Katz, 2003), we also find no evidence that losing access to a home PC plays a role. Although the coefficients are large for this factor, they are not statistically significant. Model 2.2 is perhaps more disappointing in that, despite its relatively high r^2 score, few of the variables turn out to be statistically significant. The exception is gender. Being female appeared to considerably increase the chances of being a mobile dropout. It is possible that with a larger sample size, other of these effects may turn out to be statistically significant, but it is also possible that the pattern of mobile dropout is largely random.

These are by and large expected findings regarding ICT poverty. After all, factors associated with continuous nonuse are likely to be very similar to those associated with nonuse at one point in time. The point that is often drawn from the analysis of longitudinal (financial) poverty is that far more people are touched by poverty over time than we observe at a single time. This indicates that poverty is a larger issue but is also not necessarily a defining characteristic. When we translate to ICT poverty, however, the question then becomes whether this is a defining characteristic. To put the question somewhat differently, is there a transitional state of movement in or out of ICT usage that sets these people apart from others? Are people who adopt an ICT apparently for the first time similar to those who already have it, or are they more similar to those who drop out? Is flux therefore an issue?

We test this theory not only for Internet and mobile usage but also for PCs, using multinomial logistic regression, where movement into and out of use of a form of technology is tested both against each type of technology and against continuous access, as is continuous nonusage. The main aim is to see whether the coefficients for adoption and churn tend to be mostly in opposite directions or mostly the same. If the former, we would say that adoption is a very different process from dropping out because it is more clearly associated with various characteristics; for instance, age, gender, education, work status, or leisure interests. The alternative is that the coefficients are similar. In this case, these opposite movements should both be interpreted as a single indicator of flux—of a less committed response to the new technologies than is apparent both among those early adopters and nonusers. The results (for simplicity, also not shown) partially support the flux hypothesis. Although this is only a rough indicator, in the case of computer usage, the coefficients for adoption rates and for churn, with the base category being continuous usage, are the same sign in 10 out of 17 cases, compared to 9 for Internet usage and 8 for mobile telephony. Thus, slightly over half of the variables work the same way in the two cases. This is clearest in the case of technophobia.

Both new adopters and churners are more technophobic than continuous users where computers and the Internet are concerned. Nevertheless, remembering that the comparison is, in both cases, with continuous users, the two categories of people are by no means the same. The factors that set adopters apart from continuous users are not always the same as the factors that set churners apart from continuous users. Thus the people who churn and who adopt are to some extent self-similar but not substantially so. Flux suggests an intermediate level of commitment, but the direction in which flux occurs matters.

Conclusions

So what are we to make of these results, and what implications do they have?

To return to the starting point, the chapter illustrates that examining the dynamics of ICT poverty using longitudinal data, as opposed to merely examining growth curves using cross-sectional data, produces a different picture of the processes that underlie ICT diffusion. This picture can lead us to new insights regarding who may be missing out (passing by) and who may be passing through (dropping out).

We have seen that the rates of passing by and passing through vary between the two ICTs studied (mobile telephone and home Internet use) and between European countries. Rates also vary between different sociodemographic groups within one of those countries (United Kingdom). We have seen that household Internet access is not a one-way street. A significant minority give up (or lose) Internet access or give up faster access (such as broadband) and return to modem access. We have also seen that having a mobile in the household, and therefore perhaps being exposed to its value and utility, may lead to the subsequent acquisition of a personal mobile phone, especially in countries with a currently low diffusion rate such as Bulgaria. As anticipated, we have also seen that the more developed countries have a lower rate of persistent ICT poverty. However it is noticeable that persistent household Internet poverty is much more prevalent in every country than is persistent mobile phone poverty. Internet dropout rates are more even across countries, and the net result of this, together with decreasing rates of acquisition across these countries, appears to have a slowed if not stalled Internet diffusion rate. Mobile dropout rates are also consistent across these countries, with the exception of Bulgaria, where it is remarkably high (24%). In general, mobile dropout rates are marginally lower than household Internet access dropout rates.

The data provide limited evidence that such rates change over time. The e-Living data, being only two waves, cannot do so. The earlier Home OnLine data, however, indicate that the rates of dropping out may decrease over time, as does the rate of acquisition—suggesting a plateau effect for penetration levels. In addition, the data indicate that from 1999 to 2001 in the United Kingdom, the chances of a person maintaining household Internet access were between 81% and 98%, but that the chances, once lost, of regaining Internet access were only about 50%. Those who pass out may not come back. The data for the mobile phone over the same period in the United Kingdom show remarkably similar patterns, except that the rate of acquisition increased.

Overall, we see that classic sociodemographic factors feature strongly as predictors of persistent Internet poverty. For mobile phones, however, we see far less in the way of systematic sociodemographic effects. The analysis of dropping out shows distinctly different patterns to that of persistent poverty and different patterns between the two technologies studied. Household Internet dropouts are very likely to have had little Internet experience. Age is also a factor, but overall its predictive power is low. There are no wealth effects and no computer

attitudinal effects, and perhaps of most interest, losing access to a home PC is not a significant factor.

In contrast, only a few identifiable single factors apart from gender affect loss of a personal mobile phone; here again the model gives us little insight into why women are more likely to be mobile dropouts than men.

These results indicate that dropping out was not particularly problematic in the United Kingdom between 1999 and 2001. It appears that once individuals have ICT access they tend to keep it, with the notable exception of women (in the case of mobile phones) and those with little or no Internet experience (in the case of household Internet access). This indicates that it is the analysis of persistent ICT poverty that is most crucial.

We can consider one aspect of this poverty by recasting the analysis in terms of risk. We have seen that certain groups of people are much more at risk of never having household Internet access than others. These groups are generally those who are already disadvantaged. Given that in 2003, 89% of U.K. Internet users accessed the net at home (Rose, 2003), we see that claiming near universal access in the United Kingdom is somewhat premature if that access is taken to mean actual practical and useful, everyday access, as opposed to "in principle" access. We have found strong evidence that, in terms of household Internet access, the digital divide is persisting and becoming increasingly concentrated in already marginalized groups. If social and economic benefits do flow from Internet access or, as seems more likely, access to critical social services will be increasingly online, then actions must clearly be taken to prevent useful and usable Internet access from becoming just another brick in the wall of social exclusion. Of all the factors that appear to predict persistent household Internet poverty, those that seem most amenable to change are wealth (i.e., cost of access) and attitudes toward personal computing. We do not imagine, for example, that increasing the population's educational attainment will lead to lower overall Internet poverty, unless such education is associated with developing experience of and skills in using ICTs. What seems more likely is that the provision of applications and services that motivate people to go online, at prices they can afford, will change the utility function of the Internet. In this case, those without access are motivated to acquire it despite it requiring both money and time, which, for them, might be scarce. Although this is true of public policy aspirations, it is also true of commercial market strategies. It is increasingly recognized within the industry that raising the penetration level of the Internet in the United Kingdom will require a shift in its economics and its perceived utility to a mass market.

In the case of the mobile telephone, however, there are far fewer systematic patterns of persistent mobile poverty. Since these data were collected, the penetration of mobile phones has increased still further. Although we have seen limited evidence for the experience effect for mobile telephony in the e-Living data, it seems far less significant than for the Internet. We might suggest that this is because the mobile phone's utility and value may be clearer to a broader range of users. The provision of public services via mobile devices would appear to have fewer digital divide issues than does provision via the Internet. Given the positive relationship between informal interpersonal communication, social capital, and general well-being (Li, Pickles, & Savage, 2005; Pevalin & Rose, 2003), the preliminary evidence of the value of mobile phones is in maintaining social relationships and hence mediating social capital (Ling, 2004). In addition, the fact that even those with no fixed address or telephone (and thus no fixed Internet access) can still own and use mobile devices (Goodman, 2003), means that mobiles should be more carefully considered as a technology that can bring social and economic benefits.

Our second main concern is with the nature of flux. Is adoption different from churn, or does it represent an intermediate level of commitment to or engagement with a technology between continuous users and continuous nonusers? Appropriately, perhaps, the answer is itself intermediate: We cannot be sure. The models of take-up and churn show that both categories of users differ from continuous users; the two categories of flux, however, are neither overwhelmingly different nor overwhelmingly the same. Flux is, as always, a slippery subject.

Acknowledgments.   The Home OnLine project was funded by British Telecommunications PLC and the e-Living project by the European Commission's FP5 IST Programme under contract number IST-2000-25409. This chapter has benefited from discussions with Malcolm Brynin, Roger Burrows and other participants of the iCS/OII Internet Research Symposium held in September 2002 at Balliol College, Oxford, where the U.K. results were first presented. The e-Living results were first presented at the e-Living: Life in a Digital Europe conference held in Essen, 20–21 January 2004, and the chapter has benefited from comments and discussion at that conference.

References

Anderson, B. (2004). *Passing by, passing through and dropping out. Chimera working paper.* Colchester, UK: Chimera, University of Essex.

Anderson, B., & Tracey, K. (2001). Digital living: The "impact" or otherwise of the Internet on everyday life. *American Behavioral Scientist, 45*(3), 457–476.

CEC (2002). *eEurope 2005: An information society for all—An action plan.* Brussels: Commission of the European Communities.

Gallup Europe (2002). *Flash Eurobarometer 135: Internet and the public at large—Results and comments.* Luxembourg: Office for Official Publications of the European Communities.

Gershuny, J. (2003). Web use and net nerds: A neo-functionalist analysis of the impact of information technology in the home. *Social Forces, 82*(1), 141–168.

Goodman, J. (2003). *Mobile telephones and social capital in Poland. A report for the "Digital Europe: e-business and sustainable development" project.* London: Forum for the Future.

Katz, J., & Aspden, P. (1998). Internet dropouts in the USA: The invisible group. *Telecommunications Policy, 22*(4/5), 327–339.

Layte, R., & Whelan, C. T. (2002). *Moving in and out of poverty: The impact of welfare regimes on poverty dynamics in the EU. EPAG Working Papers.* Colchester, UK: University of Essex.

Lenhart, A. (2002). *Barriers to internet access: From the non-user and new user perspective.* Proceedings of AoIR3, Maastricht, Netherlands, 2002.

Li, J., Pickles, A., & Savage, M., (2005). *Social capital and social trust in Britain. European Sociological Review 21*(2), 109–123.

Ling, R. (2004). *Social capital and ICTs. e-Living Project Report.* Oslo: Telenor R&D.

Office of the e-Envoy (2003). *UKOnline report 2003.* London: Cabinet Office.

Pevalin, D., & Rose, D. (2003). *Social capital for health: Investigating the links between social capital and health using the British Household Panel Survey.* London: Health Development Agency.

Raban, Y. (2004). *e-Living D11.1: ICT uptake and usage: Panel data analysis. e-Living Project Report.* Tel Aviv: ICTAF, University of Tel Aviv.

Rice, R., & Katz, J. (2003). Comparing Internet and mobile phone usage: Digital divides of usage, adoption and dropouts. *Telecommunications Policy, 27*(8/9), 597–633.

Rogers, E. M. (1995). *Diffusion of innovations.* New York: Free Press.

Rose, R. (2003). *Digital choice, 1st results from the Oxford Internet Survey (OxIS).* Oxford: iCS/OII Internet Research Symposium.

Thomas, F. (2002). *Dropouts—a forgotten category of Internet users.* Maastricht, the Netherlands: AoIR3.

Wyatt, S., Thomas, G., & Terranova, T. (2002). They came, they surfed, they went back to the beach: Conceptualizing use and non-use of the Internet (pp. 23–40). In Woolgar, S. (Ed.), *VirtualSociety? Technology, cyberpole, reality.* Oxford: Oxford University Press.

4

Yoel Raban and Malcolm Brynin

Older People and New Technologies

Why Older People?

Age tends to be associated with reduced health and resources, as well as diminished openness to new experiences. Yet aging is not a one-dimensional process. In the case of adaptation to new technological developments, even if the average use of new information and communication technologies (ICTs) by older people is lower than that of younger people, the behavior of older people nevertheless contains considerable variation. We should neglect neither this variation nor its possible effects. Just as with younger people, the factors among older people that influence ICT behavior are varied, including age itself (i.e., very old people are different from less old people), gender, education, social class, income, wealth, and so on. A study of people aged 70 years and over in Berlin found that although age tends to reduce variation in capacities, the latter remains considerable. Nearly 30% of the sample could be classed as "vitally involved," "socially embedded," or "active." Not all were equally fit and active, but another 23% were "satisfied with life" or "independent" (Baltes & Mayer, 1999, p. 502). Material differences are also important. In Britain, in the mid-1990s, average weekly nonessential spending was nearly £250 for the richest tenth of

two-person households with an occupational pension, compared to £50 for the richest tenth of one-person households on a state pension (Mann, 2001, p. 96). This disparity makes a huge difference to the ability to adopt new ICTs because the elderly poor are exceptionally poor.

The constraints of old age are not only material but may derive from ill health, loss of social networks, and unfamiliarity with the new. In a survey in Belgium, although 85% of those aged 18–29 years considered computers useful, only 32% of those over 65 year of age agreed (Galand & Lobet-Maris, undated). Yet it would be wrong to assume that only the young have learning curves, even if they move along these curves faster. The Berlin study mentioned above found that a majority of the elderly people in the sample wished to or were able to continue to learn. Whereas PC access declines among older people, for instance, from 57% of those in their 50s to 32% of those in their 60s, over 30% of people aged over 50 years who responded to the appropriate question in another European survey said they wished to improve their computers skills (SeniorWatch, 2002, pp. 52–58).

The "problem," if it is a problem, comes from the lack of resources to move along the learning curve inherent in the need to adapt to any new technology. This insufficiency might be material, but it also derives from reduced energy and, in the sense of perceived life span, even of available time. The last point is especially important, as it makes generational effects almost period effects: older people are exposed to new ways of doing things that belong to an era in which they will only marginally participate. Virtually all people who are young today will, when they are older, be able to operate a computer without difficulty. Yet they will face new processes when older which they will find difficult and that will not warrant their time or effort to learn to use. A learning curve is like a playground slide: although once to the top it is possible to enjoy the ride, getting up the stairs to the slide's starting point becomes increasingly difficult with age.

Older People in the Sample

The analysis used to test the place of variety in the ICT behavior of older people is based on the e-Living survey, which also appears in other contributions to this book. The survey was a household panel study carried out in six countries: Bulgaria, Germany, Israel, Italy, Norway, and the United Kingdom.[1]

The following sections of this chapter look first at the relationship between age and ICT behavior, therefore comparing the old to the less old, and then at older people only (taken arbitrarily to mean

aged 60 years and above), where processes of ICT engagement and attitudes are examined more causally.

Of course, older people differ from younger generations in a number of major, general characteristics that are in turn related to ICT behavior. We need to try to isolate the effects of age itself from those of poverty, education, a different gender balance, and so on. The proportion of the sample that is female is 50% among those aged 30–45 years and 57% for people aged 60 years or over. Only 6% of people in the first age group have absolutely no academic qualifications, compared to 22% of the older group. These characteristics are in turn related to ICT behavior. For instance, PC use among university graduates is 80%, compared to only 35% among primary school graduates.

ICT Adoption

Age is an important explanatory variable of diverse consumption patterns and is expected to be a strong predictor of ICT ownership and use. To see how older people fare, in this section we compare older people to other age groups. Figure 4.1 shows the age distribution of PC ownership. It is clear from the graph that being older, rather than being *old*, is the key determinant in this distribution. Ownership declines from the age of 40 years and up (after a slight plateau during the 20s and 30s). Figure 4.2

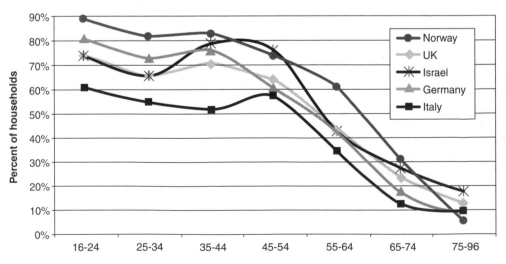

Figure 4.1. PC ownership in e-Living households.

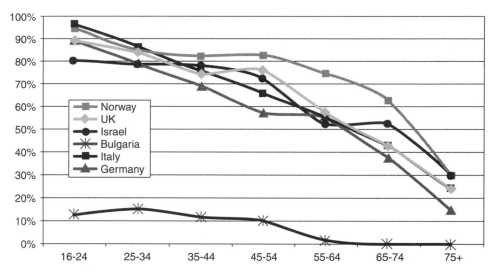

Figure 4.2. Mobile ownership by age.

shows the distribution for ownership of mobile phones. This distribution generally displays a more continuous decline by age.

But which dimensions of the aging experience cause these results? Age is correlated with income and education, both of which help determine ownership of ICTs (see, e.g., *US Department of Commerce, 2002* and *UCLA Center for Communications Policy, 2001*, both relating to the United States). PC ownership increases from 17% in *e-Living* households with a monthly income of €800 to 83% among households with monthly income of €4800 and above. PC ownership and Internet access increase from 29% and 18% (respectively) for householders with primary school education to 72% and 58% for householders with a degree.

Nevertheless, age still has an effect even when we control for these factors, which implies some sort of generational effect. The eLiving project included a question about reasons for not using the Internet. Of individuals who did not expect to acquire access, 53% were retired from work, and 49%

of these "averse" people were over 65 years of age. This effect of age is more fully demonstrated in table 4.1 for mobile ownership, PC access, and for Internet usage. The coefficients, which derive from separate analyses for each outcome, measure the effect of a being older, by 1 year, on the odds of the dependent variable occurring. In fact, this is the log of the odds, which means that we can broadly interpret the coefficients as indicating the percentage increase or decrease in the odds associated with age. The other independent variables, effects of which are omitted for simplicity, are household size, gender, education, attitudes to technology, work status, and household income. The Internet model includes use of a PC as an explanatory variable (Figuera, 1999), as Internet use is necessarily correlated with PC use. Despite the controls used in the analysis, age continues to have a statistically significant effect in reducing ICT participation.

Respondents in all six countries were asked for how many years they had been using the Internet. Transforming years of Internet experience into the

Table 4.1. Mobile ownership/PC/internet use, separate logistic results: effects of age.

	UK	Italy	Germany	Norway	Bulgaria	Israel	All
Mobile	−0.037	−0.029	−0.042	−0.033	−0.046	−0.039	−0.025
PC	−0.049	−0.106	−0.106	−0.115	−0.084	−0.106	−0.087
Internet	−0.043	−0.046	−0.062	−0.036	−0.061	−0.036	−0.042

Note: the coefficients are beta values and are all significant to $p < .05$.

first year of use enables us to build diffusion curves of Internet users. The dots and diamonds in figure 4.3 are the real cumulative and net additions, respectively, of Internet users in all six countries. The smooth curves approximate the real data by using a logistic function, allowing it to go forward in time to year 2006. We can see that, according to diffusion theory (Rogers, 1995), we are already past most of the life cycle phases (innovators, early adopters, early majority, and late majority), and are now entering the "laggards" phase. We can also see that the sample diffusion rate approaches an average saturation level of 47%,[2] whereas the sample proportion of respondents that use a home PC is in fact 55%. However, the diffusion of Internet users varies by country: Norway exhibits the fastest diffusion rate, approaching a saturation level of about 65%–70%; the United Kingdom, Germany, Israel, and Italy follow, with saturation levels of 40%–55%.

When we compare individuals according to their Internet experience, we find that "innovators" and "early adopters" aggregated together as one group belong to higher income households and have much higher average monthly personal incomes (€4,250) than individuals from the "early majority" and "late majority" segments (€3,200 and €2,700, respectively). Another demographic variable that distinguishes between diffusion segments is the level of education, in that 56% of "innovators and early adopters" have a university degree, compared to 21% in the "late majority" segment. Innovators and early adopters also differ from the other segments with respect to leisure activities and attitudes toward ICTs. They are involved in sporting activities more often, are less intimidated by computers, and find the Internet more useful than individuals in other segments.

But what is the effect of age? Innovators and those in adjacent segments tend to be younger, though there is not much difference in the mean ages of innovators and laggards (31 years for the former, 36 for the latter). However, this difference is in the aggregate. Within each age group there is considerable variety, and indeed, each group has its own diffusion profile. When we look at the slopes for different age groups in figure 4.4, we find a clear relationship between age and the steepness of the slope: Those aged 65 years and older come in particularly late and in relatively small numbers. Yet only the slope for the oldest group shows little or no change.

Net ICT adoption rates, in fact, consist of gross adoption less churn. It is of note that older people do not differ much from other age populations in their propensity to adopt the Internet relative to

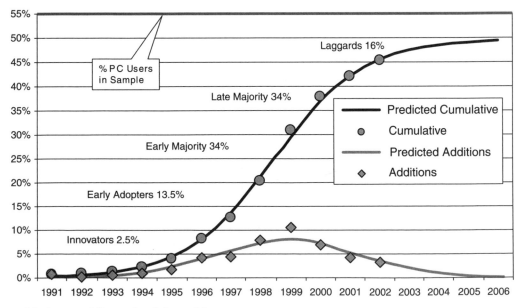

Figure 4.3. Internet diffusion (pooled sample).

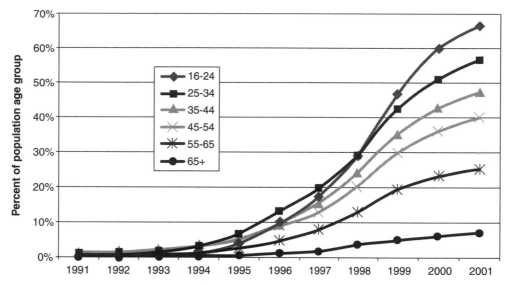

Figure 4.4. Internet diffusion by age group.

their propensity to drop out. The proportion of adopters is always roughly double the proportion of dropouts, regardless of age. The difference that age makes, however, is that after about age 50 years, both adoption and drop-out rates fall sharply.

Age has a very different effect once a technology has been adopted. The average time spent on the Internet (i.e., among Internet users) is shown by age group in figure 4.5. Usage generally declines with age. However, in the United Kingdom, Israel,

and Italy, it picks up very roughly from the age of around 50 years. In Israel, this "recovery" is apparently more extreme and starts earlier.

Thus, in Israel, Italy, and the United Kingdom, Internet use has a "U" shape, in which younger and older people are heavier users than middle-aged people. In Israel, daily use drops from more than 55 minutes in the 16–24 age group to less than 40 minutes in the 35–44 age group, and then rises to more than 55 minutes for the 65+ age

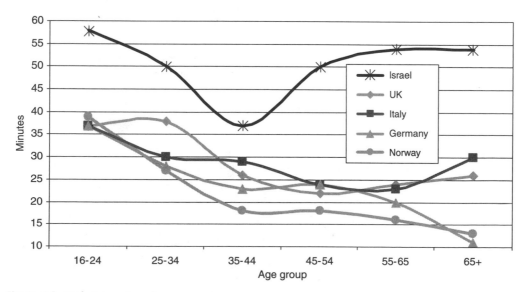

Figure 4.5. Daily Internet use by age group.

group. By comparison, in the United States, the average time spent on the Internet was 73 minutes per day (UCLA Center for Communications Policy, 2001.)

It is also of note that the age profile of specific Internet activities is fairly flat—in other words, usage varies rather little across many age groups. The main exceptions are obvious: music and education. Online banking goes down only slightly with age; online shopping even less. Moreover, some Internet uses, such as travel, banking, and shopping, increase in popularity with experience rather than with age. Over time, online users tend to become more confident and trustful, especially in regard to uses that require monetary payments. Average online spending over the three previous months tends to increase with experience, from around €200 for the least to more than €700 for the most experienced. These findings are supported by Horrigan and Rainie (2002), who report significant increase in e-mail and other activities, including online transactions, for U.S. users with more Internet experience.

Is Age Important?

This section examines the relationship between age and attitudes toward ICTs. The latter measure is based on five Likert-coded items such as "computers are intimidating to use" and "I am interested in new technologies," producing a scale from 5 to 25. The correlation between age and the scale is 0.3, which indicates only a moderate relationship. Yet, as has been shown above, age is associated with a range of factors that might constrain more positive attitudes to technology, such as reduced resources or even poverty. Table 4.2 produces an arbitrary split between people with fewer than three household goods (somewhat on the luxury side of consumption, such as a digital camera, a dishwasher, a DVD player, etc.), and those who have three to eight. It compares the mean "phobia" scores on these two dimensions across three age groups, where a higher score indicates higher phobia. (In this and subsequent analyses, the data from both waves are pooled, using robust standard errors where appropriate.)

The score is higher among older people, but it is also higher among those with fewer goods, although the difference that ownership of these goods

Table 4.2. Computer phobia scores by age and ownership of household goods.

Age, years	< 3 goods	≥ 3 goods	Difference
60+	15.1	13.7	1.4
40–59	13.7	12.2	1.5
16–39	12.8	11.3	1.5

makes is the same within each age group. In fact, respondents who are over 60 years of age and who have three or more household goods of this type have the same average phobia score as those aged 40–59 years who have three or fewer goods. Of course, ownership of this type of goods is related to computer attitudes, as ownership depends in part on age. Ownership of goods is lower among the really elderly: The oldest group's average number of goods is 2.8, compared to over 4.2 for the other age groups. Nevertheless, it is clear that a large proportion of older people are ready to adopt new technologies and have positive attitudes toward technology; however, those with limited resources, including education, are likely to do less well on both counts.

We can see more clearly what effect age has on attitudes, relative to other factors that are perhaps associated with age, by undertaking regression analysis (ordinary least squares) with the phobia score as the dependent variable, and with age as an explanatory variable (see table 4.3). This analysis incorporates several models, either including or excluding different combinations of other variables correlated with age. If the coefficient for age remains high and significant, even with the entry of these variables, then age alone can be viewed as having a strong correlation with attitudes. If the age coefficient reduces substantially (though no test of significance is introduced here for this change), then it is likely that it is these other variables that are producing high phobia scores. The high scores cannot, therefore, be attributed entirely to age. (For simplicity of presentation, the effects of some control variables used in all the models—gender, country, education—are not shown.)

In the first column of table 4.3, age when entered alone (i.e., apart from the controls) is positively associated with phobia. This effect halves when an age-squared term is introduced, which itself has a positive effect. This indicates that age has an exponential effect. Phobia rises with age, but at

Table 4.3. OLS regression coefficients with phobia score as the dependent variable.

Independent variables	Model 1	Model 2	Model 3	Model 4	Model 5
Age	0.06***	0.03***	0.06***	.07***	0.06***
Age²		0.0003***	−0.0000	−0.0002*	−0.0002*
No work			0.48***	0.37***	0.13
Manager			−0.35***	.027***	0.03
More goods				−0.39***	−0.26***
Home PC					−1.45
Work PC					−0.83***
R²	.19	.19	.19	.22	.26

*** $p < .001$ *$p < .05$.

older ages it increases even faster. However, further introduction of the occupational indicators "no work" (mainly retirement) and professional or managerial status brings us back to the original situation as shown in the first column. Thus, the effect that old age specifically has on phobia, as opposed to the effect of age in general, is related to low occupational status or to having no current occupation at all. This is because being out of employment—as in the oldest group—reduces both resources and experience. The fourth column partially addresses the issue of resources by adding the number of household goods owned. This reduces the effect of occupation, thus giving some idea of how much of the occupational effect is related to resources (primarily and obviously through having a wage). The age coefficients remain the same, however, so access to resources does not explain away the effect that age has in this fuller model. However, and most important, the age-squared coefficient is now negative. Thus, the effect of old age is, at most, neutral if we allow for differential resources. The effect of age therefore appears to begin to taper off with older age rather than, as the second column implies, increasing exponentially.

The model specification shown in the column just discussed is the preferred model, but a further variant is shown in the final column, in which use of a home or a work PC is included. These are clearly endogenous, as such usage must be associated with reduced phobia, but the model serves to show that the age and age-squared effects remain despite this further control. This indicates a degree of robustness to this previous finding. It is, of course, possible that country-wide differences in age distributions and in access to jobs or other resources in part explain this outcome, but restriction of the analysis (the results of which are not shown here) to four more homogeneous countries (Britain, Germany, Italy, and Norway) makes negligible difference, with the exception that the age-squared coefficient becomes nonsignificant, though retaining the same sign and size.

Conclusions

Age is strongly associated with reduced access to many resources, including ICTs, as well as with limited willingness to engage with new technologies. Yet there is no single cut-off point for determining what age, in this respect, is actually old. Seventy-year-old people are less positive to new technology than those who are 60 years old, who are less positive than those who are 50 years old. This means that a substantial core of people who are over age 60 years not only access new technologies but also have positive attitudes. Their response is slower, but if we take the diffusion curves as indicating an aggregate learning curve, the slope is positive. There is great variety of ICT behavior in this age group, as indeed in all age groups. Perhaps more important, much of the effect of old age on attitudes toward technology relates to secondary factors that are associated with age, such as reduced employment, diminished resources, and lower levels of education. To some extent, there is perhaps a period effect rather than a generational effect here. With the massive expansion of education in recent decades, educational differentials should not be as pronounced for future generations of older people as in the past. Insofar as inequalities are reduced by growing national incomes or governmental actions, though the latter might sometimes have the reverse effect, the effect of income differentials might also be seen as a period effect. It is possible that the digital divide will diminish simply because some of the new technologies, like television, might become standard, at least where average incomes continue to rise. Although age will always limit access to new things and adaptation to new things, these limitations are strongly mitigated by circumstances that enable older people to participate in society to the same degree as other people.

Notes

1. The aim of wave 1, conducted from October to December 2001, was to recruit a representative sample of roughly 1750 households within each country. The study used computer-assisted telephone interviewing (CATI) in all countries except Bulgaria, where telephone penetration was insufficient; face-to-face interviewing (CAPI) was used instead. The CATI method used random digit dialing to select households. In each household that was contacted, one adult (aged 16+ years) was selected for interview using a randomizing procedure. The response rates were around 40% (typical for CATI), although the response rate in Bulgaria was much higher. In wave 2, the response rates averaged 65% in the five countries excluding Bulgaria, where again the response rate was higher. Some of the analysis (below) pools both waves. The questionnaire covered standard socio-demographics and ICT ownership and use, as well as details of work, education, skills, and social interaction. The survey also contained modules on attitudes to ICTs, the environment, measures of quality of life, and some prospective questions on likelihood of purchase of ICTs. For full details see E-living deliverable D6: Wave I documentation and integrated dataset; retrieved June 19, 2003 from http://www.eurescom.de/e-living/index.htm.

2. The results reflect average levels for the pooled sample, not weighted for differences in population sizes.

References

Baltes, P., & Mayer, K.-U. (Eds.). (1999). The Berlin Aging Study. Cambridge, UK: Cambridge University Press.

Figuera, G. (1999). An analysis of international Internet diffusion. Retrieved June 19, 2003, from http://rpcp.mit.edu/Pubs/Theses/gonzalo.pdf.

Galand, J.-M., & Lobet-Maris, C. (Undated), Appropriation of ICTs by elderly people: A complex process. Namur, Belgium: University of Namur.

Horrigan, J. B., & Rainie, L. (2002). *Getting serious online*. Pew Internet & American Life Project. Retrieved June 19 2003, from http://www.pewinternet.org/reports/toc.asp?Report=55.

Mann, K. (2001). *Approaching retirement: Social divisions, welfare and exclusion*. Bristol, UK: Policy Press.

Rogers, E. (1995). *Diffusion of innovations*. New York: Free Press.

SeniorWatch. (2002). *Older people and information society technology*. An E.U. Fifth Framework Project (IST-1999–29086). Retrieved June 19, 2003, from http://www.empirica.biz/swa/reports/D51_final.pdf.

UCLA Center for Communications Policy (2001). *Surveying the digital future*. The UCLA Internet Report 2001. Los Angeles: University of California, Los Angeles.

U.S. Department of Commerce. (2002). A nation online: How Americans are expanding their use of the Internet. ESA/NTIA. Retrieved June 19, 2003, from http://www.ntia.doc.gov/ntiahome/dn/.

5

John P. Robinson and Jos De Haan

Information Technology and
Family Time Displacement

From Fear to Facts

Are we becoming slaves of our communication machines? Does new technology threaten family life? Does the Internet support our diverse, scattered social networks? Does e-mail bridge geographical distance and keep us close to those far away?

Many such questions can be raised with regard to new technology's impact on social life, with much of the intellectual discussion summarized in the distinction between utopian and dystopian views. The utopian view sees new technology like the Internet as improving the quality of our social lives, in contrast to the dystopian view which raises serious concerns about decreasing social contacts, loneliness, and the disintegration of family life. With more and more empirical research studies becoming available, the strongest of these hopes and fears have already had to be modified. Ideologically-driven discourse has given way to the more sober language of researchers, who have tested the effects of information technology (IT) in a wide variety of social contexts such as child–parent relations, contacts with family and friends, and interactions with colleagues in the workplace. Research also admitted the possibility of there being no notable new effects of IT.

This chapter examines the way in which new IT, and in particular the Internet, has affected peoples' time spent on social contacts and compares these results with the effects on other ways of spending time. How does the amount of time spent on various forms of social contact differ between Internet users and nonusers? We examine these differences in the context of the "functional-equivalence" hypothesis, as it has been used to explain the influence of television, a previous new technology which appears to have affected both social life and the use of mass media. According to this hypothesis, a new technology will replace those activities that most closely perform the same functions for users as did the older technologies.

Testing this hypothesis requires that we investigate a wide variety of uses of time. Are the uses of time on equivalent activities more affected by the Internet than the time spent on nonequivalent activities? We discuss the possible impact of the Internet on social contacts, mass media, and other activities below. Our investigation is based on time-diary studies from the United States and the Netherlands.

Comparing the United States and the Netherlands involves two of the leading IT countries in the world. In the latter half of 2001, 59% of the Dutch population could access the Internet at home, compared to 43% of Americans. At the same time, the two countries differ in several respects other than their contrasting histories, cultures, and geographic locations. The Netherlands is a smaller and more homogeneous country, with a greater population density, a factor that could stimulate face-to-face interaction—thus reducing the Internet's appeal in transcending greater distances. Time-diary comparisons also suggest the Netherlands to be somewhat of a "leisure paradise" in contrast to the United States, with shorter workweeks, less (female) employment, and longer vacations; having more free time, Dutch citizens might thus be better able to exploit the Internet's efficient and attractive features. As a "welfare state" with higher taxes and less income spread, Dutch people could be more homogeneous in the content they seek on the Internet. Finally, the Dutch are well-known for their tolerant and liberal values, which Robinson and Kestnbaum (1999) have shown to be prime predictors of going online. Nonetheless, we still expect that the Internet's time-displacement potentials should transcend these differences—much as they did when the displacement differences for television in the 1960s were found to be remarkably consistent across 12 different countries with marked cross-national variation in television diffusion and programming (Robinson, 1972).

The Functional Equivalence Hypothesis

Earliest personal communication technologies, like simple conversation, evolved into more long-distance forms, with the development of postal mail and the telephone as examples. More recently, mass "broadcast" forms of communication began to emerge, first cinema and later radio, but most prominently today television. The Internet can combine and meld the functions and features of both personal and mass forms of communication. When one turns to the question of how Internet use may affect daily activities—and communication activities in particular—it becomes clear that as Internet usage becomes more prominent, its displacement of alternative activities becomes more substantial.

As noted above, the functional-equivalence argument is the most well-known and accepted

framework in which to describe and understand how new technologies may affect communication and other behavior patterns. The development of this argument requires first a specification of functions. A prevailing distinction in media studies is between providing information, socializing, cultural integration, and providing amusement (cf. McQuail, 1994, p. 79). In principle, all of these functions can be performed by printed media, audiovisual media, and digital media like the Internet.

However, the functions are not restricted to media use, since other daily activities also can perform these functions. In this section, we first describe these functions in more detail and then describe how the Internet can perform these functions.

When television first appeared in the United States, it was immediately clear that it affected other mass media that provided light entertainment. Thus, audiences abandoned their radio sets, movie theaters closed, and magazines that featured the type of content now prevalent on television (such as the light fiction in *Collier's* and the *Saturday Evening Post*) ceased publication. The general explanation offered for these effects was that television content now more efficiently performed functions that were equivalent to those being abandoned (Weiss, 1969; Schramm, Lyle & Parker, 1961). Both Coffin (1954) and Bogart (1956) document how time spent on the movies, radio, and print fiction were displaced by television (with Coffin's study being based on a pre–post panel design that is ideal for measuring social change). In historical studies in the Netherlands, similar displacement effects of television use on movie and theater attendance, radio listening, and reading were found (Knulst, 1995; Knulst & Kraaykamp, 1996).

When complete time-diary data covering all daily activity became available in the 1965 Multinational Time-Budget Research Project (Szalai, 1972), it was clear that television's apparent impact extended well beyond these directly functionally-equivalent activities. These first diary data were collected from more than 25,000 respondents in 12 countries in which the diffusion of television ranged from 28% to 95% (Bulgaria and the United States, respectively). In the United States, as in almost each country, there were systematic differences in the daily activities of television owners versus nonowners (Robinson, 1972). These differences reflect major declines in the most functionally equivalent activities. Thus, radio listening was 60% lower, movie attendance 52% lower, book reading 41% lower, and magazine reading 28% lower. In terms of the *social* lives of individuals and families, time spent in out-of-home socializing among television owners was lower by 33%, and conversation in the home was lower by 25%, with the combined 16+ minutes of lower percentages of social life in these two activities almost equaling the 19-minute decline in other mass-media use.

Perhaps surprisingly, most other free-time activities were not significantly different between television owners and nonowners. That fact further supports the functional equivalence argument: the activities displaced are the ones to which the technology offers a functional equivalent. Other declines—in grooming, laundry, and pet/garden care—are more difficult to defend from the functional equivalence perspective, however.

Because the differences in television use are taken from single-time surveys, they can hardly be taken as causal evidence—although many are consistent with Coffin's (1954) panel results. The unanswered question remains whether these were preexisting differences among television owners that existed before their television was acquired. At the same time, the differences are consistent across countries with widely varying access to television— and widely differing broadcast philosophies about viewer choice of television programming. Although some of the activity differences in these 1965 data do not fit under the functional equivalence umbrella, most of the media-use changes predicted by it are found in these data. One should not be surprised, then, to find the present data on the Internet to have uneven predictive power.

Predicting the consequences of the rise of the Internet from the functional-equivalence perspective fits within a "neofunctionalistic" approach. Although this perspective points to some activities, such as social contacts and media use, that are expected to be influenced and to other activities that are not, it has several limitations. The concept of function is itself ambiguous.

In the literature, the functions of mass communication for society can be distinguished at four levels, first the society as a whole; second its subsystems, groups, or institutions; third, individuals; and fourth, culture (Wright, 1986). Here this rather confusing concept of functions is regarded as specifying human needs. In his neofunctional study,

Gershuny (2002b, p. 9) puts it as follows: "The functions are 'wants' for particular consumption experiences."

Even if the attention is drawn to functions for individuals, the concept is not free of problems. The equation of function with a psychological concept like need or want indicates that this attainment of needs can be a goal in itself. More often than not, this does not hold true. Maintaining social contacts, for example, is not valued as a goal in itself but, rather, as a stepping stone to valued rewards such as support, respect, or security. Therefore, it is theoretically more attractive to conceive the four functions as instrumental goals that people strive for to reach more general goals (Lindenberg, 1998). Moreover, which action is chosen from functionally equivalent alternatives depends not only on the available alternatives but on the resources of individuals that have to choose between these alternatives.

Among these resources are competencies in handling the old and new media. In particular, the new media require digital skills that not all people master to the same degree. Early adopters have more experience and capabilities in handling new media compared to late adopters (De Haan, 2003). Furthermore, using new technology for communication purposes requires knowing people who also have access to this communication technology and know how to use it. Thus, using e-mail also depends on social resources. In our final section, we return to this resources-driven explanation as an alternative to the functional-equivalence hypothesis.

Previous Studies of Internet's Impact on Mass Media and Other Activity

Speculation in initial publications on the possible impact of the Internet has tended to focus on social life and communication on the one hand, and mass communications on the other. The content of communication on both types of media channels can perhaps be more effectively or attractively conveyed by the Internet than by other media, so that there are reasons to expect many of the same sorts of differences for the Internet as were found for television. More specifically, one should find declines in social life and in usage of mass media among Internet users. Furthermore, the functional-equivalence hypothesis would be more strongly supported if no change were found for activities not considered to be functional alternatives.

Two widely publicized studies of early Internet impact report results consistent with that hypothesis of declining social life and media use. Both Cole et al. (2001) and Nie and Erbring (2000) conducted national studies with more than 2000 respondents that indicate declines in social life, television viewing, and other activities that could be considered functionally equivalent.

An issue arises with the Nie–Erbring survey—questions were asked that required respondents to report retrospectively on the changes that had occurred in their lives, rather than simpler questions on the time spent on this or that activity. It is recognized that survey respondents find it difficult to act as objective psychologists in perceiving changes happening in their lives (Robinson & Godbey, 1999). Indeed, most Nie–Erbring respondents reported that they could see no change in their media or other activities.

Studies that have used a less ambitious set of questions and research designs have produced more mixed results. The Pew Center for Public Opinion Research has been conducting national surveys related to IT since 1995, with periodic updates on certain questions on almost a monthly basis. The center's most complete surveys were conducted in 1995 and 1998, with nearly 3000 respondents in 1995 and nearly 4000 respondents in 1998 (response rate information is unfortunately not provided for these surveys). One value of these data is that they ask intensive questions about social and media activity "yesterday," as well as their behavior over longer time periods. Robinson, Barth and Kohut (1997), Robinson and Kestnbaum (1999), and Robinson, Kestnbaum, Neustadtl and Alvarez (2000) present several analyses based on these Pew data, as well as on data about Internet users from the 1997 Survey of Public Participation in the Arts. On the basis of the 1995 Pew data, Robinson, Barth, and Kohut (1997) found that in 1995, Internet and IT users were significantly more likely to use print media, radio newscasts, and movies than nonusers and were not significantly less likely to engage in social activities, nor to watch television with either entertainment or news content. These results were robust, remaining after statistical controls for gender, age, education, income, race, and marital status were introduced to the analyses.

Moreover, these results were largely replicated by Robinson and Kestnbaum's (1999) analysis of the 1997 Survey of Public Participation in the Arts national data, which asked about weekly Internet use for hobbies or recreational uses, rather than about news media use. Again, the self-described general Internet users were significantly more likely to read books and literature and to use the media for arts content, even after controlling for other factors. They were also more likely to attend arts events and to participate in a wide variety of other free-time activities, such as attending sports events or movies, playing sports, and doing home improvements. They were no more likely to do gardening or to watch less television.

In their examination of the more recent 1998 Pew data, Robinson et al. (2000) showed that the proportion of Internet users had grown in the interim, with similar results for social life, but somewhat different results for media. Print media use, although still greater among Internet users, was no longer significantly greater among Internet users. Television use was lower among users, but not statistically significantly, after introducing multivariate controls. However, when only earlier Internet users (3+ years of use) in the 1998 survey were examined, the results were much the same as in 1995. That is, Internet users' use of print media was notably higher, consistent with the 1995 results. That meant that later adopters of the Internet were neither more nor less likely to use other news media than were nonusers.

Overall, then, these analyses provide little support for time displacement following the functional-equivalence argument. Not only did Internet users not use news and other media less, but many of them used print media *more*, and they were more active in a wide variety of other more active free-time pursuits as well. While their television times tended to be lower, they were not significantly so.

At the same time, these results are based on single-time surveys that have limited capacity to identify causal processes or to monitor dynamic relations between IT use and other activity, as the Coffin study did. Moreover, they provide no clue about what other activities are being replaced by the Internet. IT time may thus be replacing other activities not covered in these studies.

Perhaps the ideal data source, then, is one that covers all daily activity. The U.S. 1998–2001 time diary study and the Dutch 2000 time diary study described below have such a feature, although these, too, are single surveys that do not allow for examination of the cross-time dynamics of activity displacement.

Study Methodology

The main American source of the time-use evidence in this article is a comprehensive set of time-diary data, as reported by a 1998–2001 national probability survey of 1775 respondents aged 18–64 years, in the form of 24-hour recall time diaries. The first half of the survey was done in 1998–1999, and the second half with a parallel but separate national 2000–2001 diary sample. Comparisons of the two data sets showed remarkably similar results across the 2 years, which forms the basis for using the combined file in the analyses below.

In these 1998–2001 diary accounts, respondents provided complete accounts of what they did for the full 24 hours of a particular day. Respondents in these surveys describe exactly when they went to bed, when they got up and started a new day, and all the things they did until midnight of that day. In these accounts, the analyst can learn not only what people did, but also where people spent their day, who they were with, and what other activities they were doing in addition to these activities. Because they represent complete accounts of daily activity, diary data collected from cross-section samples allow one to estimate how much societal time is spent on the complete range of human behavior—from work to free time, from travel to time spent at home.

Features of the Time Diary and a Sample Diary

The measurement logic behind the time-diary approach follows from that employed in the most extensive and well-known of diary studies—the Multinational Time Budget Study of Szalai (1972). In that study, roughly 2000 respondents aged 18–64 years in urban employed households from each of 12 different countries kept a diary account of a single day. The same diary procedures and activity codes were employed in each country in 1965. Respondents were chosen so that each day of the week was equivalently represented; in subsequent U.S. studies, all seasons of the year were covered as well.

Figure 5 in Robinson and Godbey (1999) and appendix 5.A (from Kestnbaum, Robinson, Neustadtl, & Alvarez, 2002) show how the diary was filled out by two (pre-Internet) respondents. Here, it can be seen that the diary keepers may have had some recall difficulties in performing this task, but a diary report is fundamentally different from the task of making longer-term time estimates. The diary keeper's task is to recall only a single day's activities in sequence. This reporting approach may be similar to the way the day was structured chronologically for the respondent and to the way most people store their activities in memory. Rather than having to consider a long time period, the respondent needs only focus attention on a single day (yesterday). Rather than working from some list of activities whose meanings vary from respondent to respondent, diary respondents simply describe in their own words the day's activities as recalled (Robinson & Godbey 1999; chapter 5)

The diary procedure thus avoids most of the pitfalls of the alternative "time-estimate" approach (Robinson & Godbey, 1999). There are still problems of memory, as when respondents have trouble piecing together a particular period of the day. However, few diary accounts are beset by such structural reporting problems once underway. Automatic procedures were built into the diary-recording protocol that was implemented using Computer Assisted Telephone Interviewing to ensure accurate reporting. Whenever respondents reported consecutive activities that involved different locations, they were reminded to connect them with a travel episode. Activity periods that last more than 2 hours automatically involved the probe, "Were you doing anything else during that time, or were you doing (activity) for the entire time?" Moreover, all periods across the day had to be accounted for so that the diary account totaled all 1440 minutes of the day (across the 24 hours).

As in earlier diary surveys, these largely open-ended diary reports were then coded with the basic activity-coding scheme developed for the 1965 Multinational Time Budget Research Project (as described in Szalai, 1972). As outlined in appendix 5.B, the Szalai code first divides activities into non-free-time activities (codes 00–55) and free-time activities (codes 56–99). Nonfree activities are further subdivided into paid work (00–09), family care (10–39), personal care (40–49), and education (50–54). Free-time activities are further subdivided under the five general headings of other education activities (55–59), organizational activity (60–69), social life (70–79), recreation (80–89), and communication (90–99).

New activity categories 56 (Internet use), 57 (computer games), and 58 (other computer use) were coded in minutes per day and then converted into hours per week, after ensuring that all days of the week were equally represented. In other words, the sampling units involved are in person-days rather than persons, as the latter were interviewed about only a single day's activities. The data are weighted by demographic variables to match 1998–2000 U.S. Census Bureau characteristics (e.g., gender, age, education, income, and employment status).

Comparing time use in the United States with that in the Netherlands is enhanced by a long-standing tradition of time use studies (TUSs) in the Netherlands that is also based on Szalai's (1972) grouping of 10 major activity fields. The Dutch Social and Cultural Planning Office has been engaged in a series of TUSs that started in 1975. This person-based survey has been repeated every 5 years (in 1980, 1985, 1990, 1995, and 2000), with a sample size of roughly 3000 respondents—except in 1975 and 2000, when approximately 1300 and 1800 respondents participated, respectively. Respondents keep a paper-and-pencil weekly diary with fixed 15-minute intervals, starting on a Sunday and ending on a Saturday. In the diary, respondents identify their primary activity, their location, and (if applicable) a secondary activity, using precoded categories. In addition to the diary, a 1-hour questionnaire is administered. For a detailed description—in English—of sampling and nonresponse issues in the TUS 2000, see http://www.tijdsbesteding.nl, and for the development of time spent on the main activity fields, see De Haan and Huysmans (2002).

Multivariate controls for demographic differences were introduced by using Multiple Classification Analysis, or MCA (Andrews, Sonquist, & Morgan, 1973). In short, MCA provides differences in average values for each category of a predictor variable that make the statistical effects of other predictors equal. Internet or IT use, the major independent measure, was operationalized in two different ways to capture both single-day and longer-term use. In sum, the aim is to use analysis of variance, first, to compare the effects on average

time spent on various activities of being either a user or a nonuser of IT, and second, to see to what extent this difference remains after controlling for factors such as age and gender. The single-day measure was developed from the time diary, defined by whether respondents explicitly mentioned Internet or IT usage as a primary activity at any time during the diary day. The long-term general Internet use measure was developed from responses to a questionnaire item asking how many hours per week respondents used the Internet.

Comparing IT Users and Nonusers in the United States

Comparison of the daily diary activities of IT users versus nonusers on that same day is shown in table 5.1 for the "yesterday" diary users and in table 5.2 for general, long-term Internet users. As shown in table 5.1, 1521 respondents (86%) did not report using the Internet or other IT in their diary, whereas 254 (14%) reported such usage "yesterday." In contrast, as shown in table 5.2 below, 889 (51%) of these respondents said they had used the Internet in a typical week, and 866 (49%) said they had not. Data are shown in extrapolated weekly hours that add up to 168 hours per week to aid in interpretation. Statistically significant differences ($p < .05$) at the bivariate level were then subjected to MCA adjustment for the demographic control measures and the adjusted differences and adjusted correlations with IT time shown in the final columns (where significant).

Daily Differences

Turning first to "yesterday" comparisons for non-free-time activities in table 5.1, it can be seen in the top row that IT users did report 6.6 fewer hours worked outside the home than nonusers across the week after MCA adjustment (correlation = –.07). IT users' time on education, however, is some 2.3 hours higher on average—a difference that is also statistically significant and can be seen to offset about a third of that work deficit (correlation = +.08). After MCA adjustment, the work difference is statistically significant and thus does show IT users doing less paid work. This could be a result of heavier IT users being interviewed on days off from work or doing work at home on that day.

In terms of household work and family care, IT users spend about one half hour per week doing more housework than nonusers, but childcare and shopping differences are very small. None of these family-care differences are statistically significant. One notable difference consistent with the differences in table 5.1 for television is that IT users sleep 4 fewer hours per week—or about one half hour per day. IT users' grooming time is also lower—significantly so after MCA adjustment at about an hour a week. Eating times are identical for the two groups.

What free-time differences, then, are found? Are there activities to which IT users devote less time—given their average 14.4 weekly extrapolated hours they spend with IT, as near the bottom of table 5.1? As Kestnbaum et al. (2002) show, the social activities engaged in by Internet users and nonusers take up about the same time. Indeed, hardly any differences exist among social activities (like religion, organizations, or attending social events) or other such free-time activities as fitness/sports, hobbies, and other media activities like radio,

reading, and movies (and other social events)—none of which are statistically significant. IT users report about one half hour less time relaxing and thinking, and about one hour less in traveling, both of which are significant but not very time-consuming activities.

The free-time activity that is notably lower among IT users is television time—3.5 hours a week (about half an hour a day) before MCA adjustment and 2.5 hours after taking the lower education, older age, and other demographic differences of nonusers into account. The main differences between users and nonusers, then, come from non-free-time activities, like sleep and work, rather than from free-time activities. Put another way, IT users have more free time, but they use less of it for TV (even if they stay home more).

Long-Term Differences

Many similar patterns are found in the comparison of general Internet users and nonusers shown in table 5.2. Here, many more of these comparisons

Table 5.1. Differences in activities "yesterday" by IT users and nonusers (in extrapolated hours per week).

	IT users (n = 254)	Nonusers (n = 1521)	Bivariate difference	After MCA[a]	Correlation with IT use
Non–free-time					
Work	26.2	31.8	−5.6*	−6.6*	−.07
Education	4.3	1.7	2.6	2.3*	.08
Housework	13.8	13.2	0.6	NS	
Child Care	4.2	4.3	−0.1	NS	
Shopping	3.6	3.5	0.1	NS	
Sleep	52.5	56.6	−4.1*	−3.0*	−.07
Eat	7.8	7.8	0.0	NS	
Groom	4.9	5.8	−0.9	−1.2*	−.05
Free time					
Fitness/sport	1.7	1.9	−0.2	NS	
Hobby	1.4	1.6	−0.2	NS	
Television	10.4	13.9	−3.5*	−2.5*	−.05
Radio	0.1	0.3	−0.2	NS	
Read	2.2	1.9	0.3	NS	
Events/movie	0.9	1.1	−0.2	NS	
Think/relax	1.0	1.6	−0.6*	−0.2	NS
Other	0.1	0.2	−0.00	NS	
Social life	7.5	8.2	−0.7	NS	
IT use	14.4	0.0	14.4*	12.8*	.60
Travel	10.1	11.3	−1.3	−1.8*	−.06

[a]Controlling for gender, age, education, income, and employment status.
*p < .05; NS, not significant.

Table 5.2. Differences in daily activities by long-term internet users and nonusers (in extrapolated hours per week).

	Internet users (n = 889)	Nonusers (n = 866)	Bivariate difference	After MCA[a]	Correlation with Internet use
Non–free-time					
Work	33.1	29.6	3.5*	4.0*	.06
Education	2.8	1.4	1.4*	0.5*	.02
Housework	11.5	14.8	−3.3*	−2.4*	−.08
Child care	4.3	4.4	−0.1	NS	
Shopping	3.7	3.3	0.4	NS	
Sleep	54.5	57.5	−3.1*	−2.1*	−.07
Eat	8.8	7.4	1.4*	−0.8*	−.06
Groom	5.5	5.9	−0.4*	0.7*	.05
Free time					
Fitness/Sports	2.0	1.5	0.5*	0.3 (NS)	
Hobby	1.3	1.8	−0.5*	0.4 (NS)	
Television	11.5	15.2	−3.7*	−4.2*	−.08
Radio	0.2	0.2	0.0	NS	
Read	2.2	1.6	0.6*	0.7*	.07
Events/movies	1.3	0.8	−0.5	NS	
Think/relax	0.9	2.1	−1.2*	−0.7*	−.07
Other	0.1	0.8	−0.7*	−0.5 (NS)	
Social life	8.5	7.9	0.6	NS	
IT use	3.2	0.5	2.7*	2.5*	.16
Travel	11.9	10.5	1.4*	0.7*	.05

[a]Controlling for gender, age, education, income and employment status.
*$p < .05$; NS, not significant.

are statistically significant. As found in Kestnbaum et al. (2002), Internet users spend more time socializing, but by less than an hour a week for all forms of socializing combined. In contrast to the uses of free time shown in table 5.1, table 5.2 shows that the free-time hours of users and nonusers are now very similar, largely because the IT-use differences are here less than 3 hours per week.In terms of non-free-time activities, table 5.2 shows that the paid work hour differences are again statistically significant, but in the opposite direction—Internet users work 4 more hours than nonusers. In addition, they spend twice as much time in classes and related educational activity, although only half an hour more after MCA adjustment.

In contrast to table 5.1, table 5.2 shows that Internet users report significantly less housework than nonusers (by more than 2 hours a week), but not significantly less time on other family care of shopping and caring for children. Consistent with

table 5.1, users again spend 2 hours less time sleeping and about 40 minutes less time grooming. The latter is offset by more eating and meal time (no difference being found in table 5.1).

Table 5.2 reveals more significant differences for free-time activities than does table 5.1. The largest difference, however, continues to be for television—more than 4 hours less television after MCA adjustment. Both tables 5.1 and 5.2 show that users spend less time than nonusers thinking, relaxing, and performing "other" free-time activities. To some extent, these deficits are offset by the significantly greater fitness/sport, reading, and cinema-going times of Internet users. In terms of overall mobility, long-term Internet users now travel significantly more than nonusers, even after MCA adjustment, but they travel less when this category is examined on a daily basis, as shown in table 5.1.

Thus, some 11 activity differences (shown in table 5.2) between Internet users and nonusers are statistically significant after MCA adjustment, compared to only seven in table 5.1. The largest and most consistent differences that are shown in both tables are the Internet and IT users' lower figures for television viewing, thinking/relaxing, sleeping, and grooming, and their higher figures for adult education. In the diary day comparisons, Internet users work and travel less than nonusers, but in the long-run comparison, they work and travel more. In the long-run comparisons, Internet users also spend significantly more time eating, doing sports/fitness activities, and reading, but less time in other activities.

Secondary Activities

Table 5.3 shows secondary activities in this data set between nonusers and Internet users who are either "yesterday" users or "general" users. In general, the differences are either insignificant or inconsistent.

The largest difference is for secondary eating, which is an hour and a half lower among IT users; however, long term, there is no difference. A similar result is found for the lower reading times among IT users on a daily basis. Conversely, IT users report almost 10% more radio listening on a daily basis, but the reverse is found long term.

The one consistent activity difference between Internet users and nonusers is that Internet users view 10% more television as a secondary activity than do nonusers—both on a daily and a long-term basis. At the bottom of table 5.3, total time on these secondary activities is summed, and it can be seen that IT users report more such multitasking, especially in the long-term comparisons.

Summary and Conclusions

In this analysis of recent differences between the daily activities of IT users and nonusers, several patterns are consistent with the 1965 comparisons between television owners and nonowners, in which television owners reported notably lower use of prior media and less time spent sleep and grooming. The more active lifestyles of IT users are further suggested by their higher reporting of reading and of all secondary activities, as well as their lower sleep time and time thinking and relaxing. Table 5.2 (but not table 5.1) also suggests that Internet users work longer hours and travel more, consistent with the "Newtonian" model of Robinson and Godbey (1999), in which "bodies in motion, stay in motion" (Isaac Newton) In other words, people who are active in one type of participation are more likely to engage in other types of participation as well.

In terms of the historical and theoretical issues raised at the outset of this chapter, then, IT in its initial stages seems to mimic certain dramatic displacement effects found with television (and perhaps earlier media). Internet use seems to function both as a time displacer (one in which people do give up other activities to accommodate it) and as a "time enhancer" (as in the case of reading, which is consistently higher among Internet users in both this study and earlier articles). Indeed, Internet use may allow one to be more productive in use of time—such as enriching uses of old media, and replacing less active forms of free time and personal care with more active and interactive uses of time.

Table 5.3. IT User vs. Nonuser differences in secondary activities (in extrapolated hours per week).

	Yesterday IT use			General Internet use		
	Nonusers (n = 1521)	Users (n = 254)	Difference	Nonusers (n = 866)	Users (n= 888)	Difference
Housework	2.3	2.7	0.4	2.3	2.4	0.1
Child care	2.3	2.2	0.1	2.5	2.1	−0.4
Eating	6.0	4.4	−1.6	5.7	5.7	0.0
Radio/stereo	9.5	10.3	0.8	10.3	9.4	−0.9
TV	5.1	5.8	0.7	5.1	5.6	0.5
Reading	2.3	1.5	−0.8	2.7	2.6	−0.1
Relax/write	0.5	0.5	0.0	1.3	0.7	−0.6
Other	33.2	34.7	1.5	28.6	37.2	8.6
Total secondary activity	61.2	62.1	0.9	58.5	65.7	7.2

Comparing Internet Users and Nonusers in the Netherlands

The Netherlands is among the forerunners in the worldwide information society. The penetration of PCs there grew rapidly from 18% in 1985 to 70% in 2000, with 18% of Dutch people having two or more PCs at home. The percentage of Dutch people with an Internet connection at home has increased from 4% in 1995 to 21% in 1998 and to 59% in 2001 (Van Dijk, De Haan, & Rijken, 2000; De Haan, 2003). In addition, the TUS provides information on the use of the PC during leisure time from the diaries. Table 5.4 shows that in 2000, 45% of the population used the PC at least for a quarter of an hour in the TUS week, almost double the 1995 percentage of 23%. The weekly use increases faster than the spread of the PC itself, implying that nonuse of PCs at home is declining. The percentage of PC owners who were active in the TUS week increased from 40% in 1995 to 60% in 2000. The rise of PC use between 1995 and 2000 has not resulted in a further increase of the number of hours that PC users are active. This number remained constant at an average of 4 hours per week. To measure the use of the Internet separately from other PC use, a distinction between these two categories was made in TUS 2000.

Internet Time

In 2000, 24% of the population aged 12 years and older used the Internet at least for a quarter of an hour in the TUS week, amounting to an average of half an hour a week among the whole population (table 5.5). Internet use is relatively low among women, the elderly, and the less educated. During a normal week, men surf the Internet twice as long as women. Working people and students also use the Internet above average, whereas the retired lag far behind. Internet use among the unemployed and disabled is remarkably high.

Given the zero-sum fixed "budget" of 168 hours per week, more IT time inevitably means that fewer hours are available for other activities. Following the functional-equivalence argument, time-displacement effects might be expected in time spent on social activities and media use, in particular, because the Internet enhances communication and the retrieval of information.

A first inspection of the time-use data does indicate that Internet users spend significantly more time on paid work than do nonusers (table 5.6), although Internet access may not be the cause of this difference. Working people are more often male, young, and highly educated—also characteristics of people who have access to the Internet at home. Although controlling for the influence of these social and demographic characteristics does not settle the question of causality, it does clarify whether these difference between Internet users and nonusers are solely a function of background factors.

After MCA adjustment, a quite different picture of the differences in paid work time emerges, in that Internet users turn out to spend 2 hours less on paid work than do nonusers. The high proportion of explained variance and the low beta indicate that the differences in paid work time are mainly attributable to social and demographic characteristics, and not so much to Internet use per se. Given the low value of the beta of the variable "use/nonuse," the original relationship can mainly be attributed to demographic differences. Taken together, the time spent on work, study, and the household is called "productive time" in table 5.6. Mainly because of paid work, Internet users seem to be busier than nonusers, but after MCA controls, it is the nonusers who are actually busier—with not only more time spent on paid work but also more time spent on childcare and household chores

Table 5.4. Computer use among Dutch population aged 12 years and older, 1985–2000 (in percentages and hours).

	1985	1990	1995	2000
Has a PC at home (in %)	18	30	51	70
Uses PC during leisure in TUS week (in %)	4	13	23	45
Uses Internet during leisure in TUS week (in %)				24
PC use among PC owners (in %)	18	33	40	60
Average number of hours spent on PC by users (in TUS week)	3.5	3.7	4.0	3.9

Source: SCP (TUS 2000). See explanation of Time Use Studies (TUS) in text.

Table 5.5. PC use of online services, population aged 12 years and older, 2000 (in percentages of PC owners).

	Internet	Other PC use
Population aged 12 years and older	0.5	1.3
Gender		
Males	0.7	1.8
Females	0.3	0.7
Age		
12–19 years	0.7	2.7
20–34 years	0.6	1.0
35–49 years	0.6	1.4
50–64 years	0.5	1.2
65 years and older	0.1	0.5
Family status		
Living with parents	0.6	2.1
Single	0.5	1.1
With partner without kids	0.5	1.0
Parent(s) with kid(s) at home	0.5	1.3
Education		
Lower	0.3	1.1
Middle	0.6	1.5
Higher	0.7	1.2
Labor market status		
Student	0.7	2.6
Worker	0.6	1.2
Homemaker	0.3	0.8
Unemployed, disabled	1.1	1.9
Retired	0.1	0.6

Source: SCP (TUS 2000).

as well—differences that hold after MCA adjustment. However, Internet users devote more time than nonusers to education, even after age controls.

Internet users do spend fewer hours on personal time (sleeping, eating, and personal care). Again, MCA adjustment makes a difference. The amount of time spent on sleeping and eating is the same for Internet users and nonusers after controlling for social and demographic variables.

In 2000, most Dutch people had less free time than in 1990 (Breedveld & Van den Broek, 2001). An increase in labor market participation (mainly part-time jobs occupied by women) is one of the reasons, and longer sleep time is another. Internet users appear to have somewhat less free time (1.3 hours) than nonusers, here again a difference largely explained by demographic factors. After MCA adjustment, however, Internet users have more free time (3.1 hours) than nonusers, and the amount of free time is also strongly related to social and demographic characteristics.

A detailed comparison of the weekly free-time activities of Internet users and nonusers is also shown in table 5.6, with statistically significant bivariate differences ($p < .05/.01$) visible for the number of hours spent on electronic media (television, radio, and stereo), on social participation, and on hobbies other than sports, culture, and church attendance. After MCA adjustment, these differences are no longer significant, leading to the conclusion that there is actually no difference in the use of free time between users and nonusers. Again, another exception appears after controls—Internet users spend more time on print media than do nonusers. This significant difference after MCA adjustment is related to the reading of books, with no differences found in the reading of newspapers, magazines, or advertisements (De Haan & Huysmans, 2002).

Regarding family life and other domestic social contacts, the changes across time are varied. Compared with 1995, people spent more time at home in 2000, ate together as a family in the evening to the same extent, and set aside just as much time for activities with children; but they spent less time in

Table 5.6. Differences in the total time budget (productive time, personal care, and leisure), population aged 12 and over, 2000 (in hours per week).

	Before MCA controls				After MCA controls[a]				
	Internet users	Nonusers	Internet difference	Eta	Internet users	Nonusers	Internet difference	Beta	R^2
Productive time	46.7	43.0	3.7**	.09	42.1	44.5	−2.4**	.06	.38
Paid work	23.9	18.0	5.9**	.12	18.0	20.0	−2.0*	.04	.38
Family care	14.8	20.3	−5.5**	.16	17.7	19.4	−1.7**	.05	.47
Education	8.0	4.7	3.3**	.11	6.4	5.2	1.2*	.04	.49
Personal care	74.9	77.2	−2.3**	.09	76.1	76.8	−0.7	.03	.07
Sleeping	59.6	61.3	−1.7**	.08	60.3	61.1	−0.8	.03	.08
Personal care	5.9	5.9	0.0	.00	6.1	5.8	.03	.03	.03
Eating (at home)	9.5	10.0	−0.5*	.05	9.8	9.9	−0.1	.01	.07
Free time	43.8	45.1	−1.3	.04	47.2	44.1	3.1**	.09	.32
Print media	3.7	4.0	−0.3	.03	4.3	3.9	0.4*	.05	.25
TV, radio, stereo	11.5	13.5	−2.0**	.10	−12.8	13.1	−0.3	.02	.13
Social contacts	9.7	10.2	−0.5	.03	10.1	10.1	0.0	.00	.05
Social participation	1.3	2.0	−0.7**	.03	1.5	2.0	−0.5	.04	.05
Going out	2.8	2.5	0.3	.04	2.5	2.6	−0.1	.01	.06
Sport and exercises	2.0	1.7	0.3	.03	1.8	1.8	0.0	.00	.04
Other hobbies	5.4	7.3	−1.9**	.11	6.8	6.9	0.1	.01	.16
Free time travel	3.1	3.0	0.1	.01	3.1	3.0	0.1	.01	.05

Source: SCP (TUS 2000).
[a]Controlling for gender, age, education, family status and employment status
**Difference significant at $p < .01$.
*Difference significant at $p < .05$.

conversation with family and other household members and devoted less time to visiting. The reduction in contact with family and visits with friends and others not in the household is part of a trend that has been visible for some time. Although people appear to spend more time at home, they have not become more homebodies in terms of outside social contacts (Van den Broek, 2001).

In the Netherlands, much of the discussion on the effects of Internet has centered on its influence on social contacts (Steyaert & De Haan, 2001; De Haan & Klumper, 2004). De Haan and Huysmans (2003) conclude, in line with most international research, that computer-mediated communication tends more to *supplement* existing social relations than to replace them (cf. Wellman, Haase, Witte & Hampton, 2001; Gershuny, 2002a; Kestnbaum, Robinson, Neustadtl & Alvarez, 2002; Robinson & Nie, 2002). Table 5.7 shows hardly any differences between Internet users and nonusers in various forms of social activity. Statistically significant bivariate differences ($p < .05/.01$) are visible for the number of hours spent on talking to household members and for the general category of contacts with others, but these differences are not statistically significant after MCA adjustment.

The results are very similar to those in the United States, although Kestnbaum et al. (2002) found that IT users spent more time on conversation at home than did nonusers. Again, a Dutch exception is that after MCA controls, Internet users spend less time on attention to children (reading to them, games, talks, and walks) than did nonusers. Among 18–64-year-old respondents, however, this discrepancy did not reach significance. In contrast, in this age group, Internet users used the telephone more than nonusers. That aggregated categories of time use do not show any significant difference between Internet users and nonusers does not imply that differences in activity at a lower level of aggregation are also automatically not significant—as with time spent on attention to children.

Summary and Conclusions

The early adopters of the Internet in the Netherlands on average had more free time than nonusers. Internet users spent less time on paid work and household tasks (including child care). The rise of the information society in the Netherlands might reinforce images of a leisure paradise, however,

Dutch Internet users did spend more time on education than nonusers.

Within the free time, hardly any differences could be found between Internet users and nonusers for specific activities. Thus, the displacement effects found with television are not replicated for the Internet in the Netherlands. Moreover, the higher book-reading time among Internet users points in the opposite direction, so that the Internet shows up as a "time enhancer" of reading in the Netherlands, much as in the United States. Both this enhancement of reading and the similarity of time spent on social life among Internet users and nonusers are inconsistent with the idea of functional time displacement.

Other Studies

The above analysis casts doubt on the usefulness of the functional-equivalence thesis in respect to IT usage. Not all the expected differences between users and nonusers are consistent with expectations, and many differences become very small after adequate controls. We conclude by placing these results in the context of other findings.

Similar to most evidence in the social sciences that attempts to integrate the results from several sources, methods, and authors, there is far less than unanimity of results and conclusions about time displacement and the Internet. At the risk of oversimplification, an overview of other study findings is summarized in tables 5.8 and 5.9. The designation "+" in these tables refers to positive relations (more Internet use is associated with increases in that activity), the designation "−" is associated with negative relations or time displacement, and "0" is associated with no significant relation. In each cell of tables 5.8 and 5.9, the bivariate or unadjusted relation is shown first, and the multivariate relation is shown after the slash (/) sign. Results are also shown separately for short-term comparisons (yesterday) and long-term comparison (weekly, monthly, or longer-run IT use). The term "NA" means that the study contains no applicable data to test the hypothesis in question.

Readers interested in further details on the settings, conditions, and methods of each the studies can find them in issue 2 of *IT and Society*, although it is important to note that almost all of the studies were conducted with samples designed to be nationally representative (including the Dutch studies, which are the same as those described in the previous section).

Following from the functional-equivalence hypothesis, it was expected that two domains of time use would suffer from the rise of the Internet, one regarding social life and the other media use. Concerning television, most studies in table 5.8 find no relation with Internet use, especially after control for other factors. This is in line with the findings from the A. C. Nielsen/NetRatings (1999) study cited by television industry executives, which found no lower viewing levels among PC purchasers.

Table 5.7. Differences in time spent on social contacts, population aged 12 and over, 2000 (in hours per week).

	Before MCA controls				After MCA controls[a]				
	Internet users	Nonusers	Internet difference	Eta	Internet	Nonusers	Internet	Beta	R^2
Total social contact time	10.5	11.0	−0.5	.03	10.8	10.9	−0.1	.01	.07
With household members	2.5	2.3	0.2	.03	2.3	2.4	−0.1	.01	.16
Talking	1.5	1.3	0.2*	.06	1.4	1.3	0.1	.03	.05
Attention to kids	0.8	0.8	0.0	.00	0.7	0.9	−0.2*	.05	.19
Playing games	0.2	0.2	0.0	.03	0.2	0.2	0.0	.01	.01
With others	8.0	8.7	−0.7*	.05	8.5	8.6	−0.1	.00	.05
Visitors	1.9	2.1	−0.2	.03	2.3	2.0	0.3	.04	.06
Visiting others	4.0	4.5	−0.5	.05	4.2	4.4	−0.2	.02	.03
Party/diner/reception	1.3	1.4	−0.1	.02	1.2	1.4	−0.2	.04	.01
Telephone	0.8	0.7	0.1	.03	0.8	0.7	0.1	.05	.09

Source: SCP (TUS 2000).
[a]Controlling for gender, age, education, family status and employment status.
**Difference significant at $p < .01$.
*Difference significant at $p < .05$.

Table 5.8. Summary of the relationship between Internet use and time spent on other media.

Study	Television		Reading		Radio/stereo	
	Long-term	Short-term	Long-term	Short-term	Long-term	Short-term
SIQSS	NA	–/–	NA	–/–	NA	0/0
Maryland	–/–	–/–	+/+	0/0	0/0	0/0
Sloan Family	–/0	NA	0/0	NA	0/0	NA
Canada	–/–	0/0	+/+	+/+	0/0	0/0
UK	0/0	NA	0/0	NA	0/0	NA
Netherlands A	–/0	NA	0/0	NA	0/0	NA
Netherlands B	NA		NA		NA	
Pew 1998–2000	0/0	0/0	+/0	+/+	NA	
GSS	–/0	NA	+/0	NA	NA	
UCLA	–/0	NA	+/+	NA	+/+	
SIQSS	–/NA	NA	–/NA	NA	NA	

Research summarized here was originally reported in *IT&Society*, *1*(1) (http://www.stanford.edu/group/siqss/itandsociety/v01i01.html). Values represent relationships unadjusted/adjusted for demographic differences, using multiple classification analysis. –, Significant negative relationship; +, significant positive relationship; NA, no available data.

Four of the other studies (the Sloan Family Time, the Dutch TUS identified above, the General Social Survey, and UCLA Internet, as identified and presented in issue 2 of IT&Society), in contrast, do find a significant bivariate difference initially, but one that is largely explained by Internet users having higher education, lower age, and the like. The U.K. panel study similarly found an overall lower television viewing figure for IT users, but one that did not hold when new users, prior users, and nonusers were examined separately. The main exceptions are the SIQSS Internet diaries and the University of Maryland telephone and Canadian telephone diary studies, which provide the most persuasive evidence of a displacement effect of television by IT.

The more interesting, and counterintuitive (given the zero-sum nature of time as a variable), findings concern the *higher* reading times among IT users. This shows up after multivariate adjustment in almost half of the studies, and the relation usually holds after these multivariate adjustments for various background predictors are taken into account. Notably, only the

Table 5.9. Summary of the relationship between Internet use and time spent on other activities.

Study	Sleep		Work/education		Family care	
	Long-term	Short-term	Long-term	Short-term	Long-term	Short-term
SIQSS	NA	–/–	NA	–/–	NA	0/0
Maryland	–/–	0/0	+/+	–/–	–/–	–/0
Sloan Family	–/–	NA	–/–	NA	0/0	NA
Canada	0/0	–/–			–/0	–/0
UK	0/0	NA	–/0	NA	0/0	NA
Netherlands	–/0	NA	–/–	NA	–/–	NA

Research summarized here was originally reported in *IT&Society*, *1*(1) (http://www.stanford.edu/group/siqss/itandsociety/v01i01.html). Values represent relationships unadjusted/adjusted for demographic differences, using multiple classification analysis. –, Significant negative relationship; +, significant positive relationship; NA, no available data.

SIQSS study shows significantly *lower* reading times among IT users, even after education and other predictors are taken into account.

There is some evidence of lower amounts of time spent in sleep in the SIQSS, Maryland, and Canadian diaries. Using an estimate question, however, no such sleep difference was found in the UCLA data (not shown in table 5.9).

There is also some evidence of lower-paid work and higher education among users—a finding that needs further study to understand whether this means Internet users are working at home, were interviewed on a day off from work, or just work fewer hours for other reasons. Almost no studies provide consistent or persuasive support that more IT use is associated with less housework or child and family care.

Overall, then, there is some evidence that Internet use is associated with lower amounts of time spent at work, in television viewing, and in sleep. However, like the findings relating Internet use and social life in the issue 1 of *IT&Society* (as summarized in table 5.10), the evidence is scattered, often insignificant, or sometimes simply explained by background factors.

Thus, most of the predictions derived from the functional-equivalence hypothesis have not been confirmed in many of the detailed national studies done to date. Time displacement has not concentrated in the domains of media use and social life, as Robinson (1972) found to be the case for television. Moreover, some uses of time that do not seem a priori to be functionally equivalent do distinguish Internet users from nonusers, and some forms of media time use, especially book reading, were higher—contrary to expectations. This raises the question of why some of these differences in time use between users and nonusers occur.

A resource-driven explanation was suggested above to account for the differences between IT users and nonusers, as an alternative to the functional equivalent hypothesis (see De Haan & Rijken, 2002). People choose between behavioral alternatives based on the resources they control. People rich in cultural resources use different media to inform themselves. Their wide diversity of use indicates that different media are not considered to be competing alternatives but, rather, complementary sources. This would account for

Table 5.10. Studies on the Internet and sociability.

	Strongly antisocial	Tending antisocial	Neither; both	Tending prosocial	Strongly prosocial
Time-diary data					
Nie and Hillygus (Stanford)	−				
Kestnbaum et al. (Maryland)			0	+	
Qiu et al. (Maryland)			0		
Gershuny (Essex)			0		
Pronovost (Quebec)			0		
Time estimate data					
GSS Social Contacts (Maryland)			0	+	
GSS Sex and Church (Maryland)		−		+	
Kraut (CM)				+	
Horrigan and Rainie (Pew)				+	
Rice (Rutgers)				+	
Wellman, Boase and Chen (Toronto)			0	+	
Cole and Robinson (UCLA)			0	+	
Coget, Yamauchi and Suman (UCLA)			0	+	
Zhu and Lee (Hong Kong)			0		
Liang and Wei (China)			0		
Mikami (Japan)			0		
Mandelli (Italy)			0	+	
Nie and Erbring (Stanford)	−				
Attitudes					
Diversity Divide (Maryland)				+	
Price (Pennsylvania)				+	+

Research summarized here was originally reported in *IT&Society* 1(2) (http://www.stanford.edu/group/siqss/itandsociety/v01i02.html). Values represent relationships unadjusted/adjusted for demographic differences using multiple classification analysis. −, Significant negative relationship; +, significant positive relationship; NA, no available data.

the positive relation between book reading and Internet use.

However, it cannot explain the negative relation between Internet use and television watching. In general, people with more resources are expected to follow different paths of action to reach the same goal, whether this is seeking information or keeping up one's social contacts. People rich in social resources (such as knowing many people who can give support, companionship, or respect) can be expected to use many different channels of communication, ranging from face-to-face contacts to computer-mediated communication. This would lead to a prediction that e-communication functions to replace or substitute for existing media for so-cial contact. Given the predominant research conclusion that no differences were found in time spent on social contact between Internet users and non-users, this line of thinking is not supported. Each of the theoretical approaches would need further elaboration, careful deduction of testable hypothesis, and appropriate data collection.

Perhaps it is too much to expect a strong influence of the Internet. Television still continues to consume 3 to 10 times as much of people's time as IT. Historically, and unlike other modern technologies, television truly revolutionized how people spent time (Robinson & Godbey, 1999). It seems doubtful that IT will ever have a similar temporal or consistent impact on our daily lives.

Appendix A. Sample of a Completed Time Diary

Female, Cook, Age 40, Married with 2 children—Friday, December 3, 1965

What did you do?	Time began	Time ended	Where?	With whom?	Doing anything else?
Watch television	12:00	12:15	Home	—	No
Got daughter from work	12:15	12:30	Transit	Daughter	No
Got ready for bed	12:30	12:50	Home	—	No
Sleep	12:50	4:00	Home	—	No
Got up—made lunches and breakfast for family	4:00	4:30	Home	—	No
Got ready for work	4:30	4:55	Transit	—	No
Left for work (car)	4:55	5:00	Transit	—	No
Work	5:00	8:00	Restaurant	Employees	No
Coffee break	8:00	8:15	Restaurant	Friend	Talked
Work	8:15	12:00	Restaurant	Employees	No
Ate lunch	12:00	12:15	Restaurant	Employees	Talked
Work	12:15	1:30	Restaurant	Employees	No
Off work—drove home	1:30	1:35	Transit	—	No
Visited with neighbor	1:35	2:00	Yard	Neighbor	Talked
Cleaned house	2:00	5:15	House	—	Radio
Got daughter from school	5:15	5:45	Transit	Daughter	No
Took shower	5:45	6:00	Home	—	No
Made supper	6:00	7:15	Home	—	—
Took daughter to school	6:25	7:00	Transit	Daughter	—
Served meal	7:00	7:15	Home	Family	—
Ate supper	7:15	8:00	Home	Family	Talked
Did dishes	8:00	8:30	Home	Daughter	Talked
Washed clothes	8:30	9:00	Home	—	No
Sat down and watched television	9:00	10:15	Home	Family	No
Got daughter from work	10:15	10:30	Transit	Daughter	No
Got ready for bed	10:30	10:45	Home	—	No
Went to bed; sleep	10:45	12:00	Home	—	No

Appendix B: Basic Two-Digit Activity Code

0–54 Nonfree-Time Activities
00–09 Paid Work
00	(Not used)
01	Main job
02	Unemployment
03	Work travel
04	(Not used)
05	Second job
06	(Not used)
07	(Not used)
08	Breaks
09	Travel/to-from work

10–19 Household Work
10	Food preparation
11	Meal cleanup
12	Cleaning house
13	Outdoor cleaning
14	Clothes care
15	Car repair
16	Other
17	Plant
18	Pet care
19	Other household

20–29 Child Care
20	Baby care
21	Child care
22	Helping/teaching
23	Talking/reading
24	Indoor playing
25	Outdoor playing
26	Medical care—child
27	Other child care
28	(Not used)
29	Travel/child care

30-39 Obtaining Goods/Services
30	Everyday shopping
31	Durable/house shop
32	Personal services
33	Medical appts
34	Govt/financial services
35	Repair services
36	Other services
37	Other
38	Other Errands
39	Travel/goods, services

40–49 Personal Needs and Care
40	Washing, hygiene, etc.
41	Medical care
42	Help and care
43	Eating
44	Personal
45	Night sleep
46	(Not used)
47	Dressing
48	Not ascertaincd activity
49	Travel/personal care

50–59 Educational
50	Attend classes
51	Other classes
52	(Not used)
53	(Not used)
54	Homework

55–99 Free-Time Activities
55	Library use
56	Internet use
57	Computer games
58	Other computer use
59	Travel/education

60–69 Organizational
60	Professional/union
61	Special interest
62	Political/civic
63	Volunteer helping
64	Religious groups
65	Religious practice
66	Fraternal
67	Child/youth/family
68	Other organizations
69	Travel/organizational

70–79 Entertainment/Social
70	Sports events
71	Entertainment
72	Movies
73	Theater
74	Museums
75	Visiting
76	Parties
77	Bars/lounges
78	Other social
79	Travel/social

80–89 Recreation
80	Active sports
81	Outdoor
82	Exercise
83	Hobbies
84	Domestic crafts
85	Art
86	Music/drama/dance
87	Games
88	Computer use games
89	Travel/recreation

90–99 Communications
90	Radio
91	Television
92	Records/tapes
93	Read books
94	Magazines/etc.
95	Reading newspaper
96	Conversations
97	Writing
98	Think/relax
99	Travel/communication

Acknowledgments.   We gratefully acknowledge the National Science Foundation, Office of Science and Technology, for support through grants NSF01523184, NSF0086143, and SBR-9602058, and the Alfred P. Sloan Foundation's Working Families Program.

References

Andrews, F., Morgan, J., & Sonquist, J. (1973). *Multiple classification analysis.* Ann Arbor, MI: Institute for Social Research.

Bogart, L. (1956). *The age of television: A study of viewing habits and the impact of television on American life.* New York: Unger.

Breedveld, K., & Van den Broek, A. (Eds.). (2001). *Trends in de tijd. Een schets van recente ontwikkelingen in tijdsbesteding en tijdsordening.* Den Haag: SCP.

Coffin, T. (1954). Television's impact on society. *American Psychologist, 10,* 630–641.

Cole, J., Suman, J., Schramm, P., Lunn, R., & Coget, J. (2001). *The UCLA Internet report 2001. Surveying the digital future.* Los Angeles: University of California, Los Angeles, Center for Communication Policy.

De Haan, J. (2003). IT and social inequality in the Netherlands. *IT&Society, 1*(4), 27–45.

De Haan, J., & Huysmans, F. (2002) Differences in time use between Internet users and nonusers in the Netherlands. *IT&Society, 1*(2), 67–85.

De Haan, J., & Huysmans, F. (2003). Revolution or eVolution, an empirical approach to eCulture. In Dodd, D. (Ed.), *eCulture: The European perspective: cultural policy—knowledge industries—information lag.* International Conference Reader, Zagreb, Croatia, 24–27 April 2003. Retrieved July 14, 2004 from http://www.culturelink.org/conf/ecult/ecultread.html.

De Haan, J., & Klumper, O. (Eds.). (2004). *Jaarboek ICT & Samenleving: beleid in praktijk,* Amsterdam: Boom.

De Haan, J., & Rijken, S. (2002). The digital divide in the Netherlands: The influence of material, cognitive and social resources on the possession and use of ICTs. *Electronic Journal of Communication, 12,* 1&2..

Gershuny, J. (2002). Social leisure and home IT: A panel time-diary approach. *IT&Society, 1*(1), 54–72.

Gershuny, J. (2003). Web-use and net-nerds: A neo-functionalist analysis of the impact of information technology in the home. *Social Forces, 82*(1), 141–168.

Kestnbaum, M., Robinson, J. P., Neustadtl, A., & Alvarez, A. S. (2002). IT and social time displacement. *IT&Society, 1*(1), 21–37.

Knulst, W. P. (1995). Podia in een tijdperk van afstandsbediening. Onderzoek naar achtergronden van veranderingen in de omvang en samenstelling van het podiumpubliek sinds de jaren vijftig. Het culturele draagvlak, deel 1. Rijswijk/Den Haag: SCP/VUGA.

Knulst, W. P., & Kraaykamp, G. (1996). Leesgewoonten. Een halve eeuw onderzoek naar het lezen en zijn belagers. Het culturele draagvlak, deel 2. Rijswijk/Den Haag: SCP/VUGA.

Lindenberg, S. (1998). Solidarity: its microfoundations and macrodependence; a framing approach (pp. 61–111). In Doreian, P., & Fararo, T. (Eds.), *The problem of solidarity; theory and models.* Amsterdam: Gordon and Breach..

McQuail, D. (1994). *McQuail's mass communication theory,* fourth edition. London: Sage.

Nie, N. H., & Erbring, L. (2000). Internet and society: A preliminary report. *IT&Society, 1*(1), 275–283.

Nielsen/NetRatings. (1999). *TV viewing in Internet households. A report by Nielsen Media Research.* Retrieved July 7, 2004 from http://www.nielsen-netratings.com/.

Robinson, J. P. (1972). Television's impact on everyday life: Some cross-national evidence (Vol. 4, pp. 410–431). In Rubinstein, E., Comstock, G., & Murray, J. (Eds.), *Television and social behavior.* Washington, DC: Government Printing Office.

Robinson, J. P., Barth, K., & Kohut, A. (1997). Personal computers, mass media, and use of time. *Social Science Computer Review, 15,* 65–82.

Robinson, J. P., & Godbey, G. (1999). *Time for life: The surprising ways Americans use their time.* University Park: Pennsylvania State University Press.

Robinson, J. P., & Kestnbaum, M. (1999). The personal computer, culture and other uses of free time. *Social Science Computer Review, Summer, 17,* 209–216.

Robinson, J. P., Kestnbaum, M., Neustadtl, A., & Alvarez, A. (2000). Mass media use and social life among Internet users. *Social Science Computer Review, 18*(4), 490–501.

Robinson, J. P., & Nie, N. H. (2002). Introduction to *IT&Society* issue 1: Sociability. *IT&Society, 1*(1), i–xi.

Schramm, W. L., Lyle, J., & Parker, E. B. (1961). *Television in the lives of our children.* Stanford, CA: Stanford University Press.

Steyaert, J., & De Haan, J. (2001). Geleidelijk digitaal. Den Haag: SCP.

Szalai, A. (1972). *The use of time: Daily activities of urban and suburban populations in twelve countries.* The Hague: Mouton.

Van den Broek, A. (2001). Sociale contacten. In Breedveld, K., and Van den Broek, A. (Eds.), *Trends in de tijd. Een schets van recente ontwikkelingen in tijdsbesteding en tijdsordening.* Den Haag: SCP.

van Dijk, L., De Haan, J., & Rijken, S. (2000). *Digitalisering van de leefwereld; een onderzoek naar informatie- en communicatietechnologie en sociale ongelijkheid; eindrapport.* Den Haag: SCP.

Weiss, W. (1969). Effects of mass media on communication. In Lindzey, G., & Aronson, E. (Eds.), Handbook of social psychology (Vol. 5, pp. 77–195). Reading, MA: Addison-Wesley.

Wellman, B., Haase, A., Witte, J., & Hampton, K.. (2001). Does the internet increase, decrease or supplement social capital? Social network, participation and community commitment. *American Behavioral Scientist, 45,* 437–456.

Wright, C. R. (1986). Mass communication; a sociological perspective. New York: Random House.

Robert Kraut, Sara Kiesler,

Bonka Boneva, and Irina Shklovski

Examining the Effect of Internet Use on Television Viewing

Details Make a Difference

The proportion of U.S. households with a computer soared from 8.2% in 1984 to 56.5% in 2001. By September 2001, over 50% of U.S. households also had Internet access (U.S. Department of Commerce, 2002). The dramatic changes now occurring in household computing have the potential to change the lives of average citizens as much as the telephone did in the early 1900s and the television did in the 1950s and 1960s. Social scientists are now attempting to document how computing and the Internet are becoming integrated into the daily lives of users and the effects that this use is having. For example, efforts to document the effect of Internet use are occurring in the domains of psychological use of time and other media (see chapter 5), establishment and maintenance of social relationships (see chapter 19), political participation (Katz & Rice, 2002), psychological functioning, health, education (see chapter 11), and consumer behavior, among other domains.

This chapter examines the methods that many social scientists deploy to examine this effect. We review prior literature to illustrate problems that are widespread in examining the influence of Internet use. We argue that much of this research reaches limited or even erroneous conclusions, both because it uses cross-sectional data to draw causal

implications and because it fails to distinguish between varieties of Internet use.

The empirical section of this chapter is based on a national panel survey of 980 individuals. We show that the Internet is used for a wide range of functions. We use confirmatory factor analysis to disaggregate overall Internet use into a set of components, which are only moderately related with each other: interpersonal communication with friends and family, interpersonal communication with strangers, instrumental information seeking, entertainment, and commerce. Just as one would expect that chatting with friends on the phone and watching entertainment on television would have different influences on those who use these earlier technologies, so too would one expect that using the Internet for different purposes will have different effects on its users.

The empirical study examines the effects of Internet use on television viewing, illustrating the time-use perspective on the effect of new media. We use hierarchical linear growth modeling to differentiate cross-sectional from longitudinal relationships. Conclusions from cross-sectional data differ from those based on longitudinal data, and both sets of conclusions depend on how people use the Internet. For example, the cross-sectional analyses show that people who use the Internet heavily tend to watch television more frequently than those who do not use the Internet at all or who use it lightly. This association is especially strong for people who use the Internet for entertainment and escapist activities and is reversed for people who use the Internet to communicate with friends and family. In contrast, the longitudinal data show that heavier use of the Internet is associated with declines in television viewing. This association is especially strong for people who use the Internet to participate in online groups and meet new people online.

Problems with the Current Research

Varieties of Internet Use

Compared to television or the telephone, the Internet is a plastic technology, amenable to a wider range of uses. According to recent data from the Pew Internet and American Life project (Pew Internet & American Life Project, 2003), Americans use the Internet most for sending electronic mail, using search engines, researching products and services before buying, and looking for information for hobbies and leisure activities. However, the range of use is very diverse and includes playing online games, listening to music, downloading pornography, developing and displaying photographs, gambling, taking a class, and seeking dates. As individuals gain more experience with the Internet, they increasingly use it for a wider variety of purposes. Subscribers get Internet access for one purpose, but then its use extends to many other areas of daily life. For example, parents may buy a computer for their children's school work but then find that the household also uses it for e-mail, instant messaging, game-playing, and online shopping (e.g., Kraut, Scherlis, Mukhopadhyay, Manning, & Kiesler, 1996).

Moreover, the potential uses of the Internet have expanded greatly as businesses and other organizations offer new content and services online. Although information sharing and communication were available from the early days of the ARPAnet (Leiner et al., 2002) the amount of information available, the topics covered, the numbers of potential online communication partners, and the services to support information acquisition and communication have all increased since the 1970s, radically expanding the options open to users. Two

popular yet recent additions include sophisticated search engines and instant messaging applications.

Despite this diversity of use, most research on the social impact of the Internet treats its use as an undifferentiatable whole. Many researchers simply compare Internet users with nonusers (e.g., Cole et al., 2000; Pronovost, 2002; Robinson, Kestnbaum, Neustadtl, & Alvarez, 2002), which is an especially crude comparison. Others compute an aggregate frequency-of-use measure without differentiating among types of use. For example, our own research used a summary index of Internet use (self-reported frequency of use in Kraut et al., 2002; machine-logged hours of use in Kraut et al., 1998) when assessing the consequences of Internet use on social involvement and psychological well-being. Others concentrate on people's history of online activity; for example, distinguishing new users from veterans (e.g., Cummings & Kraut, 2002; Howard, Rainie, & Jones, 2001; Katz & Aspden, 1997).

There is strong reason to think that different personal attributes and precipitating events will cause people to use the Internet for different purposes. For example, compared to adults, teenagers and young adults are much more likely to use the Internet for listening to music, for visiting chat rooms to meet new people, and for synchronous communication through instant messaging programs (Lenhart, Rainie, & Lewis, 2001). Consistent with their broader role responsibilities, women are more likely than men to use the Internet for communication with friends and family (Boneva, Kraut, & Frohlich, 2001). Women, people who are ill, and those who care for ill family members are especially likely to use the Internet as a course of health information (Kommers & Rainie, 2002). Extraverts are especially likely to use the Internet for social communication (Kraut et al., 2002).

There is also reason to expect that using the Internet for different purposes is likely to have differential effects on the users. McKenna (chapter 19) argues, for example, that people who use the Internet to reveal aspects of their true selves get more benefit from its use than do others. The parallels with television viewing, a much more constrained activity, are instructive. Watching dramatic violence on television in childhood leads to more aggressive behavior in adulthood (Huesmann, Moise-Titus, Podolski, & Eron, 2003). How television is used, however, makes a difference. In addition to this influence on adult aggression, using television primarily for entertainment purposes (rather than for information) is associated with declines in civic engagement. In contrast, watching the news on television, even though it is filled with violence, seems to be associated with more benign social outcomes, including increased civic engagement (Putnam, 2000).

Very little research has attempted to demonstrate that specific uses of the Internet have identifiable consequences, and most of it is concentrated in the area of health (see Bass, 2003, for a recent review). More generally, Kraut, Mukhopadhyay, Szczypula, Kiesler, and Scherlis (1999) distinguished between using the Internet for interpersonal communication and using it for acquiring information. Although using the Internet for communication led to increased time spent online in subsequent periods, using the Internet for information-gathering purposes decreased time spent online in subsequent periods. Weiser (2001) also differentiated between using the Internet for social reasons and for information purposes. On the basis of cross-sectional data, he concluded that social uses of the Internet led to reduced social integration, whereas greater use of the Internet for informational purposes was associated with increased social integration. Although valid, the distinction between communication and informational uses of the Internet is not precise enough. For example, communication with friends and family is likely to differ from communication with strangers online, both in terms of causes and of consequences. Weiser's (2001) paradoxical conclusions that social uses of the Internet were associated with low social integration may reflect his construction of a social use scale that was dominated by communication with strangers. One of the goals of the current research is to differentiate among uses of the Internet in a richer way and to identify uses that lead to changes in other media use.

Comparison of Cross-Sectional and Longitudinal Research Methods

The second goal of this chapter is to illustrate how survey research design can influence the conclusions one can draw about the effects of Internet use. To do so, our research contrasts cross-sectional designs with panel designs. Cross-sectional designs assess the association of Internet use and a variable of interest at a single time point. In contrast, panel designs collect data from the same people at multiple time periods and estimate the degree to which changes in a dependent variable are associated with Internet use.

Documenting the Effect of Internet Use

To make these issues concrete, we examine the effects that Internet use has on television viewing. The Internet's effect on the use of other media is related to earlier research in media studies that examines the substitutability of the mass media or their ability to stimulate each other (Atkin, 2001; Robinson & Kestnbaum, 1999). In addition, this dependent variable is generally representative of a research tradition that examines how the introduction of one pastime affects other uses of time (Gershuny, 2000; Robinson, 1990).

Many commentators hypothesize that the Internet will displace television or, at least, will reduce its dominance in the American household, much as television viewing did to listening to the radio, reading magazines, or going to the movies. As Robinson and De Haan (chapter 5, this volume) note, according to a functional displacement hypothesis, one technology will displace another to the extent that the new technology can be used for similar functions as the old, while offering new opportunities or reduced costs (Carey & Moss, 1985). For example, television displaced radio as the preferred source for story-based entertainment and the evening newspaper as the source for news, in part, by augmenting the earlier technologies with moving pictures. By this logic, one may expect that the Internet could displace television as a source of both entertainment and news by increasing the diversity of available material and offering individualization of schedule and content.

To date, evidence on how Internet use affects television watching is ambiguous. For example, Coffey and Stripp (1997) concluded from PC meter data that personal computer use did not reduce the time users spent viewing television. Around that same time, in a seminal study of American use of time, based on self-report diary data, Robinson and Godbey (1999) found no substitution of television watching with computer use. However, results from more recent research are mixed, with some research indicating that the Internet is displacing television watching (Kaynay & Yelsma, 2000; Nie & Hillygus, 2002) and some showing just the reverse—that

Internet use increases TV watching and other media use (Cole et al., 2000). In chapter 5, Robinson and De Haan show that Internet users watch approximately 4 fewer hours of television per week than do nonusers in the United States (table 5.2), but in the Netherlands, Internet users and nonusers do not differ in their hours of television watching (table 5.4).

The functional displacement hypothesis goes beyond merely predicting that heavy Internet use will lead to reductions in television viewing. If functional displacement is happening, then how people use the Internet should determine what other technologies will be displaced. In particular, we should expect to see greater reductions in television watching among those who use the Internet for news and entertainment purposes than among those who use it for other purposes, including communication and commerce.

Data and Methods

Data Collection

The data for this study come from a national United States panel survey conducted between June 2000 and March 2002. Respondents completed a questionnaire at time 1, starting in June 2001, and again 6–8 months later at time 2, via postal mail or on the Internet. The national sample was recruited by random digit dialing of residential telephone exchanges to secure a representative sample of United States households. Of those initially contacted by telephone, 43% agreed to participate. Of the original sample, 41% completed the survey at time 1, and 82.8% of these participants completed the survey again at time 2. Seventy-four percent of respondents at time 1 and 72.3% at time 2 had Internet access. Respondents with Internet access were asked to complete the survey online, whereas those who did not have Internet access were mailed paper surveys. If respondents with Internet access did not complete their survey online, they were subsequently sent a copy by postal mail. Of all respondents at both times, 60% completed the survey online, and all others completed a mail survey. Respondents' ages ranged from 13 to 94 years. Of those who completed the surveys, 85% were adults (19 years of age or older), 43% were men, 89% were Caucasian, and 61% were married. Of all respondents, 30% had a household income of up to $30,000, 44% had incomes of between $30,000 and $70,000, and 26% had an income of $70,000 or more.

Key Variables

Internet Use

The major independent variable for this research is the extent to which respondents used the Internet. All the measures are based on respondents' descriptions of the frequency with which they used a computer or the Internet at home for 27 different purposes, such as "communicating with friends," "getting the news online," "playing games," and so on. Figure 6.1 lists the full set of items asked. Participants responded using a 7–point, quasi-logarithmic Likert-scale, with response categories of "several times a day," "about once a day," "3–5 days per week," "1–2 days per week," "every few weeks," "less often," and "never." We then used these items to construct several indexes of Internet use. These indexes indicated whether the respondent used the Internet for any of the stated purposes and included both a binary measure—indicating whether the respondent used the Internet at all—and several continuous measures for how often respondents used the Internet, both overall and for specific purposes. We describe the creation of these Internet-use indexes in the following paragraphs.

Some research has simply compared users and nonusers of the Internet (e.g., chapter 5; Katz & Aspden, 1997), whereas others have used a measure of time spent online among active Internet users (e.g., Goget, Yamauchi, & Suman, 2002). Because the first of these approaches uses a dichotomous measure, it is insensitive. The second approach uses a measure that can only be calculated for those who actively use the Internet, truncating the distribution of Internet use and limiting the statistical power available for analysis. Our research combines these approaches by constructing two measures of Internet use: a binary measure and a frequency measure. As described later, we also disaggregated the frequency measure of Internet use to create separate indexes to measure the use of the Internet for each of several different functions, among those who use the Internet at all.

Use of Internet. We constructed a binary measure of Internet use at home at each time period. This variable was coded 1 if respondents indicated they used the Internet for any of the 27 functions listed in figure 6.1; if not, the variable was coded 0.

Frequency of Internet Use. We constructed an index to measure the frequency and range of applications for which respondents used the Internet. This index consists of the mean frequency of use for each of the 27 online functions. This was an internally consistent measure (Cronbach's alpha of .91) with high stability over time (test–retest correlation = .66). As described below, using both exploratory and confirmatory factor analysis, we examined the substructure of this index among those who used the Internet at all (i.e., those for whom *Use Internet* was true).

Components of Internet Use. Our previous work showed that one can differentiate participants' Internet use on the basis of their activities (Kraut et al., 2002). Exploratory factor analysis of a list of 28 online activities collected from respondents in the Pittsburgh area indicated that typical Internet use can be broken out into at least five components: communicating with friends and family, communicating with strangers, acquiring instrumental information, finding product information, conducting commercial transactions, and entertainment. Because in this study we added multiple items assessing respondents' use of the Internet to seek health-related information, we expected to uncover six components for why respondents used the Internet: communication with friends and family, communication with strangers, news and instrumental information, health information, commerce, and entertainment.

To examine the structure of Internet use in the current sample, we conducted a series of five confirmatory factor analyses. The single factor model (model 1 in table 6.1), in which all 27 items in figure 6.1 are presumed to reflect a single latent variable, represents the hypothesis that Internet use is

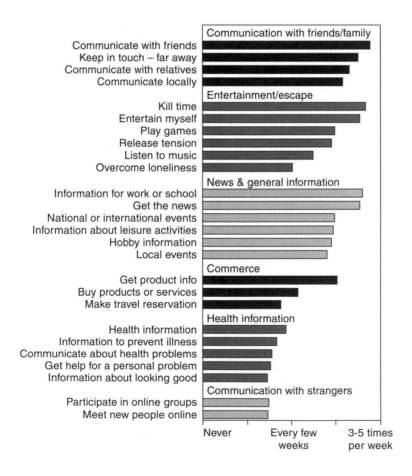

Figure 6.1. Frequency of Internet use for six distinct purposes.

best represented by a single index that taps how frequently respondents used the Internet, regardless of what they use it for. This model tests the default assumption made in the research literature as a whole. The single-factor model was a very poor fit to the data (Bentler-Bonett normed fit index = 0.79; comparative fit index = 0.81). The input data consisted of the respondents' average Internet use for each function across the two surveys (i.e., a 922 respondents with Internet access by 27-function matrix). We compared this single-factor model to several multifactor models. Model 2 tests whether differentiating between interpersonal communication and other uses explains the data well. Model 3 differentiates the noncommunication uses of the Internet but lumps communication with friends and family together with communication with strangers. Model 4 differentiates all components, except for the informational uses, and combines informational uses for news and local events with health information. Model 5 is the six-factor solution described previously. It represents the hypothesis that one can distinguish six distinct ways of using the Internet.

The six-component model (model 5 in table 6.1) was the best fit to the data. It is the model reflected in figure 6.1. It was a much better fit than the single-factor model (model 1) and significantly better than models that merely distinguished between communication and other uses (model 2), combined different kinds of communication (model 3), or combined different kinds of information (model 4).

Frequency of Television Viewing

Respondents also indicated at each time period how often they used television for each of 21 functions in the 6 months before the survey, using a logarithmic-like, Likert response scale that ranged from several times per day to never. These functions were a subset of the functions asked about the Internet, excluding the interpersonal communication activities that are impossible to perform using a television, such as joining online groups or communicating with friends or relations. The index was highly reliable (Cronbach's alpha = 0.85) and had high stability across time (test–retest reliability = 0.63).

Table 6.1. Confirmatory factory analysis of uses of the Internet.

Model no.	No. of components	Component descriptions	NFI	CFI	χ^2	DF	P-value, fit improvement[a]
1	1	Twenty-seven items as a single component	0.79	0.81	4638.3	325	
2	2	Communication with family/friends/strangers News/health information/commerce/entertainment	0.81	0.83	4212.95	324	<.0001
3	5	Communication with family/friends/strangers News Health information Commerce Entertainment	0.85	0.86	3413.19	325	<.0001
4	5	Communication with family/friends Communication with strangers News + health information Commerce Entertainment	0.88	0.89	2703.71	324	<.0001
5	6	Communication with family/friends Communication with strangers News Health information Commerce Entertainment	0.88	0.90	2660.26	325	<.0001

NFI, Normed Fit Index; CFI, Comparative Fit Index.
[a]p-value for the hypothesis that model N is a better fit to the data than model N-1.

Control Variables

Respondents provided their gender, age, marital status, level of education, race, and income, as reported at time 1. In addition, at time 1, we included Johnand Srivastava's (1999) measure of extraversion. The extraversion scale was reliable (Cronbach's alpha = 0.83). Because these variables have been associated with both Internet use and television viewing in other research, we include them in all analyses that follow

Data Analysis Methods

We use hierarchical linear growth models (Singer & Willett, 2003) to estimate how respondents' Internet use influenced their television watching. In hierarchical linear growth models, an outcome of interest (in this chapter, television viewing) is measured at multiple time periods (here on questionnaires collected in 2000 and 2001). The predictors include static characteristics of the respondent (here gender, race, education, and extraversion), time (whether the data was collected in 2000 or 2001), and the amount the respondent used the Internet. Although we collected information about Internet use both in 2000 and 2001, we use only the data from 2000 in the models to make interpretation of the data clearer. By using Internet use only from time 1, we exclude the ambiguity that may result from television habits changing as a result of Internet use.

Ordinary least squared regression techniques are not appropriate for longitudinal designs with repeated measures, because ordinary least squares regression assumes that measurement errors are independent and normally distributed and have constant variance. In contrast, hierarchical linear modeling recognizes that responses from the same respondent are not independent of each other. The hierarchical linear growth model separates out the variances associated with the respondent from the variances associated with the time period nested within the respondent. The models allow both intercepts (here, the initial levels of television use) and slopes (change in television use over time) to vary by respondent, and the analysis attempts to account for both individual differences in intercepts and slopes. It calculates the correct degrees of freedom associated with each level of the analysis (respondent or questionnaire) and provides more appropriate estimates of the standard errors than does ordinary least squares regression.

In the analyses in table 6.3 below, we distinguish between cross-sectional associations, which account for individual differences in intercepts, and longitudinal associations, which account for individual differences in slopes. Models 1 and 3 are cross-sectional analyses that test whether respondents who used the Internet at all or those who used it more frequently differ on television viewing from those who do not use the Internet at all or use it less frequency. For these cross-sectional analyses, Internet use and the dependent variable are measured on the first questionnaire. Models 2 and 4 are analyses of the panel data, adding time to models 1 and 3, respectively. The time effect in the panel analyses tests whether frequency of television viewing changes between time 1 and time 2. The time-by-use Internet interaction tests whether changes in television viewing differ among Internet users and nonusers. The time-by-Internet frequency interaction tests whether the change in television viewing varies with the amount the respondents uses the Internet.

In table 6.4, we conducted similar analyses, using the disaggregated measures of frequency of Internet use for specific purposes (i.e., communication with friends, communication with strangers, information, entertainment, commerce, and health). Because using the Internet for a distinct purpose is contingent on using the Internet at all, we conducted this analysis only among Internet users. We conducted preliminary analyses to determine whether the overall frequency of Internet use influences television viewing among Internet users (i.e., that the earlier results do not reflect only the comparison of Internet users and nonusers). We then substitute the six components of Internet use listed in table 6.1 for the overall frequency of use, including them in a single model to control for other Internet use when examining the effects of any single type of use.

Results

Preliminary Analyses

Table 6.2 shows the descriptive statistics for the variables used in the regressions in 2000.

Overall Internet Frequency

Model 1 in table 6.3 shows results from the cross-sectional modeling, predicting the frequency of

Table 6.2. Descriptive statistics in 2000.

Variable	Mean	SD	N
Age (years)	45.2	17.5	913
Education (7-point scale: 1 = elementary school, 3 = high school graduate, 5 = some college, 7 = advanced degree)	4.7	1.8	895
Income			
Marital status (1 = married, 0 = single)	0.6	0.5	963
Race (1 = white, 0 = other)	0.9	0.3	929
Gender (1 = male, 0 = female)	0.4	0.5	950
Extraversion (7-point scale: 1 = low, 7 = high)			
Frequency of Internet use (1 = never, 4 = 1 or 2 days/week, 7 = multiple times per day)			
Overall frequency (27 functions):	1.2	1.0	963
News & information	1.6	1.4	959
Entertainment	1.4	1.5	956
Commerce	1.0	0.9	958
Health Info	0.5	0.7	961
Communicating with friends and family	1.8	1.7	959
Meeting new people	0.3	0.9	955
Frequency of television watching (1 = never, 4 = 1 or 2 days/week, 7 = multiple times per day; mean of 21 functions)	1.8	0.8	958

television watching respectively from Internet frequency, the continuous measure of frequency of Internet use. In terms of control variables, poorer and more extraverted respondents watch television more frequently than do others. The significant, positive coefficient of the Internet frequency variable means that heavier Internet users, that is, those who use the Internet more frequently and for a wider range of purposes, also watch television more frequently.

Model 2 adds the time and time-by-Internet frequency interactions to model 1 to assess whether television viewing changed over time and whether Internet frequency moderated this change. Note that the estimate for the main effect for Internet frequency in model 2 is approximately of the same magnitude and significance level as it was in model 1. The main effect of Internet frequency represents the cross-sectional association of Internet frequency with the frequency of television watching (although in model 2 it represents the association of Internet frequency at time 1 with television watching at both time 1 and time 2). The statistically significant time effect in model 2 shows that television viewing increased between 2000 and 2001 for the sample as a whole. The statistically significant negative time-by-Internet frequency interaction shows that the growth in television viewing was less strong among

respondents who used the Internet heavily compared to nonusers. Figure 6.2 illustrates the interaction. Although television watching increased for respondents who did not use the Internet at all, it declined among those who used it most in the sample.

The overall frequency of Internet use is based on two components: a contrast between Internet users and nonusers and the frequency of use among those who do use the Internet. To clarify the results involving Internet frequency in model 2, we conducted two supplementary analyses that contrasted Internet users and nonusers and, among Internet users, contrasted those with compared heavier and lighter use (table 6.4). The nonsignificant use Internet estimate in model 3 shows that cross sectionally, Internet users and nonusers did not differ in their television viewing. However, the significant, negative time-by-use Internet interaction shows that television viewing increased among respondents who did not use the Internet but declined among those who did use it. In model 4, the significant positive Internet frequency estimate is a cross-sectional effect. It shows that among Internet users, people who used the Internet more frequently also watched television more frequently. In contrast, the significant negative time-by-Internet frequency interaction represents a longitudinal analysis and shows that among Internet

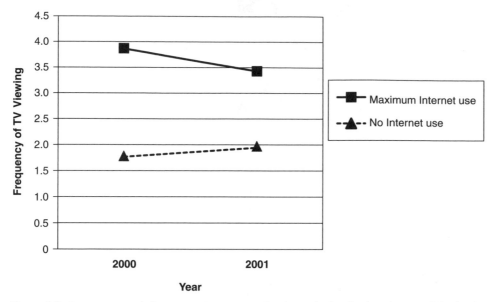

Figure 6.2. Internet use and changes in TV viewing. Plot shows the fitted values from model 2 for the amount of TV viewing at time 1 and time 2 for respondents who did not use the Internet at all compared to those used it multiple times per day at time 1.

users, heavier Internet use was associated with declines in television viewing.

Components of Internet Use

Model 5 in table 6.5 disaggregates overall frequency of Internet use into six components to determine whether different ways of using the Internet have distinct effects on frequency of television viewing. This model predicts television watching better than does the aggregated model (chi-square = 42.34, df = 10, $p < .0001$). The functional displacement hypothesis reviewed earlier predictions that cross sectionally, people who use the Internet most for entertainment would be the heaviest television viewers and that heavy Internet use for entertainment would lead to declines in television viewing as people shift their entertainment choices from one medium to the other.

The predictions from the functional displacement hypothesis were only partially confirmed. People who used the Internet for entertainment watched television more frequently than those who did not, but so did those who used it to gather health information, to research and purchase products, and to communicate with strangers. The time-by-entertainment and time by Information interactions were not significant, indicating that using the Internet for entertainment or for watching

the news and getting other information did not lead to larger than average declines in television viewing. In contrast, the significant, negative coefficient for the time-by-communicating with strangers estimate shows that among Internet users, television watching declined more among people who joined online groups and used the Internet to meet new people than it did among other users of the Internet.

Discussion

Methodological and Substantive Contributions

This research examines the role of the Internet in changing people's use of other media. Our focus in this research was both substantive, to examine the functional displacement hypothesis in the context of Internet use, and methodological, to encourage researchers to be sensitive to methodological detail when investigating the effect of this new technology on people's lives.

Methodologically, our results show that researchers must move beyond the cross-sectional research methods that characterize most of work in this area to make causal claims about the effect of the Internet in daily life. As the research reported

Table 6.3. Predicting frequency of television watching from frequency of Internet use, all respondents.

Independent variables	Model 1: OLS, cross sectional, Internet frequency				Model 2: HLM, panel, internet frequency			
	Estimate	SE	DF	P	Estimate	SE	DF	P
Intercept	1.782	.163	956	≥.0001	1.765	.154	956	<.0001
Male (0 = female; 1 = male)	−.019	.051	956		−.018	.048	956	
Age (12–97)	.002	.002	956		.004	.002	956	≥.10
White (0 = minority; 1 = white)	−.125	.084	956		−.162	.079	956	≥.10
Married (0 = not married; 1 = married)	.005	.057	956		.035	.054	956	
Education (1 = some elementary school; 7 = advanced degree)	−.058	.016	956	<.001	−.068	.015	956	≤.0001
Income (1 = $10K; 8 = >$70K)	−.058	.012	956	≤.0001	−.053	.012	956	≤.0001
Extraversion (1 = minimum; 5 = maximum))	.084	.032	956		.081	.030	956	≤.01
Time (0 = 2000; 1 = 2001)					.178	.035	791	≤.0001
Internet, frequency (mean 27 items; 0 = no use; 6 = multiple times per day)	.239	.028	956	≤.0001	.350	.042	956	≤.0001
Time × Internet frequency					−.103	.024	791	≤.0001
R^2	.118							
χ^2					409.28			
AICC					3795.40			
BIC					3805.40			

OLS, ordinary least squares; HLM, hierarchical linear model.

Table 6.4. Predicting frequency of television watching from Internet use (all respondents) and frequency of Internet use (Internet users only).

Effect	Model 3, all respondents: HLM, panel, binary Internet use				Model 4 Internet users only: HLM panel, overall Internet frequency			
	Estimate	SE	DF	P	Estimate	SE	DF	P
Intercept	2.033	.161	956	≤.0001	1.422	.167	753	
Male (0 = female; 1 = male)	.020	.049	956		.027	.051	753	
Age (12–97)	−.001	.002	956		.001	.002	753	
White (0 = minority; 1~white)	−.153	.082	956	≤.10	−.134	..086	753	
Married (0 = not married; 1= married)	−.030	.055	956		.038	.058	753	≤.05
Education (1 = some elementary school; 7 = advanced degree)	−.038	.016	956	≤.10	−.040	.016	753	<.001
Income (1 = <$10K; 8 = ≥ $70K)	−.037	.012	956	≤.01	−.046	.012	753	≤.10
Extraversion (1 = minimum; 5 = maximum)	.095	.031	956	≤.01	.061	.031	753	≤.001
Time (0 = 2000; 1 = 2001)	.141	.043	791	≤.01	.300	.056	511	≤.0001
Use Internet (0 = no; 1 = yes)	.082	.096	956					
Time × use Internet	−.112	.052	791	≤.05				
Internet frequency (mean 27 items; 0 = no use; 6 = multiple times per day)					.561	.056	753	<.001
Time × Internet frequency					−.165	.032	511	≤.0001
χ^2	426.91				243.65			
AICC					2574.1			
BIC	3874.5				2583.3			

HLM, Hierarchical linear model.

Table 6.5. Predicting television watching from components of Internet use, among those who use the Internet at all.

Effect	Model 6			
	Estimate	SE	DF	P
Intercept	1.390	0.166	746	≤.0001
Male (0 = female; 1 = male)	0.058	0.051	746	
Age (12–97)	0.000	0.002	746	
White (0 = minority; 1 = white)	–0.106	0.083	746	
Married (0 = not married; 1 = married)	–0.020	0.057	746	
Education (1 = some elementary school; 7 = advanced degree)	–0.028	0.017	746	≤.10
Income (1 ≤ $10K; 8 ≥ 70K)	–0.035	0.012	746	≤.01
Extraversion (1 = minimum; 5 = maximum))	0.082	0.031	746	≤.01
Time (0 = 2000; 1 = 2001)	0.255	0.060	505	≤.0001
Internet use for communicating with friends & family	–0.030	0.022	746	
Internet use for communicating with strangers	0.085	0.034	746	≤.05
Internet use for news & general information	–0.001	0.028	746	
Internet use for entertainment	0.102	0.023	746	≤.0001
Internet use for health information	0.306	0.042	746	≤.0001
Internet use for commerce	0.115	0.039	746	≤.01
Time × communicating with friends & family	–0.032	0.021	505	
Time × communicating with strangers	–0.072	0.033	505	≤.05
Time × news & general information	–0.015	0.026	505	
Time × entertainment	–0.021	0.021	505	
Time × health information	–0.032	0.042	505	
Time × commerce	–0.008	0.038	505	
χ^2	201.4			
AICC	2551.8			
BIC	2561.0			

[a]Hierarchical linear model, panel components of Internet frequency.

here demonstrates, cross-sectional data and longitudinal data led to different conclusions. Cross-sectional results showed that people who used the Internet more watched television more frequently and for a wider variety of purposes than did lighter Internet users. In contrast, longitudinal results show that both Internet use versus nonuse and the frequency of Internet use, among users, were associated with declines in the frequency of watching television.

The second methodological contribution of this chapter is to demonstrate that how people use the Internet makes a difference in the effects this use is likely to have. The confirmatory factor analyses demonstrated that conceptualizing Internet use as an undifferentiated aggregate fits the data poorly, even though this is the dominant approach in the research literature. At a minimum, research needs

to distinguish among the ways that people use the Internet: information seeking, communication with friends and family, and entertainment. Among informational uses of the Internet in our data set, school, work and hobbies, product information, and health information uses can be distinguished. Undoubtedly, had we asked additional questions about using the Internet for gathering political information or information in other substantive domains, those domains would also have been distinguishable. Among social uses of the Internet, distinguishing communication with friends and family from communication with strangers fits the data better than a model that lumps all communication together.

Substantively, the results of our research provide evidence that use of the Internet is associated with declines in television viewing. That is, aggregate

Internet use in 2000 predicted declines in television watching between 2000 and 2001. Although these broad results are consistent with the functional displacement hypothesis, a more detailed examination is not. According to the functional displacement hypothesis, people who use the Internet most for informational and entertainment purposes should show the strongest declines in television viewing. However, the results were not consistent with this detailed prediction. The cross-sectional data show that people who used the Internet for entertainment, for health information, and for commerce are the heaviest television viewers, indicating that people who desire particular types of information in one media will use a new media for the same purposes. However, using the Internet for entertainment or news (the dominant uses of television) did not predict above-average declines in television viewing. In contrast, using the Internet for meeting new people was associated with declines in television viewing over and above those resulting from aggregate use. Interestingly, this function of Internet use has no parallels in television viewing.

Limitations

We have shown that one reaches different conclusions using cross-sectional and longitudinal data to examine the effect of using the Internet. The hierarchical linear growth models used in our research take into account individual differences in television viewing and Internet use at the initial time period and in the covariation between these individual differences and change. We acknowledge, however, that longitudinal designs are not panaceas. They are still subject to validity threats. Other events covarying with time may drive both changes in Internet use and changes in outcomes. These covariates can be internal to the individuals, such as learning or maturation, or external, such as the business cycle or change in popular culture. In addition, because of errors of measurement, preexisting differences among participants are never fully, statistically controlled in longitudinal designs. Finally, preexisting differences among individuals may lead some of them to be more susceptible to change. Only experimental research, in which participants are randomly forced to use the Internet or are prevented from using it, can lead to pure inferences about causation. However, true experiments are difficult to perform when one is seeking to ex-

amine broad social effects in the population or when examining the effect of technology on phenomena, such as the development of friendship, that are likely to emerge only after long periods of use. In addition, as Kraut et al. (2002) demonstrated, random assignment of participants to Internet use may no longer be possible in the United States, at least among people who buy their own computer. In their study, over 80% of individuals assigned to a no-Internet control group subscribed to Internet service on their own.

Conclusion

The Internet has become common in American homes. It is used for a wide range of purposes, including communication, information, entertainment, and commerce. There is controversy about the effects that widespread diffusion of the Internet is having on the lives of its users. This chapter used a national panel to examine how Internet use changed participants' use of time. We have made three contributions in this chapter. First, we have demonstrated that cross-sectional research methods are likely to lead to misleading conclusions about the effects of Internet use. Second, we have demonstrated that measuring and analyzing Internet use at a disaggregated level leads to better models in two senses. The disaggregated models fit the data better than models based on aggregated data. Third, we have demonstrated, using longitudinal data, that heavier Internet use is associated with declines in television viewing. Although this result is broadly consistent with a functional displacement hypothesis, detailed results were not. Using the Internet for entertainment and information was not associated with above-average declines in television viewing, whereas using it to meeting new people online and to participate in online groups was.

Acknowledgments. This research was supported by National Science Foundation grant IRI-9900449.

References

Atkin, D. J. (2001). Home ecology and children's television viewing in the new media environment. In Bryant, J. & Bryant, J. A. (Eds.), *Television and the American family* (2nd ed., pp. 49–74). Mahwah, NJ: Lawrence Erlbaum.

Bass, S. B. (2003). How will Internet use affect the patient? A review of computer network and closed Internet-based system studies and the implications in understanding how the use of the Internet affects patient populations. *Journal of Health Psychology, 8*(1), 25–38.

Boneva, B., Kraut, R., & Frohlich, D. (2001). Using e-mail for personal relationships: The difference gender makes. *American Behavioral Scientist, 45*(3), 530–549.

Carey, J., & Moss, M. (1985). The diffusion of new telecommunications technologies. *Telecommunications Policy, 9*(2), 145–158.

Coffey, S., & Stipp, H. (1997). The interactions between computer and television usage. *Journal of Advertising Research, 37*(2), 61–66.

Cole, J. I., Suman, M., Schramm, P., Bel, D., Lunn, B., Maguire, P., Hanson, K., Singh, R., & Aquino, J.-S. (2000). *The UCLA Internet report: Surveying the digital future*. Retrieved December 30, 2000, from http://www.ccp.ucla.edu.

Cummings, J. N., & Kraut, R. (2002). Domesticating computers and the Internet. *The Information Society, 18*(3), 1–18.

Gershuny, J. I. (2000). *Changing times: Work and leisure in post-industrial society*. Oxford: Oxford University Press.

Goget, J. F., Yamauchi, Y., & Suman, M. (2002). The Internet, social networks, and loneliness. *IT & Society, 1*(1), 180–201.

Howard, P. E. N., Rainie, L., & Jones, S. (2001). Days and nights on the Internet: The impact of a diffusing technology. *American Behavioral Scientist, 45*(3), 383–404.

Huesmann, L. R., Moise-Titus, J., Podolski, C.-L., & Eron, L. D. (2003). Longitudinal relations between children's exposure to TV violence and their aggressive and violent behavior in young adulthood: 1977–1992. *Developmental Psychology, 39*(2), 201–221.

John, O. P., & Srivastava, S. (1999). The big five trait taxonomy: History, measurement, and theoretical perspectives. In L. A. Pervin & O. P. E. John (Eds.), *Handbook of personality: Theory and research* (2nd ed., pp. 102–138). New York: Guilford Press.

Katz, J., & Aspden, P. (1997). A nation of strangers? *Communications of the ACM, 40*(12), 81–86.

Katz, J. E., & Rice, R. E. (2002). *Social consequences of Internet use: Access, involvement, and interaction*. Cambridge: MIT Press.

Kaynay, J. M., & Yelsma, P. (2000). Displacement effects of online media in the socio-technical contexts of households. *Journal of Broadcasting and Electronic Media, 4*(2), 215–229.

Kommers, N., & Rainie, L. (2002). *Use of the Internet at Major Life Moments*. Pew Internet & American Life Project. Retrieved May 9, 2003, from: http://www.pewinternet.org.

Kraut, R., Kiesler, S., Boneva, B., Cummings, J. N., Helgeson, V., & Crawford, A. M. (2002). Internet paradox revisited. *Journal of Social Issues, 58*(1), 49–74.

Kraut, R., Mukhopadhyay, T., Szczypula, J., Kiesler, S., & Scherlis, W. (1999). Communication and information: Alternative uses of the Internet in households. *Information Systems Research, 10*(4), 287–303.

Kraut, R., Patterson, M., Lundmark, V., Kiesler, S., Mukhopadhyay, T., & Scherlis, W. (1998). Internet paradox: A social technology that reduces social involvement and psychological well-being? *American Psychologist, 53*(9), 1017–1031.

Kraut, R. E., Scherlis, W., Mukhopadhyay, T., Manning, J., & Kiesler, S. (1996). Homenet: A field trial of residential internet services. *Communications of the ACM, 39*(12), 55–63.

Leiner, B. M., Cerf, V. G., Clark, D. D., Kahn, R. E., Kleinrock, L., Lynch, D. C., Postel, J., Roberts, L. G., & Wolff, S. (2002). *A brief history of the Internet (Version 3.32)*. The Internet Society. Retrieved February 10, 2004, from: http://www.isoc.org/internet/history/brief.shtm.

Lenhart, A., Rainie, L., & Lewis, O. (2001). *Teenage life online: The rise of the instant-message generation and the Internet's impact on friendships and family relationships*. Pew Internet & American Life Project. Retrieved June 20, 2001, from: http://www.pewinternet.org/.

Nie, N. H., & Hillygus, D. S. (2002). Where does Internet time come from? A reconnaissance. *IT & Society, 1*(2), 1–20.

Pew Internet & American Life Project. (2003). *Internet activities*. Retrieved May 21, 2003, from: http://www.pewinternet.org/reports/chart.asp?img=Internet_A8.htm.

Pronovost, G. (2002). The Internet and time displacement: A Canadian perspective. *IT & Society, 1*(1), 44–53.

Putnam, R. (2000). *Bowling alone: The collapse and revival of American community*. New York: Simon & Schuster.

Robinson, J. P. (1990). Television's effects on families' use of time. In Bryant, J. (Ed.), *Television and the American family* (pp. 195–209). Hillsdale, NJ: Lawrence Erlbaum.

Robinson, J., & Godbey, G. (1999). *Time for life: The surprising ways Americans use their time*. (2nd ed.). University Park, PA: Penn State University Press.

Robinson, J. P., & Kestnbaum, M. (1999). The personal computer, culture, and other uses of free time. *Social Science Computer Review, 17*(2), 209–216.

Robinson, J. P., Kestnbaum, M., Neustadtl, A., & Alvarez, A. (2002). Information technology and functional time displacement. *IT & Society, 1*(1), 21–36.

Singer, J. D., & Willett, J. B. (2003). *Applied longitudinal data analysis*. New York: Oxford University Press.

U.S. Department of Commerce. (2002). *A nation online : How Americans are expanding their use of the Internet*. Washington, DC: Government Printing Office.

Weiser, E. B. (2001). The functions of Internet use and their social and psychological consequences. *CyberPsychology & Behavior, 4*(6), 723–743.

7

Malcolm Brynin

The Neutered Computer

Gendered Diffusion of Technology

It is widely acknowledged that men incline more to technology than do women, both at work and home (if not to the technologies associated with house-work). Given that over their lifetime most people's welfare depends on their productivity at work, and because technology is an important basis for this productivity, it is difficult to avoid the conclusion that technology provides men with a significant welfare advantage. At the most general level, a wide range of evidence indicates a strong relationship between technical innovation and productive potential (Gallie, 1994; Nickell & Bell, 1995; Machin, 1996). More specifically, there is evidence of a possible association between individual usage of technologies at work—especially computers—and both productivity and wages (Krueger, 1993; Green, 1998). Although this relationship has been disputed (diNardo & Pischke, 1997; Entorf & Kramarz, 1997), an inability or unwillingness to use computers might reduce an individual's scope for employment or for fully effective employment.

How inevitable is this? Is the male advantage the result of a response to technology, whether innate or socialized, that is positive for men and negative for women, or is the issue more transitory and

contingent than this? One strand of thought sees girls, generally considered to be closer to mothers than boys, as favoring caring and interconnectedness over competition and aggression.[1] This might ultimately feed into different responses to technology (Turkle, 1998). Girls and women tend not to undertake technical subjects in school and higher education, which has direct implications for the nature of their subsequent employment (Gaskell, 1992)[2]. This might be reinforced by differential access to domestic leisure technologies,[3] and in particular the home computer.[4] Such a difference might have direct welfare implications, as women would gain less than men from the capabilities of the computer, and in particular of the Internet (see Wellman & Haythornthwaite, 2002, for an overview of such effects). However, experience with a home PC might have a further effect on access to or efficacy with work-based technologies.

Alternatively, we might say that rather than having underlying differences in attitudes toward technology, men and women have differential experiences, especially at work (Webster, 1996), which might in turn give rise to distinctive attitudes. Thus, traditional employment demarcations cause the attitudinal gap, rather than the other way around. This seems reasonable given the long-standing male predominance in the use of technologies at work, reinforced by extensive job segregation by gender and by male dominance of skilled manual work and training (Cockburn, 1987; Shavit & Müller, 1998).

These two very different approaches do not contradict each other. Traditional demarcations lead to differential experience and to differences in both capability with and attitudes toward technology. The result is that the differences are "real": "What about all the ignorance of women, all the exclusions and failures of knowledge and skill? What about men's access to daily competence, to knowing how to build things, to take them apart, to play" (Haraway, 1991, p. 181). However, Haraway (1991), Turkle (1998), and other writers such as Plant (2000), view technology as being in some way "transformative," so that through the technology itself, the gender difference will either disappear or even turn in favor of women. These arguments can be rather visionary, but at a practical level they derive from the fact that the largely nonmechanical interface of computers can be seen as either "androgynous" (Grint and Woolgar, 1997, p. 110), or even "feminine." Some uses of computers involving design, for instance in the fashion industry, are likely to be dominated by women (Cockburn, 1985), whereas the computer's networking function is often seen as "naturally" feminine. Although an early view that the computer is inherently gender-neutral is no longer held (Woodfield, 2000), we must see the development of the work computer as part of a complex web of processes that are fundamentally human, not technological. These processes include a restructuring of work relations that might use the gender difference in new ways, not necessarily to the disadvantage of women. The decline in "male" skilled work and the growth of the office computer is one aspect of this change. There is no inevitable reason why technological change should have a male bias. Whether it actually does depends in part on the functions of the technology, whereas even a single and the simplest technology might have several functions. Moreover, it is useful to make a distinction between two aspects of the engagement with technology: everyday use of technology and the response to innovation. The former can be determined by the location of an individual within employment, as this dictates which technologies that person will use; the level of skill required for this; and the productivity effect of that work. The response to innovation, in contrast, depends in large measure on predispositions. Cockburn (1983) views the male technological advantage in part as an adaptation to cycles of technological innovation that are designed to protect their technological privileges, though employer decisions and strategies also come into play.

In the case of new domestic and leisure technologies, which are dependent on the availability of resources but also on individual choice, the effect of predispositions is perhaps clearer. Domestic technological innovations diffuse through the population on the basis of by now quite well-known patterns (Rogers, 1995). Although there has been a tendency for diffusion analysis to be undertaken at the household level, the evidence indicates that men are generally more likely to be technological innovators than are women (Norris, 2000).

Perhaps, though, men do not use technology more than women but simply *sooner*. Men are, in diffusion terms, early adopters. The issue, then, is how quickly the gender gap disappears. In 1995, 7% of Internet users in Europe and 17% of those in the United States were female. By 1998, these figures had risen to 16% and 41%, respectively.[5] Other data show a further significant rise in women's use of the Internet immediately after this study in the United Kingdom and the United States (Wellman & Haythornthwaite, 2002, p. 14). In Germany, the gender gap in usage of the home PC narrowed in a similar manner (Wagner, Pischner, & Haisken-deNew, 2002, pp. 170–171). Such degendering of the use of technology has been apparent in other cases such as driving (men drove cars before women) and the telephone. The latter was originally often an extension of the office only for men, yet Martin (1998) suggests that women helped turn the phone into a tool of mass communication. What about attitudes toward technology? Surely familiarity does the job: "if PCs are placed on kitchen tables rather than in studies, technophobia can be transformed into technofamiliarity" (Green, 2001, p. 182).

At work, men and women use computers more or less equally (Wagner et al., 2002), and it is precisely the interaction between the practical, everyday circumstances of men and women's use of technology at work, in combination with the related attitudinal and motivational aspects of this, that give grounds for the argument that the significance of gender differences is diminishing. More generally, the male hold over skilled manual work is declining in importance, and the ubiquity of the work computer provides a platform for female extension into nonmanual work (some skilled, some routine). Past socialization into a particular response to technology might therefore be of limited long-term importance, as it is probably the immediacy of the experience that counts. Measuring technological engagement at any point in time appears to give men the advantage; measuring it longitudinally renders the advantage less significant. Perhaps the sum of the differences across technological cycles is important in its social effect, but nevertheless there is no fundamental difference in the technological engagement of men and women. Though Haraway (1991) looks to science fiction for a neutered technology, at least in some dimensions of life this is happening in a more prosaic manner.

The analysis below tests whether there is a strong and persistent differential between men and women in their attitudes toward computer technology against a theoretical alternative: that other factors associated with gender, such as work experience, determine gender differentials in attitudes toward computers. Moreover, as some of these data come from a panel survey with measures taken on the same individuals on three separate occasions, causal links can be tested explicitly.

Data

The analysis uses two data sets. The first of these is based on the three waves of the 1000–household Home-OnLine (HoL) survey, which started in 1998 and was funded by British Telecommunications.[6] Interviews were sought with every member in the household aged 16 years or above. Attempts were made to trace all people who moved home between waves, and new household members became eligible for interview. Interviews were made face to face in wave 1 and by telephone thereafter. The data set is complicated by deliberate oversampling of homes with computers in wave 1. In addition, homes that dropped out of the survey in wave 2 were substituted by replacement. The household response rate was 57% in wave 1. Taking this as the baseline, plus the replacement households introduced in wave 2, produces a pool of individuals eligible for interview for at least one wave of 2500, of which 33% were interviewed three times, 30% twice, 35% once, and 2% never. (Eligibility for interview, of course, varied. For instance, new sample members in wave 3 would only be eligible once.)

The above complexities of the sample required a weighting design to compensate for the oversampling, to produce weights for the replacement households, and to adjust for household and within-household nonresponse. Separate weights were also produced to deal with nonresponse to the diary discussed below once an interview had been obtained. The analysis presented below uses different weights as appropriate.

Table 7.1 summarizes the data used in the main results table. In addition, time-use data are used in some of the analysis. This information came from a week-long self-completion diary that shows activities for each day, with 35 categories, including

Table 7.1. Means of main HoL variables used (sample of working people).

	Men	Women
Uses work PC	0.59	0.61
Uses home PC	0.55	0.46
Monthly pay	£2371 (SD: 5501)	£1242 (SD: 4741)
Age	38.8 (SD: 12.4)	38.5 (SD: 12.3)
Has a degree	0.18	0.21
Higher manager	0.17	0.06
Work autonomy scale (range 0–2)	0.53	0.52
Work hours	42.2 (SD: 12.8)	30.3 (13.5)
PC attitudes range 1–25 (high = negative)	10.3 (SD: 3.1)	10.6 (SD: 3.1)
Sport leisure scale 1–6 (low = frequent)	2.8	2.1
"Going out" leisure scale 1–6 (low = frequent)	3.2	3.3

Information and Communication Technology (ICT) usage, divided into quarter-hour slots.

The other data set derives from the eLiving project,[7] funded by the European Union's IST Programme. The project is based on a household survey of 1750 homes in each of six countries—Britain, Bulgaria, Germany, Israel, Italy, and Norway—undertaken in 2001 and then repeated as a panel in 2002. The aim was to provide comparative information across a range of European Union or associate countries on the causes and effects of different aspects of ICT behavior.

Gender Differential in Computer Behavior

This section reviews three aspects of gender differentials in engagement with computer technology: home PC usage, attitudes toward computers, and usage of computers at work.

Whether we look at frequency, intensity (time spent on an ICT activity), or change in them over time, women use home computers less than men. In wave 1 of HoL, 36% of men and 25% of women used a home PC. In wave 3, these figures were 53% and 41%, respectively.[8] This indicates a continuing and in fact slightly widening gender differential during a time when usage of home computers dramatically increased. This seems to negate any idea of rapidly converging adoption (or take-up) rates. The differential diffusion is also apparent from gender differences in the number of years of experience with a home PC. Thirty-two percent of male home PC users had been using a home PC for 10 or more years, compared to 17% of women. The disparity does not improve when we look at the functions of usage. These are of interest because women, with different preferences, might use computers for certain functions more than men do. In wave 1, using the HoL diary for information on intensity of usage, there does indeed seem to be a typical gendering of PC behavior. Men mostly use home PCs for games, work, and surfing the web, whereas women exceed the time men spend on computers for education and on e-mail.[9] However, by wave 3, men had reduced time spent on games and increased time on some other functions, with the overall result that by then they were spending roughly double the time women spent on each type of use. Moreover, total male time on computers in

wave 1 was 6.0 hours, whereas for women it was 3.9 hours; by wave 3, these figures were 7.1 and 3.3 hours, respectively. This indicates a weaker longitudinal commitment to home PC usage among women, whose intensity of usage actually falls.

Nevertheless, the gender differential in home PC usage is not as pronounced as this brief summary suggests. The figures on overall usage mask a surprising amount of fluctuation. The question asked in HoL is about current usage, but some people use a PC for a length of time, and then not at all (a process often called "churn").[10] The cross-sectional picture is therefore a net result of both new take-up and churn. These rates might differ between men and women. Adoption rates over the 2-year period of waves 1–3 were in fact high for both men and women, at around 22%, but 11% of men stopped using a home PC over the period, compared to 20% of women. Thus, net adoption by women was about zero. This indicates an initially equal—but (despite this) a less robust—preference on the part of women. It is also likely to be older women whose interest in computers is relatively limited. The gender gap is not uniform across age groups. Looking at the under-30s in HoL, the figures for home PC usage are 47% for men and 38% for women in wave 1, but 70% and 68%, respectively, in wave 3. In other words, over a very short period of time, young women's PC usage has become equal to that of young men.

We get a similar picture of male predominance being much more fragile than appears at first sight when we look at attitudes. Men have a more positive attitude to computers than do women, but HoL data show that the difference is slight. In wave 1, the mean score is 11.1 for men and 11.9 for women (with the range of 1–25, and for which a high score represents greater "phobia"). In wave 3, the figures are 10.8 and 11.7, respectively, so there was no apparent catching up over this admittedly short period. However, attitudes are not a given but are, in part, a function of experience. Tables 7.2 and 7.3 show the mean "technophobia" scores for men and women who either have no PC in the home (row 1) or who have a PC but use it in some cases (row 2) and not in others (row 3). Attitudes toward computer technology are associated with experience with computers far more than with gender, both in wave 1 and wave 3, as the difference in phobia scores between users and nonusers is much greater than between men and women. Much the same

Table 7.2. Mean "technophobia" scores for home PC users and nonusers (Home-OnLine data, UK).

	Wave 1		Wave 3	
	Male	Female	Male	Female
No home PC	12.2	12.7*	12.7	13.3*
PC user	9.1	9.8**	9.1	9.6*
Nonuser	12.1	12.4	12.6	13.2
All	11.1	11.9***	10.8	11.7***
n	793	941	700	848

***p < .001; **p < .01; *p < .05.

pattern appears in the results from the six countries of the eLiving study.

To try to get closer to the causal nature of this relationship, table 7.4 compares change in usage against change in attitudes in HoL. Attitudes become less technophobic if people become new users, and this statistic is the same for men and women. If no computer is ever used, women tend to become more phobic, but among continuous users, they become slightly less phobic. In both these cases, the attitudes of men barely change, which indicates that women adapt more to experience (or to inexperience).

It is possible to test the causal direction of this association more directly by comparing change in usage to change in attitudes across the three waves. New users, whether male or female, show a slight decrease in technophobia before adoption and a somewhat bigger positive change, though still small, after adoption. This perhaps indicates that the process is one of moving toward a decision (for whatever reason) that results in attitude change. This, in turn, is reinforced by implementation of the decision. Attitudes depend on experience; gender makes no difference. Women's slightly more nega-

tive attitudes might on average impede adoption of the home PC or any other computer experience, but gender is a far less powerful predictor of PC attitudes than is experience itself.

Men and women use computers at work about equally. HoL data show that about 59% of male and 61% of female workers used a computer at work in wave 1.[11] In respect to attitudes toward computers when a PC is used at work, women's "phobia" score is 9.8, compared to 9.3 for men.

In summary, although women tend to have less positive attitudes toward computers and use computers less at home than do men, they are equally willing to start using a home computer, though less willing to persist. Young women's take-up rates are little different from that of young men. Women also use computers about equally with men at work. Moreover, not only is the functional use of computers by men and women becoming increasingly similar, but the relationship between computer experience and attitudes is much the same for men and women. Attitudes toward computers are in both cases highly pliable and follow rather than lead experience with computers. The similarities between men and women are encapsulated in tables 7.5, 7.6, and 7.7. These tables show results from a logistic regression analysis of the factors associated with home and work PC usage. The data are pooled across all three waves. The models include some lifestyle indicators represented by frequency of leisure activities such as attendance at outside sports events or fitness classes and going to the cinema, theatre, or eating out. These controls, although of no inherent interest, have been included because computer usage itself might be considered an aspect of lifestyle, and they might therefore help produce more reliable estimates of the main processes in which we are interested. Some of the other mea-

Table 7.3. Mean "technophobia" scores for home PC users and nonusers (eLiving data, six countries).

	UK		Italy		Germany		Norway		Bulgaria		Israel	
	Male	Female	Male	Female	Male	Female	Male	Female	Male	Female	Male	Female
No home PC	14.2	14.3	12.8	13.7***	13.6	14.4***	13.6	14.3	13.5	14.2***	13.3	13.6
PC user	10.1	11.5***	10.9	11.3	10.7	11.7***	10.0	11.3***	9.5	10.1	11.3	11.6
Nonuser	12.5	14.1**	12.8	13.4	13.1	14.3**	13.3	13.3	11.4	12.7	12.9	13.4
All	11.7	12.9***	11.9	12.9***	11.8	13.2***	10.9	12.3***	13.3	14.0***	12.2	12.7***
n	763	997	710	1052	802	951	847	909	815	934	662	1089

***p < .001; **p < .01.

Table 7.4. Change in attitudes waves 1–3 (positive score = higher phobia) (Home-OnLine data, UK).

	Men	Women**	n
Never uses	0.03	0.36	616
New user	−0.71	−0.76	129
Stopped using	0.94	0.30	43
Stays user	0.02	−0.10	397
n	524	661	1185

**p < .01 (between the categories of the column).

sures that are included reflect aspects of employment that might encourage home PC use; for instance, whether the respondent has a senior management position. This might make it more likely that a computer will be used either at home or at work.

The results show the effect of each explanatory variable on the odds of using a PC at home or at work, while holding the effects of the other variables constant. If the odds are one or close to one, there is no effect, as with the age variable. If they are greater than one the odds rise, as in the case of having a degree, which raises the odds of using a computer in all four models. If the odds are less than one, there is a reduced effect on the probability of using a PC. Thus, in all four models, having negative attitudes to technology (unsurprisingly) lowers the odds of using a home computer.[12]

In most cases, there is little difference in the profile of effects when comparing men to women.

A major exception is that being a senior manager is much more likely to be associated with use of a work PC for men than for women. In addition, there is a higher correlation between use of a work and a home PC for men than for women. However, the overall picture is one of similarity. The same factors that help explain the likelihood of using a computer at home help explain work computer usage, and they do so roughly equally for men and women. It would appear that computer usage is computer usage, wherever it is undertaken and whoever undertakes it. Above all, we can see that although attitudes toward computers might differ between men and women, their effects do not.

This situation is equally apparent in a reversal of this procedure, in which the dependent variable is attitudes to computers. The analysis uses ordinary least squares because this variable is treated as interval level (though it should more strictly be treated as ordinal). The results are shown in table 7.6 (but without the controls). Using a work or a home PC reduces negative attitudes about equally for men and women. Table 7.7 looks at the effects of different types of usage. For this reason, only people who have a home PC are selected. The table shows that men who use a home PC for games, e-mail, web-surfing, or study are likely to have less negative attitudes than others (though only two of these coefficients are statistically significant). For women there is much less differentiation. Nevertheless, this does not greatly affect overall levels of association between attitudes and usage.

Table 7.5. Factors associated with home and work PC usage, those in work only (odds ratios from logistic regression: observations for men 1458, women 1459; Home-OnLine data, UK).

| | Men | | Women | |
	Home	Work	Home	Work
Age	1.0	1.0	1.0	1.0
Has degree	2.0*	2.9***	2.6***	2.0*
Senior manager	1.8*	7.3***	2.1**	1.6
Uses PC at home/work	3.0***	3.0***	1.9***	1.9***
Negative attitudes to PCs	0.8***	0.8***	0.8***	0.8***
High work autonomy	1.2	1.8**	1.4*	1.5**
Undertakes sports or fitness	0.9	0.9	1.4***	0.9
Goes to cinema/theater, etc.	1.4***	1.1	1.0	1.3**
Pseudo R^2	.24	.30	.21	.17

***p < .00l; **p < .01; *p < .05.

Table 7.6. Effect of use of computers at work and at home on negative attitudes toward computers, ordinary least squares regression (HoL; *N* as in table 7.2).

	Men	Women
Work PC	−1.8***	−1.8***
Home PC	−1.7***	−1.5"***

***p < .001.

PC Usage and Welfare

This still leaves the question of the welfare effect of attitudes to computer technology. In table 7.8, this is measured by the log of gross hourly wages, in analysis again using ordinary least squares. The aim is to see whether computer attitudes are associated with wages, and if so, whether this varies by gender. It is of note that there is a negative association between "technophobic" attitudes and wages for both men and women. This is in part because the models do not include whether or not a PC is used either at home or work. If these variables were included, they would have a positive effect, and attitudes would play less of a role. More important, the results show a larger negative effect in the case of women's attitudes. The figures can be interpreted as roughly a 4% decline in wages for women and a 2% decline for men for every increase in the scale of technophobia. It is possible that the distribution of the attitude scale might differ enough between men and women for this interpretation to be doubtful. That is, the differences in outcome might simply derive from different effects in different parts of the distribution. Nevertheless, where negative

Table 7.7. Effect of use of computers at work and at home on negative attitudes toward computers, ordinary least squares regression (HoL).

	Men (n = 423)	Women (n = 407)
Work PC	−1.3**	−0.8**
Home PC		
Games	−0.5	−0.1
E-mail	−0.4**	−0.1
Web	−0.8	−0.3***
Study	−0.9***	0.0
Work	0.0	−0.1
Other	0.0	−0.2*

***p < .001; **p < .01; *p < .05.

Table 7.8. Association of "technophobia" with log of monthly hourly wage (OLS coefficients; Home-Online data, U.K.).

	Men	Women
Age	0.01***	0.01***
Goes to sports/fitness.	0.04	0.02
Goes to cinema/theatre	−0.01	0.06**
Has a degree	0.21***	0.38***
Senior manager	0.45***	0.24***
Work hours	−0.01*	−0.01
Technophobia	−0.02**	−0.04***
Constant	3.66***	3.26***
Observations	963	1002
R^2	.19	.17

***p < .001; **p < .01; *p < .05.

attitudes exist, women are penalized at least as much and probably more than men.

To some extent, therefore, this finding contradicts the main hypothesis underlying this research—that of minimal gender differentials in the welfare gains from having positive attitudes to computer technology. The earlier tables showed that attitudes to computers do not vary substantially by gender over time, and also that attitudes adapt quickly to experience. It is therefore not clear why attitudes should have the differential effect visible in table 7.8. One explanation might be that they reflect occupational differences that have nothing to do with use of computers. Indeed, other research by the author (not reported here) shows that women and men generally gain equally from use of a computer at work.

Attitudes are only one part of the story. The analysis returns to eLiving to make use of an innovative piece of information not available in HoL: a measure of computer skills. This is based on six questions asked of those with any experience of computers: if they know how to download from the web, construct a web page, e-mail a file, cut and paste, reboot, and copy to a floppy. The range is therefore 0–6. In what follows, those with no experience of computers have been included as zero values. Averaging over the six countries, women score 2.0 and men 2.7, showing that men at least claim to know more. (This is not the result of differential access, as among those with computer experience, women score 3.6 whereas men score 4.4.)

Table 7.9. Association of "technophobia" with log of monthly hourly wage converted to Euros (OLS coefficients; eLiving data for five countries).

	Men	Women
Age	0.01***	0.01***
Graduate	0.18***	0.25***
Manager/professional	0.24***	0.21***
Work hours	−0.01***	−0.01***
Britain	0.48***	0.48***
Italy	0.02	0.09*
Germany	0.39***	0.38***
Norway	0.63***	0.71***
Computer skills	0.05***	0.06***
Constant	1.64***	1.57***
Observations	2327	2563
R^2	.47	.44

***$p < .001$; **$p < .01$; *$p < .05$.

Is this differential associated with a difference in wages? The results appear in table 7.9, again based on ordinary least squares regression where the dependent variable is the log of hourly wages. Bulgaria is excluded as being somewhat of an outlier; the remaining countries are pooled (with Israel as the reference category). "Computer skills" is the critical variable. These skills boost the hourly wages of men by 5% and of women by 6%. This difference is minimal. Thus, although confidence with computers shows a gender difference, actual skills, clearly only derived through experience, do not. This supports the idea that experience is perhaps a counter-balance to earlier gendered socialization.

A further adaptation to the general models shown above was tested on the HoL data. Number of years of experience with a PC both at home and work was entered in addition to the other computer variables already tried. It was expected that this number would show greater benefits to men through their earlier adaptation to computer technology, but none of the coefficients, whether for men or women, reached statistical significance. Number of years' experience makes no difference— it is current usage, skills, and attitudes that count.

Conclusion

Because women use domestic computers less than men do, and because women have on average less

positive attitudes toward computer technology, it is tempting to assume that the response to computer technology is fundamentally gendered. Such a concept would fit in with a wide range of theoretical and empirical literature, much of it feminist. Yet this difference might be more apparent than real. It could be read simply as a speedier willingness by men to come to terms with innovations rather than as a fundamental divide between men, who are technology-minded, and women, who are not. When a new technology arises, men get in the queue first, but women follow shortly after. The analysis has shown that the structure of the relationship between PC attitudes and PC behavior is the same for both men and women. Attitudes seem to follow experience, rather than the other way round, and to much the same degree. Furthermore, the gap in attitudes between users and nonusers is far greater than the gap across the gender divide, whereas the factors that explain the use of a PC, whether at home or at work, are roughly the same for both women and men.

Furthermore, it seems likely that differential attitudes depend in part on differential work experience. However, men have long had a hold over technologically advanced and thus better-paid work. Is this changing with the spread of computers in work processes, many of which are "feminized"? Or is there again some sort of fundamental gender divide—for instance, caused either by whatever differences in attitudes exist—or by the fact that men generally have higher levels of computer skills? The effect of computer attitudes on productivity (measured by wages) is tested in wage regressions where computer attitudes and skills are used as explanatory variables. The former do indeed favor men, but the latter are equal for men and women.

The computer is forming the basis of a reordering of the gendered basis of the advantages that accrue to the use of technology at work. We cannot go as far as to say this will lead to a substantial equalization of income from work for women relative to men, but it does mean that we should begin to dismantle ideas of an inevitable male technological advantage. This advantage derives from differential work experience, which varies over time, not from gender differences, which do not.

Acknowledgments. The author is very grateful to British Telecommunication PLC (Home-OnLine) and to the IST Programme of the European Union's

Fifth Framework Programme (eLiving) for the generous grants that enabled both data collection and the research based on the data. The work reported above also forms part of a program of research funded by the Economic and Social Research Council, the assistance of which is gratefully acknowledged. The author would also like to thank Ben Anderson and Eileen Green for their helpful comments on this chapter. Bonka Boneva, toward the end of her life, though that was not known then, invited me to give an early version of the paper in San Sebastian, Spain. We discussed the subject walking along the bay. I am grateful to her memory.

Notes

1. Some early feminists, conceding that science and rationality are "male," developed antitechnology theories (critiqued in Farganis, 1986, pp. 185–194).

2. "The second year I was the only girl in the class, and I felt really stupid, so I didn't want to go back" (quoted in Gaskell, 1992, p. 48). Referring to computer science, Turkle argues that its culture is male because success is linked to risk-taking and thrills (for the hacker in particular). The location of computer science in departments where geeks do not predominate, such as in social science, raises female participation (Rasmussen & Håpnes, 1998).

3. Male predominance in use of or control over a range of leisure technologies is well attested (Gallagher, 1987; Wajcman 1991; Morley, 1995; Stewart, 1998). The same applies to domestic usage of ICTs (Sullivan & Lewis, 2001). Men are more likely than women to be in the types of occupations in which teleworking occurs (Haddon & Silverstone, 1994).

4. Telephonic behavior is gendered, with women tending toward different call lengths but also more likely to use the telephone not only for social contacts but for "kinkeeping, nurturing, and community support" (Moyal, 1995, p. 303). Use of e-mail tends to replicate the gendering of relationship patterns. For instance, in one sample, far more women than men used e-mails to "revive family ties" (Boneva & Kraut, 2002, p. 382).

5. Intensity of usage might be stronger among men (Scott, Semmens, & Willoughby, 2001, p. 6). In the case of a quantitative example from Germany, although 73% of young men aged 16–17 years and 63% of young women used the Internet, the average weekly usage (in hours) was 12 for men and 5 for women (Wagner, Pischner, & Haisken-deNew, 2002, pp. 170–171).

6. Analysis based on this data set also appears in Anderson & Tracey (2002).

7. Available at http://www.eurescom.de.

8. The difference is also apparent across cultures. Using eLiving data, male usage varies in the extent to which it exceeds that of women across five countries, from 11.4 percentage points (Israel) to 18.5% (Italy).

9. In one U.S. sample, women spent nearly twice as long as men using e-mail (Boneva & Kraut, 2000, p. 385).

10. Dropping out from Internet usage has been measured in the United States at around 10% of a sample of current users per year (Katz & Rice, 2002: 129).

11. In Germany, there is a similar equality, although men are substantially more likely to use the Internet at work (Wagner et al., 2002, p. 172).

12. The extent to which the odds change in fact depends on the units in which the explanatory variables are measured. Nevertheless, the direction of change is always clear. Statistical significance is indicated by asterisks, in the conventional manner. The higher the number of asterisks, the greater the degree of probability that the outcome would occur in the population, not just in the sample.

References

Anderson, B., & Tracey, K. (2002). Digital living: The impact (or otherwise) of the Internet on everyday British life. In Wellman, B., & Haythornthwaite, C. (Eds.), *The Internet in everyday life* (pp. 139–163). Oxford: Blackwell.

Boneva, B., & Kraut, R. (2002). Email, gender, and personal relationships. In Wellman, B., & Haythornthwaite, C. (Eds.), *The Internet in everyday life* (pp. 372–403). Oxford: Blackwell.

Cockburn, C. (1983). *Brothers: Male dominance and technological change.* London: Pluto.

Cockburn, C. (1985). *Machinery of dominance: Women, men and technical know-how.* London: Pluto.

Cockburn, C. (1987). *Two-track training: Sex inequalities and the YTS.* London: Macmillan.

diNardo, J., & Pischke, J.-S. (1997). The returns to computer use revisited: Have pencils changed the wage structure, too? *Quarterly Journal of Economics, February, 112,* 291–303.

Entorf, H., & Kramarz, F. (1997). Does unmeasured ability explain the higher wages of new technology workers? *European Economic Review, 41*(8), 1489–1509.

Farganis, S. (1986). *Social reconstruction of the feminine character.* Totowa, NJ: Rowman and Littlefield.

Gallagher, M. (1987). Redefining the communications revolution. In Baehr, H. & Dyer, G. (Eds.), *Boxed in: Women and television* (pp. 19–37). London: Pandora Press.

Gallie, D. (1994). Patterns of skill change: Upskilling, deskilling, or polarization? In Penn, R., Rose, M., & Rubery, J. (Eds.), *Skill and occupational change* (pp. 41–76). Oxford: Oxford University Press.

Gaskell, J. (1992). *Gender matters from school to work.* Milton Keynes, UK: Open University Press.

Green, E. (2001). Technology, leisure and everyday practices. In Green, E., & Adam, A. (Eds.), *Virtual gender: Technology, consumption and identity* (pp. 173–188). London: Routledge.

Green, F. (1998). *The value of skills* (mimeo.). Kent, UK: University of Kent.

Grint, K., & Woolgar, S. (1997). *The machine at work: Technology, work and organization.* Cambridge, UK: PolityPress.

Haddon, L., & Silverstone, R. (1994). Telework and the changing relationship of home and work. In Mansell, R. (Ed.), *Management of information and communication technologies: emerging patterns of control* (pp. 234–247). London: Aslib.

Haraway, D. (1991). *Simians, cyborgs, and women.* London: Free Association Books.

Katz, J., & Rice, R. (2002). Syntopia: Access, civic involvement, and social interaction on the Net. In Wellman, B., & Haythornthwaite, C. (Eds.), *The Internet In everyday life* (pp. 114–138). Oxford: Blackwell.

Krueger, A. (1993). How computers have changed the wage structure. *Quarterly Journal of Economics, 58*(1), 33–60.

Machin, S. (1996). Changes in the relative demand for skills. In Booth, A., & Snower, D. (Eds.), *Acquiring skills* (pp. 127–146). Cambridge, UK: Cambridge University Press.

Martin, M. (1998). The culture of the telephone. In Hopkins, P. (Ed.), *Sex/machine: Readings in culture, gender, and technology* (pp. 50–74). Bloomington: Indiana University Press.

Morley, D. (1995). Theories of consumption in media studies. In Miller, D. (Ed.), *Acknowledging consumption* (pp. 296–328). London: Routledge.

Moyal, A. (1995). The feminine culture of the telephone: People, patterns and policy. In Heap, N. & Open University (Eds.), *Information technology and society* (pp. 284–310). London: Sage.

Nickell, S., & Bell, B. (1995). The collapse in the demand for the unskilled and unemployment across the OECD. *Oxford Review of Economic Policy, 11*(1), 40–62.

Norris, P. (2000). *A virtuous circle: Political communications in industrial societies.* New York: Cambridge University Press.

Plant, S. (2000). On the matrix: Cyberfeminist simulations. In Janes, L., Woodward, K., & Hovenden, F. (Eds.), *The gendered cyborg* (pp. 265–275). London: Routledge.

Rasmussen, B., & Håpnes, T. (1998). Excluding women from the technologies of the future: A case study of the culture of computer science. In Hopkins, P. (Ed.), *Sex/machine: Readings in culture, gender, and technology* (pp. 381–394). Bloomington: Indiana University Press.

Rogers, E. (1995). *Diffusion of innovations.* New York: The Free Press.

Scott, A., Semmens, L., & Willoughby, L. (2001). Women and the Internet: The natural history of a research project. In Green, E., & Adam, A. (Eds.), *Virtual gender: Technology, consumption and identity* (pp. 3–27). London: Routledge.

Shavit, Y., & Müller, W. (Eds.) (1998). *From school to work: A comparative study of educational qualifications and occupational destinations.* Oxford: Clarendon.

Stewart, M. (1998). *Cracking the gender code.* Toronto: Second Story Press.

Sullivan, C., & Lewis, S. (2001). Home-based telework, gender, and the synchronisation of work and family: Perspectives of teleworkers and their co-residents. *Gender, Work and Organisation, 8*(2), 123–145.

Turkle, S. (1998). Computational reticence: Why women fear the intimate machine. In Hopkins, P. (Ed.), *Sex/machine: Readings in culture, gender, and technology* (pp. 365–380). Bloomington: Indiana University Press.

Wagner, G., Pischner, R., & Haisken-deNew, J. (2002). The Changing Digital Divide in Germany. In B. Wellman & C. Haythornthwaite (Eds.), *The Internet in Everyday Life* (pp. 164–85). Oxford: Blackwell.

Wajcman, J. (1991). *Feminism Confronts Technology.* Cambridge, England: Polity Press.

Webster, J. (1996). *Shaping women's work: Gender, employment and information technology.* London: Longman.

Wellman, B., & Haythornthwaite, C. (Eds.) 2002. *The Internet in everyday life.* Oxford: Blackwell.

Woodfield, R. (2000). *Women, work, and computing.* Cambridge, UK: Cambridge University Press.

Technology in Context:
Home, Family, and Community

8

Maria Bakardjieva

The Consumption Junction Revisited

Networks and Contexts

In this chapter, I analyze domestic Internet use, drawing on Actor Network Theory (Callon, 1987; Law, 1987). More specifically, I follow the direction proposed by Cowan (1987), who pioneered an actor-network approach taking the user as its point of departure. Cowan's (1987) project was to understand the network that holds users and technology together from "the consumption junction, the place and the time at which the consumer makes choices about competing technologies" (p. 263). Cowan believed that this consumer-centered version of an actor-network would help to explain the success or failure of different artefacts. The consumption junction represented for her "the interface where technological diffusion occurs" and also "the place where technologies begin to reorganize social structures" (p. 263).

In a somewhat different development inspired by Actor Network Theory, Gomart and Hennion (1999) elaborate on a "sociology of attachment" through the study of music amateurs and drug users. They introduce the concept of "subject networks" (p. 220), which attempts to capture the ways that "the subject can emerge as she actively submits herself to a collection of constraints" (p. 220). These constraints are imposed by entities found in the local environment, including objects and people,

or actants and actors, which link together into a network. Making these networks the object of study, Gomart and Hennion propose, would help analysts move beyond questions like "Who acts?" and "What is the determinant and what the determined?" Instead, analysts can focus on the question, "What happens?" In this way, crude dualisms like those between agency and structure, activity and passivity, and freedom and determination would be overcome and replaced by a more fluid picture of mutual constitution between subjects and the entities of their surrounding world. Further, Gomart and Hennion invoke Foucault's notion of "dispositif" to define the focus of their analysis as "the tactics and techniques which make possible the emergence of a subject as it enters a 'dispositif'" (p. 220). Within the "dispositif," objects represent mediators, not causes. They do not carry inherent qualities but acquire qualities "contingent on the user's discovery movements" (p. 238).

I believe these ideas can yield interesting results when applied to some of the uncertainties generated by the interaction between users and technologies. Do technologies impose determinations of their own, as suggested by the numerous studies looking for the proverbial social effects of different technological innovations? Do they embody and enact the intentions of those who designed them? Are they neutral tools marshaled by users' free will toward the achievement of desired results? The various brands of actor-network theorizing quoted above indicate that we could learn more about the interaction between subjects and technologies if we abandoned the search for simple determinations. Technologies and users mutually constitute each other by joining together into heterogeneous networks. According to Actor Network Theory, objects (artefacts) represent networks of both human and nonhuman elements. Subjects, or users, on their part, emerge out of the networking of the various elements in their environment, including technological artefacts (Gomart and Hennion, 1999). Activity and passivity, freedom and determination—all are distributed across the network. They are not an intrinsic property or birthright belonging to any one of its components. Paradoxically, this relativistic approach offers valuable insights into some of the unexpected consequences of technological innovation, as well as into the transformations that subjects undergo as a result of their engagement with technologies.

In the rest of this chapter, I apply this approach to the diffusion of the Internet, a remarkable communication technology that has attracted a vast user population in recent years. I report the results of a study that focused on the integration of the Internet into the everyday lives of ordinary users who connect to it from their homes. My goal is to describe the actor networks that ensure continuation—or in constructivist terms, "stabilization" (Pinch & Bijker, 1987), of use. Tracing the dynamic of these networks, I believe, can help us grasp the Internet's social fate and significance in depth and detail. This can demonstrate how subjects changed the medium through discovering its potential properties in relation to their specific social circumstances. At the same time, it is possible to trace changes in the subjects themselves as they turn into Internet users, and thus enter new relations and alliances afforded by the technology.

An important outcome of this analysis, as it turns out, is the realization that the search for universal characteristics and effects of the Internet is misguided. Users form a variety of different relationships with the Internet. As a consequence, the effects, or changes, in ways of acting and living, in social relations and social organization that are induced by the Internet are infinitely diverse—but this is not the kind of diversity that should paralyze research. The unlikelihood of finding the one great impact, the message of the medium in McLuhanist terms, does not render analysis futile. It refocuses attention on the quest for understanding the kinds of relationships and networks that we build with and through this technology. These networks are precisely what define us as subjects, as well as the social world that we inhabit.

Research Design

The specific challenge posed by this research goal was to devise sensitive instruments for capturing the everyday practices in which Internet use is embedded. The methods of data collection included indepth interviews and site visits to the homes of 20 lower-middle class households with Internet connections in the metropolitan Vancouver area in 1998 and 1999. The research procedure consisted of four complementary and partly overlapping components: first, a structured personal (dialogic) interview in which the central questions invited respondents to produce mininarratives describing how their "domestication" (Silverstone, 1994) of the Internet happened. Second, a tour of the computer and Internet-related space in the respondents' homes. Third, a tour of the "computer space" constituted by Internet-use practices; that is, the traces of Internet use that, unlike log files, were deliberately saved in respondents' computers or in their account's server space. These files were typically bookmarks, address books, mailboxes, folders, and so on. This particular technique allowed me to examine the "electronic artefacts" created by users as they moved in and consciously manipulated the substance of cyberspace. Importantly, on this tour I was guided by my respondents, who would explain the meaning and the importance of the digital artefacts that could be found in their computer's memory. Fourth, a short group-interview session, where possible, with respondents' family members in which the latter were asked to discuss the Internet use, in their home.

Respondents were recruited through self-selection. My interview criteria stipulated that these subjects would not have a job related to the design, production, or marketing of technology, content, or services for the Internet; would be paying for their Internet connection out of their own budget;

and would use the Internet more than three times per week.

Altogether, 20 home visits were carried out. Twenty-two main respondents (11 men and 11 women) and seven additional family members were interviewed. This respondent group included people with different sociodemographic characteristics and in diverse biographical situations. Their experience in using the Internet varied from 1 to 8 years, with the mean being 3 years. Most of the people in the group had a modest household income between CAN$20,000 and $50,000 annually. (The exceptions were three families with income between $50,000 and $100,000, and one family with an income of over $100,000).[1] In practical terms, that meant that the participants in the study belonged to an economic bracket lower than the comfortable, most often professional, middle class that was commonly associated with domestic computer and Internet use at the time (1998–1999).

The following account focuses on the stories that my respondents told me about their first encounters and early experiences with the Internet. It tracks the ways in which the domestic Internet connection had emerged as a "heterogeneous network" (Callon, 1987, p. 93) of technical, social, discursive, and cognitive elements including equipment, mass-mediated messages, interpersonal relations, and interpretations of the medium's nature and usefulness. I identify the "actants" who are responsible for the emergence of this network and seek to explain how and why the connections among them arose. I argue that the penetration of the Internet into individual households, seen from the side of the user, represents a generative process of becoming a domestic Internet user. Generally speaking, this process can be mapped out as follows: It takes place in everyday microsettings and draws from public discourses, organizational practices, situated practical reasoning, and the experience of peers. It involves local interpretations of the technology and the discovery of its properties as it proves to afford new relations with entities in the surrounding world. In strategically enacting or submitting to these new relations and action possibilities, users weave different networks and thus different practical definitions of the Internet—some aligned with those anticipated by designers, some unexpected. Through this process, different user-subject types emerge and proliferate.

The Emergence of the Home Internet Connection

Technical Actants

The computer had been the first element to find a place into the future user's home. It had usually arrived there by way of a productive activity such as work or study. Most of the time, the need to use a computer at home (its relevance) had been explicitly demanded by a certain organization, or the expense of buying one had been justified by the expectation of increased efficiency in an income-yielding activity.

> We had the computer already. My wife had bought it for her research; she was doing her master's at [the university]. (Theodore, 45, parking patroller)
>
> I went into business for myself for a few years. I already had a computer, a 286. It wasn't good enough for Auto-CAD at that point. So I bought a 486; at that time it was the best and today it is already old and out of date. (Reiner, 62, retired mechanical engineering technician.)
>
> [What were you doing with your computer before you got the Internet?]
>
> Writing letters, word processing. I did some work in security business for a while, I did the basics—selling security products like cameras. So I did bookkeeping and record keeping. (Jane, 35, homemaker)

For another category of people, the desire to own and use a computer had been provoked by public discourses proclaiming the arrival of the information society or the computer age. "When we got the computer first, it was basically for the kids and for us to be upgraded, to be technically upgraded," Sophie, a 35-year-old nutrition consultant, explained. "To be technically upgraded" was an effort to keep up with computer development—not for the sake of a concrete practical application but, rather, for the purpose of identifying oneself as an adequate member of the computer age. Similarly, Martha, a meat-wrapper for Safeway, felt compelled to "upgrade" herself with computer equipment and skills:

> I bought a computer because I needed spreadsheets and word processing, and games. Not for work, for a nonprofit group. Because I

was doing bookkeeping for this group and initially I used to go to a neighbor's place to use their computer. . . . I am not afraid of computers, and I had done a lot of database stuff on a computer in my son's school when he was grade 5, that means 7 years ago. . . . Because they were looking for volunteers in the school and I thought it would be a great way to stay in the school and keep an eye on him, and get used to using a computer. And I had taken a basic programming course a year or two before that. . . . I thought, in this computer age I better stay in touch. (Martha, 41, meat-wrapper)

For a third group of users, the acquisition of a computer had been driven by mere curiosity and the ready accessibility of the equipment, even though often in outdated form. Garry, for example, had submitted himself to the call of the object:

My brother had just upgraded his computer. My brother works . . . he is an actuary, so he uses computers all the time. So, he was upgrading and he offered me this computer. He had offered it to me three or four times before and finally I said okay. (Garry, 67, retired naval radio operator)

Although a necessary component for accessing the Internet, the computer needs to be further extended, both technically and conceptually, to transform from a stand-alone machine for record-keeping or word-processing into a communication medium. What prompted respondents to take that step? What made the Internet so attractive to them that they were ready to commit resources and effort to get connected to it?

Despite the fact that the respondents in this study were not information technology profession-als, some of them had experienced pressure from their employer or educational institution to hook up to the Internet at home. This pressure had been stronger for those who were taking courses at a college or university. Others had simply arrived at the idea that it would be convenient to transfer files between their office and their home or to do work- or study-oriented research on the Internet from home. Users had seen the home Internet connec-tion as a way to more smoothly blend their work/ education and family life spaces, and that it afforded a smoother transition.

The Internet came next because I was in nursing [college program], . . . and they strongly recommended it as a research resource, for looking up all kinds of different things we'd need to do in nursing. . . . I thought I just could use the one [connection] at school to deal with the addresses that were assigned to us at school. . . . But he [husband] said that the reality was that it's easier to use it from home, from the comfort of my own home, and he was right, because as soon as I was done with classes, I wanted to come home. (Sophie, 35, part-time nutrition consultant)

Certainly, new possibilities for both work and edu-cation were opening up in the users' imagination at the same time as the Internet was entering their homes:

I am looking into taking online courses through the Open Learning Agency. . . . I would like to take a lot of courses online. I like taking courses face-to-face, but sometimes it is a nuisance, you have to catch a bus. I just finished 3 years of business admin at [college] and it was once a week getting to the school. I like the interaction, I like other people, getting the feedback. But at the same time it takes a lot of time getting there, so I'd like to take something online. (Martha)

I include a reference to my web page in my résumé when I send it out for jobs like web programming, web maintenance, anything related to the Internet. More and more businesses are going on the Internet; some of them have nothing to do with computers and the Internet itself, so they need people with this kind of experience. (Patrick, 33, electronic technician)

For another group of users, the decision to connect to the Internet had little to do with practi-cal interest or duty. "The media hype" as one re-spondent himself put it, the different kinds of discourses spreading excitement about computer networking throughout the culture, had led these people to take interest and want to check "what was really going on."

Why I wanted to have an account? Because the Internet is something of fashion, there is a lot of talk about the Internet and I can see some business possibilities. The excitement to have

something new was the primary reason.
(Patrick)

In a third type of case, the Internet's perceived possibilities resonated with a strong personal need.

> Then a friend started telling me about the Internet. He had a son in Calgary and another one in Montreal, and he told me how every night he got e-mail letters from them and he would e-mail back. And I said: "How do you do that? How much does it cost you?" And he said: "It doesn't cost me anything. Would you like to try it?" (John, 73, retired mechanical engineer)

Users such as Garry (quoted above) and Ellen (age 49) had construed the Internet as a solution to acute personal problems. In their case, the communicative function was the one bringing the computer home:

> because I had heard—I have had arthritis now since 1992—that there was a site on there on which I could meet people with arthritis. So I said, here is my chance to use the Internet for something that would be useful to me…. I'd seen them, computers, in the library and I was sort of intrigued, but I could never find how they could be of any use to me. I am not into learning something that is not useful. (Garry)

For Ellen, a former editor with a disability making her housebound, the computer had emerged as a potential gateway to the outside world:

> My friend came and he said "I'm going to set you up on the Internet, and I'm going to show you how to use it," and this specific function was different from when I used to work. The main purpose was in order for me to be able to connect to a support group. (Ellen)

So Ellen received an old Macintosh from her friend and connected to the Internet through the local Community Net for free.

Human Intermediaries and Intermediated Humans

Gaining some basic networking knowledge and skills had been a crucial condition for the home Internet connection to stabilize itself as a working domestic technology. My respondents had picked up such knowledge and skills in formal settings such as Internet-related courses or instructional sessions, or within their own homes with the help of more experienced friends and relatives. Notably, however, even when the introduction to the Internet had taken place elsewhere, the "domestication" (Silverstone, 1994) of the medium, its integration into the user's own system of values, goals and routines, had been actively assisted by a close friend.

This figure of the human intermediary came up in respondent's accounts initially in the role of someone who precipitated the encounter between the user and the technology. This was the person who "started telling me about the Internet" or insisted that the respondent get connected for the two of them to be able communicate.

At later stages, this person would visit the home of the respondent (new user) and help him or her with setting up the equipment, learning how to use the software, figuring out what sites were worth checking out, and so on. In sum, this person acted as an intermediary between the world of technology and the new user's personal world. I define the role that this character plays in the building of the home Internet connection as that of the "warm expert" (see Bakardjieva, 2005). The warm expert is an Internet/computer technology expert in the professional sense, or simply in a relative sense compared with the new user. Warm experts typically have two key characteristics: They possess the knowledge needed to operate with a reasonable degree of success in the world of technology, but at the same time, they are part of the users' life-world and share experiences, interests, and knowledge with them. Taking this position allows the warm expert to mediate between the universal features of the technology and the overwhelmingly diverse content of the medium on the one hand, and the novice user's concrete local situation, needs, and background on the other.

In Martha's story, this role had been played by a friend from a remote suburb who had stayed at her house for a few days to help her with her newly purchased computer: "We played on the computer, we just played with it and he used a lot of metaphors." Subsequently, the correspondence with that same friend would be one of the main streams in the flow of her e-mail. In Theodore's experience, the warm expert was a cousin (a professional "tech support person") who traveled like a missionary across North America and connected his relatives to the Internet. That cousin gave Theodore his first modem and pointed him to a mailing list that would prove to be of great interest to him. John's more expert friends often walked him through his computer problems on the phone. Sophie and her husband sometimes needed to call as far as California to receive personalized computer help from her husband's stepfather, a systems analyst.

Sandy hooked up to the Internet from home following the advice of one of her professors. She was planning to drop his course because it required Internet research and she found it impossible to go to the campus computer lab given her part-time job, young child, and family responsibilities:

> And he [professor] provided a guy named Stanley who came over and helped me to get hooked up to the Internet. Very nice, very nice guy, and since then Stanley and I have become friends. So we met at the university and he told me what I needed to have and then he said "I'll come over to your place" because I was confused. And he came, hooked me up and got me the software. (Sandy)

With Stanley's help, Sandy learned how to use a chat program: "I think I phoned Stanley and he told me—by that time I had Netscape and a connection thing—so Stanley told me to go to this place called www.talkcity.com." Armed with this knowledge, she went on to discover richer sources of technical help on the network itself:

> Quite often, once I had that chat line hooked up, a lot of my help came from people in that chat line, like Roland, who had a computer science degree. And he made it easy. . . . There's a lot of people online, and if you go into the computer chat rooms, that would do the same thing, you just have to ask for the help and I think asking for the help and knowing where to go for the help is the hardest part online. (Sandy)

At the time we spoke, less than 2 years after her initial introduction to the Internet, Sandy often provided help to other people who wanted to set up their own Internet connections at home. In giving assistance, she drew on what she had learned from Stanley and from her own discoveries:

> Lots of people now get me to hook them up to the Internet because they know that I hang out

there. One of the first things that I download is a chat line program and I say: "this is where you go for help"—and if they have a Macintosh I will set it up so that they just go in there—in the Macintosh room. And if you go in there and ask for help there are hundreds of people that will help you—they'll tell you where to go and what to do. Then you form relationships with other people who have computers. [My ISP] has their own software, but I don't recommend people to use it. . . . That's how Stanley taught me—"Don't use [the ISP] software, Sandy, use your own software because you are in control of it." (Sandy)

These accounts make the relations clearly visible between the human and technical actants who form the home Internet connection. The advice, words, gestures, and even phone number of the warm expert are tightly interwoven with the wire and electronic chips that make the object what it is in the user's world. Friends, relatives, and, to some degree, helpers encountered in newsgroups and chats taught my respondents not only how to navigate but also what they themselves had discovered that the Internet meant as a communication medium. The same happened later, when some of my respondents had become capable of playing the role of the warm expert for less knowledgeable new users in their social environment.

In many of the user experiences I studied, the home network connection had been composed and stabilized by allying with the intermediated humans that it brought into reach. A remarkable interlocking between the technical and the social networks of users was strengthening and transforming both kinds of networks.

> I got online for e-mail. Yes, friends and relatives. . . . I am trying to remember with whom my initial contacts were because now I have a mile-long list of contacts. I have friends in Japan and all over the place. (Martha)
>
> I have a brother who lives in Montreal and who discovered the computer about 2 years ago. He is on the Internet so we communicate regularly back and forth.
>
> [And you didn't use to do that before?]
>
> No, we didn't. I am not a writer. I never wrote letters. Typing is something different than writing. I don't know why. Probably because you have a spell checker and gram-

mar, if you wish. It is a big reason. I was somebody who never liked writing, writing letters and so on. Once I had the spell checker, the grammar checker, no problem, I felt much more secure. But handwriting is out. The typewriter was tough because you could not correct it. But here, I can correct. So it was a wonderful thing for a person like me. My brother tells me the same thing. So we exchange messages. (Reiner)

And I talk more to my brothers now. . . . If I have a question—like this one-line question—I probably wouldn't write to them. I might phone them, but the chances to get them at home is very unlikely because they are never at home, and then the time difference—they are in Toronto. That way I can just e-mail them and they can answer it whenever they want and it doesn't cost them anything. It is easy. (Jane)

The friend who already had e-mail, the arthritis support group, the son or brother living in a different province: all were connected with wire, electronics, and software to form the user's subjective version of the Internet and its main applications. At the same time, through these mediated relations with other people, the user-subjects were defining their individual self-identity and place in the world.

Network Strength: User-Technology Relations

The relations between users and the Internet, and the respective patterns of use, were an upshot of the mutual reinforcement of these interlocking object-, subject-, and social networks. A range of different user–Internet relations could be discerned depending on the strength of these heterogeneous networks and the centrality that the Internet had acquired within them. Some users remained in a strictly instrumental relationship with the Internet. The spectrum of their applications was relatively narrow. They were preoccupied exclusively with the particular goal, which was lying beyond the technology and to which the technology was nothing more than a means. These users demanded "transparency" of the technology in the sense of not having to pay special attention to it. Failure to find such

transparency was a source of frustration to them, but these users were unwilling to invest time and money in upgrading either their equipment or their own skills to achieve this transparency. Those who had old computers and low-speed connections were annoyed by these limitations but insisted that the equipment was just fine for their purposes. Put simply, they did not care about the inner workings of the technology.

For another type of user, the relation with the Internet was very intense. These people were deeply interested in the technology and strove toward a transparent understanding of how it worked, but that didn't mean they were preparing for an IT career or becoming computer hobbyists. By means of the Internet, they were pursuing particular interests and goals lying beyond the technology itself—in that sense, the technology represented an object that was mediating access to other components of their subject-network. At the same time, these users devoted considerable time and effort in keeping up with the latest technical developments and obviously found pleasure and some pride in that. This type of user involved the Internet in a whole range of different activities related to work, leisure, education/learning, socializing, and so on. No matter that most of them derived no material benefits from their computer or Internet use, and their household incomes were modest, they regularly upgraded their equipment and extended the home Internet connection with additional gadgets:

[Why did you buy the scanner?]

To scan pictures to send to family [in Britain]. It cost $150–200. The scanner is only as good as what you need it for. If you want to just capture images, throw them into a GIF file and send them to Europe or put them onto web site. Or you can scan a picture of your family and throw it into a letter to somebody. . . . Mostly for my son. He's an artist—he draws a lot and I want to get his pictures out there. It's a sort of self-esteem thing. He can feel really good about his work.

For a third kind of user, the technology of the Internet and the computer in general were exciting for what they were. The practical goals of their Internet use seemed to be overshadowed in importance by how the technology "made them feel," to evoke Turkle's (1984) formulation. Here is a short excerpt of the animated explanation that one such respondent gave me while he was leading me on a tour of his computer interior:

> In fact it is extremely simple to use my machine, but I have done some tricky things that other people just haven't. I can provide anybody with very simple little routines to do what I do. Most of my gimmicks people don't use, but I love them. There is nothing on my screen that I don't want on my screen now. It is clean and simple. The beauty of this program is that [it] will only take about 100K. (Merlin, 58–year-old unemployed mechanical engineer)

Merlin was actively and voluntary losing himself in the technology much in the same way amateur musicians and drug addicts were submitting to their passion (see Gomart & Hennion, 1999). His intensive preoccupation with reprogramming, customizing, and outsmarting the original software gave him a sense of autonomy and achievement. A similar relationship had emerged in the case of a young college student (Larry). Partly disassembled appliances lay all over Larry's room. He took pleasure in examining what was hidden underneath the cover just for the challenge of it.

In this way, three types of relationships between users and Internet technology were emerging from my observations. To make sense of them, I will draw on (and adapt) Ihde's (1990) phenomenology of human–technology relations. Discussing the different ways in which technology is taken into the subjective life-world, Ihde defined four types of relations: embodiment relations, hermeneutic relations, alterity relations, and background relations[2] (see Ihde, 1990).

In the embodiment relation expressed by the formula (I – technology) – world (Ihde, 1990, p. 73), the technology is positioned between the user and his or her surrounding environment, between the observer and the observed; between the doer and the object of his or her action. The referent of the seeing and the doing is on the other side of the technological tool or system. In this relationship, the user takes the technology as an extension of his or her perceptual and actional bodily self. The instrumental users in my respondent group related to the computer and the Internet in this way. They expected the technology to be unobtrusive and not to divert attention or energy from the referent lying beyond it. Garry expressed this sentiment through

a common dictum: "I just want the damn thing to work!" For these users, the world was on the other side of the technology and lent itself to more or less successful comprehension and manipulation, depending on how smoothly the technology was embodied. Interestingly, even the most poorly equipped and technically uninformed users seemed to have been able to work out certain routines, even if they were awkward, for handling Internet technology, so that it served their purposes without requiring too much attention itself.

Ihde (1990) points out an essential ambiguity existing in this relation: it has a necessary "magnification/reduction structure" (p. 74). Embodiment relations simultaneously magnify and amplify—and reduce—what is experienced through them. The eyes of another person met during an encounter are a different entity from the eyes of a patient examined via the instruments of an optometrist. The person experienced through the telephone is brought to me across a big distance at the expense of being reduced to a voice.

The second type of users in my study represented a relation with technology that could be described by Ihde's (1990) "hermeneutic" formalism: I – (technology – world) (see p. 86). Building on Ihde's definition of this relation, I propose that, in this case, the attention of the user is focused on the technology—but not for its own sake; rather, because it has become a critical mediator allowing the users to relate to the world. These users see the Internet as defining the world they live in: "the computer age," "the network society." Here is the place to recall Martha's remark: "And I took a basic programming course a year or two before that. I thought in this computer age, I better stay in touch." Staying in touch with a world that they perceived as highly technological, computerized, and networked was the high stake that people in this category had in the Internet. Its importance was not limited to a single goal or activity.

Alex, a jewelry designer, for example, felt compelled to orient himself to the rising tide of information to remain in control of his life. For that reason, having the Internet connection was essential to him. In Sandy's world, information technology had two quite different faces. Sandy, a telemarketer, worked in a highly computerized environment and was an object of technologically mediated monitoring and control throughout her working day. When she was being trained for this job, Sandy recalled, she was having nightmares about the computer chasing her down the street. At the time of the interview, this pressure had been relieved (to a great extent thanks to a good trade union at Sandy's workplace). Nevertheless, Sandy's relationship with technology at work remained the same: she was the object of it. In contrast, when she was at her computer at home and on the Internet, Sandy felt in charge:

> And I have set up this thing called My Yahoo which is through the search engine. I have it all programmed to load up to things that I am interested in—stocks that I own—and it tells me whether the stock is up or down and headline news stories that I am interested in—and it loads those automatically. My chat program, my ICQ, stuff is neatly organized. The work is learning the technology, after that it's easy to organize. (Sandy)

"Organizing is essential," as Martha had also stated. A substantial part of Martha's world of interests and relationships with people was consciously structured into her bookmarks and e-mail folders. Having achieved a good command of Internet technology, Martha felt she could navigate the world outside and order her relations with it in accordance with her needs, values, and priorities. In this process, she was not only extending and enriching the content of her life world, she was reinventing herself. Thus, Martha had gradually become a resource person for many of her friends and relatives. She had done research on film-related jobs in Britain for her aunt, on the Gulf War syndrome for one of her brothers, on Attention Deficit Disorder for her local parent support group, and so on. She was learning that she actually enjoyed doing research and that: "I think I would be really good at researching. That's why I want to find a job in research. I am good at finding things."

The three respondents whose experiences I have used as an example of the hermeneutic user–technology relation, unlike Garry, whom I quoted earlier, did want to know how the technology worked to be able to effectively connect to the world that it represented and constructed. However, knowing and speaking the language of Internet technology required constantly following new technical developments. Not surprisingly, a big portion of these users' bookmarks and the newsletters and newsgroups that they subscribed to were technically oriented. In terms of software and hardware, all these people were constantly "upgrading." An interesting activity–passivity paradox could be observed in the practice of these users: to be able to actively organize and control the world of information to which the Internet was giving them access, they needed to submit to a flood of information about new programs, applications, upgrades, pieces of equipment, and so on.

Finally, by his third type of human–technology relation, the alterity relation, Ihde (1990) seeks to characterize "the positive or presentential senses" in which humans relate to technology as a "quasi-other" (p. 98). In this relation, Ihde observes, technologies emerge as focal entities that may receive the multiple attentions that humans give to the different forms of the other (p. 107). This type of relation resembles what Turkle (1984) meant by her metaphor of the intimate machine: a machine or technology experienced in ways and producing emotional reactions that are typically associated with other human beings. The examples of this kind of relation in my respondent group, Merlin and Larry, were excited by the challenges that technology posed and used it as a testing ground for their own abilities. Their computers and Internet browsers were becoming central components of the subject-networks characterizing their sense of self.

These three human–technology relations are not mutually exclusive. They can coexist within the same personal experience of a user with regard to different technologies, or at different stages of the user's dealings with the same technology. Which type of relation would prevail—not only for every user but for the various stages through which users progress—is a matter of a biographically and situationally determined constellation of relationships with people, objects, and entities of the immediate surroundings and of the social world beyond the doorstep.

Amplifications and Reductions

Different combinations of both possibilities and limitations ensued for the users in these three distinct relations with the Internet. As much as their power for action grew in certain respects, they also had to submit to specific limiting conditions. Ihde's dichotomy of amplifications versus reductions captures this state of affairs nicely. For users who had taken the Internet in an "embodiment relation," the technology provided an extension of their scope of perception and action, but it also imposed limitations on what they could do and how. Theodore (an Ethiopian immigrant to Canada), for example, could gather information about the political life of his native country from Internet sources. However, because Internet protocols did not support the Amharic[3] writing system and he had only a textual web interface, he could not receive material originating in Ethiopia itself. Therefore, he had to create his radio program for the local Ethiopian community, which was his main use of the Internet, drawing exclusively on English-language publications. In this way, his knowledge and understanding of the developments he reported on remained restricted by certain perspectives and agendas.

Don could call a meeting of his voluntary organization's board of directors by sending the same message to numerous addressees, which was a clear amplification of his communicative efficiency. At the same time, he could not count on reliable feedback about who had actually received and read the message and who had not. On one occasion, when Don decided to rely on e-mail for arranging a meeting, the designated host did not receive the message and everything failed. Without the flexibility of synchronous communication, the affairs of the organization had become captive of the quirks of a technical system.

Vera felt empowered by the possibility of using online sources for the purposes of her research, but she was anxious about the amount of time she found herself forced to spend wading through irrelevant material.

In the case of the hermeneutic relation, the Internet's role in users' lives was more pervasive. The discourse of the "computer age," "the information society," and concepts like "millions of people going online every day" that stemmed from influential public sources underlay these users' perception of the medium. The people in this relation dedicated considerable effort to studying and understanding the Internet for the purpose of being able to competently navigate the "information society" in which they believed they were living. Ironically, as the information overload paradox suggests, the more they tried to be active agents in this society, the more they were giving in to technological dictate. For them, everyday Internet use was a field

of struggle to achieve a balance between personal autonomy and inevitable compliance with imposed rules. As a result, people were beginning to reflect on the means of representing the world that is inherent in Internet technology and content and the subtle ways in which these means both amplified and reduced personal agency:

> Well, I can go to McDonalds's and I can be linked then to Burger King, Wendy's, etc., etc. . . . But I can go the rest of my life there and never have a nourishing meal, but not even miss it. (Don)
>
> You can go into the American Yahoo! site and you can search a route—how to drive from one city to another by the least amount of miles—it gives you a map. Which is very limiting because it is biased, based on their criteria. On one hand it frees me up because I don't have to worry which way I go to Florida, but on the other hand, I haven't learned so much. And I am probably the only nerd who thinks about those things—most of them will print the map and drive to Florida. (Sandy)

In fact, she was not alone. Martha too was critically monitoring her own Internet use. She admitted that initially she was "addicted," and insisted that now she was trying not to take it too seriously. "I want it to become just a tool like anything else, like using the phone." She saw the attainment, or restoration, of the embodiment relation, the "technology-as-a-tool" position, as the salvation from the overwhelming experience that was produced by the hermeneutic relation.

The recognition of the reductions imposed by the Internet was giving birth to a fourth type of relation having critical questioning as its main characteristic: I call it the critical hermeneutic relation. On the basis of their intense preoccupation with the technology as an interface to a technological world, these users were gaining awareness of the limitations and distortions implicit in this interface, and they were attempting to critically evaluate its place in their lives. The competence that these users achieve with Internet technology, combined with their critical understanding of its inherent amplifications and reductions, allows them to imagine alternative technical and cultural forms. It enables them to disseminate their critical understanding of the technology along with their skills in making meaningful use of it, as the phenomenon of the warm expert indicates.

The critical hermeneutic relation does not follow automatically in the wake of gaining technical proficiency. It emerges out of hard and broadly informed work toward understanding both the inside workings of the medium and the personal and social consequences of its use. This relation is more likely to occur in users who have a higher level of education, as well as where a user has failed to accomplish a significant personal project because of the medium's limitations. I contend that the achievement of a critical hermeneutic relation with the Internet should become the conscious goal of media education. Technical instruction centered on "how-to" questions marked the early stage of educating the public about the new technology. At present, a much broader spectrum of critical issues and reflections must be allowed into the agenda. The emergence of the critical user is supported by a "dispositif," combining notions from media discourses and technical textbooks, the advice of friends, empowering or pleasurable possibilities discovered online, and annoying or debilitating impediments. It can be fostered or forestalled depending on the kind of networks to which the home Internet becomes connected. A conscious and strategic navigation of these networks can turn users into an even more powerful constructive force in the shaping of the Internet.

Final Reflections

The observations reported in this chapter invite the question: What does the microprocess of "becoming a domestic Internet user" and the different human–technology relations that emerge from it, tell us about the rise of the "network society" (Castells, 1996, 2001)?[4] When the social trajectory of Internet technology is traced at the level of everyday life, an unsuspected realm of possibilities—and hence technological indeterminism (see Zuboff, 1988; Feenberg, 1993)—opens up. The universal and predictable technological effects that were envisioned by some commentators turn out to be crude constructs that do not capture the true dynamic of the actor-networks making up the Internet as a technology and the subject as a user. In practice, a person who encounters a technical system such as the Internet faces a wide gamut of possibilities and

limitations. Depending on the local situation, the medium can be drawn into a variety of "action collectives" (Gomart & Hennion, 1999). The relation between the Internet and the user can remain instrumental or grow into a more substantive and absorbing attachment. These different relations breed different user practices and, respectively, different sets of opportunities and threats for users as individuals, workers, consumers, and citizens. Awareness of these possibilities and their reflexive navigation can contribute to the emergence of a different "network society."

The study, on the basis of which these reflections were made, was carried out in 1998 and 1999 (i.e., at an earlier stage of Internet diffusion). At present, I am directing a project similar in its goals and methodology but including a greater number and variety of respondents in Calgary, the city with the highest Internet penetration in Canada. When we asked the question "How did the Internet come into your home?" in 2002–2003, respondents started scratching their heads and asking each other: "No, really why did we want to have it; how did it really happen?" The active decision-making seems to have fallen out of the process. However, this does not mean that the process (of becoming a domestic Internet user) that made the Internet a home fixture is insignificant or inconsequential. The memory of it may have faded away, but its results have become part of the culture and are, in fact, determining of how people use the Internet today.

A focus on the process of becoming an Internet user can also be useful in understanding the social adoption of the medium in different cultural and political contexts. How does the computer and the Internet connection arrive into the home of the ordinary man and woman in a non-Western society, for example? What are the impositions and choices that drive this movement? Who are the "warm experts" in different societies? Who has access to them and who does not? What kinds of user-technology relationships take shape in the social environments that are dominated by different political discourses and daily practices? What usage modes and subjective transformations do these relationships evoke? Answering these questions through intensive ethnographic engagement with users' experiences in different cultural contexts could give rise to a new sensitivity to the nuances and complexities of Internet use across the globe.

Notes

1. At the time of research 1.40 Canadian dollars equalled one U.S. dollar.

2. This type of relation does not represent a direction of my exploration in what follows. I have included it here for the sake of completeness.

3. Amharic is a language of Ethiopia belonging to the South Ethiopic group of Ethiopian Semitic languages. Amharic employs a modification of the Ethiopic script, which is syllabic rather than alphabetic (see http://www.infoplease.com).

4. See also Wellman, 2001. For a critical version of the sociological analysis of the network society, see Robins and Webster (1999).

References

Bakardjieva, M. (2005). *Internet society: The Internet in everyday life*. Thousand Oaks, CA: Sage.

Callon, M. (1987). Society in the making: The study of technology as a tool for sociological analysis. In Bijker, W. E., Hughes, T. P., & Pinch, T. J. (Eds.), *The Social construction of technological systems: New directions in the sociology and history of technology* (pp. 83–103). Cambridge, MA : MIT Press.

Castells, M. (1996). *The rise of the network society* (*Information Age*, Vol.1). Cambridge, MA: Blackwell.

Castells, M. (2001). *The Internet galaxy: Reflections on the Internet, business, and society*. Oxford: Oxford University Press.

Cowan, R. S. (1987). The consumption junction: A proposal for research strategies in the sociology of technology. In Bijker, W. E., Hughes, T. P., & Pinch, T. J. (Eds.), *The Social construction of technological systems: New directions in the sociology and history of technology* (pp. 261–280). Cambridge, MA: MIT Press.

Feenberg, A. (1999). *Questioning technology*. New York: Routledge.

Gomart, E., & Hennion, A. (1999). A sociology of attachment: music amateurs, drug users. In Law, J. & Hassard, J. (Eds.). *Actor Network Theory and After*. Oxford: Blackwell.

Ihde, D. (1990). *Technology and the lifeworld: From garden to earth*. Bloomington: Indiana University Press.

Law, J. (1987). Technology and heterogeneous engineering: The case of Portuguese expansion. In Biker, W., Huges, T. P., & Pinch, T. J. (Eds.), *The social construction of technological systems* (pp. 111–134). Cambridge, MA: MIT Press.

Pinch, T., & Bijker, W. E. (1987). The social construction of facts and artifacts. In Biker, W., Huges, T. P., & Pinch, T. J. (Eds.), *The social construction of technological systems* (pp. 17–50). Cambridge, MA: MIT Press.

Robins, K., & Webster, F. (1999) *Times of the technoculture: From the information society to the virtual life*. London: Routledge.

Silverstone, R. (1994). *Television and everyday life*. London: Routledge.

Turkle, S. (1984). *The second self: Computers and the human spirit*. New York: Simon and Schuster.

Wellman, B. (2001). Computer networks as social networks. *Science, 293*, 2031–2034.

Zuboff, S. (1988). *In the age of the smart machine: The future of work and power*. New York: Basic Books.

Alladi Venkatesh, Steven Chen,
and Victor M. Gonzalez

Designing the Family Portal for Home Networking

The use of information technology at home is a promising area of inquiry among scholars and practitioners (Kraut, Mukhopadhyay, Szczypula, Kiesler & Scherlis, 1999; Frolich & Kraut, 2002; Harper, 2002; Lally, 2002; Turow & Kavanaugh, 2003). Since 2001, products such as home Internet appliances, intelligent refrigerators, and WebTV consoles have been released into the market with much promise but somewhat limited success (Bergmann, 2000; Edwards, Weintraub, Irene & Reinhardt, 2003). Despite slow adoption of these home-oriented technologies, commercial interest in introducing information technologies into the home is quite intense. This study reports preliminary findings on ways that the Internet and computer technology could be integrated into family life. We used a prototype that we called the family portal as a tool to help families explore the usability and applicability of information technology at home. The prototype helped us materialize the concept and define a focal point on which to base our discussion with families. This exercise resulted in findings that we believe clarify the role of information technology in servicing the needs of the home.

Background and Study Purpose

With the widespread diffusion of the Internet, there is a growing sense of its indispensability among its many users (Kiesler, 1997; Hoffman, Novak, & Venkatesh, 2004). There is also increasing use of the home computer as a link between the home and external networks, such as workplace, schools, health organizations, and commercial sites (Papert, 1996; Neibauer 1999; Magid, 2000; Ruhling, 2000; Venkatesh, Kruse, & Shih, 2003). As the computer technology diffuses and becomes gradually domesticated (Harper, 2000; Cummings & Kraut, 2002), we need to supplement traditional evaluation metrics, such as productivity and efficiency, with those that take into consideration aesthetics, convenience, family dynamics, and the social and emotional needs of household members (Di Leanardo, 1987; Frohlich & Kraut, 2002; Livingstone, 2003; Turow & Nir, 2003). Thus, the home setting affords an opportunity for a unique form of design, which considers the perspective of family members and goes beyond a mere utilitarian point of view.

In this chapter, we describe how we designed an information infrastructure that uses Internet technologies for home management and external networking as well as meeting the emotional needs of the family: the family portal. Our research objective was determining whether we could devise a system for home information/communication and management that would be usable, friendly, and efficient and that, at the same time, would satisfy family emotional and social needs. This chapter does not attempt to demonstrate the implementation of such a system but presents some initial analysis of the factors that led to its design. In the development of our ideas, our work is similar to some recent work on the design of home-based technologies and terminals (Lee, 2000; Hindus Maiwaring, Leduc, Hagstrom, & Bayley, 2001; Mainwaring, 2002; Harper, 2002; Baillie, Benyon, Macaulay, & Petersen, 2003).

This study builds on our previous work on home as a living space (Venkatesh, 1996; Venkatesh & Mazumdar, 1999). In this chapter, we sometimes use the term "domestic space" to emphasize the domestic character of the living space. Recently, Frolich and Kraut (2002) elaborated on the notion of domestic space along with domestic time within the context of home computing. Their work offers a clear analysis of how the concepts of space and time constitute the basic elements in the use of domestic technologies. Following their work, we use the notion of domestic space as a way of positioning the family portal in the spatial configuration of the home.

Home as Domestic Space: Preliminary Considerations

The idea of the home as domestic space has primarily been considered in the fields of architecture (Lawson, 2001), anthropology of space (Cierard, 1999), human–computer interaction (Hakos & Redish, 1998; Lee, 2000), and other design-oriented specialties. The notion of the family as a socially oriented domestic unit has received attention in the fields of sociology and social/cultural anthropology (Bott, 1957; Szinovacz, 1988; Scott, 1991; Milardo & Allan, 1997).

Typically, the spatial models approach the domestic environment from a spatial planning view: use of space for different family activities, designating the space for ritualized functions, and various other practices. The approach to domesticity pays more attention to the social structure of the family, power relationships, control issues, household division of labor, family dynamics, parental and spousal concerns, and relationships. Because one approach examines how family life is organized in the home and the other examines the content of interactions and sociological motivations behind behaviors, both are closely related and are critical to our study. Some recent work on home-based technologies seems to meet these dual objectives (Frolich & Kraut, 2002; Bell, Blythe, Gaver, Sengers & Wright, 2003).

In designing home-based technologies, historically, one might say at the risk of simplification that designers have taken an approach that is closer to the living space model—using activity schedules and time budget information at the expense of more domestically oriented interactions. For example, most early household technologies were targeted toward improving the efficiency of specific household maintenance activities, such as cleaning, meal preparation, washing clothes, and so on, where labor or time could be saved. With the introduction of television in the late 1950s and early 1960s, the role of domestic technology expanded to become a tool for family entertainment. In the 1980s, with the arrival of computers in the home, it was possible for people to work at home, and we see the beginnings of the home as an extension of the place of work (Ruhling, 2000). In the 1990s, new media and information technologies—and the Internet in particular—transformed the home even more dramatically. These new technologies have given rise to the perception of the home as a shopping center, as in home shopping; a communication center enhancing networking among people in the family and between the family and the outside world; an information center; and a learning center. These new developments have contributed significantly to reconceptualizing the domestic space.

A Model of Domestic Space and the Family Portal

We present a model (fig. 9.1) adapted from our previous work (Venkatesh, 1996) of home as domestic space. Broadly speaking, the domestic space can be described in terms of three main elements: social space, technological space, and physical space.

The social space consists of the members of the household, the activities performed by them in the home, the time spent on those activities, and the interactions between household members. The

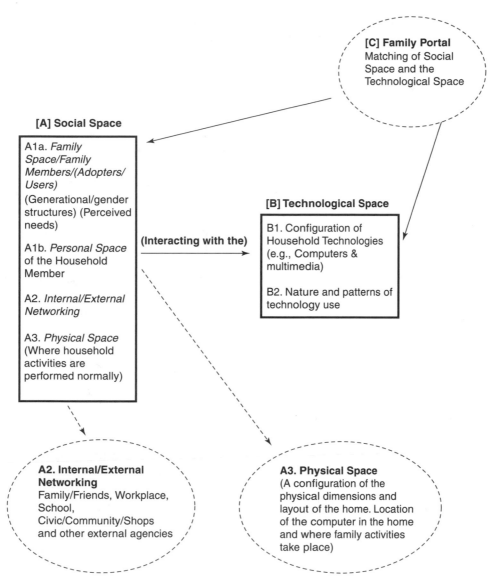

Figure 9.1. Model of domestic space and the family portal.

physical space refers to the physical layout of the home and its constituent parts (kitchen, bedrooms, bathrooms, etc.). The technological space consists of the household technologies that are embedded in the physical space and used by the members of the family as part of the social space.

This technological space consists of artifacts, such as a refrigerator, table, and stove, for example, that make the kitchen a place for meal preparation and consumption. Technological space has gained particular importance recently because of the emerging notion of the "smart home." For an inter-

action between the three spatial categories in the context of technology (e.g., WebTV) use, we refer readers to the recent work by Lee (2000), which illustrates how the notion of domestic space was used to situate Internet terminals within a family context. Here is an excerpt from Lee's research report, which elucidates the way in which spatial concerns enter into the positioning of technology in the home.

I report on a field study of introducing Internet terminals into the home. This study revealed that the acceptance of an Internet terminal such as the WebTV set-top box is dependent upon the existing social, physical, and technological spaces of the home, their interaction with each other, and their interaction with the world. Analysis of the findings showed how the new technology changes the dynamics and the relationships in and between these spaces and how the home in turn reconstructs itself as part of the process of appropriation. Analysis of the findings also suggests that theoretical conceptualization of the uptake of technologies in the home needs to consider not only the spaces within the home but also the larger social space in which the home is embedded. I conclude by drawing out some near term implications for the design of Internet terminals in the context of the home. (p. 25)

The intersection of social and technological spaces creates electronic networking opportunities within the domestic unit. At this point, one can see the emergence of the networked home. We define the networked home (see fig. 9.1, A2) in terms of two major components: an internal household network, which consists primarily of relationships with family, friends, and social circles; and an external network, which connects the home to outside agencies, such as schools, shopping centers, work/office, and other civic/community centers. Intuitively, one can appreciate the use of family portal as a tool for home networking because of its communication capabilities.

The Family Portal: A Description of the Concept and Applications

The family portal is introduced into the domestic space to facilitate various family-related activities. Its introduction rests on some key developments. Household computer use has been on the rise, especially since the introduction of the Internet. At present, the computer is used for a variety of family-related activities, including family networking. The family portal can become a means by which family members can employ the technology for domestic use. In fig. 9.1, we have shown that the family portal can link the social and technological spaces in the home.

Current information and communications technologies (ICT), with some exceptions, are designed under the assumption that they will be mainly used in workplace scenarios. Metaphors like "desktop." "files," or "personal assistant" are products of this workplace orientation. Within this context, the place and role of ICT at home will be based on how much they serve as an extension of office duties. As a consequence, the shaping of ICT to serve workplace needs makes it very difficult to appreciate and understand what the real value of ICT at home is, and how we can come out with designs that truly serve the needs of the family. We need new approaches to reorienting ICT that combine what we know about families and how they function with how we can envision appropriate technologies.

This research is based on how prototypes of appropriate ICT applications might serve these emerging family- and home-based technology needs. Prototyping permits quick testing of design concepts by potential users and helps us to refine our understanding of the needs once they are supported by technology (Beyer & Holtzblatt, 1998).

Specifically, in this research we explore how a shared repository of information and messages—a family portal—supports the domestic environment of the home and its associated activities and how it helps family members. The main method of examination is to test design ideas against scenarios of use that describe typical activities (Carroll, 2000).

Most portals on the Internet are oriented toward the individual. They provide services used by a single user, such as weather reports, finance, news, instant messaging, or e-mail, among others. These portals are not oriented toward a family. Some of them provide so-called "community features" like family-photo albums or discussion groups. Even here, however, interface elements and functionality are directed toward a single user. They are designed with the aim of personalizing the access and interface for an individual. In contrast, the aim of the family portal is to provide family access where all members can have access to a repository with a common interface and shared functionality.

There have been some recent efforts to develop technologies specifically for family use, especially in the context of family communication. Some interesting examples that use what is currently known as design ethnography include the Casablanca project (Hindus et al., 2001), shared devices for the home (Mainwaring, 2002), and cross-cultural media applications (Frolich & Prabhu, 2003). In all these cases, the motivation behind developing family-based technologies is to move beyond current technologies' individual orientation toward an orientation of family context and dynamics.

Two results of the Casablanca project are noteworthy. The digitized communication board helps families keep track of communications to make interactions more flexible. Families can stay in touch better via a shared message board that is easy to use, expressive, and aesthetic. The results also revealed that women are the "primary household communicators"; this should therefore be taken into account when designing the technology. In another study titled "Some Strategies and Challenges for the Design of Family Technology," Mainwaring (2002) proposed the notion of sharing technologies at home. He developed a fourfold typology that consists of shared devices, shared infrastructure, shared spaces, and shared activities. These items were cross-tabulated against four categories: same system, same time, same space, and joint activity. Although we do not follow his system of sharing, we concur with his argument that the next step in developing home-based technology is to position it within the context of collective use without necessarily sacrificing private access by individual members. In other words, the family portal that we are proposing in this chapter has features both for family and for the individual.

In the following account, we have identified some key features of the family portal as an initial conception. Once we test the concept and collect inputs from our respondents, we will update our conceptualization to reflect the users' input.

Family Portal as Shared Mailbox

Every family has a mailbox that contains the postal mail addressed to any member of the family. The family portal will use the mailbox metaphor as the base for its construction. It will be implemented as a web-based application to provide accessibility from any location or platform.

The family portal can serve as a way to integrate home-related information. The family portal can include a list of links to utility companies (electricity, trash, cable, phone), but it will not be just a listing. It can also help to keep track of due dates for payments and provide alerts to family members. We can think about having a historical record of past payments. Rather than replacing any existing payment web sites, it is important to note

that the family portal will serve as a gateway to those services. However, some functionality, such as reminders of payment, will be part of the family portal.

Family Portal as a Lightweight Communication Tool

The family portal can be understood as a tool for communication among the members of the family. Here we will use another metaphor—that of the kitchen refrigerator. Many families use the refrigerator's surface to attach notes for other household members about errands, reminders of appointments, telephone numbers, and so on. The family portal can serve this purpose during the time when family members are not at home. Mom can check a note from Dad while he is at work; Mom can remind Dad to bring a bottle of milk on his way home. Thus, the family portal will be a kind of lightweight communication infrastructure. In addition to this system, we envision the integration of the answering machine with the family portal in such a way that family members can be aware of messages waiting for them.

Family Portal as a Common Calendar

Many families use a calendar (usually located in the kitchen) on which they register family events: birthdays, medical appointments, and so on. The family portal can also include this kind of functionality. Here the trick is to discover what the best ways are to update it. It may just be easier to write down a family activity on the paper-based kitchen calendar. It is possible to envision an electronic calendar (touch screen) in the kitchen. In this case, the device will automatically update the family calendar in the family portal. Technology to do that is available (e.g., Smart Board), but we might want to leave the kitchen calendar in the realm of paper. In that case, we have to look for ways to facilitate users' keeping the calendar updated.

Family Portal as a Financial Organizer

An interesting application for the family portal is to serve as a financial organizer. Members of the family can use the portal to record personal expenses; this information can then be rolled up for tax purposes. In this line, we can also include direct links to banks' web sites so family members (mainly parents) can access their accounts from here. In a similar way to the utilities section, we see the family portal as a gateway to services. In this case, the family portal may provide a way to record checking balances or checks to be paid.

Family Portal as a Window to the Shopping World

As a window to the outside world, the family portal can help to present information such as the catalogs of department stores like JC Penney, Sears, Mervyns, and so on. We envision a scenario in which family members configure their family portal and subscribe to specific department stores to receive notification of their products in the portal, as opposed to by mail. One might ask what the difference is between this and current e-mail—what are the advantages? The difference is that with this mechanism, information is customized and targeted to the family.

As with other portals, the family portal can include information about local–national news and weather and can link to informational sites like driving directions, online dictionaries, and so on. These information "gadgets" can all be integrated in the interface of the family portal.

Another aim of the family portal is to support archival records. Photo albums, videos, and audio recordings can easily be stored and retrieved.

From this brief presentation of ideas, it should be clear that the goal of the family portal is not to substitute but, rather, to integrate existing communication and information infrastructure, including E-mail and instant messaging, which can still be used by family members.

To summarize, the family portal is a combination of the following features available for family use electronically:

- A shared electronic "mailbox"
- An internal communication tool
- A family calendar, with a reminder tool and event planner
- An information center
- A financial organizer, budget tool, and gateway for bank accounts and other financial services
- A gateway for shops, retailers, and other information providers to access homes

Methodology: Empirical Investigation

The data collection for the study included two main parts: in-depth interviews in the homes of 10 families, followed by a concept testing of the family portal to elicit family responses. The families were selected intentionally to ensure that a majority of them have children at home. This permits us to gather information on a wider range of activities within the home than would normally be possible in families without children. It seemed reasonable to assume that families with both spouses and children would more likely provide a more comprehensive baseline data set from which to proceed, as there are more related household members—and hence, more complex communication needs. For comparison purposes, we included one household consisting of an unmarried male to provide contrast. Because of the ethnographic nature of the study, we have to use small samples to pursue in-depth analysis. Although no generalization of the results to the larger population is attempted or warranted, the insights gained from the study will be useful in designing a major study to explore specific issues.

The whole process of interviewing and observing lasted on average approximately 120–150 minutes. The key respondent in each household (in most cases a female adult) was asked extensively about the household's management and current computer usage. After the general-purpose interview, the respondent was presented a print-out showing the façade of what we called "the family portal." This print-out was used to encourage users to talk in detail about their usage of the Internet for such purposes as surfing the web, communicating through e-mail, shopping online, or getting news. This was followed by the introduction of a more realistic version of the family portal.

The following is a representative list of questions used as our protocol in the first part of the interview:

- Do you keep a personal agenda? A calendar? A diary?
- Do you have a family organizer/calendar?
- Paper mail processing:
  Please describe for us what you do with your postal mail, where you put it, how you organize it, and so on.
- Do you save coupons for products? Where do you keep them? What about recipes?
- Do you read the newspaper? Which sections you read?
- Do you watch television? What programs you like most?

- Use of technology at home:
  Do you have computers at home? How you use them? Where do you have the computer? Do you have any portable devices? How and why do you use them?
  Do you use the computer for your home budget?
- Internet:
  Do you check the web very often? What web sites you usually visit?
  Do you send e-mail to family members?
  Do you shop online? Do you pay your bills online?
- Do you or any member of your family use a cell phone or pager?
- Do you leave paper notes to communicate with other members of your family?

In addition, the interview addressed several demographic and lifestyle questions.

Presentation of the Family Portal Concept

We introduced the family portal (fig. 9.2) through a combination of words, an illustration board, and a laptop demonstration. The illustration board served as a quick method of visually communicating the family portal concept to participants. One side of the board displayed two pictures—one of a mailbox and the other of a refrigerator door—the two conceptual bases we referred to in the framework. We explained the rationale behind the conceptual bases to our participants and asked them to keep the idea of the mailbox and refrigerator in mind when we presented the family portal software. On the other side of the board, we displayed three scenarios of possible usage for the family portal (fig. 9.3). The first showed an entrance model, in which a user can check the portal for messages on entering the home. The second scenario showed a woman eating breakfast on the kitchen table while using the portal. The third scenario illustrated a portable version of the portal located in the living room. In this particular scene, we wanted to show people that they can access the portal in any part of the home.

A small laptop was used to demonstrate the family portal. We explained the capabilities of the

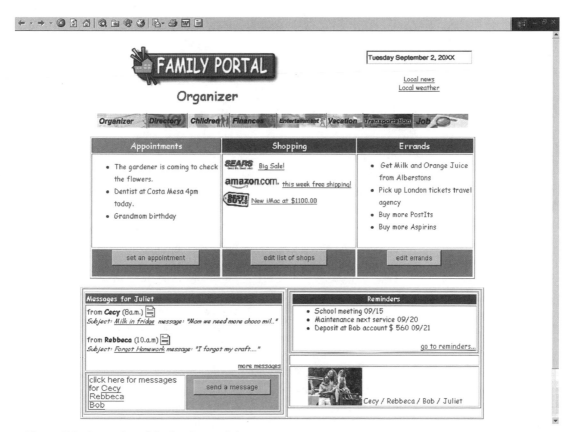

Figure 9.2. Screenshot of the family portal demo.

Figure 9.3. Three usage scenarios.

customizable to unique household needs, we developed the fictional Thompson family as a narrative device to deliver the concept and to get respondents to add their own feedback (cultural probing). So henceforth, the portal is understood to be the Thompson version, with categories that reflect Thompson interests.

The family portal demo is divided into eight sections: organizer, directory, children, finances, entertainment, vacation, transportation, and jobs. Each of these sections has categories of their own. We will briefly examine these here.

The organizer section simulates the capabilities of a paper organizer. There are separate areas in which the user can self-input appointments and errands. There is a shopping area in which out-of-home agencies can feed the family portal with service notices, news, and information. The nature of these info-feeds would be systematic (e.g., they occur on a regular, semipredictable basis) and customized to unique household needs. This is, of course, a throwback to our first conceptual basis, the mailbox. The user can edit, add, or delete agencies through a menu accessed by clicking the radio button under the shopping column. We envision the list to be a global list of vendors, agencies, and organizations. Unlike with junk mail, the user can custom-filter the information that goes into the family portal.

On the bottom of the organizer, there are two boxes, one for messages and the other for reminders. They are what we dub the "common elements," which appear in every section of the family portal. The reminders section is a simple, self-input area in which one can execute the simple reminders for that section. The messages section is an intrafamily communication center in which one member can leave a message for another member or members.

The directory is an alphabetical list of individuals and commercial services that functions like a directory in an organizer or phone book. The children section features a mix of user-fed and agency-fed information. In the Thompson portal, the subcategories were school, health, clothes, and activities. The school, health, and clothes were areas in which out-of-home agencies, such as the kids' school administration or pediatrician, could feed the family portal with updates regarding children's school activities, behavior, doctor's appointments, and clothing sales. The activities area is a self-input area.

system to the participants and did a quick walk-through of each section in the portal. After the walk-through, we let the participants explore the system for themselves. As we did to our participants, we will quickly summarize the elements and features of the family portal below.

General Overview.   One of the first things we told the participants is that the version of the family portal that he or she is seeing is the Thompson Family version of the family portal. Because we envision the portal as a system that is adaptable and

The finances section is largely agency-fed information. Banks and creditors will remind the family portal when bills and deadlines are coming up. Quick links to the family's various financial and insurance accounts are also provided for ease of access.

The entertainment section was developed with a focus on local area news, updates, and events. The family portal would deliver information such as local movie show times and local television guides, as well as local concert, drama, or sporting events.

Under the vacation, transportation, and job sections, we explored the idea of agency-fed information in more depth. Imagine receiving, through the family portal, information from Travelocity or one of the many job-search web sites. Commercial firms like airlines and employment services already provide this type of information through e-mail. However, with transportation we examine an information relationship that is more local and "neighbor friendly." Your auto mechanic would let the portal know when your car needs servicing. This approach updates the rustic model of the small town where everyone knew one another and the grocers knew your name and your buying habits, and recasts it in a new form. In addition, under transportation the user can also self-log car information such as mileage.

Findings

Household Computer Use

The grounded theory method of analyzing qualitative data permits us to extract key themes from the in-depth interviews. In analyzing the qualitative interview data on home computer use employing grounded theory, we identified 15 themes, as listed below. We will call them first-order themes.

- Household Communication (HHComm)
- Calendar/Organizer (HHCalendar/Events)
- Household Finances (HHFin)
- Entertainment/Hobbies (HHEnt)
- Job/Work Related (HHWork)
- Information/News (HHInfo)
- School Related (HHSchool)
- Social Interaction (HHSoc)
- Online Shopping (includes vacation/travel/ leisure items) (HHShop)
- Home-Based Services (HHService)

- Learning (HHLearning)
- Community Information (HHCmty)
- Parenting/Children/Family (HHPCF)
- Medical Information (HHMed)
- Everyday Routines (HHRoutine)

These themes reflect the relative frequency with which they occurred in all the interviews and refer to how the computer is currently used by the families. The variety and range of themes indicate that computers have become an integral part of the family life and are now domesticated. Table 9.1 provides the distribution of the themes across different households.

It must be noted here that the themes are conceptually distinct, but they can also be related depending on the context. So, for example, household communication (HHComm) and social interaction (HHSoc) are considered distinct in terms of the categories of computer use, but they are related because when a family member uses the computer to contact friends or family about certain matters, one can conclude that social interaction has taken place.

As the table shows, not every household uses the computer in the same fashion. That is, use patterns vary according to family priorities and needs. Most published literature on computer use at home cites three major uses for the computer: communication, information search, and entertainment. Our study certainly confirms these results (table 9.1). However, there are other uses that point to the fact that computer use is more complex or diverse; as the technology becomes more domesticated and integrated into the family life, other uses become more prevalent. Thus, families with children use the computers as part of their parenting responsibilities (HHPCF) and child-oriented activities including school (HHSchool).

In a larger sense, many household activities involve several themes. For example, when families communicate with family members, friends, shops, service agencies, banks, and so on, one way to describe this use is simply to say that the computer is used for communication (HHComm)— which suppresses a lot of finer details. This is because each act of communication has a distinct quality and content, w ticulously uncovered. For examp with family can mean family in ous matters (HHSoc) or organi; (HHCalendar/Events). Commun

Table 9.1. Home codes summary.

Respondent	Family description	Communication (HHComm)	Home information (HHInfo/News)	Entertainment, fun (HHEnt)	Work (HHWork)	School (HHSchool)
CB	Full-time housewife, two male children age 8 and 11 years, three home computers, use of computer is 40% application and 60% Internet	X	X	X		X
JP	Full-time housewife, two daughters aged 8 and 10 years and a toddler son; one desktop; one laptop for the eldest daughter	X	X	X		X
JD	Full-time housewife with infant daughter, one computer, used online services	X		X		
AB	Full-time housewife, one child and pregnant with second, one computer, use of community Web sites	X	X	X		
AMB	A mother of three children ranging in age from 4 to 21 years, more expert at the computer than husband who is intimidated, one computer in the home	X	X	X	X	X
MC	Male, shared house with another person, no children, on cutting edge, work-oriented use of computer, participant in online community club	X	X		X	
DG	Wife of a professor with a teen daughter; part-time lawyer and "household organizer"; marginal use of technology for home use, used appointment book	X	X		X	X
SB	Mother of three children; used computer as a learning device for children		X	X		
LB	Mother of two children	X			X	X
AF	Male, married, infant child	X		X	X	

dren implies some parenting activities (HHPCF) or following everyday routines (HHRoutine). Communications can also occur between parents and schools (HHSchool). Similarly, online shopping (HHShop) may involve communicating with stores (online or physical). Communication may involve seeking information (HHInfo) from community agencies (HHCmty) or medical sources (HHMed).

If we consider organizing family events (HHCalendar/ Events) (e.g., birthdays) as a key activity, it may involve several other activities, including event planning, sending invitations, shopping for the event, preparing a list of guests and ʾir e-mail addresses and telephone numbers, and ɔle list of organizing functions.

At the second stage of analysis of the themes, we go to a deeper level to see whether these discrete themes represent some fundamental aspects of family life. The logic here is that behind various themes we just uncovered are more fundamental processes or set of activities. Thus, we identify the following meta-processes that underlie the specific computer-related activities. Here is a list of such processes. Just to distinguish from the first-order themes, we label them core themes of family life (CTFL).

- Social networking (e.g., keeping in touch with family/friends/other contacts)
- Home management

Social interaction (HHSoc)	Home finances (HHFin)	Shopping (HHShop)	Services (HHServ)	Learning (HHLearn)	Community (HHCmty)	Parenting, children, family (HHPCF)	Family calendar/ events (HHCalendar)	Medical, illness (HHMed)	Everyday routine (HHRoutine)
X	X	X	X		X	X	X		
X	X			X		X	X		
		X	X			X	X		
X		X			X	X		X	
X		X	X	X	X	X		X	X
X		X	X		X	X	X		X
X	X	X	X			X	X	X	X
	X								
				X	X				
		X		X	X				

- Childcare/education and parenting
- Home finances
- Household consumption/production
- Shopping for goods and services
- Balancing work and home life
- Spatial aesthetics and comfortable living
- Civic life and community participation
- Keeping in touch with the outside world (other than the community)
- Family events and special occasions
- Family well-being/stress management
- Family entertainment/leisure/outside interests
- Travel/vacation
- Physical/financial security and safety

Although many of the terms in the CTFL list are labeled differently from first-order themes, some of the nomenclature is the same. These core activities (CTFL) can be classified in terms of four categories: maintenance activities, planning activities, expressive activities, and developmental activities. Each core activity has some element of these four categories, but the emphasis may vary depending on the context. For example, online banking (HHFin under first-order themes; Home Management under CTFL) may be more of a maintenance activity and may even involve some planning, but it may not have a high expressive or developmental content.

In a similar fashion to the way we classify family activities, we can also describe technologies as an embodiment of these four categories in varying degrees. For example, one can use a refrigerator to store food (maintenance), to make sure enough food is available at the right time for children (planning and expressive), and also perhaps to store healthy food (developmental). We can extend this type of analytical scheme for other home-based technologies. Clearly, in the design of the family portal, one should consider how this mapping fits into this complex scheme.

Finally, to conclude this section, how are these results significant to the portal? The role of the family portal in this complex set of activities is that it is an interface that permits families to plan events; contact friends, relatives, and outside agencies; keep family records; follow news; and perform various activities for which the computer is suitable. The family portal has the potential to become a central unit that systemizes family computer use—both collectively and individually. It is a meeting point for the family members and shared virtual space. At a very rudimentary level, the family portal is an information or communication portal. At another level, it permits families to use it for different organizing needs. We will now bring out these issues in some detail by presenting some key reactions of our respondents to the design considerations of the portal.

Analysis of Respondent Reactions to the Family Portal

In presenting the respondents' reactions, we select some core themes of family life (CTFL) mentioned by the respondents while discussing the family portal.

Home Management, Childcare, and Parenting
A calendar-based interface unifies the appointments, errands, reminders, and messages sections. In the current incarnation of the family portal, these sections are separated into their own areas. Respondents' feedback strongly encourages a move to create an interface that resembles an interactive calendar, in which a user can input and organize information into daily, weekly, or monthly scheme. The respondents described this new calendar-based system through words and hand-drawn pictures (fig. 9.4). In addition, we will uncover some underlying family processes in their narratives.

In the following quotation, CB implies that she likes to plan family activities in advance and views the calendar as a way to organize and make sense of her anticipated time commitment to certain ac-

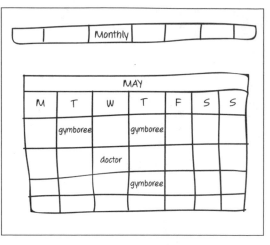

Figure 9.4. A participant's sketch of a calendar-based interface for the family portal.

tivities. Thus, the planning ahead of a week is important to her.

> CB: Something like a calendar will he helpful because, basically it will probably be like an automatic calendar. So I can say like ok, on a given day I can look and see [you know] the week at a glance, I can see the appointments for the whole week that can be automatically updated. Because otherwise it is almost like keeping two calendars.

JD has similar concerns but she is more visual and wants to see everything at glance.

> JD: See, I like this because it's all right there and it's pretty easy to access. I don't like anything that I can't type into and I like the fact that I can see everything. I see Appointments and Errands and Reminders and I see everything on one screen. I don't like not being able to see, that's what I like. I like to open my [calendar] and I can see what I have on any day, you know, I would like to see like what I have tomorrow.

SF links the calendar not only to plan her schedules but as away of caring for and controlling her children. The calendar becomes a tool in her parenting responsibilities.

> SF: Because I would rather just have them in one board, that's what I was saying, with the children . . . rather have all the appointments in one section and all the reminders. If it's an

errand or something it should be all in the Errand section. . . . It seems like those are two places to have errands and I would just rather have it in one. I would rather have it look like a calendar, so that I can see you know, tomorrow or Friday or the next week. I would like there to be like a link up here . . . then click on it and have the whole calendar of the month.

Some mothers suggested having a unique section for each child, rather than the generic "Children" section that is currently on the portal.

JP: That's neat. I would not change anything like that. Maybe if you have more than one child, would like to customize it . . . now I have two kids at school. I mean, if I am able to categorize in each child's name that way you don't have to read through everything. Because eventually I would have three kids in school and I know my sister has five kids in school…Ok, this is for Ashley, not for Christina. It would be Ashley's instead of Christina's name. About the item Health, that is . . . I would not change anything about that. The only thing I would change is to categorize in each child's name. Clothing . . . clothes that's cool.

Social Networking.   Respondents reacted positively to the possibility of having family, extended family, and friends access the calendar. In other words, the family portal will act as a networking tool for contacting family and friends.

JD: The directory is great because . . . especially if you are able to use it to print out address labels. . . . I don't know if you are able to do filtering, print out labels for Christmas cards so if you even have to write your Christmas card, your directory can sort that. What I want . . . maybe like what would be cool is to have a calendar that is accessible to your family. Not just your family at home but your friends and your brothers and sisters . . . for example I know my mom helps baby-sit my daughter and my brother's son so she can put it up on the schedule.

Family Events and Special Occasions.   There were suggestions to include indicators on the calendar-based family portal to signal new events, and alarms or visuals to indicate when an appointment

or errand needs to be run. There were no reminder systems in the demonstrated family portal.

DG's Husband: It's just your organizer? Because I see something that you click on the monthly calendar and it gets bigger and then you see the item.

DG: Oh, I know what you are saying. Yes, it's like what an Outlook calendar is now. You know you have the months and it's bolded where you have an event.

DG's Husband: Also in reminders, my phone has that little thing that pops up and starts beeping if it's something like the doctor's appointment or something.

DG: Imagine like a dialog box that it's just like you know.

In addition to reminders, there was considerable demand for being able to check things like calendar events, errands, appointments, and bills payments off on completion. In regard to checking things off, respondents said it gives them a sense of completion, productivity, and closure.

DG: It would be nice because like I said we do it manually by just check offing to make sure we have all the bills paid by a given date, say the 10th of every month. This could be done automatically?

JD: I'll put it even on a piece of paper and I'll stick it on my organizer under notes. Make a note in one section that I do for "date" stuff and one section for the "month" . . . like she's getting baptized in few weeks and so I can get the invitations out . . . make a list of people that I'm going to invite you know. And then being able to check things off, that gives me a sense of closure and productivity.

However much the families might welcome the idea of a family portal, they are not willing to give up paperwork and paper artifacts in their everyday life. Paperwork includes bills, paper notes, mail, and documents from work or school. People have an aversion for paperwork because there's too much of it, it causes too much clutter, and it requires too much maintenance.

JP: Because I lose the paper. I hate when kids get sent home tons of papers. That's what I like about *** Life [the Wired community where the informant lives and has its own Intranet] because I can read everything on a web page, instead of having everything mailed to you. . . . So much goes on in our community and I would like to keep up with it at a glance.

DG: Yes, these are all bills. This is my soccer schedule that has to go in there. This is my folder I walk around with all the time. This is a folder where I have stuff like a phone call that I've to make and a bill that I have to call about. Most of the things are like kid's things like school application I forgot to type up, some immediate thing I have to work on like my projects. And this is all calendar stuff which I haven't done yet. . . . These are for filing.

Despite their "annoyance" with too much paperwork, people still use paper to accomplish a number of daily tasks; paperwork is still a major part of their life, which is reflected in the physical landscape of their homes. For instance, we witnessed scenarios in which people would put notes around areas of high activity—around the telephone, around the computer area, and on the refrigerator (fig. 9.5).

Time and Labor Saving.   Respondents cited portability, speed, convenience, and the ability to visualize things as primary adoption factors. Paper complements household activities, such as shopping (lists), home management (calendar, organizer), and finances (receipts, bill stubs), so it is still an important and viable medium. Instead of trying to replace paper with technology, some ways to augment the portal to support the flow of paper can be investigated—systems in which paper and technology can work in harmony. Below is an example of a task that requires the tandem contributions of paper and technology:

Q: When you use Quicken what kind of things do you put together to use Quicken?

AB: Well, I just have it on my desktop, so it's a matter of clicking on it and opening it. . . . I don't keep the checkbook register so any time I go shopping or anything I just take my receipts and when I come home and I put the receipts in there and then every few days or whenever I feel like it, I check all the receipts and just input into Quicken under receipts. . . . Depending on if it is something that I

Figure 9.5. Paper artifacts are abundant in these areas. Top left: DG2's kitchen counter; right: JP's refrigerator; bottom left: SF's computer desk.

should save or not you know, I throw the receipt away or file the receipt or whatever.

Respondents suggested enabling the family portal to print out content like calendar events, tasks, appointments, and address labels from the directory.

CB: Like things you can print out of your calendar.

AB: Ok. It would be neat if you can somehow hook this up to your computer so that's almost like a PDA where you can download . . . let's say you have a calendar in your computer and you can download your appointments. It would also be neat if you can print this because I'm always writing lists of things to do . . . crossing them and rewriting them so it would be neat just to be able to do this and delete things as I go and change things, so I like that.

JD: The directory is great especially if you are able to use it to print out the address labels. . . . I don't know if you are able to do like filtering, print out labels for Christmas cards so if you even have to write your Christmas card, your directory can sort that out.

Home Finances.   Under the finance section, a family portal user can take a quick look at their bank account, credit cards, insurance, and taxes. The family portal records all financial activities, and when a deadline for a bill comes up, it will let the user know by displaying the date in red. Respondents' remarks were lukewarm. Some participants had established ways to manage bill paying, some saw the integrated family portal as something that they could use, and some saw that the home finances should be treated like a calendar event, and consolidated with appointments, errands, and messages under a calendar format.

CB: Uh, I think . . . not as much for paying the bills. Paying the bills I do twice a month, that's is just easier for me. I can just do it, what I was telling you earlier like the electronic funds transfer, that is automatic.

JP: About Finance . . . and bank account that's neat because you add links to your accounts. [As for] the bills I wouldn't change it. I mean it tells you exactly how much it is and when it's due. That is so neat because half of the time I forget

when things are due and I don't pay them on time. I guess it piles up on the table. I just forget about them, or my husband comes home, he works 12 or 13 hours and he's too tired to look at them. That's cool, I like that! Because I can tell him and I know when it's due so like we have to go in here and pay them. Because they are right next to each other, so you can look it's due and just go here and get your card, click it and bam! It's paid. Insurance . . . that would be out for me because everything is taken care of. And the taxes . . . we have our taxes done. Maybe it would be neat if they remind you . . . maybe [a] reminder when you have your tax accountant scheduling an appointment with you and a reminder that your appointment is coming up, don't forget to bring this or that, what papers to bring, so you don't forget anything.

Spatial Aesthetics and Comfortable Living. When asked where they would use the family portal, respondents suggested high-traffic areas and activity hotspots, such as the kitchen counter. Some suggested that the portal be portable, like a cordless telephone.

JD: Downstairs. You have like . . . it's funny that you have people do their mail things, right there [pointing to the location next to the kitchen]. I though it would be great to have it there, if I could because I'm always in my kitchen you know, there's where my phone is, there's where my mail is. It is just where I do a lot of stuff.

JP: I wouldn't want to have to go and stand somewhere and just have to look at everything . . . I mean it's convenient by the door I think is great. I would probably use the mobile one that you can bring around with you. If you want to do something you know, finding something when you are at bed or laying on the couch or eating dinner. I guess the second is cool but it would be attached to a table which I would be very worry about because a lot of people spill things on. Maybe at the countertop will be cool, that way it's . . . doesn't have access to liquids and doesn't damage. Food . . . we spill everyday here. So I would like that maybe on the countertop or like hang somewhere, you know maybe like on the wall by the counter.

Keeping in Touch with the Outside World, Entertainment, Civic Life, and Community Participation. People had mixed feelings about incoming information from outside agencies. There was rather low interest for information of commercial nature, which people instantly associated with e-mail spam. However, people did not mind receiving confirmation e-mails for purchases they made online. Likewise, local information for potential family events, especially movie information, was a point of interest.

JP: Area code and then you pull the theater information and then you just click on that certain theater and it would tell you what is going. I have one [theatre] just down the street. But a lot of times people don't want to go to that one. I go to that one because it's close. Some people like to go to the big ones you know like the (theater name), I don't like to go there, it's too crowded . . . well, that's neat too if you look at the movie it tells you what is playing and what times.

In contrast, there was positive feedback on receiving community-based information such as notices from schools and community clubs. Some respondents noted how normally they would throw away, ignore, or forget to read school and community notices when mailed in paper form.

JP: Right, maybe reminders of when reports are due. That's a big thing for my kids. Can't tell you how many times I do last-minute things because I don't get the paper signed you know, like my daughter brings the paper home and "Oh, your Dolphins project [referring to a science project on Dolphins] is due next week." It would be nice to have the teachers send things to you through this instead of sending a little sheet that half the time parents don't see because kids lose it . . . maybe reminders of what's happening with the school menu, what they are serving. I usually post it on the refrigerator and half the time just don't look at it. It is too confusing . . . they interchange things on menu anyway because they don't have it or they don't get the supply or whatever. I have older children and rely a lot on the school communicating more with me about things or 15 papers for me to read. That's what I do, every single day. Of course people have other activities like sports, they

got . . . my children go to Girl Scouts, a lot of Girl Scout activities we have. So that way I would like to see reminders of those things.

Q: What's the good thing about *** Life [a community web site] and iVillage? Maybe you can tell us something about those.

SF: iVillage is just for women and since I'm pregnant I got a lot of information from that. Normally I wouldn't be on it if I wasn't pregnant but I go on it just to see what's going on you know weekly in my pregnancy so it's kind of cool. *** Life: I belong to a club, a moms' group, and I go there. We have a message board where you can go on and communicate with other women in the group and find out what's going on in the community. You know, I mean it tells me about what's going on.

Q: How often do you check the *** Life site?

SF: I used to check it daily but I just don't have the time and the energy anymore. So I usually try to go on it twice a week. Just to catch up, to see what's going on with everybody.

The Family Portal: Some Final Feature-Specific Considerations and Concerns

Total Improvement

One respondent said that for her to replace the old way of doing things with a new system, the new system would have to offer total improvement. Total improvement means that the new system would have to be better in every way—more convenient, easier, faster, and more accessible.

SF: It has to be quick and totally user friendly. I mean a lot of stuff is so complicated, that's what's deterring me from doing a budget on the computer. It's taking me forever to figure out so something like this would need to just be pretty much done for me and show me how to do it. It would have to a total improvement, make my life totally easier. And it needs to be really quick.

Input Devices

Participants were asked whether or not having to type put them off, and if typing was a deterrent, then what would they suggest as a substitute as an input tool for the family portal. Most people did not mind typing, and several people actually preferred typing to writing things down by hand.

> JD: I don't like anything that I can't type and I like the fact that I can see everything.
>
> Q: With typing in stuff, does it discourage you? Bother you?
>
> SF: No because I did a similar thing when I was working. I was a personal assistant for the owner of the company and I had to type in his appointments and things what I need to write to him and e-mail to him through Outlook Express I think it was. So, I wouldn't mind typing it in.

A couple of respondents also suggested voice activation, like cellular phones.

> MC: Well, I worked for this company and they are launching a product next week called voice portal and . . . so basically you will be able to talk to it and [it] understands you. It reads back e-mails to you on the phone I'm kind of excited about it because I think that . . . you should be able to talk to your computer more versus type it in it.

The current model of the family portal leaves open the choice of an input device. Although no one has brought it up yet, touch-screen or a stylus is definitely a strong option. A keyboard will probably be needed to accommodate long text messages.

Aesthetics and Appearance

The respondents made some insightful suggestions on making the family portal more aesthetically appealing. One major comment was on enhancing the interface and making it less "businesslike" and more of a "household thing." The addition of picture icons to denote mood or an event was suggested.

> JP: No, I think it looks good. I wouldn't know how to change it . . . it is like something nice and there's like a happy face or like a heart or like a start or something like that. So I think that would be cool, I mean it could be like . . . not so businesslike. More like a household thing.

Another suggestion was to improve the interactivity of the interface. This would include check-off boxes, markers to denote new events, and having bigger text. There were also color and texture suggestions:

> JP: I would have it available in multiple colors: black, white, silver, maybe one funky you know for kids in neon colors you know green or pink. Yes! Like they have cell phones now, covers you can buy there are all different weird prints. I personally wouldn't use that but . . . me myself I would probably get a light one. Because it would blend with everything, the wood is nice . . . the wood color would be cool too, like a fake-looking wood that would be neat to put on the coffee table.
>
> Q: Do you have a favorite color? If you have a dominating color, what color could be?
>
> SF: Like this color blue, the shopping color blue. It's easy on the eyes. The red looks good too.

And finally, people suggested the size of the family portal should be no bigger than a laptop, especially if it is to be portable.

> SF: If it would be in the size that I can store it over there and could move it around. . . . Or just a tablet that's totally space saving but would depend on the size.

Overlap Between Existing Devices in Use and the Family Portal

There are a lot of direct and indirect comments that the computer already does what the family portal does in terms of calendar features, finances, and online local information. It is hard for respondents to justify another electronic device in the home that replicates the functionalities of an existing device.

> AB: Yes, because if you could do everything you know, if you have the capability then I just probably wouldn't use my regular online, but if it is limited, then I would just prefer to use the computer that could do all of it.
>
> MC: I am set up for reminders in Outlook. Like for work but for personal . . . I don't have to remind myself about the bills because that's all already set in Quicken and I just . . . every time I go it reminds me of you know, these bills are either need to be paid or they are past.

A big difference between the existing system and the family portal is the latter's visibility. There were a lot of remarks on being able to "see" the information all at once and being able to look at something and get all the visual information they need "at a glance."

Respondents noted that with computers, they had to boot up the machine, and open applications to see information, whereas in the portal, the screens are all information-loaded and ready to go:

DG: I use it [Outlook] at work a lot but I don't use it for home. I've been thinking about maybe starting or trying to move over that but that would mean you have to log on and turn on because the computer is not always on. Switch it on and then it takes like three or four minutes to log on.

Because they are "total vision people," respondents liked seeing everything at once, in one place, and alluded to having a calendar-based interface where all appointments, errands, and tasks can be logged.

AB: No. I guess I could, it just seems more like easy because you know, if you write there or wherever you can look at it while if it's in the computer I don't see it, I wouldn't be checking it frequently and it just seems like more of hassle I have to go to the program and all the different things to use it.

JO: I like the fact that I can see everything. I see Appointments and Errands and Reminders and I see everything on one screen. I don't like not seeing, that's what I like.

DG: The pro is that they have set up an alarm for me and I look it up and say "Oh my Gosh! That's right." And the con is that I'm kind of more like a total vision person, so this allows me to look at the whole month and in the other one you have to scroll.

Conclusion

The main purpose of the study is to design a family portal that would address the specific needs of families in the context of their domestic activities and routines. Data were gathered from a select group of families in two stages. First, we gathered information on their current use of computers. Second, we presented some basic ideas regarding the family portal and its characteristics, and we obtained detailed reactions and inputs from families as part of our concept testing. As a result of in-depth interviewing, we were able to identify several family-oriented themes concerning computer use (presented in table 9.1). The extensive nature of computer use

attests to its growing domestication and integration into the family life. Bearing this in mind, we asked our respondents to consider the family portal as an aid for managing various activities performed in the family context. There seems to be support for the idea on the basis of a family calendar and event organizer. It is viewed as both reducing and complementing paper-based activity, although families are not willing to give up the paper entirely. This suggests some resistance to a total virtual environment in the home. The family portal is also viewed as a useful tool for organizing home finances and for maintaining financial records. One of the families' concerns is where to locate the portal. Answers depend on where most home-based activities are performed. We also think that the aesthetics of the portal and its location should be part of the design consideration. There is less enthusiasm for a businesslike appearance; families would want the portal to blend with the home's current décor. One area of concern is that the families need to be convinced that the family portal is in any way better or superior to some existing devices. This will be one main challenge as the concept is put into practice.

Finally, this research is by no means conclusive and must be considered a work in progress. Additional work is needed in exploring the design and implementation of the family portal within the larger context of family life. Further investigation would require us to study closely the fourfold classification of activities (maintenance, planning, expressive, and developmental) and locate the portal at the center of this classification scheme.

Note

For a fuller version of our essay on the Networked Home, please refer to Venkatesh, Kruse, and Shih, 2003.

References

Baillie, L., Benyon, D., Macaulay, C., & Petersen, M. G. (2003). Investigating design issues in household environments. *Cognition, Technology & Work, 5*(1), 33–43.

Bell, G., Blythe, M., Gaver, B., Sengers, P., & Wright, P. (2003). Paper presented at CHI 2003 conference, Fort Lauderdale, FL, April 5–10.

Bergman, E. (Ed.). (2000). *Information appliances and beyond.* San Francisco: Morgan Kauffman.

Beyer, H., & Holtzblatt, K. (1998). *Contextual design:*

Defining customer centered systems. San Francisco: Morgan Kaufman.

Bott, E. (1957). *Family and social network.* London: Tavistock Publications.

Carroll, J. M. (2000). *Making use: Scenario-based design of human computer interactions.* Cambridge, MA: MIT Press.

Cierard, I. (Ed.). (1999). *At home: An anthropology of domestic space.* Syracuse, NY: Syracuse University Press.

Cummings, J., & Kraut, R. (2002). Domesticating computers and the Internet. *The Information Society, 18*(3), 1–18.

Di Leanardo, M. (1987). The female world of cards and holidays: Women, families and the work of kinship. *Signs: The Journal of Women in Culture and Society, 12,* 440–453.

Edwards, C., Weintraub, A., Irene, M. K., & Reinhardt, A. (2003, July 21). Digital homes: A special report. *Business Week, 3842,* 58–64.

Frohlich, D. M., & Kraut, R. (2002). The social context of home computing. In Harper, R. (Ed.), *Home design: Social perspectives on domestic life and the design of interactive technology* (pp. 127–162). London: Springer.

Frohlich D. M., & Prabhu, G. (2003). Fuelling the ethnographic imagination by design. In Frohlich, D. M., & Prabhu, G. (Eds.), *Contextual invention: Creative approaches to innovation in emerging markets* (pp. 39–59). Bangalore, India: Kestone Research.

Hakos, J. T., & Redish, J. (1998). *User and task analysis for interface design.* New York: Wiley.

Harper, R. (Ed.). (2000). Domestic Computing [Special Issue]. *Personal Technologies, 4(1).*

Harper, R. (2002). *Home design: Social perspectives on domestic life and the design of interactive technology.* London: Springer.

Hindus, D., Mainwaring, S. D., Leduc, N., Hagstrom, A. E., & Bayley, O. (2001). Casablanca: Designing social communication devices for the home. *CHI Proceedings of 2001, 3*(1), 325–332. New York: Association for Computing Machinery.

Hoffman, D., Novak, T., & Venkatesh, A. (2004). Has the Internet become indispensable? *Communications of the ACM, 47*(7), 37–42.

Kiesler, S. (1997). *The culture of the Internet.* Hillsdale, NJ: Erlbaum.

Kraut, R., Mukhopadhyay, T., Szczypula, J., Kiesler, S., & Scherlis, W. (1999). Communication and information: Alternative uses of the Internet in households. *Information Systems Research, 10*(4), 287–303.

Lally, E. (2002). *At home with computers.* Oxford: Berg.

Lawson, B. (2001). *The language of space.* Oxford: Architectural Press.

Lee, W. O. (2000). *Challenges and issues in the application of living space model for home-based information technology* Working Paper. Redmond, WA: Microsoft Corporation.

Livingstone, S. (2003). Children's use of the Internet: Reflections on the emerging agenda. New *Media and Society, 5*(2), 1–15.

Magid, L. (2000, June 26). Home networking: Next big thing for families with multiple PCs. *Los Angeles Times,* C3, p. 1.

Mainwaring, S. D. (2002). Some strategies and challenges for the design of family technology. *CHI New Technologies for Family Workshop.* Retrieved July 2, 2004 from http://www.cs.umd.edu/hcil/interliving/chi02/mainwaring.htm.

Milardo, R. M., & Allan, G. (1997). Social networks and family relationships. In. Duck, S. W. (Ed.), *Handbook of personal relationships, 2nd edition* (pp. 505–522). New York: Wiley.

Neibauer, A. (1999). *This wired home: The Microsoft guide to home networking.* Buffalo, NY: Microsoft Press.

Papert, S. (1996). *The connected family: Bridging the digital generation gap.* Atlanta, GA: LongstreetPress.

Ruhling, N. A. (2000). Home is where the office is. *American Demographics, 22*(5), 54–60.

Scott, J. (1991). *Social network analysis.* London: Sage.

Szinovacz, M. (1988). Series editor's foreword. In Milardo, R. M. (Ed, *Families and social networks* (p. 7). London: Sage.

Turow, J., & Kavanaugh, A. L. (2003). *The wired homestead.* Cambridge, MA: MIT Press.

Turow, J., & Nir, L. (2003). The Internet and the family: The views of parents and youngsters. In Turow, J. & Kavanaugh, A. L. (Eds.), *The wired homestead.* Cambridge, MA: MIT Press.

Venkatesh, A. (1996). Computers and other interactive technologies for the home. *Communications of the ACM, 39*(12), 47–54.

Venkatesh, A., Kruse, E., & Shih, E. (2003). The networked home: An analysis of current developments and future trends. *Cognition, Technology & Work, 5,* 1, 23–32.

Venkatesh, A., & Mazumdar, S. (1999). New information technologies in the home: A study of uses, impacts, and design strategies. In Mann, T. (Ed.), *The power of imagination* (pp. 216–220). Edmond, OK: Environmental Design Research Association.

10

Sonia Livingstone

Children's Privacy Online
Experimenting with Boundaries Within and Beyond the Family

The Internet in Everyday Life

The Internet is playing an ever-greater role in the economy, in the workplace, in education, and in our private lives. This still-diversifying bundle of technologies—including e-mail, the World Wide Web, Intranets, multiplayer games, message boards, and so forth—increasingly mediates communication, information, organization, entertainment, learning, and commerce on a global as well as a local scale. Across many industrialized countries, recent years have witnessed a rapid expansion in the domestic market as well as a significant educational market for the Internet: recent figures in the United Kingdom put domestic access at 55%, though figures for households with children are considerably higher (Office of National Statistics, 2005). The rate of Internet diffusion in the United States is such that it took just 7 years to reach 30% of households, a level of penetration that took 17 years for television and 38 years for the telephone (Rice, 2002).

What are the consequences of Internet access and use for the social practices, relations, and contexts of everyday life? One line of speculation concerns the supposed blurring of a series of traditionally important distinctions in society—between work and leisure, public and private, edu-

cation and entertainment, citizenship and consumerism, local and global, print and visual culture, and so forth. This chapter focuses on children and young people—a segment of society associated with perhaps the most speculation but only recently with a body of research (Livingstone, 2003)—and it explores their use of the Internet in relation to one of these distinctions—the relation between public and private.

Drawing mainly on the findings of an in-depth ethnographic-style project exploring children and young people's use of the Internet at home, supplemented with material from focus group interviews with children (Livingstone and Bober, 2003, 2005), this chapter focuses particularly on the experiences and practices of privacy in everyday life. Although in principle privacy is valued and protected in society, in historical and social terms children's privacy is increasingly restricted. It is argued that the media—especially the Internet—provide some key opportunities for privacy, yet policy initiatives designed to keep children safe online are (for good reasons) constraining even these opportunities. Findings reveal how children and young people understand and exercise their notions of privacy, including the range of everyday tactics by which children micromanage their privacy online.

A Matter of Privacy

The concept of privacy has been defined in many ways across many contexts. Sheehan (2002) reviews the range of conceptions of privacy evident in Western culture, which are, in some cases, instantiated in legal frameworks as rights. These include privacy as the right to be left alone, to be able to keep one's personal information out of the public domain, to be protected from control by others, to decide what personal information to share with others, to know what personal information is being collected by others, and to access one's personal data held by others. Underlying these varying definitions lies a division between definitions centered on keeping information out of the public domain and definitions centered on determining (or controlling, or knowing) which personal information is available to whom. Stein and Sinha (2002, p. 414) combine both principles when they observe that

> though conceptions of privacy vary from country to country, privacy is frequently linked to the rights of individuals to enjoy autonomy, to be left alone, and to determine whether and how information about one's self is revealed to others . . . [and, once revealed] to access and control how their personal information is used by others.

Privacy policy and regulation face some significant tensions. In reviewing the recent literacy on privacy and new information technologies, Perri 6 (1998, p. 9) locates the origin of present struggles over privacy in what he describes as

> a central fault line around which societies in the developed world are shaped. This is the continuing, and perhaps growing, tension between the impulses of economic liberalization, with its commitments to removing constraints upon trade and exchange, and of political liberalism, with its impulse to construct and then protect a conception of individual or family life from unfettered openness to trade or governance.

These regulatory debates are now being extended to the Internet. Indeed, within these long-standing tensions between private versus public, between individuals' rights to privacy versus to freedom of expression, and between freeing up the market versus protecting consumers, the Internet poses some particular challenges to the management and regulation of privacy.[2] Increasingly, it seems, "the ability of computers to collect, search and exchange data feeds a growing market for personal information and harbors the potential to erode personal privacy" (Stein and Sinha, 2002, p. 413). Or, as 6 argues, "what is distinctive about informational capitalism is that *personal information* has become the basic fuel on which modern business and government run" (6, 1998, p. 23). Hence, across industrial societies, governments are consulting, debating, and ultimately attempting to regulate the shifting boundaries of who can and should know what about whom and for what purpose. Cross-national differences are already apparent, for example, with the United States placing relatively more stress on economic liberalization and the European Union giving comparatively more weight to cultural rights and protection.[3]

A growing literature seeks to inform debate by examining the parallels and differences in public and policy conceptions of privacy between the offline and online worlds (Regan, 2002; Turow and Ribak, 2003). Both on and offline, it would appear that, as Sheehan (2002) notes, the adult population varies considerably in its level of concern over privacy. For the most part, the public is widely seen as being highly concerned, but often equally ignorant, about privacy issues. For example, in the U.K. public opinion polls, "privacy has consistently ranked above freedom of speech, inflation and equal rights for women or minorities as a public concern" (6, 1998, p. 26). Yet comparatively few people read web site privacy policies, check for cookies, or attempt to understand, or take precautionary measures against, the various threats to their privacy on the Internet (Lyon, 1994; Turow and Ribak, 2003).

However, this discussion of policy regarding online privacy rights and protection has mobilized just part of the philosophical and ethical debates over privacy, for the concern has been solely focused on external threats to privacy—indeed, mainly on state and commercial threats to individual privacy—rather than examining privacy issues in the round. Particularly, privacy as conceptualized by Internet users in their everyday lives has been considered only in relation to external threats (e.g., Regan, 2002; Turow, 2001). Important though such threats undoubtedly are, in everyday discussion it becomes clear that people are often most concerned with maintaining their privacy in relation to others within their social network. This includes peers (where the issues are those of identity and networks), parents or responsible others (where the issue is that of the balance of intimacy and independence between adult and child), and those from whom privacy is actively sought (intrusive, worrying, or even abusive adults). Moreover, although as already observed, there is only a weak relation between people's principles or beliefs and their privacy-related practices in relation to external threats to privacy, our empirical observations indicate that in relation to local or familial threats to privacy, a much closer relation exists between beliefs and practices.

Children's Privacy Online

Children and young people are usually among the earliest and most enthusiastic users of information and communication technologies, and households with children generally lead the diffusion process. Furthermore, it is often argued that children are more flexible, creative users than adults, having fewer established routines or habits and being oriented toward development, innovation, and change. Interestingly, as young people make the transition from their family of origin toward a wider peer culture, they find that the media offer a key resource for constructing their identity and for mediating social relationships. However, although research on children, young people, and use of the Internet is still in its early stages, a broad and challenging research agenda is now being mapped out (Livingstone, 2003).

Such research is best located within the now growing body of work on domestic contexts of media use, though for children connections must also be made with research on information and communication technologies in educational settings and with both developmental psychology and the sociology of childhood. Research on children and the Internet is distinctive in a further way, for although the wider literature on domestic media use tends to stress the active appropriation of media within the meanings and practices of family life, a focus on children gives rise to a strong set of anxieties among the public, policy-makers, and the research community regarding their passivity, vulnerability, and need for protection. The outcome

is a field of research structured around a strong tension between two very different, often-competing conceptions of childhood.[4]

In one view, children are seen as vulnerable, undergoing a crucial but fragile process of cognitive and social development to which the media tend to pose a risk by introducing potential harms into the social conditions for development and necessitating, in turn, a protectionist regulatory environment. In the contrary view, children are seen as competent and creative agents in their own right whose "media-savvy" skills tend to be underestimated by the adults around them, with the consequence being that society may fail to provide a sufficiently rich environment for them. Although a balance between these two positions would seem to be optimal, each position tends to be mobilized by opposing factions (protectionist vs. laissez-faire, with goals of consensus or diversity) in the public policy debates over Internet regulation and use. These in turn draw on, and take questions of children's Internet use into, the hotly fought debates regarding freedom of expression (whether defended in terms of the market or democracy) versus shared public norms (defended in terms of values and morals). Those who wish to argue for a balanced view of children's abilities and vulnerabilities can therefore seem to those in the thick of the policy debates to compromise on some crucial principles. One way forward, I suggest, is to include children's own experiences in debates about the Internet.

These broad debates are played out specifically in relation to the issue of privacy. Indeed, notwithstanding the many hopes held out for the Internet—that it will offer children new and wonderful possibilities for education, communication, and participation—there is considerable public concern over whether the Internet is, at the same time, mediating the increasing invasion of children's privacy. Concern currently centers on two external sources of risk or threat, both of which access a distinct if overlapping version of the "vulnerability" discourse about children and young people. One construes the child as naïve consumer whose privacy may be exploited by commercial bodies.[5] The second construes the child as sexual innocent whose privacy may be corrupted by harmful content or pedophilic predators (Internet Crime Forum, 2000; Livingstone, 2001). Both are serious concerns, and both are receiving considerable attention in terms of safety awareness campaigns and information and communication technology literacy training directed at consumers, as well as legislation or softer forms of regulation directed at state and commercial bodies.

In this chapter I consider a third threat to children's privacy; namely, that from parents who, generally in a well-intentioned and responsible manner, but occasionally in a less benign fashion, respond to anxieties over external threats by instituting a new, internal threat, one that risks the crucial relationship of trust between parents and children. My concern may be illustrated by the poignant observation that in a small but significant proportion of families, children need privacy from their parents precisely because their parents pose the threat through their physically or sexually abusive behavior (Russell, 1980). This makes private channels for communication—to ask for help and advice—of crucial importance, a need that conflicts with the widespread advice, and indeed policy, to devolve regulatory responsibility for children's Internet use to parents.[6] Although these cases are in the minority, the threat to children from within the family remains statistically far greater than any threat to them from outside,[7] thereby suggesting that privacy within the family is at least as important an issue as protection from external threats.[8] And as I shall hope to show below, in the vast majority of cases, and in the happiest of families, children will routinely and systematically seek to maintain their privacy from their parents (and other members of their personal network), through microlevel practices, which have the potential to shape the unfolding nature of "Internet use" more generally.

Child-Centered Investigation

Children's ideas about privacy, and especially their practices designed to maintain privacy, are not readily amenable to investigation through surveys, particularly when little qualitative work has been conducted to scope the issue from their perspective. Hence the research presented here sought to develop a child-centered approach to understanding media use (Livingstone, 1998), following Corsaro's (1977) microsociological analysis, which shows how, through daily actions unnoticed by adults, children contribute to the construction of social structures that have consequences for social

relations within the family and peer group, for media use, and for the space–time patterning of leisure (see also Qvortrup, 1995; James et al., 1998). A child-centered approach to Internet use, therefore, explores how the domestic environment affords opportunities for certain kinds of activities, including Internet-related activities, depending on social arrangements of time, space, cultural norms and values, and personal preferences and lifestyle. Crucially, it invites us to be open to the ways in which children and young people construct their own local contexts, rendering media use meaningful in specific ways, and so not only respond to but also influence their immediate environment, including their mediated environment.

In this chapter I draw first on a quasi-ethnographic project, Families and the Internet, which aimed to open up the "black box" of the home and explore what the Internet means to children and their families at the start of the 21st century (Livingstone and Bovill, 2001). The project was guided by a series of broadly ethnographic principles.[9] Specifically, 30 families, who varied in socioeconomic status, family type, and geographic location, and who had a child between 8 and 16 years old who uses the Internet, were visited on several occasions over one or more months.[10] Semistructured interviews were combined with observations of Internet use at home to explore the nature and contexts of domestic Internet use. Rather than seeking to make claims to representativeness, the research sought to "look behind" and so interpret the widely reported statistics on Internet access and use.[11] Through a series of visits, time was spent informally sitting with children while they went online, observing their decisions about what to do and where to go, as well as noting their skills in achieving their aims and the nature of the social situation thereby generated—interruptions from siblings, chatting with friends, advice from parents, the simultaneous monitoring of a favorite television program, and so forth. The analysis included both the discursive and material aspects of appropriation—what was said about going online and how this was managed in practice.

It is worth noting that, as is consistent with ethnographic methodology, the theme of privacy emerged from the attempt to make sense of children's understandings and, especially, their practices. Only once I began to recognize that questions of privacy were running through an eclectically diverse range of activities did I turn to the literature on children and privacy online, and only then did I realize that the debates are framed entirely in terms of external threats to privacy, in sharp contrast with the privacy concerns of children themselves. In what follows, I offer a portrait, doubtless selective and perhaps haphazard, of the variety of actions that reveal children's considerable concern with questions of privacy.

Interwoven with this account, I include some of the findings from a subsequent project, UK Children Go Online, which began with a series of focus group interviews with children and young people. Fourteen group interviews of around 1 hour in length were held with mostly same-sex groups of approximately four children or young people in each (a total of 55 children). These interviews were held in schools, which had been selected in turn so as to cover a range of background factors, including socioeconomic status, geographic spread, ethnicity, and school type. Each school organized two groups (usually one with boys and one with girls) of the same age from the same class, apart from one school, which provided two groups of boys and two groups of girls. The five age groups interviewed were 10–11, 12–13, 14–15, 16–17, and 17–19 years.[12] Interview topics included Internet literacy/expertise; use of different types of communication technologies, participation in global and local human networks with the help of the Internet, downloading files (e.g., music or games), undesirable online content (spam, advertising, pornography), Internet safety awareness and rules for using the Internet, Internet monitoring and filtering software, privacy online and offline, Internet nonuse and exclusion, and the role of the Internet in education (see Livingstone and Bober, 2003, in press-a).

In methodological terms, what is interesting is that children and young people turned out to be willing—indeed keen—to explain their concerns about privacy. This was interesting both because such a sensitive topic might perhaps have proved inappropriate in a group discussion format and because without the preceding observational research, it would not have occurred to me to ask about privacy, particularly in relation to internal or familial threats to privacy. On the basis of this research trajectory, and encouraged by children's articulate and enthusiastic discussions, the next phase of UK Children Go Online has translated at least

some of these concerns into survey questions, administered to a national sample of 1511 9- to 19-year-olds (Livingstone and Bober, 2004).

What Children Say and Do Online

Metaphors from familiar domains help make something unfamiliar or elusive comprehensible and stable. Some metaphors used for the Internet reveal great expectations—"it's just like life . . . you can do anything really," "a giant book about everything," "a world of opportunities," and "the future." Younger children tend to conceive of the Internet as a "place"—effectively, a new place to play—applying a spatial anchor that is comfortably familiar and appropriate to often narrow or bounded experience as users. Older children use more complex metaphors, such as "a link" or "a system," that explain the Internet's function or organization in terms of networks. Crucially, they see it as a means of connecting with others. Whether play or social relationships are foregrounded, it is worth noting that both have always been conducted in both public and private and that the very distinction between these—the choices involved, the ways in which the context frames the activity—has surely always mattered to children and young people.

Children seek privacy, but as a means to an end not an end in itself. Rather, as we shall see, they may use the opportunity of private spaces online to indulge in silly, rude, or naughty behavior; to experiment with new identities; to seek confidential advice on personal matters; to eavesdrop on the interactions of others; to meet people from far-off places or from the next street; and, most of all, to engage in uninterrupted, unobserved immersion in peer communication. Indeed, although online talk can appear spectacularly vacuous to the adult observer, for young people it is a highly social activity much valued by their peers—after all, this is "the constant contact generation" (Clark, 2005). Crucial to our present purposes, we should recognize that offline, all of these activities are customarily conducted with some conscious degree of privacy—there is no a priori reason, therefore, for things to be any different online.

Consider one particular instance, taken verbatim from our observational fieldwork notes, of a 13-year-old girl at home flirting in http://www. teen chat.com.

Candy scans the chat room options (Teen Flirt, Teen Party, The Crib, etc.) and chooses the one with most users. This room has 20 people, including London Lad, RIMO CORELONE, Majestic, 1 bubbly gal, 1 chick wanna cat, 1 fit lad, babe 2000, BIG BOY 69, Big will, Bristol_GUY, Bubbles, CHAD, Chick with attitude, Ninnie, and Cute Babe.

London Lad is in the process of insulting Big will. He writes, "big will iz gay." Babe 2000 says, "here all the guys take a <inserts 9 red roses>." RIMO CORELONE tries to get in by hitting two lines worth of unconnected letters. CHAD replies "so r u," presumably to London Lad, while Majestic asks, "is he really?" CHAD says "yes" and London Lad retorts "he asked aboot my dick!!"

After following this for a while, Candy tries to get a private one-to-one conversation going—her opening line is: "Hi r there any fit guys on here??? pm me if interested." Just after her entry, Bubbles writes "giz uz a snog" and RIMO CORELONE replies "BUBBLES YOUR A FAT SLAG." Ninnie then joins in with "ne 1 wanna chat press 123 or pm me." RIMO CORELONE is obviously trying to get a fight going and replies "**** OFF BITCH" London Lad replies "not 2day," but Silva responds to Ninnie with "123."

However, no one takes up Candy's bid for attention, and after 12 minutes, perhaps a little uncomfortable given the researcher's presence, she says she is bored and leaves the chat room.

Many things are going on here, offering some clues regarding children and young people's interest in private interactions online: the importance of identity play, their desire to push the boundaries of acceptability, the contrast with offline behavior, and the deployment of a distinctive online interaction style. I consider these in turn below.

What Privacy Means to Children

The management of private spaces involves considerable skills, and these are widely valued by young people. For example, it is commonplace to contribute to several private message conversations while also keeping an eye on what is going on in the main chat room. Young people may also retain a presence in a number of other chat rooms, minimizing some screens and only returning to them if a flash indicates that someone wishes to speak to them. In all, some keep five or six conversations going simulta-

neously. Thus, even when contributions seem trite, interest is retained by the often-demanding business of sustaining multiple conversations simultaneously; something exciting, interesting, or shocking may always happen; someone you want to talk to may come online at any minute. In addition, the skills displayed in managing the business of online communication convey the affirming message to both the child him- or herself and to observers that this is a competent individual with valued expertise.

Such competence is not so evident for teenagers in face-to-face or traditional communication, serving to add to the perceived value of online communication. Online, children feel not only private but also in control. Asked, "if you wanted to talk about something really private what would you do?" Mark, age 14 years, answers, "I don't know really. It depends what you want to do . . . my friend Nick he asked me quite a lot of times to meet him on chat at a certain time and I'd just go on there and we'd just talk and stuff like that and sometimes we phone each other or send an e-mail. It just depends really what type of mood you're in."

Online communication offers a means of managing, or avoiding, the potentially embarrassing challenges of face-to-face conversation and so of retaining control. In chat rooms, young people feel themselves to be the key node in the network—they feel themselves to be in charge—and when they feel themselves to be losing control, they can simply leave. Gus, age 13 years, compared chat room conversation with the telephone:

> On the telephone like you can be speaking but then if you don't know what to say you'll be just standing there not doing anything but with that [chat room] em it's like OK to be a bit late not be saying anything because it's not like you're waiting for them to . . . on the other end of a telephone . . . it's not so much of a rush. . . . You're not like confronted to someone. 'Cos if you say something they might not agree with they can't like hit you or say something back to you that's going to make you do something that—if they'll stand in front of you.

The Importance of Identity Play

The development of identity is not a singular or linear process—identities are performed and experimented with across a range of places. The boundaries between those spaces matter: We all act differently with different people, in different situations. Children and young people especially use the media to mark the boundaries of these different aspects of identity. As I have argued elsewhere in relation to young people's bedroom culture (Bovill and Livingstone, 2001), their use of the Walkman to block out the family, their management of multiple e-mail addresses to evade parental scrutiny, their fondness for passwords on the computer, their insistence on having a television in their bedroom, their facility with minimizing and maximizing windows—these all represent boundary marking tactics, technological updates on the injunction taped to the child's door: "Parents, keep out!!!"

The most obvious, but far from the only, way in which young people experiment with identity online is through e-mail or screen names. Although younger children tend to use their parents' or a family e-mail address, teenagers demand greater privacy and scope for self-expression. This can lead to the acquisition of a number of e-mail addresses and burgeoning communication.

On our first visit, 12-year-old Neil and his younger brother Euan, aged 10 years, had just started sending e-mails, using the family e-mail address. Their mother would open the e-mail account and call them if there was anything for them. By the second observational session, both boys had set up new, private e-mail accounts for themselves—Neil with Yahoo and Euan with http://another.com. Neil explains they are sending more e-mails now that they have privacy. Both brothers are anxious to hide their pin numbers from each other, and there is a lot of teasing over this as they try to peek over each other's shoulders. Neil now checks his mail every time he goes on the Internet, sending and receiving about three messages a week among his circle of 5–10 correspondents, all school friends.

As they get older, teens explicitly manage their interactions through different online identities. Some teens we talked to have as many as eight e-mail addresses. Some seem to keep a number in play at once, others have lost count of how many they have or have lost track of the names they have used, and others are more systematic. As Mark (age 14), says, "I normally give my own personal e-mail address out and not just—not—we've got a family one like Ted's got and I've got my own personal one so I just give that one to my friends, not the family one." Jane keeps

one e-mail address for her correspondence with friends, and the other, which she uses much less often, is the one she uses when asked to provide such information on a web site to protect herself against unwelcome junk mail, it all being directed to one site, where she deletes it when she has time.

Fourteen-year-old Manu uses both the family e-mail address and his own private Hotmail address for different purposes. He explains that he uses Hotmail not because it is his individual address but because he can access it at both at home and in school, and as he moves between these places he prefers to receive e-mail, which is available in both places. However, he admits that some of his friends can be very silly, sending rude messages to him about teachers, or insulting messages about friends, or sending him URL's to inappropriate sites, and so on. These messages he reads and then deletes straightaway, maintaining his inbox as a "clean" place for parents to see. When he accesses his Hotmail address on our first observational visit, there are two messages from a local friend. Another five are from his uncle—sent from "somewhere in Africa, don't know quite where he is, he sends messages from his laptop" (a few of these are in fact written by his aunt). His uncle e-mailed him a colorful Divali card, addressed to the whole family. Among the other e-mails, one is from a girl friend to his older brother, who does not have his own account.

For teenagers in particular, e-mail correspondence becomes part of their social construction of identity. Adopted names in chat rooms, even more than e-mail addresses, allow the trying-out of new roles as sexual beings or otherwise desirable, dynamic personalities. Consider, for example, the names of an American/English e-mail circle of 12–13 year olds: Littlelover, pixel_117, applesauce128, fireball318, actingurl, and fuel_chick. Sites such as http://another.com make it a selling point to combine anonymity with fun pseudonyms. Candy chose Kissmequick@yahoo.com, saying, "it's quite fun having a jokey name but it's privacy as well. I don't like my mum and dad reading all the e-mails I send because I write quite dodgy stuff. And when he writes back mum and dad usually read 'em and some of the things he writes are quite rude." She retaliates by reading her parents' e-mails—but "they aren't very interesting." Similarly, Manu and his older brother share seven chat room identities (the maximum allowed on the system) and alternate between them or modify them as the mood takes them. Having shown the researcher all his profiles and how to edit them, he explains that the people in the chat room "won't know who I am because I keep on changing my name. . . . It depends who I'm talking to. Say if I want to annoy someone, then I want to remain anonymous, then I'll change my name and they won't realize who it is. It's quite good."

Although this is all done in a light-hearted fashion, identity management depends on the consistency of one's self-presentation and the impression of sincerity conveyed (Goffman, 1959). Although establishing a grown-up identity offline is therefore fraught with difficulties and embarrassments, the anonymity of chat rooms and the rules of the game (where experimenting and fooling around is expected) license the trying out of new roles. There, young people, without compromising their everyday identity, can play around with the crucial boundaries between truth and fantasy, information and imagination, the real and the unreal.

Privacy is integral to the communication of identity, for identity is partly enacted through managing who knows what about us and who does not. In sustaining multiple interaction contexts online, not only are distinct aspects of identity performed (and so constituted), but they are also knowingly bounded rather than indiscriminate in their anticipated audience—intended for the eyes of certain people, for the communication of certain contents, for the revelation of certain kinds of experience. That which is made public to some is simultaneously kept private from others. When young people talk about their communication with peers, it seems that the skill and the fun stems precisely from playing with the possibilities of who knows what, taking risks with who is told what. Where Goffman (1959) wrote about the ambiguous thrill of overhearing, today's young people exploit the ambiguous thrills and puzzles of forwarding on and blind copying in of messages; the shift from chat room to private chat; the use of anonymity to construct cheeky, witty, or rude online identities; and so forth.

Pushing the Bounds of Acceptability

Although Candy, earlier, was chatting on her own, it is common practice for several friends to gather in front of the screen. When Mark and his brothers come to visit, Ted describes a lively scene in which they all shout out—"'No, don't write that,

write this.' That's what we do when all his brothers are there . . . taking different turns to type in stuff." On one of our visits, we watch while these 14-year-old friends try to disrupt the adult Yahoo chat room for police and fire officers (Police and Fire), pretending to be a blind orphan in a home with abusive carers. They type in lines like "Help!" "They're coming to get me!" Someone replies and asks if they are blind how come they can type? Mark replies "Braille keyboard" and gets the retort, "And braille screen?" They see their cover is blown and are a bit disappointed.

Similarly, Manu, also 14 years old, talks with enthusiasm about how rude he and his friends get, trading insults with each other or with other people. Particularly, they like to pretend to be other people when chatting online with friends they know from school, insulting them and then teasing at school the next day until the friends catch on as to the identity of those unknown others. One game is for the participant to be so annoying to people in chat rooms that he (or she) forces them to leave. As Manu says proudly, "I drive people out all the time, it's my speciality. When the room is empty, I feel really content with myself. . . . I just sit there and wallow in my glory and then I leave. I might go to another room."

The boundaries being pushed depend on the boundaries established by adults. Hence, as an increasing number of chat rooms are moderated, this is seen by some young people as a challenge—the game becomes seeing how far one can go before being thrown off (even in monitored chat rooms, such as those on AOL, gate-crashers can appear and create havoc before they are detected and thrown off).

Given that online information, communication, and entertainment variously blur boundaries between public and private, adult and child, normative and deviant, legitimate and illegitimate, it is unsurprising that young people enjoy using the Internet to push, to explore, to transgress boundaries that are perhaps better policed in the offline world.

Secret Language

The flexibility of e-mails allows for a customization of the correspondence, which teens use to their advantage—drawing on the icons or themes of youth culture. Where writing letters can often be seen as a chore, e-mailing is enjoyable. Among peers, e-mail has its own linguistic code, which owes much to street talk and the abbreviated language of chat rooms. Young people vary the style of their online communications according to the recipient. In e-mails, grandparents will be written to in one style (public, formal) and friends in another (private, informal). The contrast between 11-year-old Susie's e-mails to her friend Hannah and to her grandmother reveals the control children deliberately exercise in such communicative styles. Compare

——Original Message——
From: Susie J <mailto:f****@ukgateway.net>
To: Hannah M <mailto:f******@yahoo.co.uk>
Sent: 28 July 2000 19:04
Subject: howd it go?
howd the move go? i cant wate^s2 c yor new howse come round^swhen you can!!
from Devilduck
P.S. y didn't u tell me Alison had 2 dalmations? they're coming on monday i hope you'll be there to see them

With

——Original Message——
From: "Susie J" <f****@ukgateway.net>
To: <m****@talk21.com>
Sent: 03 September 2000 20:33
Subject: Thanks
> To Gran and Grandad,
> We arrived home safe and well. Helen is really pleased with her necklace and
> sends her thanks. Thank You for having us we really enjoyed ourselves.
> Thanks again for having us, love from Susie
xxxx
> P.S. I found a fossilised slipper limpet on the beach in Middlesborough

The language of online communication, as with text (SMS) language, is clearly designed both to facilitate communication among peers and to impede overseeing (the screen equivalent of Goffman's focus on overhearing) by parents, supporting the view of privacy, which stresses control over the sharing of personal information rather than, more simply, keeping personal information to oneself. As Greenfield et al. (chapter 13) note, adults are frequently floored in their attempt to follow the conversational flow in online interactions, the point being that children maintain their privacy not necessarily by keeping information out of the physical space but by rendering it symbolically inaccessible.

Relating On- and Offline

What does the online environment offer? Children come from diverse backgrounds of course, but we were struck by the contrast between one boy's online life and his offline life. Stephen, age 14 years, from a working-class home, seemed to live a tidy, organized, dutiful life offline while engaging in entertaining and slightly risqué youth culture on line. He was a good boy, working hard at school, with a very tidy bedroom containing, for example, a much prized six-volume encyclopedia from his grandmother and a shelf of computer games that he prefers not to swap with friends, as they return scratched. Outside, he plays sports, teaches karate, and swims competitively. Watching over this orderly child is a careful mother, who casually passes by several times to check on him (or on the observer) during the research—has he shown us his school work on the Internet?—perhaps compensating for a rarely present father away at work.

In one observational session, our field notes record the following. Like most young people, he checks his e-mails first (he has none). Then he briefly does what his mother told him to (6 minutes showing the researcher his homework on htttp://www.gnvqict.com). Next, typing in URLs from memory (suggesting this is his regular repertoire), he has fun, spending time on sites, which are culturally disorderly, rule or taboo breaking, and mildly improper. These include http://www.napster.com (2 minutes), laughing at the cartoons (frog in a blender, etc.), on http://www.joecartoons.com (10 minutes), downloading a game from the South Park site (http://www.spelementary.com) and looking at pictures on the site (Cartman dressed as Hitler, etc.; 19 minutes), and last, checking the music charts and jokes on http://www.mtv.co.uk, trying to download a song (19 minutes). Maybe he hopes to shock the researcher, but it is hard to avoid the conclusion that although life off the screen is heavily circumscribed for Stephen, he reacts by finding some modest privacy and freedom online.

Accessing Porn Sites

When using the Internet, young people may be physically in a private domestic space but, like television before it, the Internet brings the outside world inside. This allows in a range of unwanted intrusions—in the sense that they are judged undesirable by parents and children, although on occasion, children (and parents) deliberately seek them out—most notably, pornographic content. It is difficult to obtain reliable estimates of risk in this area—clearly, exposure to pornography online is increasing (Wigley and Clarke, 2000)—and many children have, accidentally or intentionally, encountered online pornography (Livingstone and Bober, 2004). There are good reasons to suspect their answers of both under- and overreporting, and research ethics make persistent questioning inadvisable. Whether or not these experiences are actually harmful is, of course, subject to considerable debate. For our present purposes, the point is that the belief that pornographic content harms children is a primary driver of regulation in this field, both at the national and domestic level. Let us consider, therefore, the nature and the experience of such encounters—do they appear to infringe on children's privacy, and how can this be balanced against the infringement of privacy, which occurs through attempts to prevent such encounters? We came across the following:

One 11-year-old girl, trying to find pictures of Adolf Hitler for a school project during one of our visits, innocently accessed a site labeled "Adolf Hitler pictures." She failed to note the rubric "gaysexfreepics" and found herself face to face with a porn site. As is common with such sites, it was very difficult to shut down, with the first few attempts merely producing other similar sites. She claimed not to have been upset by the site, saying that she had not found anything like it before but if she had would do as she did on this occasion—get rid of it and ignore it.

Fourteen-year-old Sally, rather than being shocked when she comes across a prostitution site at school, laughingly describes it to the interviewer as one of her "funniest experiences." She says, "one time we were going to this site where you're supposed to improve your money skills, like money dot credit UK [but] went to money dot com which [is] a prostitution site (laughs). . . . And another time I was on a Rocky Horror site. . . . There was a picture of Frank in the suspenders, not in the dress just in the suspenders and corset and sort of looking at Rocky rather admiringly and Rocky's sitting there going . . . and my IT teacher's is like . . . and now what's this? Is the sort of thing you should be looking at in school? Oh God."

Even among the youngest girls, there was some evidence that being unshockable was socially desirable. Thus, 10-year-old Anna, who confesses to have seen some "pretty rude pictures" when she inadvertently opened an e-mail of her father's, resists any suggestion that she may have been shocked: "I'm quite grown up, I know all about everything, sex life and stuff. . . . Sometimes I read stories that some people my age wouldn't be like, would be like (deep intake of breath), and I'm just like cool." These turn out to be "Buffy Angel stories, they're rated PG, 13, or R, but I just read them anyway because I like them." Clearly some of the material they see is pornographic, by common standards, although some is much milder. Reactions depend on the age and maturity of the child, expectations among the peer group, ease of discussion with parents, and so forth.

The Significance of Children's Privacy Online

The Uses of Privacy

> *Interviewer*: What do you write to them [your friends]?
>
> *Sally* (11): Sort of secrets and stuff.
>
> *Interviewer*: And why do you write secrets on e-mail and not just tell them when you see them?
>
> *Sally*: 'Cause they can make their mind up. When they've got people there, they don't always say what—when they've got people there.
>
> *Ellen* (11): And sometimes if you've got the e-mail address of the person you fancy, write it to them.

Our findings on what children say and do online indicate a series of "uses of privacy." These include feeling in control—being master of the situation—something they may experience less when under the surveillance of an adult gaze. They may use a private moment to find advice regarding, or manage the potential embarrassment of, a particular personal issue or encounter. Beatrice (13) says, "when you're like talking to them face-to-face, you're like—you've got other people around you, and they can't tell you what they really think. So like instant messaging, you can." Cameron (13) tells us, "I once dumped my old girlfriend by e-mail." When asked why, he explains, "well, it was cowardly really. I couldn't say it face-to-face." As we have seen, being children, they may wish to engage in silly, rude, or naughty behavior, experimenting with or pushing the boundaries of normatively defined expectations or identities. And they play with who knows what about them, as in Perri 6's definition of privacy, through simultaneous communications (text messaging while instant messaging, private chat while also in a chat room, etc.), precisely exploring their control over personal information.

Age matters considerably, for it is younger teens who may find face-to-face communication particularly difficult to negotiate. In our focus groups, older teenagers tended to prefer to hold private conversations face-to-face, which they think is more secure than online communication (Livingstone and Bober, 2003). They are concerned about the possibility of someone "spying" on online conversations, revealing their growing awareness of online privacy issues. As Hazel, age 17 years, points out, "if you wanted to have a private conversation, then I'm sure you'd talk to them face-to-face rather than using the Internet, because if you know they can be listened to, or someone else can see what you're doing, then I wouldn't have thought that you'd want that to happen. So you'd therefore talk to them, meet up and talk to them face-to-face."

The Value of Privacy

One may ask why the online environment is particularly important for children as a private domain. The reasons, I suggest, lie in part with the changing conditions of childhood itself (Livingstone, 2002). Consider the increasing caution parents exercise in allowing their children to go out, thus precluding access to the street corner where teens used to hang out. Consider also the introduction of central heating and the growing availability of media and consumer goods, resulting in a comfortable, safe, and private bedroom. Add to these, most importantly, the lengthening period of adolescence itself, according to which children are said to be getting older earlier in terms of consumerism,

sexual experimentation, and independence of lifestyle, while simultaneously they are getting older later in terms of financial independence and entry into employment (Hill and Tisdall, 1997). Whether or not they are changing childhood, the computer and Internet provide a flexible resource with which new freedoms can be found, new risks run, new experiments embarked on, new innocence exploited, and new expertise enjoyed, all without leaving home. Because children do live increasingly constrained lives, in terms of their freedoms in physical space, while simultaneously having greater access to images and ideas circulated by the media than ever before, it is not surprising that we are finding that children turn to the media, and increasingly to the Internet, to create private spaces for themselves. In contrast, given social tensions over changes in childhood and adolescence, it is not surprising that the means by which youth culture now finds expression—the Internet—becomes caught up in these social and moral tensions.

The Risks and Regulatory Challenges of Online Privacy

In the eyes of parents and policy makers, children's activities online are seen as being sufficiently risky to legitimate, often thoughtlessly or unwittingly, an intrusion into these private activities. When we asked parents about their concerns over their children's Internet use, the majority mentioned pornography, bad language, junk mail, and viruses (see also Turow and Nir, 2000). Giving out personal information, sometimes coupled with anxieties about chat rooms, was also mentioned. As Candy's mother said, "she's very happy to give her address or telephone number to any Tom, Dick, or Harry and you just think 'Oh no! Don't do that darling.' . . . She's a bit too trusting."

The research literature on parental mediation of media use identifies several strategies in common use in relation to television. In Livingstone and Bovill (1999), we characterized these as restrictive guidance, evaluative guidance, and conversational guidance. Whereas for television regulation we found that parents most often claim evaluative guidance, followed by conversational guidance, both strategies that rest on sharing media use with their child, it would seem that a different approach is emerging for the Internet because parents do not share the same expertise or interest with their children (Livingstone and Bovill, 2001; Livingstone and Bober, in press-b). Instead, they seem to prefer strategies of restrictive guidance (e.g., limiting time spent online, installing filtering software, keeping the password secret, and banning or blocking certain activities, most commonly young people's favorites—e-mail and chat), unobtrusive monitoring (e.g., positioning the computer in a public place, spot checking from time to time what the child is doing, and checking the history or the cache for sites visited),[13] or what we may term "benign neglect" (meaning that parents, although often well-intentioned, show a distinct lack of monitoring or engagement with their child over their Internet use, claiming a comparative lack of expertise and so, in practice, paying little attention to what their children do or what sites they access).[14]

In seeking to act responsibly, parents may or may not be aided by the market. Consider the rhetoric directed at parents by the promotional materials of Internet filtering software.[15] This conveys a message of parental concern, even fear, but not one of trust in or openness with children, and nor does it leave space for children's privacy—as is apparent in the naming of *Cybersnoop*, for example. *Cybersitter*, to take another example, "works by secretly monitoring all computer activity" so as to close the door on "unrestricted cybersmut" including, interestingly, that stored in parental files on the computer, whereas *Childsafe* allows parents to "see exactly what your children have been viewing online . . . [and to] monitor chat room sessions, instant messaging, email." Features highly valued by children, such as exercising control in choosing personal, cheeky, or flirtatious screen names, are ruled out by America Online's invitation to parents to gain control themselves by creating a screen name or e-mail name for their child.[16]

In our focus group interviews, young people reacted strongly against such practices. Anonymity and playfulness, privacy and deception, have always been vital to childhood—it is ironic that these are not only central to what children value about the Internet but also to what gives rise to parental fears for children's safety. Children and young people do not like their parents and teachers monitoring their Internet use, seeing it as an invasion of their privacy. To explain why they object to having their Internet use monitored, children use metaphors such as having one's bag searched,

having one's personal space invaded, or being stalked, which is ironic given that parental monitoring is partly aimed at precluding stalking online by strangers. In contrast, with the software named *Cybersnoop*, for example, young people's strongly expressed view that they too have privacy rights should be more clearly heard.

> My parents don't ask me "ooh, what did you go on?" because I wouldn't like it if I came from school, came home, and they search my pockets. I'd say "what are you doing—that's personal." What if I had something I didn't want them to see? Just like I wouldn't search my mum's bedroom. (Amir, 15)
>
> You just like don't want your mum spying on you and knowing everything about you. (Nina, 17)
>
> Because you want your independence, really, you don't want your mum looking over your shoulder checking what you're doing all the time. (Steve, 17)

To maintain their privacy, young people engage in a variety of tactics for evading parental or school monitoring and controls, and some clearly enjoy the challenge of outwitting adults, capitalizing on their comparatively greater Internet-related expertise. They hide folders on the computer where parents cannot find them, and they minimize or switch between screens when parents are looking over their shoulder. They are aided in these evasions by being often more expert in the use of computers and the Internet than their parents. One wonders what chance 10–year-old Anna's mother has of monitoring her Internet use when she can barely follow what her daughter is doing:

> I'll have to come up to a level because otherwise I will, I'll be a dinosaur, and the children, when children laugh at you and sort of say "Blimey, mum, don't you even know that?" . . . Already now I might do something and I say "Anna, Anna, what is it I've got to do here?" and she'll go "Oh mum, you've just got to click the" . . . "Don't do it Anna, show me what you're doing!" and she'll be whizzing, whizzing, dreadfully.[17]

This group of 14–16-year-old London schoolboys claim that they can always find a way around the school's filter—always find things they want—and they clearly enjoy engaging in this forbidden activity. On their home computers, these boys do not have filtering software because, they say, their parents would not know how to install it.

> *Amir*: The technical things there, the kids nowadays—they just know how to go onto new sites.
>
> *Prince*: This goes back to what you said earlier, like we know the computer, we're the generation of computers.
>
> *Amir*: We know how to go on something else if it isn't there, 'cause we always know how to search for things.
>
> *Interviewer*: So it's not that you can break the filter, but you can find a way round it to get—
>
> *Amir*: Yeah, to find a way around it. It's not about breaking, it's about—there's always plan B.
>
> *Prince*: There are always other options.

Although unobtrusive (sometimes secret) monitoring risks infringing children's privacy, and hence the relation of trust between parent and child, more overtly restrictive strategies may undermine children's ability to pursue the many benefits of Internet access. Hence, parents need guidance on finding a way to balance risks and opportunities, minimizing the former and maximizing the latter so that children can use the Internet safely and constructively (Livingstone, 2001). Certainly, there is something curious in the fact that, although governments have not previously advised parents to listen in on their children's phone calls or read their diary or letters, this is precisely what advice is now being given, as parents are encouraged to look over their children's shoulders as they go online and to install software to check on sites visited, e-mails sent, or chat rooms visited. Indeed, one may argue that there are many ways in which society is trading off children's freedom against protection with, it seems, a stronger sense of the dangers against which they should be protected than of the costs of such protection in terms of their privacy or freedom of expression. For example, parents advise children (and governments advise parents to advise their children) not to do precisely the things they most enjoy doing online—contacting strangers, pretending to be someone else, sending photographs of themselves. Worried parents often ban even more routine things like downloading, answering pop-ups, and visiting chat rooms.[18]

Conclusions

Fahey (1995) addresses the blurring of the boundary between public and private in relation to the family by arguing that "instead of speaking of a single public/private boundary, it may be more accurate to speak of a more complex re-structuring in a series of zones of privacy, not all of which fit easily with our standard images of what the public/private boundary is" (Fahey, 1995, p. 688). Some of these "zones of privacy," this chapter has suggested, are now to be found online, raising new challenges for parents, children, and governments alike.

I hope to have shown that children value privacy, seek privacy, and given the new possibilities afforded by the Internet, relish the chance to carve out private spaces and activities on the Internet. However, we should avoid polarizing public and private in any simple way. It is not that young people use the Internet to withdraw from public participation (and for the few that do, the reasons are more likely to be found in their lives rather than the technology). Nor do they simply use the Internet as a private medium as one thinks of reading a book in private, for the key feature of the Internet is connection not isolation. Rather, they use it to manage the boundary between public and private in such a ways as to allow them to experiment with identity, with communication, with peer culture—in short, with growing up (Turkle, 1995; see also Livingstone, 2005).

In charging parents with the responsibility to regulate that which the state itself prefers not to regulate,[19] policy risks infringing not only children's privacy[20] but also children's relations with their parents. For, as part of the longer-term cultural shifts in the conditions of childhood, we are witnessing what Giddens has termed "the transformation of intimacy" within the home. According to Giddens (1993, p. 184), intimate relationships are undergoing a historical transformation, "a democratization of the private sphere," being ever less defined according to kinship, obligation, or other traditional structures and instead being increasingly dependent on the intrinsic quality of the "pure relationship." In consequence, children—like any other participants in a relationship—have gained the right to "determine and regulate the conditions of their association" (p. 185), and parents have gained the duty not only to protect them from coercion but also to ensure their involvement in key decisions, to be accountable to them and others, and to respect as well as expect respect. This new model of parent–child relations, based on equality, respect, and rights, is difficult enough for parents without adding to the difficulty by introducing a policing role in relation to their children's online activities.

In seeking a new approach to privacy in the information age, Perri 6 invites a move away from the legalistic approach toward one focused on dignity, reframing privacy in terms of risk: "privacy can best be understood as a protection against certain kinds of risks—risks of injustice through such things as unfair inference, risks of loss of control over personal information, and risks of indignity through exposure and embarrassment" (6, 1998, p. 13). The advantage of this formulation is that one can then seek to balance risks. In other words, we need to move away from addressing the problem of privacy through balancing the protection of children against the protection of adult rights to freedom of expression. This opposes two goods for which society can brook no compromise on either, and it casts children and adults in a mutual opposition according to which protecting children infringes adult freedom. As a result of this legalistic approach, children have become a pawn in the hotly fought—even hostile—struggle between advocates of civil liberties and of censorship, and parents are being recruited as society's police in checking up on children.[21] It is this tendency against which I hope a child-centered approach effectively warns us. Instead, this chapter has proposed an alternative approach, one that balances the risks to children from unrestricted Internet use against the risks of invading their privacy when restricting their Internet use. In other words, a child-centered approach seeks a balance between children's safety and privacy.

Acknowledgment. The empirical research presented in this chapter was funded by two grants to the author: Families and the Internet (1999–2001), funded by BT, and UK Children Go Online, funded by Economic and Social Research Council grant (RES-335-25-0008) as part of the E-Society Programme, with cofunding from AOL, BSC, Childnet-International, Citizens Online, ITC, and Ofcom (see http://www.children-go-online.net).

Notes

1. The Electronic Privacy Information Centre (http://www.epic.org/ presents a strong defense of freedom of information and freedom of speech in relation to the Internet, particularly following a recent law in some states of the United States requiring the institutional adoption of filtering systems (e.g., in schools). Because the basis for such filtering is proprietary, it is difficult even to determine whether freedom of information is thereby threatened (see also Oswell, 1999).

2. As Castells (2002, p. 184) notes, "the European Union's regulation of data gathered by dot.com companies from their users protects privacy to a much greater extent than the laissez-faire environment in the United States." Note also that the EU's 1995 Data Protection Directive contrasts with the more fragmented, nonfederalized, approach to privacy in the United States (Stein and Sinha, 2002).

3. See Bingham, Valentine, and Holloway (1999), Livingstone (1998), and Oswell (1998).

4. In the United States, the Children's Online Privacy Protection Act (COPPA) came into effect in April 2000, ensuring that commercial web sites and online services directed at children cannot collect, use, or disclose personally identifiable information from children under age 13 years without a parent's permission. In April 2001, reporting on COPPA's first year, the Center for Media Education (Montgomery, 2001; see also Turow, 2001) noted that the law has significantly affected many of the marketing and business practices of commercial web sites, but that some violations of both the spirit and the letter of the law continue.

5. Oswell (1999) critically analyzes the European Commission's "Illegal and Harmful Content on the Internet" (see European Parliament, 1997) for its policy "to delegate responsibility and authority downwards" (p. 48), in this case, making parents responsible for children's domestic Internet use. By construing "a singular vision of 'good parenting', 'appropriate children's conduct' and so on" (Oswell, 1999, p. 52), a shift is effected from direct control by government to governance through "action at a distance" (and thus presenting a solution to the challenge of pan-European policy that permits cultural variation in its implementation).

6. Hill and Tisdall (1997) review evidence for the incidence of child abuse within the family that, although difficult to measure, is far more common than abuse by strangers.

7. This concern is rendered invisible by a legalistic, rather than a moral, approach to privacy. As

Perri 6 stresses, "dignity, though important to most people in every society, is not well articulated in moral languages that stress only rights and justice," for although invasions of privacy commonly undermine dignity and so matter to people, only rarely do they involve an actual injustice against which redress can be sought in law (1998, p. 36). Dignity may matter little in the relation between individuals and commercial organizations, but together with trust and respect, it is crucial to the relation between parents and children.

8. Namely, that the nature of media use is best researched more or less unobtrusively within its everyday context; the research process should be open to meanings salient to or expressed by respondents rather than those presumed by the researcher; user engagement is intimately related to the social context before, during, and after media use; a contextual approach should identify the distinctions and practices routinely performed by respondents in responding to circumstances; and last, a diversity of responses to media should be anticipated, both across individuals and for any one user over time or context (Schroder, Drotner, Kline, & Murray, 2003).

9. Specifically, 30 families were recruited, each with a child between 8 and 16 years of age who uses the Internet at home at least once a fortnight. The families were selected to represent a spread of social grades: 11 AB (upper/middle class), 11 C1 (lower middle/class), 8 C2DE (working class). Families also represented a range of ethnic origins, family types (nuclear, single parent), and geographic locations (urban, suburban, rural) across the Southeast of England. The sample contained 16 boys and 14 girls, of whom 11 were of primary school age and 19 of secondary school age (Livingstone and Bovill, 2001). The research team made four visits over a period of 1–2 months, resulting in 114 interviews/observations.

10. The methods used include both interviews and ethnographic-style observations, revealing some interesting discrepancies between self-report and observed practice. However, it should be noted that our ability to check on children's (and parents') honesty or dissembling was limited. Insofar as was practical, we checked claims about Internet use by asking to read e-mails listed in the inbox, noting which URLs came most readily to the child's mind or were listed as recently used in the drop-down address box. Any bias, therefore, is largely one-way: We saw what children showed us and drew our own conclusions; what they did not show us, we might guess at but could not see.

11. The teachers were asked to select the children at random (every fourth or fifth girl or boy from the register). The children were all asked for their written consent to participate in the group discussions, and

for children under the age of 16 years, written parental consent was sought in addition.

12. Much depends on age, of course. Father of Nell (15), is sanguine about providing a private space for Internet use: "this box room, what we call study, is a communal room. . . . So everybody can use it, and is useful in that maybe perhaps 2 years ago Gill was at home, she spent a lot of time doing homework, project work, on the computer, and now Nell is doing the same, and occasionally Chris uses the computer, and in the evening, the weekend, I use computer as well. So everyone can have their own privacy in their own little room, and yet we've got this little box room that everyone can go to."

13. The missing strategy here is, of course, the one for which more attention and resources is required; namely, safety awareness and education (Livingstone, 2001). But the problems are considerable. Recall Euan, 10 years old, unexpectedly encountering an image of anal penetration. Which parents regard it as their role to prepare children of this age for such material? And which teacher, engaged in a lesson on history or German, is ready to drop everything to address such an interruption to the lesson? For such children, parents and teachers, a technical fix is just what is wanted.

14. Online safety software is not the only technology being developed for parents to check on their children—consider the growing use of video cameras at home, even in the child's bedroom; the use of GIS software to track children's movements through their cell phone; and more recently, the development of a computer chip to be inserted under the skin to monitor where they go outside. In seeking to protect children's safety, it is evident that we risk undermining their privacy.

15. Indeed, few filtering programs flag up the value of discussing such monitoring with children (*Childsafe* being one exception that displays an optimal "Acceptable Use" policy to communicate parental rules to the child), leaving one to presume that unobtrusive monitoring, conveying little trust in the child, is generally deemed crucial. See http:// www.pearlsw.com/home/index.com (for *Cybersnoop*), http://www.netnanny.com, http://www.cyberpatrol .com, http://www.aol.com/info/parentcontrol.html, http://www.surfcontrol.com, http://www.webroot .com/wb/products/childsafe/index.php (retrieved May 29, 2003).

16. In a way that was not the case for media hitherto, many parents are learning about computers and the Internet alongside their children, and they tend to express amazement at their children's facility with the new technology. Indeed, children often find themselves much valued within the family, admired for their skills on the Internet, the use of which is an

occasion for approval and expertise that—significantly—may not have otherwise have come their way (Livingstone and Bober, 2003).

17. See Livingstone (2001). Consider also the U.K. government's recent reversal of its decision to provide every pupil with an e-mail address, having realized the risks of listing these on the school web site (indeed, the risks of making public any information about particular children—the school photo, cup winners, etc.). Children's lost opportunities—although in some cases justified—should be recognized.

18. After all, the same factors that make the media environment difficult to regulate nationally—as it becomes more complex, diversified, commercialized, and globalized, including more potentially harmful contents—also make it difficult to regulate domestically, within the home. Yet a key strategy of the present U.K. government, notwithstanding parents' avowed preference for top-down media regulation in the public interest rather than being "empowered" to regulate difficult-to-implement technology in their own homes, is to devolve responsibility for accessing and using media from the state to individual members of the public, this being framed in policy terms as a matter of media literacy (Livingstone, 2004).

19. Article 16 of the United Nations Convention on the Rights of the Child specifies that "no child shall be subjected to arbitrary or unlawful interference with his or her privacy."

20. As *Cybersitter*'s promotional materials elaborate, "parents, not censorship can help to make Cyberspace a safe place to play." (*http://www.solid oak.com/*, Retrieved September 12, 2005).

References

6, Perri (1998). The Future of Privacy. Volume 1: Private life and public policy. London: Demos.

Bingham, N., Valentine, G., & Holloway, S. (1999). Wheredo you want to go tomorrow? Connecting childrenand the Internet. *Environment and Planning D: Society and Space, 17*(6), 655–672.

Bovill, M., & Livingstone, S. (2001). Bedroom culture and the privatization of media use. In Livingstone, S., & Bovill, M. (Ed.), *Children and their changing media environment: A European comparative study* (pp. 179–200). Mahwah NJ: Lawrence Erlbaum Associates.

Castells, M. (2002). The Internet Galaxy: Reflections on the Internet, business, and society. Oxford: Oxford University Press.

Clark, L. S. (2005). The constant contact generation: Exploring teen friendships online. In S. Mazzarelle (Ed.), *Girl Wide Web* (pp. 203–222). New York: Peter Lang.

Corsaro, W. A. (1997). *The sociology of childhood*. Thousand Oaks, CA: Pine Forge.

European Parliament. (1997). Resolution on the Commission communication on illegal and harmful content on the Internet. Brussells: European Commission.

Fahey, T. (1995). Privacy and the family. *Sociology, 29*, 687–703.

Giddens, A. (1993). The transformation of Intimacy: Sexuality, love and eroticism in modern societies. Cambridge: Polity.

Goffman, E. (1959). *The presentation of self in everyday life*. Harmondsworth: Penguin.

Hill, M., & Tisdall, K. (1997). *Children and society*. London: Longman.

Internet Crime Forum. (2000). *Chat wise, street wise: Children and Internet chat services*. London: The Internet Crime Forum IRC Subgroup.

James, A., Jenks, C., & Prout, A. (1998). *Theorizing childhood*. Cambridge, UK: Cambridge University Press.

Livingstone, S. (1998). Mediated childhoods: A comparative approach to young people's changing media environment in Europe. *European Journal of Communication, 13*(4), 435–456.

Livingstone, S. (2001). *Online freedom & safety for children*. Research report 3. London: IPPR/Citizens Online Research Publication. Retrieved January 31, 2003, from http://www.children-go-online.net.

Livingstone, S. (2002). *Young people and new media*. London: Sage.

Livingstone, S. (2003). Children's use of the Internet: Reflections on the emerging research agenda. *New Media and Society, 5*(2), 147–166.

Livingstone, S. (2005). In defence of privacy: Varieties of publicness in the individualised, privatised home. In S. Livingstone (Ed.), *Audiences and publics: When cultural engagement matters for the public sphere* (pp. 163–186). Bristol, UK: Intellect Press.

Livingstone, S., & Bober, M. (2003). *UK children go online: Listening to young people's experiences*. London: LSE Report. Retrieved January 31, 2003, from http://www.children-go-online.net.

Livingstone, S., & Bober, M. (2004). *UK children go online: Surveying the experience of young people and their parents*. London: LSE Report. Retrieved September 12, 2005, from *http://www.children-go-online.net*.

Livingstone, S., & Bober, M. (2005). *UK Children Go Online: Final report of key project findings*. London: LSE Report. Retrieved from *http://www.children-go-online.net*.

Livingstone, S., & Bober, M. (In press-a). UK children go online. In B. Anderson, M. Brynin & Y. Raban (Eds.), *e-Living: Life in a Digital Europe*.

Livingstone, S., & Bober, M. (In press-b). Regulating the internet at home: Contrasting the perspectives of children and parents. In D. Buckingham & R. Willett (Eds.), *Digital Generations*.

Livingstone, S., & Bovill, M. (1999). *Young people, new media*. London: London School of Economics and Political Science. Retrieved September 12, 2005, from http://www.lse.ac.uk/collections/media@lse/whosWho/soniaLivingstonePublications 3.htm.

Livingstone, S., & Bovill, M. (2001). *Families and the Internet: An observational study of children and young people's Internet use*. Public report. London School of Economics and Political Science. Retrieved January 31, 2003, from http://www.lse.ac.uk/collections/media@lse/whosWho/soniaLivingstonePublications3.htm.

Lyon, D. (1994). *The electronic eye: the rise of surveillance society*. Minneapolis: University of Minnesota Press.

Montgomery, K. (2001). The new on-line children's consumer culture. In Singer, D., & Singer, J. (Eds.), *Handbook of children and the media* (pp. 635–650). London: Sage.

ONS (2005). *Internet Access: 12.9 million house-holds now online*. London: Office for National Statistics. Retrieved June 3, 2005, from http://www.statistics.gov.uk.

Oswell, D. (1998). The place of "childhood" in Internet content regulation: A case study of policy in the UK. *International Journal of Cultural Studies, 1*(1), 131–151.

Oswell, D. (1999). The dark side of cyberspace: Internet content regulation and child protection. *Convergence: The Journal of Research into New Media Technologies, 5*(4), 42–62.

Qvortrup, J. (1995). Childhood and modern society: a paradoxical relationship. In Brannen, J. & O'Brien, M. (Eds.), *Childhood and parenthood* (pp. 189–198). London: Institute of Education, University of London.

Regan, P. M. (2002). Privacy as a common good in the digital world. *Information, Communication and Society, 5*(3), 382–405.

Rice, R. (2002). Primary issues in Internet use: Access, civic and community involvement, and social interaction and expression. In Lievrouw, L. & Livingstone, S. (Eds.), *The handbook of new media: Social shaping and consequences of ICTs* (pp. 109–129). London: Sage.

Russell, D. (1980). The incidence and prevalence of intrafamilial and extrafamilial sexual abuse for female children. *Child Abuse and Neglect, 7*, 133–146.

Schroder, K., Drotner, K., Kline, S., & Murray, C. (2003). *Researching audiences*. London: Arnold.

Sheehan, K. B. (2002). Toward a typology of internet users and online privacy concerns. *The Information Society, 18*(1), 21–32.

Stein, L., & Sinha, N. (2002). New global media and communication policy. In Lievrouw, L. & Livingstone, S. (Eds.), *The handbook of new media: Social shaping and consequences of ICTs* (pp. 410–431). London: Sage.

Turkle, S. (1995). Life on the screen: Identity in the age of the Internet. New York: Simon & Schuster.

Turow, J. (2001). Family boundaries, commercialism, and the Internet: a framework for research. *Journal of Applied Developmental Psychology, 22*(1), 73–86.

Turow, J., & Nir, L. (2000). The Internet and the family: The view of U.S. parents. In Feilitzen, C. C., and Carlsson, U. (Eds.), *Children in the new media landscape: Games, pornography, perceptions* (pp. 331–348). Goteborg, Sweden: The UNESCO International Clearinghouse on Children and Violence on the Screen at Nordicom.

Turow, J., & Ribak, R. (2003). Internet power and social context: A globalization approach to web privacy concerns. *Journal of Broadcasting & Electronic Media, 47*(3), 328–349

Wigley, K., & Clarke, B. (2000). *Kids.net*. London: National Opinion Poll.

Linda A. Jackson, Alexander von Eye,

Frank A. Biocca, Gretchen Barbatsis,

Yong Zhao, and Hiram E. Fitzgerald

Children's Home Internet Use
Antecedents and Psychological, Social, and Academic Consequences

The HomeNetToo project (2000–2003) is a longitudinal field study of the antecedents and consequences of home Internet use in low-income families (NSF-ITR 085348; http://www.msu.edu/user/jackso67/homenettoo). Three objectives guided the design of the project. The first was to identify psychological and social factors that may contribute to the digital divide in Internet use. The second objective was to examine the psychological and social effects of using the Internet at home. The third objective was to determine whether home Internet use influenced academic performance. The focus was on African Americans because evidence indicates a persistent racial divide in Internet use. Using a longitudinal design, we obtained repeated measures of key psychological and social constructs, as well as multiple measures of Internet use that were automatically recorded (daily) for 16 months. Thus, the design permitted an evaluation of cause–effect relationships and fine-grained analyses of Internet use based on measures less susceptible to social desirability and recall biases than self-reported measures of Internet use.

Participants in the HomeNetToo project were 120 adults and 140 children who were living in a midsized urban community in the Midwestern United States. Adult participants were recruited at meetings held at their child's middle school and at the Black Child and Family Institute in Lansing, Michigan. Requirements for participation were that the child be eligible for the federally subsidized school lunch program, that the family had had a working telephone line for the previous 6 months, and that the family had never had home Internet access. Participants agreed to have their Internet use automatically and continuously recorded, to complete surveys at multiple points during the project, and to participate in home visits. In exchange for participation, families received home computers, Internet access, and in-home technical support during the Internet recording period (16 months).

Most of the HomeNetToo children were African American (83%), male (58%), and living in single-parent households (75%) in which the median annual income was $15,000 (USD). The average age was 13 years. We begin this chapter by examining the frequency and nature of HomeNetToo children's home Internet use. Next, we examine potential antecedents of these childrens' Internet use; namely, personal characteristics (e.g., race, computer skills) and situational factors (e.g., computer use by family and friends) that we expected to influence Internet use. Although previous research has considered demographic predictors of Internet use, situational factors have been largely ignored. Last, we examine the consequences of home Internet use for children's psychological, social, and academic outcomes. Specifically, we examine whether Internet use predicted changes in the affect, self-concept, social behavior, and academic performance of HomeNetToo children.

Frequency and Nature of Children's Internet Use

Numerous surveys have attempted to measure the extent to which children use the Internet at home. Estimates vary, depending on how Internet use was measured (e.g., self-report, automatically recorded), ages of children sampled, when data were collected (i.e., year of study), and how Internet use was defined (e.g., time online, frequency of use). At one extreme are estimates that children use the Internet at least 1 hour each day. At the other extreme are estimates as low as 3 hours a week (Kraut, Scherlis, Mukhopadhyay, Manning, & Kiesler, 1996; Stanger & Gridina, 1999; Woodward & Gridina, 2000). Notwithstanding the absence of definitive data, the popular opinion is that today's children, at least in the United States, spend a great deal of time online (e.g., Kraut et al., 1996; Tapscott, 1998; Stanger & Gridina, 1999; Pew Internet and American Life Project, 2000a, 2002; UCLA Internet Report, 2000, 2001, 2003; Woodward & Gridina, 2000; National Science Foundation [NSF] Report, 2001; Kids Count Snapshot, 2002).

Other research has examined the nature of children's Internet use—what children actually do when they go online. Again findings vary, depending on factors just discussed (e.g., age of children). Most studies find that children's primary motivation for using the Internet is schoolwork; specifically, searching for information needed for school projects (Kraut et al., 1996; Turow, 1999; Turow & Nir, 2000; NSF report, 2001; Valkenburg & Soeters, 2001; Pew Internet and American Life Project, 2002). The second most important motivation for going online is to communicate with others using e-mail, instant messaging, and chat (Kraut et al., 1996; Turow, 1999). However, the extent of children's Internet use for the purpose of communication is a bit unclear, in part because few studies have recorded actual versus self-reported use. The only U.S. study to do so was conducted in

1995–1996. Results for the combined sample of adults and children in that study indicated that although participants reported that e-mail was a very important reason for going online, they actually sent fewer than one e-mail a week (Kraut et al., 1996).

Relationships between sociodemographic characteristics and Internet use are less well established for children than they are for adults. For adults, sociodemographic characteristics clearly predict Internet access or location in the "digital divide" (Norris, 2001). Although the global digital divide is huge compared to the divide in the United States (Jackson, 2004a; Norris, 2001), an access divide in the United States that is based on age, race, income, and education still exists (U.S. Department of Commerce, 1995, 1999, 2000, 2002). Moreover, the digital "use" divide may be even greater than the "access" divide and may depend on characteristics other than those that determine the access divide (Hoffman & Novak, 1998; Jackson, von Eye, Barbatsis, Biocca, Fitzgerald & Zhao, 2004; Jackson, Ervin, Gardner and Schmitt, 2001a; Borgida et al., 2002; Gorski, 2002; Alverez, 2003; Cho, de Zuniga, Rojas, & Shah, 2003; Jackson, Barbatsis, von Eye, Biocca, , Fitzgerald & Zhao, 2003a, 2003b; Jackson, von Eye, Biocca, Barbatsis, Zhao & Fitzgerald, 2003c; Payton, 2003).

With respect to sociodemographic characteristics and children's Internet use, findings indicate that older children use the Internet more than younger children do, especially for communicating with peers (Turow & Nir, 2000; Pew Internet and American Life Project, 2002). Race differences in children's Internet use have yet to be examined, especially when access to the Internet is not an issue (i.e., within socioeconomic groups). Among teens, there is some evidence that African Americans use the Internet less than do Caucasian Americans (Hoffman & Novak, 1998; Jackson et al., 2001a; Kraut et al., 1996), a difference typically attributed to parental income and education (Robinson, DiMaggio, & Hargittai, 2003). However, as noted earlier, additional factors may be needed to explain the racial digital divide—factors that influence Internet use even when access is not an issue (e.g., Facer & Furlong, 2001; Alverez, 2003; Jackson et al., 2003a, 2003b, 2003c). A report by the NSF on the use of information technology (IT) in the home concluded that "Race/ethnicity disparities in home access to IT cannot typically be explained by income or level of education alone. There are deeper cultural and social factors influencing the adoption process, but these factors have not been empirically identified or isolated" (p. vii, Executive Summary, NSF Report, 2001).

Race differences in the nature of Internet use have been reported, but only for adults. According to a report by the Pew Internet and American Life Project (2000b), African Americans are more likely than Caucasian Americans to use the Internet to listen to and to download music; to obtain information about health, religion, jobs, education, and places to live; and to play games. African Americans are less likely than Caucasian Americans to use the Internet to maintain connections with family and friends. Whether children of different races use the Internet differently has yet to be investigated. It may be that when access to the Internet is not an issue, all children of the "Net generation" use the Internet equally, or it may be that the "deeper cultural and social factors" referred to in the NSF report influence the nature of children's Internet use.

Gender differences in Internet access and use are prevalent worldwide but have decreased dramatically within the United States (Jackson, 2004b). When the Internet first emerged into public consciousness (circa 1995), about 95% of its U.S. users were male. By 2002, about half the Internet users in the United States were female (U.S. Department of Commerce, 2002). Some researchers have argued that the proliferation of communication tools on the Internet is responsible for the influx of women into the online world (Roberts, Foehr, Rideout, & Brodie, 1999; Subrahmanyam, Greenfield, Kraut, & Gross, 2001). In support of this view, studies indicate that women are more likely than men to use the Internet for communication (Roberts et al., 1999; Jackson, Ervin, Gardner, & Schmitt, 2001b; Subrahmanyam, et al., 2001). Gender differences in web use have also been observed. Men are more likely than women to search for financial and sports information and to make purchases on the web. Women are more likely than men to search for information about health, jobs, and religion (Pew Internet and American Life Project, 2000a).

Studies of gender and children's Internet use in the United States are sparse and have produced mixed results. One study found gender parity in all Internet activities except the number of web sites visited: boys (ages 8–13 years) visited more web sites than did girls of the same age (Roberts et al., 1999).

Another study found that although teenage girls used the Internet less than did teenage boys, they were more likely than boys to use e-mail (56% of the girls versus 43% of the boys; Kraut et al., 1996).

In summary, research indicates that children use the Internet at home for as little as 3 hours a week to as much as 1 hour a day. The nature of children's Internet activities is unclear in part because there are so few studies and in part because even fewer measure actual Internet use (versus self-reported use). The relationships between children's sociodemographic characteristics and Internet use, in the United States or elsewhere, are similarly unclear.

Findings from the HomeNetToo Project

As noted earlier, in the HomeNetToo project we automatically recorded multiple measures of daily Internet use for 16 months. Here we focus on seven of those daily measures: time online (minutes), number of sessions (logins), number of domains visited, number of e-mails sent, number of instant message chat (IMC) messages sent, time in chats (minutes), and number of chats visited. To examine changes over time, these measures were divided into five time periods that roughly corresponded to survey administrations (3 months and 9 months), plus two additional periods to assess half-year and 1-year benchmarks. The time periods were as follows: time 1: 1–3 months; time 2: 4–6 months; time 3: 7–9 months; time 4: 10–12 months; time 5: 13–16 months.

Frequencies of Internet use for each measure and time period are presented in table 11.1. Averaged across the 16 months of recording, children used the Internet about 30 minutes a day. They participated in less than one session a day, indicating that they did not log on daily, and they visited about 10 unique domains each day. However, the children sent a negligible amount of e-mail: less than one e-mail message per week. Similarly, IMC messaging and chat activity were uncommon occurrences. Medians for all of these communication activities were zero. Also evident from table 11.1 is the high variability in Internet use, which, taken together with evidence of skewed distributions, led us to use log-transformed measures in all subsequent analyses.

Table 11.1. Frequency of children's Internet use.

	Time online (minutes)	No. of session (logins)	No. of domains visited	No. of emails sent	No. of IMC messages sent	Time in chats (minutes)	No. of chats visited
Time 1: 1–3 months							
Mean	27.09	0.75	8.69	0.10	0.20	1.53	0.03
Median	12.57	0.38	3.95	0.00	0.00	0.00	0.00
SD	37.64	0.95	11.11	0.57	1.16	5.15	0.08
Time 2: 4–6 months							
Mean	29.70	0.73	12.41	0.1	0.17	1.53	0.02
Median	11.73	0.34	6.17	0.00	0.00	0.00	0.00
SD	41.15	0.99	15.51	0.48	0.80	5.06	0.06
Time 3: 7–9 months							
Mean	27.41	0.60	10.45	0.10	0.16	1.16	0.02
Median	8.89	0.23	4.69	0.00	0.00	0.00	0.00
SD	41.04	0.91	13.65	0.63	0.63	3.84	0.05
Time 4: 9–12 months							
Mean	26.87	0.48	8.96	0.10	0.04	0.34	0.01
Median	11.20	0.26	5.30	0.00	0.00	0.00	0.00
SD	46.41	0.71	11.11	0.62	0.16	0.97	0.02
Time 5: 13–16 months							
Mean	25.63	0.45	9.27	0.16	0.12	0.19	0.01
Median	9.05	0.21	5.33	0.00	0.00	0.00	0.00
SD	48.23	0.69	12.14	1.51	0.52	0.62	0.02

Sample sizes ranged from 138 to 143. Values are per day. All measures were automatically recorded.

The percentage of children who logged on to the Internet and the percentage who were using each of the Internet's communication tools (e-mail, IMC) for each time period are presented in table 11.2. The percentage who logged on to the Internet decreased from 91% at 3 months to 84% by the end of the 16–month trial. The percentage of children using e-mail dropped dramatically from an initial low level of 41% at 3 months to only 16% by the end of the trial. IMC messaging began low (27%) and remained low (25%), as did chat activity (23%–16%). Given the infrequency of communication activities and similarity across different ways of communicating, subsequent analyses focused only on e-mails that the children sent.

To further examine changes in Internet use over time, paired contrasts were performed. Time online did not change over the course of the 16-month trial. Number of sessions (i.e., log ins) decreased between 6 months and 9 months and remained at this level for the remainder of the trial. Number of domains visited increased between 3 months and 6 months but returned to the 3-month level by 9 months, where it remained through the end of the trial. Number of e-mails sent remained the same for the first year and then increased for the handful of children still using e-mail. IMC messaging followed a similar pattern. Chat activity decreased between 9 and 12 months and remained at this level for the remainder of the trial.

Table 11.2. Percentage of children logging on to the Internet and using its communication tools.

Activity	Time 1	Time 2	Time 3	Time 4	Time 5
Logins	91	90	96	85	84
E-mails	41	39	30	28	16
IMC messaging	27	27	30	28	25
Chat activities	23	28	24	22	16

Sample sizes ranged from 138 to 143.

Because most studies of Internet use rely on self-reports, we obtained self-report measures as well and compared them to automatically recorded measures of Internet use. Means for the self-reported Internet use measures at 1 month, 3 months, 9 months, and posttrial are presented in table 11.3. Correlations between self-reported and automatically recorded measures of Internet use are presented in table 11.4. As both tables indicate, children were quite accurate in reporting their Internet use. Self-reports were highly correlated with recorded Internet use for all time periods.

Antecedents of Children's Internet Use

Personal Characteristics

The first set of potential antecedents of Internet use that we considered were sociodemographic characteristics; specifically, age, race, and gender. As discussed earlier, research indicates that older children use the Internet more than do younger children (Pew Internet and American Life Project, 2002), especially to communicate with friends (Turow & Nir, 2000). More equivocal is the relationship between children's race and their Internet use. Although African-American adults use the Internet less than do Caucasian-American adults (U. S. Department of Commerce, Internet Reports, 1995, 1999, 2000, 2002; Kraut et al., 1996; Hoffman & Novak, 1998; Pew Internet and American Life Project, 2000b; Jackson et al., 2001a), it is not known whether African-American children use it less than do Caucasian-American children, especially when both have equal access to the Internet at home. Findings for gender and children's Internet use are sparse and equivocal (Kraut et al., 1996;

Roberts et al., 1999). Thus, we predicted only that older children would use the Internet more than would younger children, making no predictions about race and gender effects.

Other personal characteristics that we considered as potential antecedents of children's Internet use were computer skills and liking for computers (Subrahmanyam et al., 2001). Because computers remain the primary vehicle for delivering the Internet, we predicted that children with greater computer skills and children who liked computers more would use the Internet more than would children who, respectively, had lower computer skills and liked computers less.

Situational Factors

Surprisingly absent from research on Internet use are studies of how situational factors influence use, either for adults or children. Of particular interest with regard to children's Internet use are the effects of parental modeling and peer behavior. A vast literature on parental modeling indicates that children learn and perform the behaviors that they observe in parental models, especially when those behaviors are reinforced (Bandura, 1977, 1986; Barone, Maddux, & Snyder, 1997). There is also a vast literature indicating that peer behavior influences children's behavior, especially during adolescence (Ambert, 1997; Harris, 1998). Thus, we predicted that children's Internet use would be influenced by their perception that parental models used and enjoyed computers and the Internet. We also predicted that children whose close friends used and enjoyed computers and the Internet would use the Internet more than would children whose close friends did not use or enjoy computers and the Internet.

Also missing from research on Internet use are studies of the effects that early successes and fail-

Table 11.3. Means for self-reported measures of Internet use.

Activity	1 Month Mean	SD	3 Months Mean	SD	9 Months Mean	SD	Posttrial Mead	SD
Logins	3.68	1.35	—	—	3.70	1.36	3.68	1.36
E-mails	—	—	1.86	0.95	1.86	1.05	1.99	1.16

Sample sizes ranged from 138 to 141. Logins were measured by the question, How often do you logon to the Internet? 1 = almost never, 2 = two or three times a month, 3 = about once a week, 4 = two or three times a week, 5 = almost every day. E-mails were measured by the question, How many e-mails do you send per week? 1 = none, 2 = one to five e-mails a week, 3 = six to 10 e-mails a week, 4 = 11–20 e-mails a week, 5 = more than 20 e-mails a week. A dash indicates that no measure was obtained at that time.

Table 11.4. Correlations between automatically recorded and self-reported measures of Internet use.

Automatically recorded Internet use	Self-reported Internet use	r
Time online at time 1	Logins: 1 month	.52
Number of sessions at time 1	Logins: 1 month	.51
Time online at time 3	Logins: 9 months	.47
Number of sessions at time 3	Logins: 9 months	.46
Time online at time 5	Logins: Posttrial	.41
Number of sessions at time 5	Logins: Posttrial	.49
Number of e-mails sent at time 1	E-mails sent: 3 months	.33
Number of e-mails sent at time 3	E-mails sent: 9 months	.66

Sample sizes ranged from 138 to 141.

ures have on subsequent computer and Internet use. There is ample evidence in the psychological literature that early performance feedback has a strong influence on task persistence. In particular, negative feedback undermines persistence and may lead to abandoning the task altogether. In contrast, positive feedback encourages task persistence and contributes to successful task performance. Thus, we examined whether early difficulties using computers and the Internet, or early successes in solving computer problems, influenced subsequent Internet use. We predicted that experiencing difficulties would undermine use, whereas experiencing successes would increase use.

Findings from the HomeNetToo Project

Descriptive statistics for personal characteristics and situational factors that were considered potential antecedents to Internet use are presented in table 11.5. As noted earlier, 83% of the children were African American and 58% were male. The mean age was 13.6 years old. Self-rated computer skills averaged just below "4," where "4" indicated "good computer skills." Seventy-five percent of the sample said they "liked computers very much—it was one of their favorite things to do."

Turning to situational factors, 76% of the HomeNetToo children said that adults in their home really liked using computers. Almost half said that most of their close friends really liked using computers, and the remaining half said that a few of their close friends really liked using computers. The mean rating of how difficult it was to use the home computer was 3.23, where "3" indi-

cated "pretty easy." The mean rating of how often children were successful in solving computer problems was 2.81, where "3" indicated "usually" successful.

Regression analyses were used to examine whether personal characteristics predicted early Internet use. All personal characteristics were entered simultaneously in separate regressions to predict each of the four measures of Internet use at Time 1 (i.e., during the first 3 months of the project). The rationale for performing separate analyses for each Internet use measure was threefold. First, time online was considered in the analyses to permit comparisons between our findings and those of previous research, which typically used time online as the sole measure of Internet use. Second, analyzing multiple measures of Internet use provided information about the limitations or generalizability of our findings. For example, it may be that findings for time online, a relatively crude measure of Internet use, will not obtain for number of domains visited—a measure of more active engagement with the Internet. Third, analyzing multiple measures facilitated a distinction between Internet use for communication (i.e., e-mail) and Internet use for other purposes (e.g., information).

Results of the regression analyses to predict Internet use at Time 1 from personal characteristics are presented in table 11.6. Except gender, all other personal characteristics predicted time online, number of sessions, and number of domains visited—although two of the 12 beta coefficients were only marginally significant. Caucasian-American children, older children, children with greater computer skills, and children who liked computers

Table 11.5. Antecedents of Internet use: descriptive statistics.

Parameter	Value	
Personal characteristics		
Race		
African American	83%	
Caucasian American	17%	
Sex		
Male	58%	
Female	42%	
Age	$M = 13.57$	
	$SD = 1.95$	
Computer skills		
1 = no computer skills	$M = 3.71$	
2 = poor computer skills	$SD = 0.83$	
3 = average computer skills		
4 = good computer skills		
5 = very good computer skills		
Computer liking		
1 = not very much.	$M = 2.70$	1 = 4%
2 = a little, but I'd rather do other things	$SD = 0.54$	2 = 21%
3 = very much, it's one of my favorite things to do.		3 = 75%
Situational factors		
Family's computer use		
1 = adults in my home really like using computers.	$M = 1.29$	1 = 76%
2 = adult in my home don't really like using computers, but use them anyway.	$SD = 0.57$	2 = 18%
3 = adults in my home don't really like using computers and don't use them.		3 = 6%
Friends' computer use		
1 = most of my close friends really like using computers.	$M = 1.59$	1 = 46%
2 = a few of my close friends really like using computers.	$SD = 0.59$	2 = 49%
3 = none of my close friends really likes using computers.		3 = 5%
Difficulty using computers		
1 = very difficult	$M = 3.23$	1 = 2%
2 = a little difficult	$SD = 0.68$	2 = 10%
3 = pretty easy		3 = 53%
4 = very easy		4 = 35%
Success solving computer problems		
1 = almost never	$M = 2.81$	1 = 8%
2 = sometimes	$SD = 0.93$	2 = 31%
3 = usually		3 = 34%
4 = almost always		4 = 27%

Sample sizes ranged from 138 to 141.

more used the Internet more than did African-American children, younger children, children with less computer skills, and children who liked computers less, respectively.

Additional analyses were performed to examine whether personal characteristics measured early in the project predicted later Internet use (i.e., use at times 2, 3, 4, and 5) after controlling for use during the preceding time period (i.e., use at time 1, 2, 3, and 4, respectively). Not surprisingly, Internet use during the preceding time period was a very strong predictor of subsequent use. Beta coefficients for previous use ranged from .41 (number of e-mails sent at time 2 from number of e-mails sent at time 1) to .67 (time online at time 5 from time online at time 4). Nevertheless, personal characteristics continued

Table 11.6. Prediction of early Internet use from personal characteristics.

	Time online	No. of sessions	No. of domains	No. of e-mails sent
Race	0.21*	0.20*	0.17†	−0.29*
Age	0.29*	0.30*	0.27*	0.02
Gender	0.03	0.06	0.07	0.17
Computer skills	0.21*	0.21*	0.16†	0.09
Computer liking	0.23*	0.19*	0.19*	0.02
Adjusted R^2	.21*	.19*	.11*	.18
F-ratio	$F(5,100) = 6.53$, $p < .001$	$F(5,100) = 5.80$, $p < .001$	$F(5,100) = 3.65$, $p < .01$	$F(5, 51) = 1.49$, $p < .21$

$*p < .05$; $†p < .10$. Values are standardized beta coefficients. Internet use is for time 1 (1–3 months).

to predict Internet use in a number of analyses. Age marginally predicted all four measures of Internet use at time 2, but not thereafter. Older children used the Internet more than did younger children. Computer skills predicted three measures of Internet use at time 3, either marginally (time online, number of sessions) or significantly (number of domains visited). Greater computer skills were associated with more Internet use. Race predicted Internet use at time 5, but only marginally. African-American children spent less time online and visited fewer domains than did Caucasian-American children.

Results of the regression analyses to predict Internet use at time 1 from situational factors are presented in table 11.7. Difficulty using computers predicted time online; children who found using the computer easier spent more time online. Success in solving computer problems marginally predicted time online—children who had more success solving computer problems spent more time online. Parental modeling of computer use and peer computer use did not predict Internet use, regardless of how use was

measured. Additional analyses to predict later Internet use from situational factors, after controlling for Internet use during the preceding time period, revealed no significant effects.

We also examined whether situational factors that were considered potential antecedents of Internet use changed over time, and whether these changes were related to later Internet use. Paired t-tests indicated that computer skills increased steadily throughout the trial, but liking for computers remained constant (and high; table 11.8). Perceptions of adult family members' liking for and use of computers changed over time in the direction of less liking and less use. The reverse was true for perceptions of friends. Thus, by the end of the trial, children were more likely than at the beginning of the trial to believe that adults in their home did not like and did not use computers and that most of their close friends really liked using computers.

Ratings of the difficulty that children experienced using the computer and success solving

Table 11.7. Prediction of early Internet use from situational factors.

	Time online	No. of sessions	No. of domains visited	No. of e-mails sent
Family's computer use	−0.14	−0.06	−0.13	−0.06
Friends' computer use	0.10	0.08	0.08	−0.08
Difficulty using computers	0.20*	0.14	0.01	−0.18
Success solving computer problems	0.18†	0.13	0.15	0.08
Adjusted R^2	.09*	.02	.01	.04
F-ratio	$F(4,122) = 4.03$, $p < .01$	$F(4,124) = 1.62$, $p < .17$	$F(4,124) = 1.40$, $p < .24$	$F(4, 52) = 0.45$, $p < .77$

$*p < .05$, $†p < .10$. Values are standardized beta coefficients. Internet use is for time 1 (1–3 months).

Table 11.8. Changes in antecedents of Internet use during the 16-month trial.

	1 Month	9 Months	Posttrial
Computer skills	3.73	3.87	4.07
Computer liking	2.70	2.67	2.67
Family's computer use			
1 = adults in my home like using computers	76.4	68.4	60.4
2 = adults in my home don't like using computers, but use them anyway	17.9	26.3	29.1
3 = adults in my home don't like using computers and don't use them	5.7	5.3	10.4
Friends' computer use			
1 = most of my close friends like using computers	46.4	50.4	50.7
2 = a few of my close friends like using computers	48.6	46.6	43.3
3 = none of my close friends likes using computers	5.0	3.0	6.0
Difficulty using computers	3.25	3.25	3.37
Success solving computer problems	2.84	2.95	3.08

Sample sizes ranged from 138 to 141.

computer problems also changed during the 16-month trial. By the end of the project, children reported less difficulty using computers and more success solving computer problems.

Additional regression analyses were performed to evaluate whether personal characteristics and situational factors that had changed by 9 months predicted Internet use at time 4 (i.e., computer skills, adult family members' liking of and use of computers, friends' liking of computers, difficulty using computers, and success solving computer problems). None predicted Internet use after controlling for use during the preceding time period (i.e., time 3).

Consequences of Children's Internet Use

Among the most fundamental of questions about children's use of IT is whether it benefits or harms them. More specifically, does IT use influence children's psychological, social, or cognitive outcomes? A number of recent reviews of the literature indicate that the answer to this question is an unequivocal "maybe." According to a report by the NSF, "Research on the actual impacts of IT [information technology] on home, family and individual household members is *extremely limited in scale and scope* . . . there is a lack of data collection on the actual impacts of computer and Internet use on homes, families and individual household members. . . . Relatively few data resources on IT in the home meet existing standards of acceptable qual-

ity for policy and scholarly analyses" (NSF Report, February, 2001, Executive Summary, pp. viii—ix; emphasis in original).

Research on the consequences of IT use has focused primarily on computer use, typically in contexts other than the home. Most studies are survey studies or other one-shot efforts that cannot establish causal relationships between IT use and child outcomes. With these limitations in mind, we briefly review the research on the psychological, social, and cognitive outcomes associated with children's IT use, and the predictions these findings suggest for the relationship between Internet use and child outcomes.

Psychological Outcomes

Does children's use of IT influence their psychological outcomes? In summarizing this research, Shields and Behrman (2000) concluded that there is no clear evidence that children's computer use is directly related to psychological outcomes. However, they note that there are few studies of this relationship, and fewer still that address the effects of Internet use rather than computer use. Two related studies that did address this relationship found that for teens, greater Internet use was associated with greater loneliness and depression (Kraut, Patterson, Lundmark, Kiesler, Mukopadhyay, & Scherlis, 1998), but these effects dissipated with Internet experience (Kraut, Kiesler, Boneva, Cummings, Helgeson, & Crawford, 2002). Overall, there is insufficient evidence for predicting whether or not children's Internet use influences psychological outcomes, such as general affect or how they feel about themselves (i.e., self-esteem).

Social Outcomes

Does children's IT use influence their social outcomes? Findings for the social domain are as sparse and inconclusive as findings for the psychological domain. In reviewing this research, Becker (2000) and Subrahmanyam and colleagues (Subrahmanyam, Kraut, Greenfield, & Gross, 2000) independently concluded that there are few documented negative social effects of using IT, and there may be some positive effects. For example, although early findings indicated that teens who used the Internet more had less social contact with family and friends than did those who used it less (Kraut et al., 1998), these effects dissipated with Internet experience (Kraut et al., 2002; c.f., Nie & Erbring, 2000). Other findings indicate that young people use the Internet to keep in touch with family and friends, thereby increasing rather than decreasing their social contacts (Pew Internet and American Life Project, 2002; UCLA Internet Project, 2000). However, researchers are quick to point out that more research is needed before drawing conclusions about the social effect of IT use for children (Katz & Rice, 2002).

Research predating the Internet has focused on two areas: the social effect of computer use in the classroom and the effects of video game playing on social behavior, particularly aggression (Dietz, 1998; Zillman & Weaver, 1999). Findings indicate that classroom computer use by young children (5–12 years old) sometimes facilitates social interaction and cooperation, friendship formation, and constructive group activities (Clements, 1987). Playing violent computer games sometimes leads to aggressive behavior, but primarily in children already prone to aggression and regardless of the amount of time spent playing these games (Fling et al., 1992). Other studies find no relationship between violent computer game playing and children's aggressive behavior (van Schie & Wiegman, 1997; Wiegman & van Schie, 1998). Thus, as was the case for psychological outcomes, there is insufficient evidence for predicting whether or not children's Internet use will influence social outcomes, such as number of close friends and time spent interacting with family and friends.

Cognitive Outcomes

Does children's use of IT influence their cognitive outcomes? After reviewing dozens of studies relating to school learning with computer-based technology, including five meta-analytic reviews, Roschelle and colleagues concluded that the findings are inconclusive (Roschelle, Pea, Hoadley, Gordon, & Means, 2000). For example, a meta-analytic review of over 500 studies (K–12 students) found that using computer tutoring applications had positive effects on achievement test scores. However, other computer uses, such as simulations and enrichment applications, had fewer positive effects (Kulik, 1994). Still other findings indicate that the benefits of computer-based instruction are clearer for math and science than for other subjects. For example, a study by the Educational Testing Service found that the use of computers to actively engage higher-order thinking skills was related to better academic performance in math among fourth and eight graders (Wenglinsky, 1998).

Roschelle et al. (2000) offered three explanations for the equivocal findings with respect to computer-based instruction and cognitive outcomes: (1) variability in hardware and software among schools participating in the research; (2) failure to accompany technology use with concurrent reforms in other areas, such as curriculum, assessment, and teacher professional development; and (3) lack of rigorous, structured longitudinal studies. The researchers suggested that computer technology can help students learn things better (how) and learn better things (what) when the technology supports the four fundamentals of learning: active engagement, participation in groups, frequent interaction and feedback, and connections to real-world contexts.

Subrahmanyam and colleagues also reviewed the research on computer use and cognitive skills, focusing on a broad array of competencies—particularly visual intelligence skills (e.g., spatial skills, iconic and image representation skills; Subrahmanyam et al., 2000, 2001). They concluded that computer use does contribute to cognitive development, at least in terms of visual skills. For example, studies indicate that playing certain types of computer games (i.e., action games that involve rapid movement, imagery, intense interaction, and multiple activities occurring simultaneously) improves visual intelligence skills, "skills that provide 'training wheels' for computer literacy," that are "especially useful in the fields of science and technology, where proficiency in manipulating images on a screen is increasingly important" (p. 128). However, they also point out that "computer game playing can enhance a particular skill only if the game uses that skill and if the child's initial skill level has matured to a certain level" (p. 128). Moreover, "much of the existing research on computer games has measured effects only immediately after playing, and thus does not address questions about the cumulative impact of interactive games on learning" (p. 128).

Other findings point to a relationship between IT use and academic performance, although causal relationships have yet to be established (Rocheleau, 1995; Cole, 1996; Blanton, Moorman, Hayes, & Warner, 1997). Several studies have shown that the presence of educational resources in the home, including computers, is a strong predictor of academic success in math and science For example, one study found that having a home computer was associated with higher test scores in reading, even after controlling for family income and other factors related to reading performance (Atwell, 2000). Still another study found that participating in a networked community of learners improved educational outcomes for at-risk children (Project TELL, 1997). In a related vein, some researchers have suggested that recent nationwide increases in nonverbal intelligence test scores may be attributable to "exposure to the proliferation of imagery in electronic technology" (; Subrahmanyam, Kraut, Greenfield, & Gross, 2000, p. 128; see also Greenfield, 1998).

Overall, it remains uncertain whether using IT contributes to children's cognitive development, as indicated by commonly accepted measures of cognitive ability (such as school grades and standardized test scores; Shields & Behrman, 2000). The limited evidence indicates that home computer use is linked to slightly better academic performance, although most studies fail to control for other factors (such as family income and education). The effects of computer-based school and after-school activities are similarly unclear, although favorable effects have been observed under some circumstances (e.g., when there is a supportive learning environment). Even more uncertain is whether

using the Internet at home has positive or negative effects on cognitive outcomes, such as school grades and performance on standardized tests of achievement (NSF Report, 2001).

Findings from the HomeNetToo Project

Psychological Outcomes

The effects of Internet use on two psychological outcomes were considered in our research: affect and feelings of self-worth. Four measures of affect were considered: positive affect, negative affect, anxiety, and feelings of being liked by others. Each affect was measured by four items rated at 3 months, 9 months, and posttrial. Coefficient alphas for nine of the 12 affect composite measures (arithmetic averages) ranged from .70 to .81. Coefficient alphas for anxiety were .67 and .58 at 3 months and at posttrial, respectively. The coefficient alpha for negative affect at 3 months was .65. Because the latter coefficients are below the conventional level of acceptability (i.e., .70), results for these measures should be interpreted with caution.

Means for the four affect measures are presented in table 11.9. Paired contrasts indicated that positive affect decreased between 3 and 9 months, $t(129) = 2.77$, $p < .01$, and then remained at that level for the rest of the trial. Anxiety increased between 3 and 9 months, $t(129) = -3.76$, $p < .001$, and then returned to its initial level by posttrial [9 months versus posttrial, $t(132) = 2.18$, $p < .05$; 3 months versus post-trial, $t(128) = -1.19$, ns]. The increase in anxiety at 9 months may be attributable to the cooccurrence of these ratings with the 2001 attack on the World Trade Center. There were no changes in negative affect or feelings of being liked by others during the 16-month trial.

Race was unrelated to affect with one exception: African-American children had less positive affect ($M = 2.33$, $SD = .49$) at posttrial than did Caucasian-American children ($M = 2.58$, $SD = .36$; $F(1,132) = 5.19$, $p < .05$). Age was unrelated to affect.

Regression analyses to predict affect from Internet use included Internet use measures that were most proximate (in time) to the assessment of that affect. Thus, Internet use at time 1 (1–3 months)

Table 11.9. Mean levels of affect.

	Positive affect	Negative affect	Anxiety	Feeling liked
3 months				
Mean	2.47	1.51	1.42	2.67
SD	0.49	0.40	0.41	0.53
9 months				
Mean	2.36	1.57	1.55	2.63
SD	0.45	0.46	0.48	0.57
Posttrial				
Mean	2.37	1.51	1.46	2.66
SD	0.48	0.42	0.39	0.56

Sample sizes ranged from 134 to 138. Measures were composites of four items rated on 3-point scales: 1 = not at all, 2 = a little bit, 3 = very, with an affect term following each alternative (e.g., very happy).

was used to predict affect assessed at 3 months. Internet use at time 3 (7–9 months) was used to predict affect assessed at 9 months. Internet use at time 5 (13–16 months) was used to predict affect assessed at posttrial (16 months). Results indicated that at 3 months, more time online was associated with less negative affect, whereas participating in more sessions was marginally associated with more negative affect, $F(3,121) = 2.58$, $p < .057$. Although the overall regression equation was only marginally significant, standardized beta coefficients for time online and for number of sessions were significant at $p < .05$ and $p < .01$, respectively. In addition, visiting more domains was associated with stronger feelings of being liked by others, $F(3, 121) = 3.15$, $p < .05$. Internet use did not predict affect at 9 months. At posttrial, participating in more Internet sessions was associated with greater anxiety, whereas visiting more domains was associated with less anxiety, $F(3, 110) = 3.24$, $p < .05$.

Thus, Internet use during the first 3 months of home access predicted affect at the end of that time period. More time online was associated with less negative affect, but participating in more sessions was associated with more negative affect. It may be that participating in more sessions is attributable to more interruptions in Internet use, either for technical reasons (e.g., disconnects) or interpersonal reasons (e.g., distractions from household members). At posttrial, participating in more sessions, which may indicate interrupted Internet use, was again associated with negative feelings, but this time with anxiety.

Feelings of self-worth were measured at pretrial, 3 months, and 9 months by Harter's self-concept scale (Harter, 1986) and at posttrial by Rosenberg's self-esteem scale (Rosenberg, 1979). For the Harter measure, children indicated on 4-point rating scales how true a statement and its opposite were of them ("really true of me" or "sort of true of me"). For the Rosenberg measure, children indicated on 4-point rating scales how true positive and negative statements were of them. All ratings were scored so that higher values indicated higher ratings of self-worth.

Mean ratings of self-worth were similar at pretrial ($M = 3.10$, $SD = .70$), 3 months ($M = 3.19$, $SD = .65$), and 9 months ($M = 3.19$, $SD = .66$) but were higher at posttrial ($M = 3.44$, $SD = .52$), which is probably attributable to using a different measure. Neither race nor age was related to feelings of self-worth.

Regression analyses to predict feelings of self-worth from Internet use during the preceding time period (i.e., use at time 1 to predict self-worth at 3 months; use at time 3 to predict self-worth at 9 months, use at time 5 to predict self-worth at posttrial) revealed no significant effects. Thus, using the Internet had no effect on children's feelings of self-worth, which began high and remained high throughout the 16–month trial.

Social Outcomes

Social outcomes considered in the HomeNetToo project were number of close friends and changes in time allocated to family, friends, and other activities (e.g., sleeping). Children provided these measures at 3 months, 9 months, and posttrial.

Mean number of close friends was 6.98, 6.73, and 6.64 at 3 months, 9 months, and posttrial, respectively ($SD = 7.13$, 10.20, 6.60, respectively). None of these means was significantly different from another. Race and age were unrelated to the number of close friends, and neither was Internet use. Thus, regression analyses to predict number of close friends from Internet use during the preceding time period (i.e., Internet use at time 1 to predict number of close friends at 3 months, Internet use at Time 3 to predict number of close friends at 9 months, Internet use at time 5 to predict number of close friends at posttrial) revealed no significant effects.

Table 11.10 presents the mean changes in time allocated to family, friends, and other activities reported at 3 months, 9 months, and at posttrial. Two

Table 11.10. Mean changes in time allocation.

	Family	Friends	Alone	Clubs/ teams	Schoolwork	Phone	TV	Reading	Sleeping	Internet/ computer
3 Months										
Mean	1.93	1.99	1.92	2.14	1.96	2.20	2.07	2.17	1.87	2.04
SD	0.68	0.67	0.71	0.54	0.68	0.75	0.73	0.72	0.70	0.66
9 Months										
Mean	1.86	1.89	1.94	2.08	1.60	2.19	1.99	2.12	1.98	2.02
SD	0.63	0.68	0.73	0.53	0.66	0.75	0.74	0.77	0.73	0.72
Posttrial										
Mean	2.07	1.89	1.85	2.10	1.77	2.14	2.07	2.05	2.07	2.10
SD	0.64	0.63	0.67	0.52	0.70	0.74	0.72	0.73	0.73	0.68

Sample sizes ranged from 134 to 138. Three-point scales were used: 1 = more time than usual, 2 = same amount of time, 3 = less time than usual.

race differences were obtained. At 3 months, African-American children reported allocating more time than usual ($M = 2.10$) to technology activities (Internet and computer) than did Caucasian-American children [$M = 1.76$, $F(1, 137) = 5.61$, $p < .05$]. At 9 months, African-American children reported allocating more time than usual to reading [$M = 2.18$, $F(1, 132) = 4.17$, $p < .05$] compared to Caucasian-American children ($M = 1.83$). Age was unrelated to changes in time allocated to various activities.

How children allocated their time changed during the 16–month trial. Children spent less time than usual doing things with family members at posttrial than at 3 months, $t(128) = -2.27$, $p < .05$, or at 9 months, $t(132) = 3.33$, $p < .001$. They spent less time than usual doing homework, $t(128) = 2.22$, $p < .05$, and sleeping, $t(129) = -2.55$, $p < .05$, at posttrial than at 3 months.

Regression analyses to examine whether changes in time allocated to various activities were attributable to Internet use during the preceding time period revealed no significant effects. Thus, using the Internet did not influence how children allocated their time among family, friends, and other activities such as sports, clubs, sleeping, and watching television.

Cognitive Outcomes

Cognitive outcomes considered in the HomeNetToo project were grade point average (GPA) and performance on standardized tests of achievement (Jackson, von Eye, Biocca, Barbatsis, Zhao, & Fitzgerald, 2006).. Descriptive statistics for GPA are presented in table 11.11. Table 11.12 contains average per-

centile ranks on the Michigan Educational Assessment Program (MEAP) tests of reading and math achievement (comprehension scores and total scores). Measures were provided by the local school district (with parental permission). Missing data are attributable to children not taking tests or changing school districts.

As revealed in tables 11.11 and 11.12, children in the HomeNetToo project were performing below average in school. Mean GPA was about 2.0, and mean percentile ranks on the MEAP tests were around 30%. However, there was significant variability in both measures.

Race differences in academic performance were obtained. For all measures, Caucasian-American children scored higher than did African-American children. Thus, race was included in the regression analyses (step 1) to predict academic performance from Internet use. Age was unrelated to GPA or to standardized test scores.

As in the preceding analyses, the Internet use measures that were used to predict academic performance were those that were most proximate in time to the assessment of that particular academic performance measure. Thus, to predict GPA in spring 2001, we used measures of Internet use during the first 6 months of the project (i.e., means for time 1 and time 2, combined; January 1, 2001, to June 30, 2001). To predict GPA in fall 2001, we used measures of Internet use during the next 6 months (i.e., means for time 3 and time 4 combined; July 1, 2001, to December 31, 2001). To predict GPA in spring 2002, we used measures of Internet use at time 5 (i.e., January 1, 2002, until the end of the project, April 30, 2002).

Table 11.11. Mean grade point averages (GPAs).

	Fall 2000	Spring 2001	Fall 2001	Spring 2002
N	70	107	108	93
Mean	2.00	2.03	2.06	2.05
SD	1.02	0.94	0.89	1.09

Grade point average ranges from 0.0 to 4.0.

To predict performance on standardized tests of academic achievement (MEAP percentile ranks) in spring 2001, we used measures of Internet use during the first 6 months of the project (i.e., means for time 1 and time 2, combined). To predict performance in spring 2002, we used measures of Internet use at time 5.

Results of the regression analyses indicated that after entering race, Internet use did not predict GPA obtained after the first 6 months of the project (i.e., spring 2001). However, it did predict GPA obtained after 1 year of home Internet access [i.e., fall 2001; $F_{change}(3, 96) = 3.09$, $p < .05$] and at the end of the 16-month trial [i.e., spring 2002; $F_{change}(4, 76) = 2.88$, $p < .05$]. More Internet sessions were associated with higher GPAs.

Regression analyses to predict standardized test scores from Internet use indicated that Internet use during the first 6 months of the project predicted reading comprehension and total reading scores obtained during that time period [i.e., spring 2001; $F_{change}(3, 86) = 2.59$, 2.83, respectively, $p < .05$]. More time online was associated with higher reading comprehension and total reading scores. Similarly, Internet use during the last semester of the project (Time 5) predicted reading comprehension and total reading scores obtained during that semester [i.e., spring 2002; $F_{change}(3, 58) = 2.86$, 2.96, respectively, $p < .05$). More Internet sessions were associated with higher reading scores. Math scores

could not be predicted from Internet use, regardless of which time period was considered.

We also examined whether academic performance predicted Internet use rather than the reverse (as tested in the preceding analyses). Children's GPAs for fall 2000 (i.e., preproject) were used to predict Internet use at time 1, GPAs for spring 2001 were used to predict Internet use at time 3, and GPAs for fall 2001 were used to predict Internet use at Time 5. In none of these analyses did GPA predict subsequent Internet use.

Similar analyses were performed to determine whether performance on standardized tests predicted subsequent Internet use rather than the reverse (as tested in the preceding analyses). Percentile ranks on MEAP tests of reading achievement in spring 2001 did not predict Internet use during the time period that followed (i.e., time 3), regardless of how Internet use was measured (e.g., time online, number of sessions).

Thus, our findings indicate that children who used the Internet more had subsequently higher GPAs and higher scores on standardized reading achievement tests than did children who used the Internet less. The reverse was not true. Children who had higher GPAs and standardized test scores did not subsequently use the Internet more than did children with lower GPAs and test scores.

Modeling the Relationship Between Internet Use and Academic Performance

We used latent linear growth curve analysis to model relationships between Internet use and academic performance (i.e., GPA and standardized test scores in reading [MEAP-R]) using LISREL 8.53 (Joreskog & Sörbom, 1993). As indicated earlier,

Table 11.12. Percentile ranks on standardized tests of academic achievement.

	2001			2002		
	N	Mean	SD	N	Mean	SD
Reading comprehension	95	31.85	28.03	75	35.03	29.72
Reading total score	95	31.93	28.55	74	33.65	28.34
Math comprehension	80	32.45	25.69	50	33.60	23.30
Math total score	91	29.15	24.85	73	30.53	25.82

Tests were the Michigan Educational Assessment Program tests.

race predicted Internet use, GPA, and MEAP-R scores and was therefore included in the models. All models were estimated on the Y-side of LISREL, using maximum likelihood methods. Model fit was evaluated with respect to the overall goodness-of-fit χ^2, the root mean square error of approximation (RMSEA), and the goodness-of-fit index (GFI). Residual plots were also inspected to evaluate fit. A model was considered tenable if χ^2 was less than 2 *df*s, RMSEA was less than .05, GFI was greater than 0.9, and the residual plot showed no extreme values.

Model fitting was exploratory in that we modified models in response to results given by LISREL runs. Specifically, we added and deleted paths in the structural parts of the model to derive the most parsimonious models that contained all of the significant relationships among the four variables of interest: Internet use, race, MEAP-R, and GPA. Separate models were estimated for each Internet use measure for two reasons. First, different use measures showed different relationships to GPA and MEAP-R in the preceding analyses. Second, sample size constraints prevented fitting a model that included all four measures of Internet use. To capture elements of the time-specific relationships of repeatedly observed variables, we freed residual covariances, based on LISREL's residual analyses. Note that the number of covariances freed was small. For each model, the maximum number that could be freed was 66, and the maximum number that was freed was 10 (i.e., 15%). Differences in the number of freed residuals among the models are reflected in differences in degrees of freedom.

In each of the four models described next, race was considered a one-indicator factor and MEAP-R a two-indicator factor. The indicators are MEAP-R (total) in spring 2001 and MEAP-R (total) in spring 2002. GPA was a four-indicator factor, with GPAs obtained for the fall semesters of 2000 and 2001 and spring semesters of 2001 and 2002. The four models differed in indicators used for the fourth factor, Internet use. For each model, the Internet use factor had five indicators from the five data waves (i.e., times 1 to 5; January 1, 2001 to April 30, 2002). This factor was specified so that each path from this factor to its indicator was fixed to an even number. Numbers are ascending, with the earliest measure assigned 1 and the last measure assigned 5. Similarly, GPA scores were assigned values from 1 through 4. Because there were only two MEAP-R indicators, the

first indicator (spring 2001) was fixed to the value of 1, and the second indicator was free to be estimated (spring 2002). The following section describes the four models.

The Models

Time Online

The model for time online is presented in figure 11.1. The path coefficients that are indicated in the model are standardized, and only significant coefficients are shown. Model fit is good, as indicated by the goodness-of-fit $\chi^2 = 66.97$ (*df* = 46; *p* = .023), RMSEA = 0.056 (*p* = .35), and GFI = 0.93.

The structural aspect of the model in figure 11.1 indicate that race is a significant predictor of time online, with Caucasian-American children showing a stronger linear trend (i.e., greater increase in time online) than African-American children. Race is also a significant predictor of MEAP-R scores, again with Caucasian-American children showing a steeper increase than African-American children. Race has no direct effect on changes in GPA. Including the latter path improved model fit only minimally and not significantly ($\chi^2 = 66.69$; *df* = 45; *p* = .19), and the path itself was positive but not significant. Therefore, we retain the model without this path.

Time online is a significant predictor of MEAP-R, but time has no direct effect on GPA. However, increases in GPA are predicted by increases in MEAP-R scores. Substituting this path with a correlation reduces model fit ($\chi^2 = 76.57$; *df* = 46). In addition, the structural paths were no longer significant. Therefore, again, we retain the model in figure 11.1.

Number of Sessions

The model for number of sessions is presented in figure 11.2. The figure also contains three nonsignificant paths (with no path coefficients indicated). Removing these paths leads to a significant reduction in model fit. This model, too, describes the data well; $\chi^2 = 78.95$ (*df* = 46; *p* = .002), RMSEA = 0.07 (*p* = .11), and GFI = .91.

The structural aspect of the model in figure 11.2 indicates that race is a significant predictor of number of Internet sessions, with Caucasian-American children showing a greater increase in

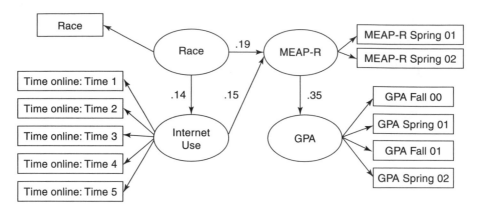

Figure 11.1. Model to predict academic performance from time online. MEAP: Michigan Education Assessment Program–Reading; GPA: grade point average. Values are standardized path coefficients.

number of sessions than African-American children. Number of sessions is a significant predictor of MEAP-R scores. None of the other paths was significant.

Number of Domains Visited

The model for number of domains visited is presented in figure 11.3. The figure displays only those paths included in the final model. Inclusion of any additional paths either reduced the model fit or created a model that failed to converge. The model in figure 11.3 describes the data well; $\chi^2 = 80.99$ ($df = 47$; $p = .002$), RMSEA = 0.07 ($p = .10$), and GFI = 0.92.

As with the model for number of sessions, the model for number of domains contains only two significant structural paths. These are the paths

from race to MEAP-R scores and from race to GPA, indicating that academic performance gains over the trial were greater for Caucasian-American than for African-American children. Visiting more domains had no effect on MEAP-R scores or GPA, and race is unrelated to the number of domains visited.

Number of E-Mails Sent

Figure 11.4 presents the model for number of e-mails sent. As with the model for number of domains visited, this model contains only two significant paths and describes the data well; $\chi^2 = 73.61$ ($df = 47$; $p = .008$), RMSEA = 0.06 ($p = .22$), and GFI = 0.92. The role of number of e-mails sent is very similar to that of number of domains visited. Race predicts MEAP-R scores and GPA. However, race is unrelated to number of e-mails sent, and the

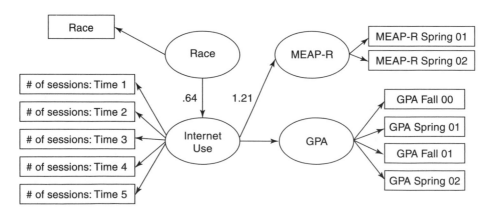

Figure 11.2. Model to predict academic performance from number of sessions. MEAP: Michigan Education Assessment Program–Reading; GPA: grade point average. Values are standardized path coefficients.

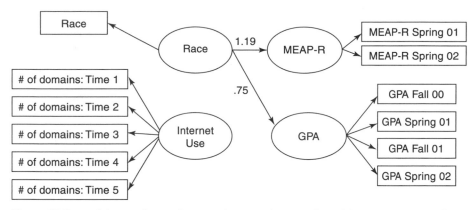

Figure 11.3. Model to predict academic performance from number of domains. MEAP: Michigan Education Assessment Program–Reading; GPA: grade point average. Values are standardized path coefficients.

latter is unrelated to improvements in academic performance (i.e., MEAP-R scores or GPA).

In sum, the four models may be categorized into two groups. The first group contains the Internet use measures "time online" and "number of sessions." In these models, we note that race has direct effects on Internet use and that Internet use has direct effects on academic performance. In addition, race effects on both Internet use and academic performance appear to be stronger for time online than for number of Internet sessions.

The second group of models is for the Internet use measures "number of domains visited" and "number of e-mails sent." In these models, there is no relationship between Internet use and improvement in academic performance. Race predicts improvement in both measures of academic performance but does not predict Internet use.

Discussion

Children in the HomeNetToo project used the Internet about 30 minutes a day. They participated in less than one session per day (i.e., they did not log on daily) and visited about 10 domains. These findings, based on continuously and automatically recorded Internet use, indicate that HomeNetToo children did not spend an excessive amount of time on the Internet. Whether they spent more or less time than the "average child" is difficult to determine because estimates of time online vary considerably from study to study—doubtless because of variability in study characteristics (e.g., year of study; Kids Snapshot, 2002; Kraut et al., 1996; Pew Internet and American Life Project, 2000a, 2002; UCLA Internet Report, 2000, 2001, 2003; Woodward, & Gridina, 2000).

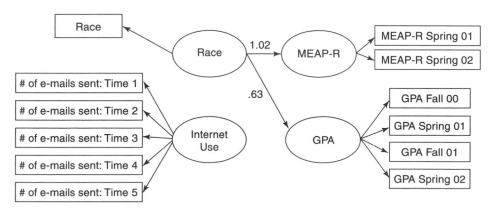

Figure 11.4. Model to predict academic performance from number of e-mails sent. MEAP: Michigan Education Assessment Program–Reading; GPA: grade point average. Values are standardized path coefficients.

Contrary to popular beliefs, media hype, and some previous research, children in the HomeNetToo project made little use of the Internet's communication tools. E-mail, instant messaging, and chat were infrequent activities at the start of the project, and the number of children participating in them dropped, often dramatically, by the end of the project. Indeed, after 16 months of home Internet access, only 16% of the children were sending e-mail or participating in chat, and only 25% were instant messaging.

Why did HomeNetToo children make so little use of the Internet's communication tools? One explanation is so obvious as to be easily overlooked. Children in the project may simply have had no one to communicate with on the Internet. HomeNetToo children were poor, and it is likely that their friends and extended family members were also poor. Poor people do not typically have home Internet access (Pew Internet and American Life Project, 2001a; U.S. Department of Commerce, 2001). Other evidence obtained from parents helps to explain why HomeNetToo children had little use for chat. Many parents in the project expressed concerns about chat activities and chat rooms in general. They viewed chat rooms as dangerous places and often prohibited their children from visiting them. Thus, with no friends or extended family online with whom to e-mail or instant message, and with parental discouragement or prohibition of chat activities, it is not surprising that HomeNetToo children made little use of the Internet's communication tools.

Another explanation for children's infrequent use of the Internet's communication tools may lie in cultural influences on communication style. The majority of the children in the HomeNetToo project were African American (83%). African-American culture is historically an "oral culture" (Hale, 1982; Keil, 1966), and consequently the text-based nature of Internet communication may not be appealing to African Americans. In support of this view, recent evidence indicates that African Americans prefer face-to-face communication to a far greater extent than do Caucasian Americans (Helms & Parham, 1990; Hollins, 1996). Thus, the impersonal and somewhat impoverished nature of current Internet communication tools may have discouraged African-American children from using them.

Children's sociodemographic characteristics were related to their Internet use. As in previous research, older children used the Internet more than did younger children (Pew Internet and American Life Project, 2002; Turow & Nir, 2000). Extending the findings of previous research (U.S. Department of Commerce, 1995, 1999, 2000, 2002; Kraut et al., 1996; Hoffman & Novak, 1998; Pew Internet and American Life Project, 2000b; Jackson et al., 2001a), Caucasian-American children used the Internet more than did African-American children. The persistence of race differences in Internet use when access is not an issue indicates that cultural factors may be operating (NSF Report, 2001). Perhaps the culture of the Internet, created primarily by Caucasian-American males, is not a hospitable culture for African-American children. Perhaps the design of web pages, again primarily by Caucasian-American males, lacks aesthetic appeal for African-American children. Systematic research is needed to examine whether cultural characteristics and technology design interact to influence technology use and enjoyment. Questions about culture and interface design become all the more urgent as wireless technology extends the reach of the Internet to the most remote corners of the globe.

In addition to sociodemographic characteristics, two other personal characteristics influenced children's Internet use: computer skills and liking for computers. As predicted, children with greater computer skills (self-rated) and children who liked computers more used the Internet more than did children with less computer skills and children who liked computers less (respectively). Findings that HomeNetToo children significantly improved their computer skills over the course of the 16-month trial speak to the importance of having a computer available in the home.

Situational factors also influenced children's Internet use. As predicted, early success in solving computer problems was related to greater Internet use, although experiencing more difficulties did not undermine use. Moreover, difficulties decreased and successes increased as the project progressed. Contrary to predictions, parental and peer modeling of computer use had no influence on children's Internet use. Thus, whether children viewed family and friends as using and enjoying computers was unrelated to their own Internet use. Interestingly, as the project progressed, more children viewed family members as not using and not enjoying the computer than at the start of the project, perhaps because they witnessed family members' frustrations with using the computer and Internet.

Home Internet use had few psychological or social consequences for HomeNetToo children. Children who spent more time online reported less negative affect after the first 3 months of home Internet access, but not thereafter. Children who participated in more Internet sessions reported more negative affect both early and late in the project. One explanation for this negative affect is that children participated in more sessions because their Internet use was more frequently interrupted, either for technical (disconnects) or interpersonal (family members wanting to use the computer) reasons. It was these interruptions, rather than Internet use, that were responsible for their negative affect. Internet use had no effect on children's feelings of self-worth, which were high and remained high throughout the project. Overall, our findings indicate that Internet use has no adverse psychological impact on children (Shields and Behrman, 2000).

Using the Internet had no adverse social effects on children in the HomeNetToo project. Regardless of how long or how often they went online, there was no change in number of close friends or in how they allocated their time among family, friends, and other activities (e.g., sports, television, reading). Two previous reviews of the literature came to the same conclusion with regard to computer use (Becker, 2000; Subrahmanyam et al., 2000). The single study that reported an adverse social effect of Internet use for teens (Kraut et al., 1998) later reported a dissipation of effects with Internet experience (Kraut et al., 2002). Other findings, most of them survey based, have suggested that Internet use may have positive social effects because it enables communication with geographically distant family and friends (UCLA Internet Project, 2000; Pew Internet and American Life Project, 2002; but c.f., Nie & Erbring, 2000).

An alternative explanation for the absence of social effects of Internet use may lie in the uniqueness of the HomeNetToo sample. Unlike the majority of research about the social effect of the Internet, HomeNetToo participants were low-income families. Neither the children nor their parents made much use of the Internet's communication tools, probably because they had no one to communicate with online. It may be that using the Internet's communication tools is necessary for its use to have social effects—positive or negative. More research

is needed, particularly longitudinal research, to determine whether and when Internet use has social effects on children and adults. Future research should include more diverse groups and better measures of social effects, such as time-sampling diaries or electronic and automatic recording of social activities.

In contrast to its lack of psychological or social effects, Internet use had significant and important effects on cognitive outcomes (Jackson, von Eye, Biocca, Barbatsis, Zhao, & Fitzgerald, in press). Children who used the Internet more had higher GPAs after 1 year and higher scores on standardized tests of reading achievement after 6 months than did children who used it less. The benefits of Internet use on academic performance continued throughout the project period. Children who used the Internet more during the last 4 months of the project had higher GPAs and higher standardized test scores in reading than did children who used it less. However, Internet use had no effects on standardized tests of math achievement.

Recall that previous research has produced equivocal findings with respect to IT use and cognitive outcomes (Shields & Behrman, 2000). At best, there is some evidence of a positive relationship between computer game playing and visual spatial skills (Subrahmanyam et al., 2000, 2001) and between owning a home computer and school performance. However, the causal nature of the latter relationship has yet to be established (Rocheleau, 1995; Cole, 1996; Blanton et al., 1997;). Whether Internet use contributes to or detracts from children's academic performance has, until now, never been systematically investigated (NSF Report, 2001). Thus, until now, there has been no evidence that using the Internet actually improves academic performance.

The next logical question is, Why does Internet use contribute to children's academic performance, and specifically reading performance? One possibility is that children who spend more time online are simply reading more than children who spend less time online. HomeNetToo children logged on primarily to use the web for information, not to communicate with others (i.e., e-mail, chat). Web pages are heavily text-based, regardless of their topical focus. Thus, whether children were searching for information about school-related projects or searching for information about personal interests and hobbies (e.g., rock stars, movies), those who were searching were reading. The time spent reading web pages may be responsible for improved performance on standardized tests of reading and in GPAs, which depend heavily on reading skills. The absence of any effect of Internet use has on mathematics performance indirectly supports this view. Because web pages do not typically engage mathematics skills, it is not surprising that spending more time on the web had no effect on standardized mathematics test scores.

Whether Internet use has a similar positive effect on academic performance for all children remains an important question for future research. Children in the HomeNetToo project were performing below average in terms of both GPAs and standardized tests scores. It may be that the academic performance benefits of Internet use are limited to children in this performance range. If this proves to be true, then the implications of the "digital divide" may be more serious than initially assumed. Children most likely to benefit from having the technology at home are the very children least likely to have it.

Future research is needed to replicate and to extend the findings of the HomeNetToo project. This research should include a large and diverse sample of children, new and more sensitive measures of social impact, multiple and reliable measures of Internet use, and longitudinal designs to evaluate change over time. Experimental research is also needed to uncover the mediating mechanism by which Internet use contributes to academic performance. New technology should be designed to examine whether similar improvements in mathematics skills might be obtained if web sites were designed to both entertain and engage mathematics skills. Finally, research is needed to examine the role of cultural factors in technology use, with an eye toward designing inclusive technology that will eliminate the digital "use" divide.

Acknowledgments. This research was supported by a grant from the National Science Foundation—Information Technology Research (085348), titled "HomeNetToo: Motivational, affective and cognitive factors and Internet use: Explaining the digital divide and the Internet paradox." September 1, 2000 to August 31, 2005. Linda A. Jackson, Principal Investigator. We are grateful to the 17 graduate students and 25 undergraduates who assisted with home visits, technical support, data collection, and other aspects of the project. We are also grateful to participants in the National Science Foundation–sponsored workshop titled "Domestic impact of information and communication technology," Estes Park, Colorado, June 5–8, 2003. Their comments and enthusiasm contributed greatly to the development of this manuscript. Special thanks go to Sonia Livingstone and Keith Hampton for reviewing and providing specific comments on this manuscript and to Robert Kraut and Sara Kiesler for organizing the workshop and coediting this volume.

References

Alverez, A. (2003). Behavioral and environmental correlates of digital inequality. *IT & Society, 1*(5), 32–45. Retrieved July 3, 2003, from http://www.ItandSociety.org.

Ambert, A.-M. (1997). *Parents, children and adolescents: Interactive relationships and development in context.* New York: Haworth Press.

Atwell, P. (2000). *Beyond the digital divide.* Working paper 164. New York: Russell Sage Foundation.

Bandura, A. (1977). *Social learning theory.* Englewood Cliffs, NJ: Prentice-Hall.

Bandura, A. (1986). *Social foundations of thought and action: A social cognitive theory.* Englewood Cliffs, NJ: Prentice-Hall.

Barone, K. S., Maddux, J. E., & Snyder, C. R. (1997). *Social cognitive psychology: History and current domains.* New York: Plenum.

Becker, H. J. (2000). Who's wired and who's not? Children's access to and use of computer technology. Children and computer technology. *The Future of Children, 10*(2), 44–75. Available: http://www.futureofchildren.org.

Blanton, W. E., Moorman, G. B., Hayes, B. A., & Warner, M. L. (1997). Effects of participation in the Fifth Dimension on far transfer. *Journal of Educational Computing Research, 16*, 371–396.

Borgida, E., Sullivan, J., Oxendine, A., Jackson, M., Riedel, E., & Gangl, A. (2002). Civic culture meets the digital divide: The role of community electronic networks. *Journal of Social Issues, 58*(1), 125–141.

Cho, J., Gil de Zuniga, H., Rojas, H., & Shah, D. V. (2003). Beyond access: The digital divide and Internet uses and gratifications. *IT & Society, 1*(4), 46–72. Available: http://www.ItandSociety.org.

Clements, D. H. (1987). Computers and young children: A review of the research. *Young Children, 43*, 34–44.

Cole, M. (1996). *Cultural psychology: A once and future discipline.* Cambridge, MA: Harvard University Press.

Dietz, T. L. (1998). An examination of violence and gender role portrayals in video games: Implications for gender socialization and aggressive behavior. *Sex Roles, 38,* 425–442.

Facer, K., & Furlong, R. (2001). Beyond the myth of the "cyberkid": Young people at the margins of the information revolution. *Journal of Youth Studies, 4,* 451–469.

Fling, S., Smith, L., Rodriguez, T., Thornton, D., Atkins, E., & Nixon, K. (1992). Videogames, aggression, and self-esteem: A survey. *Social Behavior and Personality, 20,* 39–45.

Gorski, P. 2002. Dismantling the digital divide: A multicultural education framework. *Multicultural Education, 10,* 28–30.

Greenfield, P. M. (1998). The cultural evolution of IQ. In Neisser, U. (Ed.), *The rising curve: Long-term gains in IQ and related measures* (pp. 81–123). Washington, DC: American Psychological Association.

Hale, J. E. (1982). *Black children: Their roots, culture and learning styles.* Provo, UT: Brigham Young.

Harris, J. R. (1998). *The nurture assumption.* New York: Free Press.

Harter, S. (1986). *Self-perception profile for children.* Denver, CO: University of Denver.

Helms, J. E., & Parham, T. A. (1990). The relationship between black racial identity attitudes and cognitive styles. In Helms, J. E. (Ed.). *Black and white racial identity* (pp. 119–131). Westport, CT: Greenwood.

Hoffman, D. L., & Novak, T. P. (1998). Bridging the racial divide on the Internet. *Science, 280,* 390–391.

Hollins, E. R. (1996). *Culture and school learning: Revealing the deep meaning.* Mahwah, NJ: Erlbaum.

Jackson, L. A. (2004a). The digital divide. *Encyclopedia of human-computer interaction* (pp. 171–175). Great Barrington, MA: Berkshire Publishing.

Jackson, L. A. (2004b). Gender and computing. *Encyclopedia of human-computer interaction* (pp. 276–281). Great Barrington, MA: Berkshire Publishing.

Jackson, L. A., Barbatsis, G., von Eye, A., Biocca, F. A., Zhao, Y., & Fitzgerald, H. E. (2003c). Implications for the digital divide of Internet use in low-income families. *IT & Society, 1*(5), 219–244. Available: http://www.ITandSociety.org.

Jackson, L. A., Ervin, K. S., Gardner, P. D., & Schmitt, N. (2001a). The racial digital divide: Motivational, affective, and cognitive correlates of Internet use. *Journal of Applied Social Psychology, 31,* 2019–2046.

Jackson, L. A., Ervin, K. S., Gardner, P. D., & Schmitt, N. (2001b). Gender and the Internet: Women communicating and men searching. *Sex Roles, 44,* 363–380.

Jackson, L. A., von Eye, A., Barbatsis, G., Biocca, F., Fitzgerald, H. E., & Zhao, Y. (2004). The social impact of Internet use on the other side of the digital divide. *Communications of the Association for Computing Machinery. 47*(7), 43–47

Jackson, L. A., von Eye, A., Biocca, F., Barbatsis, G., Fitzgerald, H. E., & Zhao, Y. (2003a). Internet attitudes and Internet use: Some surprising findings from the HomeNetToo project. *International Journal of Human Computer Studies, 59*(3), 355–382.

Jackson, L. A., von Eye, A., Biocca, F. A., Barbatsis, G., Fitzgerald, H. E., & Zhao, Y. (2003b). Personality, cognitive style, demographic characteristics and Internet use—Findings from the HomeNetToo project. *Swiss Journal of Psychology, 62*(2), 79–90.

Jackson, L. A., von Eye, A., Biocca, F. A., Barbatsis, G., Zhao, Y., and Fitzgerald, H. E. (2006). Does home Internet use influence the academic performance of low-income children? Findings from the HomeNetToo project. In P. Greenfield & Z. Yan (Eds.). *Developmental Psychology*, Special Section on Children, Adolescents and the Internet.

Joreskog, K., & Sörbom, D. (1993). *LISREL 8.53.* Chicago: Scientific Software International, Inc.

Katz, J. E., & Rice, R. E. (2002). *Social consequences of Internet use: Access, involvement, and interaction.* Cambridge, MA: MIT Press.

Keil, C. (1966). *Urban blues.* Chicago: University of Chicago.

Kids Count Snapshot: Connecting kids to technology: Challenges and opportunities. (2002). The Annie E. Casey Foundation. Retrieved March 23, 2003, from http://www.aecf.org/publications/pdfs/snapshot_june2002.pdf.

Kraut, R., Kiesler, S., Boneva, B., Cummings, J., Helgeson, V., & Crawford, A. (2002). Internet paradox revisited. *Journal of Social Issues, 58,* 49–74.

Kraut, R., Patterson, M., Lundmark, V., Kiesler, S., Mukopadhyay, T., & Scherlis, W. (1998). Internet paradox: A social technology that reduces social involvement and psychological well-being? *American Psychologist, 53,* 1017–1031.

Kraut, R., Scherlis, W., Mukhopadhyay, T., Manning, J., & Kiesler, S. (1996). The HomeNet field trial of residential Internet services. *Communications of the Association for Computing Machinery, 39,* 55–65.

Kulik, J. A. (1994). Meta-analytic studies of findings on computer-based instruction. *Technology assessment in education and training.* Hillsdale, NJ: Lawrence Erlbaum Associates.

National Science Foundation. (2001). Division of Science Resources Studies, The application and implications of information technologies in the home: Where are the data and what do they say? NSF 01–313. Arlington, VA: Author.

Nie, N. J., & Erbring, L. (2000). Internet and society: A preliminary report. Stanford Institute for the Quantitative Study of Society, Stanford University, Palo Alto, CA.

Norris, P. (2001). *Digital divide: Civic engagement, information poverty, and the Internet worldwide.* New York: Cambridge University Press.

Okagaki, L. & Frensch, P. A. (1994). Effects of video game playing on measures of spatial performance: Gender effects in late adolescence. In Greenfield, P. M., & Cocking, R. R. (Eds.), *Interacting with video* (pp. 95–115). Norwood, NJ: Ablex.

Payton, F. C. 2003. Rethinking the digital divide. *Communications of the Association for Computing Machinery, 46,* 89–92.

Pew Internet and American Life Project (2000a). Tracking online life: How women use the Internet to cultivate relationships with family and friends. Retrieved January 24, 2001, from http://www.pewinternet.org.

Pew Internet and American Life Project (2000b). African Americans and the Internet. Retrieved January 24, 2001, from http://www.pewinternet.org.

Pew Internet and American Life Project (2002). The digital disconnect: The widening gap between Internet savvy students and their schools. Retrieved October 16, 2002, from http://www.pewinternet.org.

Project TELL. (1990–1997). Stanton/Heiskell Center for Public Policy in Telecommunications and Information Systems, City University of New York Graduate School. Retrieved September 4, 2000, from http://web.gc.cuny.edu/Shc/docu1.htm.

Roberts, D. F., Foehr, U. G., Rideout, V. J., & Brodie, M. (1999). Kids and media at the new millennium: A comprehensive national analysis of children's media use. A Kaiser Family Foundation Report. Menlo Park, CA: Kaiser Family Foundation.

Robinson, J. P., Di Maggio, P., & Hargittai, E. (2003). New Social Survey perspectives on the digital divide. *IT & Society, 1*(5)., 24–26. Retrieved July 1, 2003, from http://www.ItandSociety.org.

Rocheleau, B. (1995). Computer use by school-age children: Trends, patterns and predictors. *Journal of Educational Computing Research, 1,* 1–17.

Roschelle, J. M., Pea, R. D., Hoadley, C. M., Gordon, D. N., & Means, B. M. (2000). Changing how and what children learn in school with computer-based technologies. *Children and Computer Technology, 10*(2), 76—101.

Rosenberg, M. (1979). *Society and the adolescent self-image.* Middletown, CT: Wesleyan University Press.

Shields, M. K., & Behrman, R. E. (2000). Children and computer technology: Analysis and recommendations. *The Future of Children, 10*(2), 4–30. Available: http://www.futureofchildren.org.

Stanger, J. D., & Gridina, N. (1999). Media in the home 1999: The fourth annual survey of parents and children (Survey Series No. 5). Philadelphia: Annenberg Public Policy Center of the University of Pennsylvania. Available: http://www.appc penn.org/pubs.htm.

Subrahmanyam, K., Greenfield, P., Kraut, R., & Gross, E. (2001). The impact of computer use on children's and adolescents' development. *Applied Developmental Psychology, 22,* 7–30.

Subrahmanyam, K., Kraut, R. E., Greenfield, P. M., & Gross, E. F. (2000). The impact of home computer use on children's activities and development. *The Future of Children, 10,* 123–144. Available: http://www.futureofchildren.org.

Tapscott, D. (1998). *Growing up digital: The rise of the net generation.* New York: McGraw-Hill.

Turow, J. (1999). The Internet and the family: The view from the parents, the view from the press. Report 27. Philadelphia: Annenberg Public Policy Center of the University of Pennsylvania. Available: http://www.appcpenn.org/internet.

Turow, J., & Nir, L. (2000). The Internet and the family 2000: The view from parents the view from kids. Philadelphia: Annenberg Public Policy Center of the University of Pennsylvania, Philadelphia.

UCLA Internet Project. (2000). Surveying the digital future: Year 1, UCLA Center for Communication Policy. University of California, Los Angeles. Available: http://www.ccp.ucla.edu/.

UCLA Internet Project. (2001). Surveying the digital future: Year 2, UCLA Center for Communication Policy. University of California, Los Angeles. Available: http://www.ccp.ucla.edu/.

UCLA Internet Project. (2003). Surveying the digital future, Year 3, UCLA Center for Communication Policy. University of California, Los Angeles. Available: http://www.ccp.ucla.edu/.

U.S. Department of Commerce. 1995. Falling through the Net: A survey of the "have nots" in rural and urban America. National Telecommunications and Information Administration, U.S. Department of Commerce Digital Divide web site. Retrieved October 13, 2001, from http://www.ntia.doc.gov/ntiahome/dn/index.html.

U.S. Department of Commerce. 1999. Falling through the Net: Defining the digital divide. National Telecommunications and Information Administration, U.S. Department of Commerce Digital Divide web site. Retrieved October 14, 2001, from http://www.ntia.doc.gov/ntiahome/dn/ index.html.

U.S. Department of Commerce. 2000. Falling through the Net: Toward digital inclusion. National Telecommunications and Information Administration, U.S. Department of Commerce Digital Divide web site. Retrieved October 4, 2001, from http://www.ntia.doc.gov/ntiahome/ dn/index.html.

U.S. Department of Commerce. 2002. A nation online: How Americans are expanding their use of the Internet. National Telecommunications and Information Administration, U.S. Department of Commerce. Retrieved October 5, 2003, from http:/ /www.ntia.d oc.gov/ntiahome/dn/index.html.

Valkenburg, P. M., & Soeters, K. E. (2001). Children's positive and negative experiences with the Internet: An exploratory survey. *Communication Research, 28*, 652–675.

van Schie, E. G. M. & Wiegman, O. (1997). Children and videogames: Leisure activities, aggression, social integration, and school performance. *Journal of Applied Social Psychology, 27*, 1175–1194.

Wenglinsky, H. (1998). Does it compute? The relationship between educational technology and student achievement in mathematics. Princeton, NJ: Educational Testing Service.

Wiegman, O., & van Schie, E. G. M. (1998). Video game playing and its relations with aggressive and prosocial behavior. *British Journal of Social Psychology, 37*, 367–378.

Woodward, E. H. IV, & Gridina, N. (2000). Media in the home in 2000: The fifth annual survey of parents and children. Philadelphia: Annenberg Public Policy Center, University of Pennsylvania.

Zillman, D., & Weaver, J. B. III. (1999). Effects of prolonged exposure to gratuitous media violence on provoked and unprovoked hostile behavior. *Journal of Applied Social Psychology, 29*, 145–165.

John M. Carroll, Mary Beth Rosson,

Andrea Kavanaugh, Daniel Dunlap,

Wendy Schafer, Jason Snook, and

Philip Isenhour

Social and Civic Participation in a Community Network

Community networks are ensembles of locally oriented Internet services and content; for example, web sites of local businesses and churches or e-mail lists of volunteer associations and recreational clubs. As with other social uses of the Internet, community networks allow people to transcend logistics with respect to their participation in discussions and activities. Thus, a community member can send an encouraging e-mail to her softball team even when a business trip takes her out of town, a father can browse projects in a high school science fair web site even if he gets home too late to attend the science fair itself, or a senior citizen can post a comment about a zoning proposal even when icy weather keeps him from attending a town council meeting.

Many studies have described and analyzed the social and civic benefits of individual participation in community associations (Homans, 1950; Edwards & Booth, 1973; Bellah, Madsen, Sullivan, Swindler, & Tipton, 1985; Putnam, 2000; Kavanaugh, Reese, Carroll, & Rosson, 2003). The network of connections among community members in their various associations enriches the social fabric of the whole community. Indeed, a key claim in the design rationale for community networks is that Internet discussion and interaction can facili-

tate social and civic engagement and participation in one's local community. The argument is that the e-mail remotely sent to the softball team increases the member's commitment, perhaps increasing the likelihood that she will show up for the game next week when she is home from her trip. Similarly, by visiting the virtual science fair web site, the father becomes more involved with his daughter and with her school and is perhaps more likely to attend a Parent–Teacher Association meeting. Likewise, the senior citizen feels more connected to his community by participating in the zoning discussion—he is less isolated by inclement weather. Perhaps he will be more likely now to read tomorrow's newspaper account of the town council meeting or to attend the next meeting in person.

But it could be otherwise. For example, a plausible alternative view is that despite all good intentions, community participation is a zero-sum tradeoff. Perhaps when the out-of-town softball player sends an e-mail, she feels that she has made her contribution, and she is accordingly somewhat less likely to show up at the game next week than she would have been had she never sent an e-mail at all. Perhaps the father feels that he has participated in his daughter's science project even though no one—perhaps not even his daughter—knows that he browsed the science fair web site. Perhaps the senior citizen is ultimately disappointed when no one replies to his posting and concludes that making the post was a waste of his time.

Our research is investigating whether and how the Internet can enhance involvement and participation in one's local community. Most basically, we are trying to distinguish and evaluate the two sorts of outcomes sketched above. Does a network of local services and content actually get used by community members? And if it is used, what effect if any does it have on their community-oriented attitudes and behaviors, such as memberships in voluntary associations, feelings of community attachment, activism with respect to community issues, and so forth?

Experiences of People, Internet, and Community

We are carrying out an assessment of the use and effects of the Blacksburg Electronic Village (BEV), a community network supporting the university town of Blacksburg, Virginia (population 47,000), and nearby areas of Montgomery and Giles counties. BEV is a mature community network, both in the sense that it has been operational for about a decade (since 1993) and in the sense that it has a high level of penetration into its community. For example, in the summer of 1999, more than 87% of Blacksburg's citizens were using the Internet on a regular basis, and more than 475 local businesses advertised online—about 75% of all businesses in the Blacksburg area. More than half of Internet users had dial-up (modem) access, and some connections are made using the public-access library computers. The remaining connections are made using Ethernet in offices and homes. Blacksburg has the highest per capita broadband access in the world; more than 60% of Blacksburg residents have broadband access at home, at work, or both. For example, over 3000 apartment units have Ethernet (BEV web site, 2003).

This level of technology adoption has helped to evoke and support a lively and diverse range of locally oriented Internet services and content (Carroll & Rosson, 1996; Cohill & Kavanaugh, 2000). Over 150 community groups maintain web sites. The BEV hosts many community-oriented initiatives (e.g., 15 community newsgroups, vari-

ous e-mail discussion and announcement lists, a town chat, a senior's nostalgia archive, and public-access kiosks). The municipal government of Blacksburg uses the BEV extensively, providing online forms for surveys, house check requests, and e-mail to town officials, as well as dissemination of schedules and other documents. All 20 county schools have been wired for Ethernet access since 1996, and many teachers have incorporated Internet activities into their curricula. As in many other communities, the youth of Blacksburg use Internet services extensively, to connect socially outside of school and to collaborate informally on homework and projects.

Our study focuses on household use and the effects of the BEV and the Internet. We recruited participants as household units. The study was multifaceted, comprising a two-wave survey, with the second survey administration taking place approximately 12 months after the first; a logging study, in which we monitored household e-mail and web activity; and an interview study, in which we carried out a series of four household interviews throughout a 12-month period. At the end of the project, an online discussion was created to share and discuss the study results within the community. The various components of this research design are summarized in a timeline in figure 12.1.

Our research design incorporated a stratified sample of 100 households, representing the actual population demographics of Blacksburg and Montgomery counties. We wanted to avoid self-selection, or "opportunity-based" recruiting practices, which can lead to systematic biases in the data. We used a random sample of 1250 Montgomery county residential addresses that had been purchased from Survey Sample, Inc., in September 2000 for a previous BEV research project; the list was prefiltered to remove 380 invalid addresses, leaving a functional sample of 870 households. We recruited households from this sample with a 10-item survey that allowed us to classify them with respect to location (residing within the Town of Blacksburg or elsewhere in Montgomery County), user type (access to the Internet from home only, from work only, from home and work, or no access), and education level of head of household (elementary school, high school, 1–3 years of college, 4+ years of college). Households were recruited to represent these three stratification variables in proportion to the actual population of Montgomery County, as

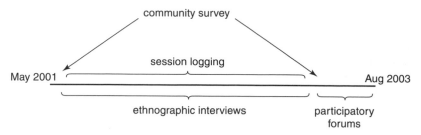

Figure 12.1. Overall research design of Experiences of People, Internet, and Community (EPIC) study.

described by U.S. Census data and other demographic studies of the local area. See Carroll and Reese (2003) for further discussion of the sample design.

Using the same selection criteria, we identified a subsample of 20 households from the overall sample of 100 to participate in the interview study (see Dunlap, Schafer, Carroll, & Reese, 2003, for additional methodological details). Only 75 households in the overall survey sample were qualified for the logging study. Ten of the households in our sample were deliberately selected to represent the 10% of the local population without Internet access, and 15 were selected to represent households with Internet access only at work or at school. In 32 other cases, we were unable to gather logging data, typically because the household's Internet service provider (AOL) employed a proprietary Internet protocol. Forty-three households participated in the logging study (see Carroll, Snook & Isenhour, 2004, for additional methodological details).

Participating households were enrolled in the study through a face-to-face visit to their homes. We made every effort to ensure that all members of the household were present for this meeting. The goals and procedures of the study were explained, and questions and concerns were answered. The survey portion of the study was distributed to participants, and if it was convenient, the participants completed the survey at that time. Otherwise, we went over the survey with members of the household and left a mail-return envelope with them. As part of this initial meeting, we installed the software to log Internet use. This included setting proxies in the household browser and e-mail clients, if this was technically feasible (see above). If the household had been selected for interviewing, we carried out the initial interview.

The final activity in our study was a participatory evaluation forum. We summarized some of

our initial results and posted them on a web forum, inviting members of the participant households to comment (anonymously). At present, we are opening this forum to the larger Blacksburg community.

Logging Home Use of the Internet

We logged participants' e-mail and web activity using proxy software running on servers in the Center for Human–Computer Interaction at Virginia Tech. The use of proxies allowed us to monitor activity without requiring the participants to change their Internet service provider or to use a different e-mail reader or web browser. Passive logging allowed us to monitor household use of the Internet without affecting participants' natural practices in any way. However, this noninvasive approach also meant that we could only monitor behavior to the extent it was articulated. For example, most of our participants had household Internet accounts; that is, one Internet account that was used by all members of the household. Thus, we are unable to differentiate the activity of individual household members.

The 43 households that we logged during a full year of interaction for each household produced 1.7 million URL requests (note that large multimedia files were not logged because of performance issues). There was substantial redundancy in people's accesses of Internet sites. A total of 369,047 unique URLs were accessed, meaning that 78% of http requests were for URLs already accessed by one or more participants, including those accessed by the same participant more than once. There was an average of 745 URL accesses of 165 unique URLs per household per week throughout the study period. There was also considerable clustering among the unique URLs accessed by our participants with respect to Internet hosts (e.g., http://www.vt.edu/academics/ and http://www.vt.edu/admissions/ are unique URLs, but share a common host: http://www.vt.edu). A total of 27,314 unique Internet host names (e.g., http://www.vt.edu and http://www.webmail.vt.edu are unique hosts) were accessed. Finally, a total of 19,390 unique domains were accessed (e.g., vt.edu is an Internet domain that includes both of the unique hosts http://www.vt.edu and http://www.webmail.vt.edu).

Most Internet traffic was not in common across different households; that is, different households accessed different hosts. More than 80% (22,161) of the roughly 27,000 unique hosts were accessed by only a single household (i.e. one household, one or more times; fig. 12.2). Conversely, only 381 hosts (just over 1%) were accessed by 10 or more households. Overall, 38% (8461) of the hosts were accessed only once (i.e., one household, one time), whereas 33% were accessed 10 or more times (i.e. one or more households, one or more times; figure 12.3).

By far the most pervasive category of http activity logged was for pushed advertising, commercial web sites accessed programmatically, not through manual user actions (sometimes called pop-ups). Pushed advertising accounted for 461,488 accesses; these records made up more than a quarter (27.7%) of all Internet activity logged in our study. Pushed advertising sites made up 28 of the top 100 top sites accessed in our study. Among the 72 sites in the top 100 that were not pushed advertising sites, 60 were dot-com sites. Of the 60 dot-com sites, the majority (22) were Hotmail or MSN servers presumably as-sociated with Hotmail traffic. The rest of the sites included search sites (http://www.google.com), banking sites (http://www.fnbonline.com and http://www.nbbank.com), and several travel sites including Orbitz and Expedia. Only 22 of the top 100 sites that we logged were neither pushed advertising nor dot-com sites (these were mainly educational sites).

Of particular interest to our project was local Internet activity by Experiences of People, Internet, and Community participants. Our goal was to create a methodology to estimate logged activity pertaining to the region within a 1–hour travel radius of Blacksburg. The BEV can be thought of logically as a neighborhood of URLs, listservers, e-mail addresses, and so forth. However, this neighborhood is difficult to define in terms of network topology—not all "local" sites are on local servers. For example, we found that movie show times for one local theater are provided by a machine in California—http://www.hollywood.com. Similarly, people in Blacksburg can order a pizza from the local Papa John's franchise, but to do this they access Papa John's national web site, http://www.papajohns.com. Conversely, not all content on local servers is actually local. For example, much of the content served from machines at Virginia Tech would contain general science and engineering material with no significant connection to Blacksburg or Montgomery County.

The first step in our method was to search URLs for distinct substrings; in this case the targets are zip codes, municipality names, and local idioms and domains, as listed in table 12.1.

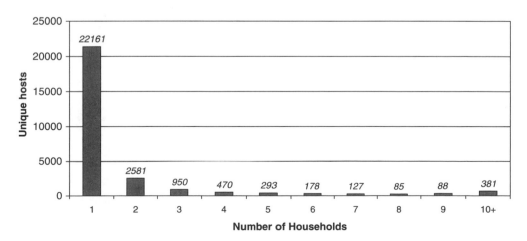

Figure 12.2. Household access to unique hosts.

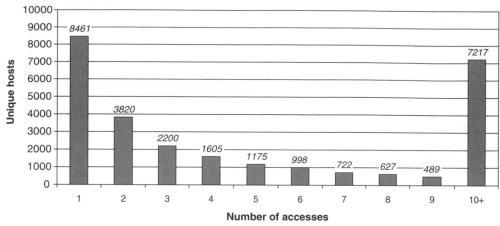

Figure 12.3. Overall access by unique hosts.

Several iterations of the keyword list were required to maximize the number of local sites identified while minimizing misses and false alarms. Several keywords originally included, such as "Pilot" (a local city name), were eliminated because they occur so much more frequently as general terms in ordinary language use. Other keywords such as "BEV" proved useful and were retained even though they produced some false alarms (e.g., we discovered that http://bevnet.com is an online beverage retailer).

We classified 79,816 URL requests to 545 distinct hosts—nearly 5% of our log data—as local. To put this in perspective, at the time of our study, the Internet consisted of more than 147 million distinct hosts (Internet Systems Consortium, 2003). Thus, requests to local hosts were approximately 10,000 times more likely than chance in our data (i.e., the 545 local hosts make up less than .0004% of the Internet as a whole). We divided local traffic into university traffic (pertaining to the three universities and colleges within our target radius: Virginia Tech, Radford University, and New River Valley Community College) and nonuniversity traffic

(civic organizations, local information). University traffic dominated, comprising 60,645 URL accesses—about 76% of local URL accesses. Local nonuniversity traffic accounted for 19,171 URLs (or about 24% of local traffic logged).

A special focus for our analysis of local traffic was visits to the BEV. Logged traffic on the BEV totaled 649 accesses for the participant pool, with just over half of the households (23) accessing it at some point during the study. On a per household basis, this is comparable to access rates for other major sites logged in our study such as Amazon (29 distinct households) and Virginia Tech (30 distinct households). The households that accessed the BEV did so about every other week during the study (28 accesses per household).

Table 12.2 presents a breakdown of BEV activity by host. Most accesses request the BEV homepage, which is updated frequently and provides headlines and pointers to community information (much of it outside the http://bev.net domain). Beyond the homepage, most of the BEV pages are portals to particular views of the community; for

Table 12.1. URL substrings used to identify local traffic.

Zip codes	Municipalities (VA)	Idioms/domains
24060, 24061	Blacksburg	montva, newriver,
24062, 24063	Roanoke	Hokie, Beamer,
24073, 24068	Christiansburg	BEV, bburg, nrv,
24087, 24111	McCoy	mcps, swva, mfrl,
24138, 24149	Montgomery, Floyd	techfcu, thelyric
24162, 24091	Shawsville, Riner	

Table 12.2. Accesses to BEV hosts.

BEV host	Accesses	Distinct households
http://www.bev.net	338	22
http://community.bev.net	97	11
http://civic.bev.net	88	9
http://www.civic.bev.net	59	3
http://arts.bev.net	33	3
http://calendar.bev.net	22	7
http://www.bburg.bev.net	2	2

example, the Village Mall is a launch pad for local commercial sites, and Neighborhoods provides links to pages maintained by local groups.

The balance of accesses to BEV pages was divided primarily between community and civic pages. Community traffic included directory listings to local products and services (http://www.bev.net/mall), local job openings, and personal homepages (http://www.bev.net/ecommunity). Civic traffic included directories of homepages for organizations such as churches, the Humane Society, and a fencing club. Twelve households collectively accessed pages on http://blacksburg.gov 295 times; the Town of Blacksburg pages are reachable via the government portal on the BEV, but apparently they were more often directly accessed (230 accesses were to the front page). The arts directory of local performances, art shows, and other events was accessed less frequently. The calendar, which lists events such as local road races, book signings, festivals, and classes, as well as art shows and performance events, was accessed even less, though by more households.

Our conclusion, based on these data, is that use of local Internet services and content in Blacksburg is strong, even though it is far from being the predominant focus of Internet activity.

Surveying Community Attachment and Involvement

Our survey asked participants about their community involvement, organizational memberships, informal group participation, Internet use, social circles, community collective efficacy, general psychological attributes, recent significant life changes, and basic demographics. We drew on existing sur-

vey instruments, particularly the HomeNet survey (Kraut, Scherlis, Mukhopadhyay, Manning, & Kiesler, 1996; Kraut, Lundmark, Patterson, Kiesler, Mukopadhyay, & Scherlis, 1998) and prior BEV surveys (Kavanaugh & Patterson, 2001). In this section, we present an exploratory data analysis of relations among demographic and general psychological variables (age, education, extroversion), community-oriented attitudes and Internet behaviors (community collective efficacy, social support, use of the Internet for social purposes, and use of the Internet for civic purposes), and community involvement and attachment (aggregating variables relating to community activism, membership in associations, staying informed, and belonging). Specifically, these analyses investigate the extent to which Internet usage mediates relationships between demographic and general psychological variables and community-oriented behaviors and feelings.

The demographic and general psychological variables we investigated were age (in years), education (in years), and extroversion (constructed from the scale of Bendig, 1962, with an obtained Cronbach alpha of .86). These variables are all acknowledged predictors of civic participation, and social interaction more generally (Bendig, 1962; Kraut et al., 1998; Putnam, 2000).

To assess residents' expectations about their effectiveness as a community, we developed a scale for Community Collective Efficacy (Carroll & Reese, 2003). Our measure of collective efficacy is an extension of Bandura's (1997) self-efficacy construct, which describes domain-specific beliefs about personal capacities to produce desirable outcomes in the face of specific obstacles. Our scale consisted of 13 items (Cronbach alpha = .86) asserting beliefs about the collective capacities of one's own community. For example, the item "Our community can greatly improve the quality of education in Montgomery County without help from the Commonwealth of Virginia" asserts that the community can improve its public schools despite the obstacle of inadequate state support. Participants rated these items on a 7-point Likert-scale with end-points from "strongly disagree" to "strongly agree."

We aggregated variables related to social support and Internet experience and use into the constructs described in table 12.3. "Social support" items include spending time with friends, being invited to do things with others, feeling that one can share worries with someone or get advice for family problems, and being able to get help and companionship. "Internet experience" is self-rated experience with computers and the Internet, along with estimated average hours of Internet use per day. "Social Internet use" includes the extent to which one uses the Internet to communicate with friends and family who are either living in the local community or living some distance away, as well as the extent to which one uses the Internet to communicate with coworkers about nonwork matters. "Civic Internet use" is the extent to which one seeks news online, posts information online, expresses opinions online, participates in online local discussion groups, and so on.

We computed correlations on the variables for each construct and conducted reliability tests. We sought to obtain constructs comprising a single factor, with reliabilities (indicated by Cronbach alpha) greater than 0.7. (We have also created and investigated other constructs in this research; see Kavanaugh et al., 2003; Kavanaugh, Carroll, Rosson, Reese, & Zin, 2005.)

The outcome variables in our analysis were a set of community involvement and attachment constructs. These variables are based on community involvement measures by Rothenbuhler (1991; Shepherd and Rothenbuhler, 2001) on how frequently respondents keep up with local news, get together with others who know what's going on in the community, have ideas for changing things in the community, and work to bring about change in the community. We aggregated these variables into two constructs, Participation and Informedness. Factor analysis (principal axis factoring) showed that the Participation construct is composed of three components we named activism, associations, and belonging (Kavanaugh et al., 2005).

As summarized in table 12.4, activism is constructed from items such as having ideas to improve the community, working to bring about local change, and working with others to solve community problems. Associations includes the participant's rating of his or her tendency to join organizations and groups, as well as the reported number of groups to

Table 12.3. Psychological and Internet variables used in regression analysis of community involvement and attachment.

Variable	Cronbach α	Example survey items
Psychological variables		
Extroversion	0.86	I am outgoing and sociable. I am talkative. I am full of energy.
Collective efficacy	0.86	Our community can greatly improve the quality of education in Montgomery County without help from the Commonwealth of Virginia.
		The people of our community can continue to work together, even when it requires a great deal of effort.
Social support	0.83	Spend time with friends; share worries; get advice for family problems; invited to do things; able get help and companionship
Internet variables		
Internet experience	0.72	Self-rated experience with computers and the Internet; estimated hours per day online
Social Internet use	0.79	Communicate with friends and family; communicate with co-workers about non-work issues
Civic Internet use	0.83	Look for news online; post information online; express opinions; participate in local online groups,
Participation	0.88	Activism; associations; belonging (below)
Activism	0.89	Have ideas to improve local community; work to bring local change; work with others to solve community problems
Associations	0.70	Belong to many organizations and groups; reported number of groups currently a member
Belonging	0.73	Spend time with friends; help neighbors in need; feel part of local community
Informedness	0.73	Keep up with news; know what's going on inside and outside local community

which the person currently belongs. Belonging includes spending time with friends, helping neighbors in need, and feeling part of the local community. Informedness includes variables such as keeping up with the news and knowing what is going on inside and outside the local community.

Prior work has shown that demographic and psychological variables predict community-oriented behaviors and attitude (Edwards & Booth, 1973); exogenous variables such as age and education have been shown to predict Internet adoption and use (NTIA, 2000). However, the BEV has been in operation for almost 10 years—enough time for more complex relations to emerge among personal characteristics, Internet use, and community behavior. Our survey was designed to assess not just Internet use in general but also the extent to which it is being used for different purposes (e.g., politics,

social interaction). Thus, our general question is, Does use of the Internet have an effect on the types of community behavior that people exhibit? More specifically, do different classes of Internet behaviors (e.g., social, civic) mediate associated classes of community behavior (e.g., group membership, activism)?

We constructed path models (Pedhazur, 1997) to summarize the correlations among the variables and constructs defined above. We began with the exogenous variables of age, education, and extroversion and regressed these variables on the community-oriented attitudes and the Internet usage constructs defined in table 12.3. We then regressed the resulting ensembles on the four community involvement and attachment constructs defined in table 12.4. We summarize our findings in the four path models shown in figure 12.4.

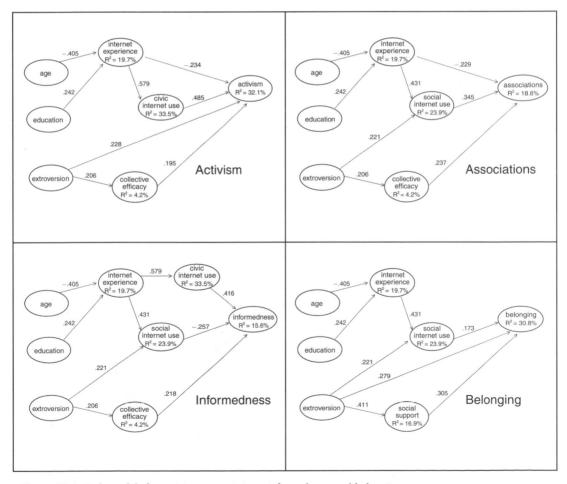

Figure 12.4. Path models for activism, associations, informedness, and belonging.

The four path models revealed several general demographic and psychosocial relationships. Younger and better-educated people tend to be more experienced and regular users of the Internet. Extroverts tend to have greater community collective efficacy and to experience more social support. Extroversion is a significant predictor of social Internet use, although it does not predict Internet experience in general, or the use of the Internet for civic purposes.

Of more interest are the relations between Internet use and community attitudes and behaviors. The upper-left panel of figure 12.4 illustrates such a relation—people who use the Internet for civic purposes tend to be more active in the community. Civic internet use in turn is strongly predicted by Internet experience. Interestingly, with the mediating effect of civic internet use removed, Internet experience is a negative predictor of activism. This suggests a two-population interpretation: some experienced Internet users have recruited the Internet for their civic behaviors, and these individuals tend to be active within their communities. In contrast, another population of experienced users may be using the Internet for other goals; these users report themselves as relatively inactive within their community.

Similar patterns can be seen in the lower-left and upper-right panels in the path models of informedness and associations, respectively. Namely, Internet experience again has a positive relation with Informedness (e.g., keeping up with community news), but only indirectly through the mediating construct of civic Internet use. In fact, experienced users who recruit the Internet for social rather than civic purposes report that they are less informed. In the case of associations, only experienced users who use the Internet for social purposes report a higher degree of membership; those whose experience comes from other uses report fewer associations. A simpler version of this pattern is apparent in the lower-right panel, showing the path model for belonging: Internet experience once again has an indirect positive effect on feelings of belonging, mediated by social Internet use.

This general pattern—in which categories of Internet use mediate its effect on community-oriented behaviors—has an intuitive interpretation: Many residents develop and pursue community-oriented goals; as their experience and use of the Internet increases, they recruit this technology in service of these goals (e.g., activism, staying informed, participating in groups). At the same time, an interesting conjecture is that when people do not have these community-oriented goals, increased use of the Internet may actually decrease their level of activity in the community.

Another general pattern across the path models concerns the mediating role of community collective efficacy in community-oriented behavior. Only the exogenous variable extroversion predicts individual reports of collective efficacy, but community collective efficacy itself is a predictor of activism, of informedness, and of associations. This is as one would expect: People who are more convinced that their community can accomplish things together are more likely to become involved with their community (although in ways that vary according to their own preferences and personal styles).

Belonging is a measure of emotional attachment (e.g., spending time with friends and neighbors), and one might not expect to see a strong relation between the achievement-oriented judgments of community collective efficacy and feelings of belongingness. However, we were surprised that the effects of collective efficacy were not mediated by the Internet usage constructs—social Internet use and civic Internet use. For example, it seems that using the Internet for civic purposes could increase one's confidence that the community can make progress. But because so many factors influence the likely success of community efforts (e.g., politics, economy), the effects of technology on such efforts may not have been strong enough to emerge in a complex path analysis.

Interviewing Critical People

We have described some of our initial results from the logging and survey components of our study. A third facet of this project was a series of in-depth interviews carried out with 20 households. Each household was interviewed four times over the course of the study. In most cases, two researchers conducted semistructured interviews in the homes of the participants. Each interview was recorded with a digital audio recorder and transcribed. Interviews lasted from about 45 minutes to several hours and covered a variety of topics relating to participants' interactions with the Internet and their involvement in community organizations and local activities.

The first interview focused on basic information about the household, their professional work, daily life, leisure activities, and feelings about the local area and community. The second and third interviews focused on their local community contacts, community involvement, and the use of the Internet in facilitating those community activities and ties. The final interview investigated the role of the Internet in the home, exploring household rules and habits relating to computers, family concerns about the Internet, and typical routines and behaviors involving their use of the Internet.

Information from the interviews was intended to support two general goals. First, rich descriptions of participants' attitudes and behaviors involving the Internet helped explain, confirm, reflect on, and augment survey findings. Second, ongoing dialog with participants provided opportunities to discover patterns and relationships that were not anticipated when developing the surveys.

The interviews provided an opportunity for participants to describe their own attitudes and understandings of the Internet in their own words. In-depth interviews were opportunities for researchers to document the discourse, language, and understandings of participants. The purpose was to describe the Internet as participants made sense of it in their lives. The stories and experiences that participants conveyed reflected the meanings that they used to understand, engage, and explain the Internet and community. The language they employed helped researchers make better sense of answers and patterns in the surveys. Participants expressed personal feelings about how e-mail, Internet chat, and the web had changed and functioned in their work, hobbies, friendships, and local government. The interviews helped researchers describe the participants even when their answers did not seem reasonable or internally consistent to the researchers.

Flanagan (1954) described the "critical incident" method for gathering vivid retrospective episodes of human performance. We tried to identify particular individuals in our interview subsample who vividly exemplify, or counterexemplify, the aggregate statistical patterns described in the prior sections. With apologies to Flanagan, we refer to them as critical people.

Living Together but Computing Differently: a Father–Daughter Contrast

In one of the interview households, we found a descriptive contrast that illustrated an unanticipated example of a local user who found particularly significant added value in Internet interaction. The family described numerous ways that they experienced and used the Internet. The most striking examples were found in the contrasts between the father and one of the daughters. Of course, younger people use the Internet more. Extroverts tend to be more active in the community, and they are more likely to use the Internet for social purposes. Interestingly, the model above also suggests that those who use Internet for social purposes also tend to be less well informed. This case provides an account of such a situation. The house shares a computer among three adults and two teenagers and they use a dial-up connection with major Internet service provider.

According to answers given on the survey, the father represents an introvert with low activism, low community belonging, and few associations and who is moderately well informed. He uses the Internet mainly at work. The daughter described his computer use from her point of view. "He's not into the Internet. . . . He knows nothing about the Internet. . . . At work, all he does is e-mail. . . . He usually just uses the computer to play games. . . . My dad is obsessed with [a certain] game." According to his wife, however, "he uses it a lot at work, a lot of communication with [business relations] and stuff like that."

The daughter, in contrast, was deemed by the survey analysis to be an extrovert with high activism, high belonging, many associations, and low informedness. In many ways, she is a typical young adult, and her Internet usage reflects that. She is an energetic high school student. She loves sports, belongs to several school clubs, and is an avid Internet user. She e-mails and chats with a large group of friends including many from clubs and church. According to the family, the father uses the computer more, but the daughter uses the Internet more.

"She will do anything to get on the computer," says her mother. Her hearing disability, in part, fueled her enthusiastic Internet usage. Challenges with oral communication shape her preference for online interactions. Typing text, although cumbersome to most, for her presents clear advantages to talking on the telephone: "[The Internet] is better for me because I can't communicate very well on the phone with certain people. It is so much better when I get on the computer with them 'cause I understand them so much better."

Useful but Detrimental

Attitudes were intriguing whether they fit expectations or belied them. Sometimes significant benefactors of technology also criticize and resist its effects. In an ironic case, a sales manager described by the belonging model discussed above expressed a strong sentiment about the change that the Internet has brought to his professional interactions. Although he was an early adopter who has used e-mail and other networked computers for many years now, he lamented the newer forms of electronic communication. He passionately described how he missed the face-to-face interactions he had with clients before e-mail. As per the belonging model, this well-educated, middle-aged extrovert has been online for several years, uses the Internet for social purposes, and shows high levels of social support. These traits and communication patterns are associated with strong feelings of belonging (such as community attachment and belonging to a group of friends) that he also indicated in survey responses. Nonetheless, in interview discussions, this individual bemoaned the erosion of face-to-face communication with the emergence of e-mail: "My biggest complaint is what [the] computer has done with social interactions . . . in my regard more business related. Where I used to do a lot of face-to-face, you know, interpersonal, now it's a lot of e-mails and phone calls, and I hate e-mails." He believes that online interactions are replacing physical meetings, and this type of communication is less personal and less valuable: "We're sending and communicating stuff that we should not be communicating by e-mail."

He strives to maintain more personal communication. He often takes day trips to visit customers within a couple-hour radius but rarely visits his company's regional office, which was about 3 hours away. His home is well connected. One computer in the house is only for work purposes, although the other is a general-purpose machine for everyone, including his wife and daughter. He uses the Internet extensively for his work, and the house-

hold has an extra phone line for a dial-up Internet connection. The company has an Intranet to connect him with the business. Recently, he and a friend organized a local youth sports event via the Internet. He communicated with his friends and most of the people involved by sending e-mail messages and attachments. This allowed them to coordinate the event with a minimal number of physical meetings. He has accepted the utility of the Internet for economizing his work and community activity, but he recognizes the costs and downsides that turn on the very same foundation that provides for the advantages.

Log on to Get Away from It All

Yet another pattern was represented vividly by a household consisting of a hard-working married couple. The husband has lived in the local community for the last 14 years and has been working in a community service related field for the last 18 years. Both work with people extensively in their professions, but neither uses computers nor the Internet extensively for social purposes. Some of the reasons are not surprising, but others are interesting.

The husband describes a 12-hour work day that he enjoys despite his feeling of exhaustion when he arrives home. After work, his typical routine has him log on to the Internet to wind down for the evening. In his spare time, he loves to read and stay current with the news and latest technology. They keep up with news from his former hometown via the web, but they do not use the Internet to get involved with politics locally or back home. As they put it, "we shy away from those kinds of issues."

Their high-speed cable access and multiple desktop computers at home play a central role in their lives but are mainly used for enjoyment and leisure activity. The husband spends most of his time on his laptop. He uses this machine for both work and personal purposes, and it contains valuable programs he has written to simplify some of his administrative work tasks. He uses the Internet to look up information and shop: "We use the Internet for information and not as a communication tool." Before the Internet, he frequently went to the library and the mall, but now he uses the web to find the information. After a long day interacting with many people at work, he enjoys sitting in the quiet of his home: "I don't want to go the mall to see people."

This case provides a picture of users experiencing relatively low use of Internet for social purposes but scoring relatively high on measures of informedness. They view the Internet primarily as a way to access and use information; indeed, the high use of the Internet for information seeking might have helped to make them even less social as suggested by their observation that they no longer visit the library and the shopping mall because of the Internet. The case also provides an account of how relatively high levels of Internet experience that is not directed at civic or social purposes can reasonably correlate with less activism and fewer associations and memberships.

The Internet as a Causal Factor in Community Participation

Can the Internet enhance involvement and participation in one's local community? We have presented evidence that people in Blacksburg do make use of their locally oriented Internet services and content, and that their general experience with the Internet, and their specific use of the Internet for social and civic purposes—along with more general community-oriented attitudes and beliefs (community collective efficacy and social support)—can affect community involvement and attachment.

As one might expect, the causal relations are complex, and we have only illuminated part of what we see as a nexus of contributory causes that includes various patterns of Internet use. We found that younger and more highly educated people use the Internet more; extroverts are more likely to use the Internet for social purposes (but not civic purposes). More generally, extroverts tend to experience greater community collective efficacy, are more active in the community, have better social support, and feel greater community belonging. People who experience greater community collective efficacy are more active in the community, belong to more community associations, and are better informed.

Our results indicate that use of the Internet can enhance community participation by mediating the link between a disposition to be civically active and the actual activity of making the activity easier. Civically engaged persons recruit the Internet for civic purposes, just as extroverts recruit it for their interpersonal purposes.

Our logging data show that "local" use of the Internet (web sites, e-mail) is a significant component of actual Internet use. Our survey data show that people who use the Internet for civic purposes are both better informed about and more active in their community. The survey data also show that people who use the Internet for social purposes belong to more community associations and feel greater community belonging.

Our results also suggest boundaries and qualifications on these relationships. We also presented results indicating that use of the Internet may sometimes undermine community participation. People who have a lot of Internet experience but who do not use the Internet for civic purposes are less active in the community. Those who have more Internet experience but who do not use the Internet for social purposes belong to fewer community associations, and those who use the Internet for social purposes tend to be less well informed.

Our study was intended to develop and refine causal hypotheses but not to provide definitive assessments. We studied a single community, but we collected a multifaceted set of data including long-term session logs, surveys, interviews, and web forums. These different sorts of data provide differing perspectives into the community and its use of the Internet. For example, we suspect that some of our senior citizen respondents understand survey items differently than do younger participants. One 76-year-old woman rated herself as dead average on everything, but when we interviewed her, we found that she belongs to eight community groups and is the leader of two. She drives other seniors around town and accessed BEV community web pages more than any other household in our study.

In our immediate future work, we will replicate and extend the results discussed here in our second round of survey data. We refined our survey instrument in several ways between the first and second waves, so our primary expectation is that similar data patterns should obtain. Because the second wave was carried out 12 months after the first, we can also use these data to examine a longitudinal question: Is the role of the Internet in community participation in Blacksburg still emerging? Although we wanted to assess the use and effects of the BEV in part because the networking infrastructure was mature with respect to adoption and dissemination, this does not necessarily mean that developmental change has ceased.

During the year, a variety of significant personal events occurred in the lives of several of the participants, and at least one seriously traumatic event occurred in the lives of all; namely the September 11, 2001, attacks on the United States. We are investigating the use of the Internet in managing life stressors (marriage, move, divorce, job change).

We are also investigating the effects of finer-grain community structures, such as personal social circles and weak-tie networks. In the Experiences of People, Internet, and Community data, people who belong to more than one community group are quite different than those who belong to only one or no community groups (Kavanaugh et al., 2003). These "bridges" are better educated, more informed, and more extroverted. They have higher levels of activism, trust, community involvement, participation, civic interest, and community attachment. Bridges have greater confidence than nonbridges in the community's ability to work together to solve common problems (measured by collective efficacy and its three dimensions—active cooperation, social services, and economic development). Moreover, people with bridging ties who use the Internet more heavily (more than 1.5 hours per day) have higher levels of social engagement and greater use of the Internet for social purposes and have been attending more local meetings and events since going online than nonbridges who use the Internet heavily. This finding emphasizes the social nature of Internet use by bridges. It suggests that in the hands of bridging individuals, the Internet is a tool for maintaining social contacts and relations and increasing face-to-face interaction, all of which help to build both bonding and bridging types of social capital in communities (Granovetter, 1973; Simmel, 1908; Wolff, 1950; Wellman et al., 1988).

As with earlier media, like the telephone, we are seeing evidence of what Ithiel de Sola Pool (1977) called "dual effects." The Internet can increase and decrease communication among family members, improve and erode writing skills, and enhance and invade privacy. New media amplify what is already going on in the household or the community. If family members are not inclined to spend time together, introducing a networked computer will not increase time shared among them, except possibly as a short-term novelty. Conversely, if family members wish to spend time together, the Internet provides new ways of sharing, meeting, and coordinating.

Our studies show that the traditional demographics associated with civic participation (higher education and income) now predict use of the Internet for civic purposes (Kavanaugh et al., 2005). However, the converse appears also to be true: People who use the Internet for civic purposes are better informed about and more active in their communities, and people who use the Internet for social purposes belong to more community associations and feel greater community belonging. We hope to further explore and develop these hypotheses.

Acknowledgments.   This research was partially supported by the U.S. National Science Foundation (IIS-0080864 to Virginia Tech, and IIS-0353097 to Penn State). We are grateful to Keith Hampton and Sonia Livingstone for their excellent discussant comments at the workshop and to Robert Kraut for guidance on finalizing the chapter.

References

Bandura, A. (1997). *Self-efficacy: The exercise of control.* New York: W.H. Freeman.

Bellah, R., Madsen, R., Sullivan, W., Swindler, A., & Tipton, S. (1985). *Habits of the heart: Individualism and commitment in American life.* Berkeley: University of California Press.

Bendig, A. W. (1962). The Pittsburgh scales of social extroversion, introversion and emotionality. *The Journal of Psychology, 53,* 199–209.

Blacksburg Electronic Village (2003). Retrieved November 12, 2003 from http://www.bev.net.

Carroll, J.M. & Reese, D.D. (2003). Community collective efficacy: Structure and consequences of perceived capacities in the Blacksburg Electronic Village. *Proceedings of HICSS-36: Hawaii International Conference on System Sciences,* January 6–9, Kona. IEEE Computer Society.

Carroll, J. M., & Rosson, M. B. (1996). Developing the Blacksburg Electronic Village. *Communications of the ACM, 39(12),* 69–74.

Carroll, J. M., Snook, J., & Isenhour, P.L. (2004). Logging home Internet use in the Blacksburg Electronic Village. Technical Report. Blacksburg: Center for Human-Computer Interaction, Virginia Polytechnical Institute and State University.

Cohill, A., & Kavanaugh, A., Eds. (2000). *Community Networks: Lessons from Blacksburg, Virginia.* Norwood, MA: Artech House.

Dunlap, D., Schafer, W., Carroll, J. M., & Reese, D. D. (2003). Delving deeper into access: Marginal

Internet usage in a local community. Paper presented at HOIT 2003: Home Oriented Informatics and Telematics, The Networked Home and the Home of the Future.

Edwards, J., & Booth, A. (1973). *Social participation in urban society*. Cambridge, MA: Schenkman.

Flanagan, J. C. (1954). The critical incident technique. *Psychological Bulletin, 51,* 28–35.

Granovetter, M. (1973). The strength of weak ties. *American Journal of Sociology, 78* (6), 1360–1380.

Homans, G. (1950). *The human group*. New York: Harcourt Brace.

Internet Systems Consortium. (2003). Retrieved June 5, 2003 from http://www.isc.org.

Kavanaugh, A., Carroll, J. M., Rosson, M. B., Reese, D. D., & Zin, T. T. (2005). Participating in Civil Society: The case of networked communities. *Interacting with Computers 17,* 9–33.

Kavanaugh, A., & Patterson, S. (2001). The impact of community computer networking on community involvement and social capital. *American Behavioral Scientist 45,* 496–495.

Kavanaugh, A., Reese, D. D., Carroll, J. M., & Rosson, M. B. (2003). Weak ties in networked communities. In Huysman, M., Wenger, E., & Wulf, V. (Eds.) *Communities and Technologies* (pp. 265–286). The Netherlands: Kluwer Academic.

Kraut, R., Lundmark, V., Patterson, M., Kiesler, S., Mukopadhyay, T., & Scherlis, W. (1998). Internet paradox: A social technology that reduces social involvement and psychological well-being? *American Psychologist, 53(9),* 1017–1031.

Kraut, R., Scherlis, W., Mukhopadhyay, T., Manning, J., & Kiesler, S. (1996). The HomeNet field trial of residential Internet services. *Communications of the ACM, 39,* 55–63.

NTIA 2000.Falling through the Net: Toward digital inclusion. A report on American's access to technology tools. Washington, DC: U.S. Department of Commerce.

Pedhazur, E. J. (1997). *Multiple regression in behavioral research*. New York: Harcourt Brace College.

Pool, I. (1977). *The social impact of the telephone*. Cambridge, MA: MIT Press.

Putnam, R. D. (2000). Bowling alone: The collapse and revival of American community. New York: Simon & Schuster.

Rothenbuhler, Eric. (1991).The process of community involvement. *Communication Monographs, 58,* 63–78.

Shepherd, G., & Rothenbuhler, E., Eds. (2001). *Communication and community*. Mahwah, NJ: Lawrence Erlbaum.

Simmel, G. ([1908] 1971). Group expansion and the development of individuality. In D. Levine (Ed.), *Georg Simmel on individuality and social forms*. Chicago: University of Chicago Press.

Wellman, B., Carrington, P. and Hall, A. (1988). Networks as personal communities. In B. Wellman and S. Berkowitz (Eds.) *Social Structures: A Network Approach* (pp. 130–184). Cambridge, MA: Cambridge University Press.

Wolff, K. (1950). *The Sociology of Georg Simmel*. New York: The Free Press.

New Technology

in Teenage Life

Patricia M. Greenfield, Elisheva F. Gross,

Kaveri Subrahmanyam, Lalita K. Suzuki,

and Brendesha Tynes

13

Teens on the Internet
Interpersonal Connection, Identity, and Information

When the *New York Times Magazine* looked to teenagers to herald the dawn of the 21st century, it found them online. In an article in the magazine's millennium issue, journalist Camille Sweeney (1999) marveled at the nature, speed, and sheer abundance of communication among teenagers whom she had observed in chat rooms and message boards throughout AOL and the Web. In the ensuing years, teenagers' use of the Internet (and in particular instant messaging [IMing]) has grown to the point at which today's youth are referred to as the Internet (Tapscott, 1998) and IM generation (Pew, 2001).

Though about 75% of young people in the United States are estimated to have Internet access, there is very little research on aspects of their Internet use, such as "its nature and quality, its social conditions, cultural practices, and personal meanings" (Livingstone, 2003, p. 159). The unique social and communicative environment of the Internet gives rise to intriguing research questions about its use among youth: How do teenagers typically spend their time online? How important is communication in this total picture, and by what means do adolescents communicate on the Internet? What is the nature of the online culture that teenagers are constructing together? These broad issues also give rise to more specific questions: Do teenagers use the

disembodied and faceless nature that often characterizes Internet communication to experiment with identities, or do they compensate for this disembodiment by developing new ways to express identity in the online medium? Do teenagers take advantage of the outreach capabilities of the Internet to seek social support and romance and discuss critical but difficult issues like race, sex, and illness with strangers, or do they intensify existing relations by communicating mostly with friends and family? In this chapter, we begin to answer these questions through ongoing research at the Children's Digital Media Center (CDMC) at UCLA.

We begin by reviewing research by Gross (2004) that, together with recent findings from national surveys on Internet use (e.g., Pew Internet and American Life Project, 2001), provides a context for closer examination of the nature of adolescent online communication. Then we review research on the nature, extent, and function of teens' online pretending. In the next section, we examine and describe the online culture constructed by participants in teen chat rooms. Here we review two studies that examine how participants in online teen chat rooms address critical developmental issues, such as identity, sexuality, partner selection, peer relations, and race (Subrahmanyam, Greenfield, &

Tynes, 2004; Tynes, 2003). Finally, we review findings from Suzuki and Calzo (2004), whose analysis of the questions posted on two teen health bulletin boards demonstrates how youth are using the Internet to ask and respond to their peers about highly personal questions involving their health and sexuality.

Varieties and Functions of Teen Internet Use

According to a survey conducted by the Pew Internet Project in the fall of 2000, at least 17 million or 73% of American youth between the ages of 12 and 17 years use the Internet (Pew, 2001). However, as several authors have recently argued (Gross, Juvonen, & Gable, 2002; Livingstone, 2003), documenting the pervasiveness of adolescents' Internet use tells us little about the functions, effect, or even critical characteristics of such use. More detailed data are needed to understand the social and developmental functions that online activity may serve (Kraut, 2003).

In 1999, Gross and colleagues set out to specify how and with whom adolescents spend their time online. Given their interest in the psychosocial context of Internet use and their expectation that much of teens' online communication occurs in private settings, Gross et al. (2002) employed a daily diary methodology that enabled them to both reduce biased recall of time use and collect highly detailed data from youth regarding their online activity that day. To examine an adolescent peer context in which Internet use is widespread, they sampled from a relatively homogenous mid- to high-socioeconomic status community in Southern California.

Participants included both seventh (mean age = 12.1 years, SD = 0.4) and tenth (mean age = 15.3 years, SD = 0.6) graders. Of the 100 boys and 161 girls who participated, 60% were European American, 19% were Asian American, 7% were of mixed heritage, 5% were Latino, and 1% were African American. A two-part data collection procedure was used: after completing an in-school survey, participants completed three to four consecutive end-of-day reports of their activities and feelings that day. Daily activity measures were obtained by asking participants such questions as "How much time did you spend after school today using chat?" Data were aggregated across study days, so that results represented adolescent participants' average weekday online activity (for a review of daily report methodologies, see Reis & Gable, 2000).

On the most basic level, it is important to know where Internet use fits into the context of young people's days. Although 91% of participants reported occasional or regular home Internet use, on a single day within the study, 40%–65% reported going online. In addition, as shown in figure 13.1, participants' after-school time was by no means dominated by Internet use. Rather, on average, time online most approximated time spent in two quintessential adolescent offline social activities: talking on the phone and hanging out with friends. Importantly, no age or gender differences were found in daily time online (see fig. 13.1). However, a gender difference in online experience was found among tenth, but not seventh, graders; among tenth graders, 88% of the boys had been online for more than 2 years, compared to only 72% of the girls, whereas among seventh graders, the same percentage (59%) of boys and girls had been online for more than 2 years.

One distinction that Gross and colleagues drew was between social and nonsocial Internet activity. In 1999, when this line of research was begun, online communication tools such as IM were commonplace on the computer screens of teenagers but remained notably absent from the pages of academic psychology journals (for an example of this distinction in the field of Information Systems, see Kraut, Mukhopadhyay, Szczypula, Kiesler, & Scherlis, 1999). In general, available data offered few distinctions among nonsocial and social forms of Internet use and typically failed to take such distinctions into account in analyses of psychological or developmental correlates of use. Gross et al. found that, on average, two of the three main uses of the Internet by teenagers involved private communication. As shown in figure 13.2, on average, participants devoted the bulk of their daily time online to three domains: IM (M = 38.97 minutes, SD = 42.8), visiting web sites (M = 33.10 minutes, SD = 39.4), and e-mail (M = 21.70 minutes, SD = 16.5). Within the broad category of web surfing, the majority of time was devoted to downloading music (M = 30.95 minutes, SD = 43.5). It should be noted that the sum of the mean time spent in specific domains far surpassed the average daily overall time participants reported spending on the Internet. This disparity indicates simultaneous activity, or multi-

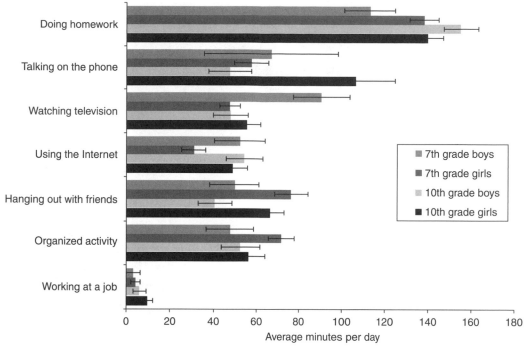

Figure 13.1. Average daily time (+SE) online and in other after-school activities (*n* = 261).

tasking; that is, of the 46 minutes the average participant may spend online daily, 36 minutes may be spent IMing, and 30 minutes may be spent visiting web sites and downloading music (although it should be noted that this inequality may also reflect other causes, including estimation biases). Furthermore, there were few significant group differences in online activity. The only group differences were that tenth-grade girls reported spending more time using IM than did all other groups, and tenth-grade girls also reported spending more time chatting than seventh-grade girls ($p < .05$).

Although private communication channels (e-mail and IM) were more frequent than public communication (e.g., chat, message boards), 18% of the respondents reported visiting at least one chat room over the course of the 3–4 days of the study. Indeed, most teenagers in the United States have explored chat rooms at one time or another. In a survey conducted in 2000, the Pew Internet and American Life Project (2001) reported that 55% of online teens had visited a chat room. In a second survey conducted in fall 2001, the Kaiser Family Foundation found that 71% of 15- to 17-year-old Internet users participate in chat rooms.

Another important psychosocial distinction in Internet use is communication with close friends versus strangers. From a social and developmental perspective, there is a world of difference between the teenager who hurries home from school to exchange e-mail with the classmates she just bid goodbye for the day (Subrahmanyam, Kraut, Greenfield, & Gross , 2000), and the Internet user who prefers playing a furry animal in a Multiuser Dungeon to living his offline life, to which he refers as "just another window" on his computer screen (Turkle, 1995). Since Turkle's landmark case studies were published in 1996, new online communication technologies that facilitate communication with known others (e.g., buddy lists), coupled with the rapid growth of in-home Internet use, mean that the Internet can now be, more than ever, a medium for both anonymous interaction with strangers and communication with established, offline friends (Kraut, Kiesler, Boneva, Cummings, Helgeson et al., 2002).

As expected, communication with people met online varied across communication modalities (see fig. 13.3). Whereas gaming was dominated by interaction with people met online, IM, the online activity to which participants devoted the most

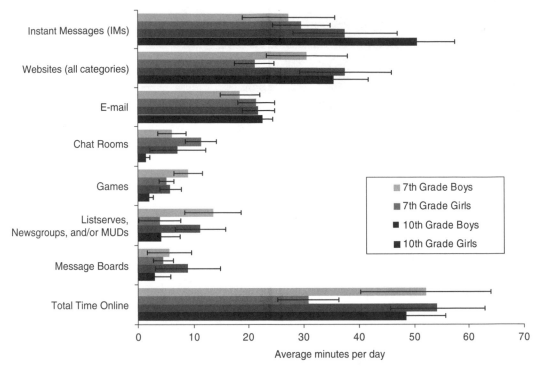

Figure 13.2. Average daily time (+SE) spent online by Internet application.

time, was dominated by communication with off-line peers. Indeed, fully 82% of IM partners were friends or best friends from school (see fig. 13.4). About half (48%) of the chat experiences involved communication with people whom participants had first encountered online; interestingly, no age or gender differences were observed in this tendency.

In summary, the youth in this study spent a majority of their online time interacting with offline friends, although a substantial minority ventured into the public space of a chat room, where they

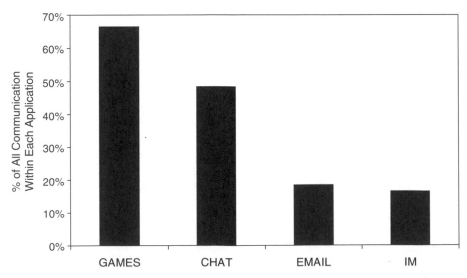

Figure 13.3. Communication with people met online by Internet application.

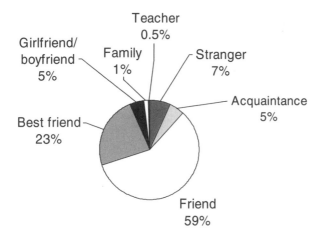

Figure 13.4. The identity of instant message partners.

would often interact with strangers. Indeed, the majority of youth, according to national surveys, have had had some experience with such public spaces.

Despite the sensationalism of online identity play, these figures would lead us to expect that pretending to be someone else would occur less frequently than claiming one's real identity. To find out whether this was the case, Gross and colleagues asked adolescent participants when, how, and why they pretended to be someone else online. Sixty percent of participants reported that they had never pretended to be someone else; 40% had. The surprise was that identity play was not limited to interactions with strangers. Rather, those who had pretended to be someone else often did so in the physical company of school-based friends. Tenth graders were more likely than seventh graders to pretend in the presence of a friend. When asked about the reasons why they engaged in pretense, 33% of youth reported that it was a joke, and 26% explicitly mentioned friends as accomplices or targets. Another 24% of those who pretended explained that they hid their identity to protect themselves and their privacy or to get past online rules. A minority of explanations (3%) appeared to involve identity exploration per se. For example, only one participant reported pretending to "to try out a personality." Not surprisingly, 82 of 95 respondents had pretended to be older; as is evident in figure 13.5, other online personas were less common. The frequency of trying to be older raises the possibility that, in a teen chat room, some participants may be younger than they say—something to bear in mind as we explore the culture of teen chat in the

next two sections. In contrast, the fact that most respondents had never pretended to be something other than what they were indicates that many participants in anonymous public communication modalities, such as chat rooms, are who they say they are.

But what do they say they are? Indeed, is identity even a subject in an anonymous space like a chat room? Identity has long been considered an important adolescent concern (e.g., Erikson, 1968). We turn to this and other important adolescent issues—sexuality, identity, partner selection, and peer relations (Subrahmanyam, Greenfield, & Tynes, 2004)—as we explore the culture of a teen chat room in the next section.

The Culture of a Teen Chat Room: Linguistic Codes and Adolescent Issues

To understand how online communication may serve as a context for adolescent development, one must start by studying the culture of teenagers' digital environments (Greenfield & Subrahmanyam, 2003; Subrahmanyam, Greenfield, & Tynes, 2004). Greenfield and Subrahmanyam broadly define culture as that which is socially constructed and shared. They focus not on the material aspects of online culture but on its symbolic aspects, such as its linguistic codes, interactions, and discourse patterns. In doing so, they documented examples of how critical adolescent developmental issues such as identity, gender, sexuality, and peer relations are socially constructed within chat environments. Because of the anonymous nature of chat rooms, no verifiable information is known about individual

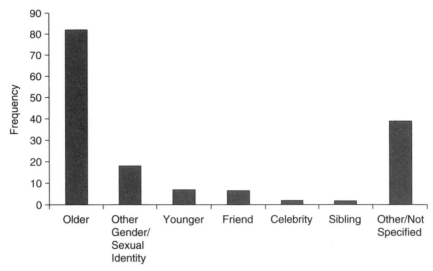

Figure 13.5. The content of online pretense: Frequency of teenagers reporting different identities (*n*= 95).

participants, and so their investigations operate at the cultural rather than the individual level of analysis. This culture is particularly interesting because it is constructed at the group rather than the dyadic level of e-mail or IM. Chat room interactions are also interesting from a developmental point of view because they offer an anonymous public window onto online adolescent culture that is not available in the private modalities of e-mail or IM. On the basis of a qualitative analysis of chat room discourse, these interactions indicate that participants in teen chat rooms are constructing and using news codes and modes of communication (Greenfield & Subrahmanyam, 2003) in the service of major adolescent developmental issues (Subrahmanyam, Greenfield, & Tynes, 2004).

In the tradition of conversation analysis (Schegloff, 1979), Greenfield and Subrahmanyam analyzed a lengthy, spontaneously produced verbal exchange in a chat room. The methodology involved Greenfield acting as a participant observer in an online teen chat room. Like the other participants, she gained access to this chat room through an account with an Internet provider. She mainly took the role of observer in the chat room, and at the end of the session, she printed out the log of the conversation. The electronic chat log was copied into a Microsoft Word document, an excerpt of which is shown in figure 13.6. Although the content of the transcript in figure 13.6 is identical to what another user in the chat room might have seen,

we have changed the formatting of the fonts to show the conversation threads. We have also changed the screen names of the chat participants.

Before returning to the theme of identity, it is necessary to say something about the communication environment of chat. The multiparty nature of the conversation makes it nonobvious to a novice how to comprehend what is going on. The first step in Greenfield and Subrahmanyam's (2003) analysis was to diagram the various conversations that were occurring. Note that the major communication issue in chat is not speed but the fact that multiple conversations are going on at once and participants are often taking part in more than one conversation. With the assistance of a 21-year-old informant who had considerable experience chatting, the researchers identified three main threads of conversation in the four-page transcript (see fig. 13.6). In contrast to face-to-face-conversations, one thing that stands out is the number of intervening turns between the relevant contributions of a conversation thread. As a consequence, related utterances are not always adjacent to each other.

Identity in a Chat Room

The expression of personal identity in a chat room is complicated because participants are disembodied online and that basic identity information about users is not readily available. Age and sex are the primary categories according to which people are assigned (Brewer & Lui, 1989). These

1 *mizrose76:*	*shut up i dont need it*
2 **morn8sun:**	**no seriously . . . the great one. . . . this ass rang my bell talking about open the door**
3 *al commands:*	*yes you do*
4 *suddenreaction:*	*i do 14/m*
5 you have just entered room «sílver»	
6 *al commands:*	*dont try to deny*
7 *al commands:*	*(shes in denial guys)*
8 blakpower1413:	/89
9 agreatonefeb74:	oh
10 *mizrose76:*	*no am not*
11 mizprude1762:	press 14 if ya wanna chat 2 a 14/f/cali
12 *mízrose76:*	*u r*
13 **morn8sun:**	**im like wrong bell. . . . if he came again i would of cussed him out good and plenty**
14 **morn8sun:**	**one time i had too**
15 **al commands:**	**what happened morn?**
16 blakpower1413:	14
17 agreatonefeb74:	kew1
18 *al commands:*	*hahahh*
19 *al commands:*	*i am what?*
20 swimteambabe:	a/s/l
21 suddenreaction:	who is f*** dany
22 *al commands:*	*the greatest?*
23 *al commands:*	*ya, i know*
24 morn8sun:	fuckdany?
25 morn8sun:	lol
26 morn8sun:	what?
27 *mizrose76:*	*al did i give u permission to talk to ne one?*
28 <u>pinkbabyangel542:</u>	<u>who believe's speedo's (on guys) aren't right</u>
29 <u>pinkbabyangel542:</u>	<u>type 3</u>
30 *al commands:*	*what!!!*
31 <u>pinkbabyangel542:</u>	<u>3</u>
32 <u>dustinknosall:</u>	<u>3</u>
33 <u>swimteambabe:</u>	<u>3</u>
34 brentjyd:	any fine ladies want to chat press 69 or im me
35 *al commands:*	*are you trying to talkback to your master*
36 *al commands:*	*??*
37 sportyman04:	hey
38 **morn8sun:**	**this ass came to myrang my bell talking about let me in**
39 <u>pinkbabyangel542:</u>	<u>it's friggin scary</u>

Figure 13.6. Record of conversation in a monitored teen chat room; see Greenfield & Subrahmanyam (2003) for the complete computer printout without altered fonts or capitalization. Note that, in the original record, participants distinguished themselves by utilizing different fonts or cases for their contributions. Italics = conversation 1; bold = conversation 2; underlined = conversation 3.

characteristics are clearly evident in face-to-face conversation but are missing online. Location, a third piece of identity-related information, is also fundamental and is taken for granted in face-to-face interactions. Location can most definitely not be taken for granted on the Internet, and users have adapted to this challenge by devising a cultural solution—the a/s/l code, which is in the form of a slot-filler code in a standard graphic format (Greenfield & Subrahmanyam, 2003). In this code, "a" stands for "age," "s" stands for "sex," and "l" stands for location. According to the Pew report (2001), online teens report that the a/s/l code is the most common question directed toward new entrants in a chat room (p. 23). The a/s/l code is used as a conversation opener to find out the characteristics of others in the room, as in the example below:

> 20 *SwimteamBabe*: a/s/l

The a/s/l code is also used to announce one's own characteristics, as in the next example, especially when looking for a conversational partner of a particular sex:

> 67 *MAKERSCLUB701*: Any girls in here wanna
>   chat im me
> 71 *MAKERSCLUB701*: 17/m/fl

This code capitalizes on the anonymity and alphanumeric nature of the chat environment, and has been developed by chat participants to give and receive fundamental information about potential conversational and/or romantic partners. Age, sex, and location have thus become important elements in the identities constructed in a teen chat room.

The Sexual Body in Cyberspace

The third thread in conversation 3 provides a good example of the social construction of sexuality in a teen chat room. The implicit topic of the conversation seems to be that Speedo bathing suits show off sexual anatomy, especially of boys. The conversation is begun by PinkBabyAngel (line 28), who wants to explore this topic, and gets agreement and encouragement from her peers in lines 32 and 33. Here, she uses a numeric code that allows her to discern who agrees with her out of the flow of multiple conversations. Requests to type a particular numeral are used frequently to identify a conversation partner who may be willing to relate in a positive manner, here by agreeing about Speedos. Typing the requested numeral indicates a desire to form a validating subgroup of peers out of the anonymous group of chatters. In this instance, PinkBabyAngel finds two kindred souls, Dustinknosall and Swimteambabe. Further on in line 39 ("it's friggin scary"), PinkBabyAngel indicates that she is not yet ready to face the male sexual anatomy. In turn, Proffich gives the male perspective in line 45. At this point, the conversation becomes a kind of an exploration of sexualized relations with the opposite sex (lines 65, 68, etc.).

Conversation 3 illustrates a central adolescent developmental issue—concern about the sexually

developing body. In this example, the special contribution of the online medium to this developmental issue is that it enables participants to have a frank discussion of a potentially embarrassing topic.

Romantic Partner Selection

It is interesting that in the midst of this discussion, Brentlyd attempts a fairly overt sexual pickup in line 34 (immediately after two female chatters have agreed that Speedos are not right on guys). No one replies in the public space, but we have no way of knowing whether anyone responded with a private message. Cyber pickup attempts in online chat are common, and because not all responses occur in the public space, it is difficult to assess how successful these attempts are. It appears that success is enhanced when participants are forthcoming with basic identity information about their age, sex, and location. An example of a successful pickup is:

> 11 *Mizprude1762*: press 14 if ya wanna
>   chat 2 a 14/f/cali
> 16 *BLAKPower1413*: 14

(For the present purposes, a successful pickup is defined as one that elicits a cooperative response.) We see here a connection between a chat convention and a developmental issue of major importance in the teen years: selection of friends and romantic partners. The use of the a/s/l code in conjunction with requests for numerals enables participants to seek and find someone who is willing to talk with them. We speculate that this enables participants in teen chat rooms to experiment with potential conversation partners in what is seemingly the low-risk environment of cyberspace.

Gender Identity

The physical disembodiment of gender in a chat room and the lack of other physical markers of identity pose particular challenges to the presentation of gender identity. Under these conditions, nicknames become the initial vehicle through which participants in chat rooms present their gender identity to others in the room—a kind of substitute for face and body. Subrahmanyam, Greenfield, & Tynes, (2004) suggest that screen names such as PinkBabyAngel542, MizRose76, Rollerbabe904590, and Mizprude1762 have a feminine connotation, whereas names such as Sportyman04, DustinKnos-All, and Al commands have a masculine connotation. Apparently, it is known in online circles that this type of name attracts the attention of the opposite sex (Ali Lexa, personal communication, December 2002). Mizprude1762 as a screen name with a feminine connotation also reflects a concern with sexual relationships, albeit reactive to much of what is going on in the sexual domain in the chat room. Many of the screen names seem to use strong gender stereotypes, or what may be called "hyper gender signals." This notion that media simulations exaggerate gender signals into a hyper form was suggested by Francis Steen (personal communication May 9, 2002). The names seem almost to be a substitute for the use of the body (Greenfield, 2002) as a signal to proclaim identity, fit in with the peer group, and attract potential partners. These playful names seem to compensate for the absence of physical identity in dealing with these important adolescent concerns.

In sum, the chat code being used by participants in a teen chat room helps the participants address important developmental issues, such as a concern with their sexually developing bodies, romantic partner selection, and gender identity in an environment in which there is no physical embodiment of physical identity. The lack of cues about basic identity also influences how participants exchange information about their race/ethnicity and how they explore their racial/ethnic identity in chat rooms—issues that we address in the next section.

Racialized Discourse and Self-Representation in Teen Chat Rooms

Adolescence is also a time when youth explore their racial and ethnic identities. In the mid-1990s, the Internet was lauded for its potential to usher in a color-blind society (Smith & Kollock, 1999; Nakamura, 2000). It was argued that this new medium could eliminate racial cues from communication and lead to more egalitarian interaction between members of different groups. Though visual signifiers of race may be removed online, recent research on adults has shown that across a range of communication settings on the Internet (Kendall, 1998; Kang, 2000; Glaser, Dixit, & Green, 2002; Nakamura, 2002), race takes on a linguistic form through text provided by participants themselves. Once made visible in the text, race has been found to be central to many computer-mediated interactions. In fact, many of the social norms and ills that exist offline

are often reproduced in adult online communities (Burkhalter, 1999). Despite the increasing availability of data on the racial dynamics of adult online communities (e.g., Bailey, 1996; Ebo, 1998; Kolko, Nakamura, & Rodman, 1999; Nelson, Linh, Tu, & Hines, 2001), there remains a dearth of research on the online race-related experiences of adolescents.

In the research study described in this section, Tynes (2003) explored whether race was salient in the online interactions of participants in monitored teen chat rooms and how they showed its importance linguistically. More specifically, this study was a virtual ethnography of racialized discourse and self-representation. As in the work described in the previous section (Greenfield & Subrahmanyam, 2003; Subrahmanyam, Greenfield, & Tynes, 2004), the researcher did not know the actual ethnic or racial identities of the participants but was studying their performed identities and the construction of these identities in the chat contexts. Like Greenfield, Tynes acted as a participant observer in the chat rooms. She made 19 visits that lasted between 20 minutes to an hour between November 2001 and November 2002. She used the copy function to record the log of the chat conversation and pasted the transcript into a Word file. In all, the transcripts were between 10 and 20 pages long.

The participants, in line with much of the literature on adolescent identity development (Erikson, 1968; Marcia, 1980; Phinney, 1989), identified themselves on the basis of race both implicitly and explicitly, using racialized discourse. Implicit forms included using African-American English or Spanish, whereas the explicit forms involved self-identification, identifying in-groups, partner selection, and expressing racial attitudes. Here, we focus on the latter form of racialized discourse.

Self-Identification

The examples below show how participants transformed or extended the traditional way of identifying the self in chat culture via the a/s/l code to include their race or ethnicity. Note that each line was taken from a different transcript.

> Mike125: 14/m/nj white/tan/buff, loves softball
> Draon: 15.italian.m.pa.pic
> CINNAMON: ne1 wanna chat wit a puerto rican hottie, press123, and im me

Here Mike125 says he is a 14-year-old male from New Jersey, who is white, tan, and buff, and who also loves softball. Similarly, Draon says that he is a 15-year-old Italian male from Pennsylvania who has a picture (pic). Cinnamon also provides information about her ethnicity as she asks if anyone wants to chat with a Puerto Rican hottie. As noted in the previous section, participants in teen chat rooms spend much of their conversations discussing/presenting their identities in terms of age, sex, and location. Adding race or ethnicity to their conversation openers or greetings indicates that it is an important aspect of their sense of self.

Identifying In-Groups

In line with research indicating that ethnicity is more salient as an identity element to members of minority ethnicities compared to members of the majority (Phinney, 1989), Tynes (2003) found that people of color often took the lead in identifying themselves and in-groups on the basis of race; however, she found that white participants also explored identity through their discourse. In the transcript shown in figure 13.7, white teens, apparently prompted by blacks, ask about race. Fake identifies himself as a 14-year-old black male with caramel skin who weighs 165 pounds and is 56 inches tall (line 1). Weeb then asks any black people in the room to press 69 (line 4). He seems to also be aware that asking this question could be inter-

1. FAKE:	if you wana chat wit a black male 56 carmel weigh 165 press 15 im 14
2. Sandy:	*is that shybrat girl out yet>>*
3. LilLauren:	**hi prepsxsuck**
4. Weeb:	**yo not to be mean or anything if u black press 69**
5. FAKE:	**56 thats my height**
6. LilLauren:	**if you are white, press 9832455**
7. FAKE:	**69**
8. FAKE:	**69**
9. Weeb:	**holla**
10. LilLauren:	**9832455**
11. FAKE:	**69**
12. Jmoney:	*69*
13. FAKE:	**lol**
14. LilLauren:	**9832455**
15. Sandy:	**9832455**
16. BIGL:	9832455
17. LilLauren:	**9832455**

Figure 13.7. Example of racialized discourse for in-group identification in a monitored teen chat room.

preted as separating himself from others. Instead of his question inciting objections, he gets only positive responses from Fake and Jmoney. Immediately following the request for black people to identify themselves, Lillauren makes a request for whites to identify themselves by pressing 9832455 (line 6). Sandy (line 15) and BigL (line 16) respond by typing 9832455. Racialized discourse, in this instance as well as others in the data set, served as a sign to other participants that race was an acceptable topic of conversation and that it was acceptable to express the desire to talk to others like oneself.

Partner Selection

As illustrated in lines 1 and 6 in the extract below, participants also identified in-groups to find conversation partners who were of a certain sex, race, or ethnicity. Ethnicity and race are clearly part of the adolescent concern with romantic partner selection.

> 1 *Na hill*: BLACKS AND HISPANIC BOYS PRESS 05
>
> 2 *Nindiri*: na hill got pic.?
>
> 3 *Na hill*: NOPE U
>
> 4 *LilRascal*: is anyone in here like really chatting or all you all just watchen the screen
>
> 5 *Vargas*: Hey ppl
>
> 6. *Nindiri*: 05 nope

Na hill asks black and Hispanic boys to press 05. In response to this request, Nindiri presses 05 (line 6). In line 2, Nindiri asks Na hill for a picture, and Na hill responds by saying "Nope U" in line 3. Nindiri then responds by typing "nope" (note he is responding to two questions at once in line 6) Race or ethnicity, for Na hill, appear to be enough to determine initial attraction and desire to speak to her interlocutors. Ten Have's (2000) paper on finding chat partners discusses the fact that chat participants log on to the chat room and enter what is akin to a market, where participants are both buyers and sellers. In this market, participants self-advertise and also shop by entering the a/s/l code. In Tynes's data, participants in teen chat rooms often asked for a person's race and indicated their own as a means of providing additional information on which to base their decisions to "buy" chat partners and initiate potential relationships.

Racial Attitudes

Participants also connected to chat partners by expressing their racial attitudes. In the extract below,

Secret1 and BigE discuss the usage of the word *nigger* (the N word).

> 1 *SECRET1*: IT BOTHER'S ME
> 2 *SECRET1*: I'M BLACK
> 3 *BigE*: how come
> . . .
> 19 *BigE*: see this is how i look at it
> 20 *Punch*: oh yeah
> 21 *JVADOK*: smurf mustangs dont suck they rock
> 22 *Kandy*: zzzzzzzzzzzzzzzzzzzzzzzz
> . . .
> 35. *BigE*: if they say it and it ends with an A and comin from another black person it doesn't bother me, but if it ends in er I get offensive

In lines 1 and 2, Secret1 states that the use of the N word bothers him because he is black (in parts of the transcript not shown here, the participants identify themselves as males). He appears to be trying to get people not to use the word at all. BigE says that the presence of the postvocalic *r* makes a difference. In African-American English, the *r* sound is often dropped so that words like player become *playa* and store become *sto*. If the N word is said without the *r*, it is often a term of endearment used by people in particular communities of African Americans. BigE argues that a person must have ethnic and linguistic membership in the black community to be able to say this word; otherwise he "get[s] offensive" (line 35).

To conclude, Tynes's analysis indicates that race is just as salient for participants in online teen chat contexts as it is for participants in adult chat contexts. Even more important, it appears that race is no longer taboo, unlike in many conventional face-to-face settings. All teens, not just teens of color as the literature suggests (Phinney, 1989), appear to be exploring ethnic and racial identities. In fact, it would appear that the prevailing interaction in chat rooms impels whites to talk about race/ethnicity and encourages interethnic interaction that may otherwise be limited in offline contexts. Her analysis indicates that through racialized discourse, teens may be socializing one another into ways of thinking about race and that much of what is learned in the monitored context may be positive.

In the previous sections, we presented research that showed that adolescents are using IM and chat rooms for daily interpersonal communication to keep in touch with friends, play, and express their emerging sexual and racial identities. In the next

section, we present research that describes how adolescents are using the Internet as an information source to address questions about their physical and sexual health. We learn that in an anonymous bulletin board setting for teens, participants ask highly personal questions and receive advice from their peers.

Peer Advice in Cyberspace: Health-Related Bulletin Boards for Teens

The many physical, social, and cognitive changes that take place in adolescence can elicit numerous health and relationship-based questions among youth (e.g., Malus, LaChance, Lamy, Macaulay, & Vanasse, 1987; Joffe, Radius, & Gall, 1988; Klein & Wilson, 2002). Unfortunately, teens are often reluctant to reveal personal problems to others (e.g., Ackard & Neumark-Sztainer, 2001; Cheng, Savageau, Sattler, & DeWitt, 1993). Teens are also reluctant to discuss personal health questions with their physicians (Ackard & Neumark-Sztainer, 2001). In one study, 86% of adolescents reported that they would go to their physicians for problems such as "a bad sore throat," but only 43% stated that they would confide in their physicians about more private health concerns such as pregnancy and substance abuse (Cheng et al., 1993).

Many teens are reluctant to seek advice about personal health concerns because of fears about confidentiality (Ackard & Neumark-Sztainer, 2001; Cheng et al., 1993; Rideout, 2002). For example, adolescents often express a fear of discussing sex with a physician—because of the potential disclosure of information to parents—out of embarrassment or inhibition (Hassan & Creatsas, 2000). Thus, the anonymity of the Internet may be an ideal place for teens to search for health information without having to reveal personally identifying information. Online health advice can be found on Web pages, newsgroups, Listservs, chat rooms, and bulletin boards (Hsiung, 2000; Sharp, 2000). Online health sites are also beneficial in that advice is available 24 hours a day (Fox & Rainie, 2000) and can be received from a huge number of peers worldwide (Finn, 1999; White & Dorman, 2001).

However, are teens using online health resources, and if so, what questions are being asked over the Internet? To address the question of teen health advice in cyberspace, Suzuki and Calzo (in press) explored the content on a popular health support Web site for teens that used a peer-generated bulletin board format to facilitate discussion about adolescent health and relationship issues. Analyses were conducted on the questions found on 273 bulletin threads (103 threads from a general teen issues bulletin board, and 170 threads from a teen sexual health bulletin board) collected on the site over a 2-month period. Visitors on this site anonymously post questions without revealing their identity (pseudonyms are used). Furthermore, adolescents can also anonymously "lurk" on the site by clicking to view the questions and responses posted by others without posting personal responses.

Content analysis was used to classify the range of topics reflected in the threads. One researcher read all 273 of the initial posted questions found on both boards. The main topic of each question was summarized briefly (e.g., side effects of the birth control pill) and inductively grouped and collapsed according to similarity of topic to form an initial set of categories. A second researcher independently took 20% of the threads on both boards and created a separate set of categories. The two category sets were then compared and collapsed by both researchers to form the final set of 14 question topic categories: Parents/Adults, Peers, Romantic Relationships, Personality/Mental Health, Grooming, Body Image/Exercise, Physical Health, Sexual Health, Pregnancy/Birth Control, Sexuality—Interpersonal, Sexuality—Preferences/Techniques, Physical/Sexual Abuse, Drugs/Alcohol, and School. (For examples of questions in each category, see table 13.1.)

Intercoder reliability was calculated by having two coders independently categorize 20% of the threads randomly selected from each board. The kappa statistic for the intercoder reliability was 0.85, which is in the excellent range (Fleiss, 1981). The content of the two boards was combined for the kappa statistic as well as for subsequent analyses. Analyses of the questions posted on these boards revealed that 181 people posted an average of 1.5 questions during the 2-month period. Table 13.2 shows the total number of posts, percentage of posts, mean number of replies, and mean number of views for each of 14 question types. (For a detailed analysis of the types of replies posted in this study, see Suzuki & Calzo, 2004).

The largest proportion (27%) of questions posted concerned sexual health and included questions about topics such as ejaculation problems, penis size and shape, menstruation, and vaginal infections. When divided into questions asked on both boards, the largest proportion of questions on the teen health board was about romantic relationships (36.9%), and for the sexual health board, not surprisingly, it was sexual health (41.8%). Thus, questions about interpersonal relationships and sexuality were the most frequently asked questions for this teen population. Questions referring to issues concerning physical/sexual abuse (0.7%) and drugs/alcohol (0.7%) were posted least frequently. This focus on sex and romantic relationships reflects a key adolescent concern and was also found in the chat room study described earlier (Subrahmanyam, Greenfield, & Tynes, 2004).

Different questions also elicited different quantities of responses. Questions about body image and exercise garnered the most replies from other posters ($M = 10.6$ replies per question). Questions about the interpersonal aspects of sex ($M = 8.9$), grooming ($M = 8.3$), physical and sexual abuse ($M = 8.0$), sexual preferences and techniques ($M = 7.9$), and pregnancy/birth control ($M = 7.7$) also averaged more than seven replies per question. Internet posters were least likely to respond to questions about parents/adults ($M = 2.5$), drugs and alcohol ($M = 4.5$), and romantic relationships ($M = 4.9$).

The number of views, or "lurks," also varied by question type. Views refer to the number of times that Internet surfers clicked on a thread to read it, even if they did not directly reply to it or participate in the discussion thread. Those who are shy about revealing themselves but who still desire information can "lurk" in online groups, reading other people's messages without active participation (King & Moreggi, 1998; Winzelberg, 1997). Thus, the number of views may be a rough measure of subject interest in the topic. Questions relating to the interpersonal aspects of sex solicited by far the greatest number of average views per question ($M = 480.9$). Also popular were questions about grooming, sexual preferences and techniques, sexual health, and peer relationships. Question types with the least number of views included pregnancy/birth control ($M = 114.9$), school ($M = 125.7$), and parents/adults ($M = 142.0$). Analyses of views for abuse could not be carried out, be-

Table 13.1. Question category codes and examples.

Thread question category	Examples
Parents/adults	"I'm embarrassed around my mom." "I lied to my parents about where I was going."
Peers	"I am not mean to anybody but for some reason nobody likes me!! HELP!!! My basketball teammates all don't like me but I don't know why. I am always nice to them!!!"
Relationships–Romantic	"I feel awkward hugging and kissing my girlfriend with everyone around." "How do I ask a girl out, or at least talk to her?"
Personality/mental health	"I feel like I'm going insane! Sometimes I feel like I want to cry about everything but I just can't" "I just want to gain the self-confidence to feel better about me . . . where do I start?"
Grooming	"I have a question about shaving 'down there'." "I am just curious, why do girls get their bellies pierced?"
Body image/exercise	"I would really like to drop 10 lbs in the next 2 months." "I feel so fat compared to some of my friends who wear such small sizes."
Physical health	"Will I get skin cancer if I only go tanning for two weeks?"" "I have a problem with a lot of sweat coming from my underarms."
Sexual health	"I have a hooked penis, do you know how to fix this?!?! PLEASE HELP ME!!!" "After having an orgasm is it normal to have white discharge looking stuff?"
Pregnancy/birth control	"Just curious, which would be better, the pill or shot for birth control?" "He came on my stomach . . . could it have went inside of me and gotten me pregnant?"
Sexuality–interpersonal	"My boyfriend wants to have sex and I agreed, but now I don't want to . . . I'm afraid that if I say no he'll break up with me." "I really don't like performing oral sex on my boyfriend."
Sexuality–preferences/technique	"Is it normal to kiss someone with your mouth open but no tongue?" "Anyone have tips for keeping the urge of ejaculating down?"
Physical/sexual abuse	"My stepsister . . . was beaten a lot by her uncle when she was young." "He took his hand across my cheek twice . . . what was I to do?"
Drugs/alcohol	"Are there a good number of people that go to high school parties that don't drink?"
School	"Should I take Human Bio or AP Bio? Which one looks better when applying for college?" "I hate going to school, I don't want to wait til I'm 16 to do homeschooling."

From Suzuki & Calzo, in press.

cause all of the subject topic headings for these threads were rated as "unclassifiable."

The results of this study revealed that adolescents were indeed using Internet bulletin boards to ask personal health questions. In fact, the most frequently asked questions referred to issues of sexual health, romantic relationships, pregnancy/birth control, and sexual preferences/techniques. Questions about sexuality were also of great interest to people who anonymously "lurked" on the site without posting responses, as indicated by the large number of views found for those threads. What makes these results particularly interesting is the fact that although teens are reluctant to seek face-to-face advice about sexuality from physicians and others (Ackard & Neumark-Sztainer, 2001; Cheng et al., 1993; Malus et al., 1987), these questions were the most popular ones posted on an online bulletin board. Thus, Internet health bulletin boards possibly help to circumvent the awkwardness associated with asking sexual and relationship questions in face-to-face encounters. It is therefore clear that teens are using the Internet to ask questions that may be embarrassing for them to ask in their off-line environments. Once again, the Internet provides a space for adolescents to explore their

Table 13.2. Frequency of question topics.

Question type	Total (N = 273)	% of total	Mean replies	Mean views
Sexual health	73	26.7	5.3	245.5
Romantic	46	16.8	4.9	170.6
Pregnancy/birth control	41	15.0	7.7	114.9
Sex, preferences/technique	24	8.8	7.9	314.0
Physical health	19	7.0	5.2	158.1
Sex, interpersonal	16	5.9	8.9	480.9
Grooming	14	5.1	8.3	349.8
Body image/exercise	13	4.8	10.6	175.2
Parents/adults	6	2.2	2.5	142.0
Peers	6	2.2	6.5	237.8
Personality/mental health	6	2.2	5.5	167.7
School	5	1.8	6.0	125.7
Abuse	2	0.7	8.0	N/A
Drugs/alcohol	2	0.7	4.5	176.3
Total/ mean total	273	100	6.4	222.0

From Suzuki & Calzo, in press.

identities and address their concerns—particularly regarding sexuality and romantic relationships—in the anonymity of cyberspace.

Conclusions

We have found that online communication is the most popular of all Internet uses among youth, with IM being the most popular of the Internet communication modalities. In other words, our research confirms that today's teenagers are indeed the IM generation. In the area of identity, we have found that a substantial group of teenagers do experiment with identities on the Internet, and equally, that they use new codes (such as a/s/l) to express identity in this disembodied medium. In the social domain, our chat and bulletin board studies show that the Internet is being used by teenagers to seek peer support and romance, and our daily report research reveals that most communication is, nonetheless, with friends and family. Indeed, contrary to popular myth, even identity experimentation is mainly with friends and family, not strangers. Concerning difficult issues, our chat and bulletin board studies indicate that adolescents do use the Internet to discuss race, sex, and illness. In the case of race, a subject that is normally taboo in social settings becomes prevalent in Internet communication.

In addition, our analysis of the codes of chat indicates that a common peer culture has been cre-ated through Internet communication. One aspect of this culture is the use of abbreviated linguistic codes such as a/s/l; another aspect of this culture is the cognitive habit of multitasking, with multiple Internet windows open simultaneously. Still other aspects of this online culture relate to conventions for keeping track of conversations in multiparty Internet settings.

Most striking perhaps is how essential concerns of adolescence are integrated into this new medium in new ways. For example, teens may be too embarrassed to seek information on sex from parents or friends, but they can openly ask these questions on a teen bulletin board. Gender identity that would normally be conveyed by body and dress is now conveyed by nicknames in a teen chat room. Racial identity, normally stronger in minority group members, is made more explicit in members of the majority by interracial discussion of ethnic membership that would usually be obvious in a face-to-face setting. What are the effects of the Internet in all these areas of adolescent development? These critical questions remain for our future research.

Acknowledgments. We gratefully acknowledge the National Science Foundation for funding the Children's Digital Media Center and HopeLab for supporting Dr. Lalita Suzuki's research. The CDMC at UCLA is part of a consortium of four centers funded by the National Science Foundation; the other three centers are located at Georgetown University, Northwestern University, and the University of Texas, Austin. Instrumental to their funding was Rod Cocking, who pushed for the scientific integration of children and their real-world environments. The goal of the CDMCs is to both carry out and seed long-term research in the area of digital media, which is a huge and understudied component of children's and adolescents' lives. We also would like to thank our collaborators and research assistants on the individual projects: Jerel Calzo and Lindsey Reynolds.

References

Ackard, D. M., & Neumark-Sztainer, D. (2001). Health care information sources for adolescents: age and gender differences on use, concerns, and needs. *Journal of Adolescent Health, 29,* 170–176.

Bailey, C. (1996). Virtual skin: Articulating race in cyberspace. In Moser, M. A., & MacLeod, D. (Eds.), *Immersed in technology: Art and virtual environments*. Cambridge, MA: MIT Press.

Brewer, M. B., & Lui, L. (1989). The primacy of age and sex in the structure of person categories. *Social Cognition, 7,* 262–274.

Burkhalter, B. (1999). Reading race online. In Smith, M., & Kollock, P. (Eds.), *Communities in cyberspace*. London: Routledge.

Cheng, T. L., Savageau, J. A., Sattler, A. L., & DeWitt, T. G. (1993). Confidentiality in health care: A survey of knowledge, perceptions, and attitudes among high school students. *Journal of the American Medical Association, 269*(11), 1404–1407.

Ebo, B. (Ed.) (1998). *Cyberghetto or cybertopia? Race, class, and gender on the Internet*. Westport, CT: Praeger.

Erikson, E. (1968). Identity, youth and crisis. New York: Norton.

Finn, J. (1999). An exploration of helping processes in an online self-help group focusing on issues of disability. *Health and Social Work, 24*(3), 220–231.

Fleiss, J. L. (1981). *Statistical methods for rates and proportions* (2nd ed.). New York: Wiley.

Fox, S., & Rainie, L. (2000). *The online health care revolution: How the Web helps Americans take better care of themselves*. Retrieved November 26, 2000 from http://www.pewinternet.org/reports/pdfs/PIP_Health_Report.pdf.

Glaser, J., Dixit, J., & Green, D. P. (2002). Studying hate crime with the Internet: What Makes racists advocate racial violence? *Journal of Social Issues, 58*(1), 177–193.

Greenfield, L. 2002. *Girl culture*. San Francisco, CA: Chronicle Books.

Greenfield, P. M., & Subrahmanyam, K. (2003). Online discourse in a teen chatroom: New codes and new modes of coherence in a visual medium. *Journal of Applied Developmental Psychology, 24,* 713–738.

Gross, E. F. (2004). Adolescent Internet use: What we expect, what teens report. *Journal of Applied Developmental Psychology, 25*(6), 633–649.

Gross, E. F., Juvonen, J., & Gable, S. E. (2002). Online communication and well-being in early adolescence: The social function of instant messages. *Journal of Social Issues, 58,* 75–90.

Hassan, E. A., & Creatsas, G. C. (2000). Adolescent sexuality: A developmental milestone or risk-taking behavior? The role of health care in the prevention of sexually transmitted diseases. *Journal of Pediatric and Adolescent Gynecology, 13,* 119–124.

Hsiung, R. C. (2000). The best of both worlds: An online self-help group hosted by a mental health professional. *CyberPsychology & Behavior, 3*(6), 935–950.

Joffe, A., Radius, S., & Gall, M. (1988). Health counseling for adolescents: What they want, what they get, and who gives it. *Pediatrics, 82*(3), 481–485.

Kang, J. (2000). Cyber-race. *Harvard Law Review, 113,* 1130–1208.

Kendall, L. (1998) Meaning and identity in "Cyberspace": The performance of gender, class, and race online. *Symbolic Interaction 21*(2), 129–153.

King, S. A. & Moreggi, D. (1998). Internet therapy and self-help groups—the pros and cons. In J. Gackenback (Ed.), *Psychology and the Internet. Intrapersonal, interpersonal, and transpersonal implications*. San Diego, CA: Academic Pres, 77–109.

Klein, J. D., & Wilson, K. M. (2002). Delivering quality care: Adolescents' discussion of health risks with their providers. *Journal of Adolescent Health, 30,* 190–195.

Kolko, B., Nakamura, L., & Rodman, G. (1999). *Race in cyberspace*. New York: Routledge.

Kraut, R. (2003). *The Internet and social life: The details make a difference*. Keynote address at the Home Oriented Informatics and Telematics Conference, April 7, 2003, University of California, Irvine.

Kraut, R., Kiesler, S., Boneva, B., Cummings, J . N., Helgeson, V., & Crawford, A. M (2002). Internet paradox revisited. *Journal of Social Issues, 58,* 49–74.

Kraut, R., Mukhopadhyay, T., Szczypula, J., Kiesler, S., & Scherlis, B. (1999). Information and communication: Alternative uses of the Internet in households. *Information Systems Research, 10,* 287–303.

Livingstone, S. (2003). Children's use of the Internet: Reflections on the emerging research agenda. *New Media and Society, 5,* 147–166.

Malus, M., LaChance, P. A., Lamy, L., Macaulay, A., & Vanasse, M. (1987). Priorities in adolescent health care: the teenager's viewpoint. *The Journal of Family Practice, 25*(2), 159–162.

Marcia, J.E. (1980). Identity in adolescence. In Adelson, J. (Ed.), *Handbook of adolescent psychology* (pp. 159–187). New York: Wiley.

Nakamura L. (2000) Race. In Swiss, T. (Ed.) *Unspoken: Key concepts for understanding the Worldwide Web* (pp. 39–50). New York: New York University Press.

Nakamura, L. (2002). *Cybertypes: Race, ethnicity, and identity on the Internet.* New York: Routledge.

Nelson, A., Linh, T., Tu, N., & Hines, A. H. (Eds.) (2001). *Technicolor: Race, technology, and everyday life.* New York: University Press.

Pew Internet and American Life Project. (2001). *Teenage life online: The rise of the instant-message generation and the Internet's impact on friendships and family relationships.* Pew Internet and American Life Project, Retrieved June 20, 2001 from http://www.pewinternet.org/reports/pdfs/PIP_Teens_Report.pdf.

Phinney, J. (1989). Stages of ethnic identity development in minority group adolescents. *Journal of Early Adolescence, 9,* 34–49.

Reis, H. T., & Gable, S. L. (2000). Event-sampling and other methods for studying everyday experience. In H. T. Reis, & C. M. Judd (Eds.), *Handbook of research methods in social and personality psychology.* (pp. 190–222). New York: Cambridge University Press.

Rideout, V. (2002). Generation RX.com. *Marketing Health Services, 22*(1), 26–30.

Roberts, D. F., Foehr, U. G., Rideout, V. J., & Brodie, M. (1999). *Kids and media at the new millennium: A comprehensive national analysis of children's media use.* Menlo Park, CA: Kaiser Family Foundation.

Schegloff, E. A. (1979). Identification and recognition in telephone conversation openings. In Psathas, G. (Ed.), *Everyday language: Studies in ethnomethodology* (pp. 23–78). New York: Halsted (Irvington).

Sharp, J. (2000). The Internet. Changing the way cancer survivors receive support. *Cancer Practice, 8*(3), 145–147.

Smith, M., & Kollock, P. (Eds.) (1999). *Introduction. Communities in cyberspace.* London: Routledge.

Subrahmanyam, K., Greenfield, P. M., & Tynes (2004). Constructing sexuality and identity in an online teen chat room. *Journal of Applied Developmental Psychology, 25,* 651–666.

Subrahmanyam, K., Kraut, R. E., Greenfield, P., & Gross, E. (2000). The impact of home computer use on children's activities and development. In Shields, M. K. (Ed.), *The future of children: Children and computer technology,* (vol. 10, pp. 123–144). Available: http://www.futureofchildren.org.

Suzuki, L. K. & Calzo, J. P. (2004). The search for peer advice in Cyberspace: An examination of online teen health bulletin boards. *Journal of Applied Developmental Psychology.*

Sweeney, C. (1999). In a chat room you can be NE1. *New York Times Magazine,* October 17, pp. 66–68.

Tapscott, D. (1998). *Growing up digital: The rise of the Net generation.* New York: McGraw Hill.

Ten Have, P. (2000) "hi, a/s/l please?": ways of finding chat partners. Retrieved February 26, 2003 from http://www.fragment.nl/mirror/Have2000/asl-mc.htm.

Turkle, S. (1995) *Life on the screen: Identity in the age of the Internet.* New York: Simon & Schuster.

Tynes, B. (2003). *"What's everyone's race": Racialized discourse and self-representation in teen chat rooms.* Unpublished Master's thesis.

White, M. & Dorman, S. M. (2001). Receiving social support online: implications for health education. *Health Education Research, 16*(6), 693–707.

Winzelberg, A. (1997). The analysis of an electronic support group for individuals with eating disorders. *Computers in Human Behavior, 13*(3), 393–407.

14

Bonka S. Boneva, Amy Quinn, Robert Kraut,

Sara Kiesler, and Irina Shklovski

Teenage Communication in the Instant Messaging Era

This chapter examines how adolescents in the United States use instant messaging (IM) to communicate with peers. Adolescents can be described as the ultimate communicators, because this developmental period is defined by a strong need for numerous friendships and peer-group affiliations. IM seems to be one new communication modality that adolescents have appropriated to satisfy this need.

IM software allows people to have real-time, private text-based conversations on the Internet. Although synchronous networked communication has a long history, IM use expanded with the introduction of the ICQ ("I Seek You") service in November 1996 by a company called Mirabilis, which made ICQ freely available to anyone with Internet access. Since that time, America Online's IM service, Microsoft's MSN Messenger, Yahoo! Messenger, and others were introduced and adopted by the public (History of Instant Messaging, 2004). All modern IM services allow users to see whether a defined group of others (often called "buddies") is logged in on their network and to send their friends messages in real time (Alvestrand, 2002, p. 1). In the United States, IM has proved to be one of the most popular applications of the Internet, induc-

ing people to stay connected to the Internet for extended amounts of time to be available for conversation (Lenhart, Rainie, & Lewis, 2001).

Teenagers have been especially attracted to IM services. In June 2001, a national study of teenage online behavior (Lenhart, et al., 2001) reported that 74% of adolescents in the United States who had Internet access used IM, and 35% used it every day. IM was the primary way to communicate with others for 19% of U.S. adolescents. Only 8% of the adolescents considered electronic mail (e-mail) a primary way to communicate with others. In contrast, e-mail was the communication medium of choice for adults—93% of adults with Internet access used e-mail, and only 47% used IM (see also Madden & Rainie, 2003).

Why do teens flock to IM? Lenhart et al. (2001) underlined the fact that adolescents have adapted IM technologies to their own needs and purposes—"the majority of teenagers have embraced instant messaging in a way that adults have not" (p. 10). In later studies, Grinter and Eldridge (2001) and Schiano, Chen, Ginsburg, Gretarsdottir, Huddleston, and Isaacs (2002) emphasized again that the popularity of IM among teens is a result of their need to socialize while confined to their homes. Yet what specific adolescence needs IM satisfies is still unclear. To answer this major question, we place teens' IM use in the larger context of adolescent culture and social interactions.

Types of Adolescent Peer Connectedness

Peer-based connectedness is especially important for adolescents (Hellenga, 2002). In the transition from childhood to adolescence, teens are engaged in defining who they are. Finding their place in the wide world creates insecurity. Peer communication is highly desirable to provide a context in which the rules of the larger world can be learned, practiced, and reinforced (cf. Samter, 2003). Communication with peers is a complementary process to private reflection for the adolescent; the social and the personal processes support one another as the adolescents make sense of life experience and construct viable relationships between self and society (McCall, 1987; Youniss & Yates, 2000). This heightened need to communicate among adolescents has rarely been acknowledged and has not been well understood when studying their communicative behavior.

Adolescents communicate with peers in two distinct modes: one-to-one and one-to-many. These modes are associated with two different types of relationships: forming and maintaining individual friendships and belonging to peer groups. It is important to distinguish analytically between these two types of connectedness, because they fulfill different functions in adolescents' development, and because each is supported by different types of communication technology. Person-to-person communication with another peer provides vital information for the adolescent to compare to similar others and to receive verification for his or her own feelings, thoughts, and actions and is crucial to self-identity formation. One-to-many communication—adolescents' connectedness to a group that creates a feeling of group belonging—is crucial to their social identity formation. The focus of our study is how IM use is associated with these two modes of adolescent connectivity: through maintaining individual friendships (that help them "decipher" the self) and through belonging to peer groups (that help them map the self onto the social categories of the larger world).

Maintaining Individual Friendships

Preadolescence is dominated by parent-based identity and inconsistency of friendships (Hellenga, 2002). Although by age 4 years children already begin to use the word "friend," during childhood, friends are defined as those with whom one plays, and thus, those who are one's "friends" change frequently (Hartup, 1983). During the transition to adolescence, in the process of switching from a parent-defined to a peer-defined identity, both the definition of friends and their value begin to change. Adolescents start to form and maintain as many friendships as possible, and these friendships tend to last longer than do those of childhood. This shift in the nature of friendship is associated with the formation of the self through social interaction (Erikson, 1968). Thus, the core of adolescents' self-formation is the communication with familiar peers—others whom they know (a basis of security) and who are similar to them (a basis of comparison; cf. Erikson, 1968; Harre, 1987).

Adolescents have more friends than do adults and interact with them more (e.g., Hallinan, 1980; Berndt, Hawkins, & Hoyle, 1986). For teens, a friendship is still mostly defined by spending time and doing things together, but friends also provide emotional support—opportunities to discuss problems, receive and give advice, and share interests (e.g., Berndt, 1986; Hartup, 1983). For adolescents, friends, not parents, are their "therapists" (Blos, 1979; Hanna, 1998). In other words, adolescence is defined by the need for intense person-to-person communication with a friend—spending a lot of time together (e.g., sharing common hobbies and spending leisure time) and self-disclosing (e.g., talking about problems and receiving emotional support).

Peer Group Belonging

A parallel process to friendship formation and maintenance is group belonging and peer-acceptance, associated with adolescent's social identity formation (see e.g., Tajfel, 1982; Turner, Hogg, Oakes, Reicher, & Wetherell, 1987). Although earlier research focused on the way that close friendships provide social support for adolescents, some recent research emphasizes the importance that belonging to groups has for adolescents' social adjustment. Teens strive to belong to one or more peer groups that are often reputation-based social categories known as "cliques" or "crowds" (e.g., Brown, 1989; Hanna, 1998; Pansini, 1996; Stone & Brown, 1999). Adolescent cliques have a well-defined core and peripheral members, and acceptance rules are quite rigid. In contrast, crowds have a looser structure and function as reference groups for adolescents. In the group, individual relationships are blurred, and there is little, if any, self-disclosure. What matters is the very fact of belonging to a peer group. Social communication can be reduced to "hanging out" with the group (see, e.g., Brown, 1989).

According to Brown, Mory, and Kinney (1994), the importance of belonging to a peer group is especially pronounced in junior high school, when the adolescents' school is likely to be bigger than it was in earlier grades, and the student body is more diverse. These changes can be threatening to adolescents' developing identities. Adolescents must negotiate their identity and structure their social world in this new context. Labeling self and others as belonging to one or another group lends structure to social interactions and aids identity formation (Eckert, 1989).

IM in the Lives of Adolescents

We have thus far argued that as children move into adolescence and away from the sheltering presence of adults, they have fundamental needs both to talk and share with close friends and to hang out with peer groups (cf. Berndt, 1996). Yet adolescents have limited time to interact with friends or hang out with in-groups at school. In particular, in early adolescence, they may not be independent enough to move around and meet with peers after school (e.g., Grinter & Eldridge, 2001; Schiano et al., 2002). Thus, face-to-face communication that supports both individual friendship maintenance and group interaction is limited at a developmental period when communication needs are highest.

If face-to-face communication is limited, then we would expect that adolescents would take advantage of communication technologies to connect to their peers (see Fischer, 1992, for a discussion of how teens adopted the family telephone at the turn of the 20th century for this purpose). The phone, however, primarily supports one-to-one communication; in addition, as Ito and Okabe (chapter 16, this volume) note, parents often restrict teens' use of the landline phone at home, and in the United

States, many teens do not owe a wireless phone. With over 73% of teens between the ages of 12 and 17 years having Internet access (Rainie & Packel, 2001), many of them can use IM at home to communicate with others.

Although IM was designed to support one-to-one synchronous communication, it also supports one-to-many communication through a variety of features, such as multiple chat windows, chat room support, and directories of contacts (buddy lists). In other words, IM could be valuable both for engaging in one-to-one conversation with a friend and for creating a sense of connectedness to a group of friends.

An Emerging Picture of Adolescent IM Use

Recent empirical studies of adolescent IM use (e.g., Grinter & Palen, 2002; Gross, Juvonen & Gable, 2001; Lenhart, et al., 2001; Schiano et al., 2002) have emphasized that adolescents most often communicate on IM with people they frequently see at school. It is not clear, however, whether IM is also used to sustain friendships at a distance, in the way that e-mail is used. Schiano and colleagues (2002) argue that, at least for junior-high and high-school teens, IM is not frequently used to chat with faraway friends, but Lenhart et al. (2001) show that it is. In their sample, 90% of the teens said that they used IM to stay in touch with friends and relatives who lived outside of their communities. If IM is used mostly to communicate with friends, we would expect daily communication to be focused on local friends. Because teens' friendships are based primarily on spending time together, the majority of their friends are local. We will cast light on these ambiguities by examining in more detail the types of relationships sustained by IM, for example, by examining with whom they communicate with via IM and where they first met their IM communication partners.

Previous empirical studies have shown that both the age and the gender of communication partners affect IM use. Both Lenhart et al. (2001) and Schiano and colleagues (2002) argue that IM use decreases with age—because older teens have less free time, the latter authors argue. However, more than free time may be at issue. It is important to further explore the effect of age on IM use in the context of adolescent psychosocial development. From preadolescence through adolescence and into adulthood, the need for intensive communication decreases because, over time, identities become more stable, and the need for constant peer comparison decreases. Older teens, for example, report fewer friends than younger teens. The decrease in IM use with age may be associated with this overall decrease in peer communication.

In both Lenhart et al. (2001) and the Schiano et al. study (2002), teens said that IM was especially useful when communicating with someone of the other gender. Similarly, Wolak, Mitchell, and Finkelhor (2002) found, in a national sample of adolescent Internet users, that 71% of the peer relationships maintained online were mixed-sex. In contrast, studies based on face-to-face interactions (e.g., Duck, 1973; Hartup, 1983; Kon, Losenkov, De Lissovoy, & De Lissovoy, 1978) have emphasized that teens' friendships, and especially close friendships, are mostly same-sex. Throughout high school, mixed-sex friendships are rare among adolescents. Why IM facilitates mixed-sex communication among teens is not well understood.

The content of IM chat could suggest some possible explanations. The female gender role is associated with more sharing, self-disclosure, and social support than the male gender role (e.g., Deaux & Major, 1987; Eagle & Steffen, 1984). As a result, both men and women tend to prefer female friends for substantial conversations; for example, sharing and emotional support. It could be, then, that male adolescents use IM for more self-disclosure with female communication partners. Male adolescents may need to share their emotions and concerns and to receive social support as much as female adolescents, despite being socialized not to, at least in face-to-face or phone communication. However, previous research (e.g., Lenhart et al., 2001; Schiano et al., 2002) indicates that IM talk is insubstantial—chatting about "anything; nothing," as one teen in Schiano and colleagues' study noted. In Grinter and Palen's study (2002), teens reported using IM mostly for planning future events, collaborating on schoolwork, and chatting about events of the day. Similarly, Lenhart et al. (2001) reported that 82% of online teens use IM for making plans with their friends. These findings suggest that IM is rarely used for substantial talk or for sharing and emotional support. It is not clear, then, why mixed-sex dyadic conversations are so prevalent on IM. It is necessary to further examine what teens talk about via IM, and with whom, in the context of their culture and psychosocial development.

If adolescents need more intensive communication than do other age groups, then it could be that the quantity rather than the quality of the communication is what makes IM valuable to teens. That is, the teenagers may need to maintain as many ties as possible, rather than striving for a few, more meaningful ones. This hypothesis is consistent with findings about the number of contacts in teens' buddy lists (i.e., IM directories). Schiano and colleagues (2002) reported that teen IM users had up to 90 contacts in their buddy lists. Of these buddies, only a few (about five) were frequently contacted "core friends," "several [were] infrequently contacted remote friends and acquaintances," and many others in their buddy lists were people "they could no longer identify" (p. 595). Ling and Yttri (cahpter 15, this volume) found a similar phenomenon for contacts in teens' cell phones. This behavior has not yet been clearly understood

In other studies on IM use (Gross et al., 2001; Leung, 2001; Grinter and Palen, 2002; Schiano et al., 2002), teenagers have described it as a way to "hang out" with peers, and Grinter and Palen (2002) call it "the network effect" of IM—the sense it creates of being part of a large community of friends. This noncommunicative function of IM has not been explored yet. The sense of belonging to a group that teens get from having large buddy lists and from one-to-many connectivity ("the network effect") may contribute to the value they place on this modality.

IM in Comparison to Face-to-Face and Phone Communication

Several researchers (e.g., Burleson, Metts, & Kirch, 2000; Cummings, Butler, & Kraut, 2002; Cummings & Kraut, 2002; Cummings, Lee, & Kraut, chapter 18, this volume) have emphasized that the association between communication and the relationship is medium specific. It is important, then, to understand the complex interplay of factors influencing IM use relative to phone use or face-to-face communication.

Some differences have already started to emerge. For example, both Lenhart et al. (2001) and Grinter and Palen's work (2002) emphasized the advantage of IM over the phone, because IM allows the user to have multiple one-to-one conversations simultaneously in individual windows. Yet the telephone seems to be the preferred medium for teens when connecting to peers. For about 70% of online youth, the landline phone is still the way they most often get in touch with their friends. It has "much more of a human aspect, less austere and sterile than cyberspace," as a 16-year-old interviewee explained (Lenhart et al., 2001, p. 21). However, it is also a fact that the majority of U.S. adolescents with Internet access use IM a lot. What makes teens choose IM? Is this communication modality chosen mostly because it can connect them to many friends at once—something that the phone cannot do? Comparing IM to phone-mediated communication (which supports one-to-one synchronous chat) and face-to-face communication (which supports both one-to-one communication and group interactions) could help further explain the value that IM has for teens.

Our empirical study is partly based on survey data in which teens describe a communication session with a friend by IM, phone and face to face. In addition, we study the use of IM in natural settings by analyzing interview data and video recordings of teens as they use IM.

A major goal is to understand how the available technological features of IM have been appropriated by adolescents to support their two distinctly different ways of connecting to peers—by one-to-one communication with a close friend and by "hanging out" with a group. First, we examine the nature of the relationships sustained via IM—where their conversation partners live, how they first met, how close they feel to each other, and how much social support they receive from the relationships—comparing them to relationships sustained by visits or phone communication. Next, we explore an IM conversation session—the content of the conversation and how useful and enjoyable the session was—compared with face-to-face and phone conversation sessions. Through the interviews and observational sessions, we examine the social environment of IM chat—who are the contacts in teens' buddy lists, how many IM buddies adolescents talk to at a time, and what other computer-related activities they engage in while using IM. Last, we study what adolescents talk about during an IM chat session.

Methods

Quantitative Data

Sample

Data come from a national sample recruited by random digit dialing of residential telephone exchanges to secure a representative sample of United States households. (For a detailed description of the national panel, see Kraut, Kiesler, Boneva & Shklovski, chapter 6, this volume.) Of all respondents who completed the survey at time 1 ($n = 1106$), 8.7% were adolescents (between 13 and 17 years old; $n = 96$); 76% of them ($n = 73$) completed the survey again, 6–8 months later, at time 2. The majority of the adolescents were Caucasian (85.4%), were attending middle or high school (97.5%) and used the Internet (91.1% reported having accessed the Internet at least once, 83.3% from home). Eighty-three percent of these teens reported using IM, and 72.4% used it at least 1–2 days a week. Fifty-two percent had an online chat/IM conversation with someone "yesterday"; 80.7% of the IM sessions were with a friend.

For this study, we selected Caucasian adolescents who reported on an IM conversation session with a friend "yesterday" at home ($n = 41$). The sample did not include enough non-Caucasian adolescents or IM sessions with relatives to be able to control for race and type of relationship in IM use. The mean age for this subsample is 14.8, with 56.6% female teens. These adolescents come from households with an average income of $40,000. On average, the respondents live in households with two computers and have been using the Internet for 2 years. At the time of the first survey, 38.7% were in junior high school and 61.3% were in high school.

Procedure

The respondents were asked to report on one online (either IM or e-mail) and one offline (either visit or telephone) communication session that they had "yesterday," the day before they completed their questionnaire. For the online sessions, respondents reported on an IM session if one occurred "yesterday"; otherwise, they reported on an e-mail session. Because the majority of the teen respondents had an IM session "yesterday," only 9% of the online sessions were via e-mail—too few to include in further analyses. For each session, respondents answered questions that described both the communication session and their communication partner. Thus we can distinguish the effects of modality and the effects of the relationship.

We examine here a total of 106 communication sessions (visit, phone, or chat/IM conversation with a friend) in which respondents reported engaging "yesterday." The 65 communication sessions reported at time 1 and 41 sessions at time 2 were combined into a single sample after preliminary analyses showed no significant differences associated with time of survey on the major dependent variables.

Measures

Communication modality is the major independent variable for this study. Respondents described communication sessions with a friend conducted through IM, during a visit, and by phone.

Variables Describing Respondent and Partner For this study, respondents reported on conversations with a "friend," defined very broadly ("close friend," "friend," "acquaintance," "coworker," and "classmate"). Respondent's age, ranging from 13 to 17 years, was dummy coded as 0 = younger teens (13–14 years old) and 1 = older teens (15–17 years old). We use these two categories based on previous findings that IM use differs between junior high school and high school adolescents. Gender was dummy coded as 0 = female and 1 = male, and household income was coded in three categories (1 = less than $30,000; 2 = $30,000–$70,000; 3 = over $70,000). In addition, age and gender of communication partner were recorded. By measuring the gender of both respondent and partner, same-versus mixed-sex communication dyads could be differentiated into categories: respondent male–partner male, respondent male–partner female, respondent female–partner male, and respondent female–partner female.

Respondents described the physical proximity to their communication partner, which was dichotomized (1 = near-by, including "same building," "same neighborhood," and "same town"; 0 = far away, including "same state," "different state," and "farther away"). They also describe where they first met their partner ("through a friend," "at school/work," "in the neighborhood," "at church/club/hobby," or "online"). Length of the relationship ("How long have you known this person?")

was measured on a 6-point scale (1 = less than a month, 2 = 1 month to less than 6 months, 3 = 6 months to less than a year, 4 = 1 year to less than 2 years, 5 = 2 years to less than 3 years, 6 = 3 years or more).

Variables Describing the Relationship The respondents described how frequently they communicated in person, by phone or by IM with each communication partner on a 7-point Likert scale (1 = never, 2 = less often, 3 = every few weeks, 4 = 1–2 days a week, 5 = 3–5 days a week, 6 = about once a day, 7 = several times a day). These measures defined a pattern of media preferences for each relationship. In addition, an overall frequency of communication score was computed for each session partner—as a mean of the communication scores across all three modalities—that measured respondent's communication intensity, independent of modality.

Respondents described their level of psychological closeness to each communication partner ("How close do you feel to this person?") on a 5-point Likert scale (1 = not at all close, 2 = not too close, 3 = neutral, 4 = somewhat close, 5 = very close). They reported their frequency of receiving social support from each with a 5-item scale ("Participate in leisure activities together"; "Discuss hobbies or spare time interests"; "Receive practical favors or help"; "Receive emotional support"; and "Receive useful advice or information"; Cronbach's alpha = .91). The frequency of each activity was measured on the 7-point scale described above.

Variables Describing the Communication Session Respondents evaluated each communication session on two dimensions: how useful the communication session was "for getting work done," "for the relationship," and "for exchanging information" (three items), and how enjoyable the conversation was. All items were measured on a 5-point scale (1 = not at all useful/enjoyable; 5 = very useful/enjoyable).

Respondents classified the general topic of the conversation as social, school- or work-related, or other. Respondents also described specific topics discussed during the conversation (dichotomous "yes/no" answers). For the purposes of this study, two scales are used: social support talk (including topics: "getting/giving support," "getting/giving advice," "asking favors," and "talking about problems"; Cronbach's alpha = .77) and small talk (including two topics: "small talk" and "killing time"; $r = .71$). The items of the scales were selected based on factor analysis of a total of 20 items and in accordance with our theoretical model.

Qualitative Data

Sample

The HomeNet Project has been conducting interviews with families in the Pittsburgh, Pennsylvania, area since 1996. Between 1996 and 1999, 40 families were interviewed, with a total of 36 adolescent children. Twenty additional families were interviewed in a 4-month period from December 2001 to March 2002. These 20 families were selected from the national HomeNet survey sample (see details above) if they met the following criteria: lived in the Pittsburgh metropolitan area, had access to the Internet at home, and had at least one adolescent live-in child. We draw some conclusions from data analyses of the 1996–1999 interviews with adolescents (n = 33), but our qualitative data analyses focus on the 2001–2002 interviews (n = 26). For the 2001–2002 sample, 14 (54%) of the interviewees were male; four (15%) were in junior high school (13–14 years old), and the rest were in high school (15–18 years old).

Procedure

Interviews were semistructured. Each interview lasted about 3 hours and consisted of two parts: a family interview in which all members of the family discussed their use of the home computer and the Internet, and individual interviews in front of the computer. The individual interviewee showed how she or he typically used the computer. All teen interviewees were asked to log in their IM account and demonstrate an IM session.

Interviews were tape-recorded, and those in front of the computer were also videotaped. All interviews were transcribed and analyzed, following standard guidelines for structured thematic analysis (see, e.g., Silverman, 2000). Interviews were systematically analyzed using NVivo, a qualitative data coding software package produced by QSR (2001). To ensure reliability, two people conducted coding of interviews, with over 90% intercoder reliability. We analyzed one-to-one IM sessions as well as the online social environment while using IM. We examined how the interviewees chose their IM partners, who was included in the buddy list, and how the contacts (screen names) in the buddy list were organized. We tried to place IM use in the context of overall com-

puter use. For example, we examined the sequence of opening computer applications and the number of windows opened during one IM session. The qualitative analyses were done to supplement the survey data analyses on one-to-one IM conversations and to develop insights about possible group processes supported by IM.

Results

IM Chat in the Context of Other Online Activities

We placed IM use in the context of other major teen computer-based activities—e-mail use and browsing the web. Comparing frequencies of use of these three applications by cohorts, we found different patterns of IM, e-mail and web use for adolescents and adults. For example, adolescents were the highest users of IM, and use of this form of communication dropped quickly with age. In contrast, respondents in their twenties were the highest users of e-mail. The decline in e-mail and Web use with age was much less steep than the decline in IM use (see fig. 14.1)

In addition, analysis of trends in our 1996–2002 interview data indicates a tendency in adolescent online behavior of switching from chat rooms to IM: 26% of adolescents interviewed in the 1996–1998 time period used chat rooms, whereas only 12% of adolescents in the 1999–2002 time period used chat (see table 14.1). This decline in the percentage of adolescents using chat was marginally significant (χ^2 = 2.3, p = .12). In the years from 1996 to 1998, IM was just starting to emerge, and for the most part, teenagers were not using IM as a communication medium. However, all adolescents used some synchronous Internet communication in the 1999–2002 time period, with all using IM and a smaller proportion also frequenting chat rooms.

IM Chat Sustains Strong Ties with Peers

According to the survey data in which teens described a recent communication session, adolescents talked primarily to friends who lived near by regardless of communication modality—their communication partner lived in their own neighborhood or town: 87.5% for IM session, 87.1% for visit, and 90.6% for phone. However, 13% of the IM partners also lived further away (i.e., in another

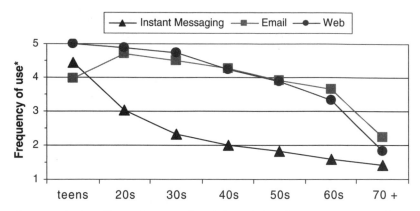

Figure 14.1. Overall use of IM, e-mail, and the Web by cohort. *1 = never; 2 = less often; 3 = every few weeks; 4 = 1–2 days a week; 5 = 3–5 days a week.

state or beyond), whereas only 6.3% of the phone partners and none the in-person communication partners lived in another state. Across modalities, adolescents were most likely to communicate with peers they first met at school: 77.5% in the IM session, 67.7% in the visit, and 62.5% in phone session. None of the visit or phone communication partners was first met online, and only one of the IM communication partners was first met online.

Teens knew their IM partners for less time than the others. In all the modalities, respondents knew their partners for over a year (85.4% for IM, 90% for visit, and 93.8% for phone), but this figure was smaller for IM partners than for phone and visit partners (χ^2 = 5.6, df = 2, p = .06).

IM sessions were more likely to involve both genders than were either phone or face-to-face sessions. Forty-one per cent of the IM sessions compared to only 13% of visits and 12.5% of phone sessions were with someone of the other gender. (see fig. 14.2). As figure 14.2 shows, boys were especially likely to use IM to initiate conversations with girls, while girls were more likely to use it to talk to their female friends.

The analyses of the 2001–2002 interview data revealed similar patterns. Fifty-six percent of the interviewees said that they used IM to speak primarily to people in the same town. Eighty-four percent of the interviewees mentioned talking regularly through IM to friends from school. Very few interviewees mentioned communicating by IM with someone they never met in person, and when they did, those were contacts ("screen names") given to them by a friend or a relative. However, our interviewees also emphasized that IM allowed them to talk to others whom they did not see on a regular basis, such as friends from previous schools, friends from summer camps, or friends from church. These friendships would have been more difficult to maintain if not for the contact through IM. Says Edward, "lots of them [peers met at church or a summer camp] live all over the place so that's how . . . [using IM] . . . that's really my only way of communicating with them because the phone bill, if I would call them all, would be outrageous." In other words, even though IM is primarily used to talk to friends from school, it also helps enlarge teens' social networks, adding more distant friends who otherwise would have been dropped or adding new contacts who otherwise would not be approached. It is a way for teens to talk to the opposite sex.

Communication Patterns

In this section, we contrast the communication patterns teens have with partners with whom they communicate primarily by IM, by phone, or in person. In the analyses that follow, sample sizes and means for the respondent and communication partner are re-

Table 14.1. Tendency in adolescents migrating from chat rooms to IM.

	Year range	
	1996–1999	2001–2002
Chat rooms	26.90%	12.10%
IM	0%	100%
N	33	26

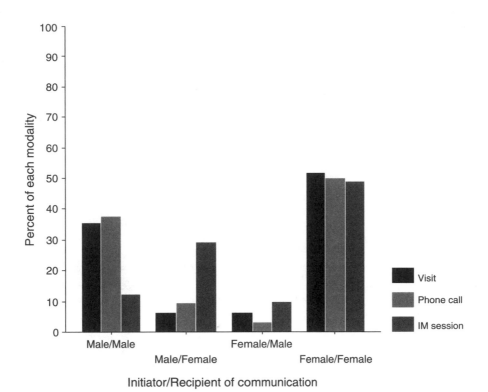

Figure 14.2. Comparing frequency of communicating with same-sex versus mixed-sex partners in each modality.

ported in table 14.2. For these analyses, we used hierarchical linear (multilevel) modeling (Bryk & Raudenbush, 1992), with communication modality treated as a fixed factor nested within respondent, a random factor. Multilevel modeling takes into account the nonindependence of the data, with each respondent describing multiple communication sessions with multiple partners. The analyses controlled for the year the questionnaire was administered, age (younger vs. older teens), household income, gender of respondent, gender of communication partner, and geographic proximity to the partner. For consistency in comparisons, mean scores for all continuous variables were standardized. Nonnormality of distributions was accounted for by using the log transformations of the mean scores for all continuous variables. Levels of significance are based on tests of whether the conversations by IM differ from conversation in each of the other two communication modalities (phone and face-to-face). Differences of least square means between IM, visit, and phone sessions are reported in table 14.3.

First, we examined how frequently respondents communicated with each session partner through each of four communication modalities (in person, by phone, by e-mail, and by IM). Teens seem to specialize in the way they communication with certain partners (see table 14.3). They communicate with some of their friends mostly via IM, supplemented by face-to-face and, to a lesser extent, by phone communication; they communicate with others primarily in person, supplemented by IM and phone communication; and with still others they primarily talk by phone, supplemented by face-to-face communication and some IM chat. These results are indicative of the complementarity of different communication modes when maintaining a friendship. Teens seem to have friends with whom they communicate mostly by IM—almost every day—but they also communicate with these IM partners in person about 5 days a week and talk to them by phone about once a week.

Psychological Characteristics of Teens' Friendships

Are the relationships teens have with their IM-session partners different from the ones they have with

Table 14.2. Sample size, means and standard deviations for respondent and partner.

Variable	By chat/IM			In person			By phone		
	N	Mean	Std	N	Mean	Std	N	Mean	Std
Respondent[a]									
Gender (% male)	41	41	50	32	44	50	33	45	51
Age	41	14.9	1.4	32	14.8	1.4	33	14.8	1.3
Income (thousands; 1 measure point = $10,000)	41	$40	0.7	32	$45	0.8	33	$35	0.8
Partner[b]									
Gender (% male)	41	22	42	31	42	50	32	41	50
Age	40	15.5	1.6	29	15.4	2.8	32	17.4	8.6
Geographic location (% nearby)	41	88	33	32	88	34	33	91	29.6
How long know partner[c]	41	5.0	1.3	30	5.2	1.3	32	5.4	1.2

[a]Not all respondents reported on all three communication sessions.
[b]Partners are different for each modality.
[c]Measured on a 6-point scale (see detailed scale in text).

their visit—and phone-sessions partners? Teens judged themselves as less psychologically close to their IM-session partners than to the visit-session and the phone-session partners. These difference remain after controlling for age, income, gender of respondent, gender of communication partner, and geographic proximity to partner for both visit-session partners ($\beta = .05$; $df = 47$; $p = .009$) and phone-session partners ($\beta = .05$; $df = 47$; $p = .007$; see table 14.3). However, there was no significant difference between levels of reported social support from friends in the IM, visit, or phone sessions. Teens reported receiving emotional support, advice, and favors; sharing common interests/hobbies, and spending time together as frequently with their IM-session partners as with their phone partners and visit partners—several times a week on average (see table 14.3).

IM Chat Not Enjoyable, Even with Best Friends

Teens judged IM communication sessions as substantially less enjoyable than phone sessions ($\beta = .64$, $df = 47$, $p < .001$) or visit sessions ($\beta = .76$, $df = 47$, $p < .001$). They enjoyed in-person communication most (see table 14.3). Because they rated their IM partner as least psychologically close, we controlled for psychological closeness by analyzing how much teens enjoyed their conversations with their best friends (partners with a score of 5 on psycho-

logical closeness). Even with best friends, teens rated IM communication sessions as substantially less enjoyable than phone ($\beta = 1.00$, $df = 18$, $p < .001$) or visit communication sessions ($\beta = .89$, $df = 18$, $p < .001$). Again, they enjoyed in-person communication most.

IM conversations were rated as less useful for getting school work done, for exchanging information, and for the relationship itself than visit conversations ($\beta = .06$, $df = 47$, $p = .06$). However, IM conversations were not rated as significantly different from phone conversations for these purposes. Both IM conversations and phone conversations were considered "somewhat useful" for these three purposes.

Self-Disclosure and Small Talk on IM

In the analyses of the 2001–2002 interviews, we found that IM conversations were usually short, with ritualized ways to start and end the conversation, but highly variable middle sections, in which the major part of the conversation occurred. The conversations started with nonspecific openers, such as "hey" and "whats up," to establish the connection. The middle portion of the conversation consisted of a variety of topics. Then conversations were consistently ended by conventional phrases such as "g2g" ("got to go") or "cya" ("see you"). A sample of typical short IM conversations follows, with translations in square brackets.

> *abc123*: hey
> *pgh1*: hey

Table 14.3. Means and levels of significance of the dependent variables, based on differences of lease square means.

Variable	IM session/partner			Visit session/partner			Phone/partner		
	N	Mean	SD	N	Mean	SD	N	Mean	SD
Frequency of communication with partner[a]									
By IM	41	5.61*	1.34	31	4.39†	2.22	32	3.81†	2.39
In person	40	5.28*	2.03	31	5.94†	1.41	32	5.22‡	1.79
By phone	40	3.45*†	2.05	31	3.84*	1.77	32	4.56†	1.54
By e-mail	41	3.34*	1.56	31	2.71*†	1.53	30	2.33†	1.71
Across all modalities	41	4.40	1.33	31	4.22	1.27	32	4.05	1.24
Attitudes toward the conversation[b]									
Useful for developing or sustaining a personal relationship	41	3.93*†	1.01	30	4.13*	0.68	32	3.56†	1.24
Useful for exchanging information	41	4.34	0.85	30	4.33	0.76	32	4.34	0.75
Useful for getting work done	41	3.24	1.22	31	3.42	1.15	33	3.27	1.33
How much conversation was enjoyed	41	1.63*	0.70	31	4.42†	0.62	32	3.84‡	0.72
Psychological dimensions of the relationship									
Psychological closeness to communication partner[c]	41	3.93*	1.10	31	4.23†	0.80	32	4.34†	0.83
Social support from communication partner[a]	41	4.22	1.35	31	4.35	1.65	32	4.30	1.57
Topics of conversation[d]									
Small talk scale	41	0.83*	0.31	30	0.77*†	0.41	31	0.61†	0.40
Social support scale	41	0.35	0.37	30	0.38	0.35	30	0.38	0.40

Means with different symbols are significantly different.
[a]Measured on a 7-point scale: 7 = several times a day; 6 = about once a day; 5 = 3–5 days a week; 4 = 1–2 days a week; 3 = every few weeks; 2 = less often; 1 = never.
[b]Measured on a 5-point scale: 5 = very useful/enjoyable; 1 = not at all useful/enjoyable.
[c]Measured on a 5-point scale: 5 = very close; 1 = not at all close.
[d]Scores vary between 0 (none of the topics was included in the conversation) and 1 (each of the topics was included in the conversation).

abc123: what r u doin today? [What are you doing today?]
pgh1: nothin u [Nothing. You?]
abc123: u wanna come over to watch the game
. . .
pgh1: ya probably
abc123: alrite, see ya round 6 then [All right. See you around 6 then.]
pgh1: k [Okay.]
abc123: cya [See you.]

When asked what they usually talk about on IM, 68% of the teens we interviewed said that they used IM mostly to pass the time, without important content. One interviewee summarized a typical conversation in IM this way: "Mostly just . . . kind of like . . . just kind of BS and . . . just talk about, you know, what you been up to—just kind of silly stuff like . . . you know, just to pass the time. Asking . . . like, I said, ask them what they're up to—just kind of chitchat—nothing real important." However, further analysis of the chat sessions we recorded suggested that in the midst of this chit-chat, teens often spontaneously shared personal information with their IM partner and offered or received emotional support or advice. Even though the initial motivation to chat on IM may not be self-disclosure, IM conversations evolve to include emotional support and self-disclosure. Here is an example of such a conversation in which a girl discloses to her friend her breakup with a boyfriend.

friend123:hey
friend123: sup [What's up?]
girl1: nm u [Nothing much. You?]

friend123: n2m chillin [Not too much. Chilling.]

girl1: kewl [Cool.]

girl1: how r things with u and jimmy r u ok?
[How are things with you and Jimmy? Are you okay?]

friend123: were friends but he was up at his camp this weeekend so haven't talked to him since late friday night

girl1: oo ic [Oh, I see.]

girl1: well do u think things r gonna be ok?

friend123: like were ok . . . but he said he waats to try being friends but he dont think its gonna work

To better understand what teens talk about, we used the survey data, in which teens described their conversations, to compare the topics most frequently included in IM, phone and face-to-face conversations. Adolescents' conversations were more often social in an IM chat than in a phone call or a visit (χ^2 = 12.3, df = 4, p < .05). Respondents categorized 87.8% of their IM sessions as social, compared to 58.1% and 54.5%, respectively, of visit and phone conversations (see figure 14.3).

Next, we examined the survey data for how frequently small talk and social support talk were included in IM conversations compared to phone and visit conversations. For this analysis, we again used hierarchical linear modeling, controlling for year of questionnaire administration, respondents' age, household income, and gender, and the ses-

sion partners' gender and geographic proximity. Across all modalities, teens' conversations involved much more small talk than supportive talk (see table 14.3). IM conversations involved more small talk than phone conversations (β = −.15, df = 46, p ≤ .07), but not more than visits. IM conversations were not significantly different from visit or phone conversations in frequency of supportive talk. Adolescents seem to receive comparable support from peers across modalities (see table 14.3).

IM Use As a Group Activity

Interviews and observations showed that teens often conducted multiple IM communication sessions simultaneously. Only one interviewee said that he never had simultaneous IM conversations. Thirty-two percent of the teen interviewees emphasized that they liked IM mainly because of the ability to talk to more than one person at a time. Twelve percent mentioned that they found the phone limiting, because they could talk to only one person at a time. One teenager, Amelia, described the appeal of multiple conversations through IM this way: "Personally I like talking to a lot of people at a time. It kind of keeps you busy. . . . It's kind of boring just talking to one person 'cause then like . . . you can't talk to anyone else."

Our interviewees reported usually conducting from two to three and up to 16 IM conversations at a time, and two of the interviewees reported even

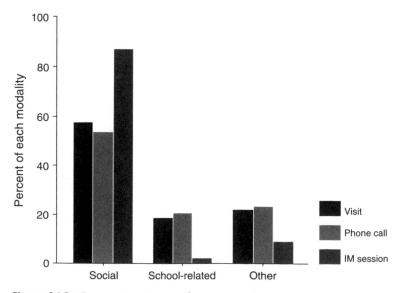

Figure 14.3. Conversation topics with communication partner.

talking on the phone while chatting on IM with several people. The intensity of IM teen communication, at least at times, is apparent in the following description, by Neil: "I'm talking to this person, this person, this person. . . . I type something to them and when they have something to say to me the . . . uh, little button down here—the icon—it . . . flashes blue, so I know that they responded and I just click on their . . . icon and talk and then click off and then . . . search some more."

Interestingly, although being able to talk to multiple friends simultaneously was one of the most revered features of IM, teens strongly preferred person-to-person chatting to using IM chat rooms, where multiple people are on the same conversation. Most IM systems support chat rooms, where users can set up "rooms" and invite others on their buddy list to talk as a group. Although most of our interviewees were aware of this option, only one had used it. It appears that teens like the privacy of one-to-one communication while "being in a group" of friends through multiple open windows.

Analyses of the videotaped IM sessions pointed to the nonselective way in which IM partners were chosen. A few interviewees mentioned that they expected some of their IM buddies to log in at about the same time as they usually did, but for most adolescents, logging into their IM account meant starting to chat with anyone on their buddy list who was available online. At the varying times of the day when our teen respondents were interviewed, all but one were instantaneously able to start chatting with several of their IM contacts. In this context, logging in to one's IM account was not a way to get in touch with a specific friend (as a phone call or an e-mail message is); rather, it was a way to join a group of peers whom the teens already knew offline and frequently met in person.

The "presence" information on IM seems to create a feel of group participation too. If anyone leaves the "group," she or he leaves a message—as in this "I'm away" message reported by an interviewee: "At the Mall shopping with mom. Back in 2 hours." In other words, although teens engaged in a sequence of one-to-one conversations during an IM session, there was always a feeling of group presence through the "presence" of others in numerous active windows and the "presence" information for those temporarily away. As illustrated below, while Amelia actively talks to some friends on IM, she is also aware of the whereabouts of other friends.

> Amelia: Okay. A lot of my friends have away messages on—they're not really like here— they're probably somewhere else. . . . If they're [away from the computer but still logged on] they usually have the yellow paper outside their name and that means they're somewhere. If you click on their name and then get information like it will say where they're at. Like, for this line, like, he says 'I'm not available.' It says he's not available because he's playing a computer game that takes up the whole screen.

Another important option of IM that enhances the sense of group belonging is the buddy list. The interviews provided insights into how adolescents organize and sustain their social networks through IM. As mentioned earlier, IM software provides a buddy list for keeping a directory of the "screen names" of their friends. Some interviewees had very few screen names in their buddy lists, whereas others had more than 100.

To explore how many friends teens communicate with on a more regular basis, we asked respondents in the survey to think of people outside of their households with whom they actively keep in touch. Teens reported actively keeping in touch with 14 friends within an hour's drive and six friends farther away. In contrast, the interview data showed that over 75% of the teens had more than 20 entries in their buddy list, with many having over 100 contacts (see figure 14.4). Interviewees who had a large number of people on their buddy lists said that they communicated by IM with a smaller number: "Whoever I talk to at school is on here [in the buddy list]. Actually, out of all these people I've probably talked to [on IM] like . . . 15. . . . That's how all my friends are—they have . . . like 100 buddies and talk to like 15. That's just the way it is, I don't know [why]."

Adolescents with a larger number of names on their buddy lists tended to customize them with idiosyncratic categories, whereas those with a few screen names left the default grouping provided by the IM software (e.g., "friends," "family," and "co-workers" in AOL IM). If customized, the new groups were often formed on the basis of major social categories (e.g., male and female or friends

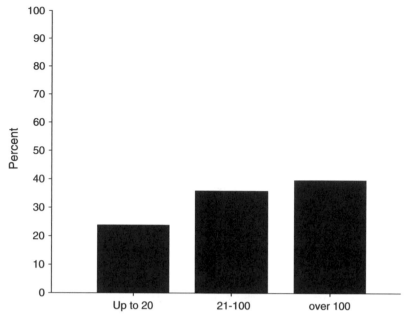

Figure 14.4. Number of contact screen names in buddy list.

and relatives) or, more often, to indicate reference groups (e.g., "my best friends" vs. "other friends" or "cool people" vs. "not so cool people"). In other words, IM contacts were classified either as "core" or as "peripheral," similar to offline "clique" members. As described by Pam, "Yeah . . . "cool people." Those are people I mainly hang out with and that I talk to a long time, like, on the phone and stuff."

Interviewees with a large number of names on their buddy lists could easily identify the screen names of "core" members but often could not do so for the "peripheral" members. Although adolescents admitted that they never communicated with certain people on their buddy list, no one reported having ever deleted a screen name from their buddy list unless they needed to do so to fit the size constraints imposed by the IM application.

Discussion

Adolescents in the United States frequently use IM programs, because doing so allows them to connect to friends in a way no other communication technology does at present: they can have a private one-to-one real-time conversation with a friend and, at the same time, "hang out" with many friends and feel part of a group. Thus, IM satisfies two major needs in adolescent identity formation—maintain-

ing individual friendships and belonging to peer groups.

Adolescence is a period of self and social identity formation. To answer the question "Who am I?" adolescents have a strong need to communicate extensively with peers and compare to them, but they also need to communicate with familiar peers and build a sense of security (cf. Erikson, 1968). When they need to talk to friends, they can generally find some of them on IM.

In a word, teens need to talk to trusted friends more than do other age groups. Internet chat rooms frequented by teens, for example, have been described as fulfilling some needs in self-identity formation (see, e.g., McKenna & Seidman, chapter 19, this volume). However, many teens recognize that chat rooms are a place in which deception is commonplace and—especially younger teens—often consider chat rooms a dangerous place (Lenhart et al., 2001). We found some evidence that teens have been abandoning chat rooms in favor of IM. IM, of course, does not eliminate online deception—approximately a quarter of online teens admit that they have sometimes used IM to pretend to be someone different (Lenhart et al., 2001). Yet, the most important aspect of IM communication is that a friend can be reached through it (Alvestrand, 2002).

Who are these friends that teens talk to via IM? Our research, like some before it (e.g., Schiano et al., 2001; Grinter & Palen, 2002), shows that IM is used mainly to supplement in-person talk with local friends. Researchers have previously emphasized that adults often use online communication to sustain distant personal relationships (see, e.g., Boneva & Kraut, 2003). In contrast, teens seem to use IM primarily for conversations with local friends. We found that teens use IM to extend their communication with friends whom they first met at school and who live nearby; they have known these partners for a comparatively long period of time, and they often talk to them in person, but rarely by phone. Teens rarely use IM to talk to someone far away. In fact, most of the teens' friends live nearby—probably because at adolescence friendships are still primarily based on doing things together.

It appears that adolescents use IM more than other communication channels to talk to the other gender. Although most face-to-face and phone communication among adolescents is with members of their own sex (e.g., Duck, 1973; Hartup, 1983), IM is used to cross the gender barrier. Previous research has also suggested that both boys and girls prefer a female communication partner (e.g., Duck, Rutt, Hurst, & Strejc, 1991). IM is a technology that teenaged boys have taken advantage of to hold these cross-gender conversations. With IM, female teens talk most often to their female friends and only occasionally to male friends, whereas boys frequently talk to girls over IM.

Interestingly, teens rated their IM communication partners as less psychologically close than their face-to-face or phone communication partners. As Cummings, Lee, and Kraut (chapter 18 in this volume) suggest, this may reflect the nonvolitional nature of much of IM communication—teens often talk to whichever of their friends and classmates is available online. Interestingly, in their longitudinal study of students who moved to college, Cummings et al.found that, even though at a given time period communicating by IM was associated with lower levels of psychological closeness than by phone, over time IM (but not in-person or phone) communication reduced the decline in psychological closeness when college students used it to stay in touch with friends. This indicates that the long-term effect of IM use may be different from that indicated by the cross-sectional snapshot.

Even though teens feel less close to their IM communication partner than to phone or face-to-face

partners, they receive as much social support from them. Similarly, teens' IM chat involved as much support talk as their visit and phone conversations.

However, even though teens use IM to receive social support from friends as frequently as in person and by phone, as well as to freely talk to others of the other gender, they find their IM conversations much less enjoyable than their visits or phone conversations. The nature of the relationship does not explain why teens do not enjoy IM chat. Media richness and social presence theories suggest that the technology may be the problem. IM has fewer social clues, clues that contribute to a satisfying communication. In a recent study, Mallen, Day, and Green (2003), for example, showed that face-to-face dyads felt more satisfied with the experience than the online chat dyads. We cannot tell from our data what inherent characteristic of IM communication (e.g., the lack of audio and visual clues) makes it less enjoyable than in-person and phone communication with similar partners.

However, the problem with IM may be may be instead be in the way that teens use it. Consider, for example, multitasking (i.e., doing other things while also chatting and not being focused on the conversation alone). If teens have several IM chat windows open at a time while also doing homework, listening to music, and possibly browsing the web, they may not be paying enough attention to any one of the conversations to enjoy it. In contrast, phone and in-person communication may capture more attention.

It is intriguing that teens flock to IM even though they do not find it enjoyable. Apparently, IM fulfills other important psychological functions that make it popular. The decline in IM use with age that we found may be at least partly because IM satisfies specific generational needs. The teens may like IM because it satisfies their heightened need at this developmental period to communicate with peers. In addition, they have a sense of being with others, of not feeling alone while physically away from friends. There is always someone out there to share with, as Grinter and Palen (2002) note. Age-specific social norms could also be involved in the popularity of IM among teens. For example, although not enjoyable, it may be "cool" to IM. Teens who do not use IM may feel excluded by peers.

IM also helps teens boost their group identity. Using IM simulates joining an offline peer "clique" or "crowd" without their rigid acceptance rules.

The abilities to talk to many friends at a time via IM and to organize buddy list contacts into social categories are both indicative of such a function. Interestingly, teens rarely invite a group to an IM session. It is not clear whether this failure to use the explicit group communication built into most IM software is the result of logistics problems of coordination or because teens value having private person-to-person conversations on IM while also maintaining the feeling of being with many friends.

The buddy list represents a teen's social world. For many teens, it includes almost all the peers they know personally or through someone else. By organizing their contacts into buddy list categories, teens label self and others as belonging to one or another group. Categorizing some peers as, for example, "cool people" or "my best friends" versus all others simultaneously places oneself into a group of peers, thus facilitating the process of social identity and boosting the sense of security. In addition, including many screen names in one's buddy list creates the feeling of building a large social network. It is well known that sense of security—essential at adolescence—is gained through building social networks (Degirmencioglu, 1995). IM facilitates extended social networks. For example, by just including a person's screen name in the "friends" category in the buddy list, a teen can make that person "a friend." This unilateral creation of friendship contrasts with offline friendships, which are generally thought of as a bilateral construct, assessed through reciprocal nominations and interpersonal communication (Asher & Parker, 1989; Masten et al., 1995).

In summary, IM seems to fulfill two separate psychological functions for adolescents. First, IM connects adolescents to peers and extends their opportunities to communicate. This is the communicative function of IM that has already been addressed in the research literature. Second, IM helps define adolescents' social identities, a noncommunicative function of IM that has not been studied and understood yet. These developmental functions may partially explain why IM use is so popular among adolescents in the United States and why its use drops off so sharply with age.

Acknowledgments.   This research was made possible by National Science Foundation grants IRI-9408271 and IIS-9900449.

References

Alvestrand, H. (2002). Instant messaging and presence on the Internet. *Background Paper Series.* ISOC Member Briefing 9. Retrieved May 8, 2003 from http://www.isoc.org/isoc/.

Asher, S. R., & Parker, J. G. (1989). The significance of peer relationship problems in childhood. In Schneider, B. H., Attili, G., Nadel, J., & Weissberg, R. P. (Eds.), *Social competence in developmental perspective* (pp. 5–24). Dordrecht, The Netherlands: Kluwer Academic.

Berndt, T. J. (1996). Transitions in friendship and friends' influence. In Graber J. A., & Brooks-Gunn, J. (Eds.), *Transitions through adolescence: Interpersonal domains and context* (pp. 57–84). Hillsdale, NJ: Lawrence Erlbaum.

Berndt, T. J., Hawkins, J. A., & Hoyle, S. G. (1986). Changes in friendship during a school year: Effects on children's and adolescents' impressions of friendship and sharing with friends. *Child Development, 57,* 1284–1297.

Blos, P. (1979). *The adolescent passage: Developmental issues.* New York: International Universities Press.

Boneva, B., & Kraut, R. (2003). Email, gender, and personal relationships. In Wellman, B., & Haythornthwaite, C. (Eds.), *The Internet in everyday life* (pp. 372–403). Malden, MA: Blackwell.

Brown, B. B. (1989). The role of peer groups in adolescents' adjustment to secondary school. In Berndt, T. J. & Ladd, G. W. (Eds.), *Peer relationships in child development* (pp. 188–216). New York: Wiley.

Brown, B. B., Mory, M. S., & Kinney, D. (1994). Casting adolescent crowds in a relational perspective: Caricature, channel, and context. In: Montemayor, R., Adams, G. R., & Gullotta, T. (Eds.), *Personal relationships during adolescence* (pp. 123–167). Thousand Oaks, CA: Sage Publications.

Bryk, A. S., & Raudenbush, S. W. (1992). *Hierarchical linear models: Applications and data analysis methods.* Thousand Oaks, CA: Sage.

Burleson, B. R., Metts, S., & Kirch, M. W. (2000). Communication in close relationships. In Hendrick, C. & Hendrick, S. S. (Eds.), *Close relationships. A sourcebook* (pp. 245–258). Thousand Oaks, CA: Sage.

Cummings, J. N., Butler, B., & Kraut, R. (2002). The quality of online social relationships. *Communications of the ACM, 45*(7), 103–108.

Cummings, J. N., & Kraut, R. (2002). Domesticating computers and the Internet. *The Information Society, 18*(3), 1–18.

Deaux, K., & Major, B. (1987). Putting gender into

context: An interactive model of gender-related behavior. *Psychological Review, 94*, 369–389.

Degirmencioglu, S. M. (1995). Changes in adolescents' friendship networks: Do they matter? *Dissertation Abstracts International, 56*(05B), 2896.

Duck, S. W. (1973). *Personal relationships and personal constructs: A study of friendship formation.* Oxford, U.K.: Wiley.

Duck, S., Rutt, D. J., Hurst, M. H., & Strejc, H. (1991). Some evident truths about conversations in everyday relationships. All communications are not created equal. *Human Communication Research, 18*(2), 228–266.

Eagle, A. H., & Steffen, V. J. (1984). Gender stereotypes stem from the distribution of women and men into social roles. *Journal of Personality and Social Psychology, 46,* 735–754.

Eckert, P. (1989). *Jocks and burnouts: Social categories and identity in high school.* New York: Teachers College Press.

Erikson, E. (1968). *Identity: Youth and crisis.* New York: Norton.

Fischer, C. S. (1992). *America calling: A social history of the telephone to 1940.* Berkeley: University of California Press.

Grinter, R. E., & Eldridge, M. (2001). y do tngrs luv 2 txt msg? In Prinz, W., Jarke, M., Rogers, Y., Schmidt, K., & Wulf, V. (Eds.), *Proceedings of the Seventh European Conference on Computer-Supported Cooperative Work ECSCW '01* (pp. 219–238). Dordrecht, The Netherlands: Kluwer Academic.

Grinter, R. E., & Palen, L. (2002). Instant messaging in teen life. In *CHI 2002: Proceedings of the ACM conference on computer supported cooperative work* (pp. 21–30). New York: ACM Press.

Gross, E. F., Juvonen, J., & Gable, S. L. (2001). Internet use and well-being in adolescence. *Journal of Social Issues, 58*(1), 75–90.

Hallinan, M. T. (1980). Patterns of cliquing among youth. In Foot, H. C., Chapman, A. J., & Smith, J. R. (Eds.), *Friendship and social relations in children* (pp. 321–242), New York: Wiley.

Hanna, N. A. (1998). Predictors of friendship quality and peer group acceptance at summer camp. *Journal of Early Adolescence, 18,* 291–318.

Harre, R. (1987). The social construction of selves. In Yardley, K., & Honess, T. (Eds.). *Self and identity: Psychosocial perspectives* (pp. 41–52). Oxford: Wiley.

Hartup, W. W. (1983). Peer relations. In Hetherington, E. M. (Ed.), *Handbook of child psychology, Vol. 4: Socialization, personality, and social development* (pp. 103–196). New York: Wiley.

Hellenga, K. (2002). Social space, the final frontier: Adolescents on the Internet. In Mortimer, J. T., & Larson, R. W. (Eds.), *The changing adolescent experience. Social trends and the transition to adulthood* (pp. 208–249). New York: Cambridge University Press.

History of Instant Messaging. Retrieved February 22, 2004, from http://www.almark.net/Internet/html/slide6.html.Joinson, A. N. (2001). Self-disclosure in computer-mediated communication: The role of self-awareness and visual anonymity. *European Journal of Social Psychology, 31,* 177–192

Kon, I., Losenkov, V., De Lissovoy, C., De Lissovoy, V. (1978). Friendship in adolescence: Values and behavior. *Journal of Marriage and the Family, 40*(1), 143–155.

Lenhart, A., Rainie, L. & Lewis, O. (2001). *Teenage life online: The rise of the instant-message generation and the Internet's impact on friendships and family relationships.* Washington, DC: Pew Internet and American Life Project. Retrieved September 8, 2005 from http://www.pewinternet.org.

Leung, L. (2001). College student motives for chatting on ICQ. *New Media & Society, 3*(4), 483–500.

Madden, M. & Rainie, L. (2003). *America's online pursuits: The changing picture of who's online and what they do.* Washington, DC: Pew Internet and American Life Project. Retrieved September 8, 2005 from http://www.pewinternet.org/reports/pdfs/PIP_Online_Pursuits_Final.PDF.

Mallen, M. J., Day, S. X., & Green, M. A. (2003). Online versus face-to-face conversation: An examination of relational and discourse variables. *Psychotherapy: Theory, Research, Practice, Training, 40*(1–2), 155–163.

Masten, A. S., Coatsworth, J. D., Neemann, J., Gest, S. D., Tellegen, A., & Garmezy, N. (1995). The structure and coherence of competence from childhood through adolescence. *Child Development, 66,* 1635–1659.

McCall, G. J. (1987). The self-concept and interpersonal communication. In Roloff, M. E., & Miller, G. R. (Eds.), *Interpersonal processes: New directions in communication research* (pp. 63–76). Newbury Park, CA: Sage.

Pansini, J. M. (1996). The experience and perceptions of interpersonal relationships with peers and peer groups in middle adolescence: A qualitative study. *DAI, 57*(08A), 347.

QSR International. (2001). *Nvivo* [Computer software]. Doncaster, Australia: QSR International

Rainie, L. & Packel, D. (2001). *More online, doing more.* Washington, DC: Pew Internet and American Life Project. Retrieved September 8, 2005 from http://www.pewinternet.org/reports/toc.asp?Report=30.

Samter, W. (2003). Friendship interaction kills across the life span. In Greene, J. O., & Burleson, B. R. (Eds.), *Handbook of communication and social*

Interaction skills (pp. 637–684). Mahwah, NJ: Lawrence Erlbaum.

Schiano, D., Chen, C., Ginsberg, J., Gretarsdottir, U., Huddleston, M., & Issacs, E. (2002). Teen use of messaging media. *CHI 2002: Proceedings of the ACM Conference on Human Factors in Computing Systems, Extended Abstracts* (pp. 594–595). New York: ACM Press.

Silverman, D. (2000). Analyzing talk and text. In Denzin, N. K., & Lincoln, Y. S. (Eds.). *Handbook of qualitative research*. Thousand Oaks, CA: Sage.

Stone, M. R., & Brown, B. B. (1999). Identity claims and projections: Descriptions of self and crowds in secondary school. In McLellan, J. A., & Pugh, M. J. V. (Eds.). *The role of peer groups in adolescent social identity: Exploring the importance of stability and change* (pp. 7–20). New Directions for Child

and Adolescent Development Series. San Francisco, CA: Jossey-Bass.

Tajfel, H. (Ed.) (1982). Social identity and intergroup relations. Cambridge, UK: Cambridge University Press.

Turner, J. C., Hogg, M. A., Oakes, P. J., Reicher, S. D., & Wetherell, M. S. (1987). Rediscovering the social group: A self-categorization theory. Oxford: Blackwell.

Wolak, J., Mitchell, K. J., & Finkelhor, D. (2002). Close online relationships in a national sample of adolescents. *Adolescence, 37*(147), 441–455.

Youniss, J. & Yates, M. (2000). Adolescents public discussion and collective identity. In Budwig, N., Užgiris, I. Č., & Wertsch, J. V. (Eds.), *Communication: An arena of development* (pp. 215–233). Stamford, CT: Ablex.

Rich Ling and Brigitte Yttri

Control, Emancipation, and Status

The Mobile Telephone in Teens' Parental and Peer Relationships

During a recent series of group interviews with teens, we recorded the following sequence:

> *Kai (15):*[1] You can't call your friends at one o'clock at night you know; that'd really piss off their parents.
>
> *Moderator:* One o'clock at night? By then I'm already in bed and asleep for a couple of hours.
>
> *Harald (15):* But it's way better at night, being on your mobile phone under the covers, instead of sitting in the middle of the living room.
>
> *Ola (14):* My cell phone's always on. I just turn off the sound. It's OK if you get an important call.

The informants describe how they prefer the exclusive individualized access that mobile telephones provide, compared to the traditional house telephone, because the mobile telephone provides new possibilities for peer group interaction. In this exchange, adolescents describe radically different ways of organizing social interaction compared to those of their parents' generation. The discipline imposed by a common family telephone—and the accompanying irritation of a parent whose child receives a call in the middle of the night—has in the last 5 years been replaced by a communication technology that adolescents themselves control. Indeed, in our recent survey of adolescents, we found that more than 20% say that they send short message system (SMS) messages at least once a week between midnight and 6:00 A.M.[2]

Today's adolescents in Norway hardly limit their interaction to a specific location or traditional business hours. As the sequence above shows, they carry out social interactions in a variety of new and unanticipated settings. Teens don't hide under the covers just for reading with a flashlight any more—they also send and receive SMS messages that might or might not meet with parents' approval. The same data cited above show that the mobile telephone is an easily accessible, nearly ubiquitous accessory for contemporary Norwegian adolescents. Owning one presents no major barriers. Indeed, from the mid-1990s to 2001, Norwegian adolescents have broadly adopted the mobile telephone. Between 1997 and 2001, mobile phone adoption rates went from approximately 15% to over 90% for those in their midteen years (see fig. 15.1).

This new form of social interaction points to a change in the functioning of the family and in how adolescents develop and maintain peer group interactions. In this chapter, we examine how mobile

219

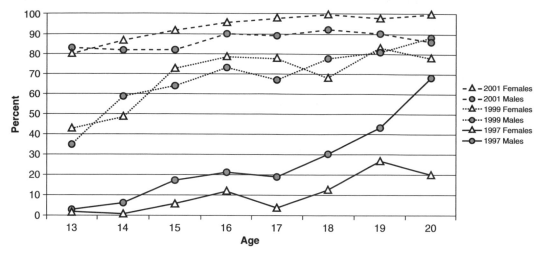

Figure 15.1. Adoption rates of mobile telephones for Norwegian teens between 1997 and 2001 by age and gender. Source: Telenor R&D.

telephony affects the power relationships among adolescents, their parents, and their peers. One of the critical issues associated with adolescent years is emancipation from their parents and establishment of their own identity. In many respects, the peer group is a type of midwife in this process, in that it provides a context within which young people can test out ideas, try out various identities, and test the constrictions and possibilities of the adult world.

The concept of emancipation implies power relationships. It assumes the individual's movement from a preexisting power structure into another status, which may indeed be as repressive as the previous one. Thus, the concept implies moving from one power structure to another. Adolescents do not necessarily have a simple moment when they move from one set of circumstances to another in a dramatic leap but, rather, two or more structures coexist, and individuals must negotiate their position within each of these simultaneously. During their teen years, however, adolescents move from being largely oriented to their family of origin to being more oriented toward their peer group. Indeed adolescence is that life period during which friends are most central (Rubin, 1985). This chapter focuses on the tension between these two groups; that is, on the adolescent's relationship to the power structure within both these family and peer groups.

Background and Method

Sociological Dimensions of Power

From a sociological perspective, Weber provides the central definition of power. He noted "In general we understand 'power' by the chance of a man or number of men to realize their own will in communal action even against the resistance of others who are participating in the action" (1958, p. 180). He also says that power "is the probability that one actor within a special relationship will be in a position to carry out his own will despite the resistance, and regardless of the basis upon which this probability rests" (Weber, 1978, p. 53). The core idea is that there is a differential in the ability to impose one's will. Beyond the basic definition of the concept, Weber further extends the issue by describing three general forms of power: that which can be associated with tradition, a legal-rational structure, or charisma.[3] In the Weberian system, individuals use various combinations of these devices to gain, assert, and legitimize power.

Another dimension to the issue is supplied by the Durkheimian tradition. We can look to the discussion of ritual and to the extensions of this approach that Collins and Goffman offer. Durkheim claims that ritual helps develop the "nomic" structure, or the common sentiment, of a society; that, in fact, the common glue holding society together is ritual. People identify themselves with the group through the collective participation in ritual acts.

> If the communication established between [individuals] is to become real communion, that is to say a fusion of all particular sentiments into one common sentiment, the signs expressing them must themselves be fused into one single and unique resultant. It is the appearance of this that informs individuals that they are in harmony and makes them conscious of their moral unity. It is by uttering the same cry, pronouncing the same word, or performing the same gesture in regard to some object that they become and feel themselves to be in unison. (Durkheim, 1954, p. 230)

It is through the participation in rituals—shared experiences that have a common focus, shared emotions, and nonpractical actions carried out for symbolic ends—that the web of society is developed and maintained. It is through situations such as this that a group becomes conscious of itself and develops a type of internal solidarity. In addition, the shared nature of the experience provides a bond for the individuals. Although it is easy to think of religious celebrations in this context, one can also consider events such as an annual family Christmas party or the studied forms of address, dress, and interaction within a peer group. Many of the same elements are present in miniature. Indeed, this insight is the contribution of theorists such as Goffman, Berger, and Luckmann. Through analysis—in particular Goffman's—of everyday life, we can see the ways in which our day-to-day activities take on ritualized form (Goffman, 1967).

Although bonding and ritualized forms of interaction are a centripetal force that increases solidarity, there is also a power dimension here. Within this type of social integration, there is an implicit form of hierarchy (Collins, 1994). Collins explicitly extends Weber's notion of power with the more emotionally based bonds outlined in Durkheim. Collins notes that "the emotional contagion that results from physical co-presence, the focusing of attention on a common object, and the coordination of common actions or gestures" is a central concept (Collins, 1974, p. 56). In this context, Collins points to the work of Goffman's microlevel analysis of everyday life and his notions of emotional solidarity. For Collins, Durkheim and Goffman provide

tools with which to examine the Weberian f. work. Collins notes that "Emotional rituals ca used for domination within a group or organization; they are a vehicle by which alliances are formed in the struggle against other groups; and *they can be used to impose a hierarchy of status prestige in which some groups dominate others* by providing an ideal to emulate under inferior conditions" (Collins, 1974, p. 56, italics added). The common sense of the group also often implies the common recognition of a "pecking order." One reading of Goffman indicates this same line of thought; specifically, that in influencing situations we manipulate symbols. These manipulations tend to either support or work against one's interests (Rogers, 1977).

Thus, power, as well as influence, prestige, and control—all of which imply the ability to impose one's will—is maintained and developed through ritual activities. These activities confirm both the integrity of the social group and its hierarchical dimensions. Whereas power has a more raw coercive interpretation, influence seems to imply a common sense of mission—as long as it develops in the appropriate direction. Beyond these ritual forms of power, and following from Weber, we can also relate these power relationships to issues such as tradition or legal–rational structures.

On the basis of this conception of power/ritual, we now turn to the examination of the adolescent within the family and the peer group. These structures are quite different in the ways they exercise power and influence and in the adolescents' different positions in each.

Family, Power, Control, and the Socialization of Adolescents

In examining power, control, and socialization processes, we note key modifications that must be taken into account. First, the discussion of power is the situation between two rather static fronts (i.e., patients and doctors, capital and labor, first world and third world, etc.). A unique issue regarding youth and their power relationships with parents is that the power relationship changes during the process of maturation; for example, the difference between a 13- and an 18-year-old person. In contemporary industrialized society, the 13 year old is often only just approaching the questions and issues arising from the transition into adulthood, whereas the 18 year old is often far into the transition, sometimes to the degree that he or she has largely completed the emancipation process. Although parents may hold most of the cards, the dealing becomes more even as time goes on (Gecas, 1981).

Adolescence is a relatively short period of life that is characterized by balancing the child's desire for freedom with the parent's desire to guide their children on a sustainable course. Thus, we place slightly more emphasis on the Weberian notion that the power in this situation needs to be legitimate (Engelstad, 2005).

Adolescence is a period in one's life in which young people gain the "ballast" that they require to become an adult. Adolescents gain insight into how to find and maintain a job, the intricacies of sexual interaction, the boundaries of socially acceptable behavior, and so on. Much of the point in adolescence is to socialize individuals, who will in turn wield power themselves. It is a period of transition—parents often sense that they are putting the final touches on their "creation" in the face of adolescents' confusion and excitement concerning their own maturation. Thus, the power relationship is dynamic, transitory, and episodic.

We have an image of children as increasingly wanting to set their own agenda and to make independent decisions. Parents have a desire to foster this process, but they balance this desire against providing their children a foundation on which to build their character, helping their children avoid pitfalls (drug use, gang participation, etc.), and helping their children out of tight situations. Thus, although at any particular moment there is an absolute power differential, the situation is dynamic. Parents and children must manage changes in that power differential to ensure that the socialization process is complete and that the child, in turn, will have the needed skills to socialize their own children.

In an absolute sense, the adolescent's participation in the family is enmeshed in a power system that is both traditional and legal–rational. Nations passed early laws that prescribe parents' rights and responsibilities, with sanctions for failing those responsibilities. Aside from legal structures, society itself prescribes roles for both parents and children. The adolescent's position is defined by traditions and by legal considerations, at least until they gain the age of majority. As noted above, however, within this absolute framework, one can also look to the rituals of power and thus move in the direction of Durkheim and Goffman (Collins, 1974; Rogers, 1977). Familial celebrations such as Mother's Day, reserving certain parts of the home for parents (i.e., father's chair in the living room), and specific times of meeting together such as the family dinner are all read as ritualized interactions that legitimize the broader institutional situation and various power relations. Within the context of the familial power structure, these rituals provide the bond that holds the family together. Further, as developed by Collins, ritual often has hierarchy as one of its fundamental elements (Collins, 1974, 1994).

The Role of Peers

Just as the role of parents is transformed during adolescence, the peer group also plays an increasingly central and necessary role in the emancipation process. In many respects it is the midwife of teen emancipation (Prost, 1991). The peer group's influence begins to be felt as the adolescent starts to move away from the family of orientation. Adolescents who use time with friends report a higher sense of self-esteem and feel happier and more powerful than those who spend time alone (Schneider & Stevenson, 1999). Adolescent friendships play many roles, including testing the degree to which various activities are seen as inappropriate, providing a safe place to discuss various routines and lore (e.g., sexuality) and developing portions of the child's social persona. This socialization is not simply received: it is created by individuals who are acting on more or less an even footing.

Using grade levels in an educational system enforces the peer group's strength; it facilitates the learning process because students are generally at the same level of maturation and development. In addition, grade levels also reinforce the peer group's internal social dynamics (Aires, 1972; Hogan, 1985, p. 2; Rubin, 1984, p. 6). Beyond facilitating adolescents' education, however, the peer groups that form as a result of the age-based grade system also provide adolescents with a context in which they are more or less free from adult supervision. In this context, adolescents can gain experience with the development of independent values and ideas. In addition, the peer group provides adolescents with a milieu that has a fluid status structure in which young people can attain affirmation (Rubin, 1985, pp. 109–111). The peer group provides the opportunity to develop an independent identity and to practice the skills of role-taking and impression management. The questions of sexual behavior and its boundaries are also at least partially learned in the peer group (Danesi, 1994; Gekas, 1981; see also Rainwater, 1970, pp. 275–315). Thus, the adolescent and the peer group are both active in shaping their own socialization (Glaser & Strauss, 1971, pp. 57–88).

The ritual interaction of the adolescent in the peer group has several interesting dimensions. The peer group can provide instruction in how to orient oneself with aplomb and reassurance in complex "adult" situations. At the same time, the peer group can demand allegiance from members and, perhaps mercilessly, make them aware of their shortcomings. In orienting themselves to the norms and dictates of the peer group, adolescents expose themselves to various tests of popularity and to a litany of specifications: how to dress, how to speak, what to consume, and generally, how to maintain their façade. The critical issue here, however, is that it is in the context of the peer group that individuals can also assert their own influence. The individual can help to determine which activities are of interest, which things should be consumed, and the rituals prescribing group interaction. In this context, the ritual machinations of power can be seen quite transparently.

In addition, the adolescent peer group trades on quickly rising and equally quickly disappearing trends and information (Fine, 1981; Lynne, 2000). This year's—or even this week's—fashion is out next year or next week. The current argot is gone, seemingly in the next news cycle. The location of this weekend's happening is quickly replaced with another.

Thus, within the peer group, young people are confronted with ideas of power or influence that are not so much based on traditional or legal–rational systems as on the ability to manipulate symbols in the Goffmanian sense. In this case, the knowledge of consumption, argot, dress, and the rituals of appropriate interaction are the basis of influence (read: power) within the peer group. In this case, power and influence are more transitory, but at any given time, there is a group or an individual within the peer group that has a greater role in the dictation of style, activities, and the general bearing of the group. It is through the application of this transitory codex that young people define their role in

the group. It is here that we see the Goffmanian notion of the presentation of self and the use of this preening to secure position and influence (Goffman, 1967; Rogers, 1977).[4]

The Role of Mobile Telephony among Teens

Up to this point, we have been looking at the adolescents' situation vis-à-vis various notions of power, their relation to their parents, and the dynamics of the peer group. Now we turn to a discussion of the mobile telephone.[5] The surprisingly fast adoption of this device has changed the dynamics of parental and peer group interaction for the adolescent. By doing so, it has also provided insight into the interaction within and between theses various groups.

Mobile telephone access seems to have polar effects. On one hand, it can help to develop social relationships within the peer group. Adolescents' very nearly ubiquitous access to modern communication technology places them into the role of being a node in a social network, and thus their access to influence in the peer group is quite dynamic. On the other hand, the mobile device can direct attention away from colocated social interaction within the family and thus dilute the potential for the coalescing effects of ritual solidarity.

From an empirical perspective, we have witnessed a profound transformation in Norwegian adolescents' access to mobile telephony. As late as 1997 very few teens had access, particularly among the youngest age groups. Mobile telephones were generally seen as being an accessory for yuppies and other nouveau riche individuals. The introduction of prepaid subscriptions and increasing access to inexpensive handsets changed this. Moreover, prepaid subscriptions reduce parental reservations regarding access because these subscriptions reduce the possibility of drastic increases in the telephone bill. Where in 1997 only a minority of adolescents owned a mobile telephone, by 2001 the device was nearly ubiquitous (Ling, 2002). In addition, there has been a gender shift: In 1997, significantly more boys owned a mobile phone; by 2001, significantly more girls owned one.

SMS or text messages provide adolescents with a form of interaction that they have adopted and shaped to their own purposes. Although some young adults and adults use this form of communication, it is largely adolescents who have adopted

SMS and turned it into a living form of interaction. Material from both Telenor R&D and also the European Union (EU) eLiving project indicate that SMS is generally a teen/young adult service (fig. 15.2). Material from the eLiving project shows that in all countries aside from Israel, heavy SMS use is generally centered among the youngest users. SMS's relatively low cost, the draw of creating unique forms of argot, and the slightly illicit ability to silently hold contact with friends (e.g., during school or in the middle of the night) have all contributed to its popularity.

Beyond noting the intensity of use, researchers might ask, whom do adolescents call? To whom do they send messages? Analysis shows that the mobile telephone and SMS "texting" are quite central for adolescents in maintaining friendships. In Europe, adolescents report contacting friends via SMS at more than three times the rate of those in the broader population.[6] The same pattern can be seen in Norwegian data. Teen girls are especially active in their SMS use: Telenor R&D research shows that in 2002, teen girls who used SMS sent a mean of 9 messages per day (fig. 15.3).

The general finding here is that adolescent friendships are maintained through more channels than just familial relationships. When looking at only teens and their friendship patterns, there is an intensity of interaction for the girls in the sample that is not as apparent for the boys. Where socializing for adolescent boys seems to take place face-to-face, adolescent girls seem more comfortable with interaction via various telephonic channels.[7]

Thus, the data point to the fact that over the last 5 years, adolescents have heavily adopted both mobile voice telephony and, to an even greater extent, texting. These channels are frequently used to communicate with friends, and both have taken their place as important elements in adolescents' lives.

Method and Data

For the bulk of this analysis, we draw on focus group material that describes the situation of Norwegian adolescents and their parents. The focus groups were held in 1999.[8] Approximately 40 teenagers, 20 persons aged 19–23 years, and 20 parents were included in 10 separate sessions. There were four sessions with mixed boys and girls, one session with only girls, and one with only boys. Finally, there were two sessions with late teens and two with parents. The transcripts from the focus groups were created and analyzed using text analysis software that categorizes sections of text. On the basis of this

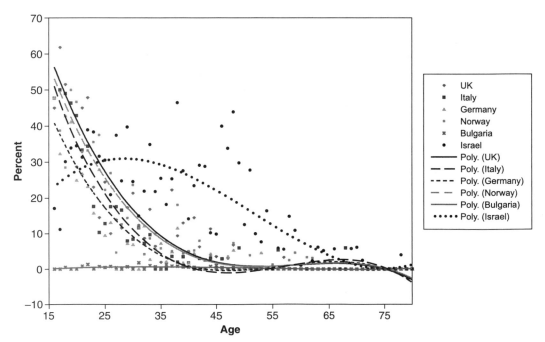

Figure 15.2. Percentage of persons who report sending five or more SMS messages per day by age for six European countries: Source: eLiving project.

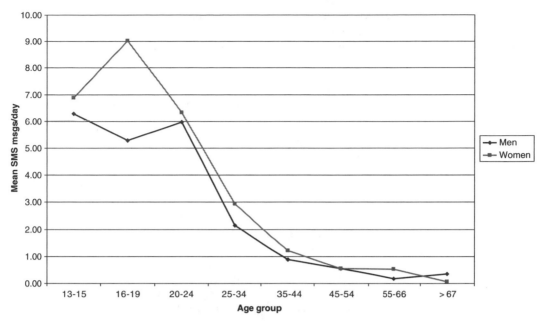

Figure 15.3. Mean number of SMS messages sent per day by age and gender for Norwegian users, 2002. Source: Telenor R&D.

first categorization, material has been reexamined for themes relevant to this chapter.

The quantitative material comes from an ongoing series of surveys carried out by Telenor R&D. The surveys contain nationally representative samples of the population and have been carried out annually between 1997 and 2002. In addition, we draw on the material from the data produced in the Eurescom P903 project that covered slightly more than 9000 interviews in 9 European countries (Norway, Denmark, Germany, Czech Republic, United Kingdom, Netherlands, France, Spain, and Italy). We also draw on the data produced in the EU-sponsored eLiving project. This project is a panel study that has been carried out in six European countries (Norway, Germany, United Kingdom, Italy, Bulgaria, and Israel).[9] There are 10,543 persons who have been included in the sample of the eLiving work.

Parental Control, Peer Group Knowledge, and the Transfer of Information in Light of the Mobile Telephone

Up to this point we have examined the sociological dimensions of power, looked into the social context of the adolescent with regard to both peers and parents, and examined the growth of mobile telephony within a Norwegian context. Now we turn to the examination of the mobile telephone vis-à-vis the family and the peer group. This provides insight into how the adolescent is simultaneously enmeshed in both a traditional/legal–rational as well as a ritual-based power system.

The Mobile Telephone and the Family

Looking first at the effect of adolescents' mobile telephone use in relation to the family, we find a type of Faustian dilemma for the parents. On the one hand, mobile telephone use provides access, a metaphorical umbilical cord that parent and child that both cherish and resent. At the same time, the mobile telephone can be used to strengthen the ties within the peer group, perhaps at the expense of parental ties. This shift in attention can trigger parental concerns that the adolescents are becoming independent prematurely, whereas adolescents think their independence cannot come fast enough.

Management of Parental Interaction

Several issues arise when considering the interaction between parents and children, particularly in the context of broad mobile telephone access.

Looking first at integrative aspects of the mobile telephone, adolescent informants thought it was important to be available for their parents and to let them know where they were.

> *Oda (18 years of age)*: It's pretty important to be available for your parents and let them know if you're going to a party or to the city or something. I usually try to let them know what time I'll be coming home.
> *Moderator*: Do your parents call you or vice versa?
> *Oda*: Usually they call me because I have a prepaid subscription so I don't bother to call so much since it is so expensive to call you know. So, we have a system where I call and let it ring three times, then they know it's me and so they just call me back.

Oda's sense that it was "pretty important" to keep her parents informed speaks to her respect for the status of the family. It also underscores the hierarchical dimensions of the relationship between parent and child.[10] This is a type of ex–post facto recognition of the institutionalized weight of the institution. It is also of note that Oda's parents call her, as opposed to her calling her parents. On the one hand, if her parents call too much, her friends will think Oda's parents are being overbearing and intrusive. On the other hand, the fact that Oda does not want to waste scarce calling time on her parents puts the responsibility on the parents to maintain the contact.

The more hierarchical and formalized relationship between parent and child is also seen in the way that the device is used. Where parents use the device instrumentally, adolescents use it more expressively (Ling & Yttri, 2002). This can be seen in the following sequence:

> *Moderator*: Do you call your parents or do they call you?
> *Nora (18)*: They call us.
> *Moderator*: What do they call about?
> *Rita (18)*: Where are you, when are you coming home?
> *Nora (18)*: Practical things, you know.
> *Moderator*: Practical things?
> *Nora (18)*: [With] friends it is more like babbling. [With] parents it is more like they call about something.
> *Erika (17)*: If I was supposed to be home an hour ago then they call me like 25 times. . . . If I

said I'd be home but then I don't come home as planned, then it's, you know, like full chaos on the telephone.

Although both parties recognize the need for access, it is sometimes a begrudging recognition. We see that interaction with parents, at least in the eyes of the teens, often focuses on the practical. Between the teens themselves, the interaction is informal. We also see that parent–child interaction can include implicit disciplinary themes:

> *Moderator*: Is it important for you to be available for your parents?
> *Lena (14)*: It's kind of dumb, if you want to do something and then they call and say that you have to come home.
> *Bente (17)*: You turn off the mobile and say that the battery was dead.
> *Annika (17)*: If you're at somebody's house and you want to be there a little longer, then they call and say that you have to come home.
> *Moderator*: So it is a little embarrassing if they call you?
> *Annika (17)*: No, it's more irritating.

Annika's expression of irritation underscores how the interaction is problematic. In addition, Bente's management of the facts shows how she can leverage the characteristics of the technology to favor interaction with peers to the exclusion of her parents. When looking at this in the context of power relationships, one can see that the ability of the parents to demand the attention of the child is not always openly accepted, and that adolescents would prefer to interact with their peer group, in which their influence holds a broader sway.

Beyond the most obvious strategies to frustrate parent's insight into their lives, the interviewees also outlined other more advanced, technologically based ruses that they could use to avoid unwanted parental involvement. The adolescents can put on an "act" and manipulate various symbolic resources to misrepresent their situation vis-à-vis their parents. Indeed, these misrepresentations can take on the appearance of clarifications when really they are a type of boundary keeping exercise. This, in turn, is recognition of the way in which power relations are being worked out regarding the use of the mobile telephone (Goffman, 1959; Rogers, 1977).

Adolescents also use the technology itself to establish generational boundaries:

Nina (18): With some telephones, you can do it
like [if a call comes] from some numbers it
goes right into voicemail, like if your parents
call then it goes right into voicemail.

Arne (17): I do that

Moderator: You do that?

Arne (17): Yeah, if I'm out on a weekend and
things like that, then I do that.

Moderator: Whom do you exclude?

Arne (17): The family.

Moderator: OK. You do that too?

Oda (18): I just don't answer the phone and then
I'll say that I didn't hear it or something.

Moderator: Have you done that?

Rune (15): Yeah.

Moderator: With whom?

Rune (15): Family.

Moderator: OK. Not friends?

Rune (15): No.

Moderator: Have you done that?

Ola (14): Yeah.

Moderator: With your family?

Ola (14): Yeah.

These comments describe technical strategies
that manage parental control. Adolescents use these
strategies to extract themselves from the family, at
least temporarily, in favor of their peer group. These
mobile telephone strategies were not available earlier. Although the mobile telephone has led to more
seamless communication, or the potential to contact another person regardless of the caller's and the
receiver's locations, the device has also provided
various ways with which one can sabotage this accessibility when it is inconvenient.[11]

The Individualization
of Mediated Communication

The individualization of the mobile telephone
streamlines social interaction because callers are
almost guaranteed to reach a specific individual,
compared to reaching a random household member with a traditional telephone. Adolescents recognize this. One, for example, noted that "It is a
little easier to call a mobile [number] that you know
that only one person answers."

One effect of this is that there is a lower threshold for interaction. Callers know that they are calling directly to an individual—not to a house
telephone, where they may have to go through the
filtering interactions of talking to a parent or an-

other sibling. Thus, it is an interpersonal and not a
broadly social interaction. A similar theme arises
when discussing the use of voicemail, a common
mobile telephone feature:

Rita (18): It's OK for somebody to leave a message
in my voicemail instead of the family's
voicemail. I can call them back. It's more
private.

Erika (17): It's like, if I'm not home and if I didn't
have a mobile telephone then my parents
would know about all the people that I hang
out with. And if friends wanted to leave me a
message but I'm not home, they'd have to
leave a message in the family's voicemail.
They'd have to quick, think about what they
should say. When you have a mobile
telephone, you have a private voicemail and a
private telephone.

The mobile telephone removes the child's social interactions from the parents' direct insight.
Adolescents control the people with whom they talk
and have more room into which they can share
thoughts and messages that might not be acceptable given a broader public. This plays on the peer
groups' ethos that their inner communications be
shielded from nonmembers, and particularly parents.

Mobile telephones allow adolescents a type of
ritual interaction. Through this shared ethic, they
can veil conversations and activities that they would
rather not expose to parents' scrutiny. Thus, the
group's knowledge and lore becomes part of a clan-
destine knowledge that defines the group's boundary. Loyalty to the group may mean respecting and
protecting the inner knowledge from others.

The physical device also becomes a repository
for different types of personal information. The text
of SMS messages is often saved, and thus the content of the interaction is recorded on the phone.
Names are recorded in the name register with the
"calling history" of who has been called, when they
were called, and how long the conversation lasted.
Thus, for example, if parents were to gain access to
their child's mobile telephone, they would have the
ability to gain significant insight into their child's
social interaction.

The Undermining of Family Rituals

The final point here is that the mobile telephone
provides young people with a way to be in touch with
friends during times that previously were exclusively

in the family realm. The adolescent is available for mediated messages during family get-togethers, meal times, and vacations. On one level, this is not a new development—other technologies have permeated these family spaces and have reformed how families interact. The television and traditional telephony are obvious examples. Nonetheless, the increase of mobile telephone usage is, to some degree, a distraction from the common focus of the ritual occasion, whether that is a common evening meal or the annual Christmas dinner. The device steals attention from the shared family experience and thus limits its effect. The technology can undercut the potential for this type of solidarity and the hierarchical dimensions that this form of social structuring implies.

Our material points to several dimensions that characterize parent–child interactions, including respect on the child's part toward the parents' roles and status. Respect, however begrudging, is indeed an indication of a power differential in the Weberian sense. Although the relationship between adolescents and their parents has affective dimensions, the marking of boundaries and the need to respect the wishes and demands of the parents indicates that there is an absolute power differential.

At the same time, adolescents expressed irritation over the possibility for control that the device represented and had a repertoire of available strategies available by which they manage their availability. However, managing their availability also requires the adolescent to manage a corresponding façade. Again, one can read these strategies as evidence of the power differential within the parent–child relationship.

Adolescents and the Demands of Peer Network

Where parents have traditional and legal positions with regard to their children, peers enjoy a different role in the adolescent's life. As noted above, the peer group is a type of midwife into adulthood for the adolescent. However, the peer group is not simply a supportive group without its own demands. Knowledge of the correct form of presentation of self, the current themes of discussion, and the correct argot are, in some respects, prerequisites for group membership (Ling, 2001). The peer group can—sometimes mercilessly—make demands that members follow certain nuanced forms in the presentation of self (Fine, 1981).

As described above, however, the peer group is described as being more fluid and changing from year to year. In the United States, adolescents report changing friendship groups because of shifts in current interests and the desire to avoid various issues considered problematic, such as drug or alcohol use. This also means that there is a more polymorphous sense of popularity. If the criteria of one group do not fit the individual, then the individual can always choose another group. In this case, though, it may be more difficult to maintain an overview over the symbolic content of interaction during the interaction. That is, the symbolic meaning of various artifacts and behaviors changes from group to group. At the same time these symbolic meanings have increasing centrality in the eyes of the teens.

Analysis shows that adolescents are aware of various status-related issues concerning the mobile telephone. In the case of Fine's Little League baseball teams, the good players leveraged their baseball skills into dominant social prestige (Fine, 1987). In other cases, adolescents who are good at telling jokes or singing have a quasi-institutionalized claim to a more influential (read powerful) position in the peer group. Putting this into the context of the mobile phone, those who are known to have a large number of names in their telephone's address book, who receive a lot of calls or messages, or who have a particularly stylish handset with reference to the type of covers and the models in their group at a particular point in time will have more influence.

The Quantification of Popularity

The mobile telephone address book has replaced owning a paper address book as the place for contact information. The address book is obviously an important and useful telephone function, but it is also a means of quantifying popularity and prestige. That is, the device provides young people with an easily comparable metric for gauging social esteem.

> *Moderator*: Do you call by entering a number or do have you the number programmed?
> *Oda* (18): It's in my phone's address book.
> *Moderator*: How many names do you have in the [telephone's] phone book?
> *Nina* (18): It's full.
> *Moderator*: Full? On your telephone, how many names can you put in?
> *Nina* (18): 100.

Moderator: 100?

Rune (15): Mine isn't all the way full, I have 80 or so.

Arne (17): I have 100 and some, about 140.

Moderator: How many do you have?

Oda (18): I have 99 or something like that.

Inger (17): My phone only has room for 50 or so.

Moderator: So you choose names in the [telephone's] phone book?

Oda (18): It's like I have my telephone with me everywhere. So, I write down the telephone numbers I get. Most of them are friends. Then there is work and home and a mobile telephone for each of them so there are quite a few.

The sequence takes on a type of "mine is bigger than yours" tone. In this way, it shows that having many names programmed into the mobile telephone is a desired state. In this context, the number of names becomes a way for young people to reckon their currency in their social network. Although the absolute number of names is important, their use seems to contradict the impression that the teens wished to portray. The material shown in figure 15.4 indicates that although teens and young adults claim to have more than 100 names in the name registers of their telephones, they call or send messages to only one or two on a daily basis. More than anything else, this points to

the symbolic use of the mobile telephone. The mobile telephone also provides other opportunities for this type of display. Just like describing the number of names in the name register function, it is possible to describe the number and importance of the messages that are received.

> *Erika (17)*: I received seven or eight text messages from him today and that means I have answered seven or eight messages, and it is not like that happens everyday you know. When I come home there are often a ton of text messages laying there but it varies a lot in relation to who you have contact with and which day it is. On Friday there are a lot more messages than on Thursday because people go out and they want to do something on Friday.

The exploitation of these symbols can be an element in assertion of influence within the peer group. Negotiation of influence is, in its most abstract form, a negotiation of power in that the person with influence is able to assert their own will in their interactions. The number of names in the phone and the number of messages or calls received are particularly powerful symbolic devices within the peer group. These elements are use as a confirmation of the individual's success in the process of establishing their own social identity, and as developed above, this is a central issue for the adolescent.

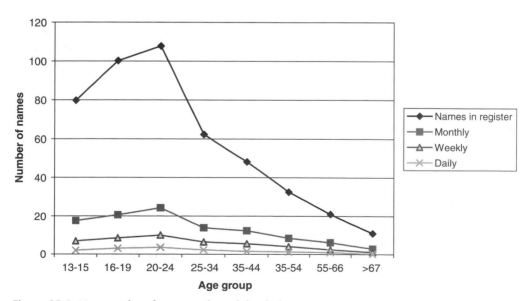

Figure 15.4. Mean number of names in the mobile telephone name register and mean number of names used to either call or to send SMS messages on a monthly, weekly, and daily basis by age, Norwegian users, 2002. Source: Telenor R&D.

Mobile Telephony as a Fashion Statement

The mobile telephone, as a physical object, is also a way to display knowledge of current fashion trends and thus garner status and influence. The device is an accessory that, beyond its functional aspects, communicates to others the owner's taste and fashion competence.

When asked in the context of a focus group to show their mobile telephones, several of the respondents demurred. On further prodding, they said that they were somewhat embarrassed by the vintage, size, or style of their mobile telephones. Thus, they were conversant with the prevailing fashion and knew that their devices were not parallel with that standard.

According to Goffman (1967), reading embarrassment allows one to read the situation. He notes that embarrassment is being caught out of the character that people wish to portray. Thus, the informants' embarrassment was an indication of how badly their façade would be threatened if peers discovered their mobile telephone's style (or lack thereof). The need to "repair" their façade undermines their ability to legitimately claim status and influence because, in effect, all can see that they are not as able to control and manipulate symbols as they would like others to believe.

In this context, a mother reported the following incident that points to the tyranny of fashion when discussing mobile telephones:

> Mia: You know, our 13 year old can borrow her father's business mobile telephone, but she absolutely refuses. She thinks it's a museum piece since it's over two years old—she absolutely can't be seen with that. I had both girls on the ferry to Denmark last weekend and I said, "Can one of you call home and say that we are landing at such and such a time?" "With that telephone? Are you crazy?" It was impossible.

It is also possible to discuss fashion in terms of interpeer group status rivalry and boundary keeping. One respondent critiqued another's mobile telephone via the use of thinly veiled condemnation of an alternative esthetic notion of mobile telephones.

> Erika (17): A mobile telephone is an expression of personality actually, because for example, I hate flowers more than anything else, but she

has a cover with flowers you know. That's something she picked out but that I wouldn't have. So, the cover shows what type of person you are. It is the same with the mobile telephones model. I know people who buy older models because they think they are better.

Erika seems to assert that the taste of another respondent is not up to snuff from the perspective of her aesthetic. She asserts that the phone (read: taste) of the other girl does not match her own.

This assertion was made with reference to various, relatively stable, notions of fashion. Although there are nuances within several general possible patterns of presentation (i.e. preppie, freak, skater, etc.), the general patterns have a relative stability (Lynne, 2000). The mobile telephone is one element in this more general picture that forms a codex of style. This codex then forms the foundation of the adolescents' knowledge/power/influence complex. To a certain degree, the codex's codification is determined in the interaction between adolescents and in their interactions with various commercial and cultural institutions. The success with which one follows this—and interprets its dictates—can be translated into positions of relative influence within the local group.

When viewed from the perspective of power relations, the degree to which a person successfully interprets the current styles can be translated to the degree of influence that one has within the group. Put into Goffmanian terms, the facility with which people manipulate symbols is an element in their more general ability to foster an impression and thereby lay a claim on influencing others within the peer group. The success or failure of this interpretation can and does hinge on nuanced elements. Details as seemingly inconsequential as the type of shoes one wears, the color of the laces, or even the way that they are laced and tied can all be a part of these evaluations. In this respect, then, it is perhaps not strange that the flowers on another's mobile telephone are deconstructed and used in the viewer's assessment of another.

It is also clear that different esthetics are characteristic of different groups. The interpretation of these flowers also points to intragroup power relations; that is, the sense that one person's own peer group is more correct or dominant than another's. What is acceptable in one clique is an anathema to another.

The quantification of popularity and the interpretation of the technology in terms of fashion show how the mobile telephone has gone beyond simply being a functional communication technology to being a type of icon in the adolescent's pursuit of their own identity.

Discussion: Adolescents and the Matrices of Power

We have examined how teens are involved in two different types of power relationships. On the one hand, there is the adolescents' relationship to their parents, which is based on tradition and legal–rational systems of power, in which the parents determine many aspects of their children's situation. Two, the adolescent's status within their peer group is more achieved than received. In the peer group, the adolescents' ability to manipulate symbols and to develop an individual identity is how they gain influence within the group.

It was into this context that the mobile telephone was introduced. The community, home, or even family are no longer units of communication; rather, it is the individual person. Thus, parents can no longer claim monopolistic control—or even oversee their children's telephone use. Enabled by the mobile telephone, children have simply debunked that assertion.

As seen from the parent's perspective, mobile telephones provide a direct channel to the child regardless of time or place. Rather than, or perhaps in addition to, coordinating interaction with their children on the basis of mechanical timekeeping, the mobile telephone allows a new type of real-time coordination. At 10:01, the parents can call a child and demand his or her presence, rather than waiting in the living room for the child's return. Seen from a power perspective, this allows the parents a new way to maintain control over their children. In addition, parents are positive that using the mobile telephone facilitates family coordination and can provide the adolescent with insight into budgeting, particularly if the teen is required to pay for his or her own telephone calls; the device can provide the child with a virtual umbilical cord.

This system, however, which provides direct access to their children regardless of time and place, requires parents to accept that the same system also gives the child parallel access to their peers. Mobile telephony, including SMS, distinguishes itself from other communication technologies in the life of the adolescent in that it allows for immediacy. With mobile telephony, adolescents orient themselves to the flux of social life, and in this way, they engage in control of the social situation. The mobile telephone provides a type of counterpoint to the family's internal structure. The device means that others (i.e., peers) can reach the adolescent regardless of the family situation. It allows the adolescent to be in touch with peers during traditional family times (i.e., vacation or family holiday meals). In addition, the mobile telephone individualizes communication.

When viewed vis-à-vis the peer group and their sometimes forced allegiance to the various forms of fashion and presentation, adolescents are often engaged in a type of symbolic power structure. In this case, extremely detailed knowledge of which type of earrings to wear, the special way to arrange trouser cuffs, or the angle of their collar speak to a type of peer-based knowledge/power that, in the most extreme cases, help to determine membership in the group. In this case, the type of mobile telephone, the way that it is personalized (ring, brand, special covers), how many names adolescents have in their mobile telephone's address book, or the frequency with which one receives or "has to" send responses are all part of this complex of significant signs that are used to participate in the economy of symbolic power.

The mobile telephone provides insight into the ritual interaction that characterizes the peer group: the ability to integrate the group via tacitly accepted consumption, the pursuit of acceptable goals such as popularity, and protecting the group's inner knowledge. Through prescriptions as to which styles and form of presentation are appropriate, peers work out the group's power relationships (Lynne, 2000, Ling, 2001). The individual teen can either contribute to the definition of these or to be bound to them. It is here that adolescents can assert influence and indeed test their abilities. Although children can influence familial decisions, the family structure does not parallel the peer group's relatively equal footing.

The mobile telephone has lowered the threshold for telephonic access. It has done this in a situation in which the adolescents are yearning to develop contact with peers and emancipate themselves from their parent's control. At the same time, parents can see both the device's positive and negative aspects.

Thus the style, content, form, and power relationships between adolescents and parents on the one hand and adolescents and their peers on the other has taken new forms and has been carried out in ways that were not possible in the recent past. Mobile telephony technology and its pervasive potential for communication mean that we are only now seeing the effects of the technology's use by sorting out the ways in which it us used, for what purposes, and with which consequences.

Acknowledgments. This chapter was published in Norwegian in an edited form [Ling, R. & Yttri, B. 2003. Kontroll, frigjøring og status: Mobiltelefon og maktforhold i familier og ungdomsgrupper. In Engelstad, F., & Ødegård, G. (Eds.), *På terskelen: makt, mening og motstand blant unge.* Oslo, Norway: Gyldendal Akademisk.]

Notes

1. In all cases the names and identities of the individuals have been changed to protect their identities.
2. Telenor R&D gathered the data for this analysis in June of 2002. Random selections of more than 2000 Norwegians of all age groups were interviewed.
3. Although we recognize the importance of charismatic power in the Weberian system, that is not the focus of this analysis.
4. Beyond the functional dimensions of adolescence, this period of life has also moved beyond simply a preparatory stage for adulthood and is a culture unto itself. It is characterized by its own parlance, dress, forms of interaction, ethos, and attendant status as a marketing niche (Franzen, 2000). Thus, in addition to being a type of apprentice adulthood and a period of emancipation, this life phase more than others is a period that is culturally unique.
5. Obviously, other theoretical approaches can be used in this context. In particular, the Bourdieuian approach is applicable because it includes the concept of symbolic power.
6. There is a small literature on adolescents and PSTN-based telephony, (Aronson, 1971; Castelain-Meunier, 1997; Claisse & Rowe, 1987; Katz & Aspden, 1998; Kellner, 1977; Lohan, 1997; Pratto & Rodman, 1993). However, the literature on adolescents' use of mobile telephony is growing (Brown, Green, & Harper, 2002; Katz & Aakhus, 2002; Ling, 2000; Ling & Yttri, 2002; Mançeron, 1997; Weilenmann & Larsson, 2002).

7. This analysis comes from data collected in the Eurescom P903 project (Mante-Meijer et al., 2001)
8. Looking further at the adolescents and their local friendship patterns, we note an intensity of interaction for the girls that is not as apparent for the boys in the sample. The more friends that a boy had, the more face-to-face meetings he had ($r = .56^{***}$). Fixed-telephonic ($r = .30^{***}$) and mobile telephone contacts ($r = .31$) both had a more modest correlation. For the girls in the sample, however, the situation was quite different. The more friends that a teen girl had, the more she reported face-to-face meetings ($r = .56^{***}$), and she also had more fixed telephone contact ($r = .44^{***}$), mobile telephone contact ($r = .42^{***}$), and SMS contact ($r = .49^{***}$). As noted above, the frequency with which subjects met face to face was only moderately correlated with the telephonic interaction (statistical significance: $^{***}p < .001, ^{**}p < .01, ^{*}p < .05$).
9. These have been supplemented with other qualitative analyses and quantitative material, most recently in 2002.
10. The inclusion of Israel slightly stretches the traditional definition of European, but in its use of mobile telephony, it is one of the most active countries.
11. There may be a type of coordination that goes on (i.e., the parents telling the child that they will be someplace). Thus, there is a line between coordination and control. Parents' ability to demand information regarding the adolescents' location and activities implies that they have the potential to either demand that the adolescent not engage in that particular situation or to create sanctions against further interaction of that type. This is control. Coordination, however, is the negotiation of when and where the activities of each party can be integrated, so that each party achieves their goals while allowing space for the other to also achieve theirs. This is a shifting issue. Younger adolescents are likely to be subject to the direct control of their parents, and perhaps displays of raw force, whereas the interaction with older adolescents is often more a negotiation of coordination.
12. On their part, parents can fight back, for example, by calling the mobile phones of their child's friends in an attempt to locate the child.

References

Aires, P. (1972). Centuries of childhood: A social history of family life. New York: Vintage.

Aronson, S. H. (1971). Bells electrical toy: What's the use? The sociology of early telephone use. In de Sola Pool, I. (Ed.), *The social impact of the telephone* (pp. 13–39) Cambridge: MIT Press.

Brown, B., Green, N., & Harper, R. (Eds.). (2002). *Wireless world: Social and interactional aspects of the mobile age*. London: Springer.

Castelain-Meunier, C. (1997). The paternal cord: Telephone relationships between "non-custodian" fathers and their children. *Reseaux, 5*, 161–176.

Claisse, G., & Rowe, F. (1987). The telephone in question: Questions on communication. *Computer Networks and ISDN Systems, 14*, 207–219.

Collins, R. (1974). *Conflict sociology*. New York: Academic Press.

Collins, R. (1994). *Four sociological traditions*. New York: Oxford.

Collins, R. (2004). *Interaction ritual chains*. Princeton, NJ: Princeton University Press.

Danesi, M. (1994). *Cool: the signs and meanings of adolescence*. Toronto: University of Toronto Press.

Durkheim, E. (1954). *The elementary forms of religious life*. Glencoe, IL: The Free Press.

Engelstad, F. (2005). *Hva er Makt?* Oslo: Universitetsforlaget.

Fine, G. A. (1981). Friends, impression management, and pre-adolescent behavior. In Asher, S. R. & Gottman, J. M. (Eds.), *The development of children's friendships*. Cambridge, U.K.: Cambridge University Press

Fine, G. A. (1987). *With the boys: Little league baseball and preadolescent culture*. Chicago: University of Chicago Press.

Franzen, A. (2000). Does the Internet make us lonely? *European Sociological Review, 16*, 427–438.

Gekas, V. 1981. Contexts of socialization. In Rosenbervg, M., & and Turner, R. H. (Eds.), *Social psychology: Sociological perspectives* (pp. 165–199). New York: Basic Books.

Glaser, A., & Strauss, B. (1971). *Status passage*. London: Routledge.

Goffman, E. (1959). *The presentation of self in everyday life*. New York: Doubleday Anchor.

Goffman, E. (1967). Ritual interaction: Essays on face-to-face behavior. New York: Pantheon.

Hogan, D. P. (1985). Parental influences on the timing of early life transitions. *Current Perspectives on Aging and Lifecycle, 1*, 1–59.

Katz, J. E., & Aakhus, M. (Eds.). (2002). *Perpetual contact: Mobile communication, private talk, public performance*. Cambridge, UK: Cambridge University Press.

Katz, J. E., & Aspden, P. (1998). Theories, data, and potential impacts of mobile communications. *Technological Forecasting and Social Change, 57*, 133–156.

Kellner, S. (1977). Telephone in new (and old) communities. In de Sola Pool, I. (Ed.) *The social impact of the telephone* (pp. 281–298). Cambridge, MA: MIT Press.

Ling, R. (2000). "We will be reached": The use of mobile telephony among Norwegian youth. *Information Technology and People, 13*, 102–120.

Ling, R. (2001). It is "in." It doesn't matter if you need it or not, just that you have it. Fashion and the domestication of the mobile telephone among teens in Norway. Presented at *Il corpo umano tra tecnologie, comunicazione e moda (The human body between technologies, communication and fashion)*, January 2001. Triennale di Milano, Milano, Italy.

Ling, R. (2002). The social and cultural consequences of mobile telephony as seen in the Norwegian context. Fornebu, Norway: Telenor R&D

Ling, R., & Yttri, B. (2002). Hyper-coordination via mobile phones in Norway. In Katz, J. E., & Aakhus, M. (Eds.), *Perpetual contact: Mobile communication, private talk, public performance* (pp. 139–169). Cambridge, UK: Cambridge University Press.

Lohan, E. M. (1997). No parents allowed! Telecoms in the individualist household. In Mante-Meyer, E., & and Kant, A. (Eds.), *Blurring boundaries: When are information and communication technologies coming home* (pp. 131–144)? Stockholm: Telia.

Lynne, A. (2000). Nyansens makt—en studie av ungdom, identitet og klær. Lysaker: Statens institutt for forbruksforskning.

Mançeron, V. (1997). Get connected! Social uses of the telephone and modes of interaction in a peer group of young Parisians. In Mante-Meyer, E., & and Kant, A. (Eds.), *Blurring boundaries: When are information and communication technologies coming home?* (pp. 171–182) Stockholm: Telia.

Mante-Meijer, E., Haddon, L., Concejero, P., Klamer, L., Heres, J., Ling, R., Thomas, F., Smoreda, Z. & Vrieling, I. l. (2001). Checking it out with the people—ICT markets and users in Europe. Heidelberg: EURESCOM.

Pratto, D. J., & Rodman, H. (1993). Telephone communication with children as part of self-care arrangement: A research note. *Sociological Spectrum, 13*, 289–302.

Prost, A. (1991). Public and private spheres in France. In Prost, A., & Vincent, G. (Eds.), *A history of private life: Riddles of identity in modern times* (Vol. 5, pp. 1–144). Cambridge, MA: Belknap Press.

Rainwater, L. (1970). *Behind ghetto walls: Black families in a federal slum*. Chicago: Aldine.

Rogers, M. F. (1977). Goffman on power. *The American Sociologist, 12*, 88–95.

Rubin, L. (1984). *Intimate strangers: Men and women together*. New York: Harper and Row.

Rubin, L. (1985). Just friends: The role of friendship in our lives. New York: Harper & Row.

Schneider, B., & Stevenson, D. (1999). *The ambitious generation: America's teenagers, motivated but directionless*. New Haven, CT: Yale University Press.

Weber, M. (1958). *From Max Weber: Essays in sociology*. New York: Oxford University Press.

Weber, M. (1978). *Economy and society*. Berkeley: University of California Press.

Weilenmann, A., & Larsson, C. (2002). Local use and sharing of mobile telephones. In Brown, B., Green, N., & Harper, R. (Eds.), *Wireless world: Social and interactional aspects of the mobile age* (pp. 92–107). London: Springer.

16

Mizuko Ito and Daisuke Okabe

Intimate Connections

Contextualizing Japanese Youth and Mobile Messaging

Ever since NTT Docomo launched its i-mode mobile Internet service in 1999, international attention has been trained on Japan as a hothouse for incubating the future of the wireless revolution. In particular, international technology communities have noted and often celebrated handset design by Japanese electronic manufacturers, third-generation infrastructures, video and camera phones, and mobile entertainment. A focus on ever-new advanced technical functionality, however, can often lose sight of the social, historical, and cultural context through which contemporary Japanese mobile media is structured and has evolved. As Richard Harper (2003, p. 187) has argued, "mobile society is not rendering our society into some new form, it is rather, enabling the same social patterns that have been in existence for some time to evolve in small but socially significant ways." In this chapter, we analyze the text messaging practices of Japanese youth as an outcome of existing historical, social, and cultural factors rather than as something driven forward by the inherent logic of new technology.

On the basis of the distinctiveness of young people's mobile media usage, we argue for the context specificity of meanings and usage of new technologies. Even as mobile phones have become common in all age groups,[1] young people use their phones more, spend more on them (IPSe, 2003), and have unique patterns of usage. Particularly distinctive is usage of mobile e-mail[2]: 95.4% of students describe themselves as mobile e-mail users, in contrast to 75.2% of the general population (VR, 2002), and they send a higher volume of messages.[3] Students also tend to be more responsive to the e-mail that they receive. Almost all students (92.3%) report that they view a message as soon as they receive it, whereas a slimmer majority of the general population (68.1%) is as responsive. Many older users say that they view a message when convenient to them or at the end of the day (VR, 2002). What is behind these distinctive patterns of usage by young people?

This chapter answers this question by analyzing ethnographic material on mobile phone usage in relation to three different contextual frames. The first of these frames is constructed by the "power geometries" (Massey 1994) of existing places of home, school, and public places. Next, we present the central social context in which youth peer messaging practice is situated—the intimate peer group. Finally, we analyze how this ethnographic material articulates with longstanding intergenerational dynamics in postwar Japan. Our focus is not on the uptake of a particular technology (i.e., short text message services on the mobile phone) but on a historically continuous set of practices that have mobilized different technologies at different times. Because of the structural location they occupy in contemporary Japanese society, youths, particularly teenage girls, have spearheaded the development of what we call "personal, portable, and pedestrian" communication media practices (Ito, Okabe, & Matsuda, 2005).

Method and Conceptual Framework

Our Research

This chapter draws from ongoing ethnographic research on mobile phone use centered at Keio University's Shonan Fujisawa Campus near Tokyo. We draw primarily from three different sets of data. One is a set of ethnographic interviews conducted by Ito in the winter of 2000 with 24 high school and college students about their use of media, including mobile phones. We have also conducted a series of observations on trains in the Kanto and Kansai regions of Japan, documenting instances of mobile phone use (Okabe & Ito, 2005). The central body of data behind this chapter is a set of "communication diaries" and interviews that we collected between July and December 2002. In these diaries, we collect detailed information on where and when particular forms of mobile communication were used by a diverse set of people. We seek direct observational records in addition to interview data, as it is notoriously difficult to capture the fleeting particularities of mobile communication after the fact. Our diary was adapted from data collection methods piloted by Rebecca Grinter and Margery Eldridge (2001) in which they asked 10 teenagers to record the time, content, length, location, and recipient (or sender) of all text messages for 7 days. As with interviews, this data collection method still relies on second-hand accounting, but it has the advantage of providing much more detail on usage than can be recalled in a stand-alone interview. We expanded the communication log to include voice calls and mobile Internet and more details about the location and context of use. Participants were asked to keep records of every instance of mobile phone use, including voice, short text messages, e-mail, and web use, for a period of 2 days. They noted the time of the usage, with

whom they were in contact, whether they received or initiated the contact, where they were, what kind of communication type was used, why they chose that form of communication, who was in the vicinity at the time, if there were any problems associated with the usage, and the content of the communication. After completion of the diaries, we conducted in-depth interviews, which covered general attitudes and background information relevant to mobile phone use, and explication of key usage instances that were recorded in the diaries. Our study involved seven high school students (aged 16–18 years), six college students (aged 18–21 years), two housewives with teenage children (in their forties), and nine professionals (aged 21–51 years). The gender split was roughly equal, with 11 males and 13 females. Five hundred ninety-four instances of communication were collected for the high school and college students, and 229 for the adults. The majority of users were in the Tokyo Kanto region. Seven were recruited in the Osaka area in southern Japan to provide some geographic variation.

In addition to our own ethnographic work, we base our analysis on Japanese popular discourse and research literature on mobile phone adoption. In particular, we draw from research compiled by Tomoyuki Okada and Misa Matsuda (2002), collected more recently in English (Ito et al., 2005), which represents over a decade of work on youth mobile media. The final section of our chapter brings this material to bear on our ethnographic material, analyzing current mobile messaging practices as an instantiation of longstanding intergenerational dynamics and a history of mobile media adoption. We turn now to the theoretical and conceptual framework for our analysis.

Conceptual Framework

Countries with widespread mobile device adoption rates exhibit cross-cultural similarities in the intersection of youth and mobile phones. Richard Ling and Brigitte Yttri (2002) have coined the term "hyper-coordination" to describe the expressive and socially active uses of mobile phones by Norwegian teens. In contrast to the more instrumental uses that older subjects described, youths describe using phones for emotional and social communications, and particularly for cementing peer relations. Ling and Yttri describe how adolescence is a unique time in the life cycle, how peers play a central role during this period, and how the mobile phone becomes a tool to "define a sense of group membership, particular vis-à-vis the older generation (2002, p. 162). A growing body of work with teens in locations such as the United Kingdom (Grinter & Eldridge, 2001; Green, 2003; Taylor & Harper, 2003), Finland (Kasesniemi & Rautianinen, 2002; Kasesniemi, 2003), Norway (Skog, 2002), and Sweden (Weilenmann & Larsson, 2002) finds similar patterns in other countries. As documented by the chapters in this body of work, text messaging, in particular, appears to be a uniquely teen-inflected form of mobile communication in these initial settings of adoption, and young people have driven adoption of the short message system across the globe (Grinter & Eldridge, 2001; Kasesniemi & Rautianinen, 2002; Ling & Yttri, 2002; Rheingold, 2002; Agar, 2003; Kasesniemi, 2003). In the United States, instant messaging appears to occupy a similar structural role (chapter 14).

Rather than locating the affinity between messaging and youth in the developmental imperatives of teens, we take a context-driven approach. In another essay, Ito (2003) argued that the practices and cultures of youth are not solely outcomes of a certain level of developmental maturity, or even of social relations, but are also conditioned by the regulative and normative force of places. In other words, rather than originating solely with the psychological, social, and developmental needs of youth, text messaging practices are structured by institutional and cross-generational surrounds. We also argue that the historical development of certain mediated communication practices also construct a key structuring context that has made mobile messaging particularly amenable to young Japanese.

Behind our approach is the "new paradigm" in childhood studies that has argued that "youth" and "childhood" are categories constructed and consumed by people of all ages and are produced in particular power-geometries (James & Prout, 1997; James, Jenks, & Prout, 1998).[4] In other words, an understanding of youth practices needs to be located within an adult social structure that limits and regulates youth activity as well as cultural discourses that often construct youth as frivolous and socially immature. Most simply put, modern teens, despite their physical and psychological maturity, do not yet have access to a full repertoire of adult rights, responsibilities, and resources, such as their own homes where they can meet friends and lovers or a workplace where they are considered productive members of society (as opposed to "consumers" and "learners"). Teens are also considered legitimate objects of external regulation, control, and redirection in a way that even young adults are not. Just as social theory has interrogated race, class, and gender, generational dynamics need to be analyzed with a similar social structural lens (Alanen, 2001). We cut our data along these lines as well. We apply the category of youth to those institutionalized as such—high school and college students who are financially dependent on adults.

In the sections to follow, we posit that the institutionalized power-geometries of place (Massey, 1994) are important factors structuring youth mobile phone usage. Youth communications are regulated by peers or adults depending on place and time of day, and access to mobile media takes a central role in managing and inflecting that control. Conceptually, our approach shares much in common with Nicola Green's in her analysis of the role of mobile phones in surveillance and monitoring, both between adults and teens and among teens (Green, 2002). Ling and Yttri (chapter 15) make similar observations of youth mobile phone usage and power relations in Norway. Cross-cultural similarities in mobile phone usage can be understood in relation to shared and different structural conditions in the lives of young people. Although this chapter does not present a comparative analysis, it does lay out conditions that contextualize Japanese youth's mobile phone use and suggests that the cross-cultural similarities in mobile phone usage are partially an outcome of the similarities in the institutionalized status of youth. Specifically, mobile messaging helps compensate for the lack of social settings and places in which youth can communicate privately among close friends and lovers.

Following our description of how mobile communications are keyed to existing power geometries, we argue that youth mobile messaging has worked to construct alternative kinds of intimate "places" or settings in which youth can be in touch with their close peer group or "full-time intimate community" (Nakajima, Keiichi, & Yoshii, 1999). In a different paper (Ito & Okabe, 2005), we have proposed a concept of "technosocial situation" to describe such settings for activity that span a range of physical locations but that still retain the coherent sense of location, social expectation, and role definition exhibited in Goffman's (1963) analyses and other practice-based studies. Our general conclusion is that youth messaging can undermine certain adult-defined prior definitions of social situation and place, but it can also construct new technosocial situations and new boundaries of identity and place. To say that mobile phones univocally cross boundaries, heighten accessibility, and fragment social life is to see only one side of the dynamic social reconfigurations heralded by mobile communications. Mobile phones create new kinds of bounded places that merge the infrastructures of geography and technology, as well as technosocial practices that merge technical standards and social norms.

Our argument is that the social outcomes of technology use are a result of social struggle over appropriate usage rather than a "natural" outcome determined by a particular technological form; mobile media usage is a site of intergenerational struggle over what should be the structuring social institutions and relations for young people. The final section of our chapter analyzes our ethnographic findings in terms of long-standing intergenerational tensions and cultural politics. Since the period of Japan's economic prosperity in the 1980s, the older generation has struggled to regulate an increasingly vibrant and self-directed set of youth cultures. Current mobile media usage is simply the latest example of young people mobilizing new technologies and consumer cultures in their struggle to claim a space of autonomy outside of the purview of adult control.

Japanese Youth and the Politics of Place

Doreen Massey has argued that "different social groups are placed in very distinct ways in relation to late modern flows of media, people, and capital" (1994, p. 61). Although the mobile phone has often been touted as an "anyplace, anytime" medium, we have found that usage is keyed to the specific structuring dynamics of particular places, and an individual's relationship to the power geometries of that place. As in most postindustrial contexts, teenagers in Japan generally find themselves in places controlled by adults with certain degrees of power over their lives, particularly their parents and teachers. Most college and high school students move back and forth from the space of the home—where they may have some privacy and discretion over their activities but lack physical access to friends—and the space of school—where they are physically copresent with their friends but have severe constraints on forms of social contact. The result, not surprisingly, is that young people have very few places in which they can have private conversations with peers and lovers. Urban spaces such as the street and cafes become key sites for gathering on their own terms. Now, the mobile phone has also become a device for young people to construct a "place" for private communication that is not monitored by adults. The low-profile, unobtrusive nature of e-mail on a small handset is particularly amenable to youth communication because it does not disrupt the norms of existing place and can escape adult surveillance. A more extended version of this argument can be found in a prior paper (Ito, 2003). Here we summarize the use of mobile e-mail in relation to places that young people inhabit.

First, in the home context, youth report that they do not see home as a place where they can congregate with their peers and significant others. Through college, Japanese youths have less private space compared to their U.S. and even European counterparts. The Japanese urban home is tiny by middle-class American standards, and teens and children generally share a room with a sibling or a parent. Most college students in Tokyo live with their parents, often even after they begin work, as the costs of renting an apartment in an urban area are prohibitively high.[5] Because of these factors, urban Japanese youth generally take to the street to socialize. For high school students, this usually means a stop at a local fast food restaurant on the way home from school. College kids have more time and mobility, gathering in cafes, stores, bars, and karaoke spots. Unlike in the United States, there is no practice of teens getting their own landline at a certain age or having a private phone in their room. The costs of running a landline to a Japanese home are very high, from $600 USD and up—about twice what it costs to get a mobile phone. It is thus extremely rare for a home to have more than one landline.

Here is an excerpt from an interview with four high school girls who are close friends:

> *Interviewer*: You all live close to each other. Do you visit each other's homes?
> *Student 1*: We don't. It's not that we are uncomfortable, or our parents get on our case, but it's like they are too sweet and caring, and you

worry about saying something rude, or talking too loud. You can't be too rowdy. So we don't meet in our homes.

Student 2: Occasionally. Maybe once a year. Actually, that's not even occasional.

Student 1: And if it happens, it is at a friend's house where they have their own room.

This stance was consistent across the youths that we interviewed. Meetings among friends almost always occurred in a third-party space run by indifferent adults, such as a fast food restaurant, karaoke spot, or family restaurant. Even for college students living on their own, their space is generally so small and cramped that it is not appropriate for hanging out with groups of friends.

The phone has always provided a way of overcoming the spatial boundary of the home, for teens to talk with each other late at night, and to shut out their parents and siblings. As noted in other studies (chapter 15; Green, 2002; Ling & Yttri, 2002; Skog, 2002), the mobile phone has further revolutionized the power geometry of space–time compression for teens in the home, enabling teens to communicate without the surveillance of parents and siblings. This has freed youths to call each other without the embarrassment of revealing a possible romantic liaison, or at hours of the day when other family members are likely to be asleep. All those whom we interviewed were consistent in stating a preference for calling a friend on a mobile rather than home phone despite the higher cost. Youths now do not have the home phone numbers of any but their most intimate friends. Parents are generally tolerant of their children's mobile phone usage, and many mothers reported using text messages for family communication. At the same time, most homes had a rule against mobile communication during meals, and peer communication can be a site of parent–child conflict. All the parents we interviewed described a sense of unease and curiosity about their children's mobile communications. Conversely, all the children took measures to keep parents in the dark about the content of their e-mail and calls. One parent voices what we take to be a typical parental stance:

Okabe: Do you have a problem with her using her mobile phone during meals, or after meals in the living room, when you are together?

Mother: I don't have a problem with it when we are just lounging around. But during meals or when she is studying, I try to tell her to tell the other person on the line.

Okabe: Are you curious or concerned about with who and what she is communicating?

Mother: I am concerned about all of it . . . though I can usually guess who it is.

Okabe: When you tell her to stop, does she stop?

Mother: She goes to her room . . . if I am strict [about her using her phone too much].

The constraints on gathering with friends in homes have driven youth to the personal medium of the mobile phone to cement peer communications. The places of school and public transportation have, more specifically, encouraged use of mobile messaging. Although the home context supports communication by both voice and e-mail, in the classroom and on public transportation, mobile e-mail, rather than voice, is by far the preferred modality.

Schools vary with respect to how teachers deal with mobile phones, but without exception, voice calls during class are considered inappropriate. Almost all schools officially ban phones from the classrooms, but most students do use e-mail during class at least occasionally. It is not uncommon for students to leave their mobile phones out on their desks during class, claiming that they use the clock function. All students, both in high school and college, voiced the rule that they would not use voice communication in class, but almost all said that they would read and sometimes send messages. The mobile phone gets used most frequently during the lunch time hour and immediately after school as students scurry to hook up with their friends.

We saw e-mail being sent during class in only two of our communication diary cases, but almost all students reported in their interviews that they would receive and send messages in class, hiding their phones under their desks. Four students we interviewed specifically described conversations with students in the same classroom, making comments like "this sucks," "this is boring," or "check it out, the teacher buttoned his shirt wrong." More commonly, students reported that they conducted "necessary" communications during class, such as arranging a meeting or responding to an e-mail from somebody with a specific query. The communications in class that we saw in the diaries involved coordinating meetings after school or receiving e-mail from friends who were absent, asking for notes or other class information. In all these cases, mobile e-mail is being used to circumvent the communicative limitations of the classroom situation, much as passing notes and glances across the classroom did in an earlier era. Perhaps more uniquely, the mobile phone in the classroom is a way to challenge the communication hierarchy of the traditional lecture format that insists that students passively listen to an active teacher. Mobile e-mail enables students to resist their role in this one-way communication and to make more productive use of their attentional "dead time" between jotting notes and waiting for teachers to finish writing theirs.

In contrast to the home and school, which are under the surveillance of adults with a personal interest in individual youth, public spaces like the street and public transportation rely on a more distributed set of strategies for regulating communication. Most trains and buses display "no mobile phone" signs, and announcements are made every few minutes specifying limitations on phone use. A typical announcement is: "Please do not make voice calls while on the train. Please turn off your mobile phone in the area surrounding 'preferred seating' [for the elderly and disabled]." The street and train platforms are open to voice calls but are generally extremely noisy, and it is difficult to have a sustained conversation in these locations. In one of our studies, we focused on uses of mobile phones on trains and subways (Okabe & Ito, 2005). Although we commonly observed e-mail use, voice calls are rare. For example, one 41-minute observation on a busy train line represented the highest volume of usage that we recorded. During the period of observation, there were 37 instances of observable mobile e-mail usage (including both receiving and sending e-mail) and only instances of voice calls. In a 30-minute observation with the lowest volume of usage, there was 1 voice call and 10 instances of e-mail use. The overall average of voice calls in any given 30-minute span is 1–2 calls.

In our interviews, almost all responded that they would freely engage in e-mail exchanges but were hesitant to make and receive voice calls. For example, interviewees described how they might decide not to answer a voice call if the train was crowded, or they might move to a less crowded location to take a call, or they might take the call but cut it right away. Most also responded that they were annoyed when somebody took a voice call on a train and talked in a loud voice. These responses were consistent across all age groups. Here is a typical response from an 18–year-old high school student from Kanagawa prefecture

> *Interviewee*: When I hear somebody's mobile phone go off on a train, it bothers me. I think, "I'll always keep mine in silent mode."
> *Interviewer*: How about e-mail in trains?
> *Interviewee*: I do e-mail a lot, to kill time. I think e-mail is probably okay. If I get a call, I do usually answer it, but I keep my voice low. I do feel bad about it and don't talk loud.

Phone ringing is also considered a violation in public space. Interviewees who were heavy mobile users almost invariably reported that they put their phones in "manner mode" (silent mode) when they left the home. In the communication diaries, we saw only one instance of a voice call being initiated on public transportation, when the subject was the only passenger on a bus. The call lasted only a few minutes and was cut as soon as another passenger entered the bus. Despite the virtual lack of voice mobile communication on trains in the Tokyo area, the announcements are relentless, attesting to a high level of social regulation work even in the absence of major transgressions.

In contrast to voice calls, mobile e-mail is considered ideal for use in public spaces. Some train announcements and signage specify no voice calls, thus implying that Internet and e-mail use is permitted. Although bus drivers will prohibit someone speaking on a mobile phone from entering a bus, we have not observed any instances of regulation of silent mobile phone uses. The private and unobtrusive nature of mobile e-mail has made it a preferred form of communication in settings where one is shielding private communications from others in the physical locale, whether in a parental home, in the classroom, or in public transportation. Largely because of the risk that their interlocutor may be on public transit, a social norm has arisen among the younger generation that you should not initiate voice calls without first checking availability with a text message. Unless certain that their recipient is at home, most youths (there were two exceptions in our study) will send a message first asking if they can call.

Tele-Cocooning in the Full-Time Intimate Community

The location-based contexts described thus far provide a picture of some of the factors that have driven Japanese youth's adoption of mobile e-mail. Now we turn to the question of the kinds of social settings, or technosocial situations (Ito & Okabe, 2005), that youth are building through their mobile e-mail exchanges. Although there are a variety of different types of situations being built through mobile e-mail, we focus here on ongoing contact in an intimate peer group.

Unlike voice calls, which are generally point-to-point and engrossing, messaging can be a way of maintaining ongoing background awareness of others and of keeping multiple channels of communication open. This is like people who keep instant messaging channels open in the background while they go about their work, but the difference is that the mobile phone gets carried around just about everywhere for heavy users. The rhythms of mobile messaging fluctuate between focused, chat-like exchanges and a more lightweight awareness of connection with others through the online space. In our interviews with heavy users of mobile phones, all users reported that they were only in regular contact with approximately 2–5, and at most 10, close friends, despite having large numbers of entries in their mobile address books. This is what Matsuda (2005b) following Nakajima et al. (1999), describes as a "full-time intimate community."

In a similar vein, Ichiyo Habuchi (2005) describes these online spaces, occupied by most Japanese youth, as "tele-cocoons." She contrasts these intimate spaces with the more extroverted spaces of online dating and encounter sites that are frequented by a small but significant minority of Japanese youth.

Although the scale of social relationships and the content of communication appears to be similar to what other studies have found in other forms of mediated communication (e.g., for instant messaging and telephone, see chapter 14), the portable format of the mobile phone affords certain distinctive usage patterns. Heavy mobile e-mail users generally expect those in the intimate circle to be available for communication unless they are sleeping or working. Text messages can be returned discreetly during class, on public transportation, or in restaurants—all contexts where voice communication would be inappropriate. Many of the messages that we saw exchanged between this close peer group or between couples included messages that informants described as "insignificant" or "not urgent." Some examples of messages in this category are communications such as "I'm walking up the hill now," "I'm tired," "I guess I'll take a bath now," "just bought a pair of shoes!" "groan, I just woke up with a hangover," or "the episode today sucked today didn't it?"

These messages define a social setting that is substantially different from the direct interpersonal interactions that are characteristic of voice calls, text chats, or face-to-face one-on-one interactions. These mobile text messages are predicated on the sense of ambient accessibility; a shared virtual space that is generally available between a few friends or with a loved one. They do not require a deliberate "opening" of a channel of communication but are based on the expectation that someone is within "earshot." From a technology perspective, this differs from PC-based communication because the social expectation is to be almost always connected. This is also not a "persistent" space as with an online virtual world that exists independent of specific people logging in (Mynatt, Adler, Ito, & O'Day, 1997). As a technosocial system, however, people experience a sense of a persistent social space that is constituted through the periodic exchange of text messages. These messages define a space of peripheral background awareness that is midway between direct interaction and noninteraction. The analogy is sharing a physical space with others whom one is not in direct communication with, but of whom one is peripherally aware. Many of the e-mails that are exchanged present information about one's general status that is similar to the kind of awareness of another that one would have when physically colocated: a sigh or smile or glance that calls attention to the communicator; a way of entering somebody's virtual peripheral vision. This kind of virtual tap on the shoulder may result in a change of setting into a more direct form of interaction such as a chat-like sequence via texting or a voice call, but it might also be ignored if the recipient is not available for focused interaction.

Of particular interest are the logs of one teenage couple in our study, which is a somewhat more intense version of couple communications that we saw in other instances. Their typical pattern is to begin sending a steady stream of e-mail messages to each other after parting at school. These messages will continue through homework, dinner, television shows, and bath and would culminate in voice contact in the late evening, lasting for an hour or more. A trail of messages might follow the voice call, ending in a good night exchange and revived again on waking. On 2 days when they were primarily at home in the evening, they sent 34 messages to and fro on one day and 56 messages on the other day. On days when they were out and about the numbers dwindled to 6 and 9. The content of the messages ranged from in-depth chat about relational issues to coordination of when to make voice contact, to thoughts or lightweight notification about their current activities. In this case, and to a smaller degree for other couples living apart, messaging became a means of experiencing a sense of private contact and copresence with a loved one, even in the face of parental regulatory efforts and their inability to share private physical space.

Although mobile phones have become a vehicle for youths to challenge the power geometries of places such as the home, the classroom, and the street, they have also created new disciplines and power geometries, the need to be continuously available to friends and lovers, and the need to always carry a functioning mobile device. These disciplines are accompanied by new sets of social expectations and manners. When unable to return a message right away, young people feel that a social expectation has been violated. When one girl did not notice a message sent in the evening until the next morning, she says that she felt terrible. Three of the students in our diary study reported that they did not feel similar pressure to reply right away. Yet even in these cases, they acknowledged that there was a social expectation that a message should be responded to within about 30 minutes unless one had a legitimate reason, such as being asleep. One describes how he knows he should respond right away but does not really care. Another, who had an atypical pattern of responding with longer, more deliberate messages hours later, said that her friends often chided her for being so slow. In another instance, a student did not receive a reply for a few hours, and his interlocutor excused himself by saying he did not notice the message. The recipient perceived this as a permissible white lie that got around an onerous social expectation.

All students who were asked about responses that were delayed an hour or more said that they would generally make a quick apology or excuse on sending the tardy response. These exceptions to the norm of immediate response trace the contours of the technosocial situation as much as do conforming practices.

With couples living apart, there is an even greater sense of importance attached to ongoing availability via messaging. The underside to the unobtrusive and ubiquitous nature of mobile e-mail is that there are few legitimate excuses for not responding, particularly in the evening hours when one is at home. Five of the 10 student couples in our study were in ongoing contact during the times when they were not at school, and all these couples had established practices for indicating their absence from the shared online space. They invariably send a good night e-mail to signal unavailability and would often send status checks during the day such as "are you awake?" or "are you done with work?" We saw a few cases when they would announce their intention to take a bath, a kind of virtual locking of the door. Him: "Just got home. Think I'll take a bath." Her: "Ya. Me too." Just as mobile workers struggle to maintain boundaries to between their work and personal lives, youths struggle to limit their availability to peers and intimates. The need to construct and mark these boundaries attests to the status of this ambient virtual peer space as an increasingly structuring and pervasive type of technosocial setting.

Cultural Politics of Youth Mobile Media

We have described how youth mobile e-mail use has grown out of the imperatives of existing places of home, school, and public space and how, in turn, it constructs a new set of technosocial places dominated by the logic of peer relations. In line with our overall context-driven approach to understanding youth messaging practices, here we analyze how these ethnographic findings articulate with long-standing cultural politics and intergenerational struggles.

Postwar Japanese urban culture has featured a succession of highly visible but transient youth subcultures, often led by young women. In their essay on Japanese women and consumption, Lisa

Skov and Brian Moeran (1995)describe how young Japanese women's central positioning in media imagery and cultures of consumption are an inversion of their weak position in the labor market. Consumption and style, particularly of youth street cultures, are one cultural arena in which young Japanese women have taken the lead, in part because of this marginal social status. Feminine consumerism represents an escape from the dominant rhythms of salaried labor. The more recent history of mobile media adoption is in line with this characterization of postwar consumer culture as an arena in which the disenfranchised have taken leadership and control. The micronegotiations that we have described though our ethnographic cases, in which young people have appropriated existing places and new technologies to create spaces of self-determination, are tied to these broader historical and structural trends. Although corporate ventures are quick to capitalize on new consumer youth trends, these emergent cultures also invite a series of efforts to reinvigorate existing (and still hegemonic) social structures and norms. The case of youth mobile media, at both the micro and the macro levels, is characterized by the struggle between youth, who may be at the social margins, discovering new means of organizing and communicating (with the help of consumer capitalism) and adults who are in the social mainstream seeking to regulate and redirect these efforts.

Although we could trace the origins of current mobile media to diary exchanges and note-passing in class, most trace current mobile messaging back to the pager cultures of the early nineties, when teenage girls first hijacked the uses of mobile media for their social purposes (Okada & Matsuda, 2002; Matsuda, 2005b; Okada, 2005). Pagers were originally conceived of as business tools for companies to beep their workers in the field, but they only became popular mobile media after teenage girls adopted them. Okada (2005) describes how 1992 was a pivotal year in the development of mobile messaging. Spurred by reductions in subscription rates and new pagers that displayed a call-back number on the terminal (as opposed to simply beeping), young users began adopting this new medium. In contrast to prior years, where business uses were central, 1993 saw individual users, mostly in their teens and twenties, begin to dominate, making up 70% of new subscriptions. Taking their cue from these trends, providers released new pager

designs that could receive text as well as numbers. At the peak of their use in 1996, 48.8% of Tokyo middle and high school students had a pager.

Mobile phone providers took note and began piloting inexpensive text messaging services for mobile phone handsets in 1996 through 1997. Young people soon jumped onto the short message services purveyed by the Personal Handyphone System and then moved on to cellular phone–based messaging. By 2002 pager subscriptions were on the decline; young users had largely switched to texting via mobile phones. When mobile Internet services were rolled out in Japan in the late 1990s, they integrated the messaging functions that had previously been restricted mostly to short messages sent between subscribers of a particular provider. Japanese mobile Internet adoption was driven forward by mobile messaging as young people, for the first time, were able to send messages of varying length across different terminal devices and mobile service providers. Within a space of a few years between 1995 and 1998, mobile phones shifted from an association with business uses to an association with teen street culture. Many of the young women we interviewed who today extensively use text messaging had used pagers for messaging in their middle school years and the Personal Handyphone System in high school and now currently use mobile Internet services. They see the different technologies simply as upgrades that support the same underlying set of social practices.

Kenichi Fujimoto (2005) has tied mobile media's usage shift from business to play to the growing hegemony of young girls in public space. He calls this transformation "The Girls' Pager Revolution." Unlike the male *otaku* (techno-geeks) associated with video games and computers, media-savvy girls have been associated with communications technologies such as pagers and mobile phones. Through the nineties, young women and girls gained more strength in defining street cultures, and in the mid 1990s, the media attached a new label to street-savvy high school girls: *kogyaru*. In the late nineties, certain *kogyaru* in urban centers sported bleached and frosted hair, extreme tropical fashions, tanned faces, heavy make-up, and customized mobile phones, becoming the object of widespread imitation by youth across the country and moral panic among adults (Cohen, 1972; Matsuda, 2005a). We started our ethnographic research in the waning years of extreme *kogyaru* street cultures. Though the high school girls we interviewed would not self-identify with these subcultures, most adopted related cultural forms, such as bleached hair, brightly colored fashions, and conspicuous mobile media use. Even with pundits declaring the death of the *kogyaru* at the turn of the millennium, this youth subculture has a lasting legacy in mobile texting cultures and related public perception of mobile media.

In line with the moral panics over *kogyaru* street cultures, public discourse has associated pagers and mobile phones with bad manners, declining morals, and a low-achievement, pleasure-seeking mentality. Mobile phones continue to be iconic of a fast and footloose street culture beyond the surveillance of the institutions of home and school. For example, there is widely reported practice called *enjo kousai* that started in the 1990s, where high school girls, particularly *kogyaru*, meet older men on the street and date them for money. Although anonymous dating and prostitution was supported with voicemail services using pay phones and landlines, public reports have associated mobile phones with the growth of these practices among minors (Tomita, 2005). In one example of public uptake, the popular weekly magazine *Aera* ran a series of articles about *kogyaru* and *enjo kousai*, depicting Lolita-complex middle-aged men and "old man hunting" teenagers meeting on the street, keeping in touch with pagers and mobile phones (Hayami, 1996). Mobile phones have been linked as well to a more general decline in morals and manners. In the late 1990s, a series of articles described the annoyance of having to listen to young people engaging in trivial chit chat via mobiles on trains and buses, and public transportation facilities started prohibiting voice calls (Okabe & Ito, 2005). A cover of a recent best seller, *Keitai wo Motta Saru: "Ningen Rashisa" no Houkai* (Monkeys with Mobile Phones: The Collapse of Humanity), features three *kogyaru* on a subway, clutching mobile phones, legs splayed, talking loudly (Masataka, 2002).

Social and cultural research paints a different picture of young people's mobile media adoption. The young people in our studies were highly conscious of mobile phone manners and used their phones to keep in touch almost exclusively with family and close friends from school. Others have argued phones have made youths' relationships ler than superficial (Matsuda, 2000), and minority of youth engage in anonymous uchi, 2005; Tomita, 2005). In an ear-

lier study of American and Japanese youth, Merry White (1994) describes highly consumerist youth cultures that are likely familiar to North Americans, but she sees fewer conflicts between Japanese parents and youths. Dependency has less social stigma that it does among Euro-American youths, and this is institutionalized in the protective functions of family that extend through college and often beyond. White also describes how youth are defined by marital and employment status rather than by age, and how "such institutional definitions have more weight than social and psychological identities" (1994: 11). Arguably, youth culture in Japan has been subject to more concern since the 1990s, after White completed her work. Yet our ethnographic research supports her overall findings, in that the regulatory and protective functions of institutions such as family and school still dominate the lives of Japanese youth into their twenties.

Conclusions

The leaders of the girls' pager revolution and the antiauthoritarian subcultures of *kogyaru* were the early adopters of a new set of technosocial practices that have infiltrated the everyday lives of mainstream Japanese youth on the backs of new mobile media. Our ethnographic findings attest to the less confrontational but more pervasive practices of micronegotiations with the hegemonic structures of home, school, and urban space that carve out new spaces of action for young people. Although the low-profile exchange of messages among full-time intimate communities is a far cry from the more extroverted practices of *kogyaru* extreme fashion and *enjo kousai*, both ends of the spectrum are indicative of young people's everyday struggles to push back at the adult-controlled structures that govern their everyday lives. Adults, too, push back through public demonization of deviant youth as well as more everyday efforts to regulate mobile phone usage in schools, homes, and public settings.

This chapter has described some of the social conditions that have contextualized the unprecedented adoption of the mobile Internet by Japanese youth. Rather than focusing on factors "inherent" in the personality and cultures of Japanese young people, we have paid attention to a broad set of historical, social, and cultural factors. Among these are the unique history of mobile messaging in their intersection with youth street cultures, as well as the power geometries of place that regulate youths' everyday lives and social contact. We have described youth messaging as a unique response to these existing patterns of social life based on their sense of connection and accountability to their peer relations. The intersection between mobile e-mail and the life situations of Japanese youth have created a new set of technosocial practices and situations in support of distributed intimacy and pervasive lightweight contact. These practices are both novel and situated within a broad set of historical, social, and cultural contexts.

Acknowledgments. Portions of this chapter were excerpted from two prior papers, "Japanese Youth, Mobile Phones and the Re-Placement of Social Contact," and "Technosocial Situations: Emergent Structurings of Mobile E-mail Use." An earlier version of this paper appeared in *The Inside Text: Social, Cultural, and Design Perspectives on SMS,* edited by Richard Harper, Leysia Palen, and Alex Taylor (London: Springer). This chapter is republished with permission from Springer. Research described here was supported by NTT Docomo and Docomo House at Keio University Shonan Fujisawa Campus, as well as by the Annenberg Center for Communication at the University of Southern California. We would like to thank Kenji Kohiyama and Hiromi Odaguchi of Docomo House and our student research assistants, Kunikazu Amagasa, Hiroshi Chihara, and Joko Taniguchi. This work has also benefited from the comments of Alex Taylor, Richard Harper, and our colleagues at the K-Times workshop at Keio University (particularly Misa Matsuda), and reviewers and participants at the conference Front Stage/Back Stage: Mobile Communications and the Re-Negotiation of the Public Sphere in Grimstad, Norway.

Notes

1. Since the late 1990s, youth have had higher rates of mobile phone ownership than the general population, but the gap is closing. In contrast to a 2001 survey that documented how young people had higher adoption rates (Yoshii et al., 2002), a 2002 national survey of mobile phone communications conducted by Video Research (2002) found that the overall penetration of mobile phones in Japan was 73.7%, with ownership by students age 12 years and up at 75.7%.

2. We use the term "mobile e-mail" to describe messages (mostly text, but sometimes images) sent via short message services analogous to the short message system, as well as mobile Internet services. Short messages can generally only be sent between subscribers to the same provider and cannot be as lengthy as those sent over the Internet. Although users make case-by-case decisions about whether to send a message via short messaging or via Internet, both types of messages are generally called *meiru* (mail).

3. Teens send twice as many e-mails as 20–somethings, sending approximately 70 a month in contrast to 30 for the slightly older set (Yoshii et al., 2002). In contrast to the general population (68.1%), almost all students (91.7%) report that they send over five messages a day.

4. In her study of Japanese youth, Merry White (1994, p. 11) describes the differences between U.S. and Japanese labels for young people. The category of "teenager" of "*cheenayja*" has been borrowed from English but is not in widespread use. The native categories are *shonen* and *seinen*, which are closer to the English term "youth" or "young person."

5. Our sample of college students for the communication diary part of our study is a bit skewed in this respect, as our student pool at the Keio campus was largely composed of youth living on their own. As a suburban campus of an elite urban university, the situation at our campus is unique in attracting students from around the country in an area with a relatively low urban density. Overall, our interviewee pool represented a range from mainstream middle class to elite.

References

Agar, J. (2003). *Constant touch: A global history of the mobile phone.* Cambridge, UK: Icon Books.

Alanen, L. (2001). Explorations in generational analysis. In Alanen, L., & Mayall, B. (Eds.), *Conceptualizing child-adult relations* (pp. 11–22). New York: RoutledgeFalmer.

Cohen, S. (1972). *Folk devils and moral panics.* London: MacGibbon and Kee.

Fujimoto, K. (2005). The third-stage paradigm: Territory machines from the girls' pager revolution to mobile aesthetics. In Ito, M., Okabe, D., & Matsuda, M. (Eds.), *Personal, portable, pedestrian: Mobile phones in Japanese life* (pp. 77–102). Cambridge, MA: MIT Press.

Goffman, E. (1963). *Behavior in public places: Notes on the social organization of gatherings.* New York: Free Press.

Green, N. (2002). Who's watching whom? Monitoring and accountability in mobile relations. In Brown, B., Green, N., & Harper, R. (Eds.), *Wireless world:*

Social and interactional aspects of the mobile age (pp. 32–45). London: Springer.

Green, N. (2003). Outwardly mobile: Young people and mobile technologies. In Katz, J. E. (Ed.), *Machines that become us* (pp. 201–218). New Brunswick, NJ: Transaction.

Grinter, R. E., & Eldridge, M. A. (2001). *y do tngrs luv 2 txt msg?* Paper presented at the Seventh European Conference on Computer-Supported Cooperative Work, Bonn, Germany.

Habuchi, I. (2005). Accelerating reflexivity. In Ito, M., Okabe, D., & Matsuda, M. (Eds.), *Personal, portable, pedestrian: Mobile phones in Japanese life* (pp. 165–182). Cambridge, MA: MIT Press.

Harper, R. (2003). Are mobiles good or bad for society. In Nyiri, K. (Ed.), *Mobile communication: Social and political effects* (pp. 185–214). Vienna: Passagen Verlag.

Hayami, Y. (1996). Toragyaru tachi no osorubeki enjo kousai (The dangerous prostitution of tiger-gals). *Aera,* April 15, 62.

IPSe. (2003). *Third annual consumer report: Survey results from research on mobile phone usage.* Tokyo: IPSe Communications.

Ito, M. (2005). Mobile phones, Japanese youth, and the re-placement of social contact. In Ling, R. (Ed.), *Mobile communications: Renegotiation of the public sphere* (pp. 131–148), London: Springer.

Ito, M., & Okabe, D. (2005). Technosocial situations: Emergent structurings of mobile e-mail use. In Ito, M., Okabe, D., & Matsuda, M. (Eds.), *Personal, portable, pedestrian: Mobile phones in Japanese life* (pp. 257–276). Cambridge, MA: MIT Press .

Ito, M., Okabe, D., & Matsuda, M. (Eds.). (2005). *Personal, portable, pedestrian: Mobile phones in Japanese life.* Cambridge, MA: MIT Press.

James, A., Jenks, C., & Prout, A. (Eds.). (1998). *Theorizing childhood.* New York: Teachers College Press.

James, A., & Prout, A. (Eds.). (1997). *Constructing and reconstructing childhood: Contemporary issues in the sociological study of childhood* (2nd ed.). Philadelphia, PA: RoutledgeFarmer.

Kasesniemi, E.-L. (2003). *Mobile messages: Young people and a new communication culture.* Tampere, Finland: Tampere University Press.

Kasesniemi, E.-L., & Rautianinen, P. (2002). Mobile culture of children and teenagers in Finland. In Katz, J. E., & Aakhus, M. (Eds.), *Perpetual contact: Mobile communication, private talk, public performance* (pp. 170–192). Cambridge, UK: Cambridge University Press.

Ling, R., & Yttri, B. (2002). Hyper-coordination via mobile phones in Norway. In Katz, J. E., & Aakhus, M. (Eds.), *Perpetual contact: Mobile communication, private talk, public performance* (pp. 139–169). Cambridge, UK: Cambridge University Press.

Masataka, N. (2002). *Keihtai wo motta saru: "Ningen rashisa" no houkai* [Monkeys with mobile phones: The collapse of humanity]. Tokyo: Chuko Shinsho.

Massey, D. (1994). *Space, place, and gender.* Minneapolis: University of Minnesota Press.

Matsuda, M. (2000). Friendship of young people and their usage of mobile phones: From the view of "superficial relation" to "selective relation." *Shakai Jouhougaku Kenkyuu, 4,* 111–122.

Matsuda, M. (2005a). Discourses of Keitai in Japan. In Ito, M., Okabe, D., & Matsuda, M. (Eds.), *Personal, portable, pedestrian: Mobile phones in Japanese life* (pp. 19–40). Cambridge, MA: MIT Press

Matsuda, M. (2005b). Mobile communications and selective sociality. In Ito, M., Okabe, D., & Matsuda, M. (Eds.), *Personal, portable, pedestrian: Mobile phones in Japanese life* (pp. 123–142). Cambridge, MA: MIT Press.

Mynatt, E., Adler, A., Ito, M., & O'Day, V. (1997). Network communities: Something old, something new, something borrowed. *Computer Supported Cooperative Work, 6,* 1–35.

Nakajima, I., Keiichi, H., & Yoshii, H. (1999). *Ido-denwa riyou no fukyuu to sono shakaiteki imi* (Diffusion of cellular phones and PHS and their social meaning). *Tsuushin Gakkai-shi (Journal of Information and Communication Research), 16*(3), 79–92.

Okabe, D., & Ito, M. (2005). Keitai and public transportation. In Ito, M., Okabe, D., & Matsuda, M. (Eds.), *Personal, portable, pedestrian: Mobile phones in Japanese life* (pp. 205–218). Cambridge, MA: MIT Press.

Okada, T. (2005). The social reception and construction of mobile media in Japan. In Ito, M., Okabe, D., & Matsuda, M. (Eds.), *Personal, portable, pedestrian: Mobile phones in Japanese life* (pp. 41–60). Cambridge, MA: MIT Press.

Okada, T., & Matsuda, M. (2002). *Keitaigaku nyuumon (Understanding mobile media).* Tokyo: Yuhikaku.

Rheingold, H. (2002). *Smart mobs: The next social revolution.* Cambridge, MA: Perseus.

Skog, B. (2002). Mobiles and the Norwegian teen: Identity, gender and class. In Katz, J. E., & Aakhus, M. (Eds.), *Perpetual contact: Mobile communications, private talk, public performance* (pp. 255–273). Cambridge, UK: Cambridge University Press.

Skov, L., & Moeran, B. (1995). Hiding in the light: from Oshin to Yoshimoto Banana. In Skov, L., & Moeran, B. (Eds.), *Women, media, and consumption in Japan* (pp. 1–74). Honolulu: University of Hawaii Press.

Taylor, A., & Harper, R. (2003). The gift of the gab? A design oriented sociology of young people's use of mobiles. *Computer Supported Cooperative Work* 12: 267–296.

Tomita, H. (2005). Keitai and the intimate stranger. In M. Ito, D. Okabe, & M. Matsuda (Eds.), *Personal, portable, pedestrian: Mobile phones in Japanese life* (pp. 183–204). Cambridge, MA: MIT Press.

Video Research. (2002). *Mobile phone usage situation.* Tokyo: Video Research.

Weilenmann, A., & Larsson, C. (2002). Local use and sharing of mobile phones. In Brown, B., Green, N., & Harper, R. (Eds.), *Wireless world: Social and interactional aspects of the mobile age* (pp. 92–107). London: Springer.

White, M. (1994). *The material child: Coming of age in Japan and America.* Berkeley: University of California Press.

Yoshii, H., Matsuda, M., Habuchi, C., Dobashi, S., Iwata, K., & Kin, N. (2002). *Keitai denwa riyou no shinka to sono eikyou* [The evolution of the uses of the mobile phone and its influence]. Tokyo: Mobile Communications Kenkyuukai.

IV

The Internet and Social Relationships

17

Irina Shklovski, Sara Kiesler, and Robert Kraut

The Internet and Social Interaction

A Meta-analysis and Critique of Studies, 1995–2003

Internet adoption in homes has grown rapidly since the early 1990s. By 2003, 63% of Americans had used the Internet (Pew Internet and American Life Project, 2003). The Internet has been hailed as a revolutionary social technology, in part because its predominant use has been informal communication (Kraut, Mukhopadhyay, Szczypula, Kiesler, & Scherlis, 1999). Even as new services, such as downloading music and movies, become available and easier to accomplish, communication remains the public's principle use of the Internet (Pew Internet and American Life Project, 2002; U.S. Department of Commerce, 2002).

One important implication of the Internet's migration to homes and its predominant use for communication is that it could change people's social interaction with their closest ties. Social interaction with family and friends is one of life's most pleasant experiences (Robinson & Godbey, 1999). It helps fulfill people's need to belong and often leads to feelings of closeness (Baumeister & Leary, 1995), to perceptions of social support (Gottlieb & Green, 1984; Peirce, Frone, Russell, Cooper, & Mudar, 2000), and to increases in the likelihood of receiving social support (Cohen & Wills, 1985; Wellman & Wortley, 1990). Social interaction is also associated with people's commitment to groups,

neighborhoods, and organizations (Mirowsky & Ross, 1989; Schachter, 1951), with their sense of meaning in life (Thoits, 1983) and with their adherence to social norms (Srole, 1956).

Some researchers have argued that the Internet improves people's ability to form new close relationships, especially if they are otherwise isolated (McKenna & Bargh, 2000). Early studies indicated that the Internet facilitated the development of group ties (Sproull & Kiesler, 1991), information exchange in organizations (Kraut & Attewell, 1997), and the creation of new groups and organizations (Sproull & Faraj, 1995). Overall, do such changes add up to an increase or reduction in people's social interaction with the most important people in their lives—their family and friends? In this chapter, we examine what is now known about the effects of using the Internet on peoples' social interaction with these close ties.

The Social Impact Debate

In 1995, Katz and Aspden conducted the first national survey of the public's use of the Internet. They reported that Internet users had more total contact with family members than did nonusers, and that they made more new friends, including those they talked with or met on the Internet. The authors concluded that using the Internet augments traditional communication and adds to people's social ties.

About the same time, Kraut, Patterson, Lundmark, Kiesler, Mukhopadhyay, and Scherlis (1998) launched a longitudinal study of Internet use in Pittsburgh, Pennsylvania. In 1995 and 1996, they recruited 96 families and provided each family with a computer and dial-up Internet access. The researchers followed these novice Internet users for 3 years. After 18 months, controlling for initial levels of the outcome variables, participants who used the Internet more showed declines in face-to-face communication with family, smaller social circles, and higher levels of loneliness, stress, and depressive symptoms. The data, the authors suggested, indicated that Internet use can displace valuable time that people spend with family and friends (Nie, Hillygus, & Erbring, 2002).

The Kraut et al. and Katz and Aspden studies framed a debate about the Internet's social impact that led to subsequent surveys examining how Internet use affects people's self-reported socializing and social involvement with others (Mesch, 2001; Cole & Robinson, 2002; Gershuny, 2002; Katz & Rice, 2002; Kestnbaum, Robinson, Neustadtl, & Alvarez, 2002; Kraut et al., 2002; Lee & Zhu, 2002; Lee & Kuo, 2002; Mikami, 2002; Neustadtl & Robinson, 2002; Nie & Hillygus, 2002; Pronovost, 2002; Shklovski, Kraut, & Rainie, 2004; Jackson, von Eye, Barbatsis, Biocca, Fitzgerald & Zhao, 2004). As these survey studies emerged in the literature, it became apparent that the debate over the Internet's social impact had not been decided. For example, Nie and Hillygus (2002) concluded from a cross-sectional diary survey that Internet use damages social interaction with family members, whereas Kraut et al. (2002) claimed just the reverse, based on a longitudinal study. Our examination of the relationship of Internet use and social interaction represents an attempt to resolve the debate by drawing from the accumulated evidence from 16 surveys completed by 2003. All of these surveys address whether Internet use is associated with more or less social interaction with family or friends.

How the Emerging Internet Shaped Discovery

When Katz and Aspden conducted their national sample survey in 1995, only 8% of their sample were Internet users. Not surprisingly, these authors asked few detailed questions about Internet use (e.g., "Have you heard of the Internet"), and their measure of Internet use was dichotomous: "Do you use the Internet [scored yes or no]?" Few people at the time imagined a time when a national sample survey would show over half of the nation to be Internet users.

Over the next decade, with the spread of the Internet and the huge growth in its services, researchers began to measure differences among Internet users. By the end of the 1990s, almost all researchers were measuring the independent variable "Internet use," using continuous self-report measures of Internet use—the amount of use, in minutes per week (or the amount of use yesterday); the frequency of Internet use per week (or yesterday), the frequency of e-mail use, the frequency of Web and e-mail use, the breadth of use (i.e., number of purposes), or number of years since respondents first went online.

Authors who studied the effect of these differences in Internet use measured the dependent variable, "social interaction," by asking people to report on their behaviors such as how frequently they went out with friends. Comparison across studies assumes similarity of the conceptual dependent variable across studies (e.g., Lepper, Henderlong, & Gingras, 1999; Albarracin, Johnson, Fishbein, & Muellerleile, 2001). The measures of social interaction in our corpus included questions about communication and going out with family and friends (e.g., time with family per week), community involvement and organizational memberships (e.g., attendance at community events), breadth of social networks (e.g., number of acquaintances or friends), and individual psychosocial well-being related to social interaction (e.g., loneliness). These concepts have different empirical and theoretical implications. For instance, perceived social support, which is critical in health and well-being, derives primarily from close ties rather than from involvement in community or acquaintanceships (Wellman & Wortley, 1990; Bolger, Zuckerman, & Kessler, 2000; Cohen, Underwood, & Gottlieb, 2000). Furthermore, some research indicates the presence of social interaction tradeoffs, where weak tie relationships can interfere with strong ties (e.g., Helgeson, Cohen, Schulz, & Yasko, 2000). If true, then we could be obscuring important phenomena if we were to compare studies across very diverse measures of "social interaction."

The authors of the 16 studies that we reviewed had one common focus that permitted us to go forward with a comparative analysis: all have an interest in how the Internet affects people's close relationships and all asked respondents about their interpersonal interactions with family or friends. Some authors asked respondents about their interactions with family and friends separately, whereas some used aggregated measures without differentiating between interaction with friends and interaction with family. Allan argued that interaction with friends is more sensitive to distance and other factors that influence frequency of communication, compared to interaction with family, which is often more obligatory and less voluntary and opportunistic (Allan, 1979, pp. 122–123). Thus, one would expect that Internet use might have a larger influence on interaction with friends than with family. Hence, our review includes an examination of the effects of Internet use on social interaction with family versus friends.

Choices of Method

The Internet's potential social impact draws research interest across the social sciences and beyond. Authors of the 16 studies we reviewed work in departments of psychology, sociology, communication, political science, information systems, human–computer interaction, computer science, and journalism. The disciplinary diversity of authors may be in part responsible for the methodological diversity of the 16 survey studies in our data set. For example, whereas all of the sociologists used national sample surveys (Gershuny, 2002; Kestnbaum et al., 2002; Neustadtl & Robinson, 2002; Pronovost, 2002), two groups of social psychologists drew comparatively small community samples (Kraut et al., 1998; Jackson et al., 2004). In two of the social psychologists' studies (Kraut et al., 1998; Jackson et al., 2004), the researchers provided Internet connections to volunteer households. These samples differed from the national samples in other ways; for example, because Jackson et al. were interested in social class effects, they oversampled Internet users with low household income.

Diversity of method is generally good for research because it improves the reliability of findings. In this area of research, though, diversity makes it difficult to compare results across studies. Authors of half of the studies used single or repeated

cross-sectional (correlation) designs; authors of the other half used longitudinal designs with repeated measures within respondents.[1] Although all of these researchers have the purpose of understanding the Internet's social impact, the cross-sectional studies can only show whether levels of Internet use were associated with levels of social interaction, whereas the longitudinal studies can show whether levels of Internet use at one time predicted changes in social interaction later.

In view of these differences, our research goal was to compare these studies statistically to reveal evidence on whether people's use of the Internet has an effect on their social interaction with family and friends. Since we claim that study methods can influence results, we coded the studies for methodological attributes. For example, we coded whether the studies used cross-sectional or longitudinal methods and for the type of social interaction they examined. We examine how these factors affect survey results.

Meta-Analysis

Study Retrieval

The main criterion to include a particular study was whether it examined Internet use and interactions with respondents' close ties. We located relevant studies by searching computerized reference databases including PsychInfo, FirstSearch, ArticleFirst, and CiteSeer by examining reference lists of studies on the effects of Internet use on social involvement, social relationships, socializing, and so on, and through personal contacts. To be included in the analysis, the researchers had to have selected participants from a real-world community or from a population that included both Internet users and nonusers. Some of these studies examined people's close relationships with family members as compared with their relationships with friends. Others did not differentiate between the two. We did not include laboratory experiments because they typically examined the effect of very short term Internet use on interaction, generally with strangers. Nor did we include surveys that solicited participants exclusively online because these studies lacked base rate and comparison data with nonusers, and were highly susceptible to self-selection bias. Table 17.1 provides descriptive information on the 16 surveys in our analysis.

Table 17.1. Study characteristics for studies of Internet use and social interaction.

Researcher[a]	Study	Year	Cross-sectional/ longitudinal	N	Research question	Internet use	Social involvement[b]	Category[c]	z_r
Katz & Aspden[n]	A Nation of Strangers	1995	C	2500	Relationship of Internet use with off-line interaction, online social interaction, and online expression	Use/non-use	Phone calls per week[23]	UCT	0.051
Kraut et al.[o]	The Internet Paradox	1996	L	261	Impact of Internet use on social involvement and psychological well-being	Amount (min/week)	Local social circle[123]	UCT	−0.150
							Distant social circle[123]	UCT	−0.150
							Time w/family (min)12	Family	−0.070
Kraut et al.[o]	Internet Paradox Revisited (Internet Paradox Sample)	1997	L	208	Impact of Internet use on social involvement and psychological well-being	Amount (min/week)	Family communication[1234]	Family	0.120
							Local social circle[1234]	UCT	−0.009
							Distant social circle[1234]	UCT	0.038
Crawford[o]	Internet Paradox Revisited (TV-buyers sample)	1998	L	403	Impact of Internet use on social involvement and psychological well-being	Internet use (freq)	Local social circle[123]	UCT	0.155
							Distant social circle[123]	UCT	0.159
							Phone communication[123]	UCT	0.063
							FtF communication[123]	Friends	0.113
							Family communication[123]	Family	0.005
Mesch[n]	Social Relationships and Internet Use among Adolescents in Israel	1998	C	927	Relationship among youth leisure activities, peer relations, and the frequency of Internet use among adolescents	Use/non-use	Out to parties w/friends[123]	Friends	−0.028
							Going out to discotheques[123]	UCT	0.018
							Going out to the movies[123]	UCT	0.012
							Going out to performances[123]	UCT	0.003
Lee & Kuo[o]	Internet and Displacement Effect: Children's Media Use and Activities in Singapore	1999	L	817	Relationship between Internet use and activities important to childhood development	Amount (min/week)	Time w/family(min)	Family	0.054
							Time w/friends (min)	Friends	0.079
Gershuny[n]	Web-use and Net-nerds: A Neo-Functionalist Analysis of the Impact of Information Technology in the Home	1999	L	2294	Impact of use of various facilities of the World Wide Web on patterns of sociability	Amount (min) (past 24 hrs)	Going out with friends (min)[12]	Friends	0.051
							Visits w/fam & friends (min)[12]	UCT	−0.037
							Phone fam & friends (min)[12]	UCT	−0.019
Cole & Robinson[n]	Internet Use and Sociability in the UCLA Data: A Simplified MCA Analysis	2000	C	1774	Relation between Internet use and sociability using both relational and attitudinal data	Amount (min)	Household socializing (min)[1234]	Family	−0.042
							Friends socializing (min)[1234]	Friends	0.064
							Number of friends[1234]	Friends	0.020

Author	Title	Year	Type	n	Research focus	Measure	Variable	Tie	Coef.
Lee & Zhu[n]	Internet Use and Sociability in Mainland China	2000	C	1798 China	Impact of Internet use on socializing with friends, household socializing, and family interactions	Amount (min)	Time w/family (freq)[1234]	Family	0.042
							Time w/friends (min)[1234]	Friends	0.042
							Talking w/family (min)[1234]	Family	-0.020
	Internet Use and Sociability in Hong Kong	2000	C	1007 HK		Amount (min)	Time w/family (freq)[1234]	Family	0.053
							Time w/friends (min)[1234]	Friends	-0.042
							Talking w/family (min)[1234]	Family	0.140
Mikami	Internet Use and Sociability in Japan	2000	C	2393	Relationship of Internet use and household socializing and socializing with family and friends	Amount (min)	Household socializing[1234]	Family	0.042
							Friends socializing[1234]	Friends	-0.075
Neustadtl & Robinson[n]	Social Contact Differences Between Internet Users and Nonusers in the General Social Survey	2000	C	1815	Incidence of other forms of communication, particularly among those who use the Internet for social communication	Use/non-use	Social evening w/friends[1234]	Friends	0.087
							Social evening w/family[1234]	Family	-0.087
							Social evening w/neighbrs[1234]	Friends	-0.075
							Going to bars/taverns[1234]	UCT	-0.031
							Social circle[1234]	UCT	0.064
							No. of people you phone[1234]	UCT	0.193
							No. of people you see FtF[1234]	UCT	0.124
Shklovski, Kraut, & Rainie[n]	The Internet and Social Relationships: Contrasting Cross-Sectional and Longitudinal Analyses	2000	L	1501	Influence of Internet use on communication and social involvement	Breadth (scale)	Visit family or friends[124]	UCT	-0.057
							Telephone family/friends[124]	UCT	0.009
Nie & Hilligus[n]	The Impact of Internet Use on Sociability: Time Diary Findings	2002	C	5738	Does Internet use impact face-to-face interactions; hydraulic theory of IT impact	Amount @ home (min) (past 6 hrs)	Time w/fam (min)[124]	Family	-0.144
							Time w/friends (min)[124]	Friends	-0.075
							Social activities (min)[124]	UCT	-0.076
Kraut et al.[n]	HomeNet 3	2002	L	1072	Impact of internet use on sociability and psychological well-being	Internet use (freq)	Interpersonal com[124]	UCT	0.023
							Spending time with family[124]	Family	0.043
							Spending time w/friends[124]	Friends	0.022
Jackson et al.[o]	The Social Impact of Internet Use on the Other Side of the Digital Divide	2003	L	117	Does Internet use in the home undermine psychological well-being and social involvement for low-income African Americans	Amount (min)	No. of close friends[2]	Friends	-0.029

n = national sample; o = opportunity sample.
[b] Control demographics included in the analysis model: 1 = gender, 2 = age, 3 = income, 4 = education.
[c] UCT = unspecified close ties.

Variables and Coding

We examined relationships reported between measures of Internet use (the independent variable) and social interaction with close ties (the dependent variable). Many authors measure more than one type of social interaction. We treat each finding as a separate result. We include any measure of interaction with family, friends, or both, even if the question asks about a particular activity, such as "going out" or "socializing" with these people.

Based on our claims about how differences in measurement and study design can affect findings, we created the following moderator variables.

Type of Relationship

Twelve studies include measures of interaction (time or frequency) with friends; 11 studies include measures of interaction (time or frequency) with family or household members; 10 others ask about interaction with "family and friends" or do not explicitly specify the type of relationship. Because family relationships and friendships may differentially be sensitive to Internet use, we created dummy variables to represent whether the measure of interaction asked about family (or household), about friends, or unspecified (which includes questions asking about "friends or family," and "friends and family.") These dummy variables are moderator variables in our analysis.

Study Design

In the cross-sectional studies, researchers customarily attempt to statistically control for preexisting differences among respondents through regression techniques. However, with or without controls, these studies do not permit causal conclusions. The longitudinal studies offer more convincing, though still imperfect, ground for causal claims. We expect that if Internet use has an effect on interpersonal relationships, longitudinal studies would produce smaller but more consistent, homogeneous effect sizes. Study design was a moderator variable in our analysis.

Other Potential Moderator Variables

Internet use was the independent variable in all of these survey studies. Based on the literature on survey methods, we coded for differences in how authors measured Internet use and conducted preliminary analyses to examine whether these differences may have affected the results of the studies. For example, Catania, Gibson, Chitwood, and Coates (1990) show that asking people direct questions about socially desirable or undesirable behavior can bias their responses in the socially desirable direction. This work is relevant because Internet use is generally a socially desirable behavior (e.g., Kraut, Scherlis, Mukhopadhyay, Manning, & Kiesler, 1996). In two studies, authors collected unobtrusive automated logs of Internet use, as well as self-report measures (Kraut et al., 1998; Jackson et al., 2004); in all of the other studies, authors collected only self-report measures of Internet use. Automated measurements of Internet use correlate fairly well with the self-report measures and do not show differential effects on dependent variables. Also, whether authors used discrete (use vs. nonuse) or continuous measures of Internet use did not affect the results. On the basis of these preliminary analyses, we exclude from the final analysis moderator variables reflecting coded measurement differences that did not affect the results.

Preliminary examination of the effects of the date of study was also not significant in any of the analyses and failed to illustrate a significant change in the effect of Internet use on social interaction over time. We omit date from all subsequent analyses.

Computation of Effect Sizes

Each suitable study in the sample contributes at least one effect size for the meta-analysis. Each effect size represents a value that quantifies the statistical relationship between Internet use and interpersonal interaction. There are several possible measures of effect size (Rosenthal, 1994). We select the Pearson product-moment correlation coefficient, r, because it best describes the relationship of interest and is understandable by most social scientists. In most cases, r is not reported directly within a study, but it can be obtained either from available raw data or by transforming other reported statistics (e.g., t, eta) that test for a relationship between Internet use and interpersonal interaction. We use formulas recommended by Rosenthal (1994, pp. 236–240) to conduct the necessary transformations. In some cases, studies do not provide enough information to calculate appropriate effect sizes. In those cases, we omitted the studies from the analysis.[2] From the 16 studies in the analysis, we were able to obtain 48 effect sizes. Before analysis, we transformed all effect sizes using the Fisher's Z transformation suggested by Rosenthal and Rosnow (1991, pp. 491–501). Table 17.1 reports the transformed effect sizes.

Once the data set was obtained and the effect sizes properly transformed, we performed a sensitivity analysis (Greenhouse & Iyengar, 1994) to identify the proper method of analysis and to identify outliers in the data. Because many of the studies provide more than one test of relationship between Internet use and interpersonal interaction, we used a hierarchical linear regression (Bryk & Raudenbush, 1992) as the method to control for nonindependence of effect sizes (i.e., multiple effect sizes could be nested within a single study). This method is similar to a regression model for stochastically dependent effect sizes suggested by Gleser & Olkin (1994). Because the use of hierarchical linear models is not well documented in the methodological literature of meta-analysis, we also conducted our meta-analysis using a combination of the more commonly used fixed-effects procedure, following the weighted-variance method in Shadish and Haddock (1994).

In our model, we use the transformed effect sizes as the dependent variable, and various combinations of predictor variables as independent variables. Each transformed effect size is weighted by an inverse of its variance (as suggested in Rosenthal & Rosnow, 1991; Shaddish & Haddock, 1994). Studies with larger sample sizes, therefore, contribute more weight to the analysis than those with a small sample size, because the large sample sizes provide effect size estimates that are closer to the true effect size of the population.

Results

The 16 studies included a total of 35,578 participants and yielded 48 effect sizes. Preliminary analysis showed a mean weighted effect size of r = –.02 with a 95% confidence interval of –.03 to –.01, indicating that overall, there is a slightly negative association of Internet use with social interaction. Figure 17.1 shows the histogram for the weighted effect sizes. This histogram clearly shows several outliers. These outliers come from one large-sample study (Nie & Hillygus, 2002). Sensitivity analysis (Greenhouse & Iyengar, 1994) was performed to identify severe outliers and to examine them separately. Figure 17.2 shows normally distributed histogram for weighted effect sizes with the single outlier study removed (three effect sizes). The mean effect size with outliers removed was .01 with a 95% confidence interval of .00 to .02, indicating no observed association of Internet use and social interaction.

The study with outliers had some unique methodological characteristics (Nie & Hillygus, 2002). The data collection method used was an augmented

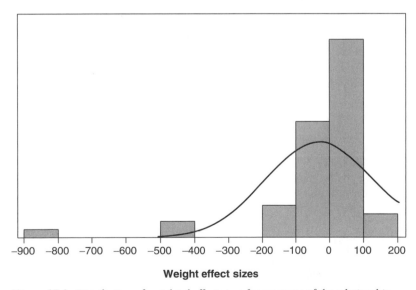

Figure 17.1. Distribution of weighted effect sizes for measures of the relationship between Internet use and interpersonal interaction with close ties in 16 studies.

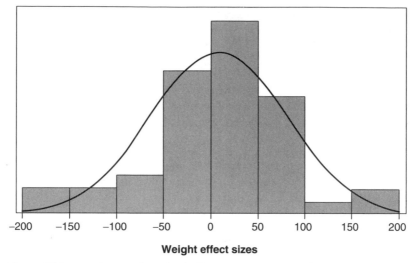

Figure 17.2. Distribution of weighted effect sizes, removing outliers (Nie & Hillygus, 2002).

diary study, in which respondents were asked to recount their primary activities, including their offline social interaction over the previous 6 hours. This reporting interval limited the number of primary activities that would fit within such a short timeframe. Assuming people cannot simultaneously do two primary activities, such as both surfing the Web and socializing offline with friends, this short time interval for the sampling period could have led to biased estimates of the association of Internet use and social interaction. For example, by limiting the sampling period to 6 hours, this method excluded cases in which the Internet was used in the morning to schedule an offline social interaction for the same evening. We concluded that this study method is biased to produce negative Internet effects and is sufficiently different from all other studies to warrant its exclusion from the analysis. We report only the analyses that were performed without this study.

We analyze the effects of Internet use on social interaction across the remaining 15 survey studies by entering the type of relationship studied and the study design method into a hierarchical mixed linear model that predicts effect size. We treated study as a random effect, with effect size nested within study. Table 17.2 shows the results. The marginally significant effect of the friends variable shows that, across all study methods, effects of Internet use were smaller or less likely to be positive when authors measured social interaction with friends as

compared with other close relationship ($b = 65.3$, $p < .09$, $t = -1.79$).

Overall, study design (cross-sectional vs. longitudinal studies) did not have a significant effect on effect sizes, but design did affect results when the type of relationship measured was considered. Table 17.2 shows a marginally significant interaction effect of study design, with the dummy variable measuring social interaction with friends versus unspecified relationships ($b = 98.2$, $p < .07$, $t = 1.86$). This interaction effect reflects the fact that cross-sectional studies tended to show negative effects of Internet use on interaction with friends, and negative effects on interaction with others, whereas longitudinal studies tended to show positive effects of Internet use on interaction with friends and no effect on others. As also shown in table 17.2, study design did not lead to different effect sizes when contrasting family interactions with other social interactions ($b = 52.9$, $p > .2$, $t = -.99$). Figure 17.3 illustrates these effects.

To investigate these trends further, we also conducted a more traditional fixed effects regression analysis. This analysis does not control for the correlations among effect sizes within a study. Within-study correlated effects can be produced when a single investigator uses more than one measure of the same variable. In our corpus, the mean number of measures of social interaction with friends within any study that measured this variable was 1.1; the mean number of measures of social inter-

Table 17.2. Hierarchical linear model weighted regression, testing the effects of study design and type of social interaction in studies of the effects of using the Internet on social interaction.

Effect	Estimate	df	t value
Intercept	38.75	13	1.52
Study method (0 = cross sectional, 1 = longitudinal)	−38.21	13	−1.16
Social interaction with friends (0 = unspecified close ties, 1 = friends)	−65.27	26	−1.81*
Social interaction with family (0 = unspecified close ties, 1 = family)	−33.80	26	−0.91
Study method × friends	98.15	26	1.86*
Study method × family	52.91	26	0.99

*$p < .1$.

action with family within any study that measured this variable was 1.3, and the mean number of measures of social interaction with unspecified close ties was 2.2. Hence, any threats to validity mainly rest with the measures of social interaction among unspecified close ties.

Table 17.3 shows the results of this analysis. The table shows that cross-sectional studies (across all measures) and measures of social interaction with unspecified others (in both cross-sectional and longitudinal studies) tend to produce significantly variable, heterogeneous effects. The only homogeneous effect sizes emerge from longitudinal studies of social interaction with family and with friends. However, the confidence limits (CL) for family in-

clude positive and negative effects, indicating that there is no significant result. The strongest trend corresponds with the finding from the hierarchical model, showing that Internet use predicts slight increases in social interaction with friends ($CL = .004–.103$). Although these effects are small, they support the findings from the hierarchical analyses described earlier.

Discussion

Our meta-analysis of 16 studies of the association of Internet use with social interaction in close relationships showed that the association is very small.

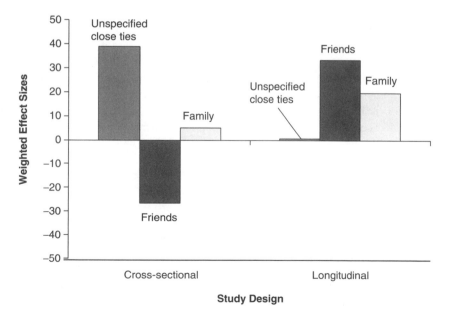

Figure 17.3. Illustrating relationship between study design and measures of social interaction.

Table 17.3. Fixed effects analysis of the effects of the Internet on social interaction, examining effects of types of social interaction and study design.

Variable and class	Between-classes effect (Q_B)	k	Mean weighted effect size (ωZ_i)	95% CI for Z_i Lower	Upper	Homogeneity within class (Q_{wi})
Interpersonal relationship type	4.01					
Friends		13	−0.003	−0.02	0.014	62.5***
Family		12	0.01	−0.01	0.028	39.64***
Unspecified close ties		20	0.02	0.006	0.039	83.05***
Study design type	1.78					
Cross-sectional		23	0.01	−0.005	0.018	135.02***
Longitudinal		22	0.02	0.006	0.039	52.4***
Relationship type by study design type						
Cross-sectional	14.22***					
Friends		8	−0.02	−0.04	0.004	46.5***
Family		7	0.003	−0.02	0.03	33.2***
Unspecified close ties		8	0.04	0.012	0.065	41.1***
Longitudinal	7*					
Friends		5	0.05	0.004	0.103	3.7
Family		5	0.037	−0.02	0.09	3.9
Unspecified close ties		12	0.001	−0.02	0.026	37.8***

Q_B = between class effect, k = number of effect sizes; CI = confidence interval; Q_{wi} = homogeneity within each class (significance indicates rejection of the hypothesis of homogeneity).
*$p < .05$ ***$p < .001$.

Once we removed an outlier study for substantive and statistical reasons, the effect was close to zero ($r = .01$, CL =.00–.03). The other primary finding was that study design influenced outcomes for different types of personal relationships. Cross-sectional studies produced highly variable effects that, on average, indicate use of the Internet was positively correlated with interaction in unspecified close relationships, but negatively related to social interaction in friendships. Longitudinal studies, fewer in number but more stable in their results, show that more Internet use predicts slight positive increases in social interaction with friends. Again, all of the effect sizes were very small.

What might account for the finding from longitudinal studies of a more positive effect of Internet use on social interaction with friends than with unspecified close ties? Assuming that unspecified close ties include family, household, relatives, and romantic partners, it seems possible that people's interactions with their friends would be somewhat less stable than their relationships with family, household, relatives, and romantic partners. Using the Internet might reduce the costs and increase the convenience of communicating with friends, and in doing so, make other types of social interaction,

such as phone calls or spontaneous outings, more likely (see also chapter 18). These effects do not hold, however, for family and relatives, especially those in the same household, because family communication already has low costs. Consistent with a possible shift to more social interaction outside the household, Gershuny (2002) reports from his longitudinal study that more time on the Internet has a small positive effect on respondents' saying they "go out" with friends.

A related possibility is that Internet communication may function as an extra source of friendship-related stimulus at home or at work—a source of reminders that friends (people outside the home) need or want attention. Friendships require consistent maintenance (Duck, 1998) and, sometimes, serious time commitment. This maintenance might be enhanced by the exchange of e-mail and instant messenger messages. Family ties, in contrast, are much more stable, partly because they are not voluntary (Allan, 1979, pp. 122–123).

These effects would be apparent in longitudinal studies and not in cross-sectional studies, because longitudinal studies are more likely to detect changes in social interaction over time. Cross-sectional studies can only detect whether a positive or negative relationship exists. The cross-sectional studies that find a negative relationship of Internet use and social interaction in friendships may be explained by a desire of those without many friends to seek friends on the Internet (see McKenna & Bargh, 1998, 2000) or a personality trait such as introversion that causes people to prefer the Internet over face-to-face contact. Unfortunately, there are comparatively few results from longitudinal studies with items that examine the effects of Internet use on social interaction in different relationships. Furthermore, the studies we reviewed were not designed to investigate factors that cause people to use the Internet more or less, and few studies measured personality traits.

The Need for an Improved Paradigm

Our results point to the need for investigators to invest their time and effort in longitudinal studies. The outcomes of our meta-analysis indicate that cross-sectional designs produce not just ambiguous results but also results that contradict those of longitudinal studies. If investigators wish to learn the social impact of the Internet, or of any new technology, longitudinal studies are far more credible. The ability to evaluate the same people over time mitigates several major threats to causal inference; first, that preexisting differences among individuals account for differences in the outcome variable; second, that the purported outcome variable affects changes in the purported independent variable; and third, that an unmeasured variable changes the relationship between the independent and dependent variables. When people answer a survey multiple times, these participants bring the same demographic and other cross-sectional differences to all surveys, effectively controlling for their own cross-sectional variation. Many statistical techniques have been developed to aid analysis and inference from longitudinal data. The best of these techniques allow investigators to separate the variability in the data that can be attributed to "before" factors (i.e., how much social interaction a person has when the study starts) and "after" factors (i.e., how much social interaction the same person had when the study ends). In our review, the longitudinal study designs may determine whether levels of Internet use predict changes in social interaction with family or friends whereas the cross-sectional studies cannot.

Longitudinal designs remain subject to some threats to validity. Other events that change with time may drive change in Internet use and, simultaneously, change in outcomes. These extraneous events can be internal to the individuals, such as learning or maturation, or external, such as the business cycle or change in popular culture. Also, because of errors of measures, preexisting differences among participants are never fully statistically controlled in longitudinal designs. Hence we recommend longitudinal studies with the caveat that they will never resolve all ambiguities.

Our findings also point to the need to study how people use the Internet, and particularly how they communicate offline and online within different types of social relationships (Coget, Yamauchi, & Suman, 2002; Shklovski et al., 2004). Few authors in our corpus differentiate the relationships within which Internet interactions take place; for instance, whether someone used the Internet to send e-mail to family members and to close friends or to meet new people in chat rooms (cf. Boneva, Kraut, & Frohlich, 2001). If the Internet does have differential social effects depending on who communicates with whom, these effects would be obscured in aggregate studies of "Internet use." Theories of social interaction in different relationships would help researchers to formulate questions and would advance the state of the literature.

Finally, variables that can moderate the effects of Internet use on social involvement and psychological well-being, such as extraversion and other comparatively stable predispositions toward social behavior, were rarely measured in the reviewed studies of the Internet and therefore were unavailable for statistical control. McKenna and her colleagues have argued that the Internet has differentially positive effects on those who are socially stigmatized or isolated and find new relationships online (chapter 19; McKenna & Bargh, 1998, 2000). Online relationships, however, were rarely measured in the studies reviewed here. It seems possible that people who are (or feel) isolated can successfully seek out new relationships online, whereas the same behavior would be counterproductive for those who already have strong ties that should be maintained (Bessiere, Kiesler, Kraut & Boneva, unpublished manuscript, 2004). Internet effects moderated by people's social context or personality could be detected if studies included these variables.

Conclusion

One decade ago, in an early proposal, we argued for studies of the social impact of the Internet:

> We lack information about the personal effects of electronic services on families and the community—and about the effects of not having such services. The answers to these questions are important if we are to spend public and private resources efficiently and effectively, if we are to understand the barriers to serving many people, and many kinds of people, and if we are to measure outcomes objectively, in a manner that informs policy. (Kraut, 1994)

Our argument, and the sentiments of many others, resulted in research supported by foundations, businesses, and the National Science Foundation and other government agencies. Over the past decade, researchers in the United States and other countries have studied the effects of the Internet. The outcome of this program of work is mixed. These studies served policy. For example, early researchers documented the superior income and education characteristics of Internet users as compared with nonusers and catalogued economic (Anderson, Bikson, Law, & Mitchell, 1995) and technical (Kiesler, Zdaniuk, Lundmark, & Kraut, 2000) barriers to Internet use. This work helped bring about and justify major federal and state programs to support Internet access in libraries and schools.

In contrast, as our analysis shows, the burgeoning literature on the social impact of the Internet has identified few consistent effects across people, relationships, and settings. Our overall finding is that the Internet has not had any broad effect on social interaction, but this finding must be tempered by the nature of the research we reviewed: survey studies looking at gross Internet use (for any purpose and across many relationships) and social interaction within broad types of relationships. The hype and expectations surrounding the Internet also may have blinded researchers to the stability of people's lives and the changes that have to take place before a technology is incorporated into, and adapted to, home, work, and everyday life (Cummings, Butler, & Kraut, 2002). The number of insignificant effects in the literature indicates that some of the most important parts of life—how people use major blocks of time, their closest relationships, and their emotional lives—are comparatively stable over time and resist change. Thus, even though the Internet may have changed many habits, the effects of those changes on fundamental relationships and psychological well-being seem to be small or at least slow in emerging. More recent research, especially theoretically driven studies, that is targeted to understand particular uses of the Internet for particular relationships will be more likely to discover how using the Internet in these ways affects our social interactions and other important aspects of our lives. This review of the literature has shown that it is time to focus on developing a more differentiated view of the Internet and its social outcomes. The Internet is a malleable and diverse technology, and its effects must differ, dependent on the purpose of its use.

Notes

1. No one has yet been able to conduct a true field experiment comparing users and nonusers (see, for instance, Kraut et al., 2002).

2. Our database included 18 published and unpublished studies. Many authors reported their results in a form of a multivariate analysis with control variables that differed across studies. They often did not include information relevant to effect sizes. We contacted authors to obtain the needed information. We were unable to obtain relevant information for two of the selected studies, reducing our study sample to 16.

References

(*Note:* Asterisks mark references used in the meta-analysis.)

Albarracin, D., Johnson, B. T., Fishbein, M., & Muellerleile, P. A. (2001). Theories of reasoned action and planned behavior as models of condom use: A meta-analysis. *Psychological Bulletin, 127,* 142–161.

Allan, G. (1979). *A sociology of friendship and kinship.* London: George Allen & Unwin.

Anderson, R., Bikson, T., Law, S., & Mitchell, B. (1995). *Universal access to E-mail.* Santa Monica, CA: RAND.

Baumeister, R. F., & Leary, M. R. (1995). The need to belong: Desire for interpersonal attachments as a fundamental human motivation. *Psychological Bulletin, 117*(3), 497–529.

Bessière, K., Kiesler, S., Kraut, R., & Boneva, B. (2004). Longitudinal effects of Internet uses on depressive affect: A social resources approach. Unpublished manuscript, Pittsburgh, PA: Carnegie Mellon University.

Bolger, N., Zuckerman, A., & Kessler, R. C. (2000). Invisible support and adjustment to stress. *Journal of Personality & Social Psychology, 79,* 953–961.

Boneva, B., Kraut, R., & Frohlich, D. (2001). Using e-mail for personal relationships: The difference gender makes. *American Behavioral Scientist, 45*(3), 530–549.

Bryk, A. S., & Raudenbush, S. W. (1992). *Hierarchical linear models: Applications and data analysis methods.* Thousand Oaks, CA: Sage.

Catania, J. A., Gibson, D. R., Chitwood, D. D., & Coates, T. J. (1990). Methodological problems in AIDS behavioral research: Influences on measurement error and participation bias in studies of sexual behavior. *Psychological Bulletin, 108,* 339–362.

Coget, J. F., Yamauchi, Y., & Suman, M. (2002). The Internet, social networks, and loneliness. *IT & Society, 1*(1), 180–201.

Cohen, S., Underwood, L. G., & Gottlieb, B. (2000). Social relationships and health. In Cohen S., Underwood, L. G., & Gottlieb, B. (Eds.), *Social support measurement and interventions: A guide for health and social scientists* (pp. 3–25). New York: Oxford University Press.

Cohen, S., & Wills, T. A. (1985). Stress, social support, and the buffering hypothesis. *Psychological Bulletin, 98*(2), 310–357.

*Cole, J. I., & Robinson, J. P. (2002). Internet use and sociability in the UCLA data: A simplified MCA analysis. *IT & Society, 1*(1), 202–218.

Cummings, J., Butler, B., & Kraut, R. (2002). The quality of online social relationships. *Communications of the ACM, 45*(7), 103–108.

Duck, S. (1998). *Human relationships* (3rd ed.). Thousand Oaks, CA: Sage.

*Gershuny, J. I. (2002). *Web-use and Net-nerds: A neo-functionalist analysis of the impact of information technology in the home.* Unpublished manuscript. Colchester, U.K.: University of Essex.

Gleser, L. J., & Olkin, I. (1994). Stochastically dependent effect sizes. In Cooper, H., & Hedges, L. (Eds.), *The handbook of research synthesis* (pp. 339–356). New York: Russell Sage Foundation.

Gottlieb, N. H., & Green, L. W. (1984). Life events, social network, life-style, and health: An analysis of the 1979 national survey of personal health practices and consequences. *Health Education Quarterly, 11,* 91–105.

Greenhouse, J., & Iyengar, S. (1994). Sensitivity analysis and diagnostics. In Cooper, H. & Hedges, L. (Eds.), *The handbook of research synthesis* (pp. 383–398).New York: Russell Sage Foundation.

Helgeson, V., Cohen, S., Schulz, R., & Yasko, J. (2000). Group support interventions for people with cancer: Who benefits from what? *Health Psychology, 19,* 107–114.

* Jackson, L. A., von Eye, A., Barbatsis, G., Biocca, F., Fitzgerald, H. E., & Zhao, Y. (2004). The social impact of Internet use on the other side of the digital divide. *Communications of the Association for Computing Machinery, 47*(7), 43–47.

Katz, J., & Aspden, P. (1997). A nation of strangers? *Communications of the ACM, 40*(12), 81–86.

*Katz, J. E., & Rice, R. E. (2002). *Social consequences of Internet use: Access, involvement, and interaction.* Cambridge, MA: MIT Press.

*Kestnbaum, M., Robinson, J. P., Neustadtl, A., & Alvarez, A. (2002). Information technology and social time displacement. *IT & Society, 1*(1), 21–37.

Kiesler, S., Zdaniuk, B., Lundmark, V., & Kraut, R. (2000). Troubles with the Internet: The dynamics of help at home. *Human-Computer Interaction Special Issue, 15*(4), 323–351.

Kraut, R. (1994). *HomeNet: A field trial of residential Internet services.* Unpublished proposal to the National Telecommunications and Information Administration. Pittsburgh, PA: Carnegie Mellon University.

*Kraut, R., Kiesler, S., Boneva, B., Cummings, J. N., Helgeson, V., & Crawford, A. M. (2002). Internet paradox revisited. *Journal of Social Issues, 58*(1), 49–74.

Kraut, R., Mukhopadhyay, T., Szczypula, J., Kiesler, S., & Scherlis, B. (1999). Information and communication: Alternative uses of the Internet in households. *Information Systems Research Special Issue, 10*(4), 287–303.

*Kraut, R., Patterson, M., Lundmark, V., Kiesler, S., Mukhopadhyay, T., & Scherlis, W. (1998). Internet paradox: A social technology that reduces social involvement and psychological well-being? *American Psychologist, 53*(9), 1017–1031.

Kraut, R. E., & Attewell, P. (1997). Media use and organizational knowledge: Electronic mail in a global corporation. In Kiesler, S. (Ed.), *Research milestones on the information highway.* Mahwah, NJ: Lawrence Erlbaum.

Kraut, R. E., Scherlis, W., Mukhopadhyay, T., Manning, J., & Kiesler, S. (1996). HomeNet: A field trial of residential internet services. *Communications of the ACM, 39*(12), 55–64.

*Lee, B., & Zhu, J. (2002). Internet use and sociability in mainland China and Hong Kong. *IT & Society, 1*(1) 219–237

*Lee, W., & Kuo, E. C. Y. (2002). Internet and displacement effect: Children's media use and activities in Singapore. *Journal of Computer-Mediated Communication, 7*(2). Available: http://jcmc.indiana.edu/vol7/issue2/singapore.html

Lepper, M., Henderlong, J., & Gingras, I. (1999). Understanding the effects of extrinsic rewards on intrinsic motivation: Uses and abuses of meta-analysis. *Psychological Bulletin, 125,* 669–676.

McKenna, K. Y. A., & Bargh, J. A. (1998). Coming out in the age of the Internet: Identity "demarginalization" through virtual group participation. *Journal of Personality & Social Psychology, 75*(3), 681–694.

McKenna, K., & Bargh, J. A. (2000). Plan 9 from cyberspace: The implications of the Internet for personality and social psychology. *Personality & Social Psychology Review, 4*(1), 57–75.

*Mesch, G. (2001). Social relationships and Internet use among adolescents in Israel. *Social Science Quarterly, 82*(2), 329–339.

*Mikami, S. (2002). Internet use and sociability in Japan. *IT & Society, 1*(1), 242–250.

Mirowsky, J., & Ross, C. E. (1989). *Social causes of psychological distress.* Hawthorne, NY: Aldine De Gruyter.

*Neustadtl, A., & Robinson, J. P. (2002). Social contact differences between Internet users and nonusers in the general social survey. *IT & Society, 1*(1), 73–102.

*Nie, N., & Hillygus, D. S. (2002). The impact of Internet use on sociability: Time diary findings. *IT & Society, 1*(1), 1–20.

Nie, N., Hillygus, S., & Erbring, L. (2002). Internet use, interpersonal relations and sociability: Findings from a detailed time diary study. In Wellman, B. (Ed.), *The Internet in everyday life* (pp. 215–243). Oxford: Blackwell.

Peirce, R. S., Frone, M. R., Russell, M., Cooper, M. L., & Mudar, P. (2000). A longitudinal model of social contact, social support, depression, and alcohol use. *Health Psychology, 19*(1), 28–38.

Pew Internet and American Life Project. (2002). *Daily Internet activities.* Retrieved October 25, 2002, from http://www.pewinternet.org/reports/chart.asp?img=Daily_A1.htm.

Pew Internet and American Life Project. (2003, December 22). *The changing picture of who's online and what they do.* Retrieved March 24, 2004, from http://www.pewinternet.org/reports/toc.asp?Report=106.

*Pronovost, G. (2002). The Internet and time displacement: A Canadian perspective. *IT & Society, 1*(1), 44–53.

Robinson, J., & Godbey, G. (1999). *Time for life: The surprising ways Americans use their time* (2nd ed.). University Park: Pennsylvania State University Press.

Rosenthal, R. (1994). Parametric measures of effect size. In Cooper, H., & Hedges, L. (Eds.), *The handbook of research synthesis* (pp. 231–244).New York: Russell Sage Foundation.

Rosenthal, R., & Rosnow, R. L. (1991). *Essentials of behavioral research: Methods and data analysis* (2nd ed.). Boston: McGraw-Hill.

Schachter, S. (1951). Deviation, refection, and communication. *Journal of Abnormal and Social Psychology, 46,* 190–207.

Shadish, W. R., & Haddock, C. K. (1994). Combining estimates of effect size. In Cooper, H., & Hedges, L. (Eds.), *The handbook of research synthesis* (pp. 261–283).New York: Russell Sage Foundation.

*Shklovski, I., Kraut, R., & Rainie, L. (2004). The Internet and social relationships: Contrasting cross-sectional and longitudinal analyses. *Journal of Computer-Mediated Communication.* Retrieved October, 2004 from http://jcmc.indiana.edu/vol10/issue1/shklovski_kraut.html

Sproull, L., & Faraj, S. (1995). Atheism, sex, and databases: The net as a social technology. In Kahin, B., & Keller, J. (Ed.) *Public access to the Internet.* (pp. 62–81). Cambridge, MA: MIT Press.

Sproull, L., & Kiesler, S. (1991). *Connections: New ways of working in the networked organization.* Cambridge, MA: MIT Press.

Srole, L. (1956). Social integration and certain corollaries. *American Sociological Review, 21,* 709–716.

Thoits, P. A. (1983). Multiple identities and psychological well-being: A reformulation and test of the social isolation hypothesis. *American Sociological Review, 48*(2), 174–187.

U.S. Department of Commerce. (2002). *A nation online: How Americans are expanding their use of the Internet.* Washington, DC: Government Printing Office.

Wellman, B., & Wortley, S. (1990). Different strokes from different folks: Community ties and social support. *American Journal of Sociology, 96*(3), 558–588.

18

Jonathon N. Cummings, John B. Lee, and Robert Kraut

Communication Technology and Friendship During the Transition from High School to College

People maintain only a limited number of personal relationships. Researchers estimate that people typically keep 10–20 important relationships out of the approximately 1000 individuals with whom they interact or can identify (e.g., Fischer, 1982; Wellman, 1992). Friendships, in contrast to family relationships, are especially fragile and require active maintenance or they die (Canary & Stafford, 1994). Although family ties exist because of the accident of birth and are often maintained through obligation, friendship and romantic relationships are voluntary. They grow, decline, and end through concrete actions (Allan, 1979).

In this chapter, we examine how young adults maintain friendships when faced with life events that threaten them, such as moving from high school to college. In particular, we examine the role that phone and computer communications play in maintaining these friendships as the parties move geographically apart.

In Duck's analogy (1988), friendships need a regular investment of effort; otherwise, normal centripetal forces cause the friendship to come apart. In this view, people develop and maintain particular relationships by enacting them (i.e., by carrying them out through regular exchanges of communication or social support; Duck, 1988). Initial factors that bring

people together, such as common interests, shared work goals, beauty, or charm, lose power with time (Berg & Clark, 1986). These factors must be supplemented with behavioral exchanges that affect whether the relationship will be valued and retained or devalued and dropped (Berg & Clark, 1986). Regular contact is at the heart of friendship (Allan, 1979). We typically grow to like others with whom we communicate and spend time, and this liking drives further companionship (Newcomb, 1961). It is in this sense that friendships are enacted. They are maintained through communication and other behavioral exchanges.

Since at least the 1930s, we have known that physical proximity increases the likelihood of friendships and romantic relationships (e.g., Bossard, 1932; Festinger, Schachter, & Back, 1950). However, when people are separated by geographic distance, it becomes more difficult to enact relationships through communication and the exchange of social support. As a result, when people change residences and move away, personal ties often fade and dissolve. Rose (1984), for example, found geographic separation to be the factor most often associated with the disintegration of friendships.

Physical proximity is conducive to the growth and maintenance of personal relationships, whereas physical distance leads to their dissolution. In part, this is because proximity decreases the behavioral costs of communication between people and hence increases its frequency, whereas distance increases the costs and decreases the frequency. Proximity not only increases the frequency of communication but also shifts the types of interactions between individuals. For instance, even if distant friends communicate frequently by phone and e-mail, the distance itself make it difficult for them to spend leisure time together, to share common activities, to be physically intimate, or to exchange certain types of social support.

When people move apart, two factors contribute to the decline of the original relationships. First, it becomes difficult to communicate with the people in the original location. Second, building relationships in the new location consumes some of the time and attention the person would need to maintain the old relationships. As a result, friendships change after a move: one may drop a friend altogether or shift that person from the active list to the list of those whom one sends holiday greetings.

Communication Technology and Social Relationships

Telecommunications technologies—literally communications at a distance—can change the amount and type of communication between people who are located remotely from each other and thus can allow them to maintain friendships at a distance. If friendships are enacted and maintained through communication, as Duck proposed, then friendships among those who live far from each other are less likely to decline the more they communicate. This hypothesis—that communication regardless of the modality leads to the maintenance of friendships at a distance—is oversimplistic and needs elaboration. In the following section, we discuss the evidence for how telecommunications affects friendship and features of the relationships and the technology that moderate the link between communication and friendship.

Differences among Communication Modalities

Phone, e-mail, and instant messaging (IM) are the three main telecommunication technologies used

by American consumers. In 1876 the phone was invented, and in 1915 the first U.S. transcontinental phone call was placed. According to AT&T, in 1945, a 10-minute evening phone call between New York and Los Angeles cost $56.80 in 1995 dollars. By 1995, the cost of this same call dropped to $1.50. At such a price, pre–World War II conversations required good reasons to call. With today's pricing, however, people call any time, just to talk. This drop in costs influences the extent to which friendships can be sustained at a distance (Fischer, 1992). The first e-mail message was sent in 1971 (Leiner et al., 2002), and the first of the IM programs, ICQ ("I seek you"), was released in 1996 by Mirabilis (*History of IM*).

Scholars have argued that these media are not equally useful for building and maintaining social relationships. In this section, we briefly review the empirical evidence that indicates that these technologies differ in their usefulness for starting and maintaining social relationship. We also identify three reasons why they differ: intrinsic properties of the media that influence both social presence and how much information is exchanged during a communication session, cost structures that change how frequently people communicate over them, and features of the technologies and communication genres associated with them that change the content of the communication.

A growing empirical literature examines the hypothesis that communication modalities differ in their ability to support social relationships. Most of this research compares text-based, computer-mediated communication with face-to-face communication (e.g., Walther, 1995), although sometimes comparisons are made to the phone as well. Cross-sectional research by Parks and Roberts (1998) and by Cummings, Butler, and Kraut (2002) has indicated that ties created or primarily maintained online are of lower quality than those sustained through other means. For example, Parks and Roberts (1998) surveyed respondents in an electronic group about their relationships with another member of the group, as well as with a matched person in their social network outside of the electronic group. The authors found that respondents spent less time, were less interdependent with, and were less committed to their online partner compared to the offline one. Cummings, Butler, and Kraut (2002) reported similar results. They asked respondents to indicate how close they felt toward two different people outside of the household. The first was the individual with whom they communicated most often by e-mail, and the second was the person with whom they reported communicating most using other modalities, including personal visits and the phone. Respondents reported feeling significantly less close to the e-mail partner.

In contrast to these survey studies, experimental studies indicate that social relationships through computer-mediated communication can be as strong as those that develop face-to-face, if participants are allowed to communicate for enough time (Walther, 2002). McKenna (chapter 19) reports research showing that cross-sex undergraduate pairs who met each another for the first time in an Internet chat room tended to like one another more compared to those who met face-to-face.

As these conflicting results demonstrate, social relationships that are maintained using different communication media do not necessarily grow at the same rate or to the same depth. Research currently presents no clear consensus about whether one communication modality is better than another for the maintenance of social relationships. The reason for these conflicting results may be that the communication media themselves may inconsistently influence fundamental communication variables; these variables may then mediate their influence on the social relationships. In particular, the communication media may influence both the frequency of communication sessions and the quality of communication during a communication session.

Cost Structures and the Frequency of Communication

Different communication modalities impose both financial and behavioral costs, which are likely to affect how frequently people use one or the other modality to communicate. For example, telecommunication providers typically charge for each long-distance phone call based on distance and duration, whereas Internet service providers' rates for e-mail or instant message sessions are independent of distance and duration. Previous research has shown that communication volume is highly sensitive to these costs and that people communicate substantially more when these costs are reduced (e.g., see Mayer, 1977, figure 7). The medium's design affects the behavioral cost of communication

as well; for example, phones require communicators to be simultaneously available before they can converse. To overcome these limitations, people play "phone tag," use answering machines to convert synchronous to asynchronous communication, or they may restrict their calling to known times of availability (Lacohee & Anderson, 2001). In contrast, e-mail is asynchronous and does not require simultaneous availability. Yet another medium, IM, requires simultaneous availability. Many IM applications provide awareness services, which inform users when a potential partner is online and available. In contrast to phone calls, however, the awareness services in IM software help to synchronize the simultaneous availability of partners and are therefore likely to increase the frequency of communication.

Quality of Communication

Communication media differ on the amount of information they transmit and their interactivity, among other features (Clark & Brennan, 1991). These features have implications for relationships that are maintained using these media (Sproull & Kiesler, 1991). Social presence theory suggests that media differ on the social presence that they afford; for example, face-to-face communication provides more social presence than the phone, which in turn provides more than text-based communication. The thesis is that media with more social presence should be better at supporting social relationships (Short, Williams, & Christie, 1976). Although many scholars contrast computer-mediated communication to face-to-face communication without differentiating among the varieties of text-based communication, the degree of interactivity is likely to be especially important both for language understanding in general (Clark & Brennan, 1991) and for companionship (Rafaeli & Sudweeks, 1997). In contrast to the relatively contemplative style of composing and reading e-mail messages, the conversational style of an IM session makes the event more engaging and analogous to "being with" a communication partner; that is, IM offers more social presence than e-mail. This interactivity encourages users to tailor messages to particular recipients (Kraut, Lewis, & Swezey, 1982) and to use an informal communication style, making it easier for communicators to quickly repair mistakes.

Media richness theory indicates that media can be differentiated on the number of social cues that they convey and their level of interactivity (Daft & Lengel, 1984; Dennis & Kinney, 1998). IM is richer than e-mail because it is more interactive. Among the interactive media, face-to-face communication is richer than the phone, which in turn is richer than IM, because both face-to-face and phone communications offer more affective and interpretive cues such as tone of voice. These richer media are better at reducing "uncertainty" and "equivocality" than leaner media such as IM and e-mail; hence, richer media are better suited to maintain relationships. Walther (Walther & Parks, 2002) argues that because writing is slower than talking, less information per unit time is conveyed in computer-mediated communication than in face-to-face and phone conversations. As a result, people need more time to develop relationships conducted over the Internet, although Walther argues that given enough time, people can develop and maintain strong social relationships online.

In contrast to research indicating that more social cues, social presence, and interactivity are better for supporting social relationships, other researchers have identified conditions under which fewer social cues, reduced social presence, and less interactivity may be better. For example, Postmes and colleagues (Postmes, Spears, & Lea, 1998, 2000) propose that the individuating information available in rich communication media interferes with identification with a group as a source of social influence. McKenna and colleagues (chapter 19) argue that the lack of social presence and superficial social cues that are available in text-based, computer-mediated communication allows individuals a better opportunity to display and learn about each others' true selves and may be especially useful for introverts or socially awkward individuals to slowly form social relationships without the pressures of face-to-face meetings.

Method

Overview

To examine the role of communication technologies in sustaining friendships, we tracked high school students as they moved to college—a situation that places existing social relationships at risk. As they move from high school to college, students go from a secure world populated with high school

friends who often attend the same school and live in the same town, to a world where these relationships disperse as both the student and friends relocate. Relationships that were once supported by geographic proximity are threatened. However, new relationships form at the beginning of college, supported by physical proximity; these new relationships may squeeze out the old ones. By following the course of old high school and new college friendships, we evaluate how communication in general—and different media in particular—facilitates the development and maintenance of relationships.

This study had two samples, representing two different high school graduation years. In both samples, we asked respondents at the end of high school to identify up to 20 friends and acquaintances from high school; at end of their first semester in college, those same respondents again identified up to 20 friendships that they formed in college. Out of these, in the first group, we sampled four high school friends and four college friends in the first sample; in the second group we sampled three high school friends and three college friends. Respondents reported on the frequency of their communication with each relationship partner in person, as well as by phone, e-mail, and IM, and on their psychological closeness to that partner. We followed these relationships for up to 3 years. We use hierarchical linear growth models to examine the influence of time and communication frequency on changes in psychological closeness.

Sampling Respondents

We collected data from two samples of high school students. Sample 1 included 500 high school students who were admitted to Carnegie Mellon University (Pittsburgh, PA) in the Spring of 2000, stratified by distance from home: 100 were students randomly selected from within 15 miles of Pittsburgh, 100 were foreign residents, and 300 were students randomly selected by U.S. zip code. Sample 2 included 500 high school students who were admitted to Carnegie Mellon in the spring of 2001, also stratified by distance from home: 100 students randomly selected from within 15 miles of Pittsburgh, 100 students randomly selected between 100 and 200 miles from Pittsburgh, 100 students randomly selected between 400 and 800 miles from Pittsburgh, 100 students randomly selected between 1700 and 5000 miles from Pittsburgh, and 100 randomly selected international students. Participants were sent a $2 bill before each survey was administered and were entered into a lottery for prizes after they completed the survey.

In each sample, survey data were collected during the spring of the students' senior year in high school (June), at the end of their first freshman semester in college (December), at the end of their freshman year in college (May), at the end of their sophomore year in college (May), and for sample 1, the end of their junior year in college (May). Of the 1000 students initially invited to participate, 62.9% completed the first survey, 48.2% completed the second survey, 39.6% completed the third survey, 31.3% completed the fourth survey, and 22.8% completed the fifth survey (sample 1 only).

Sampling Relationships

We used name generators to sample the respondents' high school and college relationships. The purpose of the name generators was to elicit a wide variety of social ties, from which we randomly selected individual relationships to follow. We used this procedure rather than allowing respondents to nominate relationships on their own, because the self-nomination would have restricted variance on the outcomes of interest (i.e., psychological closeness). People tend to select individuals who are emotionally close and currently provide support in their lives (Burt, 1986). This selection on the dependent variable would either have lead to regression toward the mean or made differences in changes in closeness difficult to observe.

The name generators were phrased, "Think about relationships with specific people in your (high school/college) social circle . . . (a) who provide you with practical assistance, (b) with whom you discuss hobbies, sports, movies, and other spare-time activities, (c) with whom you socialize, (d) who give you advice about important issues, and (e) who are in the same organizations as you." For each of the five types of relationships, respondents entered up to four names, along with the gender and age of the tie.

Respondents used a web-based survey to complete the name generators; the software then randomly selected a subset of the relationships that students identified, stratified by gender. In sample 1 were four high school relationships (two males and two females) and four college relationships

(two males and two females). Sample 2 included three high school relationships (at least one male and at least one female) and three college relationships (at least one male and at least one female). We wanted to balance the gender of partners to broaden the kinds of relationships studied and, again, to create variance on the outcome measures because people, in general, feel closer to women than to men (e.g., Duck, Rutt, Hurst, & Strejc, 1991; Wheeler & Nezlek, 1977). For the high school and college relationships, respondents were asked whether each tie was a relative, romantic partner, acquaintance, friend, close friend, or other. In the analyses reported below, only acquaintances, friends, and close friends are included as "friends" to avoid idiosyncrasies associated with relatives and romantic partner.

Measures

Psychological Closeness

Though both samples used the same questions, response options in sample 1 during the first three time periods are slightly different than those used in sample 2 and the final two time periods in Sample 1. Closeness was measured on a 5–point scale with the question "How close do you feel to [name here]." In the first sample (during spring 2000, fall 2000, and spring 2001), the response options only included (1 point) not very and (5 points) very, whereas in the second sample (and during spring 2002 and spring 2003 in the first sample) the response options included 1 = not at all, 2 = not too much, 3 = neutral, 4 somewhat, and 5 = very.

Time

The purpose of this chapter is to examine how the relationship between respondents and their partners change over time. We code time in months as the interval between questionnaires: 6 months between the first three questionnaires and 12 months thereafter. Time is 0 when a partner first appears in the data set (i.e., at the initial questionnaire for high school friends and at the second questionnaire for college friends).

Communication Frequency

For each time period, respondents reported the frequency with which they communicated with each partner in person, by phone, by e-mail, and by IM.

They answered on 7-point Likert scales, ranging from never to multiple times per day. For ease of interpretation, we transformed the Likert scales to days per months of communication. Overall communication was the sum of communication across the four modalities. Because our goal is to predict changes in psychological closeness among respondents and their partners on the basis of communication frequency, we use lagged communication frequency to reduce ambiguity in making causal claims. That is, in the analyses below, communication in the preceding time period predicts communication at the subsequent time period and changes in psychological closeness between the two periods.

Analysis

To examine how communication using different technologies influences changes in social relationships, we used hierarchical linear growth modeling, also known as multilevel modeling (Bryk & Raudenbush, 1992; Singer & Willett, 2003). Multilevel modeling takes into account the nonindependence of the data, with each respondent describing multiple partners during multiple questionnaire administrations. For the data described above, a three-level model is required. In this model, level 1 represents the respondent (e.g., the respondent's sex, age, and race), level 2 represents the relationship (e.g., partner's sex and age, communication frequency, and closeness with that partner), and level 3 represents time (e.g., repeated observations).

In these analyses, the coefficients for time-invariant level 1 variables (e.g., respondents' gender, age at the first time period, and race) and time-invariant level 2 variables (e.g., partner's gender and age at the first time period) represent cross-sectional associations. The coefficients indicate whether, for example, women report closer relationships with their partners on average than men, or whether respondents report closer relationships on average with women partners than males. The coefficients for time-varying level 2 variables (e.g., prior frequency of communication with a partner) test whether communication predicts subsequent psychological closeness. We can do this because, as shown below, both the communication variables and the closeness variable are moderately stable over time. The association of communication frequency with subsequent closeness primarily represents the cross-sectional association of communication and closeness.

The main effects and interactions with time represent the variables that predict change in psychological closeness. The coefficient for the main effect of time indicates the degree to which a participant's closeness with a particular partner changes over 12 months. A negative coefficient indicates a decline in psychological closeness. The time-by-communication interactions indicate how frequency of communication moderates the effects of time on changes in the relationship. A positive coefficient for the interaction of time with communication indicates that partners who communicate more have a slower decline in closeness. We test the effects of communication frequency both for overall communication and for the four modes of communication.

Results

Preliminary Statistics

Combined descriptive statistics for respondents from sample 1 and sample 2 are shown in table 18.1. Approximately 51% of the respondents were males; 30% were Caucasian, and 30% were Asian, and they were 18 years old at the time of the first questionnaire. Of the friends and acquaintances they described, 65% were from the high school years and 35% were added during the first semester in college. All matched the respondents in gender and age.

At the time of the initial questionnaire, when friends and acquaintances were initially described, respondents were communicating with them approximately 60 times per month, or roughly twice a day. Participants communicated most with those they felt closest to. The contemporaneous Pearson correlation between overall communication with a partner and closeness to that partner, measured on the same questionnaire, was .41, $p < .001$.

About half of this communication was conducted in person (28 times per month), with phone (15 times per month) and IM (15 times per month) occurring more frequently than e-mail communication (nine times per month). Surprisingly, face-to-face communication predicted closeness less well than phone, e-mail, or IM communication: The contemporaneous correlation between closeness and communication frequency was .10 for in-person communication, .41 for phone communication, .35 for electronic mail, and .39 for IM. Presumably, this is because phone, e-mail, and IM communication

Table 18.1. Variable means at initial time period.

Variable	Mean	SE	N	Test–retest reliability (Pearson r)
Respondent gender (% male)[a]	51.1	49.5	585	
Respondent age[a]	18.8	0.8	585	
Respondent race (% white)[a]	53.8	50.0	585	
Respondent race (% Asian)[a]	31.4	45.3	585	
Partner age[b]	19.2	14.5	2533	
Partner gender (% male)[b]	51.2	42.9	2533	
Added friend in college (%)[b]	35.2	47.9	2533	
Frequency of communication overall[b,c]	60.7	47.3	2526	.49
Frequency of communication in-person[b,c]	28.1	21.6	2526	.47
Frequency of communication by phone[b,c]	15.2	19.1	2526	.46
Frequency of communication by e-mail[b,c]	9.1	14.8	2526	.46
Frequency of communication by IM[b,c]	15.4	21.0	2526	.44
Psychological closeness[b]	3.99	1.00	2526	.65

[a]Measured at the initial questionnaire.
[b]Measured when a partner first enters the data set (questionnaire 1 for high school partners and questionnaire 2 for college partners).
[c]Communication episodes per month.
[d]For time-varying variables, communication and closeness.

is primarily volitional (i.e., at least one party intended the communication to occur), whereas in-person communication is to a degree involuntary. Whether they wanted to or not, participants talked to each other when they were in the same place (possibly to avoid being perceived as rude).

All communication dropped over time, with the largest declines for face-to-face communication.

This supports our hypothesis that geographic distance affects the patterns of communication in relationships (see fig. 18.1).

Table 18.1 also shows the intertemporal stability of the time-varying measures: communication frequency and psychological closeness. These were computed by taking the Pearson correlation between the same variable measured on adjacent

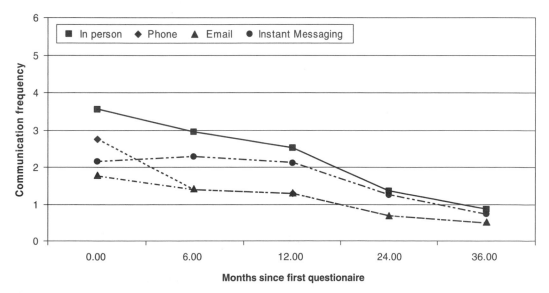

Figure 18.1. Decline in communication over time by medium.

questionnaires. The intertemporal stability is moderate. Correlations for the communication measures range from .44 to .49. Because the response rate to the questionnaires dropped over time, this stability measure is most heavily influenced by questionnaires early in the study. Because one might expect most change in communication and relationships to occur during this period, this was also the period that we sampled at 6-month intervals rather than yearly intervals.

The closeness that respondents expressed toward their partners also declined across time (see fig. 18.2). Table 18.2 shows moderate stability in the measure of psychological closeness, with the test–retest correlations being .65.

Predicting Psychological Closeness

Table 18.2 describes hierarchical linear growth models, predicting psychological closeness with a partner from respondent characteristics, partner characteristics, time, and overall communication frequency. In these models, we standardized the psychological closeness variable, with a mean of zero and a standard deviation of one. Thus we interpret the coefficients as the extent to which a unit increase in an independent variable is associated with psychological closeness, as measured in standard deviation units.

Model 1 examines the associations of psychological closeness with stable characteristics of both respondents and partners and time. Older respondents reported feeling less close to their partners than younger respondents felt to their partners (and older respondents felt less close to older partners). In addition, respondents reported feeling moderately closer to their high school friends than to the ones they met in college (by .3 standard deviation units). The highly reliable negative coefficient for time confirms the pattern seen in figure 18.2: respondents' closeness to their partners declines with time. On average, closeness to these friends and acquaintances declines a fifth of a standard deviation per year. The nonsignificant coefficient for the time-by-partner interaction that was added in college indicates that closeness diminishes approximately equally with time both for high school and college friends, even though participants felt moderately closer to their high school than college friends.

Model 2 in table 18.2 adds the overall frequency of communication to the model. The coefficient for lagged communication indicates that respondents felt closer to partners with whom they had more communication in the previous time period. Because communication frequency is measured on a log scale, the coefficient means that respondents report feeling approximately 8% of a standard deviation unit closer to partners with whom they communicate twice as frequently. The positive time-by-communication frequency interaction indicates that the decline in psychological closeness is less for

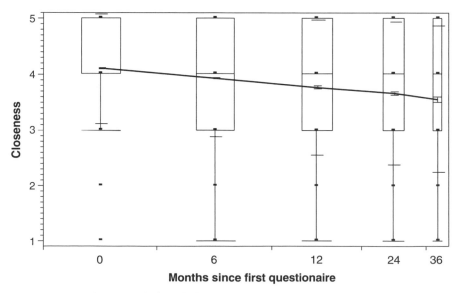

Figure 18.2. Decline in psychological closeness over time.

Table 18.2. Predicting psychological closeness from respondent and partner characteristics, overall communication, and time.

	Model 1				Model 2			
Effect	Estimate	SE	DF	Pr > |t|	Estimate	SE	DF	Pr > |t|
Intercept	−0.058	0.099	435		−0.506	0.120	435	***
Respondent gender (0 = female; 1 = male)	−0.050	0.061	435		−0.061	0.059	435	
Respondent age	−0.070	0.032	435	*	−0.072	0.031	435	*
Respondent white	0.057	0.091	435		0.049	0.088	435	
Respondent Asian	0.129	0.097	435		0.101	0.094	435	
Partner added in college (0 = no; 1 = year)	−0.365	0.067	2672	***	−0.354	0.065	2662	***
Partner gender (0 = female; 1 = male)	−0.058	0.042	2672		−0.040	0.040	2662	
Partner & respondent are same gender	0.416	0.084	2672	***	0.424	0.080	2662	***
Partner age	−0.008	0.004	2672		−0.004	0.004	2662	
Time (years since partner entered analysis)	−0.223	0.025	2672	***	−0.205	0.056	2662	***
Time × partner added in college	0.056	0.056	2672		0.046	0.056	2662	
Overall communication frequency, previous period (log)					0.079	0.015	2662	***
Time × communication frequency (lagged)					0.027	0.013	2662	*

*$p < .05$; **$p < .01$; ***$p < .001$.

partners with whom respondents communicate with more. Doubling communication with a partner reduces the decline in closeness to that person by about 13% (ratio of the coefficients .207/.205).

To predict psychological closeness, table 18.3 decomposes the overall frequency of communication into the modalities through which it occurs. We use the same analysis framework as in table 18.2 (model 2), except that we include the communication frequency for the four communication modalities in place of overall communication frequency. The coefficients for the main effects of the communication are in table 18.3, model 3; all are positive and significantly greater than zero. This pattern indicates that respondents feel closer to friends with whom they communicate using each of the four modalities. Differences in the size of the coefficients are instructive. The coefficient for phone communication is twice is high as the coefficients for e-mail and IM, the two computer-mediated communication modalities. These results indicate that respondents are more likely to talk by phone to those with whom they feel closer than to communicate to those same partners with either e-mail or IM. The two computer-mediated communication coefficients in turn are twice as high as that for in-person communication, again reflecting the frequent nonvolitional nature of in-person communication.

Model 4 in table 18.3 adds the time-by-communication interactions to examine the asso-

ciation of communication with changes in closeness. The positive coefficients for both e-mail and IM indicate that communication using these modalities reduces the decline in closeness. Doubling e-mail communication with a partner is associated with a 34% reduction in the decline in closeness with that partner (.037/.107). Similarly, doubling IM communication with a partner is associated with an 18% reduction in the decline in closeness with that partner (.020/.107).

Predicting Communication

The longitudinal results in tables 18.2 and 18.3 are consistent with the claim that communication prevents declines in psychological closeness. However, to examine the causal direction in more detail, we conducted supplementary analyses predicting changes in communication from closeness. Table 18.4 presents results from hierarchical linear growth models that predict frequency of communication (in the log scale) based on time, psychological closeness at the prior time period, and their interactions. Stable characteristics of the respondents and their partners were included as control variables. Overall, during their college years, respondents communicated 175% more with partners whom they added during college than with their high school friends. This difference depended on the media that respondents selected. The gap was larger for in-person

Table 18.3. Predicting psychological closeness from respondent and partner characteristics, communication over different communication modalities, and time.

Effect	Model 1				Model 2			
	Estimate	SE	DF	Pr > |t|	Estimate	SE	DF	Pr > |t|
Intercept	−0.465	0.106	420	***	−0.448	0.109	420	***
Respondent gender (% male)	−0.030	0.063	420		−0.029	0.063	420	
Respondent age	−0.080	0.033	420	*	−0.080	0.033	420	*
Respondent white	0.078	0.094	420		0.075	0.094	420	
Respondent Asian	0.104	0.101	420		0.105	0.101	420	
Partner added in college (0 = no; 1 = year)	−0.446	0.081	2109	***	−0.475	0.085	2105	***
Partner gender (0 = female; 1 = male)	−0.028	0.041	2109		−0.025	0.041	2105	
Partner & respondent are same gender	0.443	0.083	2109	***	0.426	0.083	2105	***
Partner age	0.000	0.004	2109		0.000	0.004	2105	
Time (years since partner entered analysis)	−0.079	0.031	2109	*	−0.107	0.036	2105	**
Time × partner added in college	0.091	0.061	2109		0.134	0.067	2105	*
In-person communication frequency (log)	0.017	0.010	2109	***	0.035	0.017	2105	*
Phone communication frequency (log)	0.074	0.010	2109	***	0.082	0.017	2105	***
E-mail communication frequency (log)	0.038	0.009	2109	***	0.009	0.016	2105	
Instant messaging communication frequency (log)	0.039	0.008	2109	***	0.022	0.013	2105	
Time × in-person communication frequency (log)					−0.027	0.016	2105	
Time × phone communication frequency (log)					−0.010	0.018	2105	
Time × e-mail communication frequency (log)					0.037	0.015	2105	*
Time × instant messaging communication frequency (log)					0.020	0.011	2105	

*p < .05; **p < .01; ***p < .001.

communication and phone communication than for e-mail and IM.

Consistent with figure 18.2, the analyses show that overall communication drops with time by about 43%, and that this effect is larger for in-person than for other types of communication. Consistent with the correlations between closeness and communication frequency that were reported previously, the multivariate analyses show that students communicate more across all modalities with partners with whom they felt closer in the previous time period.

The interactions between time and psychological closeness are the most interesting results used to assess the direction of the causal link between communication and closeness. The nonsignificant interaction between time and psychological closeness for overall communication indicates that respondents' preexisting closeness with a partner does not mitigate the drop in communication. The time and psychological closeness interactions were nonsignificant for both e-mail and IM, again indicating that respondents' preexisting closeness with a partner does not mitigate the drop in computer-mediated communication. The positive time and

psychological closeness interaction for in-person communication indicates that prior closeness mitigates the drop in face-to-face communication. We speculate that this result occurs because students make an effort to see only their closest friends when they return from school for breaks or summer vacation. In contrast, the negative interaction for phone communication indicates that the drop in calls is especially steep for partners with whom the respondent had previously felt very close. We speculate that financial costs force students to refrain from calling once-close friends—people whom they called frequently when they lived in the same town and attended the same school.

Discussion

Our findings indicate that when students move from home to college, they reduce both their communication and their closeness with their high school friends—their sense of psychological connection. This same effect occurs with new friends that students made during their first semester in college as

Table 18.4. Predicting communication frequency from respondent and partner characteristics, psychological closeness, and time.

Effect	Overall communication (log)				In-person communication (log)				Phone communication (log)				E-mail communication (log)				Instant messaging communication (log)			
	Estimate	SE	DF	p	Estimate	SE	DF	p	Estimate	SE	DF	p	Estimate	SE	DF	p	Estimate	SE	DF	p
Intercept	1.705	0.246	436	***	−0.349	0.248	435	***	−2.008	0.249	436	***	−0.657	0.272	436	*	−1.165	0.329	435	*
Respondent gender (% male)	0.091	0.093	436		0.039	0.091	435		−0.043	0.097	436		−0.144	0.112	436		0.291	0.128	435	*
Respondent age	0.056	0.049	436		−0.005	0.048	435		0.092	0.051	436		0.195	0.058	436	***	−0.038	0.067	435	
Respondent white	0.276	0.140	436	*	0.280	0.137	435	*	0.073	0.146	436		0.165	0.168	436		0.446	0.192	435	*
Respondent Asian	0.034	.149	436		0.129	0.147	435		−0.099	0.155	436		−0.091	0.179	436		0.461	0.206	435	*
Partner added in college (0 = no; 1 = year)	1.756	0.113	2969	***	4.361	0.124	2714	***	1.176	.114	2954	***	0.404	0.121	2961	***	0.547	0.153	2842	***
Partner gender (0 = female; 1 = male)	−0.037	0.064	2969		0.070	0.067	2714		−0.074	0.066	2954		−0.254	0.069	2961	***	0.013	0.090	2842	
Partner and respondent same gender	−0.109	0.129	2969		−0.129	0.134	2714		−0.045	0.133	2954		0.025	0.139	2961		−0.180	0.181	2842	
Partner age	−0.021	0.007	2969	**	−0.002	0.007	2714	**	−0.006	0.007	2954		−0.006	0.007	2961		−0.060	0.009	2842	***
Time (years since partner entered analysis)	−0.616	0.127	2969	***	−0.435	0.126	2714	***	0.375	0.125	2954	**	−0.231	0.134	2961		−0.509	0.162	2842	**
Time × partner added in college	−1.115	0.090	2969	***	−2.215	0.094	2714	***	−0.778	0.090	2954	***	−0.413	0.096	2961	***	−0.524	0.118	2842	***
Psychological closeness (lagged)	0.466	0.050	2969	***	0.188	0.051	2714	***	0.666	0.050	2954	***	0.469	0.053	2961	***	0.574	0.066	2842	***
Time × psychological closeness	0.035	0.033	2969		0.065	0.033	2714	*	−0.133	0.033	2954	***	−0.044	0.035	2961		0.002	0.043	2842	

$*p < .05$; $**p < .01$; $***p < .001$.

they got further into their college career. The purpose of this chapter was to see how these factors were causally related and to assess whether modern telecommunication technologies change the risk to relationships that distance and time can introduce.

To summarize the main results, longitudinal analyses show that although psychological closeness to high school and college friends declines with time, this decline is less steep among pairs who communicate more. This pattern is consistent with Duck's hypothesis (1998) that communication can mitigate the centripetal forces causing social relationships to split apart. Surprisingly, when we looked at the influence of different communication modalities, communication by e-mail and IM seem to retard the drop in closeness, but communication in person and by phone do not. This pattern of interactions occurs even though phone communication is the technology that best predicts psychological closeness at any given time.

Why do computer-mediated communications seem to guard against the disruption of social relationships more than in-person and phone communication for these students? This finding is inconsistent with some of the literature reviewed in the introduction, which focused on the media's intrinsic properties. Both media richness and social presence imply that communicating by phone would be most useful for guarding against threats to relationships.

Why does closeness drop least among partners who regularly use e-mail and IM? One possibility is that frequency of communication for computer-mediated media is less affected by distance than communication by phone. The technological advantages of computer-mediated communications may be irrelevant in mitigating distance as a factor; rather, this advantage may simply be the result of government regulations and corporate marketing decisions. Unlike traditional long-distance phone providers, Internet service providers do not charge more to send data packets across the country than across town. Moreover, pricing schemes used by long distance carriers are not fixed. This may change, however, if Internet phone technologies become more popular because the Internet is regulated less by the Federal Communications Commission and state agencies than are conventional phone services (e.g., Federal Communications Commission, 2003).

One strength of our research is the use of longitudinal data, which enabled us to follow relationships over time. As a result, we were not constrained by the ambiguities inherent in cross-sectional analyses of how strong ties were at a single point in time. For example, the cross-sectional results indicate that communication by phone is the strongest predictor of psychological closeness with a communication partner. This result is consistent with predictions from media richness and social presence theories; that is, that richer and more interactive media will better support social relationships. However, the cross-sectional results are also consistent with an alternative explanation: students primarily call people with whom they feel close, whereas they are more profligate with their computer-mediated communication. The longitudinal results tell a different story. They show that communication over a computer is associated with less erosion in social relationships, whereas communication by phone is not. Our conclusion from this pattern of results is that communication frequency, not communication quality, is the important element that sustains relationships; we also conclude that for economic reasons, the frequency of communication by phone is especially sensitive to distance, whereas communication by computer is not.

One weakness in this research is the lack of an identifiable mechanism by which different communication technologies had varied effects on relationship maintenance. It is likely that norms of communication technology use contribute to how using that communication will influence the relationship. For example, the norm among some high school students is to congregate on IM at specified times in the evening to "hang out" with friends, whereas college students tend to make themselves available whenever their computers are connected to a network. These norms of availability can shape how this computer-mediated communication influences relationship maintenance. Future research would benefit from measuring communication norms. Students may believe that regular use of a particular media, regardless of content, can sustain a relationship at the desired level of closeness and support.

Equally important, the communication content that is exchanged over different media will undoubted influence how a communication change influences relationships. As Lacohee and Anderson (2001) note, phone conversations are often used to exchange social support, especially among women (see also Boneva & Kraut, 2003). In contrast, as

Boneva and colleagues (chapter 14) note, much of IM communication is used for exchanging chitchat, and social support is rare with this medium.

An obvious issue raised by the discussion of maintaining personal relationships during the transition from high school to college is whether or not there are academic consequences. Are students more likely to stay in college when relationships are maintained successfully? Do students perform better in their courses? Is college more satisfying for them than high school? We do not have answers to these questions but would speculate that personal relationships contribute to a positive quality of life for students in college.

For students who move off to college, the ties with their high school friends and the friends that they make their first semester in college are fragile. On average, these relationships decline with time. Consistent with an enactment model of relationships, however, communicating with these friends prevents the relationships from declining as swiftly as they otherwise would. Communication seems to inject energy into a relationship and prevents it from going dormant. In contrast, simply feeling close to these friends does not prevent the communication from declining.

E-mail and IM seem to be the telecommunication technologies that are especially useful for maintaining friendships among young adults. The utility of these technologies may not stem from their intrinsic features—for example, their interactivity, media richness, the effort needed to type messages, or their ability to convey social presence. Rather, we suspect that arbitrary economic decisions may be more important. Unlike the phone, which costs more when talking longer to someone farther away, pricing for computer-mediated communication does not depend on either the length of a message or the distance it must travel.

Note

1. Response labels changed slightly across questionnaire administrations. In the first two administrations of Sample 1, the responses options were (0) never, (1) less often, (2) monthly, (3) biweekly, (4) weekly, (5) daily, and (6) many times per day, whereas in all other administrations, they were (0) never, (1) every few months, (2) every few weeks, (3) 1–2 days a week, (4) 3–5 days a week, (5) about once a day, and (6) several times a day.

References

Allan, G. (1979). *A sociology of friendship and kinship.* London: George Allen & Unwin.

Berg, J., & Clark, M. (1986). Differences in social exchange between intimate and other relationships: Gradually evolving or quickly apparent? In Derlega, V., & Winstead, B. (Ed.), *Friendship and social interaction* (pp. 101–128). New York: Springer.

Boneva, B., & Kraut, R. (2003). Email, gender and personal relationships. In Wellman, B., & Haythornthwaite, C., (Eds.), *The Internet in everyday life* (pp. 372–403). Malden, MA: Blackwell.

Bossard, J. (1932). Residential propinquity as a factor in marriage selection. *American Journal of Sociology, 38,* 219–224.

Bryk, A., & Raudenbush, S. (1992). *Hierarchical linear models.* Newbury Park, CA: Sage.

Burt, R. (1986). A note on sociometric order in the general social survey network data. *Social Networks, 8,* 149–174.

Canary, D., & Stafford, L. (1994). Maintaining relationships through strategic and routine interactions. In D. Canary, & Stafford, L. (Ed.), *Communication and relationship maintenance* (pp. 3–22). New York: Academic Press.

Clark, H., & Brennan, S. (1991). Grounding in communication. In Resnick, L., & Levine, J., & Teasley, S. (Eds.), *Perspectives on socially shared cognition* (pp. 127–149). Washington, DC: American Psychological Association.

Cummings, J., Butler, B., & Kraut, R. (2002). The quality of online social relationships. *Communications of the ACM, 45*(7), 103–108.

Daft, R., & Lengel, R. (1984). Information richness: A new approach to managerial behavior and organizational design. *Research in Organizational Behavior, 6,* 191–233.

Dennis, A. R., & Kinney, S. T. (1998). Testing media richness theory in the new media: The effects of cues, feedback, and task equivocality. *Information Systems Research, 9*(3), 256–274.

Duck, S. (1998). *Human relationships* (3rd ed.). Thousand Oaks, CA: Sage.

Duck, S., Rutt, D., Hurst, M., & Strejc, H. (1991). Some evident truths about conversations in everyday relationships: All communications are not created equal. *Human Communication Research, 18*(2l), 228–267.

Federal Communications Commission. (2003). *FCC to begin Internet telephony proceedings* (vol. 2004). Washington, DC: Author.

Festinger, L., Schacter, S., & Back, K. (1950). *Social pressures in informal groups.* Palo Alto, CA: Stanford University Press.

Fischer, C. (1982). *To dwell among friends*. Chicago: University of Chicago Press.

Fischer, C. S. (1992). *America calling: A social history of the phone to 1940*. Berkeley: University of California Press.

Kraut, R. E., Lewis, S. H., & Swezey, L. W. (1982). Listener responsiveness and the coordination of conversation. *Journal of Personality & Social Psychology, 43*(4), 718–731.

Lacohee, H., & Anderson, B. (2001). Interacting with the phone. *International Journal of Human-Computer Studies, 54*(5), 665–699.

Leiner, B. M., Cerf, V. G., Clark, D. D., Kahn, R. E., Kleinrock, L., Lynch, D. C., Postel, J., Roberts, L. G., & Wolff, S. (2002). *A brief history of the Internet* (version 3.32). The Internet Society. Retrieved February 10, 2004, from http://www.isoc.org/internet/history/brief.shtm.

Mayer, M. (1977). The phone and the uses of time. In d. S. Pool, I. (Ed.), *The social impact of the phone* (pp. 225–246). Cambridge, MA: MIT Press.

Newcomb, T. (1961). *The acquaintance process*. New York: Holt, Rinehart, & Winston.

Parks, M., & Roberts, L. (1998). Making MOOsic: The development of personal relationships on line and a comparison to their off-line counterparts, *Journal of Social and Personal Relationships, 15,* 517–537.

Postmes, T., Spears, R., & Lea, M. (1998). Breaching or building social boundaries? SIDE-effects of computer-mediated communication. *Communication Research, 25*(6), 689–715.

Postmes, T., Spears, R., & Lea, M. (2000). The formation of group norms in computer-mediated communication. *Human Communication Research, 26*(3), 341–371.

Rafaeli, S., & Sudweeks, F. (1997). Networked interactivity. *Journal of Computer Mediated Communication, 2*(4).

Rose, S. M. (1984). How friendships end: Patterns among young adults. *Journal of Social & Personal Relationships, 1*(3), 267–277.

Short, J., Williams, E., & Christie, B. (1976). *The social psychology of telecommunications*. New York: Wiley.

Singer, J., & Willett, J. (2003). *Applied longitudinal data analysis: Modeling change and event occurrence*. New York: Oxford University Press.

Sproull, L., & Kiesler, S. (1991). *Connections: New ways of working in the networked organization*. Cambridge, MA: MIT Press.

Walther, J. B. (1995). Relational aspects of computer-mediated communication: Experimental observations over time. *Organization Science, 6*(2), 186–203.

Walther, J. B. (2002). Time effects in computer-mediated groups: Past, present, and future. In Hinds, P., & Kiesler, S. (Eds.), *Distributed work* (pp. 235–257). Cambridge, MA: MIT Press.

Walther, J. B., & Parks, M. R. (2002). Cues filtered out, cues filtered in: Computer-mediated communication and relationships. In Knapp, M., & Daly, J. A. (Eds.), *Handbook of interpersonal communication* (3rd ed., pp. 529–563). Thousand Oaks, CA: Sage.

Wellman, B. (1992). Which types of ties and networks provide which types of support? In Lawler E., Markovsky, B., Ridgeway, C., & Walker, H. (Eds.), *Advances in group processes* (pp. 207–235). Greenwich, CT: JAI Press.

Wheeler, L., & Nezlek, J. (1977). Sex differences in social participation. *Journal of Personality and Social Psychology, 35*(10), 742–754.

Katelyn Y. A. McKenna

and Gwendolyn Seidman

Considering the Interactions

The Effects of the Internet
on Self and Society

People have been interacting with others by means of computer-mediated communication for more than 20 years, and yet the effects of such interaction for the individual, for work and social relationships, and for society are not entirely clear. Research on the social consequences of the Internet is still in its relative infancy and what we know—and what we think we know—about the effects of online interaction is undergoing a constant state of revision and qualification. Indeed, the assessment of the effects of this communication technology has sometimes seemed to change as quickly as the technology itself has advanced. A brief examination of the burgeoning research on computer-mediated interaction makes one conclusion quite clear, however: researchers have advanced well beyond the initial stage of overly simplistic "main effect" accounts. Just as there is no longer an "average" Internet user (e.g., Howard, Rainie, & Jones, 2001), simple main effects of Internet use appear to be few and far between.

Research in recent years has taken a more discriminating approach. From a wide variety of disciplines and theoretical perspectives, and using the full spectrum of available methodological tools, research has focused on the differential effects that can occur depending on the population under study, individual differences, and varying situational contexts.

In this chapter, we discuss the major findings to date of our program of research examining online group processes, the expression of self, and relationship formation and maintenance over the Internet. In doing so, we attempt to place our findings within the context of other research in these areas. The chapter is organized around two main sections, focusing first on the interactions between individual differences and online communication (the person × Internet interaction), and then on group-level interactions (the group × Internet interaction).

A secondary aim of this chapter is to synthesize the relevant existing research into a coherent framework for understanding what conditions and confluence of factors are most likely to produce particular outcomes. For instance, anonymity has been shown to produce antinormative behavior online (e.g., Kiesler, Siegel, & McGuire, 1984); it has also been shown to produce even stronger normative effects online than in face-to-face situations (e.g., Spears, Postmes, Lea & Wolbert, 2002). Yet other studies have shown that being identifiable rather than anonymous increases participants' group-normative behavior (e.g., Douglas & McGarty,

2001). These findings appear to contradict one another until moderating and mediating factors are taken into account.

The Person × Internet Interaction

The particular aspects of the Internet interaction situation interact with the goals, motivations, and personal characteristics of the individuals involved, producing effects on psychological and interpersonal outcomes. People have reasons and motivations to use the Internet just as they do other forms of communication and entertainment media. In the realm of communications research, the influential "uses and gratification" theory (Blumler & Katz, 1974) would suggest that the particular purposes of the individuals within the communication setting solely determine the outcome of the interaction, regardless of the particular features of the communication channel in which the interaction takes place. (Spears and colleagues [2002] discuss the complementary "social science" version of this theory as applied to the Internet.) According to this viewpoint, if the motivation or goal for using the media is known, the outcome can be reliably predicted—in other words, there is a "main effect" of the particular goal or motivation, and thus outcomes will hold for any and all users for whom that goal is relevant.

Yet, beginning with early research by Hiltz and Turoff (e.g., Hiltz, 1976; Hiltz, Johnson & Turoff, 1986; Turoff, 1976), the distinctive characteristics of electronic communication have long (relatively speaking) been shown to produce effects on users. Indeed, the pioneering technological and engineering models of computer-mediated research propose that it is these particular features (such as anonymity and a lack of physical presence) that are responsible for any effects on the users of the medium. A good example of this is Sproull and Kiesler's (1985) reduced social cues model. According to this perspective, the reduced available social cues in computer-mediated communication produce an impoverished communication experience, resulting in a deindividuating effect on the individuals involved, and thus inducing behavior that is more self-centered and less socially regulated than usual, such as an increase in hostile "flaming" behavior and a tendency for members of all status levels to contribute equally to the discussion. This limited band-width model assumes that the "channel" effects of Internet communication are the same for all users and across all contexts—in other words, it predicts a "main effect" of communication channel.

As it turns out, both the uses and gratification approach and the engineering approach each explain some of the effects of electronic communication, but neither, alone, is able to fully predict or account for the outcomes of social interaction that take place over the Internet. Thus, a third and more recent approach has arisen. This approach focuses on the interaction[1] between features of the Internet communication setting and the particular goals and needs of the communicators, as well as the social context of the interaction setting (see McKenna & Bargh 2000; Bargh 2002; Spears et al. 2002). This interaction perspective acknowledges that the special qualities of Internet social interaction do have an impact on both the social interaction itself and its outcomes, but it also argues that the effect can be quite different depending on individual differences and the social context.

In the text that follows, we focus on three individual difference variables that interact with the particular, unique aspects of the Internet communication situation: loneliness and social anxiety, the aspects or versions of self expressed on the Internet, and motivations for using the Internet. There are, of course, many other individual differences that interact with the electronic communication situation in a variety of ways. We focus our discussion on these three in particular, as they are among the most researched topics in online communication to date.

Loneliness and Social Anxiety

What effects Internet use and online interaction may have on introverted or lonely individuals is currently a question for researchers. For instance, do already introverted and lonely individuals become more lonely and isolated if they use the Internet, or do they become less so? (Note that this is a different question than whether or not using the Internet causes previously nonlonely people to become lonely and socially isolated).

Ameliorating Social Anxiety?
Socially anxious and shy individuals have more difficulty forming social bonds with others, and so often social anxiety and loneliness go hand in hand.

Not only do those who suffer from social anxiety feel less likeable and accepted than their nonanxious counterparts, but they actually tend to be liked and accepted less by others (e.g., Leary, 1983). However, many of the situational factors that can foster feelings of social anxiety (e.g., having to respond on the spot, talking to someone face-to-face) are absent in online interactions. One might expect, then, that interacting with others online would place introverted individuals on more equal footing, allowing them to interact more comfortably and with less reticence than they generally would in a face-to-face situation.

That is what was found in a recent laboratory study examining small group interaction among socially anxious and nonanxious participants (McKenna, Buffardi, & Seidman, 2005b). Seventy-five undergraduate students at New York University were preselected for this study on the basis of their responses on the Interaction Anxiousness Scale (Leary, 1983). Only those who scored at the high and low extremes of the scale were recruited for the study, and they were randomly assigned to interact in groups of three either face-to-face or in a specially created Internet chat room. Immediately following the interaction, participants assessed how they felt during the interaction, as well as how accepted and included they felt they were by the other group members.

Consistent with their responses on the Interaction Anxiousness Scale, socially anxious individuals in the face-to-face condition reported feeling anxiety, shyness, and discomfort during the group

interaction, whereas the opposite was true for nonanxious participants. In marked contrast, interacting online produced significantly different results. Participants reported feeling significantly less anxious, shy, and uncomfortable and more accepted by their fellow group members than did those who interacted face-to-face—but these effects were wholly qualified by differences in levels of social anxiety. That is, our extroverted participants felt equally comfortable, outgoing, and accepted interacting online and in person. For those experiencing high levels of social anxiety, however, the mode of communication proved pivotal to their feelings of comfort, shyness, and acceptance. Moreover, the self-reports of the socially anxious participants in the online condition on these measures were virtually identical to those of nonanxious participants in the face-to-face condition (see fig. 19.1).

Although the extremely shy participants in this lab study felt like nonanxious extroverts during their short online interaction, the question remains whether these feelings of heightened communication efficacy would result, over time and repeated experience, in lasting increases in self-efficacy. Research in self-efficacy suggests that such confident and successful exchanges would eventually result in increased feelings of comfort and confidence about one's ability to engage in social interactions, at least online (e.g., Bandura, 1977). However, this raises an important issue: If those with high levels of social anxiety find online interaction to be so much more comfortable, will they begin to eschew the more anxiety-provoking experience of interacting face-to-

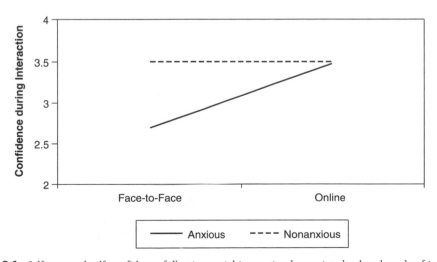

Figure 19.1. Self-reported self-confidence following social interaction by anxiety level and mode of interaction.

face with others, withdrawing even further socially? Or will they perhaps become more dissatisfied with their existing face-to-face relationships? The end result for either of these scenarios might well be increased feelings of loneliness and isolation.

Intensifying Social Anxiety or Loneliness?

A recent study by Kraut et al. (2002) suggests that increased loneliness is indeed the case for some. In a year-long study of families in the Pittsburgh area who had recently purchased their first computer, the researchers found that introverts may not fare as well as others once they go online. For both introverted and extroverted participants, using the Internet more led to larger increases in their local and distant social circles, and both groups reported increasing the amount of face-to-face contact with family and friends. And yet, despite forging new friendships in the Pittsburgh area and further afield, and despite spending more "in person" time with existing family and friends, these introverted participants reported becoming more lonely. Furthermore, although greater Internet use was associated with increased community involvement for extroverts, it resulted in declines in community involvement for introverts.

On the face of it, these findings appear contradictory: Why would using a communication medium that seems to increase one's social network and that is associated with increased face-to-face contact with close others make an individual more lonely? Introverted participants in the study reported having significantly less perceived social support than did their outgoing counterparts—a finding that is in line with previous research showing that extraversion is predictive of social support (e.g., Von Draas & Siegler, 1997). It is thus possible that increasing one's contact with friends and family members whom one does not see as particularly supportive may exacerbate one's feelings of loneliness. It is also possible that, for those who are introverted, the benefits generally associated with increasing one's social network take longer to accrue. Other findings for the introverted and the lonely are not as bleak. McKenna, Green, and Gleason (2002) conducted a study with nearly 600 randomly selected Internet newsgroup participants. We found that those who are socially anxious or lonely in traditional, face-to-face interaction settings are more likely than the nonanxious and friend-rich to feel better able to express important aspects of

self online that they are commonly blocked from expressing in their everyday lives. That is (and as is discussed in more detail in the next section), they felt better able to express their true selves over the Internet than in their nonelectronic interactions with family and friends.

For the lonely and the nonlonely, the socially anxious and the extroverted, expressing the true self more online resulted in the development of close and meaningful relationships there. When asked about their closest online relationship, more than 50% of all participants reported bringing this relationship into their face-to-face lives. Looking only at those who were socially anxious, more than 40% did so. The majority of participants (68%) reported that Internet use had increased their social circles. A 2-year follow-up with the participants in this study found significant decreases in feelings of both loneliness and social anxiety, and these decreases were not qualified by initial levels of either social anxiety or loneliness.[2] In other words, participants who were socially anxious and those who were lonely reported equivalent decreases on these measures as did those who were not socially anxious and those who were friend-rich. Of course, there may be many other reasons that Internet use may have caused these participants to become less lonely over the 2-year period. However, when explicitly asked to assess the effect that using the Internet had on feelings of loneliness, only 6% of participants reported that they felt lonelier as a result of using the Internet. Forty-seven percent thought that their Internet use had reduced their feelings of loneliness.

It is important to note, however, that there were no main effects of either social anxiety or loneliness on the formation of close online relationships. Believing that one can express more of one's real self on the Internet plays a crucial role in the formation of close relationships there, which may lead to a reduction in one's loneliness (see the following section). Indeed, for those who initially reported high levels of social anxiety, the development of a close Internet relationship was marginally predictive of decreased loneliness 2 years later ($B = .30, p = .06$). For both the introverts and the extroverts in our sample, expressing more of their true selves online was also associated with decreased loneliness ($B = .25, p < .01$). In another study, Hamburger and Ben-Artzi (2002) found that although lonely individuals do seem to use the Internet more, Internet use does not seem to have a general tendency to increase their feelings of loneliness.

Yet another factor comes into play when discussing the relationship between Internet use and loneliness: Not everyone uses the Internet in the same way. The Internet can be used for research, e-mail, online chatting, shopping, playing games, or simple "Web-surfing," to name a few activities. Some of these activities are nonsocial in nature (e.g., "Web-surfing," single-player online games), whereas others can be entirely social (e.g., e-mail, chatting). It may well be the case that using the Internet only or mainly for nonsocial activities would have the effect of increasing one's sense of isolation and loneliness. Whom one chooses to interact with online, along with one's motivations or purpose for the interaction, will also have moderating effects. For instance, Gross, Juvonen, and Gable (2002) found that when adolescents experience rejection from a peer or peers on any given day at school, when they get home and go online they generally elect to chat with strangers rather than the school friends who are also available online. Importantly, following an instance of peer rejection at school, these adolescents are seeking to engage in "one-time-only" interactions with strangers online and are not looking to form any kind of continuing relationship with them.

Taken together, the results of these studies seem to indicate that there is no simple, clear-cut answer; that there is no main effect of Internet use on social anxiety or loneliness. Rather, outcomes will depend on the way an introverted or lonely individual uses the Internet, the quality of the relationships he or she forms and maintains, and importantly, the kind of self-expression in which he or she engages online.

Aspects of the Self Expressed Online

Facilitation of Self-expression

As Turkle (1995) first noted, the Internet is a ripe venue for individuals to explore and express aspects of self, especially those that tend to go unexpressed in everyday life. There are two features of the Internet that particularly facilitate such self-expression. First is the ability to be relatively anonymous[3] in one's online interactions. This sense of anonymity can engender a sense of freedom from the constraints and expectations placed on a person by

those who know him or her. It also reduces the risks and costs of incurring social sanctions for what is said and done in the online environment. Research by McLeod, Baron, Martie, & Yoon (1997), for instance, has found that individuals are more likely to express marginal beliefs online when they are anonymous, presumably because there is less risk associated with revealing this undesirable information. McLeod and colleagues (1997) find that expressing a minority opinion within the context of an online workgroup results in the expresser of such opinions becoming a less influential member of the group (see the section on the group × interaction); however, as is discussed below, a quite different process unfolds in other social contexts online.

As Pennebaker (1989), Derlega, Metts, Petronio, and Margulis (1993), and others have noted, there can be very real costs to disclosing negative or taboo aspects of oneself to others, and even to one's family and friends. But it is not only the expression of negative or socially stigmatized self-aspects that can evoke such costs. Even expressing socially acceptable (positive) behaviors and opinions, if they do not conform to one's usual repertoire, can be met with disapproval or rejection by important members of one's social circle (e.g., Cooley, 1902; Goffman, 1959; Rogers, 1951). Yet, because people have a real need to have others see them as they see themselves (e.g., Gollwitzer, 1986; Swann, 1990), the threat of such sanctions can create tension and conflict for the individual (e.g., Horney, 1946). Concealing or being constrained in the expression of important aspects of self can be psychologically—and even physiologically—costly (e.g., Pennebaker, 1997; Smart & Wegner, 1999).

The potential for anonymous interaction enables a person to express aspects of the self to new partners that he or she is usually barred from expressing, because of these constraints or the fear of social sanctions. Theorists have long held that people possess multiple senses of self: William James (1892 p. 179) noted, "A man has as many social selves as there are individuals who recognize him"; Carl Rogers (1951) famously spoke of the disaccord that often exists between an individual's "true" or inner self and the self he or she actually shows to others publicly; Markus and Nurius (1986) spoke of the "possible selves" an individual believes he or she could become if so chosen; and Higgins (1987) described "ideal" and "ought" versions of self that a person strives to or feels obligated to express. The theme of these perspectives is the idea that people have alternative senses of self that are distinct from the "actual" or public self that they generally show to others. As is discussed below, we believe that the particular aspects of self that the typical person will be motivated to explore and express over the Internet will be his or her inner or "true" self.

A second unique aspect of the Internet is that it provides people the opportunity to readily find others who share important aspects of self, such as hobbies, beliefs, sexual predilections, and so forth. Nearly every topic and interest imaginable can be found among the tens of thousands of community mailing lists, chat rooms, topical newsgroups, Web site bulletin boards, and the like. Exotic animal owners, coin collectors, and fringe political ideologues can now find kindred spirits on the Internet. This facilitates being able to fully express these important aspects of self with similar others and to have them socially validated (see Howard et al., 2001; McKenna & Bargh, 1998).

Sharing these important aspects of self with similar others has powerful effects on one's identity and self-concept. These effects are so powerful that even if they are socially taboo aspects of self, one is strongly motivated to "come out" about them, for the first time, to close family and friends (McKenna & Bargh, 1998). The Internet is thus a potentially powerful medium by which people can express and explore their inner or true selves and thereby meet social and psychological needs that are not currently being met in everyday life.

The Relational Online Self

The potential identity-transforming nature of the "online self" is not restricted to the socially sanctioned, stigmatized aspects of self. When the true-self concept is active during online interactions there is a greater likelihood of those relationships becoming important aspects of identity. Several contemporary models of the self see it as embedded or linked with our representations of other people, whether it be with the identity-important groups to which we belong (e.g., Tajfel & Turner, 1986; Deaux, 1996) or to the significant individuals in our life (e.g., Baldwin, 1997; Chen & Andersen, 1999). To the extent that relationships with others become defining features of oneself, associational mental connections will tend to form between the self-concept and the representations of those external social entities.

This prediction was tested by McKenna et al. (2002) through structural equation modeling of survey responses provided by hundreds of randomly selected newsgroup members who take part in groups devoted to normative topics (e.g., history, computer science, astronomy, parenting, pet care, and so forth). The critical mediator of whether an individual would form close Internet relationships was his or her responses to a "real me" scale (see Bargh, Fitzsimons, & McKenna, 2002). This scale measured whether or not the participant felt better able to express aspects of self and personality in Internet interactions than in offline social life. McKenna et al. (2002) found that, compared to those who reported feeling more their true, inner selves in traditional social settings, those who felt they expressed more of the "real me" on the Internet were significantly more likely to have formed close and intimate relationships there. Further, they were more likely to have taken steps to integrate those online friends and romantic partners into their face-to-face interaction world. And, as a 2-year follow-up study showed, these close Internet relationships turned out to be remarkably stable and durable over time.

As discussed earlier, social anxiety and loneliness in one's offline life proved to be reliable predictors of who would feel better able to express the true self online and thus form close relationships. However, it was not only the socially anxious or the lonely who did so. The model also held for those who were not socially anxious or lonely but who, nonetheless, felt that their true self was better expressed over the Internet than in their offline interactions.

The Activation and Expression of the "True Self" Online

Two related effects of Internet communication on the average person have been documented: one that facilitates relationship formation on the Internet but is distinct from the effect of locating the true self on the Internet, and the other offering more direct evidence of the role played by the true-self concept. According to a number of theorists (e.g., Derlega et al., 1993; Laurenceau, Barrett, & Pietromonaco, 1998), self-disclosure is an important ingredient in the development of closeness and intimacy, as it entails being able to express and have accepted one's inner or true feelings and personality. It should be the case then that those who consistently present their inner or true selves online should be more likely than others to form close Internet relationships. The fact that people tend to more readily engage in acts of self-disclosure on the Internet has been well-documented (e.g., Joinson, 2001; Levine, 2000; Walther, 1996).

McKenna et al. (2002, study 3) therefore conducted a laboratory experiment to test whether undergraduates who were randomly assigned (in cross-sex pairs) to meet one another for the first time in an Internet chat room would tend to like one another more and develop a closer relationship (although the meeting lasted for only 20 minutes) compared to those assigned to meet face-to-face. In line with predictions, those who met online both liked each other more and felt that they had gotten to know one another better than did those who interacted face-to-face. This effect held when participants met one another twice, once in person and once over the Internet, unaware that it was the same interaction partner in both situations.

There was also a significant correlation between the degree of liking for the partner, conversational quality, and how well the participant felt he or she had gotten to know the other person for those who met over the Internet. However, there were no such correlations in the face-to-face condition. That is, the more participants in the online condition felt certain they knew their partners, felt that they could accurately predict their partner's attitudes, felt that they had moved easily from one topic of conversation to another and had covered a wide range of topics, and felt that they had been able to share intimate or personal things about themselves with the partner, the more they reported liking their partner. Thus, when participants interacted on the Internet—but not when they interacted face-to-face—the quality of the conversation, especially the intimacy and closeness attained, determined liking. In the face-to-face meetings, the quality of the interaction was not associated with liking judgments, consistent with the idea that when people meet in person, it is the more superficial dating features (e.g., physical appearance) that dominate liking and overwhelm other important interpersonal factors.

It is important to note that these effects of liking occurred for participants who had not been preselected for the study on any basis, including whether they located their true selves on the Internet versus in offline life. Along similar lines, Walther (1996, 1997) found that new acquaintances can achieve greater intimacy through online communication than they do in parallel face-to-face interactions. Further research (McKenna, Buffardi, & Seidman, 2005b) has shown, however, that there is an important caveat to the findings of heightened liking in the online vs. off-line interactions with new acquaintances. Although these findings of greater liking online hold for cross-sex pairs, they do not appear to do so for same-sex pairings. Indeed, female–female pairs like one another significantly more when they meet in person and report significantly more suspicion and distrust of new female acquaintances when the interaction takes place online.

The second major effect of online interaction concerns the degree to which the average person's true self becomes more accessible and activated during online versus offline interactions. Bargh et al. (2002) conducted several laboratory experiments to examine the accessibility and activation of the true self, as opposed to the person's actual self-concept (the person they feel they actually are with other people in typical social interactions; see Higgins, 1987), in online versus face-to-face interactions.

In study 1, participants listed the traits or other characteristics that they believe they actually possess and express to others in social settings (the actual self) and, separately, those that they possess and would like to be able to express but are generally unable to do so in social settings (the true self measure). They then interacted with a cross-sex partner either in an Internet chat room or face-to-face. Following the interaction, they privately provided a free response description of their partner. An analysis of variance on the number of matches between the descriptions of one's partner and the partner's own description of his or her actual and true self revealed that participants successfully conveyed more true-self features than actual-self features over the Internet. The opposite was true for participants in the face-to-face condition, who conveyed more actual-self features than true-self features during their interaction.

Study 2 measured the relative activation of the actual versus true self concepts during face-to-face and Internet interactions. Participants again listed the qualities of their actual and true selves and then interacted with another (randomly assigned) participant either online or face-to-face. They then, individually, took part in a speeded self-judgment task on a computer. They were asked to respond as quickly as possible with either the "me" or "not me" key on each trial according to whether they considered the adjective presented to them to be self-descriptive (see Markus, 1977). The actual and true self characteristics given by the participant at the beginning of the study were embedded within a larger list of positive and negative characteristics. Participants were significantly faster to respond to content related to the actual self following a face-to-face interaction, but following an online interaction they were faster to respond to true-self descriptors. That is, content related to the participants' true self was more accessible following an Internet interaction than following a face-to-face interaction, and content related to the actual self was more accessible following a face-to-face interaction than an online interaction.

If it is the case that the average person's true self is more accessible when interacting with new acquaintances on the Internet, that his or her inner qualities are more readily perceived by online partners, and that the Internet facilitates this greater liking for others, then why doesn't everyone who goes online locate the true self on the Internet and form close and intimate relationships there? In part, it may depend on the way in which an individual uses the Internet. For instance, we would not expect new and important online relationships to develop for people who mainly use the Internet to interact with existing family and friends and only rarely or sporadically with people they meet online. It may depend on whether an individual becomes cognizant that he or she is expressing the true self more with others on the Internet than in his or her face-to-face interactions. McKenna, Buffardi, & Seidman (2005b, study 3) conducted a replication and extension of the Bargh et al. (2002) study 2 and found that, although the true self again became more activated and accessible for participants during online versus face-to-face interactions, participants were not consciously aware of it, as indicated by their self-reports when explicitly asked. And finally, it may depend on the degree of felt discrepancy between one's inner and actual self (e.g., Horney, 1946; Rogers, 1951) and the extent to which the true self serves as an important self-guide to one's behavior (e.g., Higgins, 1987). If the true self is an important guide to one's behavior, there should be a strong motivation to find avenues for its expression.

Motivations and Goals

According to classical motivation theorists such as Lewin (1951) and Atkinson (e.g., Atkinson & Birch, 1970), all behavior is motivated in some way, and one engages in particular behaviors to further a desired end. Motivations are enduring and pan-situational, and they find expression through situationally appropriate goals. Different motives and goals may underlie the same surface behavior. For instance, someone may join and participate in an illness support group online with the goal of gathering more information about the illness. Another individual might participate in the same group to gain social support. The social and psychological consequences of participation in this group may thus be quite different for these two individuals, despite the fact that they are engaging in the same kinds of activities online (see McKenna & Bargh, 1999; McKenna, Green, & Smith, 2001).

A person's motivations and goals for using the Internet will determine how he or she generally uses the available resources online. The goals of individual group members can not only interact with Internet communication to produce social and psychological effects for that individual but, as will be discussed in the next section, can also affect the processes and functioning of the group as a whole.

The Group × Internet Interaction

In many, if not most, respects, group functioning and social interaction on the Internet follow the same rules as in face-to-face interaction. Just as membership in traditional groups becomes an important part of one's social identity, so too does membership in electronic social groups (McKenna & Bargh, 1998). The same gender differences emerge online as in real-life relationships: women are more likely both to find relationship-related activities in both domains to be more gratifying in general than do men and to maintain relationships with family and friends in distant locales (e.g., Boneva, Kraut, & Frohlich, 2001; McKenna et al., 2002). Group norms emerge in online groups in the same way as they do in face-to-face groups (e.g., Postmes, Spears, & Lea, 1999). Theoretical models developed from research on traditionally formed (face-to-face) groups, such as self-completion theory, social identity theory, and self-categorization theory, have been tested and shown to apply to online groups as well.

At the same time, there are aspects of online communication that do uniquely affect group processes, and we turn to a discussion of these issues next. There are a number of detailed reviews of the extensive literature on various aspects of electronic group functioning (e.g., McKenna et al., 2005a; McLeod et al., 1997; Spears et al., 2002). Therefore, as we did in our section on individual differences, below we selectively focus only on those issues relating to group functioning that are among the most debated or for which the existing research findings appear to be most contradictory.

Anonymity and the Salience of the Group Identity

One respect in which online groups differ from traditional groups is the ability of members to be anonymous in their interactions. Russell Spears and colleagues have argued that anonymous communication within groups leads to a sense of depersonalization by the group members (see Spears et al., 2002). That is, members feel an absence of personal accountability and personal identity, and thus the group-level identity becomes all the more important. When the group-level identity is thus heightened, Spears and colleagues have shown that group norms can have an even stronger effect than occurs in face-to-face interactions. The degree to which the group identity is salient, however, plays an important role in determining what the effects of anonymity will be on the development of group norms.

For instance, Spears, Lea, and Lee (1990) found that when members of online groups interacted under anonymous conditions and group salience was high, normative behavior increased in those groups as compared to electronic groups in which members were anonymous but the salience of the group was low. Whether group salience was high or low, participants who interacted under individuating conditions displayed an intermediate level of conformity to group norms.

One of the most interesting sets of studies from the extensive program of research demonstrating the interaction between anonymity and identity-salience examined the effects of primed behavior in electronic groups. Postmes, Spears, Sakhel and De Groot (2001) primed participants with either task-

oriented or socioemotional behavior and then had them interact in electronic groups under either anonymous or identifying conditions. Members in the anonymous groups displayed behavior consistent with the respective prime they received considerably more so than did their counterparts who interacted under identifiable conditions within their groups. Normative behavior strengthened over time in the anonymous groups, with the members conforming even more strongly to the primed behavior. In contrast, when members were identifiable to other group members, they actually bucked the norms and behaved more prime-inconsistently over time.

An extension of this study (Postmes et al., 2001) provided even stronger evidence of the effect that anonymity can have on normative behavior. In this study, only half of the participants in each group received the behavioral prime. In the anonymous groups, those participants who did not receive the prime nonetheless conformed to the task or socioemotional behavior being exhibited by their primed cohorts and did so significantly more than did the nonprimed participants in the identifiable groups. Further, those who interacted anonymously reported feeling a significantly stronger attachment to their group and to the other group members.

However, it is not always the case that being anonymous in one's interactions will tend to increase behavioral conformity or that being identifiable will decrease it. When people have the goal of being positively evaluated by other group members and they are identifiable to the in-group, then they too are motivated to act in a manner consistent with group norms (e.g., Barreto & Ellemers, 2000; Douglas & McCarty, 2001; Noel, Wann, & Branscombe, 1995). Thus, self-presentational motivations can drive identifiable participants to engage in increased group-normative behavior.

McKenna and Bargh (1998, study 1) found that an individual's behavior in online groups is shaped by the positive and negative feedback of the virtual group members, but only to the extent that group membership is important to the person's identity (Deaux, 1996). We reasoned that people with stigmatized and concealable social identities (see Frable, 1993; Jones et al., 1984), such as homosexuality or fringe ideological beliefs, would be more responsive to the feedback they received from other group members who shared that marginalized identity than would individuals taking part in nonmarginalized groups. People with stigmatized identities are motivated to join and participate in Internet groups devoted to that identity, because of the relative anonymity and thus safety of Internet (compared to face-to-face) participation and the difficulty of finding similar others in "real life." Furthermore, because their online groups are often the only venue in which to share and discuss this aspect of their identity, membership in the group should be quite important to these people. Thus, the norms of such groups should exert a stronger than usual influence over members' behavior. These members should be motivated to behave in such a way as to gain acceptance and positive evaluation from their fellow group members. This prediction was confirmed by an archival and observational study of the frequency with which members posted messages to (i.e., participated in) the group: Unlike in other Internet groups, within the stigmatized-identity groups, participation significantly increased when there was positive feedback from the other group members and decreased following negative feedback.

Anonymity and Group Status

At first pass, it may seem that anonymous communication on the Internet would make the status of group members less important than in face-to-face groups. Racial, gender, and age-related features are easily identifiable when people interact face-to-face (e.g., Brewer, 1988) but are more readily concealable when one interacts online. Accordingly, Kang (2000) and others have argued that an important social benefit of the Internet is its potential to disrupt the reflexive operation of racial stereotypes (as well as those that accompany age, gender, etc.).

Not surprisingly, much research has supported this view. Studies have found that, compared to White consumers, African Americans and Hispanics pay more for cars purchased through traditional means, but this discrepancy in pricing disappears if the car is purchased online instead (Scott Morton, Zettelmeyer, & Silva-Risso, 2001). Those holding minority opinions (and thus minority status in some sense) in the group have been shown to be more likely to express those opinions during online group discussions than face-to-face discussions (McLeod et al., 1997; Roa & Jarvenpaa, 1991). Anonymity makes power less of an issue during discussion, which will lead group members, regardless of status, to contribute more to the discussion (Spears et al., 2002).

However, as McLeod et al. (1997) note, although members do indeed feel freer to express opinions that run counter to the majority opinion of the group, those expressing these minority opinions remain less influential within the group.

Yet, despite the anonymity of online communication, cues to social category membership, such as gender (Thompson & Murachver, 2001) or social class and ethnicity (Burkhalter, 1999) can still be observed. When these cues are observed and there is an absence of other types of information about the individual, these status differences can become even more salient to the other group members (Hollingshead, 1996; Postmes, Spears, & Lea, 1998; Spears & Lea, 1994). In other words, they can exert a stronger than usual influence. Thus, anonymity can make status in online groups either more or less important than it is in face-to-face groups, depending on the type of status differences in question and whether or not such differences are easily observed.

The Character and Purpose of the Group

The kinds of effects on members that are produced in electronic groups depend to a large extent on the characteristics and type of the group in question. For instance, pioneering research in the 1980s examined the effects of e-mail communication within the workplace and organization (e.g., Kiesler et al., 1984). In line with their "limited bandwidth" model, Sara Kiesler and her colleagues consistently found that electronic communication produced an increase in hostile and aggressive exchanges and decreased conformity and group consensus, and that the usual inhibitions one would have when interacting with superiors was greatly reduced. With the birth of the Internet in the early 1990s, researchers assumed that these findings would hold for all the various kinds of groups—whether socially oriented or work related—that quickly developed online. That turned out not to be the case, as the research exemplified by Russell Spears and colleagues discussed above has shown.

In the Workplace

Although early research found that electronic communication has a tendency to produce antinormative and hostile exchanges within workplace settings, subsequent meta-analytic reviews of the literature have concluded that computer-mediated communication (CMC) does not produce such effects among participants (e.g., Walther, Anderson, & Park, 1994; Postmes & Spears, 1998). Walther and colleagues concluded that hostile exchanges between work mates (i.e., insults, name-calling) were overreported activities. Straus (1997) conducted a study comparing 36 CMC and 36 face-to-face workgroups composed of three members each and found that "the incidence of personal attacks in groups in either communication mode was exceedingly small and was not associated with cohesiveness or satisfaction, suggesting further that the impact of this behavior was trivial" (p. 255).

Within a corporate negotiation setting, however, several aspects of online communication can interact with the goals of the participants to produce disadvantageous results. Although features of electronic communications (such as anonymity, the lack of physical presence, and the ability to exercise greater control over one's side of the exchange) can lead to greater self-disclosure and feelings of closeness within social settings, these same features can lead to greater distrust between parties when it comes to negotiations.

Thompson and colleagues (see Thompson & Nadler, 2002 for a review) have conducted extensive research comparing electronic negotiations to those that take place face-to-face. These researchers argue that the main problem with "e-gotiation" is that the participants make implicit assumptions about the time delays that occur in hearing back from their opponents and the motivations they attribute to such delays. For instance, in a negotiation situation, people tend to assume that the other party will receive and read an e-mail just as soon as they have sent it, and they therefore expect an immediate response. They then tend to attribute any delays in hearing back to stalling, power-plays, or disrespect by the other party.

Research by Alan Dennis (1996; Dennis & Kinney, 1998) has shown that although members of verbally interacting workgroups tend to share less vital information than do members of electronic workgroups, and hence make poor decisions, members of the electronic groups also tend to make poor group decisions, despite exchanging 50% more of the vital information needed to make an optimal decision. Thompson and Coovert (2003) also found that electronic work teams experienced more confusion and had more trouble maintaining mutual knowledge in their attempts to reach a decision compared to face-to-face work groups. The online teams in this study were also less satisfied with the decision they reached.

Yet, as Thompson and Coovert note, whether such findings extend to all work teams is still far from clear. Galegher and Kraut (1994) for instance, found that although electronic group members experienced greater difficulty in coordinating their work and took longer to complete the task, their final product was similar in overall quality to that produced by face-to-face group members. The members of the work teams researched by Dennis and Kinney (1998) and Thompson and Coovert (2003) were assembled solely for the purpose of the study and had not worked together before the manipulations, nor did they have expectations of working together in the future. Research has shown that mature teams—those with a history of working together (e.g., McGrath & Hollingshead, 1994)—already have in place an integrated knowledge system, and that having experience working together online can moderate such effects of electronic collaboration (Hollingshead, McGrath, & O'Connor, 1993; Walther & Burgoon, 1992).

It seems likely that many of the factors that differentially affect the decision-making process and the quality of a given outcome in traditional, face-to-face workgroups (see Kerr & Tindale, 2004; McLeod, et al. 1997, for a review) will also prove to be moderators when such teams interact electronically instead. Further, as Thompson and Nadler (2002) suggest, as we gain understanding of how and why some of the negative outcomes of electronic business interactions occur, we also gain insight into preventative solutions that can be implemented. For instance, these authors found that if participants do not simply plunge into an e-gotiation but, instead, start off the interaction with a quick exchange of "schmooze-mail" to get to know one another, then the negotiation is far less likely to reach an impasse and far more likely to reach a satisfactory and integrative agreement.

Common Bond versus Common Identity Groups

In their insightful analyses of traditional group relations, Prentice, Miller, and Lightdale (1994) distinguished between groups based around a common identity and those based on a common bond. In common bond groups (such as among a group of friends), an individual's attachment to the group is based on the bonds that exist between the group members. Attachment to a common identity group (such as a sports team) is based on one's identification with the group as a whole—that is, its purpose and its goals—rather than on the bonds that exist between individual members. Prentice and colleagues (1994) found that in common identity groups, as compared to common bond groups, there is greater adherence to group norms, indicating that the former have a greater effect on individual members' behavior. Sassenberg (2002) has examined equivalent common bond and common identity groups on the Internet and found that the same distinctions and processes outlined by Prentice et al. (1994) apply to electronic groups as well. Thus, the kind of group to which one belongs (online or offline) matters. Below we discuss two kinds of common identity groups—socially stigmatized groups and social support groups—for which further distinctions can be made and for which there is contradictory evidence as to whether involvement in such groups online results in positive or negative outcomes for participants and for society.

Socially Stigmatized Groups

Especially for important aspects of one's identity for which there is no equivalent "offline" group, membership and participation in a relevant virtual group can become a central part of one's social life. According to Deaux's (1996) model of social identity, active members of stigmatized-identity Internet groups should incorporate their virtual-group membership into their self-concepts. Once the virtual group has been incorporated into the self-concept, it becomes a new and important self-aspect. We would thus expect members of these groups to want to make this new identity a social reality (Gollwitzer, 1986) by revealing it to significant others—in other words, to "come out" in public about it for the first time.

Consistent with this prediction were the results of two studies conducted by McKenna and Bargh (1998). Structural modeling analyses of survey responses, across two replications focusing on quite different types of stigmatized social identities, demonstrated the transformational power that participation in Internet groups can have on the self. The average respondent was in his or her mid-30s, and many of them, as a direct result of their Internet group participation, had revealed this stigmatized aspect of themselves to their family and friends for the first time in their lives. These participants also

benefited from increased feelings of self-acceptance, and they had come to feel less socially isolated and "different" from the rest of society as a result of their group membership. It is thus clear that membership and participation in Internet groups can have powerful effects on one's self and identity.

But is this unabashedly a good thing? The answer to that depends, of course, on one's valuation of the marginalized identity in question. Certainly in the event that the effect of online membership in a group is to encourage real-life behavior that results in physical harm to another innocent person or persons, it cannot be viewed in a positive light. For instance, consider the case of an individual with an unexpressed interest in pedophilia whose participation in an online group devoted to discussion of that interest encourages him to act out his fantasies with a real child. Although we do not have direct evidence that such would be the case, the research by McKenna and Bargh (1998), discussed above, and that by McKenna, Green, and Smith (2001) suggest that it will be true for some. Racism is also socially stigmatized—particularly in extreme forms such as advocacy of White supremacy and racial violence (see McKenna & Bargh, 1998, Study 3). Today there are more than 3000 web sites containing racial hatred, agendas for violence, and even bomb-making instructions (Lee & Leets, 2002). Glaser et al. (2002) infiltrated such a group, and their research provides telling examples of the support and encouragement given by group members to each other to act on their hatreds and not just talk about them online.

Thus, what is at issue in this instance is not whether this process of identity demarginalization will occur and whether or not it will be good for the individual—there is ample evidence showing that individuals place a high value on their respective socially marginalized online (and offline) groups, and through participation reap personal benefits of self-esteem and self-acceptance. Rather, what is at issue is discerning when such benefits for the individual will come at a cost for wider society.

Online Support

Despite the lack of face-to-face contact—or perhaps even because of it—online support groups can provide those suffering from illnesses with valuable comfort and information. In harmony with findings of McKenna and Bargh (1998) discussed above, a study of online support provision and seeking by those with grave illnesses (Davison, Pennebaker, & Dickerson, 2000) found that people used Internet support groups particularly for embarrassing, stigmatized illnesses such as AIDS, alcoholism, and prostate cancer, because of the relative anonymity of the online community. The authors point out that these patients feel anxiety and uncertainty and are thus highly motivated by social comparison needs to seek out others with the same illness. When the illness is an embarrassing, disfiguring, or otherwise stigmatized one, they prefer to do this online because of the anonymity afforded by Internet groups.

Internet support groups can be especially helpful not only for those with stigmatized illnesses but also for those who may not have other sources of support available to them. For example, participation in an online support group for the hearing impaired was particularly beneficial for participants with little "real-world" support (Cummings, Sproull, & Kiesler, 2002). However, for some individuals, this may lead them to substitute online support groups for useful support that is available from friends and family (Helgeson, Cohen, Schulz, & Yasko, 2000), with negative results.

There are two recent studies that suggest that turning to online (and offline) support groups in times of illness is not always the best policy for one's psychological and physical health. In a study with cancer patients, Helgeson et al. (2000) found that when individuals have a readily available strong and supportive network and they also join a (face-to-face) cancer support group, the results may be more negative than positive. Although participation in the discussion groups proved beneficial for those with low levels of support from their social network, participation was actually detrimental for those with existing high levels of social support. Then there is the question of what the effects may prove to be of a phenomenon that is relatively unique to online support groups—the fact that face-to-face friends and family members may also take an active part in the group along with the person in need of support. Cummings et al. (2002) first documented this phenomenon. In their study, they found that nearly half of the deaf participants in the group had real-world family members or friends also taking an active role in the group. Such inclusion of one's social network is relatively rare in offline support groups. We do not know yet whether, or under what conditions, such a blending of online and offline support will prove beneficial or harmful for the individual.

It is also clear that in many cases online support groups function just as well as—that is, neither better nor worse than—their non-Internet counterparts. For example, McKay et al. (2002) found that those who participated in diabetes self-management and peer support over the Internet experienced the same improvements in physiologic, behavioral, and mental health—especially in dietary control—as did those using conventional diabetes management. Along similar lines, Barrera, Glasgow, McKay, Boles, and Feil (2002) found that diabetes sufferers who were assigned to participate in Internet support groups reported feeling that they had received more support, in general, than did those who relied on their offline social network for support and used the Internet only to gather information or get advice about their illness. Among older adults, greater participation in community support web sites for the elderly, such as SeniorNet, was associated with lower perceived life stress (Wright, 2000).

In summary of the findings on social support groups, as with the need to express important aspects of one's identity, people will be especially likely to turn to Internet groups when embarrassment, hearing loss, or lack of mobility makes participation in traditional group settings problematic, as will those with a lack of offline support. In addition, just as with traditional groups, those who take an active role in an electronic support group are likely to reap the benefits generally associated with such group involvement. However, it may be the case that the benefits gained from group participation will be overshadowed if one uses the group as a replacement for, rather than supplement to, an existing and strongly supportive social network. Whether a blending of one's existing social network with one's online social support group will prove to be beneficial is a question as yet unanswered.

Conclusions

There appear to be few "one size fits all" effects of Internet use. People are not passively affected by technology but, rather, actively shape its use and influence (Fischer, 1992; Hughes & Hans, 2001). The Internet has unique, even transformational qualities as a means of communication, including relative anonymity and the ability to connect with others who share one's interests, values, and beliefs. But there is certainly greater ambiguity surrounding the interactions that take place online—a lot is left unsaid and unspecified. The desires and goals that an individual brings to the interaction and the goals he or she holds regarding the communication partners makes a dramatic difference in the assumptions and attributions made in that informational vacuum.

Not all interaction situations on the Internet are created alike—the context matters—and nor are all Internet users cut from the same cloth. The individual differences of the users often interact with the communication situation, as well as with the unique features of electronic communication, to produce different, and sometimes powerfully so, outcomes.

Our review has revealed many cases and situations in which social interaction over the Internet leads to equally beneficial or even better outcomes than traditional interaction venues. But the Internet is not a panacea. We have highlighted many other cases in which the Internet produces more negative outcomes. As is the case with our many and varied interactions in face-to-face venues, outcomes are sometimes beneficial and sometimes not, sometimes good for the one but not for the other. The task for researchers is now to discover the difference between the types of situations that do produce better outcomes and those that do not. There is a saying, often mistakenly reported to be an ancient Chinese curse: "May you live in interesting times." For Internet researchers and common users alike, the next decade should prove to be interesting indeed.

Notes

1. The term interaction, as used in the first instance in the sentence above, is being used in the statistical sense of the word and refers to moderating effects (i.e., when the effect of one independent variable depends on the level of another independent variable). For example, if the effect of Internet use is different for those who are lonely than it is for those who are not, then we would say that the degree of loneliness an individual experiences is interacting with use of the Internet to produce different outcomes.

2. The range and average mean of reported levels of loneliness within this sample was comparable to that of other studies using random samples (e.g., Gutek, Nakamura, Gahart, Handschumacher, & Russell, 1980).

3. More specifically, it is not anonymity in the sense of not using one's name but rather the lack of identifiability by one's interaction partners and their lack of contact with and knowledge of one's offline social network that is important for these effects on self-disclosure (Derlega & Chaikin, 1977). A person can use his or her real name and still be relatively anonymous if the interaction partner has no other identifying information about the person.

References

Atkinson, J. W., & Birch, D. (1970). *The dynamics of action.* New York: Wiley.

Baldwin, M. W. (1997). Relational schemas as a source of if-then self-inference procedures. *Review of General Psychology, 1*(4), 326–335.

Bandura, A. (1977). Self-efficacy: Toward a unifying theory of behavioral change. *Psychological Review, 84*(2), 191–215.

Bargh, J. A. (2002). Beyond simple truths: The human-Internet interaction. *Journal of Social Issues, 58*(1),1–8.

Bargh, J. A., Fitzsimons, G.J., & McKenna, K. Y. A. (2002). The self, online. In Spencer, S., & Fein, S. (Eds.). *Motivated social perception: The 9th Ontario Symposium on Social Cognition.* Mahwah, NJ: Erlbaum.

Bargh, J. A., McKenna, K. Y. A., & Fitzsimons, G. M. (2002). Can you see the real me? Activation and expression of the 'true self' on the Internet. *Journal of Social Issues, 58*(1), 33–48.

Barrera, M., Jr., Glasgow, R. E., McKay, H. G., Boles, S. M., & Feil, E. G. (2002). Do Internet-based support interventions change perceptions of social support? An experimental trial of approaches for supporting diabetes self-management. *American Journal of Community Psychology, 30*(5), 637–654.

Barreto, M., & Ellemers, N. (2000). You can't always do what you want: Social identity and self-presentational determinants of the choice to work for a low-status group. *Personality and Social Psychology Bulletin, 26*(8), 891–906.

Blumler, J., & Katz, E. (1974). *The uses of mass communication.* Thousand Oaks, CA: Sage.

Boneva, B. Kraut, R., & Frohlich. D. (2001). Using e-mail for personal relationships: The difference gender makes. *American Behavioral Scientist, 45*(3), 530–549.

Brewer, M.B. (1988). A dual process model of impression formation. In Srull, T.K. & Wyer, R.S., Jr. (Eds.), *A dual process model of impression formation: Advances in social cognition* (vol. 1, pp. 1–36). Hillsdale, NJ: Erlbaum.

Burkhalter, B. (1999). Reading race online: Discovering racial identity in Usenet discussions. In

Kollock, P., & Smith, A. (Eds.), *Communities in cyberspace*. London: Routledge.

Chen, S., & Andersen, S. M. (1999). Relationships from the past in the present: Significant-other representations and transference in interpersonal life. Zanna, M. (Ed.), *Advances in experimental social psychology* (vol. 31, pp. 123–190). New York: Academic Press.

Cooley, C. H. (1902). *Human nature and the social order*. New York: Scribners.

Cummings, J., Sproull, L., & Kiesler, S. (2002). Beyond hearing: Where real world and online support meet. *Group Dynamics: Theory, Research, and Practice, 6*(1), 78–88.

Davison, K. P., Pennebaker, J. W., & Dickerson, S. S. (2000). Who talks? The social psychology of illness support groups. *American Psychologist, 55*(2), 205–217.

Deaux, K. (1996). Social identification. In Higgins, E. T., & Kruglanski, A. W. (Eds.), *Social psychology: Handbook of basic principles* (pp. 777–798). New York: Guilford.

Dennis, A. R. (1996). Information exchange and use in small group decision making. *Small Group Research, 27*, 532–550.

Dennis, A.R. & Kinney, S.T. (1998) Testing media richness theory in the new media: The effects of cues, feedback, and task equivocality. *Information Systems Research, 9*(4), 247–259.

Derlega, V. L., & Chaikin, A. L. (1977). Privacy and self-disclosure in social relationships. *Journal of Social Issues, 33*(3), 102–115.

Derlega, V. L., Metts, S., Petronio, S., & Margulis, S. T. (1993). *Self-disclosure*. London: Sage.

Douglas, K. M., & McGarty, C. (2001). Identifiability and self-presentation: Computer-mediated communication and intergroup interaction. *British Journal of Social Psychology, 40*(3), 399–416.

Fischer, C. (1992). *America calling: A social history of the telephone to 1940*. Berkeley: University of California Press.

Frable, D. E. S. (1993). Being and feeling unique: Statistical deviance and psychological marginality. *Journal of Personality, 61*(1), 85–110.

Galegher, J., & Kraut, R. E. (1994). Computer-mediated communication for intellectual teamwork: An experiment in group writing. *Information Systems Research, 5*(2), 110–138.

Glaser, J., Dixit, J. & Green, D. P. (2002). Studying hate crime with the Internet: What makes racists advocate racial violence. *Journal of Social Issues, 58*(1), 177–193.

Goffman, E. (1959). *The presentation of self in everyday life*. New York: Doubleday.

Gollwitzer, P. M. (1986). Striving for specific identities: The social reality of self-symbolizing.

In Baumeister, R. (Ed.), *Public self and private self* (pp. 143–159). New York: Springer.

Gross, E. F. Juvonen, J., & Gable, S.L. (2002). Internet use and well-being in adolescence. *Journal of Social Issues, 58*(1), 75–90.

Gutek, B. A., Nakamura, C. Y., Gahart, M., Handschumacher, I., & Russell, D. (1980). Sexuality in the workplace. *Basic and Applied Social Psychology, 1*(3), 255–265.

Hamburger, Y. A., & Ben-Artzi, E. (2002). Loneliness and Internet use. *Computers in Human Behavior, 19*(1), 71–80.

Helgeson, V.S., Cohen, S., Schulz, R., & Yasko, J. (2000). Group support interventions for women with breast cancer: Who benefits from what? *Health Psychology, 19*(2), 107–114.

Higgins, E. T. (1987). Self-discrepancy theory. *Psychological Review, 94*(3), 1120–1134.

Hiltz, S.R. (1976). A social scientist looks at computer conferencing. *Proceedings of the Third International Conference on Computer Communication, Toronto, 3*, 203–207.

Hiltz, S.R., Johnson, K., & Turoff, M. (1986). Experiments in group decision making: Communication process and outcome in face-to-face versus computerized conferences. *Human Communication Research, 13*(2), 225–252.

Hollingshead, A.B. (1996). Information suppression and status persistence in group decision making: The effects of communication media. *Human Communication Research, 23*(2), 193–219.

Hollingshead, A. B., McGrath, J. E., & O'Connor, K. M. (1993). Group task performance and communication technology: A longitudinal study of computer-mediated versus face-to-face work groups. *Small Group Research, 24* (3), 307–333.

Horney, K. (1946). *Our inner conflicts: A constructive theory of neurosis*. London: Routledge & Kegan Paul.

Howard, P. E. N., Rainie, L., & Jones, S. (2001). Days and nights on the Internet. *American Behavioral Scientist, 45*(3), 383–404.

Hughes, Jr., R. & Hans, J. D. (2001). Computers, the Internet and families: A review of the role of new technology in family life. *Journal of Family Issues, 22*(6), 776–790.

James, W. (1892/1961). *Psychology: The briefer course*. Allport, G. (Ed.). New York: Harper & Row.

Joinson, A. N. (2001). Knowing me, knowing you: Reciprocal self-disclosure in internet-based surveys. *Cyberpsychology and Behaviour, 4*(5), 587–591.

Jones, E. E., Farina, A., Hastorf, A. H., Markus, H., Miller, D. T., & Scott, R. A. (1984). *Social stigma: The psychology of marked relationships*. San Francisco: W. H. Freeman.

Kang, J. (2000). Cyber-race. *Harvard Law Review, 113*(5), 1130–1208.

Kerr, N. L., & Tindale, R. S. (2004). Small group decision making and performance. *Annual Review of Psychology, 55,* 623–656.

Kiesler, S., Siegel, J., & McGuire, T. (1984). Social psychological aspects of computer-mediated communication. *American Psychologist, 39*(10), 1129–1134.

Kraut, R., Kiesler, S., Boneva, B., Cummings, J., Helgeson, V., & Crawford, A. (2002). Internet paradox revisited. *Journal of Social Issues, 58*(1), 49–74.

Laurenceau, J., Barrett, L., & Pietromonaco, P. R. (1998). Intimacy as a process: The importance of self-disclosure and responsiveness in interpersonal exchanges. *Journal of Personality and Social Psychology, 74*(5), 1238–1251.

Leary, M. R. (1983). Social anxiousness: The construct and its measurement. *Journal of Personality Assessment, 47*(1), 66–75.

Lee, E. & Leets, L. (2002). Persuasive storytelling by hate groups online. *American Behavioral Scientist, 45*(6), 927–57.

Levine, J. (2000). Internet: A framework for analysing online human service practices. *Human Services Online: A New Area for Service Delivery, 17,* 173–192

Lewin, K. (1951). *Field theory in social science.* New York: Harper.

Markus, H. (1977). Self-schemata and processing information about the self. Self-schemata and processing information about the self. *Journal of Personality and Social Psychology, 35*(2), 63–78.

Markus, H., & Nurius, P. (1986). Possible selves. *American Psychologist, 41*(9), 954–969.

McGrath, J. E., & Hollingshead, A. B. (1994). *Groups interacting with technology: Ideas, evidence, issues, and an agenda.* Thousand Oaks, CA: Sage.

McKay, H. G., Glasgow, R. E., Feil, E. G., Boles, S. M., & Barrera, M. (2002). Internet-based diabetes self-management and support initial outcomes from the diabetes network project. *Rehabilitation Psychology, 47*(1), 31–48.

McKenna, K. Y. A., & Bargh, J. A. (1998). Coming out in the age of the Internet: Identity demarginalization through virtual group participation. *Journal of Personality and Social Psychology, 75*(3), 681–694.

McKenna, K. Y. A., & Bargh, J. A. (1999). Causes and consequences of social interaction on the Internet: A conceptual framework. *Media Psychology, 1*(3), 249–269.

McKenna, K. Y. A., & Bargh, J. A. (2000). Plan 9 from Cyberspace: The implications of the Internet for

personality and social psychology. *Personality and Social Psychology Review, 4*(1), 57–75.

McKenna, K. Y. A., Buffardi, L. & Seidman, G. (2005a). Self presentation to friends and strangers online. In Renner, K.-H., Schutz, A. & Machilek, F. (Eds), *Internet and personality.* Goettingen, Germany: Hogrefe & Huber.

McKenna, K. Y. A., Buffardi, L. & Seidman, G. (2005b). *Interactions among friends: Defining and redefining the self* (Manuscript under review). Ben-Gurion University.

McKenna, K. Y. A., Green, A. S., & Gleason, M. E. J. (2002). Relationship formation on the Internet: What's the big attraction? *Journal of Social Issues, 58*(1), 9–31.

McKenna, K. Y. A., Green, A. S., & Smith, P. K. (2001). Demarginalizing the sexual self. *Journal of Sex Research, 38*(4), 302–311.

McLeod, P.L., Baron, R.S., Martie, M.W., & Yoon, K. (1997). The eyes have it: Minority influence in face-to-face and computer-mediated group discussion. *Journal of Applied Psychology, 82*(5), 706–718.

Noel, J.G., Wann, D.L., & Branscombe, N.R. (1995). Peripheral ingroup membership status and public negativity toward outgroups. *Journal of Personality and Social Psychology, 68*(1), 127–137.

Pennebaker, J. W. (1989). Confession, inhibition, and disease. In L. Berkowitz (Ed.), *Advances in experimental social psychology* (vol. 22, pp. 211–244). New York: Academic Press.

Pennebaker, J.W. (1997). *Opening up: The healing power of expressing emotions.* New York: Guilford Press.

Postmes, T., & Spears, R. (1998). De-individuation and anti-normative behavior: A meta-analysis. *Psychological Bulletin, 123*(3), 238–259.

Postmes, T., Spears, R., & Lea, M. (1998). Breaching or building social boundaries? SIDE-effects of computer-mediated communication. *Communication Research, 25*(6), 689–715.

Postmes, T., Spears, R., & Lea, M. (1999). Social identity, group norms, and "deindividuation": Lessons from computer-mediated communication for social influence in the group. In Ellemers, N., Spears, R., & Doosje, B. (Eds.), *Social identity: Context, commitment, content.* Oxford: Blackwell.

Postmes, T., Spears, R., Sakhel, K., & DeGroot, D. (2001). Social influence in computer-mediated communication: The effect of anonymity on group behavior. *Personality and Social Psychology Bulletin, 27*(10), 1243–1254.

Prentice, D. A., Miller, D. T., & Lightdale, J. R. (1994). Asymmetries in attachments to groups and their members: Distinguishing between common-identity and common-bond groups. *Personality and Social Psychology Bulletin, 20*(5), 484–493.

Roa, V. S., & Jarvenpaa, S. L. (1991). Computer support of groups: Theory-based models for GDSS research. *Management Science, 37*(10) 1347–1262.

Rogers, C. (1951). *Client-centered therapy*. Boston: Houghton-Mifflin.

Sassenberg, K. (2002). Common bond and common identity groups on the Internet: Attachment and normative behavior in on-topic and off-topic chats. *Group Dynamics: Theory, Research, and Practice, 6*(2), 27–37.

Morton, F., Zettlemeyer, F., & Silva-Russo, J. (2001). Internet car retailing. *Journal of Industrial Economics, 49*(4), 501–519.

Smart, L., & Wegner, D.M. (1999). Covering up what can't be seen: Concealable stigma and mental control. *Journal of Personality and Social Psychology, 77*(3), 474–486.

Spears, R. & Lea, M. (1994). Panacea or panopticon? The hidden power in computer-mediated communication. *Communication Research, 21*(4), 427–459.

Spears, R., Lea, M., & Lee, S. (1990). De-individuation and group polarisation in computer-mediated communication. *British Journal of Social Psychology, 29*(2), 121–134.

Spears, R., Postmes, .T, Lea, M., & Wolbert, A. (2002). When are net effects gross products? The power of influence and the influence of power in computer-mediated communication. *Journal of Social Issues, 58*(1), 91–107.

Sproull, L., & Kiesler, S. (1985). Reducing social context cues: Electronic mail in organizational communication. *Management Science, 11*(11), 1492–1512.

Straus, S. G. (1997). Technology, group process, and group outcomes: Testing the connections in computer-mediated and face-to-face groups. *Human-Computer Interaction, 12*(3), 227–266.

Swann, W. B., Jr. (1990). To be known or to be adored? The interplay of self-enhancement and self-verification. In Higgins, E. T., & Sorrentino, R. M. (Eds.), *Handbook of motivation and cognition* (vol. 2, pp. 408–448). New York: Guilford.

Tajfel, H., & Turner, J. C. (1986). The social identity theory of intergroup behavior. In Worchel, S., & Austin, W. G. (Eds.), *Psychology of intergroup relations* (pp. 7–24). Chicago: Nelson-Hall.

Thompson, R., & Murachver, T. (2001). Predicting gender from electronic discourse. *British Journal of Social Psychology, 40*, 193–208.

Thompson, L., and J. Nadler. 2002. Negotiating via information technology: Theory and application. *Journal of Social Issues, 58*, 109–124.

Turoff, M. (1976). Human communications via data networks. In Blanc, M. & Colton, E. (Eds.), *Computer Networking*. New York: IEEE Press.

Turkle, S. (1995). *Life on the screen: Identity in the age of the Internet*. New York: Simon & Schuster.

Von Draas, D.D., & Siegler, I.C. (1997). Stability in extraversion and aspects of social support at midlife. *Journal of Personality and Social Psychology, 72*, 233–241.

Walther, J.B. (1996). Computer-mediated communication: impersonal, interpersonal, and hyperpersonal interaction. *Communication Research, 23*, 3–43.

Walther, J.B. (1997). Group and interpersonal effects in international computer-mediated collaboration. *Human Communication Research, 23*, 342–369.

Walther, J.B., Anderson, J.F., & Park, D.W. (1994). Interpersonal effects in computer-mediated interaction: A meta-analysis of social and antisocial communication. *Communication Research, 21*, 460–487.

Walther, J.B., & Burgoon, J.K. (1992). Relational communication in computer-mediated interaction. *Human Communication Research, 19*, 50–88.

Wright, K. (2000). Computer-mediated social support, older adults, and coping. *Journal of Communication, 50*, 100–118.

20

Christian Licoppe and Zbigniew Smoreda

Rhythms and Ties
Toward a Pragmatics of Technologically Mediated Sociability

Almost a century has passed since Georg Simmel (1908) founded his sociology on a dialectic between social structure and interpersonal interaction. In Simmel's perspective, society exists wherever people act reciprocally toward each other. Social forms are woven by such reciprocal action but take on independent life and, in turn, constrain action. This perspective allowed Simmel to analyze various forms of social life. At the time he formulated his structuralist interactionism (Forsé, 2002), Simmel had in mind primarily situations of face-to-face interaction. Nonetheless, there is no reason why we cannot apply this same approach to analyze the role that different kinds of media (e.g., telephone rather than face-to-face conversation) have in interaction. Simmel's sociology therefore can serve as a framework for analyzing how forms of association are changing in a context where digital technologies have become widespread. The formats in which interpersonal interactions take place were already complex, either in the home (Albert, 1993), or in the office (Fraenkel, 1995), before the advent of information technology, as research on different forms of writing and inscriptions formats has shown. However, the massive development of IT has led to a significant increase in the range of interactional devices of which people may avail themselves. So, alongside the standard household telephone, we have public phones and portable phones—both of which today may permit the sending of text as well as voice messages—and all the communication services that can be used through a computer connected to a network (i.e., e-mail, chat sites, discussion forums, instant message services, and so on). It is therefore important to examine this dimension in which a growing number of technologies of social interaction come into play, because the sense of each of these different technologies depends not only on their suitability for a particular kind of user and a particular type of exchange but also on the position of each alternative vis-à-vis others in a technological landscape that has become increasingly crowded and varied. The concepts of "interaction" and "interpersonal exchange" are too general here, for they both lump together and obscure two distinct forms of complexity. The first concerns the contents and formats of an exchange; in other words, the contents of the conversations and the way conversations are organized in discursive genres, which make up, together with intervening face-to-face meetings, the warp and woof of social ties. The second concerns the diverse technical means that affect the sense of these discursive activities and the way they are produced, diffused, and appropriated within the framework of reciprocal relations.[1]

We define interpersonal sociability in very general terms as the flow of exchanges that people maintain with those to whom they are connected. We therefore see sociability as having three distinct poles: the social network (a set of social ties possessing one or more relational measures[2]); exchanges themselves in the strict sense, made up of a succession of embodied gestures and language acts. These may take a number of forms even within one medium—as has been shown by research on writing,[3] the telephone,[4] or on the forms of interactional reciprocity[5]; and the various technical means that are available at a given moment of historical time and that enable an exchange to happen. These poles both pose constraints on and provide resources for interactions; thus, all three poles shape the form that relational practices take.

In our tripolar description, sociability is thus a bubbling of conversations, messages, and contextualized exchanges: a process inscribed in a multidimensional space consisting of networks of ties, forms of exchange, and interactional mediations. Through the web interactions, we can identify forms of coherence or patterns in which the nature of social relations is shaped alongside the relevance of discursive forms and the implications of technological media. None of these is completely determined beforehand. Certain patterns allow particular kinds of relations to crystallize out of the interactional froth. They can then be specified and compared to the canonical models of close ties. There are distinct ways of weaving the web of interactions between, say, an intimate friend compared to a simple acquaintance. Only certain ways of communicating are appropriate to each relationship type. There are ways of managing a tie that parallel how the tie itself is developing, and these methods play on the various discursive and technical resources that are available to shape the tie in the desired direction in an acceptable time frame. Nor should we assume that there is just one way of achieving this. Sociability is malleable: a specific kind of tie can be enacted in various interactional patterns. There is much discretion with regard to the forms and formats of reciprocal exchanges that progressively define a tie in the overall web of sociability.

We draw here on a series of empirical studies and will concentrate mainly on the strong ties of family and friendship. The first set of studies contains databases of telephone traffic and interviews focusing on the use of the telephone. These provide us with both quantitative and qualitative material on ego-centered personal networks of telephone/electronic sociability,[6] plus qualitative information on interpersonal exchanges that take place through other media. The studies in question cover the way that practices of social life change with biographical events such as a move (Mercier, de Gournay, & Smoreda, 2002) or the birth of a first child (Mançeron, Lelong, & Smoreda, 2002). Despite being commonplace, these biographical events are major tests in the construction of self. They constitute particularly interesting areas in which to examine our hypotheses regarding the connections between the public representations, which are more or less shared, that organize coherence and the concrete involvement of actors in relational practices.

How do people cope with the time constrictions introduced by the arrival of a first child, and with the new family configuration that the event brings—in what way do they redistribute their relational activity to satisfy these new conditions? How do we adjust when a geographical move takes us away from friends and relatives (and perhaps puts us closer to others)?

Events such as the birth of a child or a move lead to redeployment of relational resources and a reevaluation of one's personal network, and thus to a change in the way that people keep their network together and a change in the type of both exchanges and the technical means used to make these changes. This provides an empirical opportunity to observe sociability at work in its triple inscription in social networks, forms of exchange, and uses of communication technologies.

We also draw on a second group of studies that investigate interpersonal exchange via screens —forms of "always connected" sociability. These studies provide quantitative[7] and qualitative data on uses of the Internet; for example, the way people use spaces of interpersonal communication (Beaudouin & Velkovska, 1999), and consumption and gifts (Licoppe, Pharabod, & Assadi 2003). We will also use the results of research carried out on the exchange of messages via mobile phones (Rivière, 2002; Rivière & Licoppe, in press).

We begin by examining a number of rather specific exchanges, such as the transmission of news regarding the birth of a child or the purchase of Christmas gifts, to show how actors distribute their various relations and interactional modes. This will show that it is necessary to take into account the changing technological landscape when we analyze sociability. The examples also bring out a theme that will be central in our analysis—the temporal rhythm of mediated exchanges, and the way such rhythms are stretched by various expectations and conventions.

The Rhythms of Mediated Interaction and the Production and Reproduction of Social Networks

The course of interaction is guided by conventions, but it is also constructed in the course of the interaction itself. The temporal rhythm of exchanges and the degree of attention expected from one's interlocutor differ from one medium to another. Actions and reciprocal actions can take place on the model of a dialogue, where exchanges evoke responses almost immediately or, alternatively, may leave much longer intervening pauses—intervals that may or may not be accepted as standard and may or may not be acceptable. In certain cases, the action initiating the cycle has a conventional format. For example, biographical events like marriage, moving house, or the birth of a child produce the almost ritual format of the "announcement." Because these exchanges have a generic character, they can take place on different media without changing form, and often without involving extra effort. So the choice of one medium rather than another has a social sense: The decision to use a particular way of announcing the event is a way of reaffirming and reshaping closeness and distance in the personal network. In general, the closer the relation, the more important it will be to make the announcement rapidly and to obtain a reply. In the same way, the use of a particular medium for communicating the news is taken as a statement of distance or closeness, depending on what delay a particular technical medium allows in replying. This particular type of interaction shows how the choice of one medium rather than another produces and reproduces the social structure. It shows that when analyzing sociability, we do indeed need to pay attention to the technical means used to communicate.

We can thus observe that the announcement of the birth of a first child takes place in a series of concentric circles, starting with members of the immediate family and closest friends, followed by "less close" friends and more distant family, with acquaintances, cousins, colleagues, and so on, coming last. According to whether the news comes directly from the parents or via an intermediary, whether it comes directly after the birth or with a certain delay, and whether it comes via face-to-face contact, telephone, e-mail, or letter, a hierarchy of relations emerges:

> We told our parents and grandparents first; it was Pierre who told them. And it was they who passed on the news to the uncles and aunts and cousins. . . . So they heard at 2.30 a.m. . . . Then the following day we phoned our closest friends, and they passed the word on to friends who aren't quite as close. I mean, a bit less close or who we hadn't spoken to on the phone for a while. (Woman, 28 years of age, couple with one child)

The first people chosen to hear the news thus hear it without any intermediary as a sign of the quality of the relationship.

The calls made immediately after the birth and in the following days by the people who act as relays for the news are complemented by other means of communication—written announcements and e-mail messages—that make up a second level of prioritization. Once again there is a correspondence between the means used and the content of the relationship. Friends who are seen less frequently receive a written announcement of the event, whereas colleagues are more likely to receive an e-mail.[8] These written media are less committing in terms of reciprocity compared to conversation (face-to-face or on the phone). There is more delay before these messages are sent, and a further delay is expected before a reply comes. The length of this latter delay can be read as a sign of the degree of involvement of those receiving the message, a measure of how close they feel to the new parents. Those friends who do not reply, or who reply only after a long delay, might be abandoned, whereas certain others who reply more quickly than expected might occasionally be readmitted to the circle of intimates. The differential use of particular means of communication thus lays down a space of relational practices in which ties of similar closeness are treated in a similar way, and in which this degree of closeness is publicly expressed and negotiated. Relational proximity is shown to be greater if the news comes via telephone immediately (rather than with a delay) and directly (without the mediation of another person), and depending on whether it comes in the form of a written announcement (which may or may not be followed by a telephone contact), and according to whether it comes via mail specially addressed to one individual or to a whole list of people (fig. 20.1).[9]

The question of time is ever-present. The event of a birth constitutes a testing or sounding of the network of social relations, in the sense that it is an occasion in which the relational distance between the couple and their various ties is redefined. The delay between the event and the announcement of the event can be seen as a statement of the tempo of the relationship, and thus of relational proximity. The status of relations within the personal network is thus renegotiated via a temporal metric—a timing that depends both on when the news is given and on when the reply is received. The role of different interactional media in sociability is also reaffirmed and redefined in the course of this test, which employs them to perform the same language act, but to different persons. Telephone contact comes out as having the highest status, being most appropriate for giving the news to the closest circle of family and friends—those whom one prefers to see or hear from in the immediate context of the event.

The work of sociability thus turns into a joint redefinition of relational proximities in the network and a redefinition of the sense of each of the interactional resources available for the maintenance of the relationship. This redefinition makes use of an ordinary event and a standardized interactional format: the announcement. Such a biographical event is thus the occasion for a test that concerns the most appropriate modalities of adjusting the interactional dynamics.[10]

Similar patterns can be seen in the various festivities of the year and in the gift giving that these involve, as timing is also crucial here. A mother interviewed in one of our studies, who is a frequent Internet user, says she would not consider ordering her son's Christmas present on the web—fearing that the delay in delivery might make the present arrive late, because her role as mother means that the present must be there on the day. Things are different, in contrast, with regard to the neighbor's children:

> On the other hand, for the neighbors' kids I normally order comics through Alapage.com

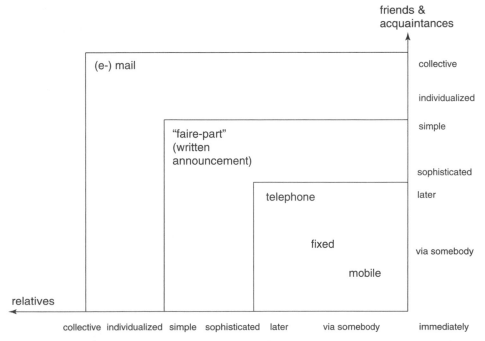

Figure 20.1. Media and timing of announcements of birth of a child, by proximity of the correspondent. Adapted from Mançeron and Leclerc, 2001.

. . . if they don't arrive, well they'll have to wait till the 26th. I'll tell them, "Look . . . " They'll have their presents from their parents. It's not the same thing for your own child. If I saw my Paul putting out his stocking and all the others had their presents, but not him, you can imagine his face. (Woman, 39 years of age, mother of three children)

Events and ritual festivities thus work as tests of a relationship. They are an occasion for reaffirming the strength of a relationship or, on the contrary, for endorsing its inevitable decline. The use that one makes of the different temporal arrangements that are implicit in various technical means of communication expresses this hierarchy.

However, a tie is woven out of many contexts, many occasions, and many technical means of communication. It is constructed through a constant point and counterpoint of interaction, a chronicle of encounters—each with a particular form of communication—in which the thread of timing stitches presence and absence according to the characteristic modes that make up a relationship. To conceptualize the three-cornered dynamic between the tie, the forms of the exchange, and the technical means used requires an analytic framework that takes account of how a tie is "tied," how interactions via various media are both ordered in time, and how they are interspersed with periods of silence or inattentiveness. How can we conceptualize this time of daily life, which beats out the rhythm of a tie and elaborates the motif that makes the tie unique?

The Music of Interpersonal Ties

Rhythms of Exchange and Dynamics of Sociability

Numerous writers have emphasized the links between time and activity, showing, for example, how industrial society brought with it more rigid forms of time observance (Thompson 1967). However, the subtle adjustment of the timing of both presence and absence in everyday social relations has attracted little attention. Roland Barthes' (2002) analysis of the conditions of a happy "living together" constitute an exception, as this discusses how an individual may alternate between periods of isolation, in which he or she follows their own

rhythm,[11] and periods of exchange and conviviality. Although Barthes's reasoning emerged out of analysis of ancient forms of the ascetic life, and of various texts of the literary canon, this construction of a "living together" is applicable to any community in which the personal rhythm of each person has its place. It connotes any enterprise that attempts to flexibly reconcile collective life and individual life—the independence of the subject and the social life of the group.

One of the principal insights that this approach brings is that it permits us to conceptualize several temporal orientations of collective action. As is well known, the question of time is closely linked to that of power—to impose one's own time rhythm on someone is to exercise power over them. In contrast, rhythm should be distinguished from what we will call cadence, which is a temporal ordering that exists outside interaction, imposed by rules and institutions. Freedom is in the rhythm: Only the subject can slow down the pressure of the cadence. Any flexible mode of association that allows individuals to follow their own rhythms is opposed to regulated communities and their imposed cadences, to the extent that these communities allow individuals the possibility of following their own rhythms. The principle, which underlies all such forms of association in which one's own rhythm can be expressed, is therefore that it is opposed to institutions, hierarchies, and rules and to their cadences that interfere with the rhythm of living together. To the metaphor of society as an anthill, Barthes opposes the alternative model of society as a school of fish: A smooth symbiosis of individuals who are nonetheless separate, equidistant, with synchronized movements.

If this living together is the flexible grouping of a limited number of subjects who try to coexist in the vicinity of each other while preserving their own rhythms, why should they group together at all? In such flexible, often elective, associations, there is not a strict causality (which would make the collectivity subject to a law, to rules, and to determinism). Rather, these associations offer a diffuse set of aims, which are often expressed via evocative and emotionally charged words. The grouping of living together defines itself in this way, in the name of ideals—which must be sufficiently vague to remain relevant in spite of changing circumstances yet sufficiently committing to hold the collective's loyalty, like a pure homeostatic machine that maintains itself.

As the metaphor of the school of fish suggests, living together is an adjusted form of collective life that rests on an ethic of distance. Its dynamic equilibrium and its maintenance presuppose that the investment of individuals takes a suitable form, particularly with regard to efforts made to articulate the time of absence and meeting; the time of being present together and coexisting. If the whole holds together too loosely, there is a strong risk that individuals will become too distant from each other and fall into isolation and exile. If the tensions of living together weigh too heavily on individuals who are subject to other exigencies, there will be friction between individuals who have become too close—and thus the risk of regulation and alienation emerges. Finding the right distance, one that is appropriate for the diffuse aims of the group and yet allows the group to endure over time, involves a double question: What form of presence lasts when the members of the group are physically separated and following their own rhythms? This absence is not a form of exile: It is a kind of solitude that "in no way means absence from society—on the contrary, it is action of society at a distance, positive determination of the individual via negative socializing," as Simmel (1900, p. 366) remarks. Second, what role do moments of exchange and conviviality play in the affirmation and maintenance of this living-together sociability, in the moments of separation that follow? To these two central questions, implicit in Barthes' original model, which opposes separate coexistence and copresence, we would like to add one more: What difference does it make to living together when we have today many possibilities to maintain contacts over a physical distance?

The dynamic approach of living together allows us to conceptualize the logics of sociability by examining the way this is inscribed in geographical space, in time, and in social forms. These questions have emerged fairly frequently since the social sciences have turned their attention to the collective seen as a set of coordinations linked by concurrent temporalities. The anthropologist Mary Douglas (1991) has analyzed the organization of the home from this point of view. She thinks of the household as a "middle way," a kind of living together between two extremes: On the one hand is the tyrannical domestic community, which forces all its members to conform to the daily rituals of its rigid cadence (justified in the name of a formally explicit domestic collective well-being that threatens to represent anyone who does not conform as selfishly pursuing their own interests). On the other hand is a model that makes the home similar to a hotel, in which the collective is dissolved by the closure of each family member in their own rhythms, which never synchronize in a moment of meeting and shared conviviality.

Focusing in this way on the rhythm of interactions in forms of association between persons provides a fruitful framework for thinking about interpersonal ties and all their forms. Describing a succession of exchanges in terms of ties provides a narrative and retrospective unity to a succession of interactions and exchanges spaced out over time. The tie thus emerges out of the tangled mass of sociability, making up a resource that leaves its mark on the interaction and that allows actors to orient themselves within the relationship. The question emerges of how a strong dyadic tie (e.g., a lasting friendship) becomes crystallized. And what reflexive relation does such a strong tie have with the temporal ordering of the course of interaction? How does the sense of the other person's presence last when they are not physically present, allowing the sense of friendship to persist?

In certain cases the dyadic interpersonal link is inseparable from a collective tie. This is the case when actors have for the other the role of "go-between" or bridgehead into a group. This situation is common when people move, perhaps even changing country or going into exile. In this situation, the emigrant may make telephone calls to a relative or friend back home, who gives the emigrant news of "all the gang," who are, however, seen collectively only on rare visits back "home."[12] Here, interaction splits into two modes—interaction while the people are present, and interaction at a distance—the conjunction of the two modes makes up a hybrid rhythm that is characteristic of the way that interpersonal ties are inserted into a wider social and geographical territory. In other patterns, each party belongs to a rule-governed community in which presence is made tangible via the imposition of cadences on each person. This means that a rhythm of social life has to be found that is compatible with each of these cadences if the interpersonal tie is to last. This is the case of friendships of members of two different households, where the people see each other as couples or as entire families.

Finally, it should be said that the approach is a dynamic one, which treats social life as a process and social structure as an emerging configuration. In advocating harmony of the rhythms of absence and presence as a condition of happiness that is common to the various forms of association and ways of constructing interpersonal ties, we attempt (without having recourse necessarily to external determinants or to the deliberate intentions of individual actors) to grapple with the question of how private sociability manages to reproduce itself or reshape itself during biographical events in which actors' environment and context changes. We will try to illustrate the relevance of this model for the description of personal sociability by examining close—indeed, very close—relationships.

Sociability with Close and Intimate Ties: An Example of the Pragmatics of Living Together

When describing their social networks, almost everyone brings into play a special category of tie— that of the intimate, those who are very close. These are often friends who have become "like my family." But this category of the intimate may also include members of the family circle itself; for example, brothers, sisters, or cousins (usually members of the same generation) with whom the interviewee has a particularly strong and lasting relationship. These elective friendships are marked by reciprocity, sharing ideas and experiences, and similarity between oneself and an intimate friend. These particularly close relationships are sharply distinguished from the general mill of acquaintances, both because one trusts them with confidences and because one has confidence in them and how they will act. Thus, familiarity shows through via the fact that it is possible to say anything and everything to each other, and to confide secrets, thus conforming to the formula of intimate outpouring: "With your friends, you talk about lots . . . with a girl I'm friendly with, really friendly, I'll tell her a secret" (woman, 40 years of age, in a couple relationship with two children). And these intimates are people who will always "be there" when needed, those whom you can count on being there when you call for help and for whom you will be there too: "people you can count on. You know that you can call them at two in the morning, waking them up. Whatever it is you need. . . . They'll still give you their shirt off their back if that's what you want . . . and they know that you'd do the same for them"

(woman, 60 years of age, couple with three grown-up children).

Friendships of this kind are meant to last. The expectation is that contacts will be maintained, and the friendship will stand the test of time: "What is a friend, well if I had to give a definition I'd even say it's people who you stay in contact with up till the day you die; and on that criterion, you probably don't have many friends" (man, 40 years of age, couple with two children). Looking back, interviewees tend to see the fact that one relationship has lasted the trials of life, whereas another has not, as proof of a sharp distinction between true friendship and simple acquaintanceship:

> [M]y best friend! She's the person I can talk the most to. She's the person I've been through the most with. I've known her since the second grade, so that's 6 years. After this friend there are people who are really fond of you. Then there are mates, then acquaintances . . . people you like, but if you lose touch with them, well, you lose touch and that's that. But, well . . . they're not like family, you know!" (Woman, 22 years of age, single)

The maintenance of friendships is not, however, deliberate or planned. It is a constant improvisation, in which the fact of thinking of the other person alternates with seeing them or hearing from them in the name of an ideal typical friendship that turns around confidences (knowing one can say everything) and being confident that one's friend will always be there to hold you if you need them. This representation is vague (in the sense that it is not precise enough to prescribe any one single kind of behavior as appropriate), but it is nonetheless sufficiently loaded with affect to seem to be the principal motor of reproduction of the relationship through the various trials of life.

To have a few relationships characterized by a high degree of proximity is seen as normal and as a right. It is in their nature that they should be few in number: "I think you can have two or three" (woman, 45 years of age, couple with two children).

> I don't think you can keep up close relationships with everyone. It's too . . . it'd be too superficial. . . . I think there are people you can have a deep friendship with, you know . . . whereas with others you don't put so much of yourself into the relationship . . . because you

don't really believe it's worthwhile, as it were—whatever you did, you couldn't change their attitudes, they couldn't change the way you think, so you don't really have anything to give them, they couldn't really give you anything, so . . . that's it." (Woman, 40 years of age, married with three children)

People resign themselves quite happily to this numerical limitation because it seems to them part of the order of things, either because they see potential candidates as soul mates being too rare to be able to imagine more or because intimacy would imply an emotional charge that was too committing. It is therefore presented as rational to concentrate relational investment on a few people, rather than to waste resources by spreading investments out over relationships that would inevitably be superficial. Another justification often cited is that these investments in close relationships need to be compatible with domestic and work commitments. Intimate proximity, which bears all the traits of these flexible and elective forms of association that we described above, come down in the end to the problem of how to adjust time—how does one maintain an intense elective tie organizing absences and moments of conviviality within the limits that allow for the cadences imposed by the home and work?

The analysis of use of the telephone after a geographical move (Mercier et al., 2002) allows us to construct an ideal type of durable relationships. Such relationships tend to start in youth in the context of wider collective experiences and then survive the first tests and bifurcations of adult life. They therefore free themselves from the context and from the social relationships in which they were originally inserted and become individualized into a particular and distinct tie.[13] This tie is kept alive through a suitably adapted flow of interactions that take place in various media: face-to-face meetings of conviviality, shared activities, telephone calls, letters, and so on. As the people in question get older, interactions become gradually rarer, the friendship becoming more and more a presence sustained in memory. An interesting aspect of this developmental ideal type is that it brings out the fact that there are different ways of maintaining the friendship link at different phases of the life cycle. The different ages of life involve different modes of "living-together," each with its periods of separation (which pose the problem of inscription in the memory, making them present "in the head") and

moments of exchange and conviviality. It is significant, therefore, that the different ages of life also involve different technical means for communication at a distance and maintenance of the relationship.

Events like a change in the configuration of one's family (e.g., with the birth of a child) or a move to another region constitute critical tests for the social tie. Biographical ruptures stress those forms of living together that have been smoothed out by routine and conventions. These ruptures threaten the equilibrium of that "right distance," which, before the change, incorporated an equilibrium between absence and interaction, within the framework of a relationship whose quality and status is expressed precisely by that adjusted rhythm of silences and exchanges.

In the case of moves, the fact that the people in question find themselves suddenly separated geographically or suddenly closer redefines the efforts that are necessary to conduct certain kinds of interaction. Face-to-face meetings become more difficult or easier to organize, the cost of a phone call changes, and so on. A way of being together as friends, based on seeing each other with a given frequency and on doing a certain number of things together, may therefore become unfeasible, and no other satisfying mode of relationship may appear. These friends may seem to be "so close yet so distant," and they risk being relegated retrospectively to the role of mere acquaintances:

> Because we only saw each other once a year, and well . . . "What have you been up to?" Well, that's all very nice, but it's not the same. It's that you simply don't share your life any more! When you're close you see each other often, you share masses of things, you know what's going on in the local area. You keep up with your news by phone. (Woman, 35 years of age, married with three children)

In the case of a birth, it is change in the status of the family that requires renegotiation of the parameters of sociability. Since the birth of her first child, Aurélie has discovered a satisfying relationship with her in-laws, who live in another town, because they have expressed their commitment via fitting modes of exchange:

> If we could live in the same town they'd be really pleased. If we could see each other all the time they'd be over the moon. That's very

different from my parents! Jean's parents need to hear and see their children. I know it's breaking their heart not to be near their grandson. And so they often ring up to ask how he's getting on, and now this weekend we're going down to see them and they're jumping up and down with joy. They really are. We're going down to Lyon soon, and taking Thomas [the baby] and they can't wait, they keep ringing up: "Do you need this, will he want that?" . . . they're really over the moon.

Aurélie's own parents in contrast do not ring much, and this hurts her. Because her parents have not changed the way they behave, the birth of a child shows up the dissonance in the relationship: absence, presence, and exchanges between mother and daughter have not adjusted to rhythms that are "right" for the new kind of tie.

My parents live nearby, yet they don't really see Thomas much more than Jean's parents. And they don't jump up and down with joy. They're pleased, but . . . My parents are very reserved and I've often thought—especially when I was pregnant—it'd be nice to have a call from time to time, that'd do me good. Yet it's often me who rings. I often ring my mother at her work, because I don't really like ringing home, because the family situation isn't very . . . well, anyway, the fact is that she doesn't ring me often, and when I left home I minded that a bit. I couldn't understand how we were supposed to form a new relationship if she never picked up the phone to ask how I was getting along. Her attitude was: no news, good news, and that was enough for her, and I couldn't understand that.

What emerges from interviews of this kind is thus a relational difficulty in finding a rhythm in the frequency of contact that suits both parties. Whether close family or friends, people seem slightly uncertain about when they should call and about what kind of reminders or demands for attention are appropriate.

It is natural that we should see our friends less now—perhaps because we make contact less often now that we have less time. Or maybe our friends, some of them, don't know quite how to react; they don't know whether they

can see us, whether they're disturbing us, whether this, whether that. (Woman, 31 years of age, couple with child)

Friends whose requests and expressions of friendship are compatible with the new daily rhythms of a couple with a young child are quickly distinguished from friends who do not adapt to a new way of being together or keep to their own rhythms.

There are two kinds of friends: there are those who understand because they've already thought about what it means to be a parent, and know that changes everything. For example, there are those who . . . well, as I said earlier, you can tell by the fact that some people talk loudly and others lower their voice. There are some who continue to talk loud, to joke and shout while the baby is howling because there's so much noise. So there are the young couples and people who go out all the time—people who've never grasped what a baby is. (Woman, 29 years of age, couple with one child)

Whether the tie will survive or not depends on being able to resolve these forms of discordance in temporal rhythms. Once again, it can happen that a strong friendship will be recategorized as a simple acquaintance because agreement on these matters seems impossible. Or, another relationship in which such renegotiation succeeds may be confirmed as a "real" friendship that will probably last all one's life. This adjustment of synchronization and coordination of the personal rhythms of various individuals inevitably involves power and an element of imposition; such power does not operate at random. Rather than allowing space for innovative social combinations, then, such renegotiation tends to work as a powerful mechanism for reimposing social reproduction and established patterns. For example we find that among the friends of a young couple, those who are themselves about to have a child not only share similar concerns[14] but are also subject to similar time rhythms. For this reason, it is easier for two sets of parents who have recently had children to adjust to each others' cadences: With births coming more or less at the same time, these cadences are harmonized with each other. This same economy that gives priority to friendships where the cadences are in harmony with each other and where domestic preoccupations (and therefore social trajectories) are similar because they also affect the formation of new ties (Eve, 1999).

At the beginning of this chapter, we introduced the idea of a sociability with three poles, consisting primarily of social networks and the metric or measure that is appropriate to them (i.e., a relational distance or the intensity of the tie); second, of conventional formats of exchange and interaction; and third, of a variety of technical and interactional means of effecting the tie. We then introduced the dynamic of living together as a principle that underlies the adjustment of interpersonal sociability. We will now go back to the question of sociability and try to identify patterns, stressing two contrasting motifs in a tapestry of interaction in which everything is both always in process and liable to come apart at the slightest negligence, delay, or interfering biographical event.

Tests of the Tie: Sociability as a Relational Economy

Actors' use of the telephone and of written communication is organized in a variety of modes. The first of these describes a modality that we call "relational." In exchanges that take place between close friends (or intimate relatives), long conversations and the exchange of long written texts mark out an interactional space that conquers absence. The people in question give and receive news, reconstructing a shared world because they have not been able to see each other or talk for some time. The telephone call, letter, or e-mail signal an intention—they show that, absence notwithstanding, *alter* is present in *ego*'s thoughts. Gestures, gifts, written messages, and conversations thus help to maintain a tie that is rendered fragile by too much separation. Without pretending to be substitutes for face-to-face contact, these means try to compensate for the rarity of such contact.

This mode of technically mediated sociability is not new. Throughout the centuries it has adapted to the transformation of interpersonal mediations. In the 16th century the exchange of gifts between peers, gentlemen, and scholars helped them keep in contact "like the stones of a good building held together by cement" (cited in Davis, 2003, p. 105). Erasmus criticized such an exchange of everyday objects and of game as a way of maintaining friendship, proposing that these gifts should be substi-

tuted in humanist circles by the exchange of books and of scholarly commentary by way of letters. However, his suggestion does not challenge the significance of this circulation of gifts; it is still a question of maintaining a tie "for fear that, in the absence of each other's company, good will may languish and even die away, under the influence of the prolonged gap of time and place" (Davis, 2003, p. 60). In the 19th century, bourgeois correspondence took up the same theme. We might even talk of an epistolary pact—a widely accepted idea that physical separation is a test for the letter writers to overcome. Letters thus filled in the absence of the other by providing news and signals of presence. Another common 19th-century theme is that of letters as substituting conversation or chat—that chat which physical separation has made impossible (Dauphin, Lebrun-Pézerat, & Poublan 1995). In defining letters as a "conversation between absent friends," contemporary manuals of writing even presented this kind of attitude prescriptively as the correct one (Dauphin, 2000). Today, the telephone is typically viewed as the most appropriate tool for maintaining an intimate tie: "You use the means of your own times. I think we would have written to each other if the telephone didn't exist. We would have kept in touch. You use whatever means is most handy . . . the easiest thing is the telephone" (woman, 35 years of age, couple with no children).

Research on networks of interpersonal sociability and in particular on friendship (Bidart, 1997) maps the direction in which patterns tend to change over the life course. For young people, friendship tends to be tied to shared places and group activities. Opportunities to see each other are frequent. Exchanges mediated by technical means nonetheless constitute an important connective tissue coordinating and synchronizing group activities and meetings. The fact of being "on the list" both expresses the fact that one belongs to the group and makes it possible to participate in group activities (Mançeron, 1997). Notwithstanding this prevalence of the group, a few friendships do detach themselves from the collective context and are cultivated with their own rhythms. Secondary school students use the possibilities provided by mobile phones and chats to communicate after school with members of their groups—thus interacting in a more elective, individually focused form of sociability, freed from the tyranny of keeping up appearances that often dominates adolescent groups.[15] As the years go by, activities diverge and friends move geographically; these changes create a tendency to extract a few privileged ties out of the original mass of collective links, and these dyadic ties are maintained for their own sake. These lasting friendships are thus immediately subjected to the test of biographical events (Bidart & Pelissier, 2002). When such events seem to place a "distance" between friends, the use of mediated forms of communication like the telephone can be crucial—and the "relational" modality of interpersonal exchange seems particularly suitable for this purpose.

The telephone, and in particular the "relational" mode of telephone usage is therefore a particularly appropriate tool to help people keep in step with each other and find a new equilibrium between periods of absence and moments of presence, fitting the cadences of everyday life with the rhythms appropriate for intimacy and thus renegotiating the "right" distance for the tie:

> Well, given the enormous mass of work I have to do, I don't notice time passing that much. As I say, it's hardest at weekends. Because everyone tries to work a bit. So you don't see each other, you see fewer people and I miss that, and yes, I spend a lot more time on the phone. And it doesn't always work; it's frustrating, I find being a long way away hard to cope with at the weekend. (Man, 20 years of age, single)

As we have pointed out, this relational significance has its effects on the form that telephone calls take: They become less frequent but longer ("You maybe make fewer calls to friends, but calls which last longer" [man, 30, couple with two children]) as people seek to reestablish via words a shared experience despite the distance that separates them[16]:

> When you move, you're in a whole new context, a new life . . . that takes more communication, to explain it all . . . yes, that's what happens, that's what happens, you have more to tell people; so when you move—at least, this is what happened with us—at least during the transition period, there's an increase in your calls and your communication. (Man, 40 years of age, couple with two children)

It is interesting to note that this does not only affect telephone interaction. All kinds of interaction take on a different relational mode when a bio-graphical event such as a move tests the relationship. Face-to-face meetings also become more charged with expectations and take on a new form, becoming longer and rarer, more out-of-the-ordinary than they were once:

> It's much more intense. Now for example we'll be seeing each other the whole weekend. They're arriving tomorrow, and they'll be going on Sunday evening. Whereas before, well, we used to see each other for a meal, or we might spend a bit of the afternoon together, then we'd both go back home, or at least in the evening. Whereas now you really take advantage of the time you have, you go for walks, we're planning a picnic on Sunday . . . you do things you wouldn't have done otherwise, it's funny isn't it? But maybe we wouldn't have done things like that when we were living close . . . we used to live 10 kilometers from each other. Or rather, the closest lived just 10 kilometers away; the others, well anyway it was, "Hey why don't you drop by, come and have a coffee," then "Oh well, I'll be getting home, I've got to put the children to bed." Whereas now there's no putting the children to bed here! So it's . . . it's more concentrated . . . it's . . . it's better. (Woman, 40 years of age, couple with two children)

In becoming more of an "event," more "concentrated," face-to-face meetings of this kind demonstrate the commitment of participants to the tie and inscribe the relationship more firmly in memory.

There is, therefore, an interdependency between the tie, the distance, and the form taken by interaction. This leads to empirical regularities that we might summarize in terms of the dictum that face-to-face meetings and telephone calls become rarer and longer the greater the distance between friends or close relatives. This is a very robust effect in our research results, as can be seen in fig. 20.2, which gives data on number of calls and length of calls by geographical distance separating the speakers before and after a move of one of the households. It can be seen clearly that the length of telephone conversations increases with geographical distance and with the infrequency of calls.

So interpersonal sociability here takes the form of a compensatory economy. In their attempts to maintain a tie that is classed, retrospectively, as a

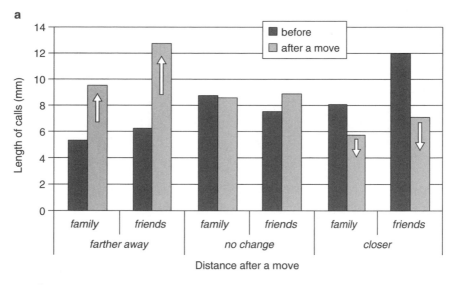

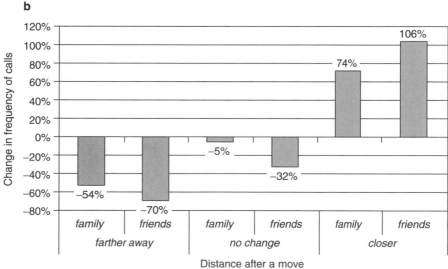

Figure 20.2. (a) Average length of telephone calls (in minutes) by change in the geographical distance separating the speakers (family and friends). (b) Change in the frequency of telephone calls by change in geographical distance separating the speakers (family and friends). "Farther away" means that people who, before a move, lived near each other (less than 50 km) and now live further away. "Closer" means that people who previously lived farther away now, after their move, live within 50 km of the friends/relatives in question. "No change" refers to ties where the frends/relatives were more than 50 km away both before and after the move. The data regard the telephone traffic of 110 households who moved home, recorded for 16 months (4 months before the move, 12 months after it). Source: Mercier et al. (2002, p. 140).

strong and lasting relationship, actors reallocate scarce resources like time, personal availability, and physical effort to find an adjustment between absence and moments of interaction and sharing that appropriately expresses the status of the tie. In other words, it creates an equilibrium that is appropriate

for a living together as friends in the new context created by the geographical move.

This relational economy is embedded in the economy in the classic sense of the word. Money constitutes one of these rare resources that have to be allocated in the household, thus necessitating negotiation over what is the collective welfare. The question is not merely a question of accounting in the simple sense—the total of costs of interaction with friends and relatives that appear at the end of the month in the form of bills—but also a question of adjusting different temporal rhythms. For example, to encourage customers to spread out calls, telephone companies usually charge different rates for different times of the day. Financial pressure is thus felt as a cadence imposed without regard to consideration of the needs of a relationship; following a move one is obliged to conform to this external cadence in relations with friends and family:

> [W]ell, every so often you really feel you need to make a call, but I hold myself back a great deal, even for calls to my family, because I think what you pay is too much. . . . So I think that the phone is a bit scandalously expensive, and it's not so easy to take advantage of the times when the rates are cheaper. I don't really take account of those, I don't manage to work it out. Anyway often it's not easy when you want to catch people when they're still up. You know, there are the children, meals, and so on and, well, after all that it's getting a bit late so you ask yourself if you can call so late. And in any case when it's late you don't necessarily have the energy to make that warm, emotional call you would have made during the day. . . . So that's the telephone, how we use the telephone. It's not something I talk about often, but it twists me up inside when I think of the bills I pay, and I feel I'm being taken advantage of. (Man, 40 years of age, couple with two children)

In this case, the dissonance is expressed by the fact that this interviewee uses the language of social injustice; he sees his right to maintain ties with family and friends as bumping up against the constraints of economic rationality.

The actor of this kind of economic rationality is a "strategic" actor who manages his or her resources in such a way as to maintain strong ties and make sure they come through the tests imposed by biographical events. Successful optimization sometimes makes people feel retrospectively that such life events constituted no threat to the relationship: "they come to see me, I telephone them, moving hasn't turned my life upside down at all, it's hardly changed anything in my relationships with the people I'm really close to" (woman, 26, single). Some people do in fact adopt this pose of strategist managing a relational rationality, but they do this after the fact, when the test has safely passed. Others take a different line: "It's true that there are times when we won't telephone or write. But I think we've got a really deep friendship, deep feeling, we really respect each other, value each other as individuals, so that's what it's all about—it's not that you think 'Oh dear, I ought to keep up the relationship'" (man, 40, couple with two children). In this case, the friend is represented as being so strongly present in the memory that there is no need for any strategy to preserve the tie. Because of this continual presence of the friend *in absentia* in his thoughts, *ego* can delegate the task of maintaining the tie to whatever contacts happen to come along, none of them explicitly aimed at maintaining the tie. The right distance is found via interactions that, because of the faith one has that each is thinking of the other, have no problem in finding an appropriate rhythm that makes up for the physical separation.

"Connected" Presence

The relational mode just discussed is only one of those that exist in the landscape of sociability via technical means. Living together has other patterns as well; for example, when the people in question share a sufficient number of places and activities so that there is no shortage of face-to-face meetings. Alongside the mode in which long conversations compensate for the days people cannot meet up, there is a kind of "interstitial" communication in which there is a proliferation of exchanges and messages regarding the coordination of activities. These act as connecting tissue and form a suitable terrain for a particular form of mediated sociability: the "always on" presence.

This interstitial communication, which consists mainly of short calls and messages for the coordination of interpersonal activities, exemplifies another pattern of presence and absence—a pattern in which absence no longer means silence. In this pattern, actors who are close socially (and often also geographically) are often in contact. With these close people who are seen nearly every day, there is the closest intertwining between situations of copresence and a connecting tissue of messages sent by phone and so on. This pattern is without doubt currently most widespread among young people whose social life and diversified use of communication resources constitute a suitable terrain for this kind of pattern. In all cases, however, shared activities—those that require numerous calls for coordination and synchronization—form the backdrop for this mode of communication. The calls are so frequent that they act as reminders of the other's presence even when the people are not actually together. It is less necessary in this mode that the messages should manifest commitment to a strong tie: the reciprocal commitment is visible in the very frequency of the calls and messages that coordination of shared activities makes necessary. In this pattern, therefore, the strength of the tie is lived rather than said.

This interstitial pattern makes heavy use of technological means of communication. It has developed considerably in recent years with the emergence of portable means of communication, which are especially suitable for coordination. It has also been encouraged by the development of various kinds of message systems such as answering services, e-mail, and the short message system. These technologies for sending messages loosen the constraints that would otherwise be imposed by the proliferation of communication because they allow the person receiving a message to delay before replying, for the more numerous communications become, the more frequently people have to interrupt the activity with which they are currently engaged to fit in with another cadence. The risk is that ties with friends will become institutionalized in the form of expectations and mutual obligations to be constantly available electronically. Mediated sociability currently seems to be countering this risk of control, preserving playful tie management, by making greater use of less intrusive means of communication. Thus, in the last 10 years there has been rapid growth of telephone and electronic contacts, but an even more rapid growth of message systems.[17]

This development has been accompanied by more subtle changes that crystallize a new way of living together in which the distinction between coexistence and copresence becomes thoroughly blurred. Calls and messages become so frequent and their formats so varied that, together with face-to-face meetings, they make up a tightly knit and seamless tissue of interaction—a real "always connected" presence (Licoppe, 2002). At the same time, short calls and messages become an emotional and expressive resource—and a resource used in a particular mode of maintenance of ties.

Constantly connected presence, in fact, makes widespread use of the possibility of making little gestures where the discursive content is less important than the act itself; that is, "phatic" communications (Jakobson, 1973). Rather than constructing shared experience by recounting small and large events of the day or the week, one sends little expressive messages, providing sensations or reactions to some event or an emotion, or perhaps asking the person to express themselves in this way. Although the exchange of letters in the 19th century required people to justify themselves if they had nothing to say and to fill the page with "I love you" or "you are in my thoughts," such condensed expressions of intimate emotion become a positive resource in "connected" living together. In the semiotic of the discourse of love, "I'm thinking of you" condenses presence and absence in the same language act, to the extent that it reveals both forgetting of the other and waking up from this forgetfulness (Barthes 2002). However, it is the repetition of these little messages that maintains the tie, filling in absence via a sort of incantation. To a considerable extent, the rhythm of the connected tie consists of this insistent psalmody of little expressive messages. In the framework of ties between close friends, they will tend to be as frequent as possible, for the more this presence-at-a-distance is continual, the more it is reassuring in terms of the tie itself.

If the "always connected" presence is most prominent in intimate ties, it is not found only where people live close to each other or see each other frequently. The availability of new technical means may stimulate this pattern in the attempt to find a solution to the problem of living together. This is illustrated by a young woman (in her thirties, married with one child) whose best friend is in Britain. They had few exchanges until recently, and only on the initiative of the friend; phoning abroad is expensive, especially for long, conversational calls, as is usual between best friends.

Before I had an Internet connection, it was usually she who called me, I didn't call because financially it's very expensive, so I didn't call, and I'm very lazy about writing letters— writing the letter, getting the paper, then going and posting it and all that, I hardly ever do it.

Whereas an e-mail is different: I connect up, I write her a little note and that's that.

To write a letter required too much organizational and cognitive investment. With e-mail, the financial cost is no longer a restricting issue, unlike the telephone; the effort necessary to initiate an exchange is minimal, unlike a letter. This makes it possible to have frequent small exchanges. These two friends have effectively turned to a "connected" mode of managing their relationship via their use of e-mail:

And I discovered how pleasurable it was to write to her, because we replied to each other. It wasn't chatting directly but we corresponded, she received my mail, she replied immediately and sent off the reply, and sometimes I would reply back. Sometimes it was just one sentence that we'd send off like that.

It can also be seen in these examples how "connected" presence, especially in its emotional and expressive register, exploits nondialogic means of communication such as voice messages, electronic message systems, or the short message system; these signal a demand for attention but allow a deferred response. Indeed, sometimes these messages do not even require any response at all, because they authorize a kind of civil lack of attention. In some extreme cases, the mere fact of knowing that a line of communication is active and that one is therefore "connected" to the other is sufficient.[18] The emotion that accompanies this knowledge makes the tie present to consciousness and the exchange of words superfluous.

E-mail or little messages sent by the mobile phone thus constitute an especially suitable resource for managing relational difficulties and making bearable expressions of aggressiveness in a relationship:

Little messages make it possible to step back a moment. Even when the person sends a very aggressive little message there is always the telephone between you. It is less violent I would say. You lose your temper less I think and you don't remember it so much as you do with verbal aggressiveness.

The availability of the short message system (SMS) as a communication resource leads to reassessment of other forms of mediated communications, mak-ing more salient the potential violence inherent in face-to-face or telephone conversation. Text messaging, or SMS, is much used in the management of intimate relationships, making it possible to negotiate very close relationships, and it helps to negotiate difficult passages without breaking the thread of mediated contact or the "connected" tie.

That happened with my best friend. We weren't getting on for two or three months and the only thing we did was to send each other SMS, but really horrific ones. I can't even begin to describe them. He called me up 2 weeks ago and said "Look, I was half joking in all those SMS. I love teasing you and all that because I know you get mad at once." . . . Well, if that had been on the telephone it just wouldn't have been possible to backtrack like that. You see, it's not the same. . . . We let it go as if he had just been taking the piss out of me, whereas if it had been on the phone he couldn't have pissed me about like that. (Woman, 23 years of age, single)

For the following man, in love with a dancer whose hours of work are very different from his (he works in the daytime, she at night), short messages are part of a strategy intended to reassure the other of a loving presence without seeming to solicit a response too embarrassingly:

Yes, I have sometimes thrown out . . . for example . . . a phrase like, for example "I miss you"—I know that if I say that on the phone there will be a pause afterward. Not because she doesn't want to reply but because she takes the sentence for herself and turns it over. So I put it in an SMS. That way at least I'm sure there won't be a pause afterward and I won't have to start the conversation up again. It's just a phrase and that's it.

There is a fantasy of living together that conditions uses of the various technical means of communication. As we have seen, what attracts in the ideal type of connected presence is the opportunity to reshape a piece of one's interpersonal sociability, where presence is always mediated and actors increasingly use nonintrusive message systems. These systems thus minimize the risk that is inherent in any interaction. Some philosophers (e.g., Dreyfus, 2001) have argued that intrinsic limits exist to the extent that electronic media, and in particular the Internet, are able to create strong ties, and that these limits have the lot to do with the way participants may be put at risk when using different communication media. The general idea is that the less interactions are embodied, and the less risk there is for participants, the less these participants will reveal of themselves. The right distance in this new configuration of connected presence may thus be a matter of finding a suitable balance between forms of interaction that minimize interpersonal risks and forms in which actors commit themselves enough to be vulnerable and to mobilize all their attention. So instead of the play between absence and copresence, we would have a play between lack of attention and absorption, between safety and interactional vulnerability.

Notes

1. Since the 1980s, a number of French studies attempted to organize these questions around the idea of uses of information technologies (Jouet 2000). Although these studies did not succeed in founding a real sociology of uses, they continue to stimulate debate among those concerned with information technologies.

2. Critiques of structuralist network analysis (Gribaudi, 1999; Eve, 2002) have emphasized the tendency present in much formal network analysis to focus on one sphere, often work relations, neglecting the multidimensional character of personal networks that tend precisely to criss-cross several social spheres. Analyses that do have data on just one sphere are unable to focus on the tensions and contradictions that stem from playing in several spheres.

3. For example, if we take correspondence in the 19th century and the particular case of letter-writing, we find a distinction between the formal, rather stilted register used to maintain relations with a range of kin and the register of intimacy (Chartier, 1991).

4. We have shown elsewhere (Licoppe and Smoreda, 2000) that systematic analysis of the length of telephone calls brings out variability in the formats of telephone interaction. We showed a continuum existed between "relational" and "interstitial" forms of telephone communication. "Relational" telephone calls are long and relatively infrequent, with people taking their time to allow the conversation to develop, to give each other their news and share intimacy. "Interstitial" use of the telephone, in contrast, is made up of frequent short calls for practical reasons such as coordinating activities, or simply to reassure someone of one's existence.

5. Rather than the conventional distinction between written and oral communication, we are thinking here of the distinction recently introduced by Peters (1999) between dialogue and dissemination. Dialogue in this sense includes quite a wide range of interaction forms, not just face-to-face meetings and telephone conversations but also exchanges via e-mail or the short message system (SMS) if the exchanges are sufficiently close in time to evoke the turn-taking of ordinary conversation. Dissemination, in contrast, covers all those forms of communication in which messages are cast into an interactional "vacuum" without having any certainty of obtaining replies. This is true for messages left on answering machines or for letters, e-mails, or SMS messages when these written forms are not thoroughly embedded in a game of interactional reciprocity.

6. Telephone sociability is defined here as that specific part of social life that passes through this particular medium. We aim to show that it is incorrect to frame the discussion on telephone sociability as though it was simply sociability that happens to make use of the telephone, because it adheres to different rules from sociability in general, as we have defined this above.

7. We have developed a platform for the statistical analysis of text suitable for the analysis of Internet communication and "access logs" (Beaudouin et al., 2002). In combination with interviews with users, these data allow us to explore the various combinations of interpersonal exchange practices on the Web.

8. Mançeron et al., 2002, p. 98.

9. "That does make it possible to keep in touch. I noticed that when, after the birth, we sent an e-mail to more or less all the people we knew, all the ones who had an e-mail address, saying he's born, he's super, and all that. I even sent the message to old addresses I didn't know were still valid or not, people I hadn't been in touch with for 2 or 3 years. And some of those people replied, so we made contact again—whereas I would never have called or written otherwise."

10. Of course the birth of a child is not the only test of this kind. Other biographical events such as a move or marriage pose similar problems. Cf. Mercier et al., op. cit., 2002; Maillochon, 2002.

11. Barthes introduced the neologism "idiorhythm" in this context.

12. Before the telephone, this pattern helped shape the form that letters took. Some letters "back home" thus constituted a kind of visit to the whole village, in that they included messages for numerous people, trusting that the person to whom the letter was sent would pass these on—or perhaps read the letter out loud in a group (Bruneton-Governatori & Soust,

1997). The classic analysis of the personal correspondence of emigrants is, of course, Thomas and Znaniecki (1918–1920). Mercier et al. (2002) describe the way that even today people keep in touch with those back home in another region via a contact who acts as a bridgehead with another community. 13.Cf. also Bidart and Pellisser (2002).

14. Our data on telephone traffic show that after birth of a first child, time spent on the telephone with friends who have children exceeds that spent with friends who do not have children (Mançeron et al., op. cit.).

15. Dominique Pasquier, personal communication.

16. Elsewhere (Licoppe and Smoreda, 2000) we have demonstrated via a logistic regression that geographical distance significantly increases the length of telephone conversations independent of the sex and age of the people concerned. The association holds, whatever type of relationship (kinship, friendship, etc.) links the two people and whatever time of day the call takes place at.

17. Pascal Perin, personal communication.

18. This is the case with instant messaging, where favorite correspondents are represented by an onscreen icon whose color indicates the availability or unavailability of a given correspondent to immediate written exchange.

References

Albert, J. P. (1993). Ecritures domestiques. In Albert, J. P., & Fabre, D. (Eds.), *Ecritures Ordinaires*. Paris: CNAC Georges Pompidou.

Barthes, R. (2002). *Comment vivre ensemble: Cours et séminaires au Collège de France (1976–1977)*. Paris: Seuil.

Beaudouin V., Fleury S., Pasquier M., Habert B., & Licoppe C. (2002). Décrire la toile pour mieux comprendre les parcours. Sites personnels et sites marchands. *Réseaux*, 20 (117), 19–52.

Beaudouin, V., & Velkovska, J. (1999). Constitution d'un espace de communication sur Internet: Forums, pages personnelles, courrier électronique. *Réseaux*, 17, 97, 121–177.

Bidart, C. (1997). *L'amitié. Un lien social*. Paris: La Découverte.

Bidart C., & Pellissier, A. (2002). Copains d'école, copains de travail: Evolution des modes de sociabilité d'une cohorte de jeunes. *Réseaux* 20 (115), 18–49.

Bruneton-Governatori, A., & Soust, J. (1997). Pourquoi écrire? Question posée à un corpus de lettres d'émigrés béarnais aux Amériques (1850–1950). In Albert, P. (Ed.), *Correspondre jadis et naguère*. Besançon: Edition du CTHS.

Chartier, R. (1991). *La correspondance. Les usages de la lettre au XIXème siècle*. Paris: Fayard.

Dauphin, C. (2000). *Prête-moi ta plume ... Les manuels épistolaires au XIXème siècle*. Paris: Kimé.

Dauphin C., Lebrun-Pézerat P., & Poublan D. (1995). *Ces bonnes lettres. Une correspondance familiale au XIXème siècle*. Paris: Albin Michel.

Davis, N. Z. (2003). *Essai sur le don dans la France du XVIème siècle* (French translation of *The Gift in Sixteenth Century France*) Madison: University of Wisconsin Press, 2000.

Douglas, M. (1991). The idea of a home: A kind of space. *Social Research, 58*(1), 287–307.

Dreyfus, H. L. (2001). *On the Internet*. London: Routledge.

Eve, M. (1999). Qui se ressemble s'assemble? Les sources d'homogénéité à Turin. In Gribaudi, M. (Ed.), *Espaces, temporalités, stratifications: Exercices sur les réseaux sociaux*. Paris: Editions de l'Ecole des Hautes Etudes en Sciences Sociales.

Eve, M. (2002). Deux traditions d'analyse des réseaux sociaux. *Réseaux, 20*(115), 185–212.

Forsé, M. (2002). Les réseaux sociaux chez Simmel: les fondements d'un modèle individualiste et structural. In Deroche-Gurcel, L., & Watier, P. (Eds.), *La sociologie de Georg Simmel, 1908: Eléments actuels de modélisation sociale*. Paris: Presses Universitaires de France.

Fraenkel, B. (1995). La résistible ascension de l'écrit au travail. In Borzeix, A., & Fraenkel, B. (Eds.), *Langage et travail: Communication, cognition, action*. Paris: Editions du Centre National de la Recherche Scientifique.

Gribaudi, M. (1999). Avant-propos. In Gribaudi, M. (Ed.), *Espaces, temporalités, stratifications: Exercices sur les réseaux sociaux*. Paris: Editions de l'Ecole des Hautes Etudes en Sciences Sociales.

Jakobson, R. (1973). *Questions de poétique*. Paris: Seuil.

Jouet J. (2000). Retour critique sur la sociologie des usages. *Réseaux, 18* (100), 487–521.

Licoppe, C. (2002). Sociabilité et technologies de communication. Deux modalités d'entretien des liens interpersonnels dans le contexte du déploiement des dispositifs de communication mobile. *Réseaux, 20* (112–113), 173–210.

Licoppe C., Pharabod A.-S., & Assadi H. (2003). Contribution à une sociologie des échanges marchands sur Internet, *Réseaux, 20*(116), 97–140.

Licoppe, C., & Smoreda, Z. (2000). Liens sociaux et régulations domestiques dans l'usage du téléphone. *Réseaux, 18*(103), 255–271.

Maillochon, F. (2002). Le coût relationnel de la "robe blanche." *Réseaux, 20*(115), 53–90.

Mançeron, V. (1997). Tribu en ligne: usages sociaux

et modes d'interaction au sein d'un réseau de jeunes parisiens. *Réseaux, 15*(82–83), 205–218.

Mançeron, V., & Leclerc, C. (2001). *La naissance du premier enfant: La mise en place d'un nouveau monde*. Research report. Paris: Communitas.

Mançeron V., Lelong B., & Smoreda Z. (2002). La naissance du premier enfant. Hiérarchisation des relations sociales et modes de communication. *Réseaux, 20*(115), 93–120.

Mercier P.-A., de Gournay C., & Smoreda Z. (2002). Si loin, si proches. Liens et communications à l'épreuve du déménagement. *Réseaux, 20*(115), 123–150.

Peters J.D. (1999). *Speaking into the air. A history of the idea of communication*. Chicago: University of Chicago Press.

Rivière, C. (2002). La pratique du mini-message. Une double stratégie d'extériorisation et de retrait de l'intimité dans les interactions quotidiennes. *Réseaux, 20*(112–113), 139–168.

Rivière, C. & Licoppe, C. (In press). From voice to text : Continuity and change in the use of mobile phones in France and Japan. In Harper, R., Palen, L., & Taylor, A. (Eds.), *The inside text. Social and cultural design perspectives on SMS*. Berlin: Springer.

Simmel G. (1900). *Philosophie des Geldes*. Berlin:Duncker & Humblot.

Simmel, G. (1908). *Soziologie. Untersuchungen über die Formen der Vergesellschaftung*. Berlin: Duncker & Humblot.

Thomas, W. I., & Znaniecki F. (1918–1920) *The Polish peasant in Europe and America*. Boston: Badger.

Thompson, E. P. (1967). Time, work-discipline, and industrial capitalism. *Past and Present, 28*, 57–97.

Author Index

Subject Index